Ho Chi Minh's
Blueprint for Revolution

Ho Chi Minh's Blueprint for Revolution

In the Words of Vietnamese Strategists and Operatives

VIRGINIA MORRIS
with CLIVE A. HILLS

McFarland & Company, Inc., Publishers
Jefferson, North Carolina

LIBRARY OF CONGRESS CATALOGUING-IN-PUBLICATION DATA

Names: Morris, Virginia, 1969– author. | Hills, Clive A., author.
Title: Hồ Chí Minh's blueprint for revolution : in the words of Vietnamese strategists and operatives / Virginia Morris with Clive A. Hills.
Description: Jefferson, North Carolina : McFarland & Company, Inc., Publishers, 2018 | Includes bibliographical references and index.
Identifiers: LCCN 2018014974 | ISBN 9781476665634 (softcover : acid free paper) ∞
Subjects: LCSH: Hồ Chí Minh, 1890–1969—Political and social views. | Vietnam—Politics and government—1945–1975. | Vietnam—Politics and government—1858–1945. | Revolutionaries—Vietnam—Biography. | Vietnam—History—1945–1975. | Vietnam—History—1975–
Classification: LCC DS556.9 .M685 2018 | DDC 959.704092 [B]—dc23
LC record available at https://lccn.loc.gov/2018014974

BRITISH LIBRARY CATALOGUING DATA ARE AVAILABLE

ISBN (print) 978-1-4766-6563-4
ISBN (ebook) 978-1-4766-3121-9

© 2018 Virginia Morris and Clive A. Hills. All rights reserved

No part of this book may be reproduced or transmitted in any form or by any means, electronic or mechanical, including photocopying or recording, or by any information storage and retrieval system, without permission in writing from the publisher.

Front cover: Hồ Chí Minh's illustration (Pixabay); topographic map of Vietnam, 1965 (U.S. Army Map Service)

Printed in the United States of America

*McFarland & Company, Inc., Publishers
Box 611, Jefferson, North Carolina 28640
www.mcfarlandpub.com*

To our beautiful daughter, Bluebelle,
and wonderful son, Albion.

Now that this book is finished,
we can spend many more enjoyable
moments together.

Table of Contents

Acknowledgments — ix
Preface — 1
Introduction: Hồ Chí Minh's Legacy — 3

Part I: Establishing the Blueprint (1890–1945)

1. The Making of a Revolutionary — 7
2. Hồ's Female Couriers — 20
3. The Seeds of Hồ's Revolutionary Strategies — 39
4. The Infant Blueprint — 63

Part II: Evolution and Application of the Blueprint

The August Revolution (1945)

5. Hồ's Road to Power — 79

The French War (1945–1954)

6. Blueprint for Revolution — 100
7. The Water Flows South — 118
8. The North: The Westward March — 132
9. The Secrets Behind the Battle of Điện Biên Phủ — 163

The American Vietnam War (1954–1975)

10. And So It Begins Again — 182
11. A Divided Country — 208
12. The Hồ Chí Minh Trail — 230
13. Tết: America's Big Decision — 257
14. The Phoenix Program: Targeting the VCI — 291
15. Total Victory — 319

Epilogue: Eyes Wide Open	345
Appendix I. Abbreviations and Acronyms	351
Appendix II. Translation of Vietnamese Terms	352
Chapter Notes	354
Bibliography	374
Index	377

Acknowledgments

My interest in the female couriers who contributed so much to this book was first awakened when Lady Borton, a historian and author of *Hồ Chí Minh: A Journey*, mentioned the subject to me in 2005 as we sat in an open air tea room in Hanoi. I had just completed my book on the history of the Hồ Chí Minh Trail and was looking for an exciting new academic research project to expand my knowledge of Vietnam and those who had wanted to control it. My curiosity aroused, I broached the subject with Lê Đỗ Huy, a Vietnamese researcher, who had been pivotal to my work on the Hồ Chí Minh Trail. He readily agreed to assist and in the first instance approached Dr. Nguyễn Văn Khoan, a renowned historian, to guide us through the various stages of the project.

I wanted the book to be based mainly on the testimonies of key players, with direct interviews being my main source. Primary and secondary documentation including documents, journals, personal diaries, maps, audiotapes as well as books would then be used to put these very rare accounts into context. This documentation not only came from private collections, but were sourced from various institutes including those in Hanoi: the Hồ Chí Minh Museum, the Vietnamese People's Army Library, Museum of Vietnamese Revolution, the Institute of Party History, the State Library of Vietnam, the Army Museum, the Women's Museum and the Hồ Chí Minh Trail Museum. Others in Vietnam were the Navy Museum in Hải Phòng and the Women's Museum of Cochinchina in Hồ Chí Minh City. In the United States institutes included the Naval Historical Center and the Marine Corps Historical Center in Washington, D.C., the U.S. Army Military History Institute in Philadelphia and the Air Force Historical Research Agency in Maxwell. Finally, those in London comprised the British Library and the National Archives.

Before listing my main interviewees, I would like to give a thank you to those who assisted me, with special reference to a few. Primarily, Clive A. Hills, my husband and co-author, whose photographs have been used extensively in the book. He also spent several years preparing the excellent maps, with assistance from Lê Đỗ Huy and me, mainly using information obtained from the interviewees. In addition, my gratitude goes to those who copy-edited or proofread the manuscript, including Christie Dickason, author and historian; Prof. David Hunt, my PhD tutor from South Bank University; Paul Middleton and Amanda Gray, freelance editors; and my former work colleague, Clare Head. Others who contributed their military knowledge were Dr. Aziz Shahab, translator and cultural expert on Afghanistan, who was very important when it came to confirming the conclusions for the book. Mark Hampton, who helped edit the text, also gave his advice based upon his military knowledge and experience of conventional and guerrilla warfare gained from conflicts in Afghanistan and elsewhere. A special thank you goes to Brenda Morris, my mother, who looked after both my newborn daughter and later my newborn son so that I could carry on writing; Louise Edwards, for babysitting; Trish Babtie and Jeremy Preston for their support; and the Society of Authors, which awarded me an Authors' Foundation grant so that I could continue with my research.

Finally, in this group of remarkable people who contributed their knowledge and time, equal gratitude has to go to Thammavong Phiphatsely (Mr. Vong) in the Lao People's Democratic Republic. He passed away in March 2015, but at the time when I was researching this book he had retired from the Lao Army and the secret police and worked as a lawyer. He guided both Clive A. Hills and me some 1,600 km in total through remote Lao, which included more than 700km along the incredibly difficult Hồ Chí Minh Trail. This enabled us not only to collate a photographic record of previously inaccessible parts of Lao, but also to discover new information about this famous route.

Now to those who contributed by granting me interviews; a rare group of people indeed, whose remarkable lives makes this book a unique and worthwhile historical record. When the wars in Vietnam finally ended and peace returned, another fight began for them, which in some ways was even more difficult. This fight was the one to rejoin society, to return to normality, and to forget their sometimes terrible pasts. Most were then, and still are to this day, trying to free their minds of what they witnessed, endured, or had to do. The majority has found solace but only with those who shared the same experience. I feel deeply privileged to have met these men and women from both sides of the conflict and for permitting me, an outsider, to enter their world.

I extend a huge and heartfelt thank you to several American men: Senior Master Sergeant Jim Burns, Staff Sergeant John Stryker Meyer, Major Mark A. Smith and Sergeant Robert Taylor. My appreciation also goes to Mrs. Phuong, who worked alongside her allies. They all not only gave freely of their time so that I could understand fully their role in the Vietnam War, but also assisted with photographs and guidance on the maps. Through Meyer, I was invited to an American Special Operations Association reunion where I was introduced to a number of highly secretive and cautious elite soldiers and pilots. Assured by Meyer that I could be trusted, they opened up and began to talk about their covert operations in Vietnam, Lao and Cambodia, and granted me full and rare interviews.

Without doubt, the biggest thank you goes to those who explained to me Hồ Chí Minh's blueprint for revolution. The man who did most to open the door to these people was General Phạm Hồng Cư, a retired high-ranking political commissar. He arranged access to the veterans as well as photographs and information relating to them. I list interviewees in chapter order. Introduction: Mrs. Ngô Thị Huệ, General Nguyễn Thới Bưng, Mrs. Lê Thị Thu, Mrs. Võ Thị Tâm, Mrs. Lê Thị Thu Nguyệt, Mrs. Đặng Hồng Dực, Mrs. Trầm Hương and Mrs. Trần Hồng Ánh. In Chapters 1 to 4: Dr. Nguyễn Văn Khoan, Brigadier General Đào Văn Trường and General Võ Nguyên Giáp. In Chapters 5 to 9: Brigadier General Lê Trọng Nghĩa and Mr. Vũ Anh. In Chapters 10 to 15 and the Epilogue: Colonel Nguyễn Trọng Tâm, Lieutenant General Đồng Sĩ Nguyên, General Hồ Đệ, Brigadier General Trần Văn Phúc, General Lê Mã Lương, Colonel Lê Hồng Vân, Colonel Đặng Xuân Thành, Major Bùi Thị Hương, Mr. Lê Quang Vịnh, Mr. Phan Nam, Mr. Hoàng Lanh, Mrs. Hoàng Thị Nở, Mrs. Nguyễn Thị Hoa, Mrs. Trần Thị Thu, Mrs. Hoàng Thị An, Mrs. Nguyễn Quý Hoàng Nhung, Mr. Nguyễn Xuân Tốn, Mrs. Trần Thi

Kim Khánh, Colonel Hùng Sơn, Mr. Lê Đình Toán, Mr. Nguyễn Hữu Thái and Prof. Hoàng Hoa.

Others General Cư introduced me to included Brigadier General Nguyễn Huy Văn (alias Kim Sơn, for information and maps on the Westward March), Prof. Bửu Nam (a former prince who helped in contacting Mrs. Trần Thị Thu), Prof. Hoang Thi Châu (who helped in contacting Phan Nam), Prof. Nguyen Quảng Tuân (who explained the importance of the poem "The Tale of Kiều") and Phan Thuận An (a Huế scholar), along with the work of Nguyễn Trọng Thanh (a deceased war photographer).

Most of the translations were provided with great skill and dedication by Lê Đỗ Huy, mainly from Vietnamese and Russian sources, with some French material. To do this work accurately he had to understand various forms of communism, North Vietnamese military terminology and have an immense understanding of Cold War history. This task of translation alone took years to complete. Once all this information was correlated, Lê Đỗ Huy then went back to the interviewees to ask them to clarify further points. It was this deeper probing by Lê Đỗ Huy into their personal experiences that enabled me to draw my conclusions for this book. Others who helped included Phan Mạnh Hùng, who translated some interviews conducted in Vietnam, as well as the daughter of Hồ Học Lãm and the daughter of Lý Phương Đức, who translated documents from Chinese.

In conclusion, I feel I should highlight some of the complications Clive A. Hills and I came across when preparing the maps and manuscript. One of the main difficulties was time span. The ever-changing geographical provincial boundaries and place name variations were key issues; in each case the most common names and provincial boundaries were chosen for the given period. Military ranks, aliases and names of people changed over time; in general no ranks are stated in the main text and the most commonly used name of the person has been selected throughout. To easily identify a woman in the text, a female name has been given a title when it helps the flow. When looking at established groups and who ran them, it was not always possible, for example, to accurately date the disbanding of a group—it invariably operated for a time after its official closure as a result of poor communications or because people voluntarily kept it running.

Looking at the interviewees, if their words were thought to be confusing, the person in question was asked to verify what they meant. Where possible, when their way of expressing things could be kept, it was. For example, some interviewees used "Brother" or "Sister" and these forms of address were preserved rather than substituting them for the more common title of "Comrade" for continuity. When the words "enemy" or "liberated zone" were used by those who were speaking, these expressions have been retained.

The most common abbreviation is the communists' political group name, which changed throughout the years. For continuity reasons the Indochinese Communist Party, the Vietnamese Communist Party and the Worker's Party of Vietnam are either shown in full or within the main text as the "Party" or the "Communist Party." Other abbreviations include, Chinese Kuomintang to Kuomintang (Vietnamese Kuomintang is always written in full) and Côn Đảo Island Prison to Côn Đảo Prison or Côn Đảo Island. (The prison complex is actually on Côn Sơn Island, but as this is part of the Côn Đảo archipelago it is the archipelago which gives the complex its common prison name). When a person's name is shortened, as a general rule only Hồ Chí Minh is called by his first name of Hồ; most other names of people have been shortened using their last name.

Finally, the Vietnamese requested that the names of people and places were written in Vietnamese script. This has been done. Nevertheless, where the words are very common in English and might halt the flow of reading if changed, these names have been kept in English, including Saigon, Hanoi and Vietnam.

I am confident that this book is a true guide to the highly complex story of the blueprint for revolution. Making this book has been incredibly time-consuming and extremely difficult. Some of the facts could only be gleaned face-to-face, meaning information about the early years was especially problematic to get because most of the people who were involved then had died. Nonetheless, it is the many new personal details obtained which, in fact, make this book valuable.

Preface

As a foreigner, I was given an unparalleled opportunity to work with important relatives of Hồ Chí Minh. This access has enabled me to present the first definitive explanation of the blueprint he and his fellow colleagues designed to allow them to fight and win a protracted asymmetric war against a superior power; in this case conflicts against the colonial French and the Americans and their South Vietnamese allies. Although there have been many other examples of such asymmetric conflicts, the Vietnamese model is crucial to understand because it has been tested and shown to be effective.

This study is intended to provide a comprehensive look at the blueprint; a history of French and American strategies is not given here, although sufficient detail is specified for the reader to understand the context of the blueprint. In Part I, the first chapters describe how the blueprint was designed, starting in the nineteenth century through to the Japanese occupation of Vietnam in the mid–1940s. In Part II, the succeeding chapters define the application of the blueprint during the August Revolution in 1945 when Hồ Chí Minh first came to power, the French War (1945–1954) and the famed American Vietnam War (1959–1975). The Epilogue concludes with the relevance of the blueprint today, highlighting the dangers it poses to the West.

There have been numerous other studies on the wars in Vietnam, but this book is distinctive because the story is told from the point of view of communist leader Hồ Chí Minh and also quotes the Vietnamese strategists and operatives, particularly the female couriers, who contributed so much to his blueprint. To achieve this unique perspective, the work is based mainly on the rare testimonies of key players, with direct interviews being the main source. A full list of participants as well as primary and secondary sources are listed in the Acknowledgments.

Anyone attempting to undertake this project today would find it impossible to do so; the academic research and analytical analysis have taken more than a decade to complete, with many visits to America, France, Lao and Vietnam. This dedication to detail means that most of the crucial people involved have since passed away, whereas other younger veterans may not be as open when talking to unfamiliar scholars.

I earned the respect of the war veterans because of my long association with the region. I first became interested in Indochina in the 1970s, when the Khmer Rouge were in control of Cambodia. Later my curiosity shifted to the historic events of the Vietnam War and why a so-called peasant army could defeat American forces. In the mid–1990s my attention turned to actual research and during my PhD in engineering I visited Hanoi University. Then, from 1997 to 1999 I lived in the Lao People's Democratic Republic; during this period I walked the Hồ Chí Minh Trail in Lao with Clive A. Hills, becoming the first Westerners to do so since the end of the Vietnam War. It was from this achievement that the Vietnamese expressed an interest in writing books with me.

Since 2003, I have worked with senior Vietnamese Communist Party members as well as veterans of the wars in Indochina. I have been humbled and honored to do so.

Introduction:
Hồ Chí Minh's Legacy

Hồ Chí Minh became the leading figure in the fight to gain Vietnam its independence. He designed his original blueprint to liberate the country, first from the French and then from the Americans and their South Vietnamese allies. The American Central Intelligence Agency (CIA) analyzed parts of Hồ's model of asymmetric warfare. The CIA directed the Afghan Mujahideen against the Soviet invasion. The Mujahideen taught the Taliban. The Taliban have influenced other extremist Islamic groups. Now key elements of the model are being used to try to radicalize countries. The author tells the story from Hồ's point of view of how a still-current model came to be designed and concludes why this story is very relevant today.

From an early stage in his political life, Hồ wanted to use diplomacy as a means to free Vietnam; in reality, he knew that other far more drastic measures were needed. He embarked on extensive foreign travels looking for answers, from Britain to Senegal and the United States to Algeria, and during this period his revolutionary path was set. His bold travels put him on a course that ultimately led him to design what was at that time a completely new form of warfare, a blueprint, known by him and those who worked with him as an All-People's War.

Few people understand the strategies behind Hồ's blueprint. The author, however, worked for more than a decade with people who personally knew Hồ. She interviewed war veterans and, importantly, had the opportunity to go back to re-address and scrutinize what they had said. She read personal diaries and was given access to recently declassified information from Party archives. These first-hand accounts, supported by rare documents, enabled this book to cover the development and use of the blueprint through the French colonial period, the Japanese occupation (mid–1940s), the French War (1945–1954) and the American Vietnam War (1959–1975).

To help the author begin to unlock the secrets of the blueprint, in 2006 General Nguyễn Thới Bưng, a former deputy minister of defense for Vietnam (1992–1996), introduced her to five female courier veterans at the Women's Museum of Cochinchina. Built in Hồ Chí Minh City in 1985, the museum formally recognizes the incredible role of women throughout various conflicts. Hồ had said that the couriers were fundamental for victory and because women conducted most of this work, for this reason they, and the architects that used them, have been chosen to be the connecting thread of the narrative to reveal Hồ's strategies.

General Bưng's piercing black eyes gave little away as he recounted the events of the

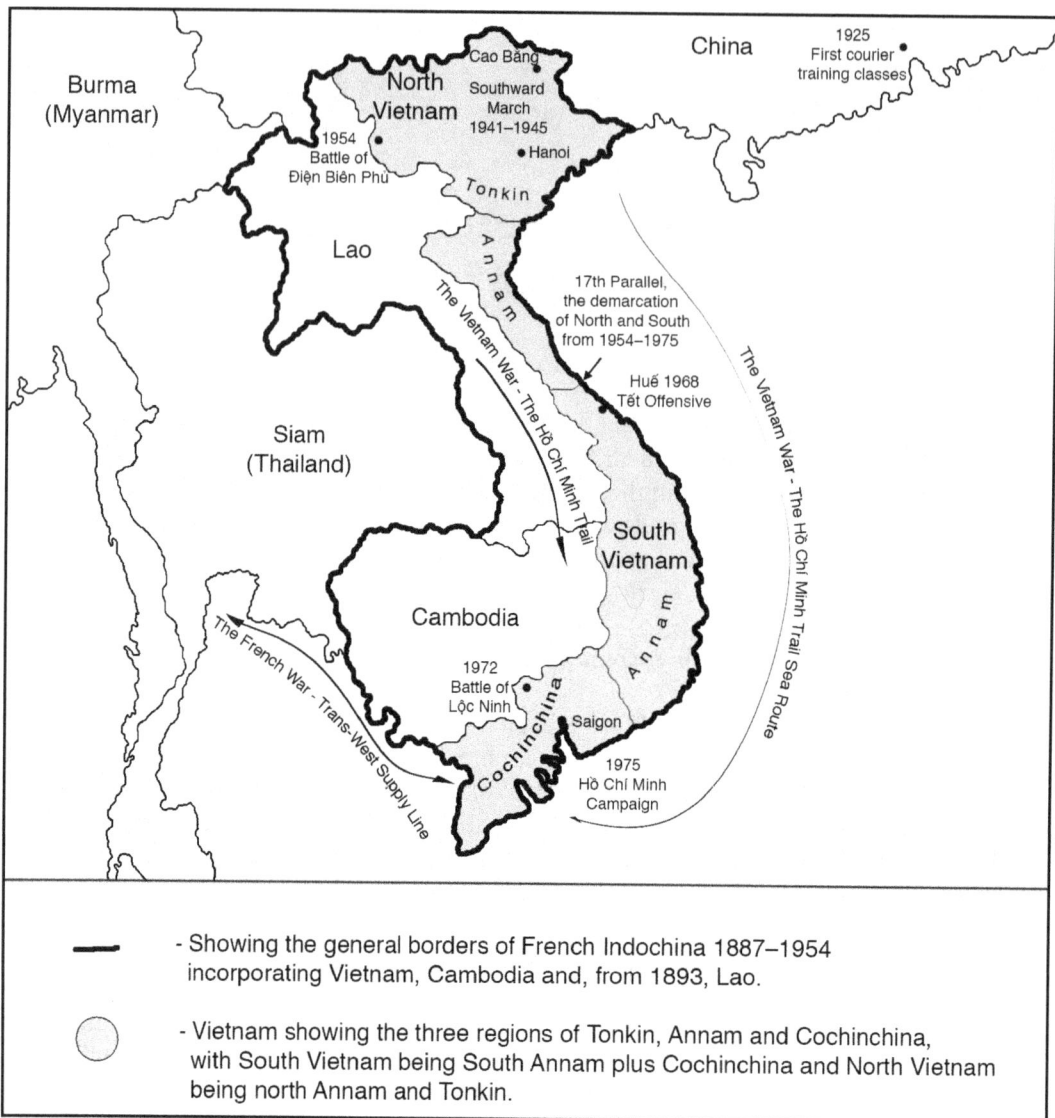

Main wartime activities, 1925 to 1975.

Vietnam War according to Party lines. Having been too young to have taken a lead role during the French War, he did play his part against the Americans, seeing Hồ's plans come to fruition. Now he had been instructed to facilitate a meeting of former couriers with the author. Behind his deadpan communist façade, you could tell he knew that the women who had agreed to speak were going to reveal the truth about some of the most compelling stories of the war era. However, one could tell by the way in which he wrung his hands, they were accounts that only heroes of the revolution could give without serious repercussion from the Vietnamese government.

The five women couriers perched delicately upon wicker seats. These former heroes greeted the author with warm smiles. Their demeanor gave few clues to the exciting, often horrific, stories they were about to tell, narratives so different from those of their

The author Virginia Morris and Clive A. Hills with their first courier interviewees, taken at the Women's Museum of Cochinchina on 15 June 2006. Sitting from left: Lê Thị Thu, Ngô Thị Huệ (widow of General Secretary Nguyễn Văn Linh) and General Nguyễn Thới Bưng. Standing from left: a member of the museum staff; Trầm Hương, a journalist; Trần Hồng Ánh, director of the Women's Museum; Võ Thị Tâm; Clive A. Hills; Lê Thị Thu Nguyệt; Đặng Hồng Dực; and Virginia Morris (Clive A. Hills).

male counterparts. They spoke about intriguing covert events, such as having to move copious numbers of weapons through enemy-held territory, to more detailed accounts including the successful planting of a bomb that led to the destruction of a military Boeing 707. They worked on what are best described as suicide assignments. What drove them to sacrifice their lives, or, more to the point, why more did not join up, are questions that can now be answered.

From interviews arranged by others at a later date came the words of those who had made use of these couriers as architects of the blueprint. They included Đào Văn Trường, one of Hồ's first guerrilla leaders, and Võ Nguyên Giáp, the supreme commander of the military. When talking to the author, Đào Văn Trường explained the difficulties they had while designing and implementing Hồ's revolutionary strategies when they had to fight both the French and Japanese in the 1940s. Giáp described the process he went through in order to develop two essential parts of the blueprint, a covert network known as the Revolutionary Infrastructure and his conventional military units. Then both men spoke of the part they played during the French War and how the revolutionaries re-established Hồ's blueprint to do it all again during the Vietnam War.

The author also interviewed Americans who had opposed the revolutionaries and fought against the spread of communism. They included men such as John Stryker Meyer, a Special Forces soldier who operated and fought along the Hồ Chí Minh Trail, and Mark A. Smith, one of the key enforcers of the notorious Phoenix Program. Meyer described how his unit had to gather intelligence, not only while being surrounded by thousands of enemy fighters, but knowing that their mission had probably been compromised. Smith spoke of how he permanently silenced hostile operatives whose names appeared on a "list."

The descriptions from all the participants changes the popular understanding of events during the various stages of the conflicts. Their detailed stories also reveal the answer to one of the most important questions: was the fight solely about the spread of communism?

Regardless of the previously unknown details in this study, countless unanswered questions on Hồ's blueprint remain unanswered. Many people who designed it have now died. Others are too old to recall their thoughts. The author's final interviewee was Lê Trọng Nghĩa, who was the former head of the Intelligence Department for both the Communist Party and the military, and who took part in major events such as the August Revolution of 1945, which saw Hồ come to power. He summarized another fundamental problem. The author had explained that she found the numerous special roles played by the couriers difficult to understand fully because there seemed to be so much information missing. He laughed and said, "Because many of the people involved were recruited and run locally by individual heads, when that head died, their network went unrecorded. Therefore, no one person will ever thoroughly grasp this paramilitary system, not even me."[1]

Hồ's legacy is the design of a new form of asymmetric warfare, which gained victory in Vietnam and opened the way for political reform across the region. There have been many other examples of asymmetric conflicts such as the American War of Independence, but what makes Hồ's blueprint important is that, although he implemented strategies and tactics that had been used previously in warfare and designed new ones, it was how he combined these and then used the population that made his unified system new.

For the world, the unwanted heritage of Hồ's blueprint or All-People's War is that he had inadvertently designed a model for fighting which is best described as a protracted asymmetric war against a superior power. The veterans who participated in this book have not only enabled a crucial part of world history to be recorded and understood, but have also unintentionally laid bare the potential threats to countries today.

PART I: ESTABLISHING THE BLUEPRINT (1890–1945)

1

The Making of a Revolutionary

Early Years

In the picturesque region of Annam, Vietnam, in 1890, a future leader was born. Known by more than 170 aliases throughout his life, he is best recognized as Hồ Chí Minh. For those who supported his way to gain Vietnam its independence, he was a hero, but those who opposed his methodology hunted him down and labeled him their "most wanted man."

Born Nguyễn Sinh Cung, Hồ was one of four children of Nguyen Sinh Sắc (1862–1929) and Ms. Hoàng Thi Loan (1868–1901). His family was raised in his father's village of Kim Liên, which typified a very poor settlement of that period, with dusty tracks leading from a large cluster of simple houses, and grubby children hanging around in dark corners getting up to no good.[1]

In 1887, just three years before Hồ's birth, French Indochina had been formed from Cambodia and Vietnam.[2] The French divided Vietnam into the two protectorates of Tonkin (north) and Annam (middle), and the colony of Cochinchina (south). Hồ's province of Nghệ An, Annam, became a region known for persistent resistance against French rule.

Poor farmers inhabited Hồ's village and, with little encouragement around them to change their impoverished situation, life remained as it had been for decades. Undeterred by this environment and the expectations of others, Hồ's father Sắc studied for a doctorate degree and became the first native of the village to achieve such a qualification. This allowed Sắc not only to educate his boys formally but he could teach them by example the power of extensive knowledge and diplomacy.

One observation by Hồ was that his father earned the admiration from his peers and the disadvantaged people because, although educated, Sắc had refused the honor of a mandarin post at the royal court of Huế to serve the emperor and took up teaching among the people instead. He told the authorities the reason was that he was still mourning the death of his wife and infant child. More probably, he did not want to align himself with the French and a corrupt royal court, saying privately to trusted friends and family, "Mandarins are slaves among slaves but their slavishness is even more than that of the slaves."[3] He meant the mandarins were slaves within the royal court whose own monarchy were slaves to the French. For his son, Hồ, the message was clear: stay loyal to your nationalist beliefs if you want to win over the people.

An elderly scholar giving village children a lesson in Chinese ideograms, a tradition that lasted until 1919 (courtesy Lê Đỗ Huy).

Learning from Phan Bội Châu

Another influence on Hồ was Phan Bội Châu (1867–1940), who had also declined a prestigious role at the royal court. A nationalist and celebrated scholar throughout the country, Châu too had an impact on Hồ through his writings and ideas.

Châu used to visit Hồ's father and the two men chatted long into fire-lit evenings about freedom and how to gain independence for Vietnam. Sắc's vision of how to free the country from a suppressive colonial grip is unknown, but it is documented that Châu believed nationalist scholars could be the catalyst. While the two men engaged in impassioned talk, Hồ busied himself with his duties or played, or simply pretended to sleep. However, all the while he was listening intently to Châu explaining his arguments and describing his experiences as a founder of various patriotic groups and his travels to foreign lands.

Châu had originally been a part of the Save the King Movement. Started in 1885, it is generally recognized as the first group to raise arms against French rule.[4] In 1904, Châu then led the group that created the Vietnam Modernization Association. They elected Prince Nguyễn Cường Để (1882–1951) as the figurehead.[5] This association became the first anti-colonial movement in Vietnam to acknowledge that the country needed to modernize. On this premise, they proposed moving from a monarchy to a constitutional monarchy.

1. The Making of a Revolutionary

An annual ceremony set up by the ruling Vietnamese Nguyễn Dynasty to elect mandarins, a tradition that lasted until 1919 (courtesy Lê Đỗ Huy).

Châu got much of his inspiration for the Vietnam Modernization Association from Japan, praising its culture through his writings and teachings. The Japanese script and race were akin to that of the Vietnamese, he said, and he wanted the Japanese to be role models for the youth of Vietnam. Although China might have appeared the more natural ally, with parts of the country being a safe haven for the Vietnamese resistance movement, Chinese power had waned in contrast to the growing strength of Japan. On these grounds, Châu ruled out asking for help from China, and remained impressed by the initial success of the Japanese in the Russo-Japanese War (1904–1905).[6]

This admiration for Japan raised an important question for Châu and other members of the Vietnam Modernization Association. They needed to know whether the Japanese would help militarily to free the Vietnamese from colonial rule by sending troops or through financial assistance, or whether they would decline to get involved. To find the answer to this question, the Vietnam Modernization Association sent Châu to Japan in 1905.[7] Đặng Tử Kính, a man known for his anti–French activities, traveled with him. Tăng Bạt Hổ acted as their courier, a man trusted implicitly by Châu because as early as 1872 and at just fourteen years old, Tăng had participated in fierce uprisings against the French.

Châu had no connections in Japan. Undaunted by this, he swiftly made contact with Liang Qichao, a Chinese activist who had taken refuge in Japan after a *coup d'état* in

China in 1898, and whose reformist writings had inspired members of the Vietnam Modernization Association. Qichao gave Châu frank and open advice about his hopes for Japanese assistance, "Once Japanese troops [have] entered within your country's borders it [will] surely be impossible to find an excuse to drive them out."[8] Qichao furthermore introduced Châu to many prominent politicians, including Okuma Shigenobu, a well-liked statesman who had previously served as prime minister of Japan for a few months in 1898. Châu asked Shigenobu for financial assistance. The Japanese government did not want to damage its own relationship with France and so refused.

From his experiences in Japan, Châu initiated the Go East Movement, aimed at encouraging the youth of Vietnam to study abroad. His idea was that the youth studying with the movement could take their newfound knowledge and external perspective on the world, and go back to Vietnam with a greater understanding of how to oppose the French. Part of Châu's thinking behind the movement came about because, although the Japanese government had said no to assistance, opposition government party members had promised financial aid to Vietnamese students wishing to study in Japan.

Châu's journey in 1905 bore other fruit to help the Go East Movement operate smoothly. While on an English ship traveling from Hải Phòng to Japan via Hong Kong, he met a cook named Lý Tuệ.[9] After talks with Châu, this new contact agreed to create a courier sea route. By the end of 1905, this route became the main and safest system for couriering, not only documents but also students, to and from Japan.[10] From 1905 to 1908, the new line carried a total of about 100 students from Tonkin and 200 from Cochinchina to the schools in Japan.[11] Eventually the French and Japanese governments suppressed the movement and expelled Châu from the country in 1909.

When in Vietnam, Châu had asked the young Hồ and his brother to join the Go East Movement. Hồ rejected the offer. Some suggest that his father persuaded him to decline based on what he had heard through his long conversations with Châu. Others say that Hồ had been influenced by Liang Qichao advising Châu not to allow Japanese troops to enter Vietnam, because later Hồ said that relying on the Japanese to oust the French could be likened to "driving the tiger out of the front door while welcoming the wolf in through the back door."[12] Châu's experience had clearly swayed Hồ's decision not to pursue the Japanese for help, but also motivated Hồ's quest to seek an alternative. Years after, Hồ wrote that he preferred to go to France to observe the secret of Western success at its source because when he had asked Châu how the Japanese had managed its own technological achievements, Châu replied, "They learned it from the West."

Hồ never joined the Go East Movement but he admired Châu's drive to liberate Vietnam. Hồ respected Châu's ability to amass support through his patriotic groups and writings, but all the while being mindful of the concepts of secrecy and security. Consequently, when former students of the Go East Movement, or close work colleagues of Châu's, wanted to join with Hồ, he took them in as trusted revolutionaries.

Useful Inheritance

Hồ Học Lãm is probably the most famous of the students Hồ inherited from Châu. For three decades Lãm worked covertly for Hồ under the disguise of a high-ranking officer in the nationalist Chinese Kuomintang Army.[13] Lãm personally knew high-up people because, for instance, in 1908 he had studied in Japan in response to the Go East

Movement.[14] In one establishment, his classmate had been Chiang Kai-shek (1887–1975), who went on to lead the Kuomintang from 1926, after the death of Sun Yat-sen (1866–1925).[15]

Nevertheless Lãm could not enjoy the privileges of his important Chinese connections. Instead he lived in daily fear, because shortly after Chiang Kai-shek took office he started to eliminate the communists and their associates. Although Lãm himself did not subscribe to communism he knew he could still become a target. He was famous among both the Vietnamese communists and nationalist parties because he put his politics aside to give cover and assistance to anyone whom he regarded as a patriot. Hồ also directed Lãm to steal information from the Kuomintang to give to the Chinese Communist Party. Hồ provided the information as a way of showing his gratitude for the many years of help he had received from Sun Yat-sen and now from members of the Chinese Communist Party.

Another example of a useful man inherited by Hồ was Lê Thiết Hùng (1908–1986). Hùng worked with Lãm as his personal Vietnamese courier from around 1930 to 1936. His cover, like Lãm, was as a Kuomintang officer. Hồ had appointed Hùng to this work because he had been one of his trainees in Guangzhou in 1926 and a loyal communist.[16] Although Hồ himself never joined the Chinese Communist Party, he had asked Hùng to enroll in 1926. This enabled Hồ to widen his group of communist allies; he also knew that Chinese Communist Party members would trust Hùng more than they did the non-communist Lãm. Hùng went on to become a central general in Hồ's revolutionary army.

Networking with Phan Chu Trinh in Paris

Highly focused and with a sense of adventure, Hồ wanted to search for a bold new approach to help liberate Vietnam. With only a primary school education behind him, on 5 June 1911 Hồ (now Văn Ba) set sail from Saigon, heading for Marseilles, France. In the following years he traveled through, and lived in, many countries, including the United States, Spain, Portugal, Algeria, Tunisia, Benin and the Congo.

On the occasion when Hồ's ship entered the port of Dakar, the capital of Senegal, a fellow passenger had recorded[17]: "At Dakar there was a great storm. The ship couldn't enter the port and the life boats couldn't be lowered into the sea. In order to make contact with the ship the French onshore forced some Africans to attempt to swim out to the ship. One, two, three then four jumped into the sea and one after another each was dragged under by the waves and drowned. It was a terrible sight for everyone on board including Ba [Hồ], who was deeply affected to such an extent that he cried. I was surprised and I asked him why? He said, 'The French in France are all good. But the French colonialists are very cruel and inhuman. It is the same everywhere. At home I witnessed similar events in Phan Rang. The French burst out laughing while our compatriots drowned for their sake. To the colonialists, the life of an Asian or an African is nothing.'"[18]

It is not known exactly when Hồ arrived back in France to settle. Vietnamese sources suggest that Hồ arrived in 1917, but French police documents record it as June 1919.[19] Hồ went to Paris to meet Phan Chu Trinh (1872–1926), a family friend and also the acknowledged leader of the Vietnamese community there.

While formulating his political ideas, Trinh lived in Paris. He had been exiled there by the French because, along with two others, Trinh had initiated the Modernization Movement.[20] Established in his native province of Quảng Nam in 1906, the group publicized the need for independence. To spread their patriotic message through peaceful means, the Modernization Movement established life improvement schemes in villages, such as economic help and education for all. Trinh was arrested in 1908 because the authorities wanted the Modernization Movement closed, and they sentenced him to life incarceration in Côn Đảo Island Prison. However, the French Human Rights Association and the French Section of the Workers' International successfully lobbied members of the French Parliament. The outcome of which meant that Trinh did not have to endure desperately grim confinement within Vietnam; instead, the colonial French authority exiled Trinh to Paris.[21]

Hồ wanted to understand fully Trinh's views on an independent Vietnam because they differed so much from those of Châu. Trinh had backed the Go East Movement, even though he opposed turning to other countries for support; instead he believed in attaining liberation by educating the population in Vietnam. Châu had also retained links to the monarchy, whereas Trinh favored French democratic principles and made it very clear that if the system of monarchical autocracy was not abolished, simply restoring the country's independence would not bring happiness.

Likewise, Trinh advocated non-violence, when Châu did not. Châu was prepared to build an army through his new Vietnamese Restoration League (1912–1925), a nationalist organization that had replaced the Vietnam Modernization Association.[22] The association had been regarded as outdated by members because its agenda focused on assistance from Japan. The new Vietnamese Restoration League took its inspiration from China's Wuchang Uprising in 1911, which served as the catalyst to the Xinhai Revolution, known as the Chinese Revolution. This action saw the end of the Qing Dynasty and in 1912, within areas controlled by the rebels, the leaders declared the Republic of China. These revolutionary acts in China inspired Châu, who now looked to develop armed units and form an interim government to create a democratic republic for Vietnam, albeit with royal connections.

On moving to Paris, Hồ wasted no time in tracking down Trinh. When Hồ arrived, the city was the scene of mass social unrest following the First World War. In such turmoil, with few jobs available for him, Hồ lived in dirty hotels and worked for long hours to make ends meet. His life improved when Trinh found a job for him as a photo retoucher in a shop managed by him. With the two of them working so closely together, they became trusted friends. Trinh introduced Hồ to Phan Văn Trường (1875–1933), another well-respected Vietnamese patriot living in France. Phan Văn Trường, now a French citizen, had trained as a lawyer and first settled in France in 1910. As he spoke French, while Trinh did not, it was he who introduced Hồ to Paris society.

Hồ enjoyed the company of both Trinh and Phan Văn Trường and they made a strong impression on him. Phan Văn Trường influenced Hồ more than Trinh because he supported Hồ's political views; remaining in contact with Hồ until Phan Văn Trường died in the 1930s. Although Hồ was more aligned to Phan Văn Trường, both Trinh and Phan Văn Trường had established movements to end French colonialism, which they discussed with Hồ. They had different styles: Phan Văn Trường was a man of action and Trinh a man of ideas. Even though neither man moved Vietnamese independence forward significantly, Hồ could see that if their skills and passion for Vietnam were nurtured correctly, they could both be very useful to him.

Hồ's First Bold Revolutionary Act

In early 1919, at the Palace of Versailles, leaders of the victorious allied powers gathered to negotiate the Treaty of Versailles, to conclude the state of war between them and Germany to end the First World War.[23]

This gathering should have been a great opportunity for nationalist groups from across the world. U.S. President Woodrow Wilson (1856–1924) issued to the conference his now famous Fourteen Point Declaration, originally announced in January 1918 in his address to the joint session of the U.S. Congress. His speech, under fourteen separate headings, formulated his ideas for the essential nature of a post–First World War settlement. He outlined a policy that included addressing self-determination for colonial countries, the removal of economic barriers between nations and the establishment of a general association of nations under specific covenants.[24] The nationalist groups liked the idea of self-determination and they issued manifestos and lobbied those at the negotiations to promote their fight for self-rule against their colonial masters.

Prince Cường Để, a close associate of Châu, had written to President Wilson on 12 February 1919.[25] His letter requested now that Germany had been defeated he should be given immediate assistance by the United States to free Vietnam from the French. It is not known whether Wilson received the letter or whether any action was taken. What is clear is that the French somehow found out, and that the letter's contents shook their colonial administration. Prince Cường Để and his cause became ever more hated.

For Hồ the negotiations at Versailles focused his mind on his message of independence. In mid–1919 he formed the Association of Annamese Patriots, calling it Annamese because the people of Tonkin, Annam and Cochinchina were often jointly addressed by this name.[26] Still relatively unknown, Hồ listed his close friends Trinh and Phan Văn Trường as the directors, with himself as the secretary. In Paris, the Association of Annamese Patriots recruited Vietnamese intellectuals and people considered to be working class; they also approached other nationalist groups seeking an end to colonial rule in their respective countries.

Hồ's new Association of Annamese Patriots submitted the document, *Demands of the Annamese People*, to those at the negotiations. It listed eight points that needed addressing, including an amnesty for all indigenous political prisoners. The document intended to appeal to the allied leaders to apply President Wilson's ideals to French colonial territories across Southeast Asia. Apparently Hồ drafted it, but Phan Văn Trường contributed by improving Hồ's then-inadequate written French. Hồ signed the *Demands of the Annamese People* as Nguyen Ái Quốc (Nguyen the Patriot) and dated the document 18 June 1919. Historians still dispute the contribution that Hồ made to the text and question the effectiveness of this petition. Some say it boosted Hồ's position among the Vietnamese community overseas, others noted his personal bravery; having put his name to it, if he were caught and extradited to Vietnam he could have been sentenced to death.

Hồ delivered the petition personally to the president of France and other key ministers of state. He received no reply from the French authorities but did receive confirmation from President Wilson's senior advisor that it had arrived. Other contacts confirmed that the document had been brought to the president's personal attention. In fact, by then Wilson had encountered strong opposition to his Fourteen Point Declaration at Versailles, so ultimately he was obliged to compromise. To preserve his prized, general association of nations, Wilson made sacrifices on many of the other thirteen points, including self-determination. This concession seriously angered the citizens of the colonies and blunted their ambitions for independence.

The *Demands of the Annamese People* did cause some agitation both in Paris and much further afield. Not only had Hồ arranged for his document to be posted to individuals and hand-delivered by activists across Paris, it was also published in the radical socialist newspaper *L'Humanité* and 6,000 copies were couriered overseas. These latter copies were distributed by sympathetic French sailors serving in the French Navy and by Vietnamese soldiers returning home after the First World War. The majority of copies ended up in Vietnam but other leaflets were sent to areas such as Madagascar (500 copies), Dahomey (400), North Africa (200) and Oceania (100).[27]

Nguyễn Viết Ty, a sailor acting as a courier for Hồ, carried his copies to Ô Cấp, Vietnam, by hiding them within layers of eggs and straw.[28] When his ship arrived he then used flour mixed with water and half-baked it, in order to form a crust over the copies. This meant that to the bystander the final results looked like normal fresh bread but for Ty the copies inside were safe. To distribute Hồ's demands, he placed the fake bread with real bread in one of the many hand baskets stacked in a sampan.[29]

This early post-war era in Paris was a turning point for Hồ and his revolutionary activities, specifically his couriers. Hồ had known about the importance of safe passage for secret documents because of his own experience as a young boy when he had acted as a messenger between his father and Châu. Furthermore, secrecy and security had been an issue during his travels. Letters that he had sent to his father in Vietnam and to Trinh in Paris had been intercepted by the *Sûreté* (French security), alerting them to his anti-colonial activities.

Hồ drew on all this invaluable first-hand experience to enable him to ensure the safe distribution of the *Demands of the Annamese People*, a landmark delivery for his couriers. For the first time, revolutionary documents had been organized, en masse, with specific intent and delivered to Vietnam. This delivery of documents by couriers ultimately set a precedent for both national and international clandestine communications as well as laying the foundations for establishing a system of legal and illegal courier liaison work.[30]

International Political Framework

These days in Paris moreover saw Hồ find his political path, a route that led back to the powerhouse of communist ideology in Moscow, and the imposing walls of the Kremlin. Hồ himself said that he changed to a radical political view, not only because of the constant harassment by the *Sûreté* but also his disillusionment with the French left wing. The *Sûreté* were clearly against his anti-colonial views. The role of the French left wing was far more entangled in colonial politics and the growth of communism.

The seeds of left-wing tendencies were already planted in Hồ before he left Vietnam in 1911. He believed that the socialists were more sympathetic to the subjugated people of the world under colonial rule. These political views developed in his mind and accompanied him to England in 1913. Here a young Hồ immersed himself in an environment of socio-economic and cultural change, a trend spreading throughout the world and forming a platform for political theories and revolution.

It is unknown whether Hồ actually visited the grave of Karl Marx (1818–1883) in Highgate Cemetery, one of the most known political theorists. Hồ worked in London at the Carlton Hotel in Pall Mall and purportedly at the Drayton Court Hotel in West Ealing, so he had a clear opportunity to visit the grave if he had wished. He definitely knew of the works of Marx because he had joined the UK Overseas Workers Association and also met communist figures such as Tom Mann (1856–1941).[31]

The Drayton Court Hotel in London (2009 photograph), where Hồ Chí Minh was supposed to have worked in 1914. It opened in 1894 as one of West Ealing's most palatial venues with vast gardens and about sixty bedrooms on offer. It has long since ceased to be a hotel and is now a busy pub with function rooms (Clive A. Hills).

In early 1919 when he was in Paris, Hồ naturally found comfort with left-wing thinkers. There he had asked Jean Longuet (1876–1938), the grandson of Marx and the chief editor of the newspaper *Le Populaire*, if he could become a trainee journalist. Longuet welcomed Hồ as they had been previously acquainted around 1917 or 1918. Longuet asked campaigner Hồ to produce articles about the horrific oppression of the Vietnamese by the French in Indochina. The friendship blossomed; Longuet became the first Frenchman to address him as "Dear Comrade" and he encouraged his political activities.

In the middle of July 1920, one of their friends gave Hồ a copy of the *L'Humanité*. Within its pages was Vladimir Ilyich Lenin's *Thesis on the National and Colonial Questions*. According to Hồ, this thesis converted him from a socialist thinker to a Leninist revolutionary. The time was right for him to absorb this new political view. He had witnessed that the Versailles conference had ended with no favorable conclusion for the oppressed citizens of colonial countries and, Hồ recognized, that when pushed too far against wider French interests, his so-called friends within the French left-wing adopted a non-committal, apathetic approach to colonial issues.

Hồ recorded on reading Lenin's thesis, "What emotion, enthusiasm, clear-sightedness and confidence it instilled in me! I was overjoyed to tears. Though sitting alone in my room, I shouted aloud as if addressing large crowds, 'Dear compatriots who are being harshly exploited! This is what we need, this is the path to our liberation.'"[32]

Lenin's thesis acknowledged the importance of the colonial countries in the larger world revolutionary scheme. It also hypothesized that, as the source of raw materials and cheap labor, the colonial countries were crucial to the ascendancy of Western capitalism. If the Western working class could ally with the oppressed people of the colonies and help them achieve independence, together they would strike an important blow against Western capitalism and support the spread of communism. Another key aspect of the thesis was the idea that during the first bourgeois stage of this colonial revolution, communists had to work with, and even within, the nationalist parties, as there was not a sufficiently large colonial working class to bring about revolution on its own. Only after the goals had been attained, with feudalism ended and national independence established, could the socialist revolution begin, led by the working class.[33]

Hô and Longuet discussed their political views and, on occasions, exchanged poignant accounts. In his memoirs, Hô writes that Longuet had told him that his grandfather loved him very much. When he was a small boy, Longuet said, they often played together, with his grandfather pretending to be a horse so he could ride him. Hô recalled that apparently when Friedrich Engels (1820–1895), a close friend of Marx, saw a young Longuet riding his grandfather he had commented, "This is a donkey riding a lion!"[34] Longuet was a donkey riding on the lion Karl Marx. For Engels or Leninists this image represented the foolish "donkey" bourgeoisie riding high on the back of the mighty "lion" laborers. Others took the words at face value: a clumsy young fool on the back of a great man. Hô interpreted these words as the foolish colonialists riding the back of the mighty suppressed nations.

Sadly, the once open friendship between Hô and Longuet soon became highly strained. Both had joined the French Section of the Workers' International, the French socialist party that had helped Trinh get to Paris. In December 1920, members went to the city of Tours to participate in the Eighteenth National Party Congress. They debated whether they should join the Third International or stay with the Second International. The First International had been founded in London in 1864, with Marx as the leader. He had to unite a variety of international left-wing socialist, communist and anarchist political groups and trade union organizations that had their roots in the working class and class struggle. The Second International was formed in Paris in 1889 and united the socialist and labor parties. It continued the majority of the work of the dissolved First International but this time excluded the still-powerful anarcho-syndicalist movement and unions. The Third International (known as the Communist International or abbreviated to Comintern) was established in 1919 under the leadership of Lenin.

Hô chose to side with Lenin and the Comintern because they offered assistance in helping to free colonial states from suppression. He recalled later how sad he felt when he noticed that even his best friend Longuet was among the leaders of the faction opposing the Comintern.[35] Longuet rejected it, saying, "I have already put forth the idea that we should protect the indigenous peoples."[36]

The decision, whether to side with the Second International or with the Comintern, split the French Section of the Workers' International. Hô left his friend Longuet and went with the majority who wanted the Comintern, becoming a founding member of the French Communist Party.[37] Others remained with the Second International and a now weakened French Section of the Workers' International.

A 2009 photograph of the final resting place of Karl Marx in Highgate Cemetery. This monument was paid for by the British Communist Party. The original resting place of Marx was paid for by Friedrich Engels and is now just a broken gravestone in the underbrush (Clive A. Hills).

Top: Hồ Chí Minh (as Nguyễn Ái Quốc) on 26 December 1920, addressing the Eighteenth National Party Congress of the French Section of the Workers' International at Tours (courtesy Lê Đỗ Huy). *Bottom:* 2007 photograph of the tomb of Nguyễn Sinh Sắc, Hồ Chí Minh's father, whose views influenced Hồ as a child. It is in Cao Lãnh City, Đồng Tháp Province (Clive A. Hills).

From now on, Hồ veered towards Lenin, viewing him as a strong political thinker with regards to the colonial question and his determination to solve it. Contrary to popular belief, Hồ did not subscribe wholly to Leninism. He was similarly persuaded by the nationalistic views of Prince Cường Để, Trinh and Châu, as well as having an ongoing admiration for the Three Principles of the People (Nationalism, Democracy and People's Well-Being) developed by Sun Yat-sen as part of a philosophy to make China a free, prosperous, and powerful nation. Nevertheless, reading Lenin's work not only moved Hồ away from the apathy of members of the French left-wing, but it also made him realize that the honorable and largely diplomatic and peaceful approaches of his fellow countrymen could not achieve independence for Vietnam.

In addition, Leninism gave Hồ the ability to gain powerful international help, which he knew he needed to achieve his goals. Sadly, Hồ never foresaw the decades of bloody war ahead. His fight for Vietnamese independence became entangled with the wider Cold War. The West rightly feared the spread of communism across Asia and they believed Hồ, his association with Lenin and his revolution, to be a threat.

What is not known is whether independence could have been achieved before the Cold War started, and if it had been, could this fact have stopped the spread of communism across Indochina? Hồ did want some form of political and social change for Vietnam, but it is unclear what he truly intended because he died before the fall of Saigon. Would he have stayed on the road to world revolution or would he have taken a detour before its end, to follow an alternative branch of socialist thinking more acceptable to the West? This question can probably never be answered, but what is known is that the new radical approach of the Comintern and Leninism, despite the misery surrounding its use, assisted Hồ in throwing the foolish colonial donkey off the mighty lion's back.

2

Hồ's Female Couriers

Role of Women

For many centuries China played a major part in Vietnam's history. Vietnam even came under Chinese rule for more than a millennium, with early independence movements from this, such as those of the Trưng Sisters starting in AD 40, being only temporarily successful.[1] The Vietnamese finally became independent from China in the tenth century. Thereafter successive Vietnamese royal dynasties flourished as the nation expanded, until the French colonized the region in the nineteenth century.

Like the Trưng Sisters before him, Hồ needed to use couriers to support his revolutionary movement, but he wanted to change the old-fashioned skill base of couriers of the past, who were merely guides or individuals who transported documents, into something more specialized. Although still referred to by the Vietnamese name *giao thông*, translated as "communications agent," his new operatives needed not only the skills of a traditional courier but also the extra abilities of fighter, spy and propagandist. It was these new so-called couriers and their courier corridors that Hồ said were the most important element for victory because they served the revolution in much the same way as blood vessels and a nervous system served the human body.[2]

Hồ spent many hours observing how his courier networks, inherited mainly from old-time revolutionary Phan Bội Châu, could be improved to meet his developing requirements. Importantly, he looked at ways to expand them. Children were an obvious choice to increase numbers and had been used as couriers before; adults simply ignored their playful inquisitive antics and so did not question their seemingly innocent movements. Hồ intended to keep the tradition and use children, but he knew that they did not suit most of the demanding positions he had in mind. Young men were another possibility, but the battlefield awaited them. This left another sizable part of the population: females.

In traditional Vietnamese society women were viewed as subordinate to men. This attitude could be summarized by two sayings. Firstly, a female must adhere to the Four Virtues of hard work, good physical appearance, appropriate speech and proper behavior. Secondly, she must adhere to the Three Submissions of childhood, marriage and widowhood, in which she was obligated to obey three masters in sequence: father, husband and eldest son.[3] An old Vietnamese expression still heard in modern Vietnam further belittled women, "One boy and you can inscribe a descendant; ten girls and you will write nil."[4] This means you can have ten girls in your family but without a boy you cannot carry on the family lineage. This almost godlike status of males gave them an unwritten carte blanche to inflict inhuman acts on women simply to get what they wanted. Such male cruelty could include bullying, sexual abuse or even selling a woman into slavery.

Hồ did not subscribe to these outdated attitudes and was a vehement advocate of women's emancipation along the lines of Soviet thinking. He had observed that women were more private, accurate, cautious, patient, better at withstanding torture and more loyal than men. Vietnamese tradition had always prepared women to fight and resist foreigners, a sacrifice summed up in the ancient proverb, "When invaders come to the house, even the women must fight." Although Vietnamese culture defined women's roles in terms of childbearing and taking care of their home and family, as defined by the Four Virtues and the Three Submissions, the need to protect their family from invaders who threatened them turned these women into warriors.

The fact that most French and Vietnamese men did not support Hồ's thinking on women enabled him to exploit this feature. In spite of the tradition of female warriors, Hồ recognized that the chauvinistic French and uneducated bigoted Vietnamese men still looked on women as incapable of operating in, or being pivotal to, a theatre of war. This meant that a female courier could get a casual job as a domestic worker in a French camp and, with her enemy in denial, gather visual or hard copy intelligence. She could then carry this material out past the apathetic male guards without great fear of being stopped and searched because society protocol dictated that men and women could not have physical contact with each other in public, even when married.

The specifics about women that Hồ had observed, and the chauvinistic traits in Vietnamese society, both made for the perfect argument as to why females could be, and must be, recruited for courier work. To persuade the numbers needed, Hồ devised a course of action. He offered high-society women, but also the vast numbers of illiterate peasant women, freedom from a feudal and a Confucian society if they joined him. Not all of Hồ's close followers wanted women's emancipation, nor did they want women working so closely with men, but he was undeterred. When Hồ eventually set up his first courier training program in China in 1925, his first trainee was a female.

The Right Credentials

To find Hồ's first courier, his fellow revolutionaries initially approached Cửu Tuấn (?–1928).[5] Living in Siam (Thailand) at the time, Tuấn was a strong-willed man with anti–French tendencies.[6] His daughter, Ms. Lý Phương Đức (1909–1986), has now been recorded by Dr. Nguyễn Văn Khoan, the author of her memoirs, as the very first official courier trained by Hồ.

In the 1910s, Ms. Đức lived with her family in Hong Ho Village, Nakhon Phanom Province, Siam. Built by her father and his colleagues, the village operated as a strategic hub linking a number of Vietnamese communities. Even after four years of being immersed in revolutionary life, Tuấn knew that he had to move the family to a region where his children could learn Chinese. He had to prepare them for any future training they might be required to do, presuming this to be in China rather than Siam owing to the strong historical links between the Vietnamese and the Chinese.

In 1920, Tuấn wanted to move his family from Hong Ho and find a village where his children could take Chinese lessons but in an area known for its anti–French activities. Some of the most capable youths from the village refused to go, only the following went:

A rare group photograph taken in 1926 showing Vietnamese soldiers in the Kuomintang Army, Vietnamese students at Whampoa Military Academy and students from Hồ Chí Minh's training courses in Guangzhou. (1) Lý Trí Thông, (2) Nguyễn Sơn, (3) presumed to be Lê Thiết Hùng, (4) Lê Hồng Phong, (5) Hồ Tùng Mậu, (6) Lý Phương Đức, (7) Lê Hồng Sơn, (8) Ngô Chính Quốc and (9) presumed to be Trương Vân Lĩnh (courtesy Nguyễn Văn Khoan).

Lý Tự Trọng (1914–1931), Tuấn's foster son, who had lived with his family from the age of three, and Ms. Lý Phương Thuận (1906–1995), his foster daughter. They both joined Tuấn's children, Ms. Đức and her brother, Lý Trí Thông (1915–199?).[7] Tuấn's eldest son, Ngô Chính Quốc, is believed to have been living away from home in China at this time.

In her memories Ms. Đức recalled:

When my family arrived at Ban Dong Village, Phichit Province, Đặng Thúc Hứa [Châu's ambassador for the Vietnamese Restoration League] built a hut for us children to have lessons in. Everyone enjoyed the community atmosphere. Children studied all day whereas the young adults worked and then studied into the evening. We learned both Chinese and *quốc ngữ* script.[8] Our peers taught us children Vietnamese, and Đặng Thúc Hứa educated us in Chinese. He was extremely strict.

My father realized that after six months of studying, our understanding of Chinese was still not proficient enough, and so he began to look for a Sino-English primary school. My father set off to Chiang Mai Province, Siam, close to the border with Burma, in order to look for a good school. He finally located a primary school that had been founded and run by a Chinese community.

My father made an appointment to see the headmaster and his deputy.[9] They told him that the school had official status and that 600 students attended it. They went on to emphasize that the teaching was of exceptional standard because when the staff had applied for their jobs, they had to pass a competitive examination in China before they left for Siam. Finally, the headmaster and his deputy offered us a place at the school, free of fees, as if we had been children of a local poor Chinese family. In fact, they knew that we were children of Vietnamese patriots but they wanted to help.[10]

The family moved to Chiang Mai in the autumn of 1921. While the four children studied and learned, both Tuấn and his wife worked as cake sellers to make ends meet, from 4 a.m. to 10 p.m. Then, at the start of 1924, loyal patriot Phan Bội Châu sent Lê Hồng Sơn to Siam from China to live and observe the family for six months, before moving on to Vietnam. Ms. Đức's father, Tuấn, acted as his courier for the long arduous journey to Siam.

Hồ became aware of Tuấn when the former arrived in Guangzhou and, in December 1924, Châu gave Hồ a confidential list of established revolutionaries. On the list, Hồ paid great attention to Châu's lieutenants in China. Hồ then turned to those who now lived in Siam because they had built a powerbase in the region, since being forced into exile after their involvement in the Save the King Movement in the provinces of Nghệ An and Hà Tĩnh.[11] Hồ trusted the movement, he had heard stories about it as a child including one from his teacher whose own brother had been actively involved. Tuấn was a perfect choice to help find Hồ's first couriers, not only because of his involvement in the Save the King Movement but because his family lived in Siam, and his children studied at a Chinese school and learned English.[12]

Ms. Đức explained in her memoirs:

> My journey to being a female courier of Uncle Hồ started at the beginning of 1925. Brother Lê Hồng Sơn was back in Guangzhou and speaking to Brother Hồ Tùng Mậu.[13] Uncle Hồ overheard them saying, "In Chiang Mai there are some children who are actively working for the revolution under the guidance of Tuấn and Đặng Thúc Hứa." Uncle immediately sent my brother, Ngô Chinh Quốc, to Siam in order to take us to Guangzhou.
>
> I remember the events of the summer of 1925 vividly. Ms. Thuận and I had just completed primary school. Lý Trí Thông and Lý Tự Trọng had moved to the 6th grade. Our group of six from Siam included us four as well as Lý Thúc Chất [1911–194?] and Lý Thúc Tự [1912–194?]. When we arrived in Guangzhou Lý Văn Minh joined us as the seventh person.[14]

Ms. Đức recollected that she had been told some time later that the night before they had all left for Guangzhou, her mother had cried herself to sleep. Her mother understood why the group had to go, but her heart ached because they were all so young, some not yet even in their teens.

Ms. Đức said:

> My father held a magnificent banquet to see us off. Đặng Thúc Hứa and some others were invited to it. My headmaster gave a rousing speech to the representatives of the local Chinese Overseas Association. In the speech he stressed that we must go to the Fatherland [China] to study at the teacher training college for three years. Then, on our return to Siam, we must then teach at the local school. "This will be an incredible achievement, especially for the girls," he had said, because women did not do this type of work at that time. Those of us who later left for China knew that his speech was a cover for us revolutionaries. It was delivered so convincingly that everyone cheered and tried to give my father money to support our landmark studies. Yet he refused to take it, knowing that this groundbreaking act was a smokescreen for other work.
>
> To give us safe passage, we had a letter of recommendation from our headmaster. It explained that, as overseas Chinese children returning home in order to study, we must be allowed to travel. The letter enabled us to buy tickets, first to travel on a train from Pacnampho Town to Bangkok and then by ship to Guangzhou.[15] After eight days of travel we reached Guangzhou. It was June 1925.[16]

Tuấn took a long-term approach when it came to the education of his children for the revolution. Hồ always said that the war of independence would be protracted. With both men understanding the need for long-term planning, this careful selection of candidates gave Hồ solid foundations on which to build his revolution.

Sustainable Training Program

Hồ needed his new trainees specifically to serve members of the emerging Vietnamese Revolutionary Youth League (Vietnamese RYL, 1925–1929).[17] In the words of Ms. Đức, they were raised as the "first communist children of Uncle Hồ."[18]

Ms. Đức recalled:

> As the work ahead was highly skilled, Comrade Wang [Hồ Chí Minh] trained Ms. Thuận, Lý Trí Thong, Lý Tự Trọng and me personally. I remember how he began our first session by opening a map of Guangzhou and asking us to pinpoint where we now lived and worked. Once we had done this, Comrade Wang then went on to explain how to reach these locations via alternative routes, so that the enemy could not detect a pattern in our movements. He then asked us to find other key locations, such as news-stands, parks and theatres. This gave us a variety of meeting points, to completely confuse the enemy.
>
> On one of our practical exercises, Comrade Wang told us to buy newspapers and magazines from a variety of outlets, while adhering to rigid time schedules. Upon our return, Comrade Wang gave us remarks such as, "Stopped too long at this crossroad, you looked uncomfortable when buying the newspaper, and when faced with an acquaintance you failed to hide the fact that you knew them…" He also stressed other points such as that when going to or from a place we must use the fastest and safest way, minimize the number of people involved, and when a message needed a reply, where possible the answer should be returned via a different route.[19]

Even when Hồ's students were taking a break, going out with friends, Hồ tested them. On their first Lunar New Year, Hồ arranged for Ms. Đức and her brothers and sister, Thông, Trọng and Ms. Thuận, to see the Lion and Dragon Dance performance in town. They had all been so excited, Ms. Đức recalled. They had gone with Lê Hồng Sơn, now a trusted colleague. However, sometime during the outing, he purposely lost Ms. Đức, Ms. Thuận and Trọng in the crowds, on the instructions of Hồ, who wanted to test how the group would handle themselves in a foreign environment, going from a happy comfortable atmosphere to one of panic. They all got back safety, and during their debrief Hồ congratulated them. Hồ likewise asked each of them a question, "Did you notice anyone following you?" Each had said they had not. Although Hồ had praised them, he knew that they had all failed to realize that Hồ Tùng Mậu had trailed them back.

Ms. Đức continued:

> Every tiny fault they spotted. Once, Lê Hồng Sơn gave us each a mysteriously styled bag, consisting of many pockets [for carrying documents]. With so many compartments to sort out, we embroidered a label on each pocket to help us remember what it held. When Comrade Wang arrived at our next training session, he asked to see our new bags. Innocently we proudly showed him our ordered compartments, only for him to tell us firmly that by tampering with the bag in such a way we had left ourselves wide open and easily identifiable if under surveillance. We had seriously compromised ourselves. He showed us firstly how to arrange and tidy our bags in an orderly fashion and secondly how to keep the coded documents safe inside. This second point meant disguising the secret documents as schoolbooks and notebooks written in Chinese, so if the Chinese police searched us, they could not find anything suspicious.
>
> Furthermore, our memories had to be perfect. One such example is that I had to remember coded sentences passed on to me by a stranger, who then instructed me to pass them on to a person wearing a coat of a certain color, in a named park, who was reading a newspaper…. In another instance, I was asked to meet someone disembarking from a carriage of a train, wearing a particular hat…. Once contact had been made, I helped them out of the train, all the while having to remember exactly what message the stranger had whispered to me. This was a complicated process, because the passwords or message might be in a number of different languages, depending on where the visitor came from; many were Comintern functionaries who had been sent to the Far East.[20]

We all felt that the course had been too complicated and we had failed, until we received feedback from one difficult covert mission. Comrade Wang had called to see Ms. Thuận, Lý Tự Trọng and me urgently, one after the other. He informed us all individually that there were credible rumors that someone had been killed near the Soviet Consulate. We had to go there quickly and collect intelligence about the incident, as well as to take a piece of evidence away from the scene. We then all met Lê Hồng Sơn, again independently, and he gave us all a sanitary towel, saying that this made the collection of blood more practical if that was our chosen piece of evidence. Each of us selected our own routes and set off at different times and by various means. It was spring, and I distinctly remember all these years later that some parts of my chosen route were lit well and full of people, while others were dark and deserted. On returning, each of us managed to show that we had reached the given location and come back safely. We all produced our sanitary towel soaked in the blood left from the victim, we had done well.[21]

To further assess his students, Hồ asked his recruits to deliver a newspaper called *Youth* issued by the Vietnamese RYL, which they did successfully. In July 1925, he instructed them to enroll in a traditional Chinese government-run school of some 3,000 pupils; they soon led the revolutionary movement covertly among the pupils there.

Once trained, what made the first tranche of students so important to Hồ was not only had they acquired the new courier skills of professional guide, fighter, spy and propagandist but they spoke various languages as if they were their own native tongues. Now they could communicate clearly with Comintern apparatchiks, Chinese Communist Party members and with people in other countries in Southeast Asia where the Comintern had cast its net; Ms. Thuận eventually became fluent in English, French, Thai, Chinese and Vietnamese. It was this combined skill base that enabled Hồ to extend the reach of the Vietnamese RYL swiftly.

Official Courier Categories

Hồ's first students graduated from his training course and, from this skill base, Hồ founded the first regular courier networks for the revolution. How these networks would be run was hinted at in a letter Hồ had written on 19 September 1924 to Albert Treint (1889–1971), a Comintern functionary. It read, "I need to work more or less illegally in this place as it is full of French *Sûreté* agents."[22]

The start of legal and illegal courier operations dated back to 1919 and the distribution of the *Demands of the Annamese People*, but at that point there was no official distinction between these groupings. It was only in the late 1930s that two formal sections started to emerge: one comprised illegal operatives and the second had both legal and semi-legal operatives.

Those acting legally outnumbered the semi-legal and illegal operatives. They were given the name "legal" because they functioned using identification permits issued unwittingly by their opponents. A good example of one of these operatives during the Vietnam War was Nguyễn Văn Lém (alias Lốp the Seventh or Tyre the Seventh).[23] He and his wife traded car tires ("tyres," hence one of his aliases), and he was authorized to do so with a permit issued by the Saigon authorities, his enemy. This cover gave him a relatively free hand to smuggle weapons and explosives for the revolutionaries within various shipments of tires.

The "semi-legal" aspect was much less common. These people worked as legal couriers; what gave them their semi-legal status was that a person or persons with whom they worked knew that they were revolutionaries or had links to them. Their work colleagues used these semi-legal couriers to liaise with the revolutionaries, to pass on or receive information or to help negotiations. It was highly dangerous work because the semi-legal courier could be arrested by the enemy at any time, if his or her services became surplus to requirements. Their numbers peaked at key times, such as from 1936 to 1939, because in 1936 the Popular Front (an alliance of left-wing movements) came into office in France, meaning that the known communists in Vietnam could operate more openly for a time. The semi-legal courier operated openly again for a short period after the French War had ended, from the end of 1954 to the beginning of 1955, in anticipation of the promised elections to unify North and South Vietnam. Their numbers again increased during the Vietnam War; one time period was prior to the start of the Tết Offensive in 1968, when the National Liberation Front (NLF) in South Vietnam sent messengers to the U.S. Embassy in Saigon to start negotiations with the Americans. Semi-legal operatives again became important prior to the fall of Saigon in 1975, when they had to probe in order to gauge U.S. reintervention.

Operatives who worked as couriers "illegally" carried out duties that had less everyday contact with their opponents and generally worked at night. This illegal grouping guided and guarded their comrades but were also instructed to fight to the death to protect them if needed. Prior to this illegal status they had typically worked legally or semi-legally but had since been flushed out by the enemy. In the main, they could not just move to another region of Vietnam where their faces were not known or be issued new fake identification papers because these couriers still had to use their knowledge of the local terrain. Although this group always existed, it only became especially widespread and clearly defined during the Vietnam War, when the American computer data files on individuals made using multiple identities, or working with fake identification, harder.

These official groupings enabled couriers to operate and penetrate every area of society. When looking at Hồ's first communist children, Ms. Thuận, for instance, acted as a legal courier gathering intelligence under the guise of a hostess in a hotel in Hanoi, frequented by Kuomintang officers. She had taken the role because at the end of 1945 Hồ had recommended that she became one of the first secret policewomen of the Việt Minh.[24]

In contrast to Ms. Thuận's long revolutionary life, in 1931 Lý Tự Trọng died, the first in the original group trained by Hồ to do so. He had been arrested by the Sûreté as he tried to keep them from Phan Bôi (1911–1947), a communist, who at the time was delivering a revolutionary speech in Saigon.[25] At his trial, Trọng announced to the courtroom, "The only path for the youth is that of revolution, there is no other way." When walking to the guillotine, he sang the "Internationale."[26] Today, sites around Vietnam have roads named in his honor and parks have statues of him. His death was a massive loss for the revolution because by the time the French executed him, he had become responsible for controlling a large number of courier lines for the Comintern. He died for the cause when just seventeen, the first of many couriers to do so.

The exact numbers of people who worked as couriers of all kinds throughout the wars is unknown. This is not only because there were high casualty rates but self-imposed survivor's guilt and an inability by the personnel involved to truly understand their own crucial importance, gave them a profound reluctance to talk. Those who did want to disclose their role could not do so because they were forbidden by the Vietnamese equivalent of the UK's Official Secrets Act. Now many have since died.

On a practical level, the majority of revolutionaries became couriers in one or more of the categories at one time or another during their careers. Nevertheless, it was unpaid peasant women who were by far in the majority. The overall network peaked through the French War but then reduced in size as advanced technology became more available, but couriers were always retained for security reasons because radio signals, for example, could still be intercepted. Despite fluctuations, during the period from 1925 to 1975 the total numbers ran into hundreds of thousands and covered areas such as Indochina, China, Hong Kong, Siam (Thailand), Malaysia and Japan.

The Bond of Kinship

When studying the details of the first communist children of Hồ, it is clear why they became such strong links in the revolutionary chain: they were all either actual relatives or part of his wider extended family.

Take for example, Lý Thúc Tự, who went to Guangzhou with Ms. Đức. Vietnamese and Soviet sources say that the real name of Lý Thúc Tự was Hoàng Tự, and that he originated from Hoàng Trù Hamlet, in Kim Liên Village. This made him a direct descendant of the Hoàng, the clan of Hồ's mother. Another distant relative of Hồ's was Lý Thúc Chắt; both men were born in the same district.[27]

Continuing the theme of lineage, it can now be seen why Ms. Đức became Hồ's first courier. From records her family is linked to Hồ's extended family in many ways; Hồ Học Lãm being the uniting person.

The first link was the father-in-law of Hồ Học Lãm, a man known as Ngô Quảng, and a famous general who worked with Phan Đình Phùng during the Save the King Movement. This was the same movement that Ms. Đức's father, Tuấn, fought in. Consequently, father and father-in-law knew each other well. When Tuấn moved to Siam and his son was born, Ngô Quảng adopted the child and he lived with his family. At this point Ngô Quảng's alias was Ngô Chính, a name that he gave in part to his newly adopted son, Ngô Chính Quốc.

A further connection came via Trần Thị Trâm (alias Mrs. Silk, 1860–1930), the mother of Hồ Học Lãm. Trâm used to be an important courier for Phan Đình Phùng, supplying him with weapons and crucial documents. She smuggled them concealed under rolls of cloth and silk and then, to help her cover, she sold the rolls as she traveled on to Siam or China. Trâm was such a trusted revolutionary that she became the adoptive mother of Nguyễn Thị Thanh, the sister of Hồ.

So the link between Hồ Chí Minh and Ms. Đức is: Hồ—Thanh (Hồ's sister)—Trâm (adoptive mother to Thanh and mother to Lãm)—Hồ Học Lãm—Quảng (Lãm's father-in-law)—Quốc (Quảng's adopted son)—Đức (Quốc's sister).

Typically, Hồ's first female courier, Ms. Đức, never knew her father's true name was Hà Huy Tuấn (not Cựu Tuấn). She found out only when she met historian Dr. Nguyễn Văn Khoan in the 1980s. If her father's full background could be examined there would probably be further links to other noted people; this too would be the case of many celebrated revolutionaries.

Wife and Mother

Clearly not all couriers were related to Hồ. The communists had to look outside the direct lineage of senior revolutionaries to increase their courier numbers. Ms. Trần Thị

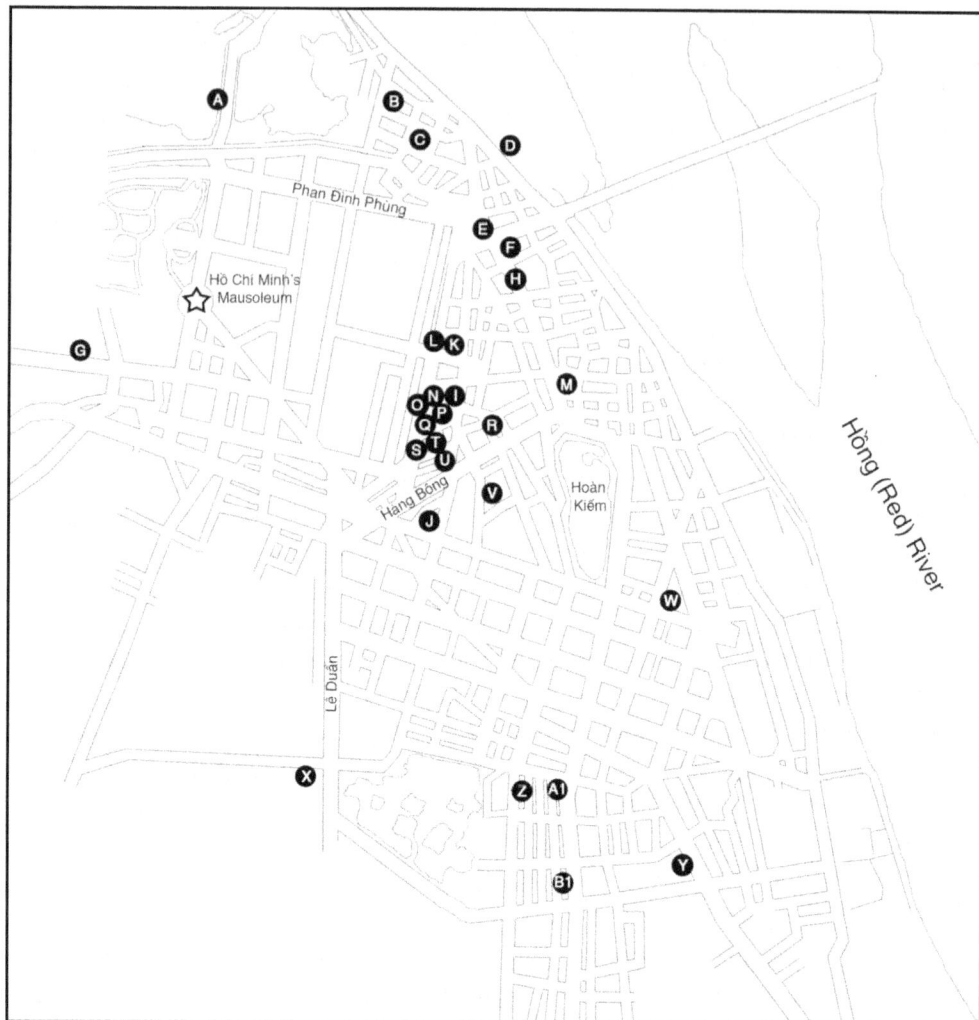

A - Ave. Marechal Lyautey (now Thanh Niên Street) - In May 1940 Võ Nguyên Giáp bid his final farewell to his wife Nguyễn Thị Quang Thái from here before leaving for China with Minh the Teacher. This location was also a meeting place for cells of the Indochinese Democratic Youth.

B - Ave. Đỗ Hữu Vị (now Cửa Bắc Street - Northern Gate) - This was the location of the central power plant and it was here that Lương Khánh Thiện built the main cell of his courier network in the late 1930s. Born in 1903 he joined the Vietnamese RYL in 1927. He was jailed in Côn Đảo Island Prison from 1930 to 1936. On his release he became a member of the Tonkin Regional Party Committee and then the secretary of the Hanoi City Party Committee until 1940. He then moved to Hải Phòng to be secretary there, after which he was arrested by the French. He had two death sentences handed to him. The French allowed the family to pay for one to be lifted. He was therefore executed in September 1941.

C - 40 Rue de Vermicels (now Hàng Bún - Rice Noodles) - A safe house for Lương Khánh Thiện from 1936 to 1939.

D - Phúc Xá (Indian Corn Plain) - A safe house of Mr. San and used by Nguyễn Văn Cừ from 1936 to 1940. Nguyễn Văn Cừ (1912–1941) was the general secretary of the Indochinese Communist Party from 1938 to 1940, until he was arrested in 1940 and executed by the French in 1941.

E - 11 Rue de Takou (now Hàng Cót - Bamboo Mat St.) - Office of the editorial board of *Hồn Trẻ Tập Mới* (*Soul of Youth*, new edition) which published twelve issues starting from No. 1 on 5 June 1936 to finishing with No. 12 on 27 August 1936.

F - Rue du Papier - Nguyễn Văn Cừ worked in a laundry, named Nam Hải along this street, as a cover to conduct his covert activities.

G - Gia Thịnh Alley on Route Du Champs de Course (now Đội Cấn St.) - The house of Mrs. Nam; the mother of Nguyễn Văn Đắc who was a trainee in Guangzhou but later killed by the French. He conducted some of his covert work from this address.

Above and opposite: **Clandestine and semi-legal networks of the Indochinese Communist Party in Hanoi (mid-1936 to 1939).**

H - Rue du Riz (now Đồng Xuân Street) – Đồng Xuân Bookshop was both a courier station and publishing house between 1936 to 1939. It was used to import Soviet literature from Paris, which was then distributed across Vietnam, and it printed some of Võ Nguyên Giáp's books at the time. It had branches in Lao and Cambodia.
Ms. Trần Thị Nguyệt Lãng operated from Đồng Xuân Bookshop in 1938, and when there, established the first courier lines in the south of Hanoi. She married Đào Duy Kỳ. Prior to this he was the leader of the Indochinese Democratic Youth at Thăng Long School, where in May 1938, his workers numbered some 100 students, after in 1941 he became the secretary of the Tonkin Regional Party Committee. When she married she was known as Mrs. Minh Châu (the Americans called her Minh Chou). In early 1944 she led the first female guerrilla team as part of the National Salvation Troops and in May 1945 she headed the cabinet at Tân Trào when the OSS team were present.

I - 21 Rue de la Citadelle (Street of the Citadel - now Đường Thành) - One of the places for the editorial board of Le Travail, for issues No. 24 to No. 30, with 30 being the last. For issues No.1 to No. 23 the editorial board was in a corner house at 24 Phạm Phú Thứ Street (now Nguyễn Quang Bích Street) and 28 Nguyễn Trãi Street (now Nguyễn Văn Tố Street). This paper operated from 16 Sep. 1936 to 16 April 1937 and was important because from it came the name, Le Travail Group; the French knew them as an organ of the communists.

J - 30 Rue Richeau (now Quán Sứ Street) - Location for the editorial board of Rassemblement. This weekly publication released five issues from 16 March 1937 until 4 May 1937 under the direction of Phan Tử Nghĩa.

K - 35 Rue de Eloffs (now Hàng Vải Street) - From 20 August 1937 to 29 October 1937 this was the editorial office of En Avant.

L - 105 Boulevard Henry d'Orlean (now Phùng Hưng Street) - From 10 April 1938 to 30 April 1938 this was the editorial office of Tin Tức (News) the paper of the Indochinese Democratic Front/Indochinese Communist Party.

M - Rue des Changeurs (Street of Silversmiths, now Hàng Bạc Street) - A hiding place for General Secretary Trường Chinh.

N - 6A Rue de la Citadelle (now Đường Thành) - One of the places for the editorial board of Bạn Dân (People's Friend). The manager was Đào Duy Kỳ for issues No. 1 to No. 29, first published on 24 April 1937 to November 1937. Then Kỳ left so it no longer served the revolution and the numbering started from issue No. 1 again.

O - 14 Phạm Phú Thứ - One of the places for the editorial board of Thế Giới (The World), with the chief editor being Đào Văn Trường. Issues No. 2 to No. 14 were published at this address. Issue No. 1 was published on 15 September 1938 at 7B Nhà Thương Khách Street (now Hòe Nhai). A further four issues were published after No. 14, at various addresses, on 1 August, 17 August, 25 August and 13 September 1939.

P - 16A Rue de la Citadelle (now Đường Thành) - One of the places for the editorial board of Đời Nay (This Life). There were a total of thirty-eight issues from 1 December 1938 until September 1939. Prior to this it was not a revolutionary newspaper.

Q - 44 Nguyễn Trãi (now Nguyễn Văn Tố Street) - The second location for the editorial board of Notre Voix, which published issues No. 19 to No. 32, the last edition being on 25 August 1939. Notre Voix was first published on 1 January 1939, from 18 Boulevard Douderd de Lagree for a total of eighteen issues.

R - 1 Rue de Stores (now Hàng Mành Street) - The barbershop located here was owned by Nguyễn Bá Song and used as a courier station by the Hanoi City Party Committee. Hoàng Văn Thụ worked undercover on the shop floor fanning clients with punkahs, all the while taking in customer gossip.

S - Location for the publication Tiếng Trẻ (Youth Voice) a weekly newspaper. Although issued before December 1936 it was not until 22 December 1936 that it was first published as a revolutionary paper. It continued for five issues until 19 January 1937.

T - Thăng Long School - This is where Võ Nguyên Giáp's professors worked until 1945, when many of them joined Hồ Chí Minh's government. Thăng Long School was founded by radical intellectuals and revolutionaries such as Phan Thanh, Hoàng Minh Giám, Đặng Thai Mai and Võ Nguyên Giáp, later they invited Bùi Kỳ to teach there.

U - 40 Rue de Cuirs (now Hàng Da) - Location for the publication Thời Thế (Times) a weekly paper managed by Trần Đình Tri. It was first issued as a revolutionary paper on 30 October 1937 and the last issue, No. 13, was published on 12 February 1938 from 69 Boulevard Rolland (now Hai Bà Trưng Street). Before the issue on 30 October 1937 it was not a revolutionary paper.

V - 49 Rue de Julien Blanc (now Phủ Doãn Street) - One of the locations of the editorial board of Hà Thành Thời Báo, and where issues No. 34 to No. 38 were published. Prior to this it was located at 16 Nguyễn Trãi (now Hai Ba Trung Street) for issues No. 1 to No. 33. After, issues No. 39 to No. 45 were published from No. 60 Boulevard Rollands (now Hai Bà Trưng Street).

W - Rue Paul Bert (now Tràng Tiền) - Location of the Taupin Printing House a clandestine base for supplying materials for revolutionary newspapers. Today the building is the French Cultural Centre.

X - Alley Khâm Thiên Market, Lane 2 (now Ngõ Chợ Khâm Thiên) - A safe house for Hoàng Văn Thụ from 1938 to 1939.

Y - Boulevard Armand Rousseau (now Lò Đúc Street) - Another safe house for Hoàng Văn Thụ, used towards the end of 1938. Situated near the Hanoi Winery, he lived here with Phí Văn Bái's relatives and Phí Văn Bái himself, before moving to a house in Rue Duvigneau. Hoàng Văn Thụ would continue to visit through 1938 and 1939 until Bái was arrested.

Z - Rue Duvigneau (now Bùi Thị Xuân Street) - Another safe house for Hoàng Văn Thụ who lived on the second floor from the end of 1938 until October 1939. He shared the accommodation with three members of the Indochinese Democratic Youth: Phí Văn Bái, who acted as his bodyguard but also worked as a clerk to earn money for food, and Kiều Văn Tu and Ms. Trần Thị Thanh who were both students at Thăng Long (where Võ Nguyên Giáp currently taught). Ms. Trần Thị Nguyệt Lãng came and lived there from September 1939 when she had to leave Đồng Xuân Bookshop because the French had discovered it as a revolutionary hub.

A1 - 22 Route de Hue (now Huế Street) - Another safe house used by Hoàng Văn Thụ from October 1939 to December 1939 after Rue Duvigneau had been discovered by the French. It was very convenient as there was a secret room at the back of the house. To protect the others at Rue Duvigneau, in October 1939 Hoàng Văn Thụ summoned Bái, Tu, Thanh and Lãng to a meeting and told them to disperse from Rue Duvigneau. Bái moved in with Hoàng Văn Thụ at Route de Hue with other revolutionaries, but in late 1939, the French Police raided this house and arrested everyone but Hoàng Văn Thụ who was able to escape.

B1 - 200 Route de Hue – The location of Bình Minh Bookshop and courier station from 1942. Vũ Quý used this address as a meeting place for members of the Indochinese Democratic Youth.

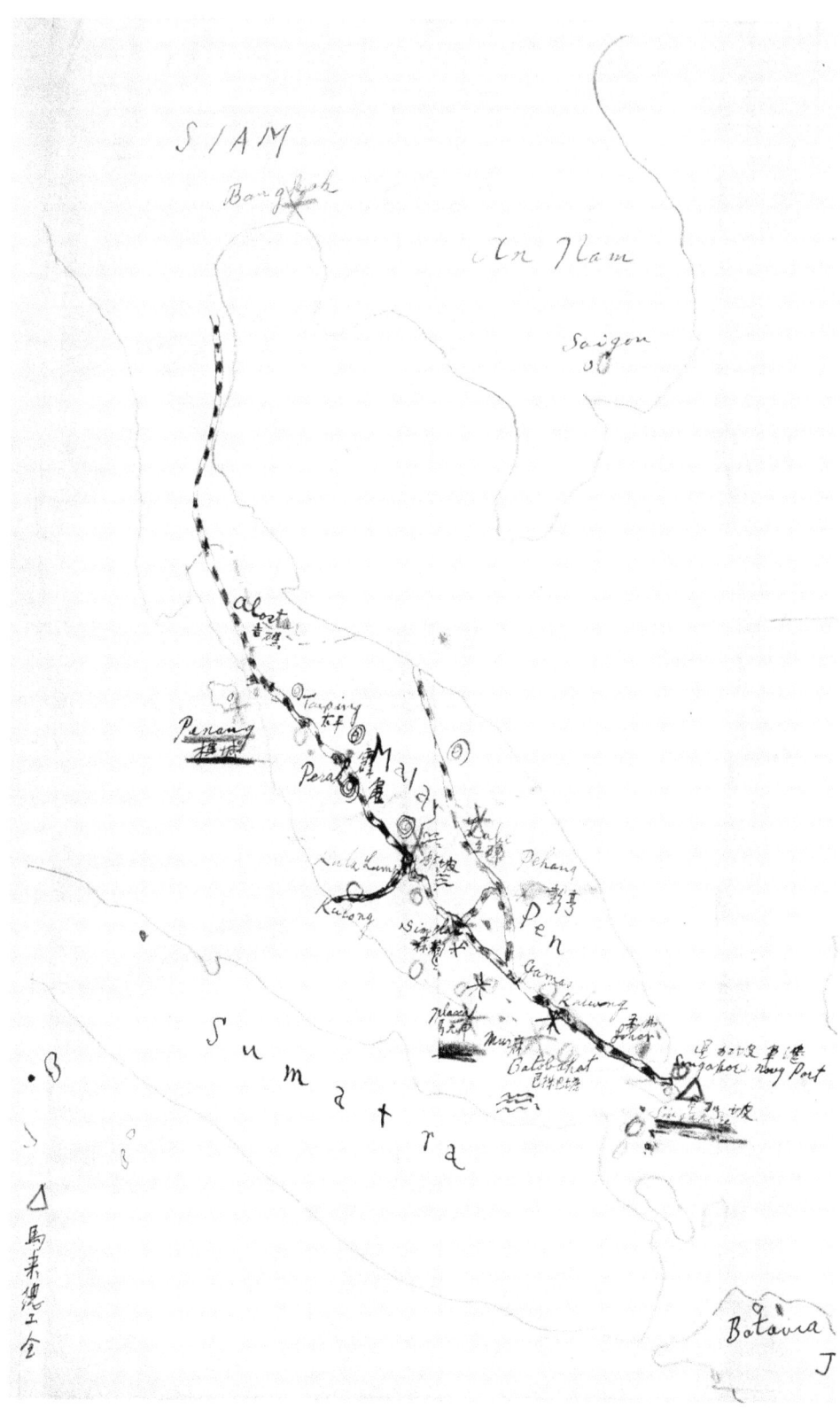

Sáu (191?–198?) was brought into the flock through the intensive education program offered to peasants. Her rare story highlights the complexities of being a family lady.

Ms. Sáu lived in the suburbs of Hanoi in Liên Mạc Hamlet, nestled on the bank of the Red River, which is today a leafy inner-city area. Her family was the poorest living there and the hamlet itself the most deprived, when compared to the neighboring hamlets of Chèm and Hoàng.[28] She married a good-natured man called Ba, but he had no wealth, not even paddy fields, and therefore lacked the ability to grow rice, so the family often went hungry. Remarkably, unlike many other men, he never drank or argued with anyone. This rare sobriety and peacefulness did not help the desperate situation for Ms. Sáu, who just wanted to continue her education.

While still single, Ms. Sáu had made friends with a literate woman whom she asked to teach her to read. According to Ms. Sáu's own memoirs, she learned fast and within twenty days she could understand basic written Vietnamese. Having taken the decision to better herself, Ms. Sáu now began to experience the prejudices that most women in Vietnam faced under a Confucian feudal system. In her case, the youngsters in her village began to speak ill of her saying, "We know your reasons. When girls study hard it is only because they want to know how to write love letters to boys!"[29] For these belittling sexist reasons, Ms. Sáu's father banned her from continuing to study. Fortunately for Ms. Sáu, her mentor ignored this prohibition and carried on secretly giving her books to read.

Both educated and married, Ms. Sáu could not live her life in limbo; she wanted to move to a Buddhist temple. To appease her husband into agreeing, she looked for a second wife for him. The perfect opportunity arose when she met a woman working for an abusive employer as a wet nurse in Hanoi. This woman agreed to the marriage and Ms. Sáu made plans to leave home. Just prior to her exit, Ms. Sáu's conscience struck, and she chose to pay the family debt off before departing. Unfortunately, adding to the pressures of living, wife number two had a child, a baby girl named Sự, and when she was just six months old her mother upped and left, leaving Sự and with no forwarding contact details. Further anchoring Ms. Sáu to the village was the horrific famine of the early 1930s, because at this time she acquired her second daughter, Dzung, when a woman begged her to take her baby.

This persistent state of poverty and famine took its toll on society, playing into the hands of Hồ's patriots. In Ms. Sáu's case it was her brother, Tuy, who became the first to be awakened to revolutionary ideas and in 1936 he brought Mr. Hét to her house. Mr. Hét enticed Ms. Sáu over by offering her literature; sometimes this was in the form of poetry written by revolutionaries, and she recalled, "I still remember these poems by heart, decades on."[30] She went on to note that, "Mr. Hét also sat down and explained to me why my family was in grinding poverty, why we had to pay high taxes and fees to the French, and why we had no fields to grow rice. He said that, 'I must love my country.' After reading and hearing what he had to say, over time things became very clear. One day, Mr. Hét said, 'You must work.' 'For what?' I asked. 'For the revolution.' 'Me, a woman?' 'Yes even women can be involved.' So I started my life as a revolutionary."[31]

The recruitment of Ms. Sáu was similar to that of Ms. Đức, and was conducted via

Opposite: When Hồ Chí Minh was arrested in mid-1931 in Hong Kong he was responsible for Comintern duties in Malaysia. This map shows his underground network within the Sumatra region. Although the map does not have any signature, it has been authenticated through his writings by the Hồ Chí Minh Museum, Hanoi (courtesy National Archives UK).

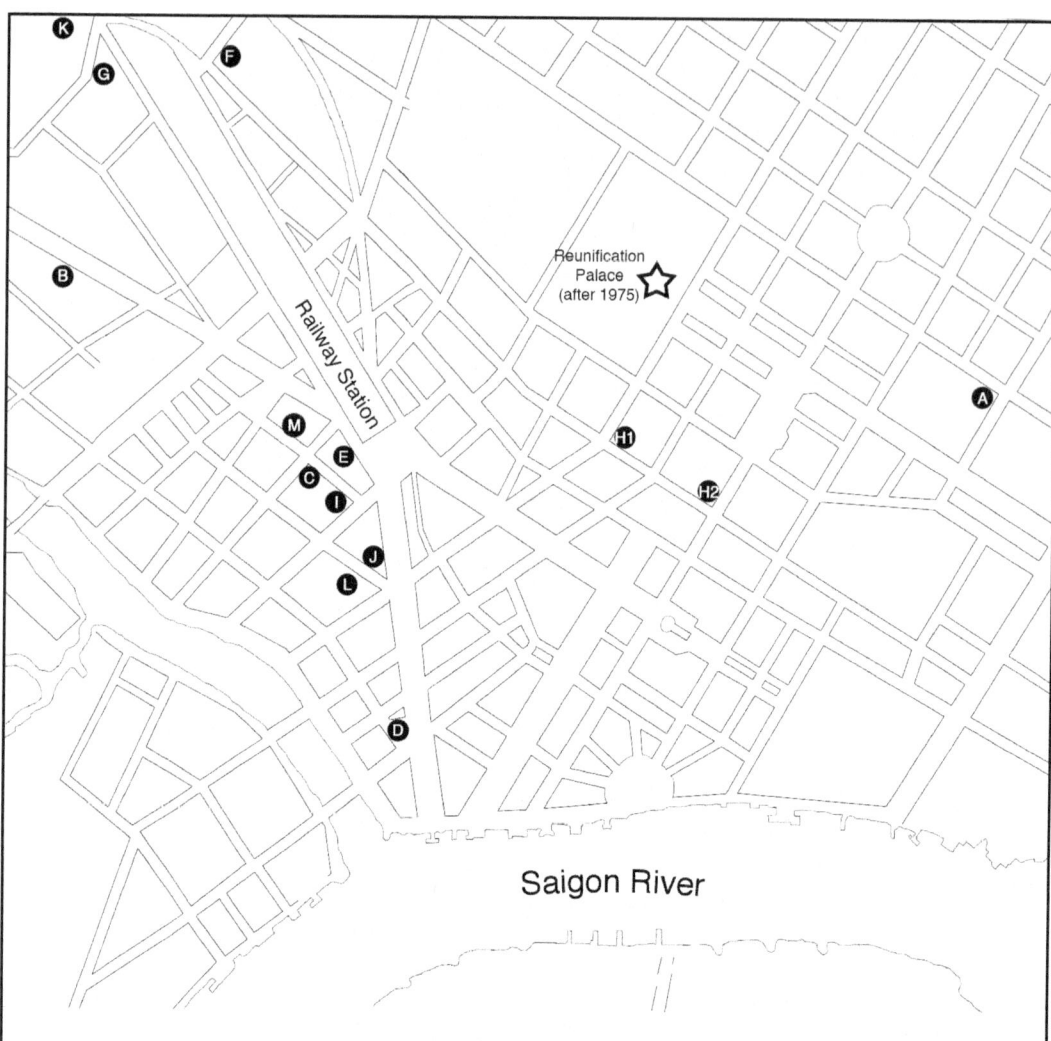

The main role of these addresses was for communications between the Comintern and the revolutionaries.
Source: A letter from Hà Huy Tập (as Sinitchkin) to the Comintern at the end of 1937, and today stored at the Russian Center for the Preservation and the Study of Documents of Modern History, Vietnam.

A - 63 Massigers Street (now Mạc Đĩnh Chi Street) - The address of Madame A. Rivera who was the wife of a rich French comrade. She was the channel for which funds from Moscow came through. This money was able to get to Vietnam as it was sent on the premise that it was for the purchase of embroidered goods from Tonkin. At times up to 10,000 francs per month came through this address.

L'Humanite, Inprecor, Bolshevik, Workers of the Soviet Union and *Viewpoint* are examples of literature sent to the following three addresses so that it could then be further distributed across Saigon.

B - 222 Boulevard Galierri (now Trần Hưng Đạo Boulevard) - Home of Trần Hữu Độ (1887–1945) a writer and revolutionary who was twice detained by the French. The first time around 1930 and the second time for a period of 18 months between 1941 to 1943.

C - 43 Hamelin Street (now Lê Thị Hồng Gấm Street) - Mr. Bernard was a Frenchman whose house was a semi-legal courier way station and the location of the editorial board of *L'Avant Garde*. Although a French language newspaper it was the voice of the Indochinese Communist Party Central Committee. The secretary of the board was Nguyễn Văn Nguyễn (1910–1953). The first issue published was on 20 May 1937, the eighth and last issue was printed on 14 July 1937 as it had been closed by the French. *Kịch Bóng* was then set up at 42 Rue de Alcase Lorraine but lasted for one issue only. After this *L'Avant Garde* was reopened but under the new name *Le Peuple* which again became the voice of the Party Central Committee but only for issues No. 1 to No. 25 or 26 and from No. 29 until it was closed by the French date unknown.

D - 10 Lefevre Street (now Nguyễn Công Trứ) - The barbershop of Le An Minh which was a way station for couriers arriving in Saigon.

Above and opposite: Semi-legal courier networks in Saigon under Hà Huy Tập from 1937 to 1940.

> Addresses of editorial offices used to print radical newspapers, which doubled as semi-legal courier way stations, some serving the Comintern.
> Source: *Revolutionary Newspapers in Vietnam 1925–1945*. Hanoi: Social Science Publishing, 1984.
>
> E - 51E Rue Colonel Grimaud (now Phạm Ngũ Lão Street) - Address for the editorial board of *Le Peuple* for issues No. 26 or 27 to No. 28.
>
> F - 14 Guillerault (now Tôn Thất Tùng Street) - Address for the editorial board of *Thanh Niên* (*Youth*). Only one issue of this paper was printed, this being on 6 March 1939.
>
> G - 38 Rue de Arras (now Cống Quỳnh Street) - Address for the editorial board of *Tiến Tới* (*Advance*). There were four issues published from 5 February 1939 until 26 February 1939.
>
> H - (H1) 25 BIS Rue de la Grandiere (now Lý Tự Trọng Street) and later (H2) 95 Rue de la Grandiere - These addresses were home to the editorial board of *La Lutte* (*Struggle*), a newspaper run by both the communists and the Trotskyists. The communists were: Nguyễn Văn Tạo (1908–1972), Dương Bạch Mai (1904–1964) and Nguyễn Văn Nguyên. The Trotskyists were: Tạ Thu Thâu (1906–1945), Phan Văn Hùm (1902–1946), Huỳnh Văn Phương (1906–1970), Trần Văn Thạch (1903–1946), Phan Văn Chánh (1906–1945) and Hồ Hữu Tường (1910–1980), all under the influence of the nationalist Nguyễn An Ninh. However, the two teams split in mid-1937. One source says that the Comintern instructed the split, whereas Nguyễn Văn Trấn said that the Trotskyists seized the paper from them.
>
> I - 42 Rue de Alcase Lorraine - Address for the editorial board of *Kịch Bóng* (*Theatre and Cinema*). Managed by Nguyễn Văn Trấn, Hà Huy Tập bought this ongoing newspaper but was only able to print one issue on 28 August 1937.
>
> J - 38 Rue d'Ayot (now Nguyễn Thái Bình Street) - Location of the editorial board of *Lao Động* (*Labor*) for issue No. 1 on 29 Nov. 1938 to No. 13.
>
> K - 33 Rue de Arras (now Cống Quỳnh Street) - Location for the editorial board of *Labor* for issues No. 14 to its last, No. 20 on 14 June 1939.
>
> L - 1 Rue d'Ayot - Location for the editorial board of *Mới* (*New*) newspaper. This was the newspaper of the Cochinchina Democratic Youth. Only one issue was published at this address; printed on 1 May 1939.
>
> M - 62 Hamelin Street (now Lê Thị Hồng Gấm Street) - The address for the next ten issues of *New*, which terminated with No. 11 in Sep. 1939.

a male contact and a male sibling. Fortunately for Ms. Sáu, the other dominate male in her life, her husband, supported her revolutionary duties and on the odd occasion even stood guard when senior communists chaired meetings. On the one hand, the fact that he kept out of front line revolutionary duties himself could have strained her relationship within her circle of leaders, because they could view both her and her husband as not being committed to the revolution and therefore weak links. On the other hand, the less he knew the better, because in a society where a wife was replaceable her husband might have revealed classified information, obtained from his spouse about high-ranking revolutionaries, to gain favor with the French, whether freely, boasting or under torture.

A mother child working union became another focus for Ms. Sáu's Party leaders. Ms. Sáu recalled that one evening Hoàng Văn Lúa brought to her house a stranger who had a fair complexion, bright eyes and looked about thirty-plus. Lúa told her to arrange shelter for Brother the Seventh. This stranger delegated two tasks to her: to convey secret documents and establish safe houses in her local hamlets of Chèm and Hoàng. Only later did she find out that this man was in actual fact Hoàng Văn Thụ (1906–1944), the secretary of the Tonkin Regional Party Committee. Thụ pushed her hard in order to ingrain in her important clandestine rules, one being what she should declare if arrested. He said, "If the enemy discovers a document on you, you must say that someone hired you to take it. No matter how many times they interrogate you, your answer must be the same. They will continue to torture you in the hope that you will give information but keep the same answer, this way they will grow weary of your reply and give up. Your loss is that they will throw you into prison but the revolution will be safe and continue to operate."[32] With Ms. Sáu trained Thụ then recruited her daughter, Dzung. She was very agile for a seven-year-old and idea to act as a courier. He tested Dzung, drilling into her, "If the French find a letter on you, what will you say?" She would reply what she had been taught, "I found the paper on the edge of the street. I took it home so that my mother could use it to wrap tobacco in."[33]

The Party did not worry that Ms. Sáu's children were not hers by birth. The borrowing of a child or children to gain safe passage was commonplace, going on the principle that no one would search a woman with a needy child in tow. This scenario existed because many foreigners thought the Vietnamese all looked the same; they could not tell if the adult accompanying the child was the parent or not. This meant that Ms. Sáu could conduct high risk activities such as conveying weapons using her children as cover.

Sadly for Ms. Đức, even though she came from noted stock and had married for the Party to help her work, having children left her and her husband, Lê Hồng Sơn, open to criticism. Her leaders accused them both of failing to dedicate their time to the revolution as before; in spite of the fact that on occasions Ms. Đức left their children to fend for themselves for days on end, when she went out to earn money but also to work for the cause. In Ms. Đức's case she had to accept an absent husband but, more poignantly, she lost her first child as a result of being vital to the revolution. Like so many women revolutionaries, being a wife and mother, meant great sacrifices, willingly or not.

The Most Important Element

With such significance put on couriers by Hồ it is ironic that they rarely speak of their experience. Nevertheless, Hồ knew that the sum of all courier work enabled the revolution to function across a whole spectrum of needs. His principle was that to undertake any of the immense tasks ahead, each task had to be broken down into smaller workloads to achieve the objective.

In Ms. Sáu's case, Hoàng Văn Thụ asked her to help promote the new Trust Bills; developed by the leadership in the early 1940s to raise much needed cash.[34] One woman she targeted was a single mother living a frugal life catching crabs from rice fields. Although she was virtually penniless, Ms. Sáu won her over because she spent time making it clear how the French had exploited the people and why the poor had to support the revolution. The woman understood and purchased two bills. Although labor intensive, Ms. Sáu used these small gains to buy rice for her leaders, including Hoàng Văn Thụ and Trường Chinh (1907–1988).[35] Money obtained by others helped train former Bắc Sơn guerrilla fighters because the revolutionaries did not want to see such an uprising fiasco again. It is not known if anyone was ever compensated for buying the Trust Bills but printing and then selling them became a common way to get funds from the people.

From selling Trust Bills, Ms. Sáu moved to playing her part in establishing a safe zone. She had been asked to do this by Hoàng Văn Thụ and Trường Chinh, who at the time was the acting general secretary of the Communist Party in Vietnam. This process began at the end of 1941 because the French started to conduct intensive searches of her area. Not long after they had, customs officers barged into Ms. Sáu's house to search it for bootleg products. They found no such illegal goods but did discover two worn books on the revolution, which she insisted she found in the street. Eventually they left, and she acted fast to hide all her documents. The next day the French *Sûreté* came back looking for incriminating evidence. On finding nothing they became incredibly angry. Worried, Hoàng Văn Thụ and Trường Chinh sent Mrs. Vẻ the Second to confirm that Ms. Sáu was safe. Mrs. Vẻ had been recruited by Ms. Sáu and now Hoàng Văn Thụ and Trường Chinh were residing with her. When the two men met with Ms. Sáu, she told them that although her house had been ransacked by the French, it was still possible to shelter comrades.

Ms. Sáu's husband felt differently and that Liên Mạc Hamlet had now been compromised. Indeed, one day Ms. Sáu fell ill on her way home. To recover she sheltered at a safe house in Phú Gia Village. The next day she moved on but as she reached Đông Ngạc Village, Chèm Hamlet, a woman waved frantically, "My goodness, why have you returned, the French have arrested your husband!"[36] Ms. Sáu hurried back to Phú Gia. Forgetting the secret principles, she rushed into the house of Mrs. Vẻ and told Trường Chinh and Hoàng Văn Thụ that they must leave at once; the French had hung wanted posters everywhere, including portraits of the two of them.

The two men decided that Ms. Sáu had to move. She was distraught thinking about leaving her daughters with relatives. Mrs. Vẻ said naively that she would not allow Ms. Sáu to go nor the enemy to arrest her. Shortly after Hoàng Văn Thụ came to get her. They both crossed the Red River to take shelter in Đông Anh. Within this district and Từ Liêm, Ms. Sáu established courier networks to form part of a safe zone.

Safe zones, known as ATKs, supported revolutionaries so that they could carry out their everyday duties more freely, even holding conferences for supporters, and enabling their leaders to set up their headquarters.[37] Ms. Sáu's networks became part of ATK 1, and that was used by General Secretary Trường Chinh and Party Central Committee members who operated in the Red River Delta. ATK 1 eventually covered the northern and western parts of Hanoi and became critical in aiding Hồ to come to power during the August Revolution in 1945. ATK 2 was located in some of the villages in the districts of Hiệp Hòa, Phổ Yên and Phú Bình, covering the mountainous midland provinces of Bắc Giang and Thái Nguyên, and is where the Party Central Committee of the Communist Party held its important meetings and conferences.

What gave a safe area, ATK status, was that the region had to have a covert revolutionary administration strong enough to support the TW.[38] The TW was just a code given to a location where the nerve center of the revolutionaries resided and was usually the headquarters of Hồ or the general secretary.[39]

Each ATK had its own specific risks. During the French War the revolutionary army and the local guerrillas defended Việt Bắc Revolutionary Base, and there were limited French soldiers within the region. The combination made it safer and easier for individual revolutionaries to carry weapons and work more openly. In contrast, the ATKs closer to Hanoi or within Hanoi were considered to be in the enemy's rear base area and they did not have such a degree of protection as their counterparts in the mountains. The presence of the French made working within them far more complex; those operating in these ATKs became extremely sought after because they had learned to adapt to a hostile environment.

To stabilize ATKs, paramilitary teams were formed, known as "action units." There were many types of action units being created at the time because most communist leaders designed what they needed individually, rather than adhering to a central coordinated template. Consequently, the functions of an action unit depended on who ran it or where it operated. Action units comprised generally small groups, and collectively their duties went beyond those of regular couriers and could include escorting communist leaders or building a revolutionary administration in hostile territory. The numbers of units grew throughout 1942; by the end of the year, to consolidate the action units, the Communist Party dedicated a department to their activities.[40]

Ms. Sáu set up the first action unit to serve as bodyguards for General Secretary Trường Chinh. This small group of patriots operated as a team of guards, dealing with the associated administrative work of the general secretary, such as arranging accommodation and food, escorting communist leaders, conveying vital articles to printing offices, delivering newspapers and documents as well as establishing courier lines. Formed around the end of 1942 or the beginning of 1943, her unit operated inside ATK 1.

Ms. Sáu might not have been as powerful as some whom she had helped operate but her work was exceptional. Along with the many thousands of other couriers, it is very evident why these females were vital for Hồ and his workforce.

Agitprop as a Tool of War

Although in some instances the action units were armed, agitprop was their main weapon; this used art, literature or music to promote a political message. Hồ attributes much of their recruitment success to nationalist agitprop because most of the populace could relate to the arts rather than to the written word, especially those people within the tribal villages, the peasantry and women. Hồ used it not only to support the quest to gain independence but secretly to achieve local socialist political reform in parallel.

Ms. Sáu had been recruited through agitprop and now she adopted this method to build ATK 1. To reach out to women, she organized gatherings where they read patriotic poetry together and engaged in political discussions. Having used this skill to attract keen women patriots, she then proceeded to the next stage, which meant teaching them how to conduct agitprop and clandestine techniques themselves. For a cover for her work, Ms. Sáu became a hired laborer and earned money doing needlework to sell.

During this period Ms. Sáu secured safe houses on both sides of the Red River. She had found some worthy people. In Võng La, the French discovered that Mrs. Lờ, the wife of the village mayor, ran a courier station out of her home.[41] To extract information, they arrested, tortured and jailed her son but he gave nothing away. After his release, Mrs. Lờ refused to shut operations down so the French came again and arrested another son. Determined to defy the French she continued to give shelter to the revolutionaries. Ms. Sáu greatest achievement was establishing the village of Vân Nội as a safe region. It was here that Trường Chinh moved in, making it the TW until 1945. This allowed him to publish the newspaper *Liberation Flag*.[42]

Ms. Sáu eventually took a highly dangerous role as a proselytizing agent. Proselytizing was a method used to convert or attempt to convert someone from one religion, belief or opinion to another. In her case she worked as a *địch vận* agent, which meant agitation and spreading propaganda among the enemy. She targeted pro–French Vietnamese mandarins, to switch them to work for the revolution as double agents. Again, her main weapon was agitprop.

Targeting key people such as mandarins was not easy. For a start, it relied on the fact that a covert revolutionary administration and a courier network had been established in a village or its wider community. Only then could the local mandarin be approached, in order to try to persuade him to join the revolution. If he did not want to join, the revolutionary administration then forced him into neutrality or to work covertly for the revolution against his will. The mandarin had no choice but to succumb to this pressure because he feared for his safety and that of his family.

The communists called these mandarins "two-faced puppet local administrators," and they valued this technique highly. They could control vast areas of the population through their revolutionary administration, but with the figurehead being a person trusted by their enemy and accepted by the people. Then, when the time was right and they needed full control over the area, the revolutionary administration simply replaced the "two-faced puppet" with one of their own, a person who had been operating covertly alongside the so-called puppet pulling their strings. This replacement might be made when the revolutionary army had to enter a village and they needed total governance of the area and its people. If a mandarin refused categorically to cooperate at anytime, the communist apparatus arrested him, and after a people's tribunal conducted by the revolutionary administration, as a last resort they executed him.

During the time that Ms. Sáu operated, the communist leaders could see that nationalist agitprop delivered by women expanded networks rapidly and the tactic of targeting mandarins through agitprop was very successful. Consequently, these techniques were used throughout both the French and the American Vietnam wars.

Couriers' Lost Children

Like Ms. Đức, Ms. Sáu survived the wars. With the sky now filled with the sound of birdsong instead of guns, what troubled Ms. Sáu the most was not any horrific flashbacks to her life as a courier, and what might have been, but the decision she had made decades before with regards to her first natural child.

This much-loved child had been the product of a fleeting reunion with her heartbroken husband in the early 1940s. He had been released from prison and had headed back to their home village to find her. On one occasion he had seen Hoàng Văn Thụ walking in the fields. He asked Hoàng Văn Thụ if he had seen Ms. Sáu. Hoàng Văn Thụ warned him not to continue searching because the French probably trailed his every move, waiting for an opportunity for him to lead them to her. After about five months Ms. Sáu returned to her village, desperately homesick and wanting to be with her family. She spent just one night in her village with her husband and then left in fear of arrest. Within days the French Sûreté came. Someone had tipped them off.

Ms. Sáu gave birth to her first natural child, but the joys of motherhood were short-lived. Mrs. Vẻ visited her and said, "Brother Trường Chinh is waiting for you at the banyan tree in Cao Hamlet."[43] While Ms. Sáu and Trường Chinh talked, Mrs. Vẻ nursed the newborn girl. What they said is not recorded, but Ms. Sáu knew that when working for senior Communist Party members she could not afford a dependent. Ms. Sáu announced the unthinkable and insisted she give her daughter away. To make sure her daughter's new mother could not be linked back to her, Ms. Sáu chose a total stranger. Shortly thereafter Trường Chinh, Hoàng Văn Thụ and Ms. Sáu all went their separate ways. At the end of 1943, Hoàng Văn Thụ was arrested by the French and swiftly executed.[44] In contrast, Ms. Sáu lived out the rest of her days in her home area.

In the early 1980s, historian Dr. Nguyễn Văn Khoan went to visit her; he knew that Trường Chinh had arranged to do the same. They both wanted to know how she coped and whether they could assist in any way. She had already refused an offer to have a new house built, even though her present one fell down around her. She had also declined improvements to her living conditions as she viewed herself as one of the lucky ones who had been given good fields to grow crops during the first Land Reforms.

What troubled Ms. Sáu in her latter years was not a failed government and their policies, or her place in history, but her personal loss. Like so many other women in her position, she now pined for the child she had given away. For years she searched, but people had died and villages changed locations, so no one could point her in the right direction. Finding her daughter was a battle she never did win.

If she had her time once more, would she have sacrificed her child? Collectively, if women like Ms. Sáu and Ms. Đức, had not made personal sacrifices for the revolution, could the outcome of the war have been any different? These questions will probably never be answered but, thanks to their rare stories, it is known that women did play an important part in Hồ's blueprint.

3

The Seeds of Hồ's Revolutionary Strategies

The First Communist Cell

Hồ arrived in Guangzhou on 11 November 1924, wanting to begin training courses across a number of disciplines.[1] The cosmopolitan port in Guangzhou had been the focus of sea trade within the region. During the nineteenth century it was one of the top three cities in the world; ships came and went with goods between Europe and Asia. Hồ saw that the still bustling harbor would give his new students the cover to operate relatively unchallenged. Now he could advance his model for the liberation of Vietnam, not only to develop his courier networks but to form his three strategic fronts: political, propaganda and the military.

Hồ worked as an interpreter at the Bureau of Press and Information, Soviet Consulate, Guangzhou. No sooner had he got the job, than he began to use Soviet secret service networks to develop his revolutionary activities. Through their help and mutual ties to the Consulate, Hồ tracked down Phan Bội Châu, because he needed to make contact with the Society of Hearts (1923–1925). Hồ had been attracted to this organization because it had little ideological focus, which could see its members open to adopting the philosophy of Marx and Lenin.

Hồ liked the radical activities of the Society of Hearts. Its initial mission had been to assassinate Martial Henri Merlin, the French governor general of Indochina who had been in China in June 1924; the first attempt by Vietnamese revolutionaries to kill such a senior Frenchman. Phạm Hồng Thái had thrown a bomb into the room where the governor general was attending a banquet. The act wounded some Frenchmen and some died, but Merlin survived, resulting in rumors throughout the Society of Hearts that there had been a traitor within their group. Phạm Hồng Thái died trying to escape.[2]

Disillusioned members of Châu's Vietnamese Restoration League had founded the Society of Hearts. They felt Châu had wrongly associated himself with the slogan, Franco-Vietnamese Collaboration in Harmony, first promoted by Albert Sarraut, a previous governor general of Indochina.[3] The slogan meant different things to different people. Many elite Vietnamese took the slogan to denote new interaction between parties producing equal benefits to both. For Sarraut and his colleagues the main intention of the slogan was that French-inspired ideas should help to convert millions of Vietnamese into willing colonial subjects.[4] In apparent further confirmation of Châu's perceived alliance with the French, in 1917, he had written that the Japanese must be viewed as "a dangerous enemy" to Asia, and that for the Vietnamese to survive a Japanese onslaught, they and the French had to unite for mutual benefit, to keep the Japanese at bay.[5]

In 1924, Châu tried to recover his tarnished reputation by transforming the Vietnamese Restoration League into the Vietnamese Kuomintang; Hồ had advised him to do so.[6] Initially Hồ supported it. Later the group became anti-communist when Chiang Kai-shek took power as the Chinese nationalist leader, and the group became a genuine threat to Hồ during the August Revolution of 1945.

Without doubt Hồ gained overall from Châu's fall. The loss of support for him provided Hồ with a pool of disillusioned politicized patriots, who needed a new direction and revolutionary group to join. In 1925, Hồ and nine members of the Society of Hearts established a secret organization called the Communist Youth Corps. Later in 1925, with other members of the Society of Hearts, Hồ established the Vietnamese RYL. By founding it, Hồ had his first pro–Marxist political organization that had broad public appeal. Importantly though, its covert controlling nucleus, was the Communist Youth Corps. This wide appeal type party, controlled through a covert communist cell, became an important part of Hồ's blueprint.

Expanding the Vietnamese RYL

Hồ ran his training courses for the Vietnamese RYL in Guangzhou from 1925 to 1927. He held three principal courses, with other classes operating in parallel. It is not known exactly how many students attended, but in 1926 there are believed to have been around 300.[7] Hồ gave lectures himself. Fellow instructors briefed in the needs of the Vietnamese RYL taught too. They included Soviet military advisors from the Whampoa Military Academy, Chinese Communist Party officials and some leaders of the Comintern.[8] Representatives of the French Communist Party are also believed to have attended; it is unknown whether they gave lectures. Each lesson might be taken by Russian, Indian, Korean, Thai, Chinese or Vietnamese lecturers.

Hồ's Vietnamese RYL seemed to appeal to those people disaffected with the old ideals of Phan Chu Trinh, Phan Bội Châu and Prince Cường Để, among others. Based upon Bolshevik doctrine, the Vietnamese RYL aimed to carry out a national revolution (to defeat the French authority and regain independence for the country), and thereafter to help accomplish world revolution (by toppling imperialism and adopting communism).[9] To put these complicated aims across, the main material taught was collated to form the book *The Road to Revolution*, which Hồ had written in Guangzhou in 1926, and published a year later. Its fifteen chapters defined the revolutionary needs of farmers, laborers, women and the youth, and outlined a theoretical strategy for revolution in Vietnam.[10]

Hoàng Văn Hoan (1905–1991) gave a vivid account of his time studying during a training course held by the Vietnamese RYL.[11] He had originally been sent to China in 1926 to attend the respected Whampoa Military Academy. With Chiang Kai-shek appointed as the first commandant, the academy produced a large number of prestigious commanders, who went on to fight in many of China's conflicts throughout the rest of the century. It is not surprising that Hồ endorsed the institute, but in the end Hoan did not end up there, instead, along with colleagues in China, he joined the third course of the Vietnamese RYL.

Within Hoan's class there were more than twenty trainees, most of them students and intellectuals. The training lasted about two months, and the lectures fell into three different categories: problems of world revolution, problems of the Vietnamese revolution and problems related to methodology of revolutionary movements. Lectures on the problems of world revolution concentrated on a study comparing the Russian Revolution with the bourgeois revolutions in Britain, France and the other capitalist countries. Lectures on the problems of the Vietnamese revolution analyzed the oppression and exploitation of the people by the French imperialists, and pointed out that the main forces for overthrowing colonial imperialism and feudalism were the workers and the peasants. In many passages the ambiguous line adopted by Phan Bội Châu was criticized, for instance, he had classified a revolution into "civilized revolution" and "brutal revolution" and he proposed to make Cường Để the emperor and later life president. In some passages, Mahatma Gandhi was condemned for attempting to realize national liberation through "non-cooperation" and "non-violence."[12]

Hoan went on to record that a part of the political training for all students was to attend a ceremony in front of the tomb of Phạm Hồng Thái, the man who had failed to assassinate Merlin, the French governor general. Hoan remembered the passion in the student's voices as they made their solemn collective vow, "[We will] fight for the rest of our lives for the cause of not only Vietnam's liberation but also for world revolution."[13]

Another student who attended the third training course was Ms. Bảo Lương (1909–1976).[14] She was the first and only woman to study under the Vietnamese RYL in China. Ms. Thuận and Ms. Đức might have been present as staff members, but Ms. Lương became the only officially designated, full-time female trainee.

Young and initially daunted by the situation, she had been chosen more because of whom she knew rather than for any innate ability; she was a relative of the wife of Tôn Đức Thắng (1888–1980).[15] Hồ had met Thắng when they were students at a technical school in Saigon, learning the art of seamanship, just before Hồ left Vietnam in 1911. Thang had established the Labor Union in Saigon in 1920. Ms. Lương worked there with Thắng, and it was during this period that he convinced her to go to China, hoping that she could then go on to study in the Soviet Union.

The decision to leave Vietnam could not be taken lightly; as a woman she risked bringing shame on her family and being ostracized, even by loved ones. Women were homemakers; any deviation from this meant that society viewed them as being up to no good with boys. Nevertheless, she made her choice, packed her bags, and left on her long journey to China in late 1927. In those days, a woman could not travel alone, and in most circumstances had to be accompanied by her husband or by a male family member. On this occasion she dressed as a man.

Years later she recalled in her memoirs her experience during her training for the Vietnamese RYL course in Guangzhou. Hồ did not teach her class because he had fled to Hong Kong in 1927 to avoid being arrested by the Kuomintang. This meant that she had not started training immediately on arrival in China; her group had to wait for Hồ Tùng Mậu to arrive back from his travels. To kill time, Ms. Lương socialized with Ms. Đức, Ms. Thuận and the two boys, Lý Tự Trọng and Lý Trí Thông.

When Hồ Tùng Mậu finally returned, training started. To open events, senior leaders held an inspiring opening ceremony; trainees were joined by a large number of branch representatives from the Vietnamese RYL and from Whampoa Military Academy. First they elected the chairman of the ceremony. Lâm Đức Thụ won the vote. Ms. Lương recalled that he was an imposing man who dressed well, and that he made an impassioned speech in an urgent voice. Like others in the room, he won her over. Hồ Tùng Mậu followed Lâm Đức Thụ, and through another imposing performance, Mậu made Ms. Lương see that nothing was more precious than freedom, and that only one path was possible for anyone who held dear the virtues of loyalty, filial piety, virtue, and chastity: that of revolution.[16] When they had finished, the senior leaders asked candidates to give a speech of introduction.

The now enthused students started classes the following day. Senior figures held lectures throughout the week, both in the mornings and afternoons. The only exception was Sunday, which meant that the students had free time to talk openly about their thoughts.

During the first month, lecturers taught the students about the origins of various ideologies. Then the day came when the lecturers asked the students to choose their ideology. Ms. Lương recorded in her memoirs that they were all given a piece of paper, presented like a ballot. This paper gave no party names but the students were asked to indicate one of the "isms," as Ms. Lương called them, that best represented their interests, such as nationalism.[17] The ballot listed six examples: the Three Principles of the People; labor and capitalist collaboration; nationalism; monarchy or constitutional monarchy; anarchy; and finally, socialism.

Although those present had been free to air their political views, because of the intense internal security that surrounded the organization and its hierarchy, the completion of training did not automatically mean that they became a member of the Vietnamese RYL. In fact, it was never clear who was and who was not a member. Ms. Lương had chosen socialism in the ballot, a choice that is now known to have opened the door to membership of the Vietnamese RYL. Just as Hoan had recalled during his training, at their closing ceremony Ms. Lương and her fellow patriots were instructed to stand at the tomb of the man who had failed to assassinate Merlin, the French governor general of Indochina.

Having graduated, and with membership of the Vietnamese RYL, Ms. Lương could undertake further training overseas. With classes at an end, she chose not to stay abroad, citing the cold weather in China and the Soviet Union as her reason for wanting to return to Vietnam. Trầm Hương, when interviewed in Saigon in 2006, suggested that Ms. Lương actually wanted to return to Vietnam because she had fallen in love with one of Hồ's male couriers, known as Lê Duy Điểm (1906–1930).[18]

Whatever her reasons, Ms. Lương returned to Indochina along with many fellow students. Their superiors sent them to different strategic areas, to conduct tasks that could include establishing Vietnamese RYL political cells and being propagandists, as well as expanding their organizations by inciting the masses and recruiting. The Vietnamese RYL courses were not for the faint-hearted, and not all students made the grade to be authorized to build courier lines.[19] Ms. Lương had done well. After returning to Vietnam, she focused on forming a courier network in Cochinchina, but also on expanding the Women's Emancipation Association; as a woman it was more culturally acceptable for her to approach other women not related to her, so she was more qualified than a man to recruit females.

The founding of the Vietnamese RYL is viewed by scholars as being a significant turning point. Hồ now had a politically educated base on which to start building the revolution. For the first time, a revolutionary group had emerged with a coherent and practical approach. Their influence had spread fast. It had group cells in Lao, Cambodia, China, Hong Kong, Siam and the three regional committees of Vietnam: Tonkin, Annam and Cochinchina. However, its success did not last.

Strategic Political Front: The Communist Party

A real decline in support for the Vietnamese RYL had begun at a conference held in Hong Kong in May 1929. Members attended from Hong Kong, Siam and the three regional committees based in Vietnam. At this meeting Ngô Gia Tự, Nguyễn Tuân and Trần Văn Cung, along with other members of the Tonkin and Annam committees, stated they wanted the Vietnamese RYL to be a "proper" communist party. They accused the Vietnamese RYL Central Committee, and other representatives, of being "false" revolutionaries, with their nationalist-communist approach. The Central Committee argued that they had to proceed slowly, and by using nationalism a wide range of people had rallied behind the Vietnamese RYL. Hồ could not attend as he had fled to Siam after being pursued by a Kuomintang general, but he remained a great believer in the Vietnamese RYL.

Disheartened that the Vietnamese RYL had not reinvented itself as a communist party, within a short period, after the May conference, radical northerners established a new organization called the Indochinese Communist Party. The growth of this new party threatened the Vietnamese RYL leadership, because they had no authority over it. In mid–1929, the Vietnamese RYL split. In their stronghold in South Vietnam, the Vietnamese RYL agreed to dissolve and transform the group into the Annamese Communist Party. The Vietnamese RYL Central Committee in Hong Kong supported this move because it enabled them to control the process.

The increase in support for communism in Vietnam and the decline of the Vietnamese RYL can partly be explained by the situation in Vietnam at that time. Right-wing political parties had turned their backs on the colonial people and their quest for independence, and the French had recently conducted extreme White Terror on nationalists. (White Terror was a phrase used by revolutionaries to refer to the continuing repression and murderous acts inflicted on them by the French.) Communism gave the people a voice, one supported by Moscow.

For security reasons Hồ still resided in Siam, but he had to be brought back. Tension had reached critical levels, the Indochinese Communist Party and the Annamese Communist Party warred with each other, and a third Vietnamese communist group not rooted in the Vietnamese RYL had emerged, called the Indochinese Communist League. Members of the Vietnamese RYL sent two couriers to track Hồ down.[20] Once found, Hồ was asked to go back to Hong Kong to talk to the leadership there. They needed Hồ's advice on how to take back control of the revolution in Vietnam. Discussions concluded that to sweep away any rival groups, an all-uniting communist organization had to be founded.

In February 1930, Hồ established the Vietnamese Communist Party at a conference in Hong Kong, with approval from the ever-imposing Comintern, to facilitate revolutionary activities in French Indochina. Five men took part in the meeting, Hồ representing the Comintern, two members from the Indochinese Communist Party and two from the Annamese Communist Party. Members of the third communist group, the Indochinese Communist League, had been invited but were unable to attend; they had been arrested just prior to the event.

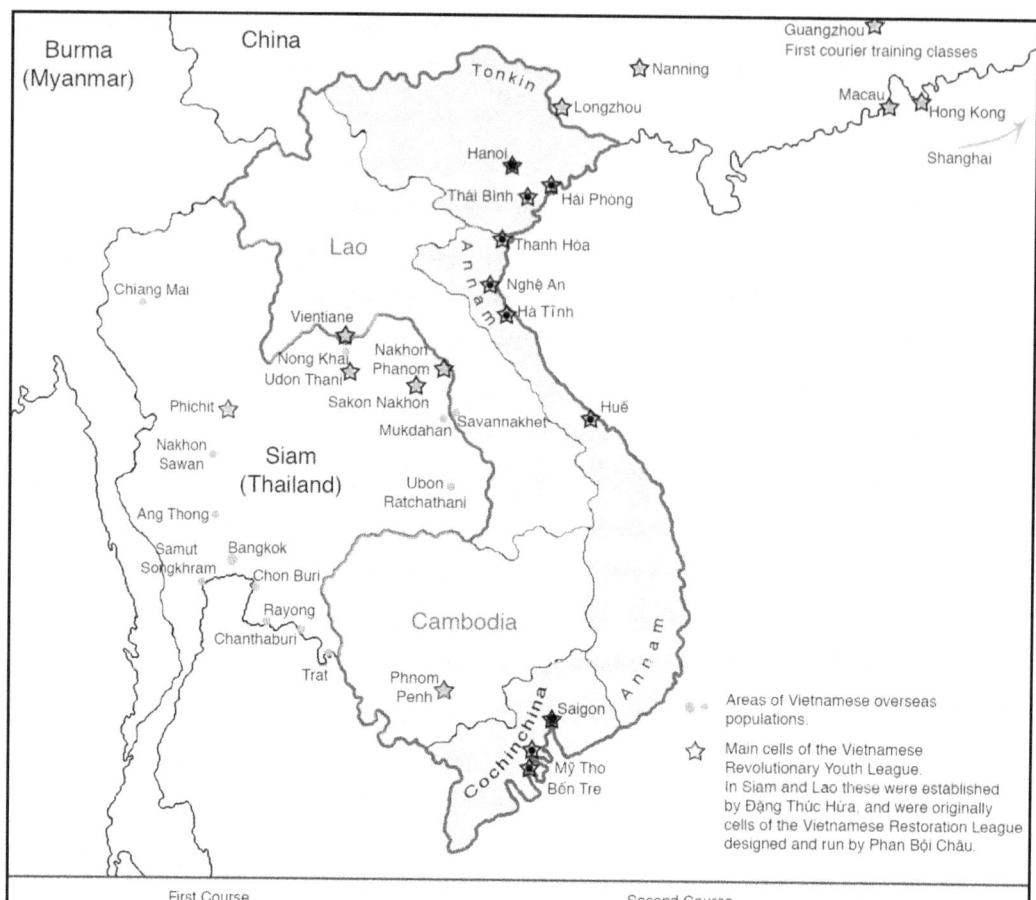

First Course Beginning of 1925		Second Course Sep 1926–Nov 1926	
Ngô Chính Quốc (1903–1990). Born in Siam. AKA: Xintechcoong (name in Siam). Ngô Tâm Ngô and Lý Tôn. Operated in Siam, ran a courier line to China, became leader of the Siamese Communist Party.	Lê Quang Đạt (190?–193?). Born in Nghệ An, Vietnam. AKA: Hoàng Cao and Lê Văn Chinh. Served in Chinese Kuomintang Army and worked as a courier for Hồ Chí Minh.	Trần Phú (1904–1931). Born in Hà Tĩnh, Vietnam. AKA: Lý Quý and Giao. Operated in Annam before going to study in Moscow.	Đặng Thái Thuyến (1897–1931). Born in Nghệ An, Vietnam. AKA: Đặng Thái Nguyên, Đặng Cảnh Tân and Ty (The Rat). Operated in Udon Thani and was the communist leader for all of Siam.
Lê Duy Điếm (1906–1930). Born in Hà Tĩnh, Vietnam. AKA: Lê Lợi. Operated in Tonkin, China and Siam.	Lê Hữu Lập (1897–1934). Born in Thanh Hóa, Vietnam. AKA: Hoàng the Short and Cậu Ấm. Operated in Thanh Hóa, established courier lines in the city and districts of this province.	Nguyễn Ngọc Ba (190?–199?). Born in Hà Tĩnh, Vietnam. AKA: Ngọc. Operated in China, then Cochinchina.	Lê Thiết Hùng (1908–1986). Born in Nghệ An, Vietnam. Courier and covert operative in the Chinese Kuomintang Army.
Trần Ba Giao (1902–1934). Born in Nam Đàn, Vietnam. AKA: Vũ Nam Hồng and Nam Hồng. Operated in Udon Thani, Siam, and Vientiane, Lao.	Trần Tích Chu (1897–1933). AKA: Chu the Pockmarked and, Đào. Operated in Siam and China, responsible for communications with the Siamese Communist Party and the Indochinese Communist Party when founded.	Phan Trọng Bình (190?–199?). Born in Hà Tĩnh, Vietnam. Operated in Saigon and recruited trainees for the third course.	Nguyễn Lương Bằng (1904–1979). Born in Hải Dương, Vietnam. AKA: Big Brother and Red Star. Operated on the sea route between Guangzhou, Shanghai and Hải Phòng, then moved to Saigon.
Ngô Chính Học (1900–1946). AKA: Trần Bảo. Operated a courier line between China and Siam.		Nguyễn Văn Lợi (1907–19??). Born in Hà Tĩnh, Vietnam. AKA: Lộc. Operated in Saigon and recruited trainees for the third course.	Nguyễn Sinh Thản (1910–1941). Born in Nghệ An, Vietnam. AKA: Lam Giang and Lý Nam Thanh. Went to Russia and died in the defense of Moscow.
		Võ Tùng (1889–1964). Born in Quảng Ngãi, Vietnam. AKA: Mr. Sixth and Lưu Khải Hồng. Operated in Udon Thani.	Phan Trọng Quảng (190?–1983). Born in Hà Tĩnh, Vietnam. AKA: An and Quan. Operated in Thanh Hóa.

Above and opposite: Vietnamese Revolutionary Youth League, mid to late 1920s. Main post-course activities of key trainees including courier and agitprop roles.

> **Third Course**
> **1927**
>
> Phạm Văn Đồng (1906–2000).
> Born in Quảng Ngãi, Vietnam.
> Led operations in Saigon.
>
> Hoàng Văn Hoan (1905–1991).
> Born in Nghệ An, Vietnam.
> Operated in Siam.
>
> Trần Ngọc Giải (1904–1931).
> Formed courier lines in Bến Tre and Mỹ Tho.
>
> Trần Văn Cung (1906–1977).
> Born in Nghệ An, Vietnam.
> AKA: Quốc Anh.
> Led local operations mainly in Nghệ An and Hà Tĩnh. Led the group that formed the first communist party in Tonkin that split the Vietnamese RYL.
>
> Lý Hồng Nhật (190?–1935).
> Operated as a courier between Hong Kong and Hải Phòng.
>
> Ms. Nguyễn Trung Nguyệt (1909–1976).
> Born in Tiền Giang.
> AKA: Bảo Lương.
> Operated in Saigon.
>
> Lê Mạnh Trinh (1896–1983).
> Born in Thanh Hóa, Vietnam.
> AKA: Tiến the Bacca.
> Led local operations in Phichit, Siam.
>
> Nguyễn Danh Đới (1905–1943).
> Born in Thái Bình.
> AKA: Điền Hải.
> Led operations in Tonkin, mainly Hanoi, Hải Phòng and Thái Bình.
>
> Nguyễn Văn Tây (1910–1996).
> Born in Cần Thơ, Vietnam.
> AKA: Nguyễn Thanh Sơn.
> Operated in Cochinchina as General Secretary from 1931; arrested later that year.
>
> Ngô Thiêm (1906–1931).
> Born in Hà Tĩnh, Vietnam.
> AKA: Huệ.
> Led local operations in Saigon. Executed by the French due to the Rue Barbier murder.
>
> Nguyễn Văn Đắc (1909–1930).
> AKA: Cao Hoài Nghĩa.
> Operated as courier between China, Saigon and Siam.
>
> Trần Tư Chính (1909–193?).
> Born in Bắc Ninh or Hà Tĩnh.
> AKA: Bàng Thống, Chính the Fifth.
> Operated as a courier between Hanoi and Saigon.
>
> Nguyễn Vĩ (1901–1941).
> Born in Nghệ An.
> AKA: Phùng Chí Kiên and Mạnh Văn Liễu.
> Operated in China, became a commander in the Chinese Red Army.
>
> Nguyễn Thái (1908–19??).
> Born in Nghệ An, Vietnam.
> AKA: The Fifth and Võ Phong.
> High-ranking courier operating between Saigon and Hong Kong.
>
> Vương Thúc Oánh (1899–19??).
> Born in Nghệ An, Vietnam.
> AKA: Tống Oanh, Chất Tống and Lương the Fat.
> Operated in Hanoi, Huế and Saigon.
>
> Nguyễn Sĩ Sách (1902–1929).
> Born in Nghệ An, Vietnam.
> AKA: Kim Phong.
> Led local operations in Annam.

At first, the new Vietnamese Communist Party comprised only members of the groups present and other Vietnamese exiles living in China. Shortly afterwards, the Indochinese Communist League accepted the suggestion that they merge with the Vietnamese Communist Party.

By establishing a unified Vietnamese Communist Party, Hồ had secured the nucleus of his strategic political front. The Party not only gave him a local political framework to work with inside Vietnam, but it opened the gateway to greater international help. Hồ used the name Vietnamese rather than Indochinese, because the former name represented a national party focusing on the one nation, whereas the latter name echoed French colonialism.

On the direction of the Comintern, the name soon changed to the Indochinese Communist Party. Frustrated Comintern functionaries had pointed out to Hồ's Party Central Committee that when Hồ had established the Vietnamese Communist Party he had emphasized within his manifesto an independent Vietnam, a phrase akin to promoting nationalism, with little emphasis on the wider international communist movement. This to them had been unacceptable. They felt that the name Indochinese reflected a wider world vision; with this change favorable terms of reference could then be compiled to emphasize the communist movement. Hồ could not attend this October meeting in Hong Kong, but he knew that thereafter Comintern meddling would become part of everyday life.

Establishing a Courier Department

Hồ described the couriers and their corridors as the most important element for victory, because without them none of his revolutionary activities could operate or expand. Things had come a long way since the days of the first training programs in

China. Fundamentally, events had become more complicated in Vietnam. The revolutionaries might have had the support of the Comintern and formed a united communist party but the French were becoming ever more ruthless in the early 1930s, and courier networks needed to adapt to deal with this threat.

The Indochinese Communist Party discussed and agreed upon their first major reforms to the courier system at the meeting held in Hong Kong in October 1930. The official document which mentioned the changes was called *The Political Thesis of the Indochinese Communist Party*. The restructuring aimed to expand the Party networks, as well as consolidate what was already there. At present it was a mismatch of political cells and sporadic courier lines because the Party had its roots in the Vietnamese RYL as well as other communist parties, each with its own independent courier operations.[21]

One part of the thesis read, "The Party apparatus must keep in close contact with the masses when conducting any operation. [To do this, the Party] must organize and expand its courier system to all areas of the Party, but especially to remote cells." The thesis went on to mention safeguarding with specific orders to find more advanced protection methods, such as strengthening procedures around safe house operations and improving access to Party cells at regional and provincial levels.[22] Operators experienced at running important existing networks were named Dynamic Comrades, and they and others who joined them, were sent to design these new lines. By 1932 the Party had worked out effective ways to tackle French aggression.

International events influenced the next substantial change to the courier system. On 27 March 1935, the Indochinese Communist Party held their First National Party Congress in Macau.[23] The Party Central Committee discussed who should go to Moscow for the 7th World Congress of the Comintern, scheduled for 25 July to 20 August 1935. At the World Congress one of the main agenda items was to be the official endorsement of the Popular Front policy, first introduced by the Comintern in 1934. The Comintern wanted to counter the growing threat of fascism by allowing communist parties to form alliances with almost any political party willing to oppose this threat, regardless of their attitude towards socialism and working class roots.

To prepare for the new Popular Front for Indochina, those present in Macau further went on to discuss the courier networks. With such a diverse number of nationalist groups coming together under the new Front, the Party's clandestine work had to be further safeguarded. Members passed a new Resolution saying, "No one person must know more than one Party network. Party courier lines must remain separate from those of the new Front, which could include groups such as the Communist Youth and the Labor Union," and groups with individuals who had at one time opposed the revolutionaries.[24]

These changes to the courier system in the mid–1930s gave Hồ the means to support any new Popular Front for Indochina. Eventually the new group formed at the Party Central Committee's conference in Shanghai in July 1936, and was called the Indochinese Democratic Front. It did indeed unite a broad coalition of different political organizations, predominantly centralists and left-wing elements opposed to fascism. However, the Front was, in fact, a ruse. Unknown to the public who supported it, the Front and the organizations it represented were actually run covertly by the Party, and was therefore being guided towards socialism.

In 1936 the Popular Front in France won the elections and came to office. This meant that in Vietnam the Indochinese Democratic Front and other revolutionary organizations of Hồ's could operate more openly, and in doing so they expanded their semi-legal courier activities, such as revolutionaries working in editorial offices and distributing literature. One newspaper printed was the *Le Travail*, a socialist paper written in French and run by the students of Lycée Albert Sarraut in Hanoi. When the first issue was published on 16 September 1936, Võ Nguyên Giáp (1911–2013) was the editor in chief, at that time a registered journalist operating semi-legally, but later to become the supreme military leader of the revolution.[25] Anticipating the closure of *Le Travail* by the French, Giáp and his colleagues published the newspaper *Rassemblement*, but again the French shut it down. A few months after that Giáp and his colleagues set up yet another paper, *En Avant*.[26]

In Hanoi, each publication not only spread Communist Party propaganda but their editorial offices and bookshops served as courier way stations. This combination allowed the Party to bring its illegal, semi-legal and legal activities together as well as connect them to its wider urban and rural movements. Furthermore, it made the Party accessible, because the general public could walk off the street into an editorial office or bookshop to report anything of relevance.

In the autumn of 1938, the French Popular Front dissolved itself, confronted by internal dissensions related to the Spanish Civil War, opposition of the right-wing, and the persistent effects of the Great Depression. A new coalition formed but this time it included right-wing parties. Any leniency towards colonial countries soon reversed and the revolutionaries in Vietnam again became a target of French White Terror.

In view of the French aggression, at a conference in June 1939, the Party Central Committee concluded they needed to set up agencies across Vietnam to again consolidate their activities. The Courier Department was one of these agencies. Part of its task was to oversee the policy first discussed at the Macau Congress in 1935, which demanded the separation of Party courier lines from those of other organizations. Another principle of the Courier Department, was that the networks should no longer work semi-legally, but be ordered to operate completely covertly.[27]

Throughout the 1930s, Hồ's couriers had matured to form a department, but their strength still mainly lay in Tonkin and the network had not been tested in combat.

Humble Beginnings of the Strategic Military Front

Hồ only ever wanted to use military action as a last resort; he did not want to damage public relations and his opponents had far greater military strength than his followers. Still, he did recognize that ultimately he would have to structure the revolution to initiate full armed resistance at some point. His main objective was that any military action by the revolutionaries must force his enemy to make political decisions in favor of the resistance. In the late 1930s, Hồ predicted that military action might now be needed; there were new threats on the horizon with turmoil from the Second World War (1939–1945) and the Second Sino-Japanese conflict (1937–1945).[28]

Đào Văn Trường, a journalist and staunch ally of Hồ, is one of the few surviving men who not only witnessed, but became actively involved in, the emergence of the strategic military front.[29] In 2008 he was ninety-two years old. The author had the privilege of interviewing him at his home in Hanoi, a modest house fronted by a mature garden. Originally from a rich background, some of his family had been well-educated and laureate Confucian scholars. Despite his wealth and the opportunities that money brings,

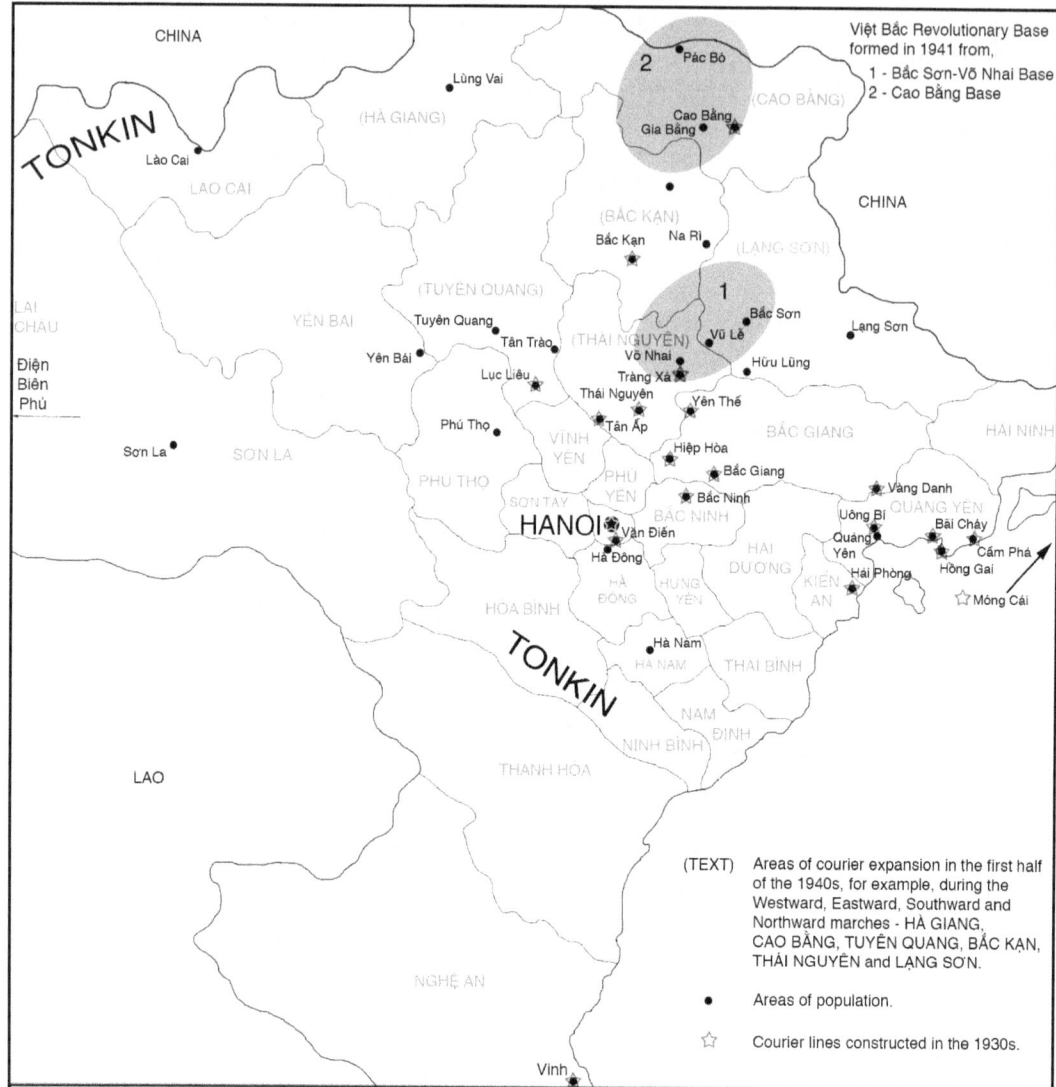

Việt Bắc Revolutionary Base formed in 1941 from,
1 - Bắc Sơn-Võ Nhai Base
2 - Cao Bằng Base

(TEXT) Areas of courier expansion in the first half of the 1940s, for example, during the Westward, Eastward, Southward and Northward marches - HÀ GIANG, CAO BẰNG, TUYÊN QUANG, BẮC KẠN, THÁI NGUYÊN and LẠNG SƠN.

● Areas of population.

☆ Courier lines constructed in the 1930s.

Examples of Courier Lines and their Designers and Operators

Constructed early part of the 1930s as a result of the document, *The Political Thesis of the Indochinese Communist Party*.

- Trần Bảo - Hanoi to Hải Phòng.
- Ms. Nguyễn Thị Nghĩa - Vinh to Hanoi.
- Ms. Hoàng Thị Ái - Huế to Đà Nẵng.
- Mrs. Hoàng Ngân - Hanoi, (around 1940 she took over the line Huế to Đà Nẵng from Ms. Hoàng Thị Ái).
- Ms. Trần Thị Dư - Quảng Nam Province to the headquarters of the Annam Regional Party Committee.
- Ms. Nguyễn Thị Lưu - Hồng Gai (coal mining area) to Hải Phòng and a bridgehead station in Hồng Gai to link with Party courier lines in China.
- Bùi Đức Minh - Saigon to Hanoi via Vinh as well as lines from Hanoi to regions of China.
- Dương Quang Đông - in charge of lines for the Cochinchina Regional Party Committee.

Constructed late part of the 1930s after the Courier Department was founded.

- Lê Trung Đình, Nguyễn Văn Cương, Nguyễn Văn Phúc and Hoàng Minh Đạo were sent to strengthen old networks and establish new ones, with their main area of operation being in the coal mining regions. One new route they established was from Uông Bí to Hồng Gai on to Đồng Đăng railway station and finally Bãi Cháy. Sometimes Hồng Gai was not used owing to French suppression.

- Hoàng Văn Trạch - mainly used merchant boats to travel along the waterways to construct lines from Hải Phòng to Hồng Gai and Móng Cái Town. This operation did not run smoothly and it was not until 1940 that lines linked up and became fully operational between the Party Committee of B-Inter-Provincial Zone, the cells within the Zinc Factory (Quảng Yên Province) and the mines of Ranh Dong, Uông Bí and Vàng Danh.

- Lê Hoàng - led the movement in Bắc Ninh Province and Bắc Giang Province, focusing on lines to the mountainous areas.

- Hoàng Quốc Việt - starting in 1938, he designed the lines between Bắc Giang, Tân Ấp, Lục Liễu and Thắng Market. It was only in 1940 that these networks had safe access to Hanoi.

3. The Seeds of Hồ's Revolutionary Strategies

Trường became a communist in 1936 and went on to join the Association of Marxist Research at the end of 1938. He opened his interview by stating his position concisely, "Thanks to patriotism being part of Vietnamese tradition, and my family teaching me to love my country, I was drawn to revolutionary ideas and to communist ideology."[30]

Good connections undoubtedly helped Trường's career. He worked with Trường Chinh, who became the general secretary of the Communist Party; with Hoàng Quốc Việt, a courier who became a high-ranking Party leader; with Ms. Hoàng Ngân, a renowned courier and guerrilla commander, and with Ms. Nguyễn Thị Quang Thái (1915–1944), Võ Nguyên Giáp's first wife, who worked as a courier for the Party Central Committee.

Trường began the interview with his recollections of when the Party still focused on political and propaganda agitation as their main strategy to gain independence. Trường described in detail his most memorable attempt at agitation against the Japanese, when he was a member of the Indochinese Democratic Front.

Đào Văn Trường as a prisoner in 1942, when he had been sentenced to death after being arrested with his courier known as Little Dương (courtesy Đào Văn Trường).

Trường said:

> At the end of 1938, I became a standing member of the Indochinese Democratic Youth, a section of the Indochinese Democratic Front. At the same time I was chief editor of *The World* newspaper of the Democratic Youth.... *The World* issued many articles promoting our anti-fascist spirit around the time of the outbreak of the Second World War.
>
> During this period there was an event that became a crucial turning point in my life as a revolutionary. In 1939, a Japanese delegation, led by Mishera, arrived in Vietnam. They openly advocated their further invasion of China and what would be known as their Greater East Asia Co-Prosperity Sphere, which represented Japan's desire to create a self-sufficient bloc of Asian nations, free of Western powers.[31]
>
> In the *Olympia Cinémathéque* the Japanese held a gathering to promote their ambitions for the region. They only invited the Vietnamese upper classes, including landlords, bourgeoisie and the intelligentsia. The workers and the peasantry could not enter. As a journalist, using my press card, I too had access. The atmosphere inside was tense, as the French *Sûreté* and their Vietnamese partners guarded the cinema. The Japanese tried to encourage the people to spread their message.... It was a coordinated propaganda exercise, not only were speeches made but films shown with the same slanted message.
>
> I waited until the Japanese had finished describing their grand vision. Then, with my heart pounding, I jumped on stage shouting anti–Japanese slogans against their invasion of China, and against their plot for further invasions under their Sphere.... With precision the Japanese and the French *Sûreté* rushed to arrest me. To confuse matters, the people surrounded me like a fence, to defend me. I took off my coat so I could not be recognized. In only a shirt and trousers I made my escape.

Opposite: Crucial courier lines opened in the 1930s and their relationship to the courier expansion in the first half of the 1940s.

A copy of a newspaper managed by Đào Văn Trường called *The World*. This is a special issue published on 15 October 1938 opposing the German and Italian fascists and promoting peace (courtesy Đào Văn Trường).

The last issue of *The World* written by Đào Văn Trường in 1939 after giving his speech in the *Olympia Cinémathéque* and before he operated underground. This issue opposes the Japanese invasion of the south of Asia (courtesy Đào Văn Trường).

I fled by the back door to Nguyên Sinh Street, arriving at a courier post disheveled but excited. Here I met both Comrade Trường Chinh, a member of Tonkin Regional Party Committee, and Comrade Nguyễn Văn Cừ [1912–1941] the general secretary. I told them and their associates what I had done for the communists. They all listened intensely, then hugged me, before explaining my next task. I was to publish within *The World* newspaper articles denouncing the Japanese plot to invade us, calling the people to struggle against the war and against fascism. Once I had published *The World* I then had to work totally covertly, since operating as a semi-legal radical courier and journalist would be too dangerous.[32]

In the latter part of 1939, Trường left his cover as a journalist and moved to B-Inter-Provincial Zone, a transfer that led to his military career. This zone included Hải Phòng, the location of the largest worker movement. As secretary of Hải Phòng City and, soon afterwards, secretary of the B-Inter-Provincial Zone, Trường was tested at once.

On 22 September 1940, the Imperial Japanese Army invaded Vietnam from the land, sea and air, and some of the troops arrived in Lạng Sơn Province, part of Trường's jurisdiction. This Japanese invasion took most people by surprise, because earlier that day an apparent peace agreement had been made between the Japanese and the French Vichy government.[33] Vichy France was formed when France conceded defeat and surrendered to Nazi Germany; thereafter they collaborated with the Axis Powers, which meant that French Indochina opened negotiations with the Japanese.

The Japanese needed to enter Indochina, to enable them to cut off the Chinese Kuomintang in Yunnan Province from American supplies coming in from Hải Phòng. Japan had previously pressurized the Vichy government, but without success, to close a strategic railway being used to supply the enemy. Frustrated, on 5 September, the Japanese Army organized troops to move into Indochina. Faced with invasion, the Vichy government yielded. On 22 September, Japan and Vichy Indochina signed an accord; this allowed up to 6,000 Japanese troops to be stationed in Indochina but with no more than 25,000 troops stationed or in transit at any given time. All Japanese land, air and naval forces were barred from Indochinese territory, except as authorized in the accord.

In spite of the agreement the Japanese military invaded on 22 September. The French protested vehemently; firstly because the brand new agreement had been breached, but more to the point, the Japanese units included pro–Japanese Vietnamese troops loyal to Prince Cường Để. What particularly incensed the French was that, as these pro–Japanese troops advanced, they sent out appeals to Vietnamese units under French command to support the invasion and to turn on their colonial masters.

After a few days of intense fighting, the French and the Japanese agreed a ceasefire. This permitted loyal French troops to return to the posts they had abandoned or been forced out of during the fighting, but left the pro–Japanese Vietnamese troops at the mercy of the enraged French. Although the fighting had been ended swiftly, it set a precedence of aggression. Thereafter, the Japanese took an ever increasing role across Indochina; they kept the colonial Vichy French in place to administer the region, but on many occasions this was in name only.

Just as Hồ had predicted, the revolutionaries now had two oppressors to fight: the French and the Japanese. Having two enemies complicated the preparations for the Cochinchina Uprising, however, this new situation would precipitate the all-important Bắc Sơn Uprising, named after a rural district of limestone peaks and sweeping valleys of Lạng Sơn Province where the fighting eventually took place.

The Bắc Sơn Uprising was a spontaneous assault by the revolutionaries. When the Japanese attacked Lạng Sơn Province, this left a temporary power vacuum, giving locals sympathetic to the revolution the opportunity to ambush their enemies and seize more advanced weaponry. The communists took advantage of the breakdown of authority to implement the Resolution issued at their Sixth Conference. The Resolution had called for an uprising against French imperialism and, when possible, to oppose all invaders, no matter whether they had white or yellow skin. The revolutionaries could act upon this Resolution because, when the Japanese originally struck, several communists broke out of Lạng Sơn Prison. Thái Long led this escape; although this in itself was an achievement, he went on to arm the prisoners and then, with local support, harass the enemy in areas such as Mỏ Nhài, in the center of Bắc Sơn District. The revolutionaries finally captured Mỏ Nhài thanks to Thái Long, who then lay in ambush and on 27 and 28 September killed several French soldiers. The Bắc Sơn Uprising stalled when the French reclaimed the region.

The Cochinchina Uprising, on the other hand, had been planned action against the French by the Cochinchina Regional Party Committee, to start in November 1940. At the Macau Congress in 1935, members had discussed the formation of a military wing to the Indochinese Communist Party, to be called the Military Self-Defense Group. In the late 1930s and into 1940 the Cochinchina Regional Party Committee established these rudimentary armed units across some southern provinces in readiness for the uprising.

Keen to complete the plans for the uprising, the Cochinchina Regional Party Committee sent Phan Đăng Lưu (1902–1941) north to Tonkin to discuss them with senior Party leaders.[34] The main point of discussion was how the uprising fitted with the agreed Party line; any local insurgencies had to be supported by nationwide action. When Phan Đăng Lưu explained that the Cochinchina Regional Party Committee had prepared to execute the uprising, the Tonkin contingent stated they had no time to mobilize nationwide support; the action must be halted.

Unfortunately, to deliver the new counter-order to halt the uprising, a comprehensive courier network needed to be in place, but this did not yet exist. This not only caused Phan Đăng Lưu to arrive back in the south too late to stop preparations, but once he had persuaded the leaders to delay, there was no effective method to spread the news on to others.

This inability to communicate across Cochinchina exposed the revolutionaries. Not only had they not received the counter-order to halt the action, but the French had intelligence on the uprising and individual Party members could not be warned that they had been exposed. These factors led to most of the leaders being killed, with other participants being captured and imprisoned; this situation compromised the courier lines already in place and set the network back for years.

When analyzing these two uprisings, the Party reached the following conclusions. They acknowledged that the Cochinchina Uprising had been very damaging, and officially recorded the Bắc Sơn Uprising as a defeat. They had not anticipated that the courier lines were not strong enough to react to such an abrupt change of orders, nor were they developed enough to support and maintain the insurgents. Where lines did exist, they had been too easily compromised by the French due to the hostile environment.

These failings during military action resulted in the creation of what the Party called "corridors," a significant development of several courier lines running in parallel but completely isolated from each other. The principle was that a message would go out along one line and come back on another. Corridors made it far harder for the enemy to predict which route to target, and if a person was arrested, as they only knew their small link, that person would not be able to expose anyone operating in another parallel line. To make the lines stronger and more capable, the Party agreed to arm the couriers. This made the traditional system more military-based.

Trường explained:

What Bắc Sơn did successfully achieve is that the Party could see that they were capable of orchestrating insurgencies, and that, with this capability, they could now move towards armed struggle. It also focused the leader's attention in on Bắc Sơn, and the area eventually become our military capital.

The question that could not be answered directly was who would command our up-and-coming guerrilla fighters. We had several leaders who had graduated from the Whampoa Military Academy or from the Soviet Union, but they could not get to Vietnam because the Japanese had closed the border.

To understand this period, and who was behind the growth of our guerrilla fighters, we have to go back to the start of the Bắc Sơn Uprising.[35]

The First Official Units

Hồ's initial fighters did not graduate from noted military academies but rose to prominence swiftly because they had played their part in the Bắc Sơn Uprising.

When the uprising started in September 1940, Chu Văn Tấn was the secretary of the Bắc Sơn Party, and it was he who had informed the Tonkin Regional Party Committee of events. The Party ordered the temporary command at Bắc Sơn to cease activities until two Tonkin Regional Party Committee members could be sent to assess the situation. The two revolutionaries given this task were Trần Đăng Ninh (1910–1955) and Nguyễn Thành Diên (191?–194?).

Trường said:

Both men had been very skilled in Party matters. Trần Đăng Ninh held the position of temporary member of the Party Central Committee. Nguyễn Thành Diên had studied at the third course of the Vietnamese RYL as well as studied Chinese martial arts, a good skill to have. Neither Ninh nor Diên, however, were militarily trained. [They had been chosen by the Party Central Committee more for their position within the Party rather than for their military skills.]

On 14 October 1940, Ninh and Diên convened a meeting in Sa Khao, Bắc Sơn District, to found our first official armed unit. Called the Bắc Sơn guerrillas, they were created by consolidating the armed insurgents of the uprising. Ninh became responsible for political goals and Diên for the military activities of these guerrillas. Chu Văn Tấn, the secretary of the Bắc Sơn Party, stayed at Võ Nhai so that he could help build a base area there to support the movement at Bắc Sơn.

By the end of October, the guerrillas had managed to spread propaganda within their area of operation, as well as to engage in some military action.[36]

It was at the Seventh Conference in November 1940, that the Party Central Committee agreed two military training courses. These were to be held in November and December, in the hilly remote area of Đức Thắng, Hiệp Hòa District.

Trường said:

Chu Văn Tấn returned with a team to Bắc Sơn to spread propaganda and build up the Party networks there. It was very dangerous work, as the French had entered the regions of Bắc Sơn and Võ Nhai to execute terror.

The Party assigned me to complete my training at Đức Thắng, because I was the youngest member of the Tonkin Regional Party Committee and keen on martial arts. They recognized my previous Party involvement and made me political commissar for the course, and concurrently the secretary of the course's communist Party cell.

With regards to my military training, in fact I did not acquire much knowledge at all, after studying military tactics, at most, I could only command up to company level. Our course had just two textbooks: *Manuel de l'Infanterie Coloniale* and a military training book issued by the Chinese Kuomintang, which had been stolen by the revolutionaries. Yet thanks to these books the Party now regarded me as a military revolutionary and one of the first soldiers of Hồ Chí Minh.[37]

That December, the Party had the chance to send Lương Văn Chi (1910–1941) to command operations in Bắc Sơn.

Trường recalled:

> Comrade Lương Văn Chi had a lot of military experience. He had attended the Whampoa Military Academy, although at the alternative branch in Yunnan. He had trained at the Kuomintang Military School and had fought as a battalion commander in Chiang Kai-shek's army. Politically he was a standing member of the Tonkin Regional Party Committee.
>
> On 23 February 1941, Hoàng Văn Thụ [who operated with Ms. Sáu] declared the formation of the National Salvation Troops at a meeting in Khuổi Nọi, Vũ Lễ Commune. Thụ was in overall control whilst Lương Văn Chi took over the operational command.
>
> Although not declared in the October or February meetings, when the war-time history was being officially documented, the Party agreed to recognize the guerrillas formed at the meeting in Sa Khao Village, Bắc Sơn District, in October 1940, as the first platoon of the National Salvation Troops.[38]

Hồ Forms the Việt Minh

Hồ now returned at last from China to Vietnam to chair the Eighth Conference at Pác Bó, Cao Bằng Province, in May 1941.[39] The delegates sat in rudimentary conditions to discuss and approve three key issues.

Primarily, the members present finally agreed the political direction of the revolution: the demands of ideology and class war must be subordinate to those of the anti-imperialist struggle for national independence.[40] This meant that all anti-colonialists, from communists to capitalists, including workers, peasants, landlords and bourgeoisie, could now be united under one organization. To show that all members of society would be viewed as allies, those present adopted as their symbol a red flag with a yellow five-pointed star, the five points representing the workers, farmers, soldiers, intellectuals and traders. In addition, Hồ suggested the formation of a democratic republic, contrary to the Workers' and Peasants' program proposed in 1930.

To take forward the struggle for national independence, the second main area agreed was the creation of the League for the Independence of Vietnam. Hồ could see that he needed a new all-encompassing organization because his Indochinese Democratic Front might have seemed outwardly very strong, but structurally it was weakening. His new organization had to be there to fill any power vacuum that might arise from the collapse of the Indochinese Democratic Front.

The League for the Independence of Vietnam was commonly known as the Việt Minh Front, Việt Minh or VM to the French, the name and its abbreviation came from the ineffectual non-communist organization built by Hồ Học Lãm in 1936 in China. Hồ purposely wanted to use the name as a ploy in order to cause confusion among the enemy and blur any links to communism.

Under the umbrella of Hồ's Việt Minh, the members at the Eighth Conference agreed to establish various organizations to appeal to different areas within society; to be known collectively as the National Salvation Organizations. This meant that people could either join the Việt Minh or could join one of the organizations if they did not want to be directly associated with them. From a security point of view, by having so many different organizations, it made it incredibly difficult for their enemy to penetrate them and destroy the Việt Minh. One recognizable group was the National Salvation Troops, shaped by the Tonkin Regional Party Committee to be the engine of the Việt Minh.

The third point was the formation of two base areas, which could only now be done because of the continuous progress made since the Bắc Sơn Uprising. The first one was in the Bắc Sơn-Võ Nhai region and the second in Cao Bằng. Indochinese Communist Party members called the combined region the Việt Bắc Revolutionary Base.

The establishment of the Việt Minh was a breakthrough; crucially there seemed to be unity. Members present at the conference had finally agreed to link with others outside the communist or socialist sphere to achieve Vietnam's liberation. Originally an approach tried during the days of the Vietnamese RYL, but until this present conference it had been greeted with limited enthusiasm because it had not been viewed as "true" communism. Now skeptical so-called "proper" communists accepted the model; they were members of a recognized communist group, the Indochinese Communist Party. They also knew that by having communist cells throughout the structure of the Việt Minh they had the ability to control vast sections of the population. The revolution had taken another move forward.

The First Việt Minh Guerrilla Commanders

Trường did not attend the founding of the Việt Minh. When he reached Võ Nhai on his way to the conference, senior Party members instructed him to return to Bắc Sơn at once. The French had sent thousands of troops into the region.

Trường explained:

To lead the National Salvation Troops at Bắc Sơn-Võ Nhai Base area, the Eighth Conference appointed Comrade Phùng Chí Kiên [1901–1941] commander, with Lương Văn Chi in operational command.[41] Phùng Chí Kiên had been Hồ Chí Minh's right-hand man in China and a seasoned Party member who had attended the third course of the Vietnamese RYL. Militarily he had graduated from Whampoa Military Academy, participated in the Sino-Soviet armed uprising in Guangzhou and Baise, China in 1929, and in late 1930 had graduated from a military school in the Soviet Union. The Party instructed both men to build Bắc Sơn-Võ Nhai Base in accordance with the policies of the newly founded Việt Minh. From July 1941 onwards the guerrillas at Bắc Sơn-Võ Nhai became more established.

Problems arose. The French and Vietnamese auxiliary troops played dirty tricks to crush us. The French ordered the Vietnamese troops to mingle in with the local civilian population so that these troops could spy on us. They transferred these Vietnamese troops between provinces to areas we occupied; these troops laid siege to us, to cut off our supplies so that we could not operate. In addition, the French punished the villagers to stop them from helping us. The French ruined any crops the villagers had and where possible undermined their local economy with the aim of making these communities so poor that they would have little food, if any, to give to us. The French built what could only be described as concentration camps for the villagers, in an attempt to separate us from the general population. We found it hard to recruit.

To safeguard our troops from French aggression, on 27 July 1941 the commanders of the National Salvation Troops decided to divide up our guerrilla unit so that the majority of them could withdraw from Bắc Sơn to Cao Bằng. At this time our unit was around a platoon in size, with Phùng Chí Kiên in command. The first group from the unit headed to Cao Bằng, and were led by Phùng Chí Kiên himself. The second group was led by Hoàng Văn Thái [1915–1986].[42] Chu Văn Tấn took the remaining guerrillas who were not in these two groups back to Tràng Xá, Võ Nhai District, so that they could guard the rest of the members of the Party Central Committee, who had remained there.

This decision to divide up our unit was a catastrophic error; each smaller group became more vulnerable to French aggression. The group led by Phùng Chí Kiên did indeed fall into a French ambush in Na Rì, with few survivors. The French killed Phùng Chí Kiên and captured Lương Văn Chi, who later died in prison. The second group succeeded, they went through Lũng Vài and headed to Lạng

3. The Seeds of Hồ's Revolutionary Strategies

Sơn instead of Cao Bằng and then on into China. It was to here that the battle weary survivors of the first group headed.

Fortunately, we recovered from this mistake. During a meeting in Tràng Xá, held on 15 September, Hoàng Quốc Việt established the second platoon of the National Salvation Troops. It consisted of forty-seven troops, including three women, with Chu Văn Tấn temporarily in command. Although we expanded, it could have been a different story, as we had lost some very important people.

But with this loss of men came my opportunity. The Tonkin Regional Party Committee held a conference in the Red River Delta in October 1941. They were looking at the detail of the Resolution from the Eighth Conference. While this present conference progressed, Hoàng Quốc Việt appeared. He was a member of the Party Central Committee and had just returned from Bắc Sơn-Võ Nhai. Comrade Việt had bad news, "The commanders of the Bắc Sơn guerrillas have been put out of action." He was referring to the French ambush in Na Rì.

General Secretary Trường Chinh decided that I, the only militarily trained person, should be sent to command the guerrillas so that we could continue fighting the enemy in their rear base area.

After I received the order to command the guerrillas, the members present told me to, "Keep the gunfire of the Bắc Sơn Uprising alive." All night long my leaders told me what to do. Trường Chinh put his old coat on my shoulders saying, "From now on, you will take on a new alias, Trung Kiên [translated as Faithful]. At all costs please try to rise to the challenge and emulate what Comrade Phùng Chí Kiên left." Hoàng Văn Thụ put his scarf around my neck saying, "When returning to report to the Party Central Committee, your alias is Xuân Trường [translated as Immortal Spring]." Hoàng Quốc Việt gave me a new Chinese pistol he had been presented with at the Eighth Conference.

My mission moved all of us and I knew that from now on I didn't have the right to die! In Vietnamese tradition, when a warlord or emperor puts his own armor on the shoulders of his chosen general, it means that the mission given to that general is as significant as his own. With such an important task ahead I never forgot either the recommendations of my Party leaders on what I should do, or the warmth they showed me as a young communist undertaking a military task for the first time. Their kindness will never leave me for as long as I live.[43]

From October 1941 to February 1942, Trường operated in Bắc Sơn-Võ Nhai commanding the second platoon, now with fifty-seven guerrilla fighters. On this appointment he become one of the first commanders of Hồ.

In parallel, Trường took on the further task of military proselytizing operative. This job was far more dangerous than being a covert agent because he had to reveal his identity to his enemy when persuading them to join the Việt Minh and bring their essential weapons with them. He also delivered leaflets and produced banners to spread his propaganda. His background in journalism and his knowledge of the French language led to a higher success rate than his colleagues.

Trường described how he started this second area of responsibility:

At that time, those operating in Tuyên Quang did not have good courier lines; they could only conduct business because they used networks in other provinces. This was not an ideal situation. I knew that the border areas between two or more French administrations meant that a French post in one province would think that the other was responsible for policing the region. Using this void in enemy activity my team established such strong new courier lines in Tuyên Quang Province that Tân Trào, Sơn Dương District, was chosen as a base for Hồ Chí Minh's future government.

I also sent guerrilla units to Hữu Lũng and Bắc Giang. This left just forty-seven guerrillas at Bắc Sơn-Võ Nhai Base. Even with such low numbers we still managed to keep the spirit of the Bắc Sơn Uprising alive until the formation of our army at the end of 1944.[44]

Further Compartment Rules for Couriers

In 1942, Trường's luck ran out, triggering a compartment rule change to the courier network. Basic compartment rules had been around since Hồ's first training camps in

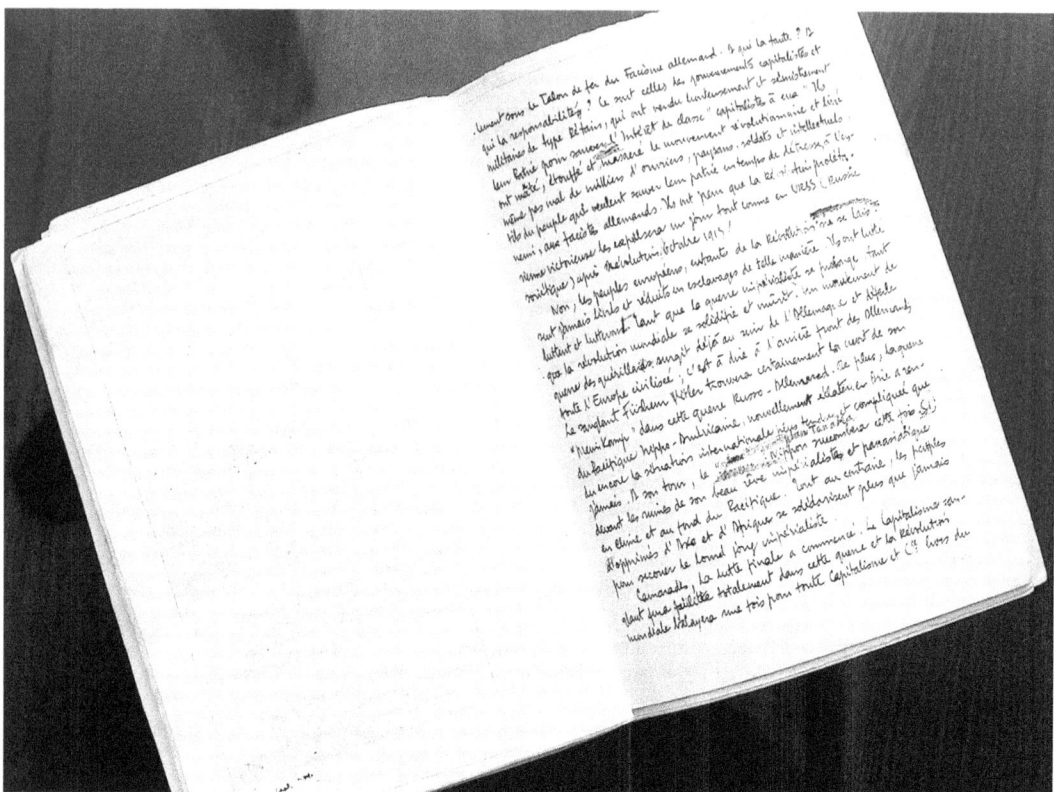

Đào Văn Trường's notes on military proselytizing, written in French and dated 1941 (courtesy Đào Văn Trường).

China, in 1925, such as a courier must only know their immediate link person. More recently another appeared after the Cochinchina Uprising and the Bắc Sơn Uprising in 1940, and the establishment of parallel lines known as corridors either between various groups or within the Communist Party hierarchy.

Now in 1942, Trường had to convey an urgent message to his superiors about guerrilla movements. That February, Chu Văn Tấn, a key participant in the Bắc Sơn Uprising and now the commander of the Võ Nhai Base, confirmed that he would temporarily move his guerrilla fighters to the Vietnam-China border. Tấn insisted that this should be done to draw the French away from Võ Nhai, thus preserving its networks from French White Terror. He chose the border region because not only were other guerrilla fighters there, but some of his guerrillas could ask their Chinese relatives for help.

Trường wanted to report Tấn's intentions to the Tonkin Regional Party Committee. On his way to meet with them, Trường and his courier, known as Little Dương, reached a market in Thái Nguyên Province. Unfortunately, a local resident acting as an agent for the French *Sûreté*, recognized Little Dương, and the French arrested both men. Little Dương's fate is not known, but Trường received three life terms and one death sentence, although the French commuted the latter one.[45]

Trường's arrest interrupted contact between the guerrillas and the Tonkin Regional Party Committee. To prevent communication breakdown again, the Party instructed; where possible, a courier and the revolutionary being guided must not appear to be traveling together. The compartment rule change that resulted from Trường's misfortune, undoubtedly went on to save many lives.

Betrayal: The Most Evil Act

Hồ had now laid the foundations for his courier network and his three strategic fronts: political, propaganda and the military. Although incomplete, it was not this that worried him most. Hồ spent his precious time building strong relationships, but with the success came betrayal.

Hồ himself had his fair share of let-downs. His wife was purportedly the younger sister of Lâm Đức Thụ's wife.[46] Lâm Đức Thụ was well respected and his father, Nguyễn Mậu Kiến, a noted scholar and a friend of Hồ's father. He was held in such high regard by Hồ that he convened the first meetings of the Vietnamese RYL at Lâm Đức Thụ's palatial home in Guangzhou. Lâm Đức Thụ still fell from grace. Lê Thiết Hùng, the son-in-law of Hồ Học Lãm, discovered large sums of money in his house around the end of 1926. Hồ intended dealing with the matter at the right time, so he asked Hùng not to disclose this to other Vietnamese RYL members.[47] When this matter finally surfaced, members reacted differently. Some wanted Lâm Đức Thụ disciplined as they suspected him of being the collaborator Agent Pinot, who is blamed for foiling the assassination attempt on Merlin, the French governor general. Others favored his continued participation because he had run trusted courier stations.

The fact that members viewed Lâm Đức Thụ as a traitor not only tarnished Hồ and his wife, but other family members, such as Nguyễn Công Thu. He had worked as a courier for the Vietnamese RYL, and had recruited a high number of trainees for Hồ's political courses in Guangzhou. Perceived to be so loyal, Hồ had trusted him to take the first copies of his book, *The Road to Revolution*, into Vietnam. Nevertheless, Nguyễn Công Thu was the brother of Lâm Đức Thụ, and so associated with alleged traitorous actions, but furthermore in the 1950s New Revolutionaries accused Nguyễn Công Thu of being a spy.[48] Although the Party did not arrest him or any family member, being linked to the words traitor and spy are still failings that hang over the family name, even today.

Ms. Lương, the first and only woman to study at the Vietnamese RYL, became another victim. Her path to betrayal started in Saigon, when she met the high flying revolutionary Trần Tư Chính, and a mutual admiration for each other grew.[49] Later he became her second guarantor so that she could attend the third political course of the Vietnamese RYL. He had studied there with her, and on one moonlit night he had told Ms. Lương that he loved her. On her return to Saigon after the course, Trần Tư Chính was not there to greet her, but still rumors circulated between some revolutionaries that they had been seeing too much of each other. He had, in fact, been in prison, but the gossip persisted because, once released in early 1928, Ms. Lương could not contain herself for him, and on one occasion she openly displayed her fury and dismay when Vietnamese RYL members called Trần Tư Chính back to Hanoi.

The Party disapproved of any relationship not sanctioned by them, so on Trần Tư Chính's return to Cochinchina in 1929, he knew he had to quash any rumors about the two of them. If he did not, he feared that these might get in the way of his orders, which were to dissolve the Vietnamese RYL and help establish the Annamese Communist Party.

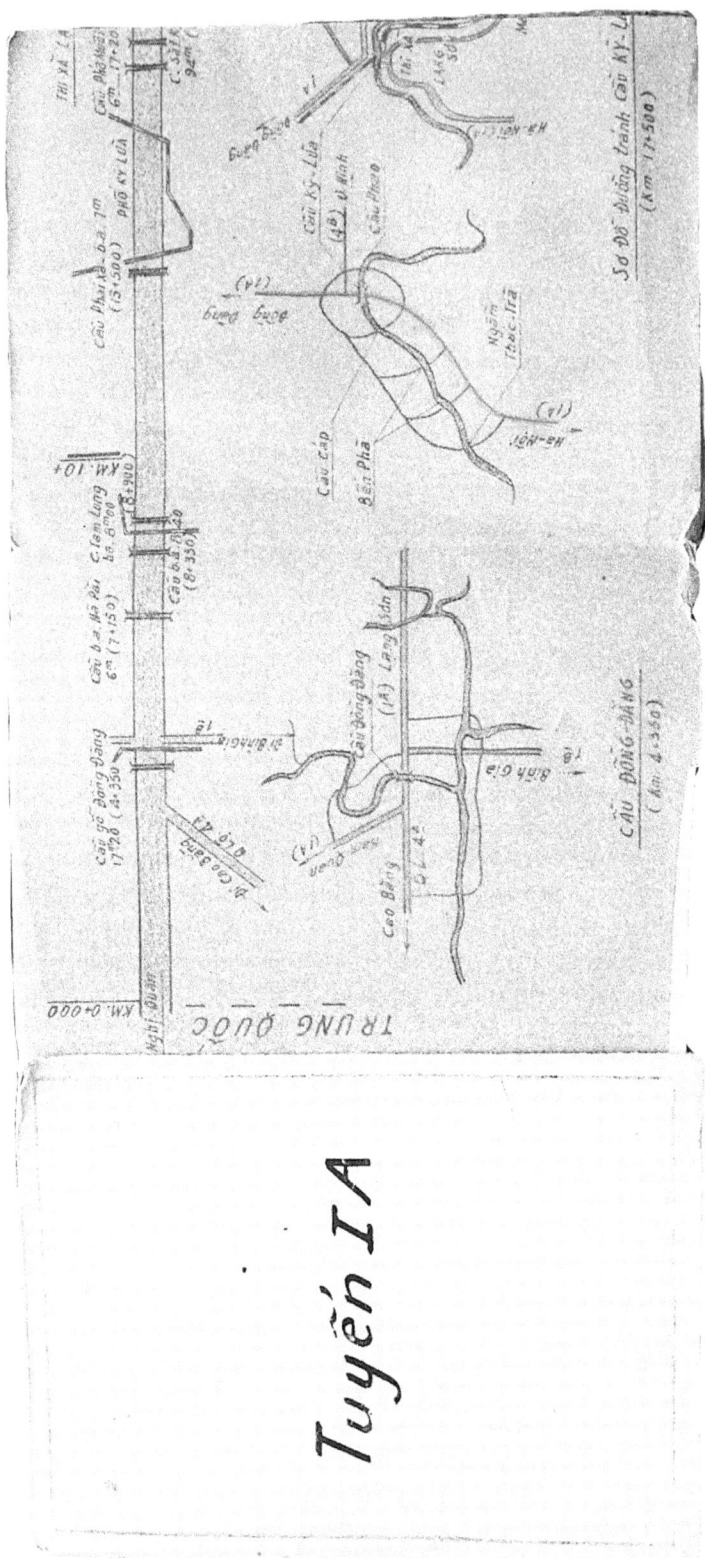

A page out of Đào Văn Trường's personal notebook from the Vietnam War when he was deputy commander of the B Department of the Ministry of Communications (A = North Vietnam, B = Southern Battlefield Vietnam and C = Lao Battlefield). The department covered the road system from North to South Vietnam including routes from China. This notebook shows all the bridges across land and over waterways that had to be kept open to traffic in North Vietnam. This particular page shows the former bridges on the border with China where the Vietnamese provinces of Cao Bằng and Lạng Sơn meet. Trường's job was to monitor constantly which bridges were still passable after being attacked (courtesy Đào Văn Trường).

An early 1968 photograph: the first man is Deputy Commander Đào Văn Trường of the B Department of the Ministry of Communications and after him Deputy Commander Nguyễn Tường Lân, a civilian responsible for volunteers and their links to the Ministry of Communications. Lân was later deputy commander to Đồng Sĩ Nguyên, who was the commander of the Hồ Chí Minh Trail (courtesy Đào Văn Trường).

To quash the gossip and any feelings that they might have for each other, it is believed he falsely and cruelly blamed her for the Rue Barbier case, which had seen the murder of Lê Văn Phát in December 1928.

There is no evidence that Ms. Lương was involved in the case, and there are differing accounts as to what happened. Nevertheless, seven months after Phát's murder the French arrested Ms. Lương.[50] This left her colleagues to question how the French knew her whereabouts. Some nationalists suspected Trần Tư Chính of informing the French, others have seen it simply as the work of the enemy gathering intelligence on the Vietnamese RYL, thanks to spies such as Lâm Đức Thụ. If the latter is true, the Rue Barbier case could have been a well-executed French plot designed to cause friction within the crumbling ranks of the Vietnamese RYL. Irrespective of which scenario is correct, the killing allowed the French to flush out revolutionary leaders such as Tôn Đức Thắng, Ms. Lương's former boss, and saw Trần Tư Chính himself fall from grace.[51]

Once convicted, Ms. Lương spent eight years in prison. Tortured severely and living in brutal conditions, nothing surpassed her loss of faith. On release she turned to writing rather than revolution and died soon after the fall of Saigon.

Trường was sidelined by colleagues, but in his case for reasons linked to China taking an ever greater role in Vietnamese politics at the start of the 1950s. China advised Hồ that he had to build re-education camps in order to reform the wealthy classes and those not engaged in the revolution. This meant that, although Trường and some fellow revolutionaries fought their way out of jail during the August Revolution of 1945, freedom was short-lived. He and many others were sent to be brainwashed in Marxism and Leninism.

The Chinese policy went further and stated that those from the wealthy classes should not hold high office even if talented and best suited for the role available. On leaving re-education Trường went on to become a teacher for the Party at one of their schools. Võ Nguyên Giáp managed to free Trường, as he never forgot his friend's military talents. Giáp assigned him to be acting commander of the 351st Engineer and Artillery Division for the Battle of Điện Biên Phủ in 1954.[52] Following his key participation during this battle, the Party did not promote Trường to be commander of the Artillery of the Vietnamese People's Army. Instead, in 1956, they promoted the less experienced Lê Thiết Hùng to that position, and drew on others, who came from peasant stock, to fill high-ranking posts in the new artillery unit. During the Vietnam War, Trường had again to accept the less prestigious but taxing position of deputy commander of the Civilian Supply State Department for the Southern Battlefield (B Department).[53] It seems that however much Trường embraced re-education and promoted communism, living up to his designated name of Mr. Faithful, he did not have, and would never have, laborer's blood.

From the 1920s, Hồ developed his model for liberation with his courier networks and his three strategic fronts: political, propaganda and the military, thanks to loyal comrades. Sadly the Party betrayed some of these most loyal revolutionaries, either by their lamentable in-house fighting or misapplication of talent, and this threatened stability, playing into the hands of its enemies. Hồ stood strong to unite when others divided; he recognized that without trust and unity he could not take the revolution on to the next stage, and the formation of his blueprint.

4

The Infant Blueprint

The Rise of a Military Leader

Võ Nguyên Giáp led the strategic military front as commander of the army and chief political commissar.[1] Hồ appointed him for two clear reasons. Firstly, Giáp was intelligent, keen and willing to put freedom before family life. Secondly, moreover, he could produce results. One remarkable achievement was during the Southward March, when Giáp designed armed security units for his couriers and their corridors. This impressed Hồ, and from then on he could see the general in Giáp.

Giáp's journey, from designing courier lines to becoming one of the twentieth century's greatest military leaders, was long and dangerous. He is best known for his victory against the French at the Battle for Điện Biên Phủ in 1954, which marked the end of French colonial rule in Indochina and aided the collapse of the world colonial system. Although a key military figure, towards the end of the Vietnam War the Communist Party played down his role. Some cite in-house fighting within the Party, with people devaluing Giáp's importance to protect their own vested interests, and position themselves within a post-revolution Vietnam. Others say that senior Party members believed that no single person should be credited with two unbelievable victories, in case he became too powerful and well-known. Giáp was further marginalized after 1976 because Soviet influence strengthened and Giáp disagreed with some of their policies for Vietnam (namely marginalizing China). Whatever the reasons, it is now accepted in military and political circles that the strategies and tactics Giáp formulated are being followed, even today, by resistance groups outside Vietnam.

Giáp was born into a humble family on 25 August 1911, in An Xá Village, Quảng Bình Province. His father, Võ Quang Nghiêm, never passed his doctoral examination.[2] Through persistence, he did become a noted Confucian scholar, who used his knowledge to teach in his local village. Nghiêm and his wife, Nguyễn Thị Kiên (1887–1961), had seven children. Their first child, called Toai, died of cholera. The next, a girl named Chau, was swept away in floods and never seen again. The following two children were girls, named Võ Thị Điểm and Võ Thị Liên. They became hired farm laborers working the fields and selling goods in the market. Giáp was the fifth child, followed by his brother, Võ Thuận Nho, and finally his sister, Võ Thị Lài, who took a job in a local warehouse. Both Giáp and his brother went on to achieve greater things, with Nho completing his baccalaureate, and eventually becoming the deputy minister of education of the Democratic Republic of Vietnam. Giáp studied Law at the University of Hanoi from 1934 to 1938, and the rest of his career is reasonably well documented.

From left, Professor Đặng Bích Hà (Võ Nguyên Giáp's second wife), Giáp and the author. She visited them at their home in Hanoi on the sixtieth anniversary of the founding of the VNPA on December 23, 2004 (Clive A. Hills).

Grinding hardship was seldom far from the family's door. Võ Quang Nghiêm never owned his own land; he could only farm plots distributed from publicly available fields. This ancient policy of dividing public land every three years did not favor very poor farmers. After the land was divided, those with capital and labor worked the land; those without resources tried to raise money from their land by selling or renting it to others. Thus, wealthy families gained control of fields belonging to the poor. Giáp's family fluctuated between living comfortably when they received good fertile land, which they could tend, to very badly when the opposite happened. This latter scenario was usually the norm, and under these circumstances they were forced to raise money on their land to make ends meet. This exploitation, by which the rich became richer and the poor stayed forever poor, Giáp later acknowledged would "mold his political thinking."[3]

His parents made nationalism part of Giáp's life. His mother often spoke of the Save the King Movement while his father regularly recited the poem, *Collapse of the Capital*, when the two of them lay next to each other in bed.[4] The poem remembered those who had died resisting the French in the Imperial Capital of Huế, during a brief uprising on 4 and 5 July 1885. Giáp did not hear his father's patriotic words again until he studied in Huế City in 1925, and attended the Ceremony for the Souls held on 5 July each year, the day that Huế had finally fallen to the French in 1885.

His time in Huế not only polarized his political views but showed his willingness to protest publically. Although different ages, Giáp became good friends with Phan Bội Châu who, since 1926, had been exiled to Huế by the French. Giáp visited Châu at his house and became fascinated by the posters of Lenin on his wall and enthralled by his motivational words. Châu could see Giáp's willingness to study and promised, "When I pass on, I'll leave my collection of books to you."[5] Giáp's rebellious streak accelerated with the passing of another noted patriot, Phan Chu Trinh, in March 1926. Giáp and his fellow students went against the wishes of their school management board and held an emotional ceremony to remember Trinh. The French police watched Giáp and his fellow students thereafter.

Giáp looked for like-minded people. His nationalist activities and socialist politics found a suitable home when he joined the New Việt Party.[6] Giáp's first main role in this organization was as an alternate member of the Central Executive Committee, with responsibilities for propaganda and courier activities.[7] New Việt leaders advised Giáp to acquire a good understanding of communism; an essential tool when dealing with the peasantry and women of Vietnam. Giáp went on to manage a number of areas, including propaganda among the school youth and organizing female activities.[8]

In a short period of time, Giáp went from rudimentary courier activities to establishing his first major networks. His appointment came about because in July 1928 Phan Đăng Lưu was elected to the Central Executive Committee at the New Việt Congress and was given responsibility for political propaganda. Giáp worked with him and under his guidance learned how to write training documents on Marxism and on the world history of women and worker movements. Now a trusted compatriot, Giáp involved himself in discussions with Vương Thúc Oánh, the son-in-law of Phan Bội Châu, to unite the Vietnamese RYL with the New Việt. Uniting the two groups proved difficult, so Phan Đăng Lưu left for China to resolve the impasse.[9] In Phan Đăng Lưu's absence, Giáp had full control of propaganda as well as becoming head of the courier underground for the New Việt.

It became apparent that a merger between the Vietnamese RYL and the New Việt was not possible right now. The lack of progress with this merger caused a split within the New Việt. Some members wanted to follow Đào Duy Anh's action plan and become a Bloc National, whereas others opted for a communist organization.[10] With debates continuing, in early 1929, Đặng Thai Mai, Nguyễn Chí Diểu and Giáp took the decision to form a covert nucleus within the New Việt, called the Union of Vietnamese Communists; the first communist group formed in Vietnam. Giáp was responsible for political propaganda within the New Việt, so when Đào Duy Anh asked him to spread the word of the Bloc National it gave him the opportunity to preach communism; eventually his cladestine communist cells sprang up in various regions.

With such strong communist feelings rising to the surface within the New Việt, members decided to rename the party the Indochinese Communist League at a conference on 1 January 1930. The following month, the Vietnamese Communist Party invited members of the League to join them. Giáp now had tested revolutionary credentials.

Dedicated to Revolution

Testing times lay ahead for Giáp. In 1935, he married the young and beautiful Ms. Nguyễn Thị Quang Thái, a fellow revolutionary and Communist Party member. The Party that had first brought them together now asked them to part because Giáp had orders to go to China. He had already put the fight against colonialism before family requirements when he refused to marry a local girl in the late 1920s, saying that he was already wedded to the ideal of revolution more than marriage. This time things were different, Quang Thái and he were very much in love, a situation happily reinforced when in January 1939 she gave birth to a baby girl called Hồng Anh (1939–2009). Now as they sat by the West Lake in Hanoi in May 1940, Giáp cradled his daughter in his arms, his heart torn by the ever-increasing demands of his revolutionary duties.

Giáp recalled, "Acquaintances were passing, greeting each other, but we became increasingly unaware of the activities around us as we focused on each other. We were deep in conversation when our thoughts were disturbed by a voice from behind, '*Monsieur*, would you come for a ride please?' I turned around and saw Minh the Teacher [my courier] with his rickshaw.[11] I parted from my wife and rode through Hanoi unaware at the time that we had just made our last farewell."[12]

Quang Thái knew that her husband's departure had to occur, not only for Party needs but because the French net had closed in on him. She wanted to go to China with him but first needed to find a safe place for their daughter. While she found this she operated illegally so she could continue her new work of leading the women's movement among the intelligentsia, workers and traders. In addition, she operated one of the most important courier routes serving the Party Central Committee in Vinh City; a bridgehead region linking the two regional party committees of Tonkin and Annam to the Party Central Committee in Saigon.

Quang Thái found her work challenging but second nature. Her home with Giáp had been a courier way station.[13] To create a cover for Party leaders to come and go, the brother of either Giáp or Quang Thái stayed in their house so that there was always another person visiting. One noted Party operative who stayed was Le Duẩn. In the late 1930s he couriered letters to and from the houses of Quang Thái and Ms. Nguyễn Thị Minh Khai (1910–1941), her sister, as he traveled on missions from the north of the country to the south.[14]

Like her sister, Minh Khai had herself become a courier, her initial task being, in September

Ms. Nguyễn Thị Quang Thái, holding daughter Hong Anh in about 1940 (courtesy Võ Nguyên Giáp).

1930, to develop further a covert line within Shanghai, recently built by Ms. Đức, Hồ's first courier in China.[15]

Both sisters, Quang Thái and Minh Khai, remained faithful to the Party regardless of the danger to their lives. One memorable occasion in fact changed the course of Vietnamese history. In September 1940, the French arrested Minh Khai, now the Party secretary for Saigon. In May the following year, Quang Thai visited Minh Khai when she was on trial with a number of other leading communists. Lê Duẩn (1907–1986), arrested for a second time, was in court. During his interrogation he had denied that he had worked with leading revolutionaries, including Minh Khai, and vice versa.

While in court, Quang Thái spoke to Lê Duẩn because Minh Khai had been desperate to communicate with him, to inform him of a traitor in the court room. For whatever reason, Minh Khai threw a folded piece of paper to him, but it missed and landed at the feet of his French guard. Swiftly, Quang Thái stooped to pick the paper up and put it into her mouth. Then, speaking in French, she persuaded the guard that the message held no meaning and intended for her anyway. If the guard had read the Vietnamese message, and then linked Lê Duẩn with Minh Khai, both could have been sentenced to death.

Lê Duẩn said later, when he had become a top Communist Party leader, "If Quang Thái had not been so quick-witted, I would not be meeting you today."[16] Saving his life allowed him to go on to make unpopular decisions, both within the Party and for the populace, such as after 1975 adopting communism across Vietnam and implementing a controversial collective farms Land Reform Program (although land was distributed to peasants in liberated areas from the 1960s).

Minh Khai was not as fortunate as Lê Duẩn, who received a ten-year sentence; the French executed her in August 1941. She was not the only member of Giáp's family to die in French hands. The French arrested Quang Thái for revolutionary activities and she died in 1944 in Hỏa Lò Prison, Hanoi, leaving their daughter with Giáp's parents. The French also took Giáp's father in the late 1940s, and he died in prison.

It is not surprising therefore, as the wars went on, that a deep-rooted hatred festered against each and every invader, and that Giáp grew ever more willing to put freedom before family life.

Traveling to Meet Hồ in China

In the spring of 1940, Giáp started a remarkable journey that led to the formation of the nationwide Revolutionary Infrastructure and saw him become Hồ's supreme military commander. This journey started with Giáp being guided to China by Minh the Teacher. The union between Giáp and Minh was unusual. Minh was a high-ranking revolutionary, as a member of the Tonkin Regional Party Committee, contrary to Giáp's low-ranking position. He escorted Giáp personally only because of the importance of the task ahead. Giáp left Hanoi in May accompanied by Phạm Văn Đồng (1906–2000).[17]

The two men were to be sent to China because of a change in Party policy. Before departing, Minh the Teacher insisted that Giáp meet with Hoàng Văn Thụ (the same Thụ that Ms. Sáu had worked for) because, as the secretary of the Tonkin Regional Party Committee, he knew the details of this policy change. Thụ waited for Giáp at Chèm Hamlet. On arriving, Thụ spoke about the Resolution issued at the Sixth Conference, which stated that for the first time armed struggle (*bạo động*) was needed; seeing the revolution go from a predominantly political and propaganda fight to a military one as well.

The Communist Party held the Sixth Conference at Hóc Môn, near Saigon, in November 1939. Following this Party conference Hồ had asked Hoàng Văn Thụ to search for suitable candidates to command any future regular army. Hoàng Văn Thụ viewed Giáp as a contender because he was educated and incredibly keen. Hồ agreed to the selection. Hồ probably knew of Giáp through reading his works.[18] Giáp, on the other hand, had known of Hồ through reading his articles when he had been a student in 1925. Although keen to go to China in hope of meeting Hồ, Giáp did not know the full reason for his summons.[19]

Now with their departure day drawing near, Minh the Teacher came and told Giáp to meet again with Hoàng Văn Thụ. So one evening, after teaching his lessons, he got a tram heading to Hà Đông. As it reached Cầu Mới, he got off. With the night setting in, and after checking that there was no one following him, he went to Quảng Thiện Cemetery. There, wearing a turban, dressed in black robes, and holding an umbrella, was a man lounging about, this was Hoàng Văn Thụ. Hoàng Văn Thụ stressed, "Sooner or later the Japanese will invade Indochina, which could see the allied armies arrive here as well. To be ready for this event, our revolutionary movement must have armed forces. We have to prepare in every possible way to wage a guerrilla war, but only when the time is right."[20] From this point on Giáp started to think of armed struggle, not as a scholar or journalist but as a soldier.

Giáp's departure from Hanoi to China had been purposely timed to start on a Friday. Giáp taught at a private school called Thăng Long and, as a general rule, had both Saturday and Sunday off, giving him two clear days before anyone raised questions about his absence from classes the following Monday morning. Nevertheless the general situation was still problematic. Not only was Phạm Văn Đồng still very weak from his time in Côn Đảo Island Prison, but the French *Sûreté* were keeping them under close surveillance.

On Giáp's last day in Hanoi Minh the Teacher drove him to a small restaurant at the end of Yên Phụ Road. This location meant that they could avoid any document checks by the *Sûreté*. Shortly afterwards Đồng arrived and the group settled down for the night. The following morning they went to Đầu Cầu because it was an auxiliary railway station to the main one in Hanoi. Đồng and Giáp took a train heading to Lào Cai, with tickets that had been previously purchased for them by Minh. They were both without luggage and sat separately. Giáp put his dark glasses on. They got off the train at Yên Bái, the station before Lào Cai. As Minh had caught a different train from them, Đồng and Giáp stayed overnight in Yên Bái waiting for his arrival.

When the three of them met up, Minh led them on foot to the bank of the Nậm Ti. This river served as the border between Lào Cai of Vietnam and Yunnan of China and was the location of an historic courier crossing point. The atmosphere was tense, they barely wanted to breathe while they hid under a cane bush waiting for Minh to prepare the next stage. From a well-disguised location, Minh found his small boat and rowed it to the Chinese bank to scout out a good place to disembark. No sooner had the ripples settled than a French customs motorboat appeared. The men became anxious waiting for it to pass; the customs officers on board did not notice that someone had just crossed the river.[21]

The route across the Nam Ti was not a pleasant experience. Small and cramped, the boat had room for just two people; Minh the Teacher had to take both Giáp and Đồng across separately. The seasonal rains had swollen the river and they had to fight against the current while the fast flowing water lapped over the sides. Giáp recalled that he took this time to look back and reflect upon the fact that he had just left behind his enemy-occupied country to escape imprisonment.

Once safely across, Minh the Teacher escorted the party to the home of a Chinese family. Here they changed into grey Sun Yat-sen attire, to help identify them as overseas Chinamen.[22] Giáp and Đồng took the Chinese names of Zhang Hoai-nan (Giáp) and Lin Po-kie (Đồng) and stayed with Hồ Học Lãm, a trusted colleague of Hồ.

The group was called to Kunming and boarded a crowded train at Hokou. For the entire journey they had to dodge Kuomintang controllers, there to check identification. The controllers started from one end of the train and to keep in front of them the group gradually made their way to the far end carriage hoping the controllers would not catch up with them. They never did. When the train stopped the group got off and walked coolly back to the first carriage, which the controllers had recently passed through. This kept these revolutionaries on their toes as the train took two days to arrive. Once there, Vũ Anh (1905–198?) and Hoàng Văn Hoan met them at the station. They guided the men through the ticket barrier to prevent detection by the controllers. Exhausted, they arrived at the house of Phùng Chí Kiên; he was a member of the Party Central Committee working abroad.[23]

While Giáp waited to meet the mystery man known only as Comrade Wang (Hồ Chí Minh), he studied Chinese by reading Chinese newspapers. He also translated from Chinese into Vietnamese, the history of the Soviet Communist Party. At the beginning of June, after nearly two weeks of waiting, Phùng Chí Kiên arrived to take the group to Cuihu, Kunming.

Having arrived at Cuihu the party were greeted by Vũ Anh, who lazed in a boat. Alongside him sat a thin, middle-aged man with bright eyes, dressed in a grey Sun Yat-sen, with a felt hat on his head. This trademark hat made Giáp recognize him as Nguyễn Ái Quốc (Hồ Chí Minh). From memory, when comparing the figure now with a photograph Giáp had seen before in his student days, the only change was that he had grown a distinguished beard. Giáp had come with the preconception that he would be an extraordinary and complicated person. When seeing him sitting there Giáp found him the opposite. Within the first few minutes Giáp felt that he had known him for ages, familiar and warm with pure and simple mannerisms. Giáp said, "This feeling has remained with me until this day. I think that all great people are pure and simple."[24]

Hồ did not compliment Giáp, he turned to Vũ Anh and whispered, "This boy looks like a girl!"[25] Even so, behind Giáp's delicate features Hồ could see a military figure. Hồ sent Đồng, Cao Hồng Lĩnh and Giáp off to study at the Xian Political-Military Academy. It was not to be. Before they had even arrived, Hồ called them back again because in mid–1940 France had finally conceded defeat and surrendered to Nazi Germany, and the French Vichy government formed. With this dramatic change of events, Hồ decided that the three men would best use their existing skills to begin training others, rather than being further trained themselves. Hồ clearly saw potential in Giáp.

The Southward March: Giáp Impresses Hồ

Giáp had been instructed to establish training programs in Jingxi, with Phùng Chí Kiên and Phạm Văn Đồng. Starting in January 1941, each lasted for two weeks and used a training manual drawn up by Hồ called *The Road to Liberation*, which covered topics such as methods of propaganda and how to organize the masses.

To enable the students of Jingxi to attend advanced military training, in late 1940, Hồ, Giáp and others had opened a local Việt Minh office in Guilin, Guangxi Province. This office was a forward thinking ruse because the Việt Minh in this case were Hồ Học Lãm's non-communist organization. Hồ anticipated that the Kuomintang would give access to their training schools to members of this Việt Minh because they would think that they were students under Lãm; not connected to the communists at all. It worked, and Giáp's students of Jingxi were funneled through the Việt Minh in Guilin, which gave them access to the superior training they desperately needed from the Kuomintang.

Giáp recruited the students for the courses from Vietnam, most of whom came from Cao Bằng Province. Their courier route ran from Cao Bằng to Guangxi; to gain free access across the border the students carried Kuomintang documentation. Although the new courier route crossed high mountains and transited dense forests it became the main route for revolutionaries going to and from Vietnam, instead of Lào-Cai-Yunnan or Lạng Sơn-Longzhou (Guangxi). This change of policy had come about because, after assessing intelligence data, Hồ Học Lãm believed that if the Kuomintang invaded Vietnam their army would go through Cao Bằng. By making Cao Bằng to Guangxi their main courier route, the region could be prepared to repel the enemy. Hồ agreed.

Giáp did not know at the time but Hồ had assessed him to see if he was capable of taking on one of the most important plans formally agreed at the Eighth Conference in 1941: the Southward March. Throughout the course of Vietnamese history there have been many southward advances by various armies, all with the same mission: to join the north with the south. Starting with Văn Lang in 500 BC, the Viet ethnic groups in the north of Vietnam began to fight or migrate their way south, efforts that peaked from the eleventh to the eighteenth centuries. Regardless of who entered Vietnam, the Chinese, French, Japanese, Cambodians or the Americans, the northern Viets would not stop until Vietnam was one country, only then would the Southward March be completed. Although today both north and south Viets are considered the same people, their cultures are quite distinct. More notably, their politics are still very different; this is why some people in South Vietnam will say, "One country, two people," in a show of historic defiance towards the northerners.

Giáp and colleagues for now worked unofficially on the Southward March; they had not been told of the name or of the gravity of their mission, they had just been instructed to develop courier Party networks from Cao Bằng Province towards the Red River Delta. This would connect Cao Bằng Base area right through to Bắc Sơn-Võ Nhai Base area, and join them with ATK 2. Giáp still shuttled back and forth between China and Vietnam, but he managed to open his first training course in a cave in the middle of Hòa An District, Cao Bằng Province in Vietnam, at the end of 1941.

Most hill tribes were self-governed and had no interest in any political events that occurred outside their village environment. They pledged loyalty to their family and their land, and not to any other regions of Vietnam, which were completely alien to them. Furthermore, most were animist. In their daily lives they passionately followed individual spirits, usually ancestral, which inhabited a natural object around them; they also looked at natural phenomena with great significance. This animist system caused many problems for the teachers. It was only a matter of time before a teacher entered an area of the village or of the surrounding region that was out of bounds. To appease the offended spirits animal sacrifices had to be carried out; in some cases these sacrifices forced a village into bankruptcy. Such complications of using the tribal farmers to fight outside their spiritual homeland are evident as far back as the time of the Trưng Sisters; the defenders of Vietnam.[26]

Hồ told Giáp that to connect this patchwork of hamlets to the nationwide revolution he had to keep his classes basic and tailor them skillfully to each tribe: a simple message put over in a simple manner. Hồ had at one time commented that Giáp tended to be wordy when putting policy across. To get the tribes to relate complicated wider events to their modest local environment he advised Giáp to give them a sense of ownership of the revolution through a message of nationalism, "Love your country." Slow progress blighted the courses, because many ethnic minority groups could not communicate with their teachers. Although Giáp did make a great effort to learn the minority languages, Hồ suggested drawing pictures to get his point across to the recruits.

Giáp opened a second class within weeks of the first in Nước Hai, Hòa An District, near the border with China. Giáp reported to Hồ how effective the courses had become. Hồ ordered him to open his next set of courses in the mountainous regions of Nguyên Bình District, Vietnam, where the revolutionary movement was still less developed. Hồ observed Giáp from afar. If Giáp passed this last rigorous test, Hồ could then inform him of the enormity of his southward mission.

Giáp's posting to Nguyên Bình, and not back to China, almost certainly saved his life. When in China he worked under the guise of Hồ Học Lãm's non-communist Việt Minh. Nguyễn Hải Thần (1878–1959) had discovered that Giáp and Đồng were actually both communists and he had informed the Kuomintang, who subsequently viewed both men as enemies.

Now unimpeded by his work in China, in January 1942 Giáp made his way to Nguyên Bình. Guided by a blind courier, Giáp trekked for two days over steep mountains. Fortunately, his sightless companion came from an ethnic group that worked better at night than during the day, and knew every twist and turn of the route in his mind's eye. The small party arrived at dusk at Gia Bằng Commune and went to the house of Xích Thắng, the secretary of the Nguyên Bình District Party Committee.[27] Giáp went on to open several political training courses in this district, the first in Kéo Quảng Cave (or Karl Marx Cave) Gia Bằng Commune.[28]

Hồ no longer resided in Pác Bó when Giáp reported back to him in March 1942, but had moved to a new base codenamed Lam Sơn at Lung Hoài.[29] For months on end Hồ had been moving locations to avoid capture, first staying in one sympathizer's house and then moving to another in a circular path of around 20km. Each time he moved, he went to a different ethnic group. Where possible he not only led a political training course there but published the Việt Minh newspaper, *Vietnam's Independence*.[30] During this time Hồ purposely remained close to Giáp; to supervise the development of his training classes from afar but also when they spoke face to face to get first-hand knowledge of progress and assess his reliability.

In July 1942, back again in Pác Bó, Hồ officially initiated the Southwards March, putting Giáp in charge of the Advancing Southwards Bureau and asking Lê Thiết Hùng to join him.[31] Hồ could see that Giáp had a unique ability to win over villagers, train them, and then personally command them to carry out their given task. He told the two men, "Brother Văn [Giáp] you should now pay greater attention to military activities and Brother Hùng to political activities."[32] It was a crucial turning point for Giáp; previously the Party regarded him as a political person, whereas they viewed Lê Thiết Hùng as the professional high-ranking officer in the Kuomintang Army, and so seemed the more likely military leader. Hùng linked up with Giáp and set up classes in Kim Mã.[33] Revolutionaries came from all over, including from Tam Lọng and Tĩnh Túc. Although the classes in Kim Mã were established after the Southward March received official status in July, today the classes at Kéo Quảng Cave have been formally recorded as the first training sessions of the Southward March.

Satisfied that the Southward March was in safe hands, Hồ decided to head back to China a few weeks later. He wanted the Việt Minh to link up with the allied forces to see if they could help the revolutionaries, now that the Germans had overrun France. He nearly did not see a unified country because en route the Kuomintang arrested him and imprisoned him in China. They did not know who he was, just an elderly man who was highly intellectual and called himself Hồ Chí Minh. After months of observing him in detention, the Kuomintang officers concluded that Hồ could be an important contact inside Vietnam and they freed him in September 1943. On his release, and reflecting back on recent successes, Hồ again predicted, "Revolution will surely win, and very soon, in 1945."

Giáp Shows His Military Credentials

Hồ viewed protecting his courier apparatus, and those who used it, as a high priority. He could not afford Communist Party leaders to be arrested, nor himself for that matter. When Giáp had told Hồ about his proposals on how to guard the courier network, he had been suitably impressed.

Giáp had allocated his new trainees to positions under three clear categories. In the first category, trainees who preferred not to stray far from their native land were simply sent back to protect their villages and to find additional trainees to attend the classes. In the second category, trainees who had grasped the concepts of guerrilla warfare during training were formed into either "self-defense teams" or "honorary fighting teams." The self-defense teams defended the corridors, whereas the honorary fighting teams neutralized spies and informers who got too close to the corridors for comfort.

Within the third category, the very best students formed paramilitary groups called "advancing propaganda teams." These were action units and classed as part of the wider action unit family. Giáp's action units are better described as advancing propaganda teams, because the word "advancing" is important. His teams contained combatants from ethnic minorities who traditionally did not want to leave their families and local areas, but had agreed to do so, in order to complete their given tasks. Namely advancing with their message of nationalism across Vietnam, opening more courier routes, and guiding revolutionaries along them, defending these revolutionaries with their lives if need be.

With such small numbers being recruited, each advancing propaganda team consisted of just three to five people. Giáp initially established two teams, one was all male and the other all female, and instructed them to go to their neighboring communes of Thượng Ân and Cốc Đán, Bắc Kạn Province. Since most trainees were reluctant to leave their homeland, only around 100 students were ever suitable for advancing propaganda teams during the Southward March.

These advancing propaganda teams, along with other groups of this kind, evolved into units called "armed propaganda teams," a term not used until 1944. The main difference between the advancing propaganda teams and the armed propaganda teams was that the latter was not solely made up of ethnic minorities. The word "armed" referred to their duties as guards, and the word "propaganda," also known as "agitprop," referred to their work in mobilizing the masses.[34]

Initially these armed units had responsibilities similar to those of the advancing propaganda teams. Over time their role went far beyond just building and guarding the underground network, and some members were chosen to form part of Giáp's first regular unit of his People's Army.

The Birth of the Revolutionary Infrastructure

Giáp's methods of guarding the courier network became a turning point for the revolutionaries because, when added to the pre-existing courier system, it formed what would be called the Revolutionary Infrastructure.

The Party apparatus defined the Revolutionary Infrastructure as generally comprising three elements: "Communist Party cells," which were then linked together by more advanced so-called "couriers" using a high number of corridor routes, and "guards." When available, these guards could be mass sympathizers from a given area or specific teams, such as those assembled during the Southward March.

This Revolutionary Infrastructure was the official title used by the Communist Party for the system but their enemies referred to it by other names. The French did not understand the mechanisms of the system to any great extent, but labeled what they did know *l'infrastructure Clandestine Việt Minh*. The Americans were more *au fait* with the mechanics of this system towards the end of the Vietnam War, and referred to it as the Việt Cộng Infrastructure (VCI).

The infrastructure was also called a "shadow government." It was not an opposition government in a parliamentary system. On the contrary, it was a covert parallel administration which operated in enemy occupied areas and aimed to control the masses and administer the war; to eventually become the overt government body in liberated areas. Due to its scale of operation, Hồ's Revolutionary Infrastructure thus gave birth to the original notion of a covert shadow government. The French made the first known mention of the term shadow government in the early 1940s, when they witnessed its spread across the northern provinces in Vietnam.

The shadow government operated everywhere and tried to control everything. The communists had Party cells at hamlet, district, provincial and national level. These cells provided various services for the people depending on how established the cells were: land control, local agriculture, schools, medical facilities, a legal system, re-education, war administration, the economy and printing their own banknotes. To fund operations, the Party implemented a number of methods such as selling Trust Bills, raising taxes and running a service known as Business-Finance; this term referred to front businesses that had been set up and run in areas occupied by the enemy to make money covertly for the revolution.

The Revolutionary Infrastructure was so widespread and efficient that it became a comprehensive shadow government with all the associated services there to support, control and expand a "shadow nation." This shadow nation was extremely significant

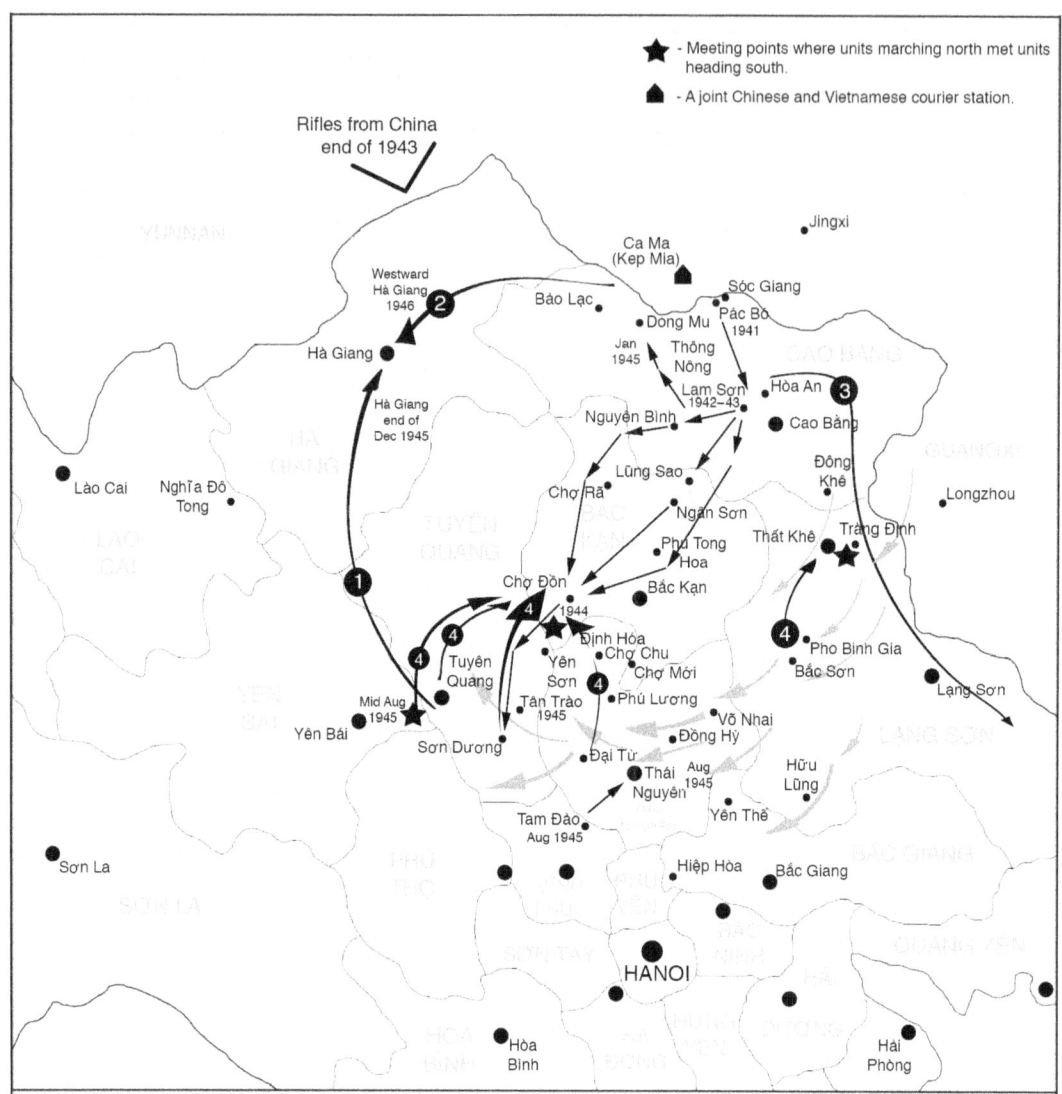

1. Mai Trung Lâm - led his platoon from Tuyên Quang to Hà Giang where the pro-French authorities still held power.

2. Westward March - led by Phạm Văn Đồng, going from Cao Bằng, Bảo Lạc to Hà Giang (in 1946) and Tuyên Quang. Đồng fell ill so Võ Nguyên Giáp did much of the work including the route Thông Nông to Bảo Lạc, which helped create the Thiện Thuật War Zone of the Man and Hmong ethnic groups. This area became the headquarters of the Cao Bằng Provincial Party Committee.

3. Eastward March - led by Hoàng Văn Hoan, starting from Cao Bằng, he went through the eastern regions including Đông Khê to Lạng Sơn.

4. Northward March - in February 1943 at Lũng Hoài, leaders decided to open the Northward March. The team would be made up of guerrilla fighters who had not gone to the Chinese border with Chu Văn Tấn in 1942. They started from the base at Bắc Sơn-Võ Nhai and were instructed to meet units from the Eastward March and Southward March.

Southward March - led by Võ Nguyên Giáp and Lê Thiết Hùng, going from Cao Bằng, Ngân Sơn, Bắc Kạn and Tuyên Quang. This latter area became the location of Hồ Chí Minh's headquarters established to fight the Japanese.

National Salvation Troops - they had left for the Chinese border in 1942, but after February 1943 they had all returned to Vietnam. From there they marched across the provinces of Lạng Sơn, Thái Nguyên, Tuyên Quang and Bắc Kạn.

because the Party knew that, in order to win total victory, they had to control the critical mass of the people, or "masses," at the decisive moment.

This so-called shadow nation was complex, just as any normal state is. In Vietnam, there were a large number of ethnic groups, most of which had their own ideas about the direction in which their part of the country should be heading. In addition, the many political parties and the religious sects in Vietnam, who were powerful in their given areas, wanted their views heard, as did the different social classes from the bourgeoisie to the intelligentsia.

Although the communists won some of the populace over by their nationalist propaganda there was always a subsection within the shadow nation that refused to switch. This subsection might oppose the revolution or they might simply not want to take part. For the French and later the Americans, it was this subsection of the shadow nation that they should have been trying to win over, rather than just labeling them all communists or bombing them.

The Revolutionary Infrastructure could be viewed as part of the strategic political front, however, if the three strategic fronts of political, propaganda and the military were adjoining cogs in a machine, the infrastructure would be best described as the oil, there to lubricate the mechanism to function proficiently. Therefore with the development of the infrastructure the Party not only had a method to wed the revolutionary fronts together, but regardless of whether or not the people wanted to be a part of the revolution, through the infrastructure all people under its control became part of the revolutionary masses.

Hồ Nearly Loses Giáp

On 4 August 1942, Giáp's good fortune nearly ended. The French now conducted White Terror with the intent on arresting Communist Party leaders. They encircled Gia Bằng, a commune in which Giáp and Lê Thiết Hùng ran courses. Giáp was at Nà Dú, Tam Long Commune, and became aware of the threat when compatriots came to inform him. Giáp managed to escape only because he had seen that the nearby stream was bulging from the recent downpour. He saw that these fierce waters could be crossed by him, but that the French, bogged down with their equipment, would have difficulties.

Giáp managed to evade capture this time, but Hồ thought that next time he might not be so blessed. Hồ sent Quang Hưng to escort Le Thiết Hùng and Giáp out of the area. On their way to Nà Áng, Cẩm Lý Commune, Giáp told Lê Thiết Hùng in confidence, "We must not leave this area. The infrastructure has only just been built. If the villages see their leaders running away, it will damage local morale." Lê Thiết Hùng agreed. So Giáp instructed Quang Hưng to go to Gia Bằng and speak to Hồ, requesting permission to stay.

Just hours later, on the afternoon of 5 August 1942, there was another breach of security. Several ethnic Tai activists from Kim Mã sought out Giáp and Hùng to ask advice on how to deal with French suppression. Giáp briefly questioned that if the tribes had found them that easily, then so could the French. Unnerved by this event, the Nguyên Bình District Party Committee wanted to move the two men far away, but Giáp refused, and said that better security was needed, concluding, "We must strike while we can and

Opposite: Building the Revolutionary Infrastructure, 1941 to 1945.

stay with our local Việt Minh revolutionaries, who are being harassed. The Party sent us here to work. I would rather die here than run away."

It was Giáp's determination and stubbornness that helped him to push the southward corridors as far as Ngân Sơn District at the beginning of 1943. Finally, the Southward March met the Northward March at Nghĩa Tả Commune, Cho Don District, the latter being led by Chu Văn Tấn, one of the first guerrilla leaders. This historic meeting point was renamed Thắng Lợi, meaning Victory Commune. The Northward March had begun in 1943, after the Eastward and Westward Marches that were coordinated to start at the same time as the Southward March.

Although these surges across the countryside were vital to spread Hồ's revolution, he always viewed the Southward March as the most important. Fundamentally, Giáp had started the great push from the base on the Chinese border to ATK 1 in the Red River Delta region, which assisted directly in the formation of the Democratic Republic of Vietnam in 1945. The death of Giáp for Hồ would have been more than a tragic loss of life.

Giáp Changed Hồ's Fortunes

Since its formation, the Revolutionary Infrastructure had spread from hamlet to hamlet like an "oil spill on a map"; this reach empowered three changes that aided Hồ in coming to power. Initially, by designing ways to protect the courier network, Giáp started to build what would be known as a People's Army, meaning that everyone, from a child to an elderly villager, could be recruited and used in some practical way to fight against an invader. His motto was, "Propagandize the masses to build the Revolutionary Infrastructure, arm the revolutionary masses to build a People's Army." So successful were Giáp and Hồ in using their fellow countrymen to fight that eventually the concept of a People's Army became synonymous with the conflict against the Americans, now commonly referred to as the Vietnam War.

On the second point, Hồ had found his top general to lead the military, and appointed Giáp to be the commander of a new regular army. On 22 December 1944, Hồ founded the Vietnam Propaganda and Liberation Army with just two sections: Combat and Intelligence. It had the word propaganda in the title because Hồ needed each battle to produce a political propaganda outcome. Part of Hồ's written instruction on founding this army stated that, when executing guerrilla warfare the units must be "invisible in arriving and departing." Giáp implemented this instruction with such precision that some in the West named his forces the "undetected enemy."

Initially the army comprised only thirty-four men chosen for their fighting abilities; they came from the northernmost provinces and a few of the men had been recruited during the Southward March. This new regular army was called a "standing army" by the revolutionaries because its recruits had stood up, left their farming lives behind and fought away from home, just as the advancing propaganda teams had. Some of those with this regular army were known as mobile units; emphasizing that these troops could move to a place to conduct a tactical battle or to a better camouflaged position, but also now that they had left their villages they had to locate a place to grow or find food.

On 15 April 1945, participants of the Military Conference of Tonkin, held in Liễu Ngạn Village, Hiệp Hòa District, decided to merge the National Salvation Troops

4. The Infant Blueprint

A photograph taken at Việt Bắc Revolutionary Base and thought to be at the Army Political-Military Training Conference, May 1949. Pictured are (1) Nguyễn Văn Hiếu (Võ Nguyên Giáp's secretary from the end of the 1940s until 1968), (2) Lê Trọng Nghĩa, (3) Võ Nguyên Giáp, (4) Hồ Chí Minh, (5) Vương Thừa Vũ (commander of the 308th Division), (6) Tạ Xuân Thu (a political commissar who directed the Westwards Front), (7) Đào Văn Trường, (8) Lê Liêm (a political commissar during the Battle of Điện Biên Phủ), (9) a European, Hồ Chí Dân (Ernest Frey, a Việt Minh officer) (courtesy Đào Văn Trường).

currently under the command of Chu Văn Tấn, with the thirteen companies of Giáp's Vietnam Propaganda and Liberation Army. This amalgamation formed the Vietnam Liberation Army, eventually to be known as the Vietnamese People's Army (VNPA). The official ceremony to combine the two was held a month later, on 15 May 1945.[35] The earlier April event was especially memorable for Giáp because Trường Chinh informed him that his wife had died in the previous year. Giáp recalled, "The brutal shock left me speechless and deathly pale for many long minutes." This heart-wrenching news put his life suddenly into perspective. He realized that although he had been successfully promoted to high office, he had in the process lost the one person most dear to him.

The third important area that grew out of the formation of the Revolutionary Infrastructure was the strengthening of Việt Bắc Revolutionary Base. This robustness had given Hồ the confidence to train and then establish the Vietnam Propaganda and Liberation Army. Now, with the army's ability to protect the area, the enemy found it difficult to reoccupy the region for any great length of time, and in June 1945, Việt Bắc was considered a liberated zone; prior to this it had been only an area of Việt Minh presence, with some liberated areas scattered within it. In August 1945, the Communist Party officially decreed Việt Bắc a liberated zone at the National People's Congress. Việt Bắc covered the vast mountainous provinces of Cao Bằng, Bắc Kạn, Lạng Sơn, Thái Nguyên, Hà Giang and Tuyên Quang. The core was the former three provinces Cao-Bắc-Lạng, which in the main had been Giáp's area of operation during his Southward March. Later, he referred to the region as a "powder keg ready to explode." On 2 September 1947, Hồ wrote to the leaders of this area, "The [August] Revolution was a success, thanks to Việt Bắc."

Clearly no revolution relies on just one man, or indeed two, Hồ and Giáp; there are many central architects. Yet, this was undoubtedly a unique partnership that grew in ability, and it is debatable that, if it had not happened, Hồ might never have come to power, and subsequently the Communist Party rule a united Vietnam. What is known, is that by creating the infrastructure, Hồ had the four elements he needed to define his blueprint: the Revolutionary infrastructure and his three strategic fronts of political, propaganda and the military; but they were most certainly not close to maturity.

PART II: EVOLUTION AND APPLICATION OF THE BLUEPRINT

• *The August Revolution (1945)* •

5

Hồ's Road to Power

The New Enemy

During August 1945, the Việt Minh finally ended decades of foreign domination when they grabbed political power across targeted areas of Vietnam, in what would be known as the August Revolution. The West attributed this achievement mainly to chance, an opportunity seized in the power vacuum left by the end of the Second World War.[1] For Hồ it was a combination of both opportunity and effective long-term planning for that very moment. If one tracks the events from the coup of 9 March 1945, when the Japanese overthrew the French, to the declaration of independence by Hồ on 2 September 1945, the August Revolution provides the first proper look at Hồ's infant blueprint and how vulnerable it was to enemy aggression.

With the Second World War coming to an end, Hồ had to answer two urgent and fundamental questions. First, should the Việt Minh use the chaos associated with the Japanese coup of 9 March as their strategic opportunity to try and take Vietnam or not? Hồ made the decision to wait. He knew that his forces were too weak, in comparison with the Japanese forces, to initiate a counter-coup. Instead, members of the Việt Minh agreed that they should take local power in targeted areas using guerrilla activity.[2]

The second question that needed to be continually reviewed was who was their main enemy, the French, the Japanese, the Chinese or another indigenous nationalist party within the country, or a combination of all of these? Without the answer to this question, the Việt Minh risked wasting precious resources against perceived threats, which did not in fact exist.

On 9 to 12 March 1945 the Party Central Committee held a conference for covert operatives working in Tonkin.[3] The main question to address was which group posed the most threat? Those at the conference agreed that their main thrust had to be against the Japanese. On the last night General Secretary Trường Chinh wrote an instruction along these lines, which had to be distributed to all Party organizations, titled, *Our Action when the French and Japanese are Fighting* (against each other). To support this document he wrote an appeal to the people on behalf of the Việt Minh, explaining the implications of the Japanese coup just days earlier. It called upon the people of Indochina to oppose the Japanese, bringing it to their attention that the French were no longer the main enemy. Trường Chinh printed his appeal on 150,000 leaflets and delivered them throughout Tonkin and Annam. He hoped others might be distributed in Cochinchina.[4]

The likes of Hồ and Trường Chinh were correct about the Japanese. With the conference still ongoing, the Japanese swept away the French administration and started to change the arrangement of the ruling body. On 10 March, they asked Emperor Bảo Đại (1913–1997) to head a government dedicated to maintaining social order. The emperor had been relieved because he had thought the Japanese might have insisted instead on Prince Cường Để, who now lived in Tokyo.

On 11 March, the Japanese instructed Bảo Đại to proclaim an independent Vietnam within their Greater East Asia Co-Prosperity Sphere. In a stroke, this proclamation ended decades of French rule. The word Vietnam originated from nationalist writers, in the 1920s, to describe the regions of Tonkin, Annam and Cochinchina; now it would be used formally from this point on.

In April, the Japanese made Trần Trọng Kim the prime minister of the royal Vietnamese government. In May, they appointed Phan Kế Toại (1892–1973) the Imperial Delegate of Tonkin, also known as the King's Special Envoy.[5]

For the Party Central Committee, these few days defined who their enemy was. The men the Japanese had put into power had once been viewed by the revolutionaries as puppets of the French; now their strings were being pulled by the Japanese.

Wooing International Support

The Communist Party viewed the Japanese as the new enemy. To get rid of such a powerful force from Vietnam, Hồ had to think radically, and get the Americans onside. He had viewed them as a potential ally ever since they had joined the Second World War in 1941. Part of his thinking was that, as a powerful nation, they would be vital in ousting foreign armed forces from Vietnam. He also anticipated that they and their allies would have the advantage over the Germans in about 1945, consequently it would be the U.S. he would have to negotiate with in a post-war Vietnam.

For Hồ, the Americans had made the right noises publically. President F. D. Roosevelt (1882–1945) had disclosed that once the Japanese had been eliminated from Indochina he would be against the French returning after the war, mainly because of his anti-colonial philosophy.[6] Indeed in 1941, he and Prime Minister Winston Churchill (1874–1965) signed the Atlantic Charter, which covered the restoration of self-government to those deprived of it.

The direction of American thinking after the Japanese coup gave Hồ and the U.S. common ground on two points: the wish to prevent the return of the French and the elimination of the Japanese. As power shifted among the various players, this era presented Hồ with a strategic opportunity to gain a degree of support from the Americans, or at least to present it that way to others.

Contact between the Việt Minh and the Americans had begun as early as December 1942, when the Việt Minh approached the U.S. Embassy for help in securing the release of Hồ from a prison in China. Nothing came of this request or others, such as appeals made by the Soviets. Hồ was released late 1943 by the Kuomintang and he eventually made his way back to Vietnam.

A tentative American–Việt Minh alliance opportunity came when events outside Vietnam started to favor allied advances. From June to November 1944, allied forces liberated France from Nazi occupation; soon after this the French pro–Nazi Vichy government lost control of Indochina. This enabled agents from the anti-Nazi Free French movement to conduct clandestine operations in the region and become one of a number of groups supplying intelligence to allied headquarters in Kunming, China.[7] The base in Kunming was home to the American Fourteenth Air Force, which ran bombing raids into enemy-held areas. The success of their missions depended upon the intelligence data collected, including accurate weather reports from within Indochina as well as data on Japanese troop movements, their bases and storage facilities. In addition, these French agents within Indochina were necessary in order to help rescue downed American pilots and, if possible, smuggle them out of Indochina and back to Kunming.

Two of the most effective intelligence groups operating in the region at the time were the GBT and the Office of Strategic Services (OSS).[8] The GBT was a private group of Anglo-Americans based in southern China who operated in Indochina (the name was made up from the initials of the three men who operated within it: Laurence "Gordon" or Laurie; Harry "Bernard"; and Frank "Tan" or Frankie. Gordon gave information to the Americans, Bernard to the British and Tan to the Chinese Kuomintang). The men of the newly formed OSS were involved in information gathering activities from Kunming. Their mission was to help bring about the defeat of the Japanese and to end their brutal iron rule they meted out within their Greater East Asia Co-Prosperity Sphere.

Initially, both the OSS and GBT had extended networks of French agents in Indochina, and relations between these two groups were both good and complementary. This arrangement started to unravel at the end of 1944 when William Donovan, the director of the OSS, tried to bring the GBT fully under its control. Although tensions had resulted, both groups recognized that they needed to put aside their differences and look for alternative, more efficient, ways to gather intelligence. This was a vital requirement because the majority of French troops and civilians were now imprisoned after the coup, and therefore the flow of French information to the allies had all but ceased, like a tap turned off. Hồ intended to make sure that the Việt Minh would fill this intelligence void.

Hồ's opportunity to make contact with the Americans came on 11 November 1944, when American reconnaissance pilot Lieutenant Rudolph Shaw encountered engine problems and had to bail out of his small aircraft, parachuting into the vicinity of Cao Bằng. The pro–Japanese French had dispatched patrols into the area to find him, but the Việt Minh reached him first and took him to Pác Bó, Vietnam, where Hồ resided. When Shaw asked Hồ for assistance to reach China, Hồ took the opportunity and agreed to take him personally. Faced with such kindness, Shaw invited Hồ to his base in Kunming.

When Hồ finally arrived in Kunming, on foot, he deftly manipulated the situation to win over American assistance. Rudolph Shaw had since left because he had flown to Kunming and then returned to America. Nevertheless, on 17 March, a determined Hồ and Phạm Việt Tử, who spoke fluent English, managed to meet with Charles Fenn, an OSS officer working with, and reporting to, the GBT.[9] At this appointment, Hồ made sure that the rescue of Shaw gave a lasting impression on Fenn, and that this image of cooperation would filter down to other GBT and OSS operatives and further expand the net of goodwill towards the Việt Minh.[10]

In the following days, Fenn had an important question to answer. He had to decide whether Hồ should be approached for intelligence work in Indochina for the GBT. From past experience Fenn knew that the OSS had been wondering if they should use and train natives of Indochina to fight the Japanese.[11] What planted a small element of doubt in his mind about using Hồ was that he knew Hồ and others within the Việt Minh had communist views. On refection, Fenn believed that these views were a combination of rudimentary Marxist philosophies and strong patriotic ideals, and he concluded that the

Việt Minh could not be considered as puppets of either the Soviets or the Chinese communists.

On 20 March, Fenn, Harry Bernard and Frank Tan had a meeting with Hồ. They proposed that a Chinese-American GBT radio operator, Mac Shin, be sent to Vietnam. They naively presumed that, as he was racially Chinese, he would blend in. Hồ expressed great concerns over this choice as any American would stand out from native Asians.[12] Still, Hồ did not want to damage his fledgling relationship with the Americans and he agreed that Mac Shin could accompany him to his headquarters.

Hồ knew that when he finally arrived back in Vietnam he had to show his countrymen that he had allied support. Before the group departed, Hồ asked to meet with General Claire Chennault, the commander of the American Fourteenth Air Force. Charles Fenn reluctantly agreed. On 29 March, Fenn, Bernard and Hồ met with Chennault. After small talk, Hồ requested an autographed photograph of the general, who was happy to provide one. Later, Hồ asked Fenn for six new Colt .45 pistols, a seemingly insignificant number, so Fenn obliged.

That May, Hồ and his courier escorted Mac Shin and Frank Tan across the Vietnamese border to his new headquarters; a place close enough to Hanoi for them to communicate with their city operatives via couriers and where this new Vietnamese-American alliance would fight the Japanese. To gain safe passage across the border, Hồ disguised himself as an elderly man and carried his prized autographed photograph given to him by Chennault. Each time the Kuomintang stopped him, he produced this photograph, and through his charming elderly talk he convinced the Kuomintang officers that he had American support and that he should be given free passage, which they gave him. For Shin and Tan their arduous route must have seemed slow and more or less random. In reality, Hồ had led them along a well-designed route established during the Southward March by Giáp.

What actually hindered the group was that the final location of the headquarters had not been finalized when they first set out. For security reasons, Hồ had to gather intelligence from the villagers on enemy activity and, in coordination with Giáp and Song Hào, choose the location just days before the group were expected to arrive. In fact, Giáp and Hào had already decided upon Tân Trào when the two men had camped just outside the area, near a place called Chợ Chu. Now agreed, Giáp and Hào designed two safe routes for Hồ to reach Tân Trào. Giáp protected the main route and Chu Văn Tấn and the one-time National Salvation Troops protected the second; a reserve and decoy. Hồ chose the former because Giáp built it and Hồ trusted him implicitly. Nevertheless, if there had been a breach in security, Hồ had the option to use the other one.

On arrival in Tân Trào, Hồ hastily called a private conference for his Việt Minh associates to persuade them that he was the man chosen by the Americans to lead the resistance. He handed out the brand new pistols, purposely kept in their original wrapping so that those present knew the guns were U.S. supplied. To further cement his authority he produced the autographed photograph of Chennault, proving he had met the head person.

With his authority confirmed, Hồ authorized Mac Shin to begin daily, or even twice daily, radio transmissions to Kunming. Shin's liaison work with his Kunming counterpart, Fenn, ensured regular airdrops of supplies and materials. Frank Tan and Shin routinely sent back intelligence from the Việt Minh base camp, reporting on weather conditions

Opposite: Hồ Chí Minh's journey to Tân Trào with Mac Shin and Frank Tan in May 1945.

5. Hồ's Road to Power

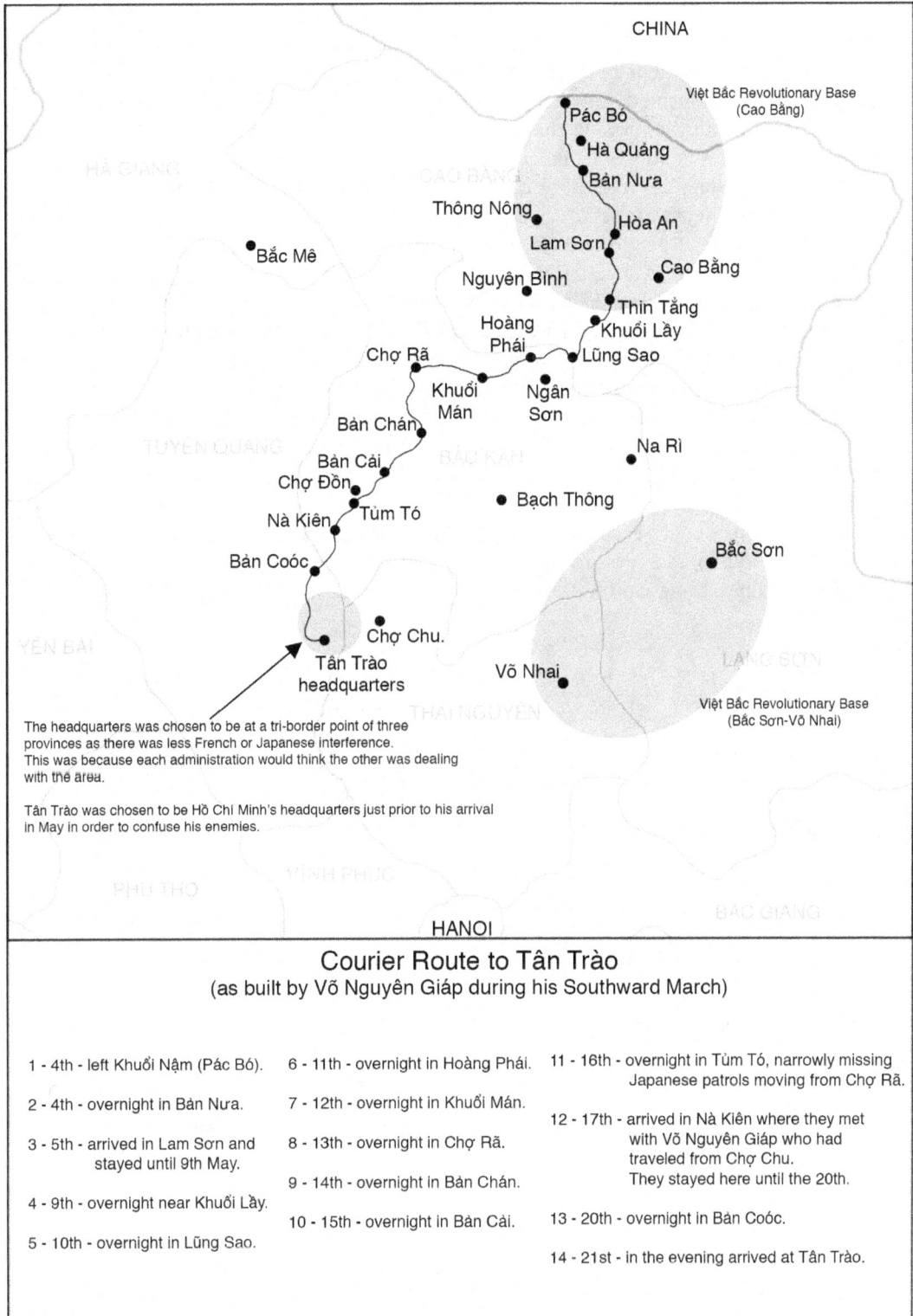

The headquarters was chosen to be at a tri-border point of three provinces as there was less French or Japanese interference. This was because each administration would think the other was dealing with the area.

Tân Trào was chosen to be Hồ Chí Minh's headquarters just prior to his arrival in May in order to confuse his enemies.

Courier Route to Tân Trào
(as built by Võ Nguyên Giáp during his Southward March)

1 - 4th - left Khuổi Nậm (Pác Bó).

2 - 4th - overnight in Bản Nưa.

3 - 5th - arrived in Lam Sơn and stayed until 9th May.

4 - 9th - overnight near Khuổi Lầy.

5 - 10th - overnight in Lũng Sao.

6 - 11th - overnight in Hoàng Phái.

7 - 12th - overnight in Khuổi Mán.

8 - 13th - overnight in Chợ Rã.

9 - 14th - overnight in Bản Chán.

10 - 15th - overnight in Bản Cải.

11 - 16th - overnight in Tùm Tó, narrowly missing Japanese patrols moving from Chợ Rã.

12 - 17th - arrived in Nà Kiên where they met with Võ Nguyên Giáp who had traveled from Chợ Chu. They stayed here until the 20th.

13 - 20th - overnight in Bản Coóc.

14 - 21st - in the evening arrived at Tân Trào.

and Japanese troop movements as well as putting in place tactics for retrieving downed American pilots. To get vital documents to the Americans, including letters, maps and intelligence, courier lines operated from Tân Trào to Kunming. Through this work, a good relationship formed between the Americans and Vietnamese. Hồ viewed Shin as being so critical to the mission that he allowed him to live in his special security zone set up about a km or so from Tân Trào.

Now that the allies had more confidence in the natives, one of a number of joint OSS-French projects were set up in China in June. It aimed to train ten to twenty French officers of European origin and 100 Vietnamese troops in sabotage techniques. These men were split into two teams, Deer and Cat, the former commanded by Major Allison Thomas. In July, on seeing the benefits for the Việt Minh, Hồ agreed that Thomas and a small group of his men could parachute into Tuyên Quang Province to visit Tân Trào.

Thomas told Hồ that his team had to gather intelligence on Japanese troop movements and then, after evaluation, Hồ had to instruct his troops to harass the Japanese; specifically to disrupt reinforcements moving from Indochina to China, where the allies were planning major offensives. To accomplish this Thomas agreed to supply Hồ with modern military equipment and train his forces in advanced combat tactics and weapons use.

This project could easily have failed. Within the Deer Team sent to the base were one French soldier and two pro–French Vietnamese, whose loyalty so incensed Hồ that he ordered these three men to leave immediately, before they could see anything of sig-

Issued on 25 May 1945, this sketch drawn by Hồ Chí Minh shows Vietnamese suppression under different nations and his plan to gain independence for Vietnam (courtesy Phạm Hồng Cư).

5. Hồ's Road to Power

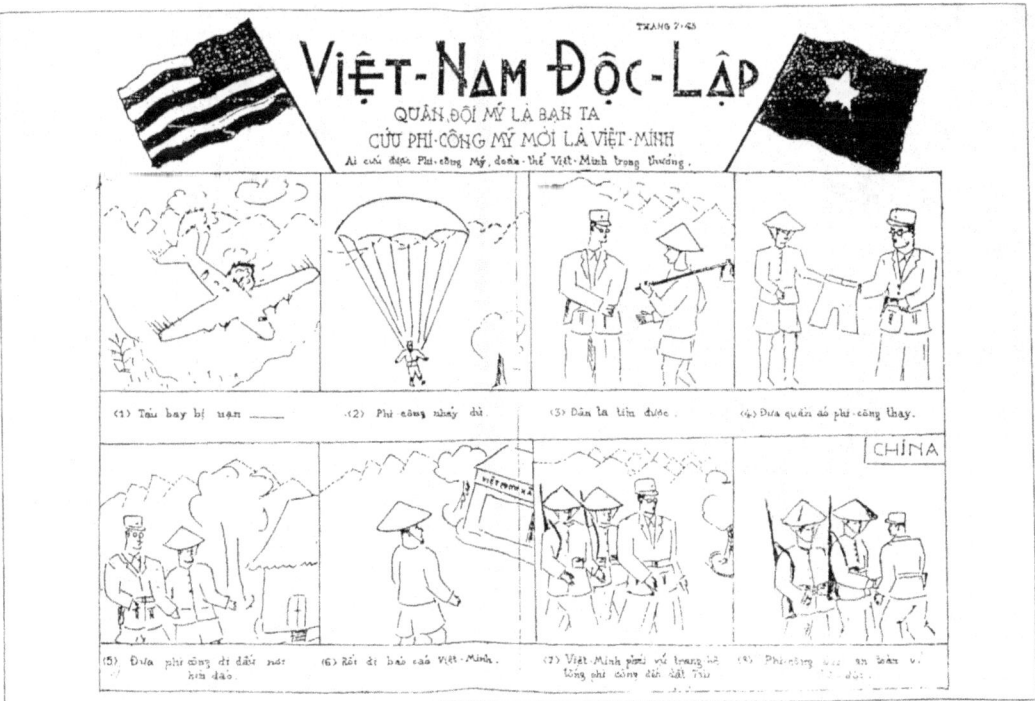

Top: Issued on 25 June 1945, this sketch drawn by Hồ Chí Minh shows the structure of the Việt Minh in the provinces of Cao Bằng, Bắc Kạn and Lạng Sơn (courtesy Phạm Hồng Cư). *Bottom:* Issued in July 1945, this sketch drawn by Hồ Chí Minh shows local people how to rescue downed American pilots. At that time they were allies (courtesy Phạm Hồng Cư).

nificance. Fortunately, between the Americans and Hồ there was a mutual need for each other and the relationship continued.

Preparing Hanoi

When France conquered Vietnam, it ultimately made Hanoi the capital of French Indochina. Hồ understood that he had to take the city if he were to control any of Vietnam. To prepare for the right opportunity to seize power, the Communist Party ordered revolutionaries to conduct various covert tasks. Lê Trọng Nghĩa (1921–2015) was one of those chosen.[13]

The author met Nghĩa in Hanoi in 2008. Born in Quảng Yên Province and part of an affluent family of eight, he had joined the revolution in 1938 when a student, becoming a communist in 1941. He started his interview by saying that his work in Hanoi for the August Revolution was the most memorable and poignant part of his career. This is despite the fact that he had been the head of the Intelligence Department for both the Party and the military from 1951 to 1968, playing lead roles in battles such as Điện Biên Phủ.

Nghĩa viewed his role in the August Revolution as important because after this revolt Vietnam gained a degree of independence for the first time. He felt that he and his colleagues had set in motion the founding of what he called a "fledgling nation" and the eventual independence it sought. Giáp confirmed his feelings on the taking of Hanoi years later, saying, "Prior to events unfolding, the Việt Minh were happy to seize any local power during the August Revolution, but once the uprising started, everyone was relieved and grateful that Hanoi had been taken so quickly."

Nghĩa explained:

> On 11 March 1945, I had escaped from Hỏa Lò jail in Hanoi with fellow political prisoners. I took shelter at the house of Trần Quảng Kiến; an old friend from Bonnal School. Soon after, in Hanoi, Lê Đức Thọ [1911–1990] sent Nguyễn Đình Thi to meet me.[14] Nguyễn Đình Thi used to be my classmate. We had been caught distributing leaflets on 6 January 1941. He was released in June 1942 whilst they sentenced me to four years. Nguyễn Đình Thi had said to me, "The organization has sent me to see you. Spend some days visiting your parents in your homeland, then come back to receive your new assignment."[15]

Lê Trọng Nghĩa, who became the head of the Intelligence Department for both the Communist Party and the military. Photograph February 26, 2008 (Clive A. Hills).

Back from his home visit, Nghĩa met Lê Đức Thọ and the communist Vũ Quý. This latter gentleman helped found the Democratic Party, a group that sat under the umbrella of the Việt Minh.[16] From its founding Vũ Quý operated covertly within it to get members to adopt communist ideology along with the principles of the Việt Minh.[17]

Nghĩa said:

> After my initial meetings with Lê Đức Thọ we met again in a safe house in Rue Rollande.[18] At that time Thọ was the Việt Minh representative liaising with other political groups such as the Democratic Party. Thọ was tasked with issuing new guidelines from the Communist Party to other revolutionary organizations, to prepare them for any armed uprising. Thọ gave me the job of running a section of the Democratic Party, not only in Hanoi but also in Tonkin. He then handed me a Browning shotgun. I felt very proud that the Party trusted me with such an important role.
>
> Within Hanoi I chose 101 Rue Gambetta to be our secret office for the Việt Minh.[19] The house belonged to Nguyễn Bá Chinh, a high-ranking officer within the Vietnamese government, who along with his three children were all revolutionary sympathizers. I chose his house because it was a big villa, which meant that the French and Japanese police generally ignored any activities associated with it as they presumed that the people who owned it were affluent and therefore against the revolution. The villa was also close to the enemy and I hoped that they would never suspect that the Việt Minh could be so near to them, as it was near to the French Freemason's head office as well as the house of Dr. Trần Văn Lai, whom the Japanese and their puppet government had appointed to be the mayor of Hanoi.
>
> Hanoi was dangerous to operate in, which meant that at that time the Tonkin Regional Party Committee and the Hanoi City Party Committee worked within ATK 1 safe zone. Now well established, as it was one of the first areas to have advancing propaganda, self-defense and honorary fighting teams, the Party had a degree of protection. I was in Hanoi, and the links between where I operated and ATK 1 were slow and sporadic. Consequently, I knew that I had to operate alone.[20]

To prepare for any uprising, Nghĩa and his colleagues took the decision to undertake targeted proselytizing; by controlling groups or individuals any uprising could be manipulated in favor of the Việt Minh. Nghĩa had also heard that Emperor Bảo Đại debated whether or not to fight against the Việt Minh. Nghĩa knew that Bảo Đại would not be the only one wanting to destroy them. By controlling associates of key individuals, this threat could be reduced or eliminated. Nghĩa targeted the middle classes, such as middle and high-ranking government officials, students and private sector businessmen. He did not target landlords to the same degree because they were seen by some as the enemy of the working class.

Nghĩa said:

> One example of how we aimed to control the situation was when the Japanese handed over various government departments to Phan Kế Toại. Student members, sympathetic to us, and within the Democratic Party, lobbied officials working for Toại when these officials looked to appoint a new chief of police for Hanoi. These students wanted Lê Văn Lăng appointed, arguing to the officials that he qualified because he had just graduated in law. In fact, they knew he was secretly a member of Việt Minh. Lê Văn Lăng was duly appointed.
>
> Other groups such as the Trotskyites approached us. I met with their leader, Hồ Hữu Tường, who expressed an interest for his group to join us.[21] They were big in Cochinchina but much less influential in Hanoi. Still, the Party recognized that if we got their northern branch under our control, we would have more influence over their southern arm. There were problems because the Trotskyites had previously heavily criticized the Việt Minh. After great thought we agreed that the Trotskyites in Hanoi could not come under the canopy of the Việt Minh, however, individual members within the Trotskyites could be admitted. These trusted members could then build an agent network within the Trotskyites, in order to control the group or to get other members over to our side.
>
> I thought that this was a good signal as, although the Trotskyites had criticized our policies, the fact that they had approached us meant that the status of the Việt Minh had risen.[22]

The Party had instructed Nghĩa and his colleagues to create systems to enable the Việt Minh to drive any people's uprising, remove the Japanese and destroy the puppet Vietnamese government. Throughout the early to mid–1940s they had achieved some of these instructions.

Seizing the Strategic Opportunity

Valuable months had passed since the coup of 9 March 1945 and the Japanese taking of Vietnam. To address a way forward, Hồ planned a large meeting of the National People's Congress to be held on 16 and 17 August, in Tân Trào.[23] The invitations went out to delegates on 4 June welcoming them from the six liberated northern provinces of Việt Bắc Revolutionary Base.

Events changed rapidly. While delegates made their way to Tân Trào, the Americans bombed Hiroshima and Nagasaki in Japan with nuclear weapons on 6 and 9 August respectively, and the Soviets invaded Japanese-held Manchuria on 9 August. The Americans in Kunming promptly radioed those at Tân Trào, informing them that the Japanese might surrender. This message is thought to have been as early as 11 August. For Hồ, and others organizing the National People's Congress, they sensed that the international unrest was the strategic opportunity they had been waiting for.

On 12 August, Communist Party members issued their General Uprising Order signed by Giáp. The objective was to distribute it to Việt Minh forces, who in turn would send ultimata to Japanese troops and Vietnamese government Civil Guard Units stating, "Surrender or be annihilated." This order was a risk because it announced prematurely that Japan had asked to surrender, and asserted that the allies had accepted Tokyo's formulation.

Members could not wait for the National People's Congress, so from 13 to 15 August, the Party hastily put together a meeting called the All Country Conference. At that meeting, members officially agreed to stage a General Uprising. They discussed the Revolutionary Infrastructure and if it was capable of supporting a General Uprising, since the courier system had failed to do so during the unsuccessful Cochinchina Uprising.[24] They then went on to appoint a new Uprising Committee that comprised Trần Đăng Ninh, Giáp, Chu Văn Tấn, Lê Thanh Nghị and Trường Chinh. At 11 p.m. on 13 August the Uprising Committee issued Military Order No. 1. This instructed the armed forces of the Việt Minh to fight the enemy, namely the Japanese Army, cut off their routes of retreat and seize their weapons.[25] Party members stated that these tactics would "lead to complete victory and national independence."[26]

On 15 August, the Japanese finally surrendered but, despite the urgency of the work in front of them, the Party held the planned National People's Congress. This meeting focused on bureaucracy and officially recognizing the decisions of the past few days. Delegates present elected a National Liberation Committee and formally approved the Uprising Committee, now referred to as the Nationwide Uprising Committee. The National Liberation Committee gave full command over to the Nationwide Uprising Committee, and delegates sent a General Uprising Appeal to the entire nation. It stated that to incite the General Uprising, it was not just the responsibility of the military but revolutionaries had to covertly agitate crowds, take advantage of any spontaneous uprisings and control the people for the benefit of the Việt Minh.

The National People's Congress had been important but poorly timed. Key provincial members had left their groups, meaning any local action could not be directed by them. What the meeting did give those delegates who had arrived was the opportunity to witness part of the training of nearly 100 men and women of the Vietnam Liberation Army, under the guidance of the Deer Team.

This military display was short-lived. Giáp and Major Allison Thomas agreed to terminate training because the Second World War had reached a critical point. On 16 August, Giáp headed to Thái Nguyên Town with his army, with instructions to destroy the Japanese stronghold there. Thomas accompanied him.

Before the various meetings finished, Hồ iterated that this was their strategic opportunity; the Việt Minh must seize power promptly to enable them to welcome the allied occupiers in a position of strength. "We will be forced to deal with the Japanese, but we should try to negotiate, if possible."

The Taking of Hanoi

What put Nghĩa at the heart of events that August were his instructions to remain in the vicinity of Hanoi, whereas his associates had gone to Tân Trào. Nghĩa had been

OSS veterans visiting the former base in Tân Trào in 1995, fifty years after they parachuted into Tân Trào just prior to the August Revolution: (1) Mac Shin, (2) Alison Thomas, (3) Henry Prunier and (4) Nguyễn Kim Hùng, the head of the Việt Minh–OSS team (courtesy Nguyễn Huy Văn).

told to stay in contact with Nguyễn Khang (1919–1976), a standing member of the Tonkin Regional Party Committee and a key decision-maker. During the lead up to the August Revolution, Nghĩa acted as a semi-legal courier.

On 13 August, Nghĩa was at 101 Rue Gambetta, now a semi-official Việt Minh office. That day, officials representing Toại, the King's Special Envoy, came to the address. They had made contact via a trusted channel, in order to deliver a verbal message from Toại to Nghĩa. Toại wanted to meet the Việt Minh to discuss power sharing. The officials went on to say, "The King's Special Envoy has just been entrusted full power by Huế."[27]

Nghĩa left and went to Hà Đông ATK, in Hà Đông Town, to relay his news to Nguyễn Khang and Trần Tử Bình. The men deliberated whether to accept the invitation. It could be a plot to arrest the Việt Minh leadership at this critical time. After thinking about the different outcomes, they agreed that Nghĩa should meet Toại. From late July, the two men had met each other on several occasions.[28]

Nghĩa continued:

During this period all Việt Minh contact with government and mandarin officials in Hanoi had to go through me. Little did Toại know, and those within his circle, that his son was an undercover Việt Minh operative and had smoothed the way each time. In spite of this vital contact, I never dropped my guard and never revealed my communist tendencies to Toại. If I had done so he might not have agreed to meet with me, although I am sure his intelligence officers knew my political views. Therefore, officially he met with the Việt Minh, not with a communist.

The aim of the meeting on 13 August, was for the puppet government to consolidate their position so that they could work with us. They wanted to invite the Việt Minh to hold important positions in office, such as ministerial posts that they even listed to me. When we shook hands they were excited about the future and the plans they intended to initiate. I knew we couldn't agree to such requests as our aim was to take full political power. I also met with Prime Minister Trần Trọng Kim, but at no time did I compromise our position.

On the morning of 15 August, Nguyễn Khang rushed into 101 Rue Gambetta, forgetting the basic principles of security: waiting for a signal for safe entry and then exchanging passwords. He looked different from usual, explaining with great emotion, almost apologetically, that the Tonkin Regional Party Committee had failed to make contact with members of the Party Central Committee in Tân Trào. From this we knew that we had to act alone.

Later on that day, Party members gathered in Vạn Phúc Village, Hà Đông ATK. This was now the home to the Hanoi City Party Committee, run by Nguyễn Khang. We had to finalize our decisions that had been agreed that morning, including mounting attacks in the provinces and establishing the Hanoi Revolutionary Military Committee, whose role was to take political power in Hanoi.

There were only five members of this Military Committee, all communists, although we kept this secret from our audience, and from the people, because at that time the face of communism was not acceptable. I represented the Democratic Party, as the leader of the northern part of Vietnam, which included Hanoi.

The other four members were Nguyễn Khang, who acted for the Việt Minh; Nguyễn Huy Khôi, who was a worker agitator revolutionary and represented laborers; and Nguyễn Duy Thân [192?–1951], who in turn represented the National Cultural Salvation Association.[29] This had been established with the arts in mind and acted as a tool with which to recruit urban intellectuals to the Việt Minh. The fifth person was Nguyễn Quyết, the secretary of the Hanoi City Party Committee, which represented the communists in Hanoi. Trần Đình Long [1904–1945] only advised us. A true Marxist veteran who had graduated from a school in Moscow in early 1930, he was now a member of the Party. Our group meant that each member represented a class of person who had joined the Việt Minh Front at the Eighth Conference in 1941.

On 16 August, I arranged for Trần Đình Long and Nguyễn Khang to meet with Toại. Again we could not agree on power sharing, so we were bold and asked Toại to hand over full control to the Việt Minh. It appears that he did not have the authority to take such a decision. We parted amicably, Toại saying, "The two sides should meet again very soon."

> For us we had to act concisely. According to rumors, another nationalist party called the Great Việt wanted power. We made the decision to stage the General Uprising in Hanoi. Nguyễn Khang, Trần Tử Bình and myself made this decision, in Vạn Phúc Village, but only on the afternoon of 17 August.[30]

The next day Minister Hoàng Xuân Hãn of the official Vietnamese government showed an interest in meeting with the Việt Minh.[31] Hãn informed Nghĩa that the allied forces of the British and Chinese Kuomintang were en route to Vietnam, which could leave the country split.

Knowing the threat, Nghĩa met with Dr. Nguyễn Xuân Chữ, who had replaced Toại as the King's Special Envoy.[32] Toại had voluntarily resigned his post that day because he now aligned himself with the Việt Minh. It had been important for Nghĩa and Chữ to meet because, along with his colleagues, Chữ had expressed an interest in cooperating with the Việt Minh. Chữ said to Nghĩa that he wanted to meet again the next day. Nghĩa became suspicious and thought that Chữ might have got wind of their plans because this was the proposed start date of the General Uprising.

Nghĩa returned to 101 Rue Gambetta to discuss his concerns with Nguyễn Quyết, the secretary of the Hanoi City Party Committee. They both decided to stop any spontaneous acts that might spoil their main plans. Nghĩa made no further contact with Chữ. The time for meetings, negotiations and planning had finished, Hanoi had to be taken and this was their strategic opportunity to do so.

On 19 August, the Hanoi Revolutionary Military Committee made their move to destroy the government and take power from the occupying Japanese. Committee members believed that they had to combine peaceful negotiations with armed struggle to force the Japanese out. More emphasis had to be placed on peaceful negotiations, as the Japanese Army was still very strong and could at any time destroy their chance of success. The leadership in Hanoi authorized Nghĩa to fire a gunshot from the Opera House, to start the Việt Minh's takeover.

Nghĩa explained:

> Nguyễn Khang requested that I take charge of the team instructed to occupy the office of the King's Special Envoy.[33] In front of the building, swarms of people demonstrated and vented their anger about decades of oppression. They forced the main gate open and people flooded in, despite the fact that the Civil Guard Units briefly shot at them in a vain effort to stop them from entering.
>
> We took the offices with no opposition and we arrested Dr. Nguyễn Xuân Chữ.[34] On arrest, we regarded this as a clear sign that political power now belonged to the Việt Minh, giving us great confidence.
>
> It was a different story at the Civil Guard camp itself, where Nguyễn Quyết led the occupation as a member of the Hanoi Revolutionary Military Committee. The Japanese Army intervened directly. They used tanks and troops in an effort to disarm the revolutionary forces, even though Quyết and his men were already occupying the building.
>
> The dilemma that developed was whether or not Quyết and his men should open fire on the Japanese troops. Quyết decided to ask other members of the Hanoi Revolutionary Military Committee for assistance. In response to his urgent call for help, Nguyễn Khang, Trần Tử Bình and Trần Đình Long asked me to take a limousine immediately from the offices of the King's Special Envoy and drive to the Civil Guard camp. They had instructed me to meet with the Japanese commander so that I could defuse the situation; a proud moment because the limousine flew our new flag, a red background with a yellow star, a banner soon to become the national one.
>
> On arrival I met with the commander at the Majestic Cinema opposite the camp and was able to persuade him not to take any further action. Before withdrawing to their military base, the commander told me, "You should talk to my superior." All of a sudden, I got the impression that they were willing to open discussions.[35]

That evening, Trần Đình Long and Nghĩa tried to make an appointment to meet the Japanese ambassador in his residence at 55 Rue Gambetta.[36] They had received a tip-off via a Vietnamese woman, who was married to a Japanese man, that a meeting might be possible. For the Việt Minh, the aim of the meeting was for both Nghĩa and Long to say to the Japanese ambassador, "We won't bother you if you just leave." On arriving at the ambassador's address, his staff told Nghĩa and Long that he was not at home; his staff advised them to go instead to the General Headquarters of the Japanese Army, at 33 Rue de la Concession.[37]

Nghĩa continued:

We met with Lieutenant General Yuitsu Tsuchihashi [1891–1975], the commander of the 38th Army of Indochina, and introduced ourselves saying we were key figures representing the new political order.

I was worried when we first met, in case he suspected us of being communists and revolutionaries, and therefore eliminated us. From our intelligence we knew that the Japanese Army had been told to oppose any such meeting.

We exchanged no names between each other, we just sat and talked. It took about two hours of negotiations but finally we got him to agree to hand over political power to the Việt Minh.[38]

The intelligence gathered by the *Kempeitai* could well have helped Lieutenant General Yuitsu Tsuchihashi with his decision to hand power to the Việt Minh.[39] His advisors would have made it clear that there had been some form of military union between the U.S. and the Việt Minh in Tonkin. If those in Hanoi had such a union, which felt challenged by the Japanese, there could be American reprisals.

Nghĩa went on:

In Japanese headquarters in Hanoi, a formal policy of non-intervention into Vietnamese affairs was discussed; once agreed, their authorities reported this to Tokyo. As a consequence of this and as representatives of the new administration, the Japanese in Hanoi assigned liaison officers to work with us and any pro-Japanese government services such as the police and guards were dissolved. Japanese and other foreigners within Hanoi were informed about these events.

Undoubtedly the Japanese recognized that once we had seized the offices of the Kings Special Envoy things were irreversible. We had achieved an unexpected but great victory: we were no longer seen by the Japanese as enemies or as just bandits.

We had political power but this did not mean we had independence. We could only say this when the people recognized Việt Minh authority. We arranged to address the people on 20 August from 8 a.m. to 9 a.m. in front of the former office of the King's Special Envoy. In readiness, we formed the Tonkin Revolutionary People's Committee, which would have its inauguration ceremony at this meeting. As this was going to be a public event, those involved, who had been acting covertly under pseudonyms, now had to pick new names in order to work overtly. I chose Lê Trọng Nghĩa, one of many that I used for my revolutionary duties.

Today there are two theories about our talks with the Japanese. The first is that the Việt Minh begged the Japanese not to interfere, and the second that the Japanese were so weak that they could not fight us. Neither is correct.

The truth is that we took the initiative above all other parties and met the highest ranking Japanese official to get recognition through negotiations. We did not fight them, we did not beg them, we went to take power from them as the new owners of Hanoi.

We had obtained power from the Japanese and we had destroyed the Vietnamese puppets. Now with strength the Việt Minh could meet the allied troops entering Vietnam, sent to disarm the Japanese.[40]

Nghĩa must have felt some reservations about the allied troops because on 22 August an American Mercy Team arrived in Hanoi, establishing their headquarters at the Metropole Hotel. Archimedes Patti, of OSS intelligence, led this Mercy Team, which had been sent to release allied Prisoners of War (POW) now the Japanese had surrendered.

However, when Patti arrived, he was accompanied by a small French contingent, led by Major Jean Sainteny, who planned to establish a French presence in Hanoi, under the *Direction Générale des Études et Recherches* (DGER).

That evening, Patti met with Nghĩa, who represented the Hanoi Revolutionary People's Committee. Patti cleverly glossed over details and assured Nghĩa that Sainteny's team was only on a "humanitarian mission" to look after the French POWs at the Citadel. He continued by saying that no French troops were anticipated, and that the United States did not support colonialism.[41]

Patti had not been transparent with Nghĩa. On 22 August, Admiral Thierry d'Argenlieu authorized a parachute drop of French intelligence agents across Indochina, with the aim of restoring French sovereignty. Argenlieu was an unfortunate choice of official. Unsympathetic to Vietnamese wishes, he is now blamed for undermining communications between Hồ and the French government, thus destroying any chances of peace.

The key man to oversee these parachute drops was Pierre Messmer. Designated as the high commissioner for Tonkin, he operated under the DGER.[42] Unfortunately for Messmer, most of the three-man teams were captured or killed by locals. He stated, after the event, "As a matter of fact, if our seven groups had dropped together, that is to say twenty-one people, we could have got through [the Việt Minh lines] because they were not well organized, and we should have succeeded in entering Hanoi. Without question: from a military point of view there is no doubt at all in my mind. The [the Việt Minh] were not organized; they had small groups with old weapons, and no wireless, no telephone, no communications. With twenty-one people we should have passed through."[43]

Messmer went on to say that if the parachutists had released the several thousand French soldiers held by the Japanese in Hanoi Citadel, then they could have regained control of the city. It appears that Messmer had seriously misread the situation.

Nghĩa tells his own story:

The taking of political power in Hanoi was very problematical. The General Uprising should have been under the Party Central Committee, but it was actually an uprising driven by the spontaneous actions and decisions of the people only—this people's action was not directed from above.

People drove the action, not the Việt Minh on the ground. We benefited from the uprising because the people of Hanoi thought that the Democratic Party controlled it. People were more aware of the Democratic Party because it had reached its peak of development on the eve of the August Revolution. This rapid expansion, as well as a high-profile standing, was partly because most of its members came from the bourgeois and intelligentsia classes. People listened to them as they called for popular change such as democracy and a republic. Hanoi was the heartland for this educated elite.

That August, when a political group declared power in Hanoi, the masses went along with it because they just presumed it was the Democratic Party behind the announcement, not the communists.[44]

How the Việt Minh replaced the Vietnamese puppet government has always divided opinion, according to Nghĩa. Some historians today suggest one of two alternative paths: firstly that the government was eager to cede power to the revolutionaries or, secondly, that power just fell into the hands of the revolutionaries. Both are incorrect.

Nghĩa said:

The government did not hand over power or collapse, the Việt Minh made the decision to destroy what was there, the entire administration. We were bold. Approaching the Japanese, harnessing the energy around the popularity of the Democratic Party to influence the outcome of the people's uprising, and using our covert operatives within the puppet apparatus to collapse things within.

It all hinged upon the fact that Communist Party members in Hanoi had not received Military

Order No 1. If we had received this then we would have been instructed to fight the Japanese Army, probably seeing us all killed and leading to a very different outcome. Acting alone was the key to our success because we could read the situation on the ground, so we put all our strength into destroying the puppet government instead.

If the revolutionaries had hesitated for even twelve hours waiting for an official order from the Party Central Committee, the circumstances would have been very different. The child was just born but at any moment the Japanese could have cut its throat to kill it.[45]

Giáp's Fighting Units

The Vietnamese-American partnership in Thái Nguyên was a display of unity designed by Hồ to show publicly that the Việt Minh were part of the allied forces, forming a Vietnamese-American Company. He hoped that from this the allies would agree to supply his units with weapons, but importantly recognize a new state of Vietnam under Việt Minh rule when he finally declared independence.

Prior to any fighting, the Japanese had been asked to concede to the Việt Minh. This request came via two ultimata, written in accordance with Military Order No. 1. These ultimata had authority. One had been signed by Giáp, and the other, in English, was signed by Allison Thomas. When these ultimata received no positive reply, hostilities erupted.

Nghĩa noted, "In Thái Nguyên Town the joint Vietnamese-American Company had to fight the Japanese. Under the command of Đàm Quang Trung, and his deputy Allison Thomas, they opened fire on the morning of 20 August." Further fighting occurred in Tam Đảo, an area where Messmer had parachuted some of his men, into what he recorded to be a disorganized battlefield.[46]

The fighting started even though the Japanese Emperor had surrendered because some Japanese units had been unwilling to admit defeat. This meant that the Vietnamese-American Company could not predict how the local Japanese would react to them but they knew that they could rebut any Japanese onslaught because they had a well-formed battle plan. Thomas later admitted he had helped his new friend, Giáp, prepare it.

Nghĩa concluded:

From 23 to 25 August the Tonkin Revolutionary People's Committee and the Hanoi Revolutionary People's Committee secured the area for the return of Hồ and other senior colleagues from Tân Trào. Hồ at the time was the chairman of the National Liberation Committee and president of the Provisional Government.

To improve security, the Hanoi Revolutionary People's Committee had to normalize relations with the Japanese Army. The fighting in Thái Nguyên had angered the Japanese in Hanoi and they demanded that the Việt Minh accompany them to the region to settle matters. This they did and, on 26 August, the Việt Minh gained Thái Nguyên its independence from the Japanese.

Preparing for Hồ to enter Hanoi had helped smooth the way for independence.[47]

Success had only really been achieved locally in Hanoi but the taking of the city was the catalyst that led to the Việt Minh coming to power across Vietnam.[48] It gave hope to other Việt Minh fighters, by showing them that they could win against a powerful enemy, because the story was different outside Tonkin.

In Huế the revolutionaries found it hard to move the people towards the Việt Minh. There was not such a large working class population there, in comparison to other parts of the country. In some instances, the upper classes had even aligned themselves with the French or the Japanese.

To support the Việt Minh in Huế City, on 23 August, the Tonkin Revolutionary People's Committee sent Emperor Bảo Đại a telegram requesting his abdication. This bold move saw Bảo Đại stand down. He cited that he could see a groundswell of dissatisfaction against his reign, and that the Việt Minh would make no concessions to him.[49] With Hanoi and Huế in their hands, on 25 August Saigon fell.

Careful Use of the Population

Before the Việt Minh took power in key areas they gauged the strength of any opposition. If deemed weak, then the Party issued the order to take political power. To understand the potential opposition, the Việt Minh penetrated and embedded their agents deep inside pro–Japanese and pro–French organizations. This infiltration had been done with such precision that even Emperor Bảo Đại cited Việt Minh agents among his staff members as one of the reasons he had decided to abdicate when he did. Worker and trader associations were target groups, along with youth movements such as the Frontline Youth in Huế and the Vanguard Youth in the south.

This Frontline Youth had been set up in Huế after the Japanese coup and were considered a fledgling military force for the Trần Trọng Kim government. Đặng Văn Việt and Cao Pha were two men within the Frontline Youth that the Việt Minh recruited.[50] The Communist Party ordered them to test what opposition the Việt Minh might face when they made their move to take Huế. These two men chose to see how the royal guards would react if they took down the royal banner from the flagpole opposite the main entrance to the Citadel and replaced it with a Việt Minh flag. The flagpole was very exposed but on 21 August, Đặng Văn Việt and Cao Pha carried out their task and met with no opposition from the guards.

From this flagpole test, Việt Minh leaders knew they could push ahead to take Huế. When Emperor Bảo Đại reflected back on this flagpole event, he said that he had not ordered his guards to shoot at the Việt Minh. He had suspected the guards would be reluctant to do so and would quite possibly have disobeyed him. He went on to say that the removal of his royal banner from the flagpole was another pivotal reason for him to take the decision to abdicate.

Whereas the Frontline Youth had been used in Huế, the Vanguard Youth did the same for the Việt Minh in Saigon. The Japanese founded the Vanguard Youth in April 1945 as a paramilitary group. When the French surrendered to the Japanese, youth programs now had to be run by pro–Japanese activists, so they asked Dr. Phạm Ngọc Thạch (1909–1968) to be president. His blood ties to the royal family and many Japanese acquaintances made him seem a good choice. Unbeknown to the Japanese, he was a communist and he soon set to work to plant Party cells, or at least sympathizers, throughout the structure of the group across South Vietnam.

The Vanguard Youth had expanded rapidly, having tens of thousands of members by August 1945. One explanation for this growth was that those within the Vanguard Youth could recruit from the well-established, formerly French-run organizations. One group, called the General Commissariat for Physical Education, Sport and Youth, aimed to channel energies away from politics and into sporting activities. Maurice Ducoroy had run it and he had set up two training institutes in Annam to accommodate youth from across Indochina. He had also established smaller schools in eleven provincial towns. By 1944, Ducoroy could claim 1,109 new sports instructors and 86,075 registered members of sporting societies. Some of those members came from groups such as the Associations of Youth Buddhists, Boy Scouts, Girl Guides, Red Ribbon Youth, Christian Workers Youth and Jeannettes.[51] By taking control of the Vanguard Youth the Việt Minh had access to many other organizations.

That August, thousands of people demonstrated in the streets of Saigon. The revolutionaries took advantage of this unrest to assess any opposition they might encounter when they went for power. The demonstrators nearly all flew the flag of the Vanguard Youth—a red star on a yellow background, the reverse of the colors of the Việt Minh flag. The Việt Minh leaders had purposely not swamped the demonstration with their flag because they wanted to monitor the Japanese reaction to seeing the Việt Minh flag at all. Demonstrators for the Việt Minh who were observing along the route reported that the Japanese did nothing but watch the crowd.

With this intelligence, Dr. Phạm Ngọc Thạch, Trần Văn Giàu (1911–2010) and Dương Bạch Mai (1904–1964) officially took office for the Việt Minh in Saigon as the unrest took hold. They instructed that their operatives in the Vanguard Youth must replace the yellow flag of the Vanguard Youth with the red flag of the Việt Minh. When the instruction had been carried out, according to eyewitnesses, the new red flags produced a spectacular color change along the route of the demonstration.[52] Again the Japanese did nothing but continued watching the crowd. This might not have been the case if the Việt Minh had not been so moderate in their initial approach. Hồ had now mastered the strategy of infiltrating into opposition organizations; something his rivals always underestimated.

Luck or Good Judgment

It is clear that victory during the August Revolution was not just the result of luck as some have contended, although an element of good fortune did play a part.

In the first instance the coup by the Japanese on 9 March was lucky for the Việt Minh, as it undermined the French and their plans. Before the coup the French had informed the Japanese that they intended to move against the Việt Minh in force. The coup put a stop to this. Luck also decreed that another nationalist army such as the Vietnamese Kuomintang did not fight the Việt Minh.[53] A third stroke of luck was the downing of American pilot Lieutenant Rudolph Shaw, as this led to the eventual American involvement with the Việt Minh. A fourth point was that, because the Việt Minh had waited until after Hiroshima to strike, many of the Japanese in Indochina switched sides to grant the Vietnamese independence. Most notably, it was lucky that the Communist Party in Hanoi did not receive Military Order No. 1. If they had received it their actions might have resulted in their defeat, and the Việt Minh would probably never have come to power.

When looking at Hồ's good judgment during the August Revolution, he recognized that the political and propaganda fronts were the most important, with the military being used more as a tool to support any political-propaganda action. Primarily, to take political power, Hồ used the uncertainty at the end of the Second World War as his strategic opportunity. If he had used the earlier coup as his opportunity then he would probably have seen the revolutionaries annihilated.

On propaganda, Hồ's seeking of a Việt Minh–American alliance enabled him to elevate the Việt Minh above other nationalist groups wanting to take power. This alliance had a profound impact on the Japanese, and the fear of U.S. reprisals helped lead to their decision not to fight the Việt Minh in Hanoi. This saw to the transfer of power to the Việt Minh and Hanoi becoming a beacon city of victory for Communist Party members who had not journeyed to Tân Trào, encouraging them to rise up and take power in their local areas. In addition, the Vietnamese-American Company made the tiny Vietnam Liberation Army appear big and powerful to the Japanese, and because the attack was not just military, but a message of propaganda and liberation, it made out that the revolutionary army represented the people of Vietnam to any onlookers. Likewise, the alliance gave the revolutionaries the means to expand their army through access to modern weapons and training.

What of the Revolutionary Infrastructure? Hồ had predicted that his Communist Party would achieve victory in 1945; recorded through his writings as far back as the early 1940s. The key to Hồ's prophecy, was that by 1945 the Revolutionary Infrastructure would have penetrated most key areas of society, giving him control not only over any opposition but a sizable part of the population. Victory could then be achieved by harnessing and controlling any nationalist uprising in favor of the Việt Minh.

His taking of political power was not a matter of *if*, but more likely *when*. Nevertheless, although the taking of power relied on the much-used and needed Revolutionary Infrastructure, during the August Revolution it failed to keep pace with unfolding events. It held better than the courier system during the Cochinchina Uprising, but this slight miscalculation during that August, did put great strain on the individuals coordinating both political and propaganda activities for the Việt Minh.

This vital point was explained by Nghĩa:

What was the role of the Indochinese Communist Party that August? Party involvement was less than people think. The uprising was driven by the people, and the Việt Minh were there to control this surge in their favor

Any Party achievements were through the Việt Minh because the Việt Minh were working for national independence and had broader political appeal.

In contrast, the Communist Party were part of the wider vision of international class struggle and world revolution, with the role of communism being to completely destroy what went before.

So, changing our appearance from solely that of the Communist Party to that of the Việt Minh was very important. People would not have risen with us if we had just kept the face of communism, because they did not want to follow this line of politics.

This changeover was agreed in 1941, when the establishment of the Việt Minh became the turning point, from the international to the national interests of Vietnam. Before 1941, you could not say this, as we were only communists.

You can see that Vietnamese patriotism won the August Revolution, not communism. The Việt Minh came to power because we harnessed this patriotism.[54]

On balance, during the August Revolution there was more judgement than luck, but for Hồ the lessons learned were clear. Undermine the enemy; infiltrate into pro–Japanese organizations to disable them and combine this with patriotic anti–Japanese propaganda. Do not use armed violence as a tool with which to encounter a powerful enemy. Do not take the rural areas in order to encircle urban regions, as Maoism states, but seize power in urban areas step by step by building the Revolutionary Infrastructure near and inside the urban areas; crucially the organs of power and within key areas of society.[55] Grasp opportunities.

Obviously, where the focus was on the Japanese during the August Revolution, it would be on the French and the Americans and their allies when war broke out during the French War and later the Vietnam War.

Hồ Establishes a Nation

On 2 September, President Hồ declared the independence of Vietnam in Hanoi.[56] Crowds of thousands listened to his speech that founded the Democratic Republic of Vietnam. Hồ established a Provisional Government that served from 27 August 1945 to 3 November 1946. Within this government, six of the fifteen ministers of state were members of the Indochinese Communist Party.

However, just prior to Hồ's declaration, the British disembarked in Vietnam to disarm the Japanese in French Indochina south of the 16th Parallel. The Chinese Kuomintang had arrived to take responsibility for the north, some coming as early as 20 August from China. This had been agreed at the Potsdam Conference in Germany, held from 16 July to 2 August; one of its aims being to divide up the post-war world.[57]

The August Revolution might have gone in Hồ's favor but his fledgling government was now under threat. Hồ predicted that next time he would be fighting a foreign conventional army, thus immediately following his declaration, he established a section of the military titled the Communications Liaison Service (Signals Service). Before this the Vietnam Liberation Army had been a light infantry force only with just two sections: Combat and Intelligence.[58]

The mausoleum that houses Hồ Chí Minh's body. It is in the center of Ba Đình Square, Hanoi, and is the historic location where Hồ read the Declaration of Independence on 2 September 1945, establishing the Democratic Republic of Vietnam. 2003 photograph (Clive A. Hills).

Furthermore, Hồ foresaw he needed to expand further beyond his borders. Looking back at history, old-time revolutionary Trinh had written a letter to Hồ when in Paris, on 18 February 1922. In this letter Trinh had expressed concerns about Hồ's strategy, namely to establish himself outside Vietnam (in order to mobilize and train young talent) and then, when the right opportunity arose, to enter Vietnam unexpectedly and take political power. Ironically, Hồ's vision had actually been realized during the August Revolution. Now, with France set to reclaim Indochina, a reappraisal of old tactics was much needed. Just after he formed the Democratic Republic of Vietnam his government signed agreements with both the Lao and Cambodian authorities. For the Lao this was an Agreement of Military Alliance, a settlement for a joint Việt-Lao Army. Hồ's government also signed a joint declaration, Việt-Cambodian-Lao Solidarity against France, with Cambodia, which resulted in the creation of a Việt-Cambodian Army.

With foreign military forces arriving across Indochina, and Hồ expanding his blueprint accordingly, when the French War started it would be known as the First Indochina War.

• *The French War (1945–1954)* •

6

Blueprint for Revolution

Hô's Objectives

As soon as the French made their intentions clear, Hô started to plan to foil them. There were two pressing matters. First he had to secure his fledgling powerbase.[1] This meant removing any potential rivals, appealing to the Vietnamese population and winning over international opposition. Of equal importance, if war was imminent, Hô recognized that in parallel to the first point he had to further fortify his strategies to give the people of Vietnam the means to fight a protracted asymmetric conflict against a superior power. Those parts of his strategies that had appeared promising, or had proved unbeaten, during the August Revolution, he would expand and develop to suit forthcoming events. It was during this process that Hô produced a successful blueprint to win this type of warfare.

Asymmetric warfare is a concept that has been around for some decades. The popularity of the term dates back to Andrew J.R. Mack's 1975 article titled, "Why Big Nations Lose Small Wars: The Politics of Asymmetric Conflict."[2] Here the term "asymmetric" referred to a significant difference in power between enemies in a conflict, roughly taken to be material power such as high-tech weapons, a large army and an advanced economy. Mack argued that in certain types of conflict conventional military superiority is not merely useless, but may actually be counterproductive because the cost of such a conflict to the public back home might end any domestic political capacity to continue the war. Scholars largely discounted his work, but by the end of the Cold War there was fresh interest in understanding this particular theory.

Ivan Arreguín-Toft researched a modern approach to this concept and published his book, *How the Weak Win Wars: A Theory of Asymmetric Conflict*, in 2005. He argued that the likelihood of victory and defeat in asymmetric conflicts depends upon the interaction of the strategies that the opposing players apply. Using statistical and in-depth historical analyses of conflicts spanning 200 years, he showed that irrespective of regime type and weapon technology, the interaction of similar strategic approaches favor the strong, while opposite strategic approaches favor the weak.[3]

Against Hô's forces, the French and Americans applied conventional warfare strategies based mainly on their experiences during the First and Second World Wars. If both opposing sides had drawn on conventional warfare, then this would have been a symmetrical fight. Meaning both sides having well defined troop formations and using conventional weaponry, with other strategies playing supporting roles. On the battlefield they would have targeted each other in open confrontation and applied set piece battle tactics, which generally involved large troop numbers moving according to a plan and responding to the opposing force, also by plan.

Hồ decided that he would not play by these conventional rules and consequently the wars in Vietnam are examples of opposite strategic approaches. Although some of Hồ's methods had been used to varying degrees in previous warfare, his strategies and their combined use were unique and a new form. He called this an All-People's War and key to understanding it was to comprehend the principle that you cannot win a war through military means alone.

Hồ used the people for his All-People's War. His vision, to get the whole nation to oppose the enemy, working on the principle that although each person was individually weak the combined opposition of the masses would eventually bring down the mightiest enemy and drive them out of power. His saying was, "If you have the people, you'll have everything." Although the concept of an All-People's War suggests that all the public supported Hồ's quest for the nation, clearly not everyone did; consequently what Hồ meant was, through various parts of his framework, he could at least control the critical mass of the populace.

The aim of the All-People's War was to fight a protracted war of attrition; grinding the enemy down. Nevertheless, Giáp saw that total victory could only be achieved through conventional units and when they had symmetry on the battlefield. To establish these conditions, Giáp used the blueprint to build his units and diminish the strength of the opposing army. Then, at a strategic opportunity, he would inflict one swift death blow on the conventional units of his enemy, so forcing them into unconditional surrender because they would have nothing to fall back on.

Although the strategic military front became dominant leading up to the death blow, the rest of Hồ's All-People's War blueprint remained important. In the first instance, if the military blow was misjudged and applied too soon then the opposing army might be stronger than expected and could destroy the conventional forces of the revolutionaries. In this case, Giáp needed the rest of the blueprint to rebuild his conventional units, and if this was not developed enough it might leave the communists in a very weak position. On a second point, if the death blow were indeed well timed and the opposing army destroyed, then the revolutionaries required the rest of the blueprint to secure the liberation of Vietnam with the Communist Party as the sole ruling power.

The revolutionaries administered two death blows, one against the French at Điện Biên Phủ in 1954 and the other against the South Vietnamese in 1975 when Saigon fell. In this latter case, what the Western broadcasters presented to the world was the symbolic end to the war, with the tanks of the revolutionaries crashing through the gates of the Presidential Palaces—conventional troops of the revolutionaries annihilating the conventional troops of the Southern Army. What actually happened was the annihilation of the Southern Army as described, but then the shadow government became overt, taking the population with them, and the rest of the clandestine people of the All-People's War revealed themselves to take over the domestic, military and administrative apparatus of the South, from the post office to the Presidential Palace.

The All-People's War formed what is best described as a blueprint for protracted asymmetric warfare against a superior power. Though it was designed solely to liberate Vietnam, this blueprint now forms a framework for this type of warfare. However, as Hồ's story shows, it takes a lot of dedication and might to implement.

Strategic Propaganda Front

Hồ was a master at propaganda and within days of forming his government, his revolutionary sympathizers within the administration set to work covertly using policies to their advantage. One high profile example was the literacy program, implemented by the government in September 1945 to educate the populace, 90 percent of whom were illiterate. People who could read were tasked with teaching their families, work colleagues and associates. It is estimated that within the first year, 2.5 million people in Tonkin and Annam had benefited to some extent, with only Cochinchina missing this opportunity owing to the outbreak of hostilities.

The revolutionaries could see other benefits to the literacy program. Principally, once educated the masses could then read their propaganda literature. Similarly, it gave the revolutionaries the means to spread nationalism and to recruit young blood. Teachers sympathetic to the revolution could keep nationalism at the heart of every class, but furthermore, alongside this nationalist drive, socialism could then be served up in digestible forms depending on the target audience.[4]

The literacy program focused on the masses and government policy, but in addition the revolutionaries conducted targeted propaganda. Military proselytizing became a clear favorite of Hồ's. Described as the act of carrying out agitation and spreading propaganda among enemy troops, Hồ termed it, "to win without fighting," and any switched person within an enemy camp became a type of Trojan Horse. Senior revolutionaries generally accepted that the core of their resistance strategy was a combination of political and military proselytizing. "Using great causes to win over cruelty" became the adopted motto, which came from *Proclamation of Victory over the Wu*, by Nguyễn Trãi (1380–1442), and meant that it was better to conquer hearts than citadels.

Another category of propaganda comprised *địch vận*, a more general agitation and propaganda tool used among the enemy, including government members, civilians and the military. During the Vietnam War those conducting this type of propaganda included presenter Hanoi Hannah, who broadcasted in English so that U.S. servicemen could listen in to Radio Hanoi; but the majority of operatives were tasked with escorting U.S. prisoners along the Hồ Chí Minh Trail to North Vietnam.

Those conducting international propaganda wanted to undertake political mischief and exploit any weak points in their enemy. Hồ, Giáp, Phạm Văn Đồng and Trường Chinh mainly drove this because they knew their enemy well; they had either been educated in the West or had studied with their colonial masters. Their overall objective was to make the wars so politically unworkable that any foreign governments could not justify to their own people their presence in Vietnam.

Other forms of targeted propaganda involved *trí vận*, which covered agitation and propaganda among the intelligentsia, and *hoa vận*, which targeted the Chinese communities of Vietnam, especially in Chợ Lớn. The Soviet term "special propaganda," which came into common use from 1978, was employed earlier as a generic term to cover all the above, as well as any other kind of secret communist manipulation that helped to shift things in favor of the revolution.

These modes of propaganda developed into a bewilderingly complex mind-manipulation tool applied by special propaganda operatives, who were from a different service to those of any secret agents. They targeted key people such as a leader of a political party or a high-ranking military individual. Operatives used various techniques to implement propaganda. For example, to distance himself from the target, an operative first approached a relative of the target, and then got the relative to approach them instead. If the target seemed to soften to the revolutionaries the operative then got a specialist to meet and socialize with him and, through pressing the nationalist button continually, the specialist tried to entice the target over to the revolutionary cause. If persuaded to switch allegiance, the targeted person could then destroy or manipulate the enemy from within. If, on the other hand, the target refused to comply, the specialist warned, "You are either with us, but if not, then do not oppose us." If the target still neither joined the revolution nor became neutral, the target could be blackmailed to do so, or eventually killed, referred to as neutralized, to preserve the specialist's cover.

By conducting mass or targeted propaganda the Việt Minh minimized their losses in manpower and financial outlay; just two clear advantages that this finely tuned system of persuasion offered.

Hồ the Diplomat

Hồ had to achieve government legitimacy both inside and outside Vietnam by persuading his rivals that elections were the best way forward. By doing this, peace could be maintained for as long as possible, giving the Việt Minh time to strengthen their blueprint, in case of war.

In Vietnam, Hồ faced a bleak situation. At a grassroots level, the morale of the general population was very low owing to high unemployment across the country. Furthermore, there was famine in Tonkin that had started the previous winter but had been made far worse because the Japanese had forced the peasants to plant jute instead of rice and that harvest had failed. Likewise, across Vietnam there were shortages of goods because the occupying forces had consumed much of the remaining food. To urgently address local concerns, the Provisional Government implemented proposals that included tax reductions and the seizure of land from French colonials.[5]

Internationally, Hồ had to be politically engaged because in August 1945 the first of the 180,000-strong Chinese Kuomintang forces had arrived from China; the majority arriving in November.[6] These troops posed a direct threat to Hồ's Provisional Government. Fortunately, General Lu Han and General Xiao Wen commanded these troops and Hồ knew General Wen. When Chinese Kuomintang forces had arrested Hồ in the early 1940s, it had been General Wen who had been ordered to check on the prisoner; unbeknown to him at the time it was Nguyễn Ái Quốc (who now openly called himself Hồ Chí Minh).

To gain government legitimacy and be the head of a permanent administration, Hồ needed to persuade the two Chinese generals to agree to elections. To accomplish this, Hồ made concessions. He changed the name of the Vietnam Liberation Army to the National Defense Guard that September. Hồ anticipated that by not using the word army it signaled to the generals that his units were non-aggressive and therefore not a direct threat to them.[7] Later in 1945, Hồ made it seem that he had closed down the Indochinese Communist Party in North Vietnam, with the south following suit in 1947. Not surprisingly, this was all a pretense. The Communist Party would, of course, still operate, but covertly.

To further advance the idea of elections, the Chinese Kuomintang generals asked

Hồ to negotiate with nationalist groups, a request designed to reduce Việt Minh domination in any administration. Hồ understood this had to be done but it would not be easy. A number of competing groups had set up a counter-revolutionary bloc, dominated by members of the Vietnamese Kuomintang and the League for Revolution. To stop any rival bloc damaging the revolutionaries, Hồ's agents penetrated them in order to eliminate people who showed more interest in their own power than in the future independence of Vietnam, and remove those who had aligned themselves with the Chinese and were happy to be governed by them.

On 6 January 1946, Vietnam held general elections to vote for its first National Assembly. The Việt Minh took the majority of seats, but so as not to alienate the other two main groups that had expressed dissatisfaction with Việt Minh rule, Hồ negotiated with the Vietnamese Kuomintang and the League for Revolution to reserve them fifty and twenty seats respectively, out of the 330 plus available.

Again, this sign of goodwill by Hồ was not all it seemed. His embedded agents within the Vietnamese Kuomintang and the League for Revolution now tried to either occupy these designated seats or position weak people into them, called "political human shields" or "puppets."[8] In this particular case, the revolutionaries looked for weak people who were non-communist and pro–Chinese, again to mollify the generals. Political human shields were used throughout both the French War and Vietnam War, and were a significant factor when it came to the negotiation of treaties or power sharing.

Hồ had given himself government legitimacy, and shown that he was a skilled diplomat and a master of four-dimensional thinking, because he understood the significance of achieving political stability when engaged in a protracted revolution.

Tactical Peace Negotiations

Hồ's new government had not pacified everyone and civil unrest had ignited across Vietnam. Equally, Vietnam had only been independent since August 1945 and no country had recognized it diplomatically. To protect and reinforce the new administration's national and international position, in March 1946 Hồ signed a *modus vivendi* in Hanoi.

This *modus vivendi* had taken great skill to negotiate but the alternative to this was war, which Hồ recognized the Việt Minh was not prepared for. The Việt Minh had to recruit more people and Hồ had noticed that many individuals already within the Communist Party had not taken their achievements seriously. They had been shocked by actual success, resulting in a collapse in certain sectors of the revolution through complacency and a loss of fighting spirit. Hồ reasoned that by him signing the document, the people would rally behind his new government and Party members might grow up and govern.

This preliminary agreement between the Vietnamese and the French covered points that included creating a favorable climate necessary for the immediate opening of friendly but frank talks, and negotiations for a referendum to unite Tonkin, Annam and Cochinchina into one Vietnam. Likewise, it covered the French recognizing the Democratic Republic of Vietnam as a free state and having its own government, parliament, army and treasury, although it still belonged to the French Union and the French-sponsored Indochinese Federation.[9]

One part of the *modus vivendi* was highly controversial. It requested that the government of Vietnam declared itself ready to accept the French Army in an amicable way when it relieved the Chinese Kuomintang. This meant replacing 180,000 Chinese Kuomintang with 15,000 troops to be located in Tonkin for a five-year duration, 800 of these garrisoned at Điện Biên Phủ.[10] Some Party members considered allowing French troops into Vietnam as a very negative concession. For Hồ it was an essential political maneuver. Hồ feared a war with China far more than he did with the French, and by having some say as to where these French troops would be positioned he could draw them away from a weak Việt Minh in Cochinchina. Although the French replacement of the Chinese Kuomintang was in conformance with international negotiations, so fearful was Hồ of the Kuomintang going back on this agreement that he gave the generals sweeteners to get them to take their troops out of the country faster.[11]

In July 1946, a French-Vietnamese conference opened at Fontainebleau, near Paris, to continue negotiations. This was just one month after High Commissioner of Indochina Admiral d'Argenlieu, violated the March agreement and proclaimed the far south of Vietnam as the Republic of Cochinchina. To rally support against this breach, Hồ had even gone to see former colleagues in Paris from his days in the French Communist Party in the 1920s. Unfortunately they were too nationalistic to damage French interests and backed away. The conference ended that September, partly because all parties failed to reach an agreement on Cochinchina. The Vietnamese delegation left France but Hồ stayed on fearing he might depart with "empty hands." Just before going he signed a second *modus vivendi*, but again it did not achieve total independence from France.

President Hồ arrived back in Hanoi knowing that some of his own Party members were critical of what he had achieved; conveniently overlooking that just over a year ago the Việt Minh had no official international legitimacy and resided in the jungle. In Hồ's eyes they had grossly failed to see that, with tensions in Vietnam growing, he had suitably weakened the enemy while at the same time preparing the Việt Minh for any conflict.

The Start of War

With Hồ's propaganda and political strategies under way, he looked to construct his military front. Two men assigned by Hồ to take this forward were Trần Văn Giàu (1911–2010) and Nguyễn Bình (1908–1951).[12] Their initial task was to consolidate the situation in Cochinchina and lead the resistance there because Hồ's powerbase was less developed in that region.

Giàu would authorize the first gunshot that started the French War, as recorded by the Việt Minh. On 23 September 1945, revolutionary Dương Quang Đông took aim, exerted sufficient pressure with his trigger finger, and this historic round left the barrel of his weapon and sped on its way towards French troops. It was a shot approved because the French now attempted to take back Saigon from those Vietnamese who had tried to defend it.[13] Three days later, Hồ sent his first units south to "save" Saigon.

Not only had the French threatened Saigon but that month British forces had started to disembark under the command of General Douglas Gracey (1894–1964), there to take control of the region below the 16th Parallel as agreed at the Potsdam Conference in Germany. Gracey was unsympathetic to the Vietnamese desire for independence and had used a very heavy-handed approach from the outset to police the unstable city; arming the French, who had remained in Saigon, and later issuing guns to Japanese troops who had surrendered. Once in-country he began a six-month process of handing back Cochinchina to the French.

Hồ had predicted a flood of foreign troops. To greet the British on their arrival in Saigon, on 25 August Party members officially established the Cochinchina Provisional Administrative Committee (CPAC). Giàu was its chairman as well as holding the position of secretary of the Cochinchina Regional Party Committee.

Trần Văn Giàu in 2007. He led the revolution in Cochinchina in the mid–1940s (courtesy Trần Văn Giàu).

The Communist Party established this committee to give them an element of control over any situation. It was meant to be made up of nationalist groups, but the Party selected the participants carefully

A temple of the Cao Đài religion, a faith officially established in the city of Tây Ninh in 1926. The main feature is the Divine Eye, which symbolizes God. This was one of the many sects that the Việt Minh continually tried to get onside, with varying degrees of success. 2007 photograph (Clive A. Hills).

because out of the nine initial members, five aligned themselves with the Indochinese Communist Party and four had already expressed their willingness to obey them. No attempts had been made to include the religious sects such as the Hòa Hảo, Cao Đài or the Catholics.[14]

With hostilities escalating, the committee members demanded of their former allies that the independence they had gained in August be reinstated. These demands fell on deaf British ears and all attempts between the committee and the French to arrange a ceasefire collapsed. The acceleration of fighting seemed inevitable.

The Opening of a Logistics Line

The Communist Party did not view Giàu entirely as the golden boy. Saigon was lawless, divided and horrifically dangerous, and the Việt Minh had few groups they could align themselves with, an overwhelming situation blamed partly on his particularly brutal campaign.

One clue as to why Giàu used sadistic methods can be traced back to his Bolshevik roots. He had graduated from the Communist University of the Toilers of the East, under Stalin's influence. As a graduate of this so-called Stalin School, he advocated the elimination of anyone against the Việt Minh and who did not conform to his view, including some armed resistance groups fighting the French. This was contrary to the general policy that looked more for non-opposition rather than immediate eradication.

What further tarnished Giàu's reputation with the Party was that the French, British and Japanese now pushed harder against any opposition. In Party eyes, he had failed to contain this and consequently a number of Việt Minh members had retreated to the Plain of Reeds, the Tây Ninh rubber plantations and the U Minh forest. Poorly equipped and with no means to support themselves, they lived off the land. Việt Minh power was now as weak as it had been after the failed 1940 Cochinchina Uprising.

Party members summoned Giàu to Hanoi at the tail end of 1945 to answer for his extremely harsh methods. At the same time, Hồ looked for colleagues that he could send to regions where the population had since become disconnected from the revolution. Hồ hoped that by sending his colleagues to regions where he had once personally lived, the population would be more willing to rejoin the revolution and supply goods. Knowing Hồ's requirements, Giàu asked to be sent to Cochinchina, Cambodia or Siam to reconnect with the people and establish logistics bases.

Officials chose to send Giàu to Siam as their ambassador. Hồ wanted to make contact with the Russians who lived there and Soviet Embassy staff, so that through them he could communicate with Moscow and ask them for aid. Giàu had not only studied with the Soviets but spoke their language. Giàu had also been at school with Pradi Phnom Yong, a Vietnamese sympathizer who now worked for members of the government of Siam, most noticeably Pridi Banomyong who briefly became prime minister in 1946. Through Pradi Phnom Yong, Giàu could see if Siam was willing to support Vietnam and their cause.

Giàu went under the guise of an official representative of the Vietnamese News Agency and traveled via Cambodia to Siam.[15] On his way he met his colleague, the prominent revolutionary Dương Quang Đông, who had been sent by the Cochinchina Regional Party Committee to buy weapons and had left for Siam on 20 February 1946.[16]

The chance meeting between the two colleagues saw them initiate the Research Bureau, to investigate the opening of the Trans-West Supply Line. By March 1946, this sea and land route, starting at the Cà Mau Peninsula, had its first two courier stations, one in Ko Kong, Cambodia and the other in Mayluot, Siam. To establish these, Đông had worked with Sơn Ngọc Minh (1920–1972).[17] The Research Bureau achieved a good track record and in mid–1946 officials supplied the team with money to purchase a 20 ton sailing boat.[18]

The logistics line grew sufficiently to support major tasks, and in mid–1946 the prime minister of Siam offered 50 tons of weapons and chemicals to make landmines; a gift to the Vietnamese resistance, thanks to negotiations in which Giàu had played a role. Once the prime minister had authorized the weapons, his men promptly transferred them to the residences of the minister of interior and the minister of foreign affairs, and then secured them in containers at Bangkok harbor, along with other goods.

On 20 June 1946, Đông set sail on his first weapons transportation assignment. In total, two boats left for Bangkok, one of 4 tons and the other of 10. Sơn Ngọc Minh sailed in one and Đông and Bông Văn Dĩa (1905–1983) traveled in the other. With the containers loaded safely, the smaller vessel arrived back with little difficulty but the larger one encountered a strong headwind and the crew ran out of food. Hungry and exhausted, they arrived weeks later at the dock at Rạch Gốc Village, Cochinchina; an inlet that became a port along the Hồ Chí Minh Trail Sea Route.

Overseas Vietnamese revolutionaries often bought weapons in Bangkok, and during these early years it was not difficult to do so. They used three pagodas to store the armaments; Thi Oa Thi Pagoda inside China Town eventually became Đông's headquarters. From here Đông purchased goods and opened courier routes, including the way stations at Buon Kieu Kachis and Mai Rout. In April 1947, the Marine Department of Cochinchina was established with Đông as its deputy head. With Bangkok now hostile to the revolutionaries because Pridi Banomyong was no longer prime minister, Đông operated covertly, his cover being as the head of an import-export company. Nevertheless, throughout his time in charge of logistics, from 1946 to 1954 Đông dispatched 97,543 tons of weapons and equipment along his lines, which reached all the battlefields of Indochina.[19]

The aims and principles of the Trans-West Supply Line had clearly been met. This corridor had enabled high troop numbers to secretly journey from one place to the next, secured the means to transport high volumes of materials and given individuals safer routes to travel. All this was possible because the couriers that served these lines were trained fighters, as a direct result of Đông being instructed to open a new front in Cambodia. The routes also traversed land, crossed rivers and transited coastal routes, and at their disposal they had oxen, elephants and a fleet of boats. Still, those using the lines or building them endured horrific illnesses, shortages of food, horrendous weather conditions and lived under constant fear of being attacked by wild animals or even by bandits. Yet thanks to those who sacrificed their health and lives, this strategic corridor earned its place in history because from lessons learned other lines were built, including the now famous Hồ Chí Minh Trail, the little known Hồ Chí Minh Trail Sea Route and, of course, the bigger brother to the Trans-West Supply Line, the Sihanouk Trail.

Top: The seaport of Rạch Giá Town, Rạch Giá Province (now Kiên Giang Province). These fishing boats typify the type of vessels used by units operating along the Trans-West Supply Line or this section of the Hồ Chí Minh Sea Route. *Bottom:* A monument to the Hồ Chí Minh Trail Sea Route, in Năm Căn Town, Cà Mau Province (both photographs 2009, Clive A. Hills).

Relying on Couriers

Hồ selected Nguyễn Bình as the second man to expand his strategic military front and in fact nominated him personally to act as his ambassador in Cochinchina. The Communist Party tasked him with forming the Armed Force of Cochinchina. Whereas Giàu had already been in Saigon when hostilities broke out, Bình arrived in the troubled city later, by train, in October 1945.

Born into a peasant family in Hưng Yên Province, Bình first participated in revolutionary activities in 1925 when he joined the Vietnamese Kuomintang. He moved to communism when serving time in prison in 1945, and once freed he formed a Việt Minh war zone in the north-east of Tonkin.

That October, Bình's initial task was to unite dissident groups and consolidate their numbers. These included the religious sects of the Cao Đài, the Hòa Hảo and the Bình Xuyên, the latter group being more appropriately described as river pirates. The Party viewed uniting these groups as essential because many had fought against the French.

Like numerous covert operatives in his position, Bình had to outwit his opponents to survive; taking on chameleon-like qualities. To this very day many of those who were trained in covert work by the communists still do not know who their fellow operatives really were; Hồ being the master of disguise and deception. Key traits that had to be grasped included learning a provincial dialect, taking on new mannerisms, altering their facial features, such as growing a moustache, and changing their name.[20] These traits altered depending on the situation, such as when traveling between provincial borders, from the jungle to the city, or from a liberated zone to those areas controlled by the enemy.

To carry out their duties operatives had to work with a courier. Officials assigned Miss Hoàng Thị Thanh to escort Bình when he operated on reconnaissance work in those early days in Saigon-Chợ Lớn. The Communist Party viewed her as ideal for the position as, although originally from the northern province of Hải Dương, she knew the streets of the city well. According to some sources, before 1945 she had worked for the Japanese as a geisha girl there. Or, in her own words, as a fashion model in a photography shop. Additionally, she looked like an overseas Chinese resident, but more importantly she knew how to act like one, as she had previously stayed in a large Chinese community when living in Hải Phòng. The ability to be viewed as a Chinese resident was a massive advantage; the Chinese were assumed to be neutral about, or at least disengaged from, the resistance war.

Miss Thanh did not feel as enthusiastic or at ease with the task as her leaders did. She believed that her presence in Saigon brought suspicion upon her. In September, city sympathizers had seen her engage in battles against the French, and now that the revolutionaries had been pushed out to the suburbs, those who returned were most likely to be traitors against the revolutionaries, and she could be killed. She also felt that she lacked self-confidence in tight situations, such as having to talk her way through military checkpoints. Bình had approached her at the end of October, when she was an ambulance woman in the militia.

At their initial meeting together, Ambassador Bình explained that he had to find a young woman with knowledge of the city so that she could take him on missions to maintain communications between the command of Cochinchina and his city units. Miss Thanh noted that when he had greeted her he had not clasped his hands together as if in prayer, to avoid body contact, but had shaken her hand like a Westerner to show that the revolutionaries were modern and respected equality.

Bình said to her, "I am very glad to see a fellow comrade from Tonkin in Cochinchina. Will you take on the task of being a city courier? Let me explain. I have just arrived from the north and have not been to Saigon for twenty years. The city has changed so much. I need a courier to guide me. The task seems so simple, yet my courier must have a number of qualities: be a resident of Saigon, have excellent self-control for dealing with high-stress situations, and be brave; but more to the point, have evidence that they have taken part in the fiercest battles. However, it is your decision. The revolutionary cause is for volunteers."[21]

He then gave Miss Thanh her first task, to purchase two Chinese dresses (*Cheongsam*), an attire he wore, because if she put one on people would think that she was an overseas Chinese resident. He had stressed that the dress would suit inner-city operations as the secret police agents working for the French did not bother Chinese residents even though there were tens of thousands of overseas Chinese in Hải Phòng and Chợ Lớn. Miss Thanh recorded that she had burst out laughing. During her city days she had always followed the latest fashions but had never worn Chinese dress. Smiling Bình had said, "Perhaps you think that these dresses will make you look ugly. This is unfounded. A chasuble won't create a priest—beauty can't be created by a dress. With such looks, dear comrade, you will be pretty no matter what you wear."[22]

With Miss Thanh now onside and dressed for the occasion, their initial reconnaissance tour could be conducted, but they had seriously misjudged the dangers. No sooner had Bình and Miss Thanh started out than their bus was boarded by a Japanese patrol searching for weapons. She had documents in one trouser leg and a shotgun in the other; so she was terrified. The Japanese military police were not fooled by her disguise as they could tell that she was a Vietnamese girl in Chinese dress. If this had been a French patrol they would not have noticed her Vietnamese features and taken her to be Chinese. Seeing Bình as a Chinese merchant, she had heard the Japanese call him "*tai ho*" or "*tai*," which means Sir or Senior.[23] They questioned why she traveled with a Việt Minh suspect. She thought that they might kill her so she denied all knowledge of Bình. She claimed he had been on the bus when the driver picked her up hitchhiking. They were clearly not convinced and arrested the two of them plus Dương Bạch Mai and Huỳnh Văn Nghệ (1914–1977) who were in their party, on suspicion of opposing British and French troops.

The Japanese soldiers started to drive the group to their barracks for questioning. On the way Bình winked at Miss Thanh. She knew that this was their prearranged secret signal, to instruct her to request the truck to pullover so that she could relieve herself. With the truck stopped, and the Japanese off guard, Bình shouted "run!" This was a petrifying situation, one which took her by surprise when the Japanese opened fire, spraying the air with bullets.

Miss Thanh lost the others when she escaped. Not knowing what to do, she accidentally ran straight into the hands of Trịnh Khánh Vàng, a hated local guerrilla commander who would soon switched sides to fight for the French. Facing Vàng, and still dressed as a Chinese woman, she feared that he would try her for spying. He might suspect her of working undercover for the French, as a Vietnamese national but with a poor choice of clothing. Or he might mistake her for a genuine Chinese resident but think she was an informer for the Japanese, because the two nations could read each other's script. Without a convincing argument to explain her situation, he sentenced her to death.

Her luck changed only when Bình tracked her down. On establishing her whereabouts he sent one of his express couriers to hand Vàng an urgent letter requesting her release. He obliged and freed her, and she fled to a sympathizer's house where Bình waited. They must have been followed. Before she had time to relax, the Japanese surrounded the hamlet, hoping to arrest both Bình and herself. To make their final bid for freedom, Bình dressed as a farmer and left by the front door, whereas she changed her clothing and fled as a peasant through the back. They had managed to evade detection and escaped.

Bình used many couriers to assist him in his work, especially when he traveled to the city from the countryside or he met people such as French communists and socialists living in Saigon. Sometimes he went undercover as Minh Hương, a writer, while other covers saw his courier disguised as a wealthy Chinese lady and he as a rickshaw driver. On one occasion, to aggravate the French and to undermine their confidence in their high-security area, he had a courier approach a Saigon newspaper to publish an article to boldly announce his arrival in the city. In another instance, he instructed a shoe-shine boy to pass a note to the chief detective of Saigon, which read, "Dear Chief Detective, I came to Saigon for a few days but sadly I was too busy to come and see you. Sorry. See you next time! Bình."[24]

The type of escape and evasion that Bình pulled off with Miss Thanh that day became everyday life for those serving as couriers or relying on them in order to operate. Likewise, it highlights the fact that, however much preparation was made for every eventuality, the most important tool at a person's disposal was the ability to think on their feet; not only to protect themselves but also their colleagues.

Designing Long-Lasting Tactics

Bình had formed and now commanded the Armed Force of Cochinchina, a position awarded to him at the Cochinchina Military Conference in November 1945.[25] Later that November, field commanders attending a military conference asked him to be commander of the 7th Zone as well. It was around this point in his career that he established the noted D War Zone and eventually set up his headquarters there, making D War Zone a very important area and the 7th Zone the most significant region in the south.

Once Bình had formed his Armed Force he designed new military tactics; his best remembered was his city action units. These were the first urban armed groups tasked with conducting covert missions in the city. To create his initial units he held a meeting in Vĩnh Lộc at the beginning of January 1946 for commanders of dissident groups.[26] He urged these rebels to unite under his new City Action Unit Department, a section of his Armed Force of Cochinchina. This new department promoted guerrilla warfare in Saigon, a rear base area for the French. With the majority agreeing to sign up, Bình announced, "We now have the means to mastermind guerrilla warfare within the enemy's heartland. Our troops must integrate into the civilian population of this city." On the same day he appointed city couriers tasked to serve this department and aid high-ranking commanders secretly visiting the region.

The concept of fighting in the city had not been suggested by other commanders. In Vietnam there had always been a clear geographical division between the highlands and the lowlands. The highlands comprised the mountainous jungles that the French found formidable and impenetrable. This is where the communists built most of their bases. The lowlands included disputed, as well as French-controlled areas, the latter being regions such as the deltas and the cities.

The revolutionaries did try to build bases in the lowlands, but found it difficult to recruit in some areas. As a general rule, the people of the Mekong Delta were far wealthier than those in other parts of Vietnam; they had rich soil to grow food and an abundance of fish so did not align themselves with communist ideology. Even when peasant farmers were recruited, as with their northern counterparts, the communists found it hard to persuade them to fight away from their homes and families due to their animist beliefs. The recruitment problems were especially true in the urban areas as these had been created mainly in their present forms by the French, and people had adopted that lifestyle.

Bình's city action units evolved over the years. In the early days they were known as Saigon *Biệt Động*.[27] To run their operations, in March 1948 Bình established the Standing Bureau 200/CT, later to be renamed Command of the Inner City Action Units. These units were the forerunners of the wider *biệt động* fighters (urban underground elite armed force) and to some extent the *đặc công* (an elite force intended to conduct operations across Vietnam). Both the *biệt động* and the *đặc công* became elite forces of the VNPA and the Americans collectively called them "commandos," although the two used very different methods to conduct their missions.

The *biệt động* units fought by using hit-and-run guerrilla tactics, from street battles to covert death blows on French and later American nerve centers in built-up areas across Vietnam. They could not carry heavy weapons but were well armed. They only truly showed their full potential during the Tết Offensive in 1968; most of the commanders and troops had been trained by Bình. During Tết they sustained punishing losses and their ranks never fully recovered. For the Vietnam War the courier and liaison arm of the *biệt động* fighters were called the *giao liên biệt động*, and tasked to convey weapons, conduct military proselytizing as well as act as reconnaissance units to prepare for a forthcoming battle and then guide the troops during the fighting.

Whereas the *biệt động* were units, *đặc công* was initially a tactic only and used by many different units. The *đặc công* tactic had been designed by the Việt Minh to attack French watchtowers in Cochinchina. With no substantial weaponry available to them, they aimed to infiltrate enemy bases secretly and, having gained access to the center, they then expanded and assaulted back outwards. To achieve a complete element of surprise, those involved used unarmed combat and could have lain in wait for days, poised for the signal to carry out their missions. Those who used this tactic had the distinguishing features of wearing black underwear-like clothing and painting their bodies black to match. This so-called body paint of mud or oil could be smeared over their skin to hide any odor that might have been picked up by a dog during an operation. At the end of the 1950s, as the southerners regrouped to the North to be trained and then returned to the South, the *biệt động* fighters adopted the *đặc công* tactic as one of their fighting methods.

During the Vietnam War *đặc công* became a tactic used by all three levels of the communist military in the south: irregular forces, local regular forces and the main regular army. From 1961 to 1967, elite units trained in *đặc công* methods were attached to infantry forces. From this partnership a new approach known as "blooming lotus" was designed and used with the motto, "To strike from both the outside and the inside." This meant that the elite unit trained in *đặc công* tactics still fought from within a base outwards, as they always had done, but they now also aimed to meet an infantry regimental-sized unit attacking the base from outside inwards. During 1967, amid the preparations for the Tết Offensive, Giáp looked for these elite units to be the spearhead of the campaign. For this he committed elite đặc công forces to each regiment and created the Command of the Đặc Công. From this point on, đặc công was not only a tactic but an official service and the units under this service were specially trained as đặc công only.

In the early days, under Bình's meticulous leadership his city action units did achieve success. On 3 June 1946, a unit attacked Gia Định Police Station and secured twenty rifles for the Việt Minh.[28] This action unit comprised both French and German soldiers sympathetic to the revolution.

Giàu and Bình ended up being fundamental to Hồ's plans because both men designed and built new military systems that the revolutionary forces used against their enemy until the eventual fall of Saigon in 1975. Their work showed how developed Hồ's military systems were, long before the majority of the American public had even heard of Vietnam.

First Vietnamese American Hostilities

The largest operation designed by Bình was his disobedience campaign of 1949–1950. To accomplish disorder, Bình infiltrated his agents into various groups and got these operatives either to start or to expand protests. His operatives whipped up the population by honing in on their anger towards the increasing number of American military units in the region and their support for the French. The people were also angry about the return of Bảo Đại, the former emperor, whom the French had persuaded to come back to Vietnam in 1949 to serve as chief of state.

Public demonstrations demanding the release of prisoners further boosted disorder. On 9 January 1950, the French tried to control and disperse the angry crowds and opened fire. In the process they shot Trần Văn Ơn dead and wounded many others. On 12 January, family members held his funeral but half a million took to the streets, including students from across Vietnam. Bình's operatives encouraged the crowds, who carried protest banners and shouted slogans demanding that the French and the Americans leave. This was the largest gathering in Saigon since the funeral of nationalist Phan Chu Trinh in 1926, and the biggest action taken in Saigon until Tết 1968.

Nevertheless, it was the events of 19 March, which held higher historical significance than the funeral crowds. On this day, 300,000 inhabitants of Saigon demonstrated against U.S. involvement in the war and the presence of two of their vessels anchored in the city port. The people shouted, "U.S. imperialists, go home!" and "Down with puppet Bảo Đại!" among other slogans. The demonstrators prevailed in the central part of the city from morning to noon. On that same night, the two U.S. vessels silently withdrew from the port. Although it is not officially known why the vessels moved, the Communist Party has marked this occasion as the day when hostilities officially started between the Vietnamese people and the Americans.

Further Defining the Infrastructure

With the changing state of war Hồ had to further outline his Revolutionary Infrastructure. Bình and Giàu played their part in this process in Cochinchina, which began around the time of the signing of the first *modus vivendi* in early 1946 because this was a relatively quiet period and allowed the Communist Party to consolidate.

To start this process, a temporary Cochinchina Regional Party Committee was launched in the latter part of 1946. Members made this permanent a year later, with Lê Duẩn as the secretary of the Cochinchina Regional Party Committee. Initial duties included expanding the Cochinchina Resistance Administrative Committee; originally founded in November 1945. Giàu had been the chairman of this administrative committee, but when Party members summoned him north, the brother of Phạm Ngọc Thảo, Gaston Phạm Ngọc Thuần, became the temporary chairman throughout 1946 and 1947. The position changed hands again and in February 1948 Phạm Văn Bạch became chairman and appointed two deputies, Gaston Phạm Ngọc Thuần and Bình.

To serve new Party cells, in July 1947 the Cochinchina Regional Party Committee issued a Resolution to found a courier department, named the Cochinchina Communications Liaison Department.[29] This functioned under the Cochinchina Resistance Administrative Committee and those who operated as couriers in this new department were given the modern job title: *giao thông liên lạc* (communications liaison agent); *giao thông* (civilian) and *liên lạc* (military).

Cochinchina Resistance Administrative Committee members instructed this new department to build courier networks across the whole of Cochinchina. They had to connect between the Party cells of the Cochinchina Regional Party Committee and the Cochinchina Resistance Administrative Committee, down to the provincial party committees and provincial resistance administrative committees, and on to districts and villages. To assist the Cochinchina Communications Liaison Department in re-establishing damaged lines, they created the courier *Giao Thông Liên Lạc* Supervision Team.

On 30 December 1949, Hồ signed Decree 149, which granted the *giao thông liên lạc* in Cochinchina a Resistance War Medal. He noted that this honor had been granted to them because they had managed to construct their networks under incredibly difficult circumstances, and he paid particular tribute to the civilian *giao thông* part. He went on to confirm that both the service and job title of those operating under the Cochinchina Communications Liaison Department would continue to be, *giao thông liên lạc*.

Around this time, those in the south started unofficially to abbreviate this cumbersome designation to the more concise courier title *giao liên*. The northerners still used the full name *giao thông liên lạc* to refer to the service, and those who operated under this still kept their designated titles of *giao thông* (civilian) and *liên lạc* (military). The difference in the way that Tonkin and Cochinchina described the same communications and liaison role was most probably because in the south there was more of a blurring between civilian and military activities; the abbreviations reflected this difference.

During the Vietnam War in the south, although *giao liên* was still used as an umbrella term, there was now a greater distinction between civilians and the military. For instance, on the regular military side individual job titles existed such as "military postmen" (*quân bưu*) or the more encompassing title "information soldier" (*thông tin*), which covered all telecommunications and military postmen personnel, whereas a civilian postman in a liberated zone was known as a *bưu điện*. Although most of these courier roles did exist during the French War they were not as defined; the changes made by Hồ during this late 1940s period began the process to give greater clarity.

A statue commemorating the work of the couriers and military postmen, which stands outside the main post office in Hồ Chí Minh City. 2007 photograph (Clive A. Hills).

The Murky End to Giàu and Bình

Both Giàu and Bình served the revolution well but their time at the top soon ended. In 1948, Party members again ordered Giàu back to Việt Bắc Revolutionary Base because he was still considered to be too harsh by some. This brutality eventually saw him sidelined by the Party, and from that point on he worked as a moderate scholar researching Western mythology.

In contrast to Giàu, Bình felt the squeeze directly as a result of the Chinese and Soviets. Historically Hồ had ties to the Soviets, yet after the Border Campaign in 1950, Vietnam also became linked with the recently victorious Mao Zedong and his Red China. However, Soviet and Chinese support came inseparably attached to their class struggle. One requirement of this was that the Chinese insisted that those who held high posts, but had been involved with groups other than a Communist Party or had privileged backgrounds, must be punished or sidelined. Bình had at one time been connected to the Vietnamese Kuomintang.

Nevertheless, this alone did not end his career but instead it was an unforeseen act of war. In 1951 he was called back to North Vietnam as Giáp planned a nationwide attack; he never arrived having been ambushed and killed by a Cambodian, pro-French patrol. There is great controversy and mystery surrounding Bình's life and untimely death. In some ways it echoes that of the hero in "The Tale of Kiều," Vietnam's national poem. People often refer to it to describe happenings in their life. In the poem, General Từ Hải is strong and handsome, as Bình. Like the heroine, Kiều, a beauty who used to work as a geisha and who falls in love with Từ Hải, Miss Thanh the geisha and courier had fallen in love with Bình.

This is not the only parallel. Từ Hải is also a prime example of a man who is the victim of a plot. Bình too was probably betrayed by an opportunist. If rumors are to be believed there was an individual within Party ranks striving to maneuver himself into a high position of power. This individual is understood to have been Lê Duẩn and it is thought that one of his men from his secret political camp tipped off the French about the route Bình was to take.

This traitorous act might have seen this opportunist reach the highest rank in the Party, but the act led directly to a comrade's death and as a consequence, due to Bình's importance to Hồ, it set the blueprint in Cochinchina back for years.

7

The Water Flows South

Entering the Secret Service

To win the type of protracted asymmetric war that Hồ designed you need to use the people to survive in your enemy's rear base area. Giáp had once said to Hồ, "If my regular forces were the 'fish,' then the people were the 'water' in which they would swim." A "fish" and "water" metaphor had once been used by Mao Zedong, who had said, "The guerrilla must move amongst the people as a fish swims in the sea." Both men used water and fish to describe surviving in the enemy's rear base area but Mao referred only to his guerrilla fighters (fish) and the mass population (water). Giáp was talking about his regular units (fish) but his metaphorical water was the people and included services such as guerrilla fighters, security operatives, secret agents and the Revolutionary Infrastructure.

In the 1940s, the revolutionaries needed to complete a strategic courier corridor to aid this metaphorical water to flow south, continuing the Southward March first instructed by Hồ in 1941. Although Hồ had identified Tonkin as the main battlefield and most of Annam a rear base for the Việt Minh, he had designated Cochinchina an important area of resistance and earmarked it for large combat operations because the French viewed all Cochinchina as their rear base area.

To service these three regions, on 25 October 1945 the Communist Party structured the Staff (known later as the General Staff). Chief of Staff Hoàng Văn Thái ran the Combat Operations and Cartography Department; Hoàng Đạo Thúy (1900–1994) the Communications Liaison Service; and Hoàng Minh Đạo the Intelligence Department.[1] In March 1947, Đạo's fledgling Intelligence Department became the Intelligence Directorate of the General Staff. There were a number of new departments under it masterminded by Nguyễn Văn Địch (1914–1997), one of six Vietnamese trained by British intelligence before the August Revolution.[2] Although intelligence gathering had become an official service, the main source of information was limited to people reading the foreign press or listening to their radio broadcasts. In mid–1947, the Communist Party focused attention on security in Cochinchina and began to dissolve the Southern Intelligence Department of the Southern Military Command to make way for a new service: the Cochinchina Secret Service Department.

Phạm Ngọc Thảo (1922–1965) had been ordered to open the new all-important strategic courier corridor to Cochinchina and simultaneously establish the Cochinchina

Opposite: **Việt Minh regions in Cochinchina and parts of southern Annam, from late 1940s to early 1950s.**

The Murky End to Giàu and Bình

Both Giàu and Bình served the revolution well but their time at the top soon ended. In 1948, Party members again ordered Giàu back to Việt Bắc Revolutionary Base because he was still considered to be too harsh by some. This brutality eventually saw him sidelined by the Party, and from that point on he worked as a moderate scholar researching Western mythology.

In contrast to Giàu, Bình felt the squeeze directly as a result of the Chinese and Soviets. Historically Hồ had ties to the Soviets, yet after the Border Campaign in 1950, Vietnam also became linked with the recently victorious Mao Zedong and his Red China. However, Soviet and Chinese support came inseparably attached to their class struggle. One requirement of this was that the Chinese insisted that those who held high posts, but had been involved with groups other than a Communist Party or had privileged backgrounds, must be punished or sidelined. Bình had at one time been connected to the Vietnamese Kuomintang.

Nevertheless, this alone did not end his career but instead it was an unforeseen act of war. In 1951 he was called back to North Vietnam as Giáp planned a nationwide attack; he never arrived having been ambushed and killed by a Cambodian, pro–French patrol. There is great controversy and mystery surrounding Bình's life and untimely death. In some ways it echoes that of the hero in "The Tale of Kiều," Vietnam's national poem. People often refer to it to describe happenings in their life. In the poem, General Từ Hải is strong and handsome, as Bình. Like the heroine, Kiều, a beauty who used to work as a geisha and who falls in love with Từ Hải, Miss Thanh the geisha and courier had fallen in love with Bình.

This is not the only parallel. Từ Hải is also a prime example of a man who is the victim of a plot. Bình too was probably betrayed by an opportunist. If rumors are to be believed there was an individual within Party ranks striving to maneuver himself into a high position of power. This individual is understood to have been Lê Duẩn and it is thought that one of his men from his secret political camp tipped off the French about the route Bình was to take.

This traitorous act might have seen this opportunist reach the highest rank in the Party, but the act led directly to a comrade's death and as a consequence, due to Bình's importance to Hồ, it set the blueprint in Cochinchina back for years.

7

The Water Flows South

Entering the Secret Service

To win the type of protracted asymmetric war that Hồ designed you need to use the people to survive in your enemy's rear base area. Giáp had once said to Hồ, "If my regular forces were the 'fish,' then the people were the 'water' in which they would swim." A "fish" and "water" metaphor had once been used by Mao Zedong, who had said, "The guerrilla must move amongst the people as a fish swims in the sea." Both men used water and fish to describe surviving in the enemy's rear base area but Mao referred only to his guerrilla fighters (fish) and the mass population (water). Giáp was talking about his regular units (fish) but his metaphorical water was the people and included services such as guerrilla fighters, security operatives, secret agents and the Revolutionary Infrastructure.

In the 1940s, the revolutionaries needed to complete a strategic courier corridor to aid this metaphorical water to flow south, continuing the Southward March first instructed by Hồ in 1941. Although Hồ had identified Tonkin as the main battlefield and most of Annam a rear base for the Việt Minh, he had designated Cochinchina an important area of resistance and earmarked it for large combat operations because the French viewed all Cochinchina as their rear base area.

To service these three regions, on 25 October 1945 the Communist Party structured the Staff (known later as the General Staff). Chief of Staff Hoàng Văn Thái ran the Combat Operations and Cartography Department; Hoàng Đạo Thúy (1900–1994) the Communications Liaison Service; and Hoàng Minh Đạo the Intelligence Department.[1] In March 1947, Đạo's fledgling Intelligence Department became the Intelligence Directorate of the General Staff. There were a number of new departments under it masterminded by Nguyễn Văn Địch (1914–1997), one of six Vietnamese trained by British intelligence before the August Revolution.[2] Although intelligence gathering had become an official service, the main source of information was limited to people reading the foreign press or listening to their radio broadcasts. In mid–1947, the Communist Party focused attention on security in Cochinchina and began to dissolve the Southern Intelligence Department of the Southern Military Command to make way for a new service: the Cochinchina Secret Service Department.

Phạm Ngọc Thảo (1922–1965) had been ordered to open the new all-important strategic courier corridor to Cochinchina and simultaneously establish the Cochinchina

Opposite: **Việt Minh regions in Cochinchina and parts of southern Annam, from late 1940s to early 1950s.**

7. The Water Flows South

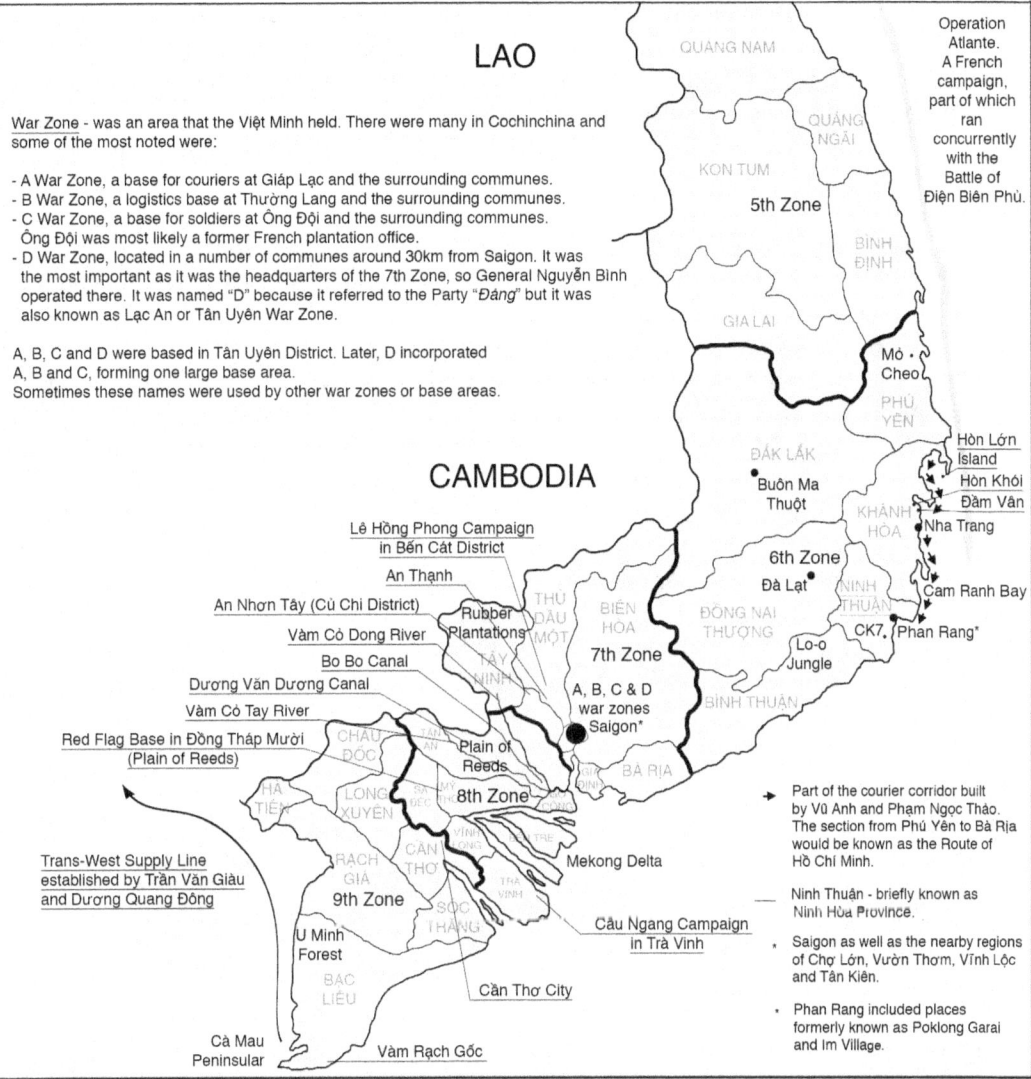

Divisions of Regions

This map should be used as a guide only. The most common province names have been taken but these changed throughout this period. The provinces drawn above are from a book by Greg Lockhart reference, *Nation in Arms, The Origins of the People's Army of Vietnam*. Australia: ASAA Southeast Asia Publications Series, 1989.

Zone - referred to a military area. Nine were first established in October 1945. Only the 7th, 8th and 9th covered the same areas throughout the French War. A year later, the other six altered their boundaries and continued to do so thereafter along with further zones being added. The zones stated above are listed in, *History of the Vietnamese People's Army, Volume 1. Hanoi: People's Army Publishing House, 1974*. This book lists twelve zones in total so is referring to a later stage of the French War.

Inter-zone - was an administrative area for the Party. In 1946 during the fighting in Hanoi the city was divided into the 1st Inter-zone, the 2nd Inter-zone and the 3rd Inter-zone. In 1948 till 1958 the Party established larger inter-zones but again borders changed from time to time.

The most common inter-zones were:
- 3rd Inter-zone, included Hanoi and a number of surrounding provinces.
- 4th Inter-zone, included provinces in the middle and north of Annam and linked with central Lao.
- 5th Inter-zone, included provinces in the middle and south of Annam and linked with lower Lao.
- 10th Inter-zone was the north-west of Vietnam and linked with upper Lao.

During the Vietnam War era an administrative area was called a "Zone" and a military area was called a "Military Zone" (or Military Region).

Secret Service Department. Born Albert Phạm Ngọc Thuần, he was one of eleven children and had originally come from Vĩnh Long Province. His father, Adrian Phạm Ngọc Thuần, had long ties to the revolution, despite his family holding French citizenship. After Albert Phạm Ngọc Thuần attended French schools in Saigon, he changed his name to Phạm Ngọc Thảo and in 1945 joined the revolution. Two of his brothers, Gaston Phạm Ngọc Thuần and Lucien Phạm Ngọc Thuần, likewise played an active role in ousting the French.[3]

Thảo's rapid promotion within the intelligence service in the south is thought to be linked to his involvement with noted revolutionaries including Lê Duẩn. Thảo's connection to Lê Duẩn came through Nguyễn Thanh Sơn (1910–1996), who knew Thảo's parents well.[4] At the time Nguyễn Thanh Sơn was deputy head of the Southern Resistance Committee, with Nguyễn Sơn (1908–1956) as the head, until it dissolved around December 1946 and the Cochinchina Resistance Administrative Committee took over.[5] Both Nguyễn Thanh Sơn and Nguyễn Sơn were trusted colleagues of Hồ because they had trained in Guangzhou for the Vietnamese RYL, although they attended different courses.

Nguyễn Thanh Sơn concurrently headed the Southern Military Command, which meant Thảo fell under his jurisdiction.[6] Thảo learned the art of covert work in Phú Yên Province in 1946, and with his abilities noted Nguyễn Thanh Sơn sent him for intensive training in Sơn Tây Province. His class was the first course run at the Trần Quốc Tuấn Military Training School, located at the site of the former French Tông Military School. After just two months, Nguyễn Thanh Sơn called Thảo back to Annam, where it is believed he became a guard to Lê Duẩn, although some sources note he had wider obligations to

Phạm Ngọc Thảo, second from left, was a top communist operative. This photograph was taken in 1952 when he was the commander of the 410th Battalion (courtesy Phạm Hồng Cư).

Lê Duẩn as his trusted courier. At the time, Lê Duẩn headed the militia in parallel with other high-ranking positions.

With such distinguished revolutionaries nurturing his talents Thảo learned fast and in February 1947, he became deputy head of the Southern Intelligence Department. Working under the guidance of Nguyễn Sơn, one of his first duties was to create an office for the department in Quảng Ngãi Province. The position of head of the Southern Intelligence Department eventually went to Nguyễn Duy Khâm (1912–1977) because at the time Thảo was not a Party member and Khâm was. Despite failing to make head, Thảo was in fact given the more respected duty of preparing Cochinchina for large combat operations.

Vũ Anh Becomes Thảo's Aide de Camp

In May 2007, the author met with Vũ Anh (1928–2015) in Cần Thơ City.[7] He had become a renowned artist and held the record in Vietnam for cutting paper silhouettes in the fastest time. The author asked him about his association with Thảo. She hoped that he would reveal details of some of their covert missions that helped to launch the revolutionaries in the south. As they chatted, he studied her from time to time and calmly, and very deftly, cut an uncanny likeness of her from black paper. Despite his hectic schedule, this elderly grandfather was only too willing to share his memories of his early days. He described in detail the highly complex world of espionage so she could understand elements of the metaphorical water.

Anh started by bluntly denying that he had been a courier, still feeling after all this time that his fighting experience and education put him on a par with Thảo. He said that Thảo always held a higher rank than he, putting this down to the fact that Thảo was a Roman Catholic, a communist, a member of the intelligentsia and had good connections.

Although communism and religion did not sit well together, the Party could see that, as a Catholic, Thảo could persuade fellow Catholics to join the revolution. The French had not only used them to establish an armed puppet administration and to build a rather dangerous spy network across Vietnam, but they had even set up an Autonomous Catholic Zone in Tonkin. This French Catholic partnership had to be broken. Similarly, the fact that Thảo was from the intelligentsia sat well. Many of this class in Cochinchina were

Vũ Anh in Cần Thơ City, May 19, 2007. He was Phạm Ngọc Thảo's mainstay in the second half of the 1940s and a top intelligence officer of the Cambodian Front during the early 1950s (Clive A. Hills).

Vietnamese French citizens; as Thảo had been a French citizen himself, he could relate to them with the aim of loosening their tongues to extract information. Notwithstanding all this, the main reason that he seemed to be liked by Party members was that high-ranking leaders trusted him.

The Party did not view Vũ Anh as being as beneficial to them. Anh had not joined the Party, he did not have good connections, could not claim to be a Catholic and, being a liberal artist, he never hid his eagerness for feminine beauty, both in art and life. Above all, he came from the despised bourgeois class; the Party did not mobilize this class group to any great extent because those within it generally aligned themselves with the French. Unfortunately for Anh, he had tried to join the Communist Party but his bourgeois roots prevented his application from proceeding on the grounds that he was not of the peasantry. This rejection occurred around 1950 and resulted from the demands of Red China that any bourgeoisie be sidelined. His vetoed application meant that Anh could not be put on the list of troops called north for regroupment in 1954, something that clearly niggled at him even to this day.

Anh said:

Nguyễn Sơn was the headmaster of the Quảng Ngãi Land Force School where I trained from April to November 1946. One of my classmates was the traitor Trần Ngọc Châu, who helped design the Phoenix Program during the Vietnam War.

After training I joined the armed forces and became a political commissar at platoon level. Other students went back to their respective home provinces to establish army stations. After fighting several battles, my commanders reviewed my history. They noted that I had a diploma from a junior high school, so they pulled me out from the platoon and sent me to study intelligence in Phú Yên Province. It was March 1947 and the course started soon afterwards.[8]

Nguyễn Thanh Sơn ran this six-month intelligence course. Anh joined it along with more than two dozen other students.[9] The teachers covered a variety of subjects: history of intelligence, foreign intelligence organizations, experience of Western and Eastern espionage, counter-intelligence, double agents and techniques such as disguises, cryptography and photography. Anh came second in the final exam, while Hoàng Hà came first. Party members cut short the training, ending it before August 1947 and after only four months, because the war had intensified.

Anh explained:

Whilst I was doing my training, Thảo, as deputy head of the Southern Intelligence Department, was given three very important tasks. In the first instance, he was to escort important delegates to Cochinchina who carried essential documents and 20kg of gold, collected during Gold Week, so that they could buy weapons. Then, he was told to establish the Cochinchina Secret Service Department so that he could run his network of agents and associated services. Lastly, he was ordered to simultaneously open a new courier corridor through Khánh Hòa Province and on to war zones in Cochinchina.

On being given this task, he requested an aide, a revolutionary with knowledge of this area. Things did not work out initially for Thảo and that is why my leaders sent me to assist him and act as a guard.[10]

Thảo had originally tried to complete his given tasks with Hoàng Hà but, according to Anh, he had been asked to step in and take over for two reasons. Anh had military experience from his work within the Dương the Third Battalion but, more to the point, there had been a personality clash between Hoàng Hà and Thảo.[11] Hoàng Hà believed that Thảo did not have enough experience for the position he had been given; contrary

Vũ Anh in front of his shop in the late 1950s where he carried out silhouette cutting. He was the first artist in Vietnam to practice this art and it turned out to be a perfect cover for meeting people and carrying out his intelligence work for the revolutionaries (courtesy Vũ Anh).

to this, Thảo did not think that Hà was best suited for a national secret service position and should be limited to a local one.

Consequently, when Thảo and Hoàng Hà reached Nha Trang City, Thảo made the decision to leave him there. Thảo then went back to the headquarters of the Southern Military Command currently in Phú Yên Province. Here he linked up with Anh, who had been waiting for him there, so that he could help Thảo with his mission south.

The Route of Hồ Chí Minh

Hồ needed a strategic corridor built to give the revolutionaries access from North Vietnam to Cochinchina. Thảo and his colleague, Hoàng Hà, had started reconnaissance work on his part of this route earlier in 1947. At the same time a number of other action units had tried to develop ways to reach Cochinchina from the north. They had used off-road routes because the French controlled the main roads but despite these measures, most of these action units had been intercepted by the French. Now in late 1947, Thảo and Anh made preparations to head south.

Anh explained:

> I remember that Thảo put a 1:1,000 map on the table and described to me the plan for our journey, a plan that only the two of us knew. He explained that he had to open a new corridor, set up a new department in the south, as well as escort delegates. He said that to maximize the mission he would try whenever possible to interview and appoint new intelligence workers in locations of southern Annam and Cochinchina. He emphasized that this must not compromise our plan to see that the elderly delegates arrive safely.
>
> The important delegation from Hanoi part walked and part went by train to Phú Yên Province. It included intellectuals who had been training in France but had since come back to Vietnam after the failed conference in Fontainebleau in 1946, and high-ranking members such as Minister of Agriculture Ngô Tấn Nhơn and Ca Văn Thỉnh [1902–1987], who had been the minister of education, and was now being sent south to join the Cochinchina Resistance Administrative Committee. Most notably, Võ Sĩ came with us, who we discovered was being sent south to be the secretary of Saigon-Chợ Lớn for the Party.[12] When Thảo finally met them, he was skeptical. They were too old and unhealthy to take on such an arduous trip.
>
> Much work had already gone into securing our safe passage. The Dương the Third Battalion had been instructed to travel in parallel with us and operate inside the enemy's area of operation to create an unexpected distraction. Thảo said that the French would focus their attention on the mainland where the battalion traveled, leaving our group to go in relative safety along the coast.
>
> Thảo then gave me two batteries for our radio, a camera and ammunition for my Browning pistol as well as two secret codes, so that I could maintain communications with the secret service in Phú Yên by coded radio messages. Then we all left.
>
> We all found it a harsh existence: always tired, thirsty and hungry. Not long after we left, our group had to crawl up and down steep hills. On one occasion I remember that we had to traverse a very steep slope called Mỏ, in Phú Yên, and one delegate called out in desperation, speaking in French, "It's terrible, my God!" Thảo looked stressed and exhausted after having to help the ageing members of the party, and answering back in French, with a hint of frustration, "I have had to go up and down this slope two times already!" After everyone finally reached the other side we got to the courier station at Đầm Vân, near Nha Trang, here the delegation rested for five days.[13]

With the delegates presumed safe, Thảo and Anh planned the next stage of their journey. First they had to confirm that the "security belt" region in the mountains had not been compromised. This belt was not a courier corridor as such, but land that, although known to have a French military presence, also had hill tribes friendly to the Việt Minh. This belt had to function correctly because the Dương the Third Battalion operated there, and if they had been attacked and killed by a rouge local tribe, they would be unable to distract the French and draw their troops away from the islands where the important delegates headed next.

Thảo and Anh found the battalion and met with their commanders. Commander Y Blok Edan had been chosen to keep the courier stations operating within this belt.[14] Not only did he understand military needs but the locals trusted him; the Việt Minh viewed him as a brilliant link man between them and the ethnic hill tribes.

Confident that the security belt region functioned, Thảo and Anh needed to examine the courier stations on the coastal islands for the next stage of their journey. Thảo had established these previously. On this present trip Thảo and Anh took with them Mr. Ba, who ran a local courier station in Hòn Khói, close to Đầm Vân Village. The three of them left Đầm Vân and rowed all night, narrowly avoiding a French patrol boat. On making land near Poklong Garai, they walked to a courier station in Im Village. The head of this village arranged for a coded letter to be sent to CK7 (guerrilla base 7 in Ninh Hòa Province), requesting that a battalion be sent to guard a specific part of Route 1; the French patrolled the road heavily and the delegation had to cross it to get to CK7.

On the way back to collect the delegation, Thảo expanded his secret service network. He diverted to Hòn Lớn Station, located on an island off the coast of Khánh Hòa. Here Thảo held a meeting to gauge the mounting threat from the French in the region. After assessing the capabilities of the individuals he had met on the island, he instructed those in the station to form armed propaganda teams and expand the Revolutionary Infrastructure in the three provinces of Khánh Hòa, Bình Thuận and Ninh Hòa.

To ease relations, Thảo assigned his former colleague, Hoàng Hà, to run this operation, making him the head of intelligence for the three provinces. Hoàng Hà had to not only counter a French spy network that operated throughout these three provinces but provide information to Thảo on the French Military Intelligence Service of Annam, based in Nha Trang.[15] On leaving Hòn Lớn, Thảo said they must both keep in touch through coded radio messages.

Before heading back to Đầm Vân Village where the delegates had taken refuge, Thảo traveled alone to Nha Trang to check on his intelligence network there. The French now occupied Nha Trang and as his operatives were either Vietnamese French or sympathetic French citizens, he had to reassure himself that his recruits still operated for the Việt Minh. Disguised as a Chinese cake seller, his extensive travel around the city became a balance of risk; if he did not keep his network alive French intelligence would have a free hand in Nha Trang, but if he were caught or killed the important delegation would find it extremely difficult to reach safety without him. According to Anh, Thảo survived these high-risk situations by taking on a sort of wild, adventurous character that held no fear.

Now with the five-day rest period coming to a close, Thảo and Anh returned to Đầm Vân, only to find total devastation. The French had gleaned some intelligence on the Việt Minh and then raided the village. The two of them frantically rounded up the disorientated delegation, which had fled and hidden in two separate groups. On witnessing the shocking events, the local head of a Việt Minh army station approached Thảo; he believed there to be a traitor amidst them, and knew who it was. Angry that their mission could have been compromised, without hesitation Thảo gave instructions for the culprit to be executed, and he was.

Anh said:

With the French onto us, Thảo obtained three sampans to move us away from the area. Each sampan carried up to six men but they were small and unstable in rough seas. With our elderly delegates becoming fearful of the violent waters from an approaching typhoon, we headed for land at Hòn Khói; losing us valuable time. That night Thảo went off to meet with Ba, who had traveled with us as our guide. Thảo made him head of intelligence in Hòn Khói and instructed him to coordinate with Hòn Lớn Station. Thảo ordered Ba to build an intelligence network within this area so that he could guide delegates passing through to Cochinchina as well as monitor and investigate French activities.

The French patrolled constantly. At 8 a.m. the next day, through the early morning light, a French warship sailed close to the cave, located 20m above the sea, and where we now hid. I held my nerve and in a forceful whisper said, "No one open fire. It is not necessary to do so if the enemy hasn't discovered us." We froze waiting for the ship to go past. Finally we set sail again. On approaching Cam Ranh Bay the water raged, pounding the cliffs and producing huge swells. The relentless sea was a natural enemy, making our sampans difficult to pilot correctly when we then headed to Poklong Garai. Our inability to have full control over navigation put us all at risk. We could have drifted into the line of sight of one of the many checkpoints manned by the French along the coast, sunk, or run the danger of being captured by one of their regular patrol ships.[16]

When the party reached shore near Poklong Garai, they proceeded to Im Village. From there the commander of the battalion from CK7 accompanied the important delegates across Route 1 and on to their guerrilla base. Thereafter, they went back to the mountain trails, and the delegation had an arduous day of climbing through thick vegetation before they began to leave the Lo-o Jungle behind. They went on to D War Zone and Thủ Dầu Một War Zone, before eventually arriving at Đồng Tháp Mười War Zone.[17]

At the end of 1947, Thảo reached an area just outside Saigon. Two of his tasks had been completed; the delegates had arrived safely and could go on to conduct their business and Hồ had a strategic courier corridor to link the Việt Bắc Revolutionary Base to the resistance in Cochinchina. From all the action units that had originally set off, only two of them, including Thảo's, eventually managed to get through. Thảo's line became the most important, because as part of it used islands off the coast of Vietnam, it took only weeks to transit, rather than months via the mainland.

The revolutionaries eventually named Thảo's coastal courier corridor E300, after the unit of about regimental-size that managed troop and supply transportation along it from 1950 onwards. The troops operating along E300 relocated to North Vietnam in 1954. After that time, owing to the large number of American patrol boats and attacks on the coastal region, the route E300 fell permanently out of use.

Two interesting points came out of Thảo's work. Primarily, he was the first person to open such a comprehensive courier sea route, thus his work contributed to the understanding of how these corridors could be built in the future, including the Hồ Chí Minh Trail Sea Route during the Vietnam War. Moreover, later in 1947, the 81st Regiment expanded his new courier sea route and eventually it stretched to an estimated 300km from Phu Yên Province to Bà Rịa. This new longer corridor was named the Route of Hồ Chí Minh, presumably the origin of the name the Hồ Chí Minh Trail.[18]

Voices from the Cochinchina Secret Service

Once Thảo had arrived in the south in late 1947, he launched the Cochinchina Secret Service Department in Vườn Thơm, near Saigon, with just fifteen people.[19] It was a small department that had to expand rapidly if the large combat operations Hồ required were to be conducted.

2007 photograph of the Ngọc Hiển District, Cà Mau Province, is one of the areas of the Hồ Chí Minh Trail Sea Route (Clive A. Hills).

Anh explained:

In March 1948, the Communist Party sent the secretary of Bến Tre Province, Phan Triêm [1916–2001] to be the deputy head of the Cochinchina Secret Service Department. He was under instructions to create a communist cell inside the division [possibly looking to recruit Thảo, who became a communist soon after].

In July, the leaders of Cochinchina assigned several new revolutionaries to join us. Our numbers swelled. To illustrate, Nguyễn Văn Châu, a graduate from the military school in Sơn Tây, served as head of the cabinet and Việt Sơn worked as a propagandist and trainer. I was the main assistant to Thảo and not even I knew who all his people were.

For our agents to operate, a personal courier served them, in accordance with our compartment rules. This tight relationship enabled information to be smuggled out and acted upon by our relevant military units, at incredible speed. [This led Colonel Đinh Thị Vân to comment on the closeness of this tight relationship, saying, "An intelligence agent and their courier were like the two wings of a bird."][20]

Throughout 1948, our underground system developed with branches in the 7th, 8th and 9th zonal areas of Cochinchina. We had spies in the office of High Commissioner of Indochina Emile Bollaert [April 1947–October 1948], in the office in Đà Lạt of Bảo Đại when this former emperor was chief of state, and in the General Staff office of the French Army based in Indochina.[21]

To enable expansion in these early days, Thảo had to raise money. One method that Anh recalled Thảo used was to publish and sell books, but he had no access to a printing press. To resolve this, in early 1948 Thảo, his brother Gaston Phạm Ngọc Thuần, and Nguyễn Ngọc Bich approached Miss Vương Thị Trinh (1920–2008). They asked if she could hand-write 100 copies of a book they had written titled *Variétés du Maquis*. They viewed Miss Trinh as ideal; she had joined the revolution in 1945, was intelligent, served as a nurse on the front line and had worked on the newspaper *La Voix du Maquis* (*The Voice of the Guerrilla Base*). Most importantly, she had impeccable handwriting.

Variétés du Maquis contained the memoirs of revolutionary intelligentsia. It covered life on a guerrilla base or as a Việt Minh fighter and drove home the fact that, however many battles the French reported the Việt Minh had lost, the revolutionaries would fight on: join the fight. Miss Trinh commented, that they were the most expensive books that she had ever seen. The bourgeois in the city paid hundreds of Indochinese Piastres for a copy of a book consisting of fewer than thirty pages.[22]

Thảo's workforce sold copies of the book to the upper classes or relatives of Việt Minh fighters within the French-controlled suburbs of Saigon. Thảo also targeted wealthy Vietnamese French citizens because he thought that the book might strike a nationalistic chord with them. When socializing with this group he had come across people who had supported the principle of independence but did not want to be involved directly. The book addressed the issue. By purchasing a copy the buyers could tell themselves that they had supported the revolution, albeit indirectly, with funding, so could not be branded traitors by the Việt Minh. Importantly, the purchaser could not be branded a collaborator by the French because, after all, it was just a book of little stories. For Thảo personally, he could use the book to communicate with his family or his agents inside French ranks. He wrote instructions in copies in invisible angelica ink between the lines of a story; the words being revealed only when the pages were wiped over with tincture of iodine.[23]

Shortly after working directly for Thảo, Miss Trinh was promoted to the 7th Zone and their newly founded secret service offices. Nguyễn Bình was commander of the Zone; the same Zone that Miss Hoàng Thị Thanh, Bình's trusted courier, operated. The two women did not work together but soon became love rivals, both admiring their handsome commander and not always from afar.

Nguyễn Bình trusted Miss Trinh and she became the head of his Cryptography Department, a service to encode messages covering both military and Communist Party matters, but at the time no personnel understood the subject well.[24] Her staff consisted mainly of females and relied heavily on the Revolutionary Infrastructure to operate. The cryptologists, as well as the radio operators, had to be on a rota of duty that ran twenty-four hours a day in order to maintain radio communication with the TW. The TW in this case meant both the General Headquarters of Giáp and the Party Central Committee.[25] When Nguyễn Bình was in Cochinchina he had to keep in regular contact with them by telegram. In communications Bình's codename was DLW, Giáp's was CFZ.

Miss Trinh's leaders initially asked her to run the mobile radio station codenamed VMA2; located within the headquarters of the 7th Zone. When intelligence arrived from a given source, she then sent out an encoded message to a Việt Minh commander so he could counteract French operations. This mobile unit had first come into operational use in September 1945 when British and French troops captured the government radio station in Saigon.[26]

To protect the mobile unit, the cryptologists had to be ready to move or hide at any time. They concealed secret documents or cipher key books in containers that they buried in the ground and surrounded with booby traps, such as mines and punji stakes. In the Plain of Reeds, where the land is waterlogged, they hid these in the trunks of large evergreens trees called *mù u*, and to create a hole in their trunks they burned the sap in the wood. In contrast, the cryptologists consigned to fighting units did not need secret hideouts to the same extent; they had to learn the cipher key by heart so that they could instantly decode or encode a message. The cipher key was codenamed the secret horse.[27]

Thảo's Cochinchina Secret Service Department also covered special propaganda. Anh had said that his most memorable mission with Thảo of that time was when the two of them made an approach to Nguyễn Tôn Hoàn [1917–2001].

Anh said:

> It was 1948, I think. Prior to this, in the mid–1940s, Thảo and Nguyễn Tôn Hoàn socialized in similar upper class circles as each other, the intellectual scene of Saigon. Hoàn was a doctor.
>
> At the time of our mission, Nguyễn Tôn Hoàn worked as a National Assembly member of the pro-French regime as well as being the leader of the French-backed southern Great Việt Party. He ran a propaganda program for the pro-French puppets, which caused difficulties for the Việt Minh.
>
> Thảo wanted to inflict a psychological blow on him. To do this we had to scout out the location beforehand. From this initial work we decided that to do the job we should hire a three-wheeled taxi, which we did from Tân Kiên in the south-west of Saigon. Then, just before reaching the office of Nguyễn Tôn Hoàn, we would change to motorbikes to make it harder for people to follow us.
>
> On the day of execution, I remember it was 5 p.m., we arrived when some Great Việt Party members were still working. The atmosphere was tense. There were four of us. We had one gunman positioned to cover us from the outside of the building and the rest of us entered. I carried a Mauser shotgun. Việt Sơn held a British Sten submachine gun. Thảo carried a weapon as well. We walked into the building right at the moment when Nguyễn Tôn Hoàn and his gang prepared to leave. Thảo signaled to me that this was the man we wanted. Việt Sơn was left to keep guard and Thảo and I then entered the cabinet room. As I reached the door, I stood and held my gun ready.
>
> Fortunately, it seems that Nguyễn Tôn Hoàn had not prepared for such an attack. He had no bodyguards and most of his fellow members had already left. Thảo coolly spoke to Nguyễn Tôn Hoàn, saying in French, "Hello, my old friend. All Vietnamese people are standing against the French to topple them and release us from the shackles of slavery. All of us are going with Uncle Hồ to gain food, clothing, freedom and independence. Think long and hard on this issue. Why would you consciously want to be a henchman for the French colonialists?"
>
> Nguyễn Tôn Hoàn could see the gun in my pocket was aimed at him. In French, he answered in a hesitant way, "I see, I see." I stood ten steps away. I noticed that the two other members, still with him, wanted to pull out their guns. Việt Sơn tapped his gun on the glass of a half-opened internal window to get them to stop. Thảo warned them, "Do not move. You are surrounded. I will not be forgiving with my actions if you betray the resistance." I confiscated their weapons.
>
> Thảo talked to Nguyễn Tôn Hoàn in French for about six to seven minutes, warning him not to align himself with the enemy and betray the homeland. Thảo continued, "We reap what we sow. I will instruct the urban underground elite armed forces of this city to keep close watch on you. I hope you will move towards the resistance." Thảo showed Hoàn his gun. Thảo forced Hoàn to turn his back to him. Then Thảo walked off several meters. We both understood that this was the moment to withdraw. We exited the offices and drove away on our motorbikes towards Tân Kiên. Another motorbike protected us from behind in case someone broke down or we were being followed.
>
> Nguyễn Tôn Hoàn had been warned and, with pressure coming in from all directions, he might not have joined the Việt Minh, but he slowed downed his aggressive actions against us.[28]

Not everything went as smoothly and the secret service asked Anh to spy on a fellow revolutionary. According to Anh, the French had caught Hoàng Thành, one of his classmates at the Quảng Ngãi Land Force School, when he had carried out an assignment for the Việt Minh in Nha Trang. At the same time, the French arrested another man, Thái, a graduate from Tông Military School. Thảo became suspicious; the French released Hoàng Thành after only a week in jail but not Thái. Nguyễn Thanh Sơn posed the question, "Why was he released so quickly, did he talk?" To keep watch on Hoàng Thành, the Party sent him to Anh to be under his control.

Anh explained that he never conclusively proved either way whether Hoàng Thành had been a traitor or not. Anh did hint that he suspected that he was because today he is inexplicably rich and the only logical explanation is that this money was originally paid to him covertly by the French for information, and hidden until recently.

Anh went on to say:

> To identify an informant was not hard. My team used to observe them coming out of French offices. Once identified, someone approached them; a risky operation because as soon as you had done so you had inevitably exposed yourself. Now they could kill you instead.
>
> Sometimes Thảo used other methods. He might write letters to traitors with a bullet attached and the word "ingrate" on the side, warning them that if they continued to oppose the revolutionaries he would go in with harder measures. Or, as a final option, he would send in the security service to take them out, namely a unit of urban underground elite armed forces. We never killed them straight away.[29]

From planting interrogators in French prisons to kill any revolutionary who might talk, to those whose job it was to spy on a fellow spy. This is why, when the French War ended and the Vietnam War raged, those who switched willingly from the Việt Minh to the Southern regime thought twice about speaking out against their former communist allies because they could never be sure who to trust and what would be the consequences. This meant that those who had operated within Hồ's blueprint became transferable between wars.

In late 1948, Hoàng Minh Đạo took over from Thảo as head of the Cochinchina Secret Service Department. Thảo and Anh parted company months later. Anh was assigned to the Cambodian Front as an intelligence officer under the command of Nguyễn Thanh Sơn, whereas the Party sent Thảo to be commander of the 410th Battalion. There he became well versed in army matters, which complemented his strong political and propaganda background. Before their departure, both men had without a doubt contributed greatly to the secret service in Cochinchina.

The South Fights

The expansion of covert operations ultimately meant that the revolutionaries could realize larger military operations, fought with regular forces, within the enemy's rear base area. Two such successful operations were executed in the 7th Zone and the 8th Zone in 1950. In the first case, the 7th Zone opened with the Bến Cát operation, titled the Lê Hồng Phong Campaign. It is now known that this was the first and only major campaign launched in Cochinchina that used a number of troops equal to that of regimental-size. Its core mission was to cut Routes 7 and 14 and by doing so open up supply routes to the Mekong Delta to support guerrilla warfare there. In the second case, the 8th Zone launched the Cầu Ngang Campaign at Trà Vinh. This operation saw Routes 1 and 13 damaged, with watchtowers and blockhouses destroyed along the way.

Hồ's metaphorical water had clearly flowed south, which had enabled Giáp's "fish" to swim. To administer these larger operations in Cochinchina, in June 1951, the Central Office for South Vietnam (COSVN) took over from the Cochinchina Regional Party Committee. The headquarters of COSVN was coded R and was directly under the leadership in Hanoi. At the time, Lê Duẩn headed COSVN.

Not everything went to plan in the South as Hồ had envisioned. He later noted about Lê Duẩn's leadership that because he had not managed a regimental-sized attack in Cochinchina between 1953 and 1954, partly as a result of the lack of infrastructure, he had not met expectation. Hồ's comments must have sent Lê Duẩn into a sulk; in 1954 he refused to regroup to the North.

8

The North: The Westward March

Giáp: The Right Man for Hồ

Hồ undoubtedly was the most influential political leader and Giáp the greatest military general of the resistance war. Hồ had chosen Giáp to lead the military for many reasons, recognizing his genius as a proactive ideas man. It is not surprising then that when historians discuss the wars in Vietnam, out of all the strategies designed and used by the revolutionaries, it is the military that is most scrutinized.

On balance, most researchers have concluded that Giáp's military strategies alone could not have won the communists their massive victories against the French and later the Americans and their Southern allies. In spite of this, the researchers do not offer any substantial explanation as to why the wars ended as they did. A factor is they have not acknowledged that what the French and Americans were actually up against was a brand new form of warfare, and that the military strategies that helped mold this new warfare were themselves new and unique.

The most common error made by current Western historians about Giáp's military thinking is that he based much of it on that of Mao Zedong and the taking of China. On the contrary, some of Giáp's first military advisors were German and French Marxists who had changed sides from the French Foreign Legion to the Việt Minh in 1945. Prior to this he had studied and written articles. Starting in 1939, Giáp wrote military works reporting on the fighting between Japan and China, and after having met Hồ in 1940, Giáp researched Eastern European and Western military art extensively. Then in 1959 to 1961 a couple of Russian teachers based in Hanoi taught him how to speak Russian before he studied at the Military Academy of the General Staff of the Armed Forces of Russia in 1961 and again in 1962. Nevertheless, Giáp did research Vietnamese generals and it was this interesting mix of European thinking, classical Asian knowledge and Vietnamese traditional military art that led to his visionary strategies.[1]

Ironically, in 1939 the French authorities did recognize Giáp's academic ability and wanted to send him to France to do a PhD. Giáp declined the offer and they sent Vũ Văn Hiền instead. Hiền went on to become a renowned lawyer. Although Giáp turned down the opportunity to become a Doctor of Philosophy, it could be said that this reluctant academic became a predominantly self-taught professor of war.

The Westward March

Giáp proved his worth to Hồ leading up to the August Revolution in 1945. Hồ credited Giáp's Southward March as being one reason the Việt Minh came to power. Now the two men could see that key to staying in government was the completion of the Westward March.[2]

The Westward March had started when Giáp carried out his Southward March in 1941. Initially Phạm Văn Đồng, his partner in China, had been given the responsibility of organizing this westward push, but as he had been dogged with illness, Giáp had actually carried out much of the work. Giáp's objective had been to develop the Revolutionary Infrastructure from Bảo Lạc Town and on to the provinces of Hà Giang and Tuyên Quang.

The aim of the Westward March in late 1945 was to first reduce, and then eliminate, French aggression against Việt Bắc Revolutionary Base, so creating a buffer zone to its north-west. Then it was to give Giáp access to Cochinchina via newly established corridors of strategic importance through Lao, Thailand and Cambodia. The overall name given to these corridors to Cochinchina was the Trans-Indochina Link.

The objective of the Trans-Indochina Link through Lao was not only to allow supplies to travel south, but by using the corridors his main regular armed units could advance on Cochinchina along the Mekong River valley. Giáp deemed going via Lao better than just thrusting down the full length of Vietnam. More troops could be moved in greater secrecy through Lao, whereas Annam was geographically thin and slightly overcondensed, which could leave the revolutionaries vulnerable to any French aggression.

To begin the process of unblocking the westward section of the Trans-Indochina Link, Giáp had to get ground troops into the north-west of Vietnam to take Lai Châu Province. Free passage through this province meant Giáp would have a direct route from Việt Bắc Revolutionary Base into Lao. Unfortunately, Lai Châu had never been captured by the Việt Minh during the August Revolution and so was still under French influence.[3]

Giáp made Lê Hiến Mai (1918–1992) responsible for conducting the first military skirmishes of this new Westward March in a procedure Giáp called, "Attacking the enemy from the rear."[4] Giáp ordered Mai to push a courier corridor through to Lao and then, once in the country, harass the returning French there to loosen the enemy's grip on Lai Châu.

Mai left for his mission at the end of September 1945 with around 150 troops. He was a perfect candidate for the post because he had been a commander of a unit within the north-west and before that had escaped from a French prison located in Sơn La. His troops headed on foot for Pa Hang, which borders Lao. On entering the country they crossed the Mã River by dinghy at a point between Sop Bao and Sop Hao. The group then walked to Muong Liet, where the advanced detachment waited.

From Muong Liet, Mai and his men planned to attack Sam Neua Town, Sam Neua Province, where French troops were based.[5] Just prior to their first assault that October, they learned that the enemy had withdrawn for some unknown reason into the jungle. Taking advantage of this situation, Mai infiltrated his whole unit into Sam Neua Town. There they learned that Marcel Alessandri had moved about 200 Vietnamese and French soldiers to Sop Nao, where they received airdrop supplies of arms and food. Mai planned to attack. Again, the French inexplicably left just prior to any confrontation. Whether informed by French intelligence, or just pure coincidence, the French leaving before

Part II. Evolution and Application of the Blueprint (1945–1954)

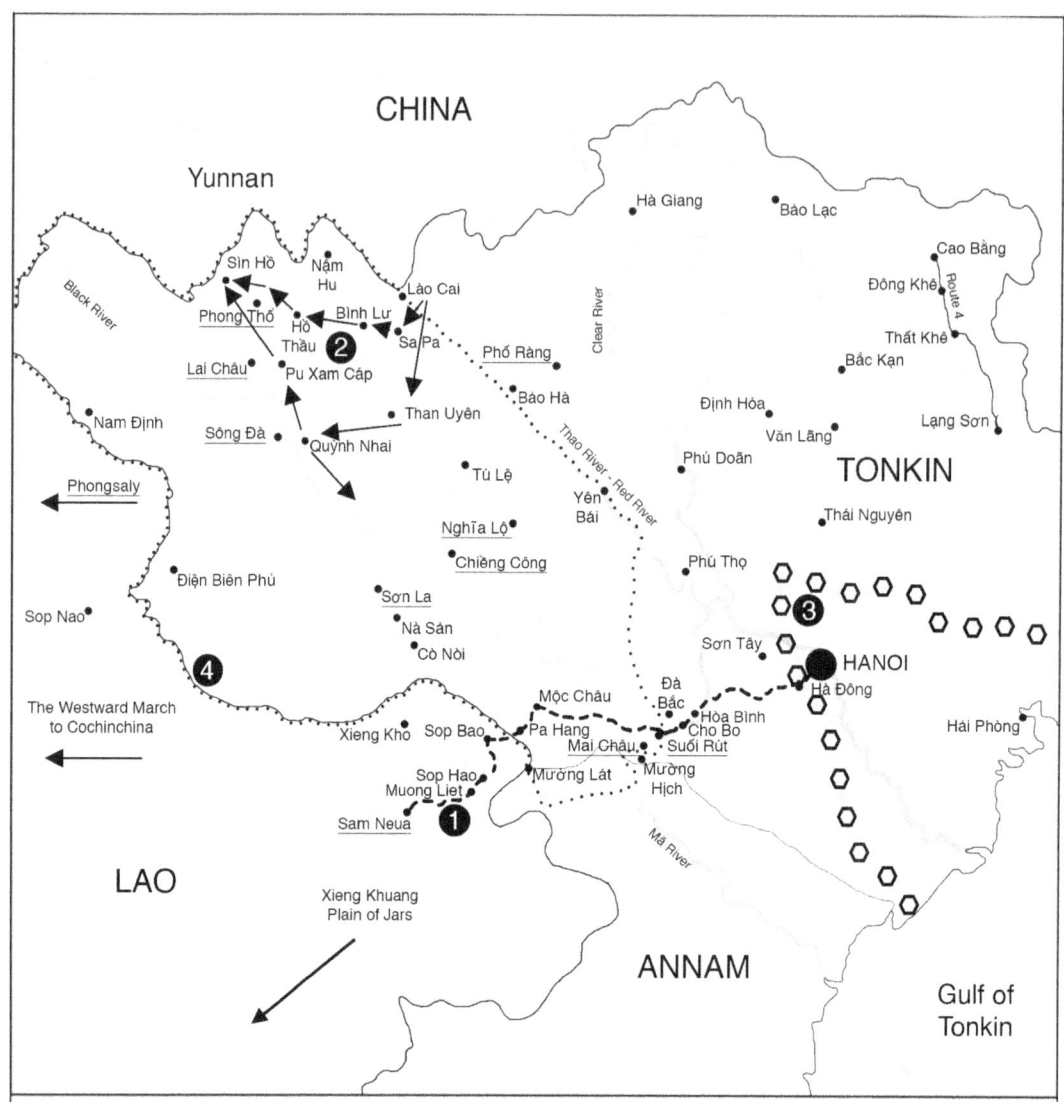

- - - - 1 - Lê Hiến Mai's journey to Sam Neua in 1945, the aim of which was to harass the returning French. His actions were part of unblocking the Trans-Indochina Link to Cochinchina.

→ 2 - Nông Văn Lạc and Hoàng Đông Tùng were sent to Lai Châu Province after the Border Campaign in 1950. First Tùng built courier corridors for independent companies to then use to clear the area. Once completed, Lạc headed the group to develop the Revolutionary Infrastructure.

○ ○ 3 - *De Lattre* Line got its name from General de Lattre. He built this fortified line to stop the Việt Minh gaining access to around 20,000 sq km of Tonkin.

········ 4 - The general boundary of the Tai territory in Tonkin.

The underlined place names show the main areas of the North-West Autonomous Zone, the French stronghold in Tonkin and upper Lao.

Top: Wat That Luang in Vientiane, which is the national symbol of Lao. It dates to the third century, according to the Lao people. At the beginning of the eighteenth century Lao (known as Lan Xang) was divided into three kingdoms; Vientiane (Vieng Chan) was one. Under the French, the region once again became a united Lao state, and in 1953 Vientiane was designated the administrative capital. *Bottom:* A classic image of cloudy mountains in the region of the Westward March. It shows the beautiful but hostile terrain that these revolutionaries had to traverse when they finally reached remote upper Lao (both photographs Clive A. Hills).

Opposite: Key activities in Tonkin leading to the Battle of Điện Biên Phủ, late 1990s.

contact, led one Việt Minh fighter to prematurely comment, "When they hear that the Việt Minh will attack, they use their legs, not guns!"[6]

Just after Mai, Giáp sent Hoàng Sâm (1915–1968) and Trần Quang Thường (1917–2013) to Sơn La Province.[7] Giáp hoped that by doing this these men could stop or slow the French fanning out past Lai Châu and occupying the fertile lowlands; a highly valued agricultural food production area for the communists. Both men had strong experience; Sâm was the commander of the 2nd Zone and Thường the political commissar of the Bắc Sơn Company.[8] To support the mission, Sâm obtained 300 rifles from a Chinese Kuomintang general who had just disarmed some Japanese troops.

Sâm and Thường started by moving their unit towards Lao, and as they did they dropped off troops in strategic locations to secure the area. In Suối Rút, Hòa Bình Province, Sâm appointed Trần Đình Khiết (?–1951), the brother of Thường, to be commander of a platoon he wanted positioned there. Sâm and Thường continued on to Bản Vặt Village, Mộc Châu District, where they met with Mai and Nguyễn Anh Đệ (1925–1985).[9] Mai was now political commissar of the 2nd Zone. Sâm made the decision that he and Mai needed to go back to their headquarters, whereas Nguyễn Anh Đệ must lead the armed forces in Lao. Thường was assigned to Son La Province.

Following the success of a number of early military actions, the Westward Front formed at the beginning of 1947, its headquarters located in Mường Hịch, Sơn La Province. Sâm and Mai became the commander and political commissar respectively. Not long afterwards the Communist Party made the decision to expand further and formed a second headquarters.

An ethnic Tai Dam Village in Sam Neua in the late 1990s (Hua Phan Province today). This would be similar to those found in the ancient Tai Federation through which those of the Westward March passed (Clive A. Hills).

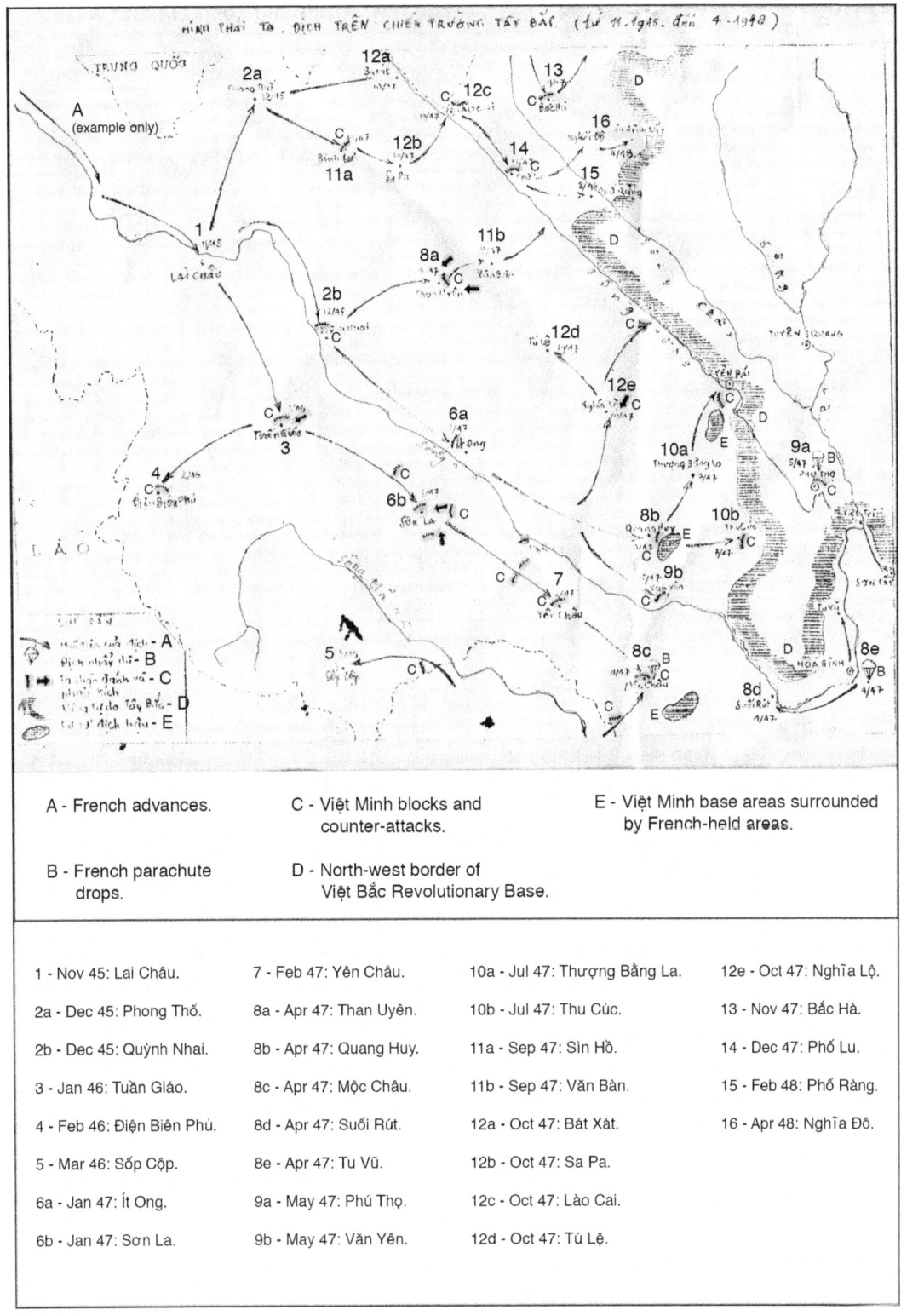

A - French advances.

B - French parachute drops.

C - Việt Minh blocks and counter-attacks.

D - North-west border of Việt Bắc Revolutionary Base.

E - Việt Minh base areas surrounded by French-held areas.

1 - Nov 45: Lai Châu.
2a - Dec 45: Phong Thổ.
2b - Dec 45: Quỳnh Nhai.
3 - Jan 46: Tuần Giáo.
4 - Feb 46: Điện Biên Phủ.
5 - Mar 46: Sốp Cộp.
6a - Jan 47: Ít Ong.
6b - Jan 47: Sơn La.
7 - Feb 47: Yên Châu.
8a - Apr 47: Than Uyên.
8b - Apr 47: Quang Huy.
8c - Apr 47: Mộc Châu.
8d - Apr 47: Suối Rút.
8e - Apr 47: Tu Vũ.
9a - May 47: Phú Thọ.
9b - May 47: Văn Yên.
10a - Jul 47: Thượng Bằng La.
10b - Jul 47: Thu Cúc.
11a - Sep 47: Sìn Hồ.
11b - Sep 47: Văn Bàn.
12a - Oct 47: Bát Xát.
12b - Oct 47: Sa Pa.
12c - Oct 47: Lào Cai.
12d - Oct 47: Tú Lệ.
12e - Oct 47: Nghĩa Lộ.
13 - Nov 47: Bắc Hà.
14 - Dec 47: Phố Lu.
15 - Feb 48: Phố Ràng.
16 - Apr 48: Nghĩa Đô.

Activity in the north-west of Vietnam from November 1945 to April 1948 (original map by Nguyễn Huy Văn, explanations in English by Clive A. Hills).

The growth of the Westward Front stemmed partly from the arrival of the French Army in Tonkin, due to the signing of the *modus vivendi* in March 1946. These French troops occupied pivotal areas and in November had attacked Hải Phòng and took the port, with fighting breaking out in Hanoi on 19 December 1946. When Giáp's units retreated from Hanoi to the surrounding countryside over the Tết New Year in late January 1947, Giáp sent Việt Minh forces from Hanoi, the 2nd Zone and the 3rd Zone to join the new Westward Front. On 27 February 1947, these troops formed the 52nd Regiment, better known as the Westward Regiment. Giáp assigned them to the battlefields of Lao and based them in Sam Neua War Zone.

Through Giáp's Westward Front, Hồ had a tentative foothold in Lao to underpin the Trans-Indochina Link and the push to Cochinchina. Neither men could have predicted that this westward push would lead to a final confrontation with the French.

Giáp's Vision to Hồ

Prior to the signing of the *modus vivendi* in March 1946, Hồ needed to understand how Giáp intended to tackle the arrival of the French Army if the agreement were to go ahead. The signing of this document initiated the official departure of 180,000 Chinese Kuomintang forces, but the reluctant acceptance of 15,000 French troops. Hồ needed to know that Giáp could rebut the French so that they could be confident in justifying the agreement to the Vietnamese people.

Hồ called a meeting with Giáp on 18 January 1946, and after discussions he ordered Giáp to go to the south of the country to evaluate the situation. Hồ requested before he left, "Your main task is to research the battlefield. You must also support your comrades in the three fronts of southern Annam, the Central Highlands and Cochinchina. They have to keep the resistance spirit alive. They must develop guerrilla warfare so that they can pin down the enemy. They must energize their civilian compatriots' and soldiers' zeal to fight the enemy for national salvation."

Giáp traveled through the provinces of Thừa Thiên, Quảng Nam, Quảng Ngãi, Bình Định and Phú Yên. On reaching Diên Khánh, Khánh Hòa Province, he stopped because Hồ had sent him an urgent telegram requesting his return. Giáp never reached Saigon, but to be as of much value to Hồ as possible, en route north, he headed back from Ninh Hòa Town, Khánh Hòa Province, via the Central Highlands to conclude his findings.

Giáp arrived back in Hanoi and just before Hồ signed the controversial *modus vivendi*, the two men discussed the ramifications of the agreement versus Giáp's findings on Hồ's initial requests. Giáp assured Hồ that he had seen much of the country and believed that he had a solution to the French Army problem, and he went on to spell out three imperative military strategies.

Giáp first pointed out that, because the southern revolutionaries used static warfare to stop the limited French troops already in the country, they had failed. Giáp agreed with Hồ's views and that the south must focus on guerrilla warfare.

Giáp then went on to state that another strategic corridor had to be built from the provinces of Nghệ An and Hà Tĩnh to Lao and on to Siam (Thailand). In addition to the normal use of a courier route, this new line would give Hồ access to Bangkok where the Soviets and Americans had embassies that could be approached, and help Hồ seek assistance from the government of Siam, who supported independence for Vietnam. Hồ and

Giáp agreed that the routes to Siam could run along the old courier lines used by nationalists revolting against the French in the 1900s and those attending Whampoa Military Academy in China in the mid–1920s. The nationalist Phan Bội Châu had constructed these routes and one of the founders and designers included Tuấn, the father of some of the first "communist children" of Hồ. The same routes would be used during the Vietnam War as part of the Hồ Chí Minh Trail.

For the third point, Giáp proposed his "war without boundaries"; a term he used only after 1975, when describing his military methodology to others. This was initially of most significance because it led Hồ to sign the *modus vivendi* that March. Giáp assured him that with the limited French troop numbers permitted in the country, he could force the French High Command into an impossible task. The French would have to split their resources, either focusing their main efforts on completely occupying and pacifying the vast territory of Vietnam, which would entail garrisons and outposts being located everywhere, or concentrating their forces in order to fight large offensives to destroy Việt Minh units. Giáp told Hồ that his war without boundaries would spread the French Army so thinly against his units that the French would fail in Vietnam.

Hồ accepted all three points and in doing so signed the *modus vivendi* and unleashed in Giáp the confidence for him to design many more innovative military concepts.

Guerrilla In-Front Warfare

The first real test of Giáp's military abilities was the defense of Hanoi in December 1946. He had to harass and pin the enemy down so that Hồ's revolutionary government had time to escape to Tân Trào. If successful, this campaign would set a positive example for the rest of the resistance movement throughout the country.

There was limited precedent in Vietnamese history for fighting inside a city. Giáp drew on his recent experiences such as at Tam Đảo against the Japanese, which ended with a ceasefire, as well as the failed defense of Saigon and Nha Trang. From his understanding of fighting in these built-up areas, Giáp saw that his troops had to keep the initiative, be active, rapid, avoid risks and make his units ever more elusive to his opponent.

Giáp reflected on general principles. Looking at his forefathers, they had used "weaker forces to overcome stronger ones" and "smaller numbers to oppose larger forces." To accomplish this, Giáp had to fight on his own terms. Instinct dictated that he should not fight when his enemy was prepared to fight, that he should only attack when they least expected him to do so and only after he had identified his enemy's weak points.

Prior to the battle, Giáp analyzed intelligence data from across the city. One personal observation he made was that, although both he and Hồ had tried to sell the rationale behind the signing of the *modus vivendi* of that March to the people, the general population still wanted to fight the French now stationed in Hanoi. Giáp also witnessed that the people had opposed French encroachment by building barricades made from old furniture, felled trees and anything else they could get their hands on. While amateur in their construction and unmanned, they did hold back the French for some time. The barriers served another purpose. The French did not know who had built them, which had undermined their confidence in the citizens and sapped French morale; any man, woman or child, no matter how innocent looking, could be a potential danger to them.

These people's barricades that Giáp wanted to include within his battle plan, concurred with Hồ's thinking. Hồ recognized that since the French Army had started to reoccupy Vietnam, the resistance movement did not have the weapons to fight them as regular forces would. Consequently, the revolutionaries needed to use anything at their disposal to slow down the enemy until the lack of weapons could be resolved.

On looking at all the evidence, Giáp planned to defend Hanoi and pin the French down in a strategy he termed "guerrilla in-front warfare." An amalgamation of guerrilla warfare and pitched battle, the former used hit-and-run tactics and the latter static defenses based loosely upon the defensive trench front line warfare of the First and Second World Wars. To implement guerrilla in-front warfare, Giáp's units had to prevent the French in the city center from attacking the outer suburbs, by using his troops to attack the enemy inside the city whilst surrounding the enemy from the outside.

To execute his plan, Giáp constructed several parallel lines of barricades and ditches to support the existing obstructions built by the residents of Hanoi. Then Giáp deployed his guerrilla fighters; each detachment being of limited size to aid mobility and secrecy. Giáp instructed them to use the barricades for protection when they targeted the enemy's weak points; intercepted the enemy through a series of small carefully prepared battles; protected strategic locations including the City Hall; and destroyed isolated French posts, important bases and service areas such as the power and water plants.

By using guerrilla in-front warfare Giáp's forces fought successfully in a city environment and rebutted French tanks and armored vehicles; by doing so they held Hanoi for some sixty days before having to retreat. This battle is now recognized by most scholars as the point at which the nationwide French War actually started.

Mobile Guerrilla Warfare

Out of a combination of fresh experience and research came Giáp's next hybrid concept for his war without boundaries, "mobile guerrilla warfare." He wanted to destroy the French rather than just to harass them and limit their superiority in weapons and war material, especially the firepower of their tanks, artillery and aircraft.

Giáp had studied the success rates of both his guerrilla units and regular forces. As had been discussed with Hồ in early 1946, whenever his small guerrilla units in Cochinchina harassed the French, no matter how strong the French forces, as long as his men adhered to hit-and-run guerrilla tactics the French found it incredibly frustrating and very hard to destroy them. On the other hand, his larger regular units, now organized up to battalion or regimental level, should have had the numbers to destroy an advancing enemy, but actually found it difficult to do so. Giáp put this down to inadequate equipment and training, as well as their more static approach, which left them vulnerable to being targeted, pinned down and possibly annihilated.

Giáp acknowledged that mobile guerrilla warfare would not be widely understood to be traditional guerrilla warfare; guerrilla units were small and fought locally whereas his mobile units would be larger in number. It was not conventional mobile warfare either, which involved fighting in big operations using large military units in set piece battles. Giáp went on to say, "In the course of a conflict, guerrilla warfare must develop into conventional mobile warfare; consequently my new mobile guerrilla warfare units are midway through this development process." At the first military conference, convened in mid–January 1947, those present agreed that the entire regular army should be converted to the new mobile guerrilla warfare system. The Party issued the formal edict stating this the following month.

Giáp's initial defining tactic was how he designed and then implemented mobile guerrilla warfare, which he did by forming "independent companies." Although Giáp understood that there were many different types of guerrilla fighter, later in life he recalled what had inspired his thinking for independent companies.

In 1945, Giáp had a book by Prussian general, Carl von Clausewitz, called *On War*, and he had taken it to the front as the war broke out. It was written mostly after the Napoleonic wars of the nineteenth century and published posthumously in the 1830s. Giáp's version had been translated into French by Marxist advisors. Giáp noted that he liked the chapter about "arming the people" and what Clausewitz noted as a "small war," writing, "A small war is characterized by the fact that small units can go to any place, that they can supply themselves, keep their presence secret, move rapidly, withdraw even in places which have no roads, and so on."[10]

Giáp then recollected that in September 1947, he went to the 12th Zone and noticed an innovative phenomenon. He observed that a regular unit of Bắc Ninh Province had become a self-formed independent company. They were originally a 100-strong city self-defense team, many of whom were ex-employees at the Gia Lâm Railway Factory, Hanoi. Self-defense teams formed from groups of factory and office workers as well as villagers from the suburbs, with the objective to agitate the masses and defend their workplace or street with vigor. When the fighting broke out in Hanoi, this unusual self-defense team had to withdraw to southern Bắc Ninh. There, Giáp noted, they held their ground and fought in the enemy's rear base area until the Tết New Year of 1947.

When listening to this unit recount their fighting experience, Giáp could see that their system allowed them to be very flexible. They could concentrate smoothly or disperse from company strength to platoon or section level depending upon the circumstances they faced. Although the French knew that parts of this elusive unit remained within their area of operation, they could not actually flush them out because the local villagers supported them. With this unit living with the people, it meant that the local guerrilla movement was not only maintained but expanded because they trained others. This format permitted this unit to remain far behind enemy lines, conducting ambushes and surprise attacks.

Giáp made each independent company consist of up to 100 men. One important factor that dictated the size of unit was that 100 men could be accommodated within a village and fed by them; any larger a unit would stand out or be a burden on the locals. To reduce encroaching on village life, this number of fighters could supplement their food by foraging and growing crops in the forest.

Giáp sent his independent companies behind enemy lines to operate freely. Tasked with much of the same duties as armed propaganda teams, their orders comprised: mobilizing the people; safeguarding them from the enemy; helping them with their production work; recruiting the best trained local fighters from the villages and grouping them to form more independent companies, local regular forces or local guerrillas; re-establishing people's power wherever possible; destroying the enemy's administration, eliminating spies, conducting military proselytizing, dissolving puppet organizations working for the enemy or turning them to be two-faced puppet local administrators; and building the Revolutionary Infrastructure. These mobile guerrilla units had to spawn guerrilla warfare across Vietnam like cancer cells mutating to infect a body.

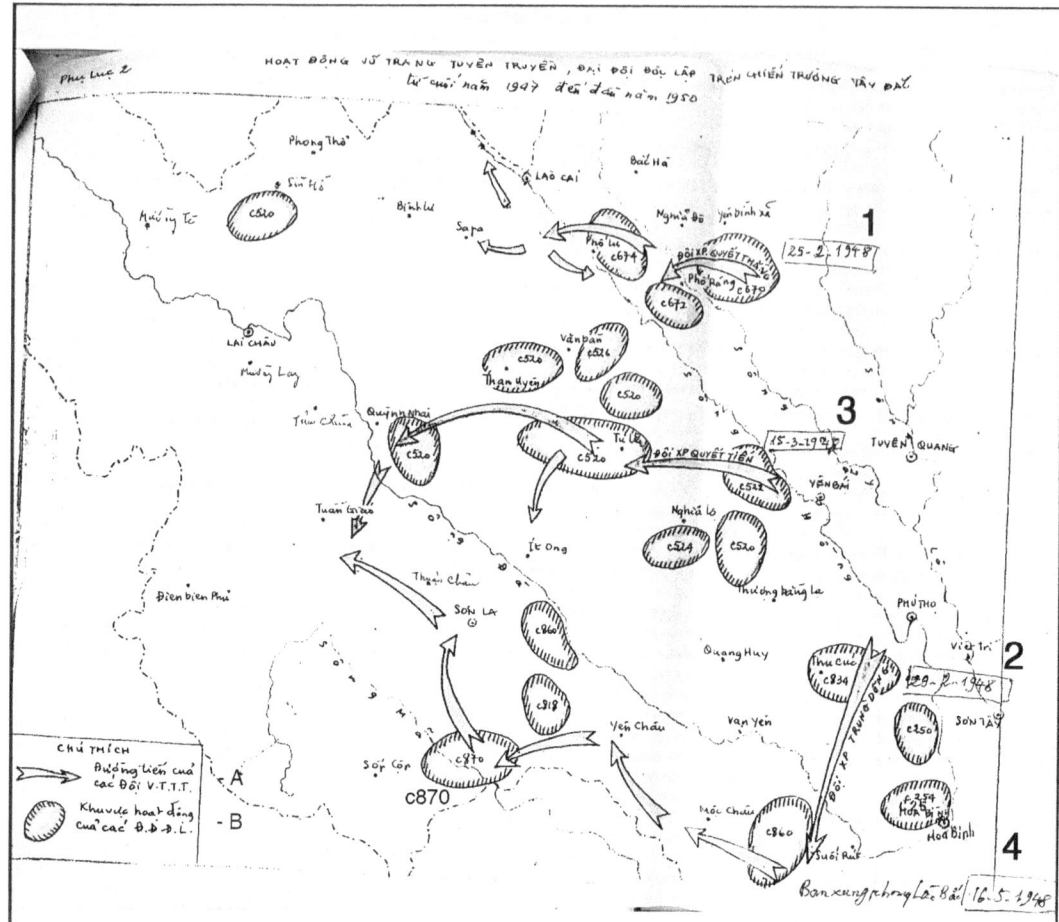

A - Showing the movements of the armed propaganda teams.

B - The operating areas of the independent companies.

C - "c" is the codename for company c870, for example.

1 - Quyết Thắng Company (Determined to Win) - formed 25 February 1948 and moved through Phố Ràng, Phố Lu and on to Sa Pa.

2 - Trung Dũng Company (Fateful and Brave) - formed 29 February 1948 and moved through Suối Rút, Mộc Châu, Yên Châu, Sốp Cộp, Sơn La, Thuận Châu and on to Tuần Giáo.

3 - Quyết Tiến Company (Determined to Advance) - formed 15 March 1948 and moved through Tú Lệ, Quỳnh Nhai and on to Tuần Giáo.

4 - Ban Xung Phong Lào Bắc Company (North Lao Advancing Team) - formed 16 May 1948. Led by Hoàng Đông Tùng and, working with Kaysone Phomvihane a future leader of the Pathet Lao, moved through Northern Lao. (There are no arrows to show these movements on the map as Lao is to the south).

The development of armed propaganda teams and independent companies from late 1947 to 1950 (original map by Nguyễn Huy Văn, explanations in English by Clive A. Hills).

Fighting Villages

One high profile objective of the independent companies was to recruit and then train villagers to turn their community into a "fighting village." Giáp's motto, "Each village forms a fortress." This concept had been around prior to the August Revolution to fight the Japanese.

A fighting village meant that each settlement had a guerrilla base; these units were known as static guerrilla fighters and were made up of locals who remained in their community and got on with daily life, such as farming. A fighting village also had a battle area filled with tunnels, trenches, fortifications, mines, spikes and booby traps, and a self-defense team strictly controlled the comings and goings of strangers. Again, Giáp had designed a new concept because these static guerrillas contradicted the more general idea of a small band of fighters constantly on the move and striking as and when the opportunity arose.

A fighting village supported Giáp's regular units, who could be caught in the middle of enemy sweep operations. By utilizing the tunnels and trenches, even with a scarcity of arms and ammunitions, the regular units could hide themselves from bombing and artillery, and seriously hinder the advance of any attacker. Giáp used fighting villages throughout the wars, and the concept is often depicted in Hollywood movies such as *Platoon*.

A typical ethnic Akha family in upper Lao in the late 1990s. Their livelihoods and culture would have changed little since the days of the Westward March when revolutionaries came to these remote locations to spread propaganda among the masses (Clive A. Hills).

Concentrated Battalions

Giáp's vision of independent companies gave him the means to form differing fighting units within an area in order to realize diverse combat configurations. The local guerrillas or local regular forces recruited by the independent companies now could initiate numerous small actions to thwart the French in enemy-occupied areas. The larger more mobile independent companies could execute small battles against the French, either with or without local help. Though, it was how Giáp proposed to fight larger battles which made his concept of mobile guerrilla warfare complete.

For larger battle arrangements Giáp grouped independent companies into battalion-sized units.[11] Due to their flexible nature, after the battle they could quickly disperse into independent companies again and rapidly disappear into the forest or back into the population. This made it very hard for the French to destroy an entire battalion. Giáp's motto for his new military strategy was "independent companies—concentrated battalions." In his own words, this final approach aided him to "transform the enemy's rear base area to be our front."

Attuning Tactics

After several months of action, Giáp and his colleagues studied how the mobile guerrilla units had operated. They discussed the questions of day versus night attacks, fighting the enemy at a distance or at close range and in different types of terrain.

Giáp's working group concluded that victory for the mobile guerrilla units was gained mostly at night because they could move close to the French without being spotted. They observed that close range fighting, namely hand-to-hand, was most effective. When fighting took place in a mountainous region, blanketed by forest, the mobile guerrillas held the advantage. Giáp remarked, "Fighting in mountainous regions meant that our troops were covered by the forests whilst the enemy was surrounded by them." The group went on to observe that in open terrain the mobile guerrilla units were less effective and could only wage small battles when using careful, rapid surprise attacks, from which they could then withdraw quickly.

With observations conducted, Giáp laid down a set of rules to which all his fighters had to adhere, whether as their primary or secondary duties. The first rule he ordered was harassment. This could include letting off a flare to startle the enemy, placing a piece of cast iron by the road in such a way that it looked like a mine, firing a round from an old flintlock at the right moment (which would be better than not firing a shot at all), or making booby traps and land mines to kill a few enemy troops. As Giáp's second rule, he instructed that isolated battles must be fought and where possible a trophy of one rifle or some bullets should be the objective. A third rule was that the enemy's logistics must be hampered by destroying roads and cutting their cable and telephone lines. Fourthly, spies have to be eliminated and, finally, fighters must annihilate enemy forces; even small numbers represented great victories.

With Giáp's new mobile guerrillas in place he had given Hồ a way to overstretch French troops and their resources. So successful were his independent companies that Giáp applied the military strategy during the Vietnam War to build up his guerrilla base again after much of it had been wiped out during the Tết Offensive in 1968.

The More We Fight: Operation Léa

The first major test of strength for Giáp's newly arranged military units came in October 1947 during the French campaign called Operation Léa. It was a campaign that targeted the region of Việt Bắc because French intelligence suspected the base was again being used by the Việt Minh. To achieve their goals, the French had to cut Việt Bắc off from any supplies coming in from China along Route 4, and then surround the area to capture its leadership and completely destroy the budding shoots of their regular forces.

French intelligence had been correct. Anticipating the French takeover of Hanoi, in October 1946, the Việt Minh prepared to make the vast area of Việt Bắc a revolutionary base again. They established an ATK (safe zone) in the area, so that in early April 1947 Việt Bắc could become the capital for the resistance.[12] To safeguard senior Communist Party members, the General Staff made a decision as to where branches of the Party Central Committee, the government and other mass organizations were to be located, and whether they should be within the ATK or the wider Việt Bắc area. For most of the time, the military headquarters was in Định Hóa District, whereas the Party apparatus and government normally located to Sơn Dương.

The French started Operation Léa on 7 October with an airborne operation. They parachuted troops into the provincial center of Bắc Kạn, which they believed was the communists' headquarters. Leading communist government officials and support staff were concentrated in the surrounding area. They included those running the Treasury Service and the units that actually printed the banknotes, as well as revolutionaries such as Trường Chinh, but not Hồ, whom the French later claimed to have captured but quite clearly had not.

A French victory did not materialize. French ground forces failed to link up with their paratrooper partners; they had become disorientated in the thick forest as a result of being attacked both from the jungle and the rivers. This meant the troops could not completely surround Việt Bắc and had to call off the assault early in November. Fighting did continue under Operation Ceinture; translated as "belt," this action did temporarily succeed in clearing a belt area from Việt Minh fighters between Hanoi, Thái Nguyên and Tuyên Quang.

Giáp had been warned about Operation Léa and a smaller auxiliary operation. On 9 October, an aircraft carrying a number of French officers was shot down in Cao Bằng Province. Nguyễn Danh Lộc, a courier, had run for several days and nights with limited rest to take the retrieved classified documents to Communist Party officials.[13] Giáp received the documents from Nguyễn Danh Lộc on 13 October.[14] Although having the advantage of gaining access to these plans surely helped, Giáp did not consider it the sole reason why General Jean Etienne Valluy (1899-1970), the commander in chief of the French Far East Expeditionary Corps, failed to destroy the capital of the Việt Minh.[15] Giáp said that he had been surprised by Operation Léa and that Valluy had been correct in targeting Việt Bắc but he had been greatly mistaken in believing that the little town of Bắc Kạn was the new headquarters of the resistance. Throughout the anti–French War and later the Vietnam War, no central organ of the command leadership was based in a town. It had always been divided into small parts, which were on the move and were mixed in with, and protected by, the people in isolated villages.[16]

Success in defeating the French during Operation Léa was a turning point for the Việt Minh. Giáp assured Hồ that despite the French misreading the situation, the main reason why they failed in their objectives was because his troops had used their experience to successfully counter-attack and spread the French too thinly. His motto, "The more we fight, the stronger we become," ("more" here meant frequency) had proved correct.[17]

Expanding in Lao

Building on the triumph of Operation Léa, Giáp now looked to continue his Westward March to destabilize the French in the north-west of Vietnam and the adjacent provinces of Lao.

Since Giáp's early tentative incursions into the region, the French had proclaimed the north-west and the adjacent parts of Lao as their own. In the late 1940s, the French set up the North-West Autonomous Zone, with the primary mission to protect the Tai Federation.[18] Furthermore, the region consisted of very fertile land and the crops grown helped to feed their armed units. It had excellent transport routes and inter-changes, such as roads that ran to upper, central and southern Lao and then west to Thailand and Burma; another route ran north to China.

To crush the enemy in the North-West Autonomous Zone, Giáp planned to initially send in small-sized armed propaganda teams to establish the infrastructure, base areas and local guerrilla units there. Then follow these with larger independent companies; each company sent to one locality only and instructed to expand on what the armed propaganda teams had already done. Like a spider's web, these localities could then be linked to each other by yet more infrastructure, to eventually form a network of secure base areas within the North-West Autonomous Zone. Where the French threatened communist control of land, and their ability to expand, Giáp would instruct concentrated battalions to stage a number of battles to force the enemy out to allow the communists in.

To liberate the North-West Autonomous Zone, Giáp not only had to attack from Vietnam but from the north-east of upper Lao. Fortunately, he had been entrusted with assisting the Lao revolution and monitoring the Cambodian revolution. This gave him control over a complex situation because, like in Vietnam, the resistance in Lao was diverse and there were many factions fighting to gain control. The ruling Royal Lao government was supported by the French and led by King Sisavangvong (1904–1959). One

Mr. Vong (Lao), the author's guide, when she walked some 1,600km across remote areas of Lao, including escorting her to parts of the Westward March and along the Hồ Chí Minh Trail in the late 1990s (Clive A. Hills).

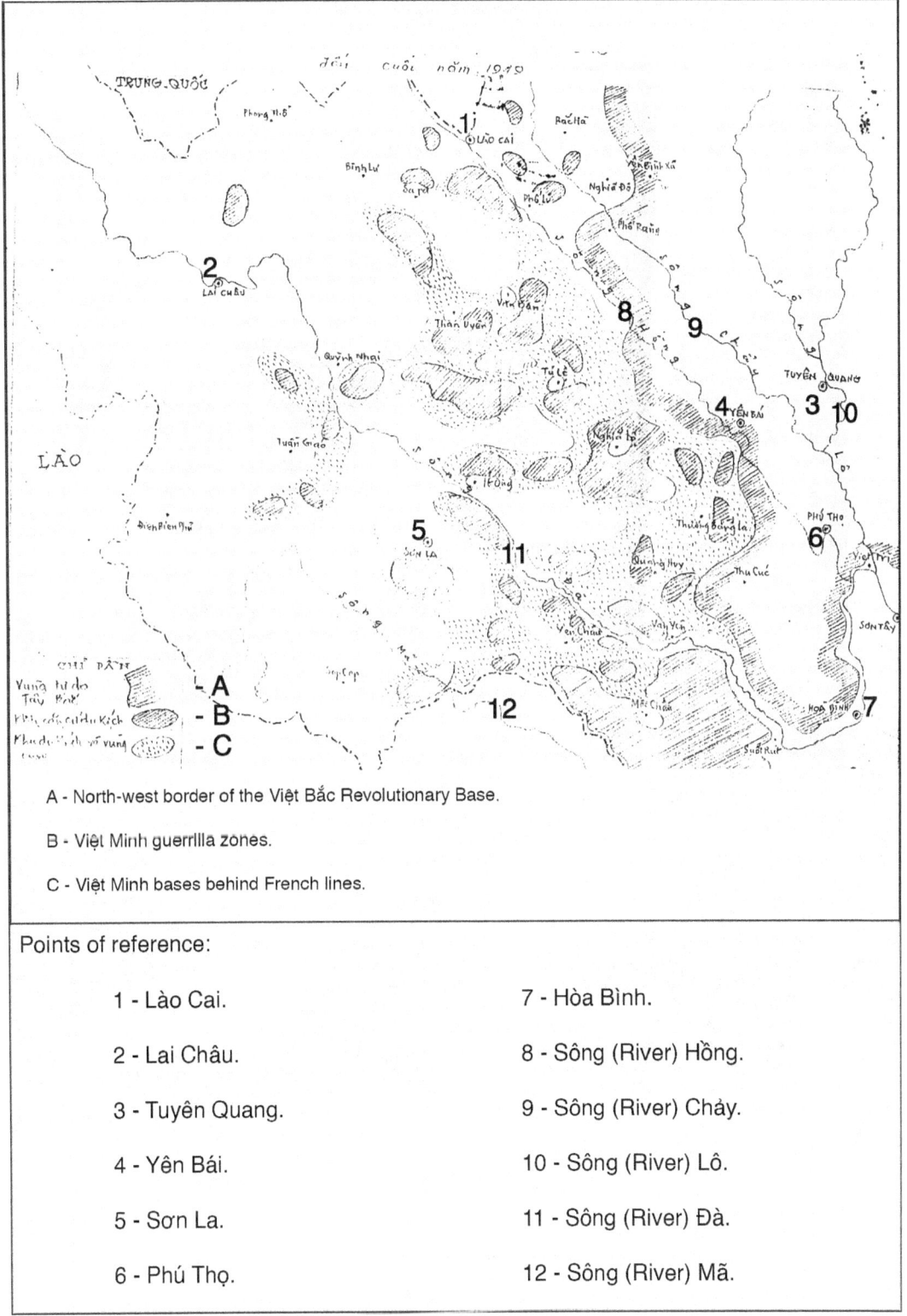

A - North-west border of the Việt Bắc Revolutionary Base.

B - Việt Minh guerrilla zones.

C - Việt Minh bases behind French lines.

Points of reference:

1 - Lào Cai.
2 - Lai Châu.
3 - Tuyên Quang.
4 - Yên Bái.
5 - Sơn La.
6 - Phú Thọ.
7 - Hòa Bình.
8 - Sông (River) Hồng.
9 - Sông (River) Chảy.
10 - Sông (River) Lô.
11 - Sông (River) Đà.
12 - Sông (River) Mã.

Locations of Việt Minh base areas behind French lines in the north-west region until the end of 1949 (original map by Nguyễn Huy Văn, explanations in English by Clive A. Hills).

opposition group was a communist resistance movement, eventually to be known as the Pathet Lao.[19]

To aid his plan, Giáp intended to establish a revolutionary base for the Lao communists and ultimately to set up a fully liberated zone. To secure loyalty, he approached a Lao national, Kaysone Phomvihane (1920–1992), in Văn Lăng Village, Thái Nguyên Province, in 1948. This young student expressed to Giáp that he wanted Lao to be at peace but with independence and freedom.

Giáp concluded that Kaysone had the personality to cope with the hardships of the Westward March. He had already gained some experience of revolutionary life when commander of an armed propaganda team of the 2nd Zone, called the Northern Lao Team, which operated in Sam Neua. To reduce the risk of shortfalls in his knowledge, Giáp spent three days personally teaching Kaysone how to approach his new role, including how to mobilize the masses, create the Revolutionary Infrastructure, train people, expand armed forces and construct a liberated zone. Giáp then sent Kaysone to Mộc Châu to join the Bế Sơn Cương Regiment, whose commander was Bế Sơn Cương. Here a new independent company formed, called the North Lao Advancing Team, which Kaysone joined. The Party assigned Kaysone to the political side, whereas a Lao called Thao Ma became responsible for the military section.

Giáp instructed the North Lao Advancing Team to open a courier corridor towards Phongsaly Province and form a revolutionary base area; Giáp suggested Xieng Kho, Sam Neua Province, as a good location. Starting on 20 May, the team entered north-west Lao with armed propaganda teams and Lao combatants. On 20 January 1949 they took Xieng Kho, and indeed the area served as a revolutionary base, codenamed D.[20] Here, the team

Phongsaly Town, Lao, in the late 1990s. In 1954, the provinces of Phongsaly and Sam Neua were set aside for the Lao communists as a regrouping area under the terms of the Geneva Accords (Clive A. Hills).

Taken in 1950 at Xieng Kho, this was the location of the first headquarters of the Lao revolution. From left, Kaysone Phomvihane (Lao), Tạ Xuân Thu, Prince Souphanouvong (Lao), Bế Sơn Cương (commander of the regiment) and Nuhac Phumsavan (Lao) (courtesy Nguyễn Huy Văn).

held a ceremony to declare the formation of the Lat Xa Vong armed unit, now officially recognized to be the first unit of the Lao People's Liberation Army.

Building on the Lao success, in 1949 Giáp ordered his first regimental-sized attack in the North-West Autonomous Zone, called the Thao River Campaign (19 May to 16 July).[21] It targeted part of the French Thao River defense line, which included outposts and entrenched camps (fortified defensive positions). If successful, the Việt Minh could establish corridors to connect new and existing base areas deep behind enemy lines in the provinces of Sơn La, Yên Bái and Lào Cai. It could also reduce pressure on Việt Bắc Revolutionary Base from the west and consolidate a springboard to upper Lao. The campaign did accomplish its task and French positions were destroyed along a 70km stretch of the river.

With this victory, Giáp launched a number of other campaigns similar to this throughout the rest of 1949 to enlarge footholds in the north-west of Vietnam and consolidate his achievements in upper Lao. Another step change in circumstances came in 1950 when Red China and Hồ engaged as allies.

Hồ's Fight and the Cold War

The Cold War was a state of political and military tension after the Second World War between powers in the Western and Eastern Blocs. Although Eastern Bloc generally

150   Part II. Evolution and Application of the Blueprint (1945–1954)

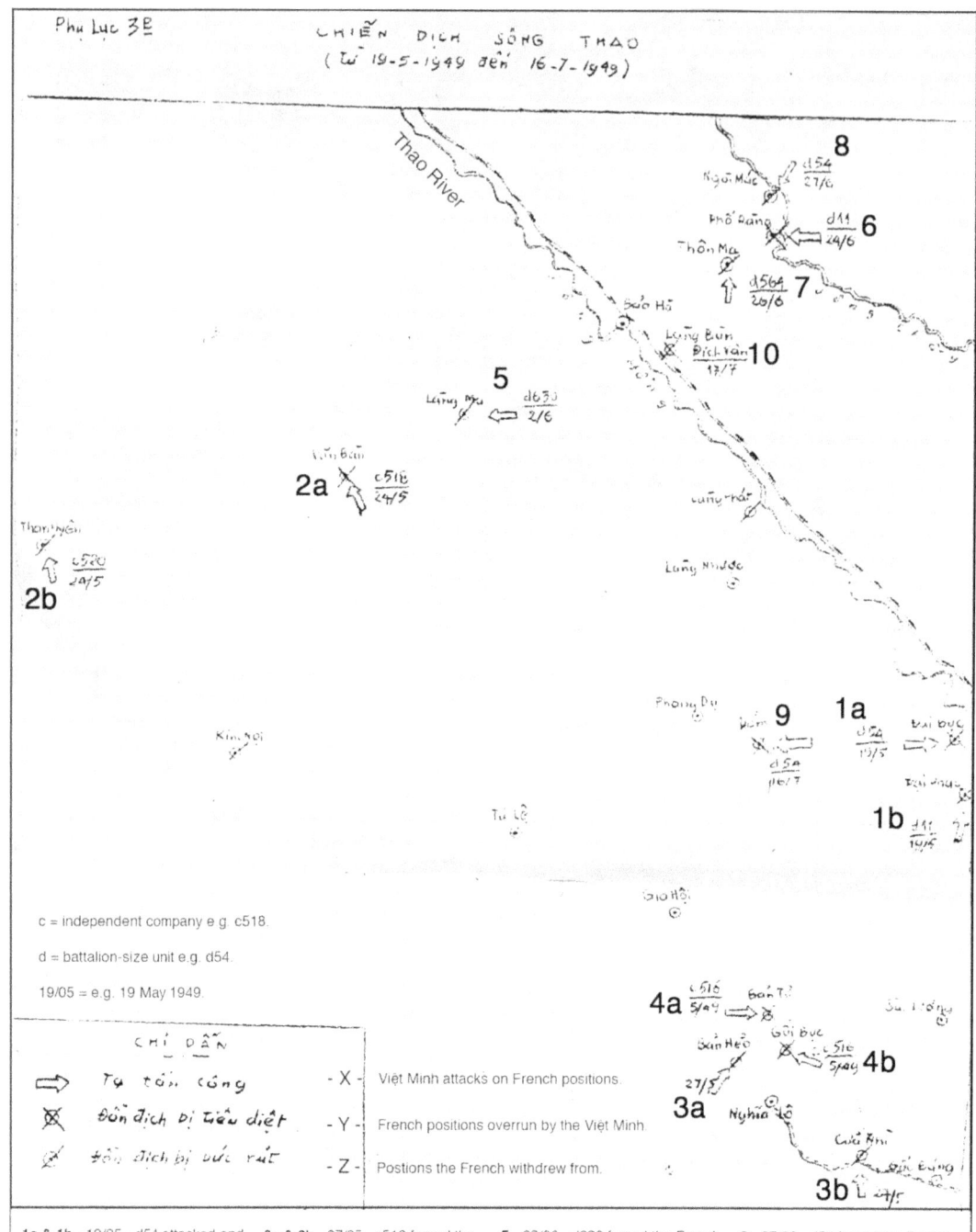

c = independent company e.g. c518.

d = battalion-size unit e.g. d54.

19/05 = e.g. 19 May 1949.

- X - Việt Minh attacks on French positions.
- Y - French positions overrun by the Việt Minh.
- Z - Postions the French withdrew from.

1a & 1b - 19/05 - d54 attacked and destroyed the French position at Đại Bục and d11 overran Đại Phác.

2a & 2b - 24/05 - c518 attacked and destroyed the French at Văn Bàn and c520 forced the French to withdraw from Than Uyên.

3a & 3b - 27/05 - c516 forced the French to withdraw from Bản Heo and Cửa Nhì.

4a & 4b - May 1949 - c516 attacked and destroyed the French at Bản Tú and Gói Bục.

5 - 02/06 - d630 forced the French to withdraw from Làng Mạ.

6 - 24/06 - d11 destroyed the French position at Phố Ràng.

7 - 26/06 - d564 forced the French to withdraw from Thôn Mạ.

8 - 27/06 - d54 forced the French to withdraw from Ngòi Mục.

9 - 16/07 - d54 destroyed the French position at Dóm.

10 - 17/07 - Good military proselytizing destroyed the French position at Làng Bún.

referred to the communist states of Central and Eastern Europe, some applied it to countries such as the People's Republic of China but then also used the wider name Communist Bloc.

Friendly relations between the Chinese revolutionaries and the Việt Minh grew from tentative exchanges. In early 1948, Zhuang Tian was instructed by Zhou Enlai (1898–1976) to meet leaders of the Việt Minh, which he did in Lục Giã, Việt Bắc Revolutionary Base. Zhuang Tian gave an account of the war in China. He said that Chinese Kuomintang troops had intensified sweeps against the revolutionary forces, which meant the revolutionary guerrilla units were in difficulty and had insufficient food. Hồ discussed with Zhuang Tian how best the Việt Minh could help and the two men agreed to support the others forces when needed.

Hồ held to his word of mutual assistance. In early March 1949, the Chinese Kuomintang forces launched fierce attacks against the Chinese revolutionaries, and to escape capture some of the insurgents crossed unhindered into Vietnam for safety. Then, in mid–1949, their first joint operation occurred at the suggestion of the Chinese; several Việt Minh units fought alongside the Red Army in Guangxi Province, China, and successfully built base areas there. To cement ties, when Mao Zedong came to power and the People's Republic of China formed in October 1949, within a month he officially recognized the Democratic Republic of Vietnam and proposed that the Vietnamese send an ambassador to Beijing.

In early 1950, Hồ needed to expand support for the Việt Minh and traveled first to China and then on to the Soviet Union, where he met with both Joseph Stalin and, for the first time, Mao. Both men agreed to supply weapons to the Việt Minh. Stalin said, "Vietnam's requirements are not so great. There must be a division of labor between China and the Soviet Union. Just now, the latter has to fulfil its task towards the Eastern European countries. China will help Vietnam with what it needs. Whatever China has not got in its depots [to supply Vietnam], China can take from the articles the Soviet Union has supplied to them in its aid program for China, and the Soviet Union will [then reimburse China]." He added, "China won't lose in this deal because, even if it provides Vietnam with second-hand articles, it will be given back new ones by the Soviet Union."[22] Stalin even joked, "If China gives Vietnam an egg, the Soviet Union would give her [China] a hen."[23] With the Soviet Union not being directly involved, they could distance themselves from events but it left Hồ with a headache because it meant he had to become more dependent on China.

Sadly for the Vietnamese people, this offer of support came with strings attached, and was linked to the Soviet Union's and China's class struggle. For Giáp, he had to accept Chinese military advisors, which tied one arm behind his back when it came to decision-making. For the general public, it meant that extremely harsh Land Reforms had to be implemented. For the individual revolutionary, Hồ remembered one event in which he had to draw up a form of census, listing names of people who had privileged backgrounds. Those on the list could now no longer hold high office in the Việt Minh, while low-ranking people from similar backgrounds were merely ignored. Purportedly when Hồ had read the original list written by the Chinese, he had looked at all the names of the so-called privileged background people on it and thrown it on the fire, saying to the Việt

Opposite: **Thao River Campaign from 19 May 1949 to 16 July 1949, Võ Nguyên Giáp's first regimental-size campaign in the north-west of Vietnam (original map by Nguyễn Huy Văn, explanations in English by Clive A. Hills).**

Minh staff member who had handed it to him on behalf of the Chinese, "If we do so, we will have no more people for the resistance."

At the same time that China, the Soviets and the Việt Minh formed closer ties, the French became ever more reliant on their allies within the Western Bloc, namely the Americans. In France the government was divided over how to proceed; the war dragged on with no quick victory in sight. On the battlefield, one view advocated occupying and maintaining Tonkin and northern Annam at any cost; the region was the hub of the war. Others wanted to concentrate military efforts on occupying and controlling southern Annam and Cochinchina; they regarded these areas as central to controlling the whole of the Indochina Peninsula.

With disputes on going in France, the Americans looked at this as a good opportunity to become more involved in the war. They needed to bring it into their strategies for the region, which were to prevent the spread of communism. Equally, now Mao had taken China, the balance of power in the region and the wider Cold War had changed. America had to blunt the influence of both China and Soviet Union in the area.

The Cold War might have been named as such because no large-scale fighting directly occurred between the Western and Eastern Blocs. Nevertheless, there were major regional wars supported by the two sides and Hồ's war for independence had become one such conflict: things heated up.

Three-Layered Military

In early 1949, just prior to China supplying weapons to the Việt Minh, Hồ's Communist Party founded a division-sized unit and with this authorized the formation of the third layer to Giáp's armed forces. This change from independent companies to the three layers of the military did not happen overnight. This switch in policy just made official what had occurred naturally. It was around this structural change that the name Vietnamese People's Army (VNPA) first came about.

Giáp's armed forces now comprised: irregular forces, predominantly guerrilla fighters operating at village and hamlet level; local regular forces within regular units and operating at district and provincial level; and a main regular army subordinate to zone authorities as well as to higher authorities and more like a traditional conventional force.

Divisions had been proposed before but Giáp had not been convinced; his forces had quite simply not been ready. At the beginning of the war he considered the 10th Inter-zone to be the best equipped but only 52 percent of their combatants actually had a rifle, whilst those without still used spears. Now, in 1949, his units were prepared; they had refined logistics, more in-depth training, and designed and manufactured sophisticated home-made weapons, such as bazookas. This first division was called the 308th Division, known as the Vanguard Division. Its commander and political commissar, Vương Thừa Vũ (1910–1980), was appointed in mid–1949. Once the weapons from China arrived other divisions formed in close succession.[24]

In mid–1950, Giáp told Hồ he had more than 160,000 troops in regular divisions and regiments with local regular forces accounting for an additional 45,000 men. French troop numbers may have matched those of the Việt Minh, but the French did not have the additional 2 million local guerrillas.[25]

Giáp's three-layered military was a defining moment in his career but he always stressed, "Guerrilla warfare is fundamental, mobile warfare is supplementary," mobile in this case referring to the main regular army. This phrase emphasized the importance of guerrilla fighters because they were the mainstay of his war without boundaries.

Beginning the Final Stage of the War

With the establishment of their first division, the Communist Party recognized that in 1949 they had the military power to move on to the final stage of their war. During the French War Giáp had both a private and a public way to describe the conflict. The private way came from Giáp himself and included his personal thoughts and his overall assessment of the current military and political circumstances. In his mind there were only two periods of combat. In the first period, his troops had to avoid a heavy blow from the enemy to preserve their strength. The second period would only be executed when the enemy had been bogged down through his war without boundaries, at which time he then planned to fight a decisive battle to end the war; the timing of which had to be kept secret so that even those closest to him did not know.

The public way came in the form of general guidelines from the Communist Party; to help both the military and the people understand that the war against the French had three stages. In stage one, the enemy was to use mobile troops to launch rapid large-scale operations and expand their zone of occupation. The Việt Minh would strive to slow down the French but at the same time preserve their strength by avoiding non-productive battles. In stage two, the French were to use sweeping operations and blockades as well as set up a puppet government to force the Việt Minh to surrender. Meanwhile, the Việt Minh would strengthen and expand their mobile guerrilla warfare strategy against the French and continue to mobilize the masses to fight an All-People's War. Again, the Việt Minh would avoid a crippling blow from the French to preserve their forces. Stage three would begin when the enemy was bogged down because they had been dragged into a war without boundaries and the Việt Minh had forged links with the Communist Bloc. The Việt Minh would then go on to wage the counter-offensive and the offensive until their strategic opportunity arrived to fight a decisive battle to end the war.

To advance on to stage three of the war, the Party chose to continue their Westward March. Giáp prepared the North-West Campaign in early 1950, his aim being to destroy part of the North-West Autonomous Zone to strengthen links with China.[26] When the fighting started, the Việt Minh made reasonable progress, taking out a string of French outposts and entrenched camps. The French pushed back robustly and brutal fighting ensued. The North-West Campaign had to be halted, temporarily Giáp thought, but in fact it was never resumed. Hồ returned from overseas in April 1950, after seeing Mao and Stalin, and on Chinese advice the direction of battle had to be changed; the ensuing battle was to be known as the Border Campaign.

The Border Campaign (16 September to 14 October) saw a new chapter in battle tactics, with some French historians going as far as saying that this was the first time that Europeans had been defeated in a land battle by Asians. For many years the French had wanted to draw the Việt Minh into a decisive set piece battle so they could destroy Giáp's army and achieve victory. So far they had failed. Now Giáp would grant them their wish but the set piece battle shoe would be on the other foot. Giáp planned the Border Campaign to be the largest coordinated operation ever launched by his main regular army because he now had sufficient forces to face the enemy the way he wanted and to win on his terms, if all went well. To aid him, he had both Chinese advisors and large quantities of weaponry from China.

The specific objective of the Border Campaign was to thrust northwards and open up access to the Communist Bloc by liberating Cao Bằng Province and unblocking Route 4. Although Việt Bắc Revolutionary Base included this province the French still had large, isolated, entrenched camps in the region. The French had kept a presence there to keep a buffer zone between Vietnam and communist China, hoping to stop supplies reaching Việt Bắc Revolutionary Base.

One of the biggest French camps was in the town of Cao Bằng. For this reason, the Chinese advisors said that this camp must be the main area of attack for any campaign. Giáp was uneasy; his forces had never attacked such a large stronghold and felt the operation might fail. Giáp wanted to strike Đông Khê, he knew the French were weaker there, but privately he did hold some reservations. Earlier that year Đặng Văn Việt and his unit had successfully attacked the post but later withdrew. On hearing about the attack, Giáp had been very irritated; the operation had not been officially authorized. Now he feared that the French had strengthened their position at Đông Khê, but on balance he knew that he could not take the risk of attacking Cao Bằng.

Giáp designed a four-phase plan to clear Cao Bằng Province. To open phase one of the campaign, Giáp insisted on attacking Đông Khê first; the only other time Giáp went against Chinese advice was at the Battle of Điện Biên Phủ. In the second phase of his plan, Giáp looked to create conditions to protect his own troops but annihilate or seriously cripple a high number of enemy units, forcing surviving soldiers to retreat. Giáp instructed his forces to attack enemy reinforcements sent from other camps to save Đông Khê, in a strategy he called, "Attacking a post and annihilating the reinforcements." In phase three he instructed his troops to assault Thất Khê, to draw away yet more French units from other camps as they tried to reinforce the area. Phase four was an attack on Cao Bằng Town, now less defended as a result of the other phases.

By adhering to his plan, Giáp won the Border Campaign and in doing so the Việt Minh now controlled two thirds of the Vietnam-China border, which ended "fighting under siege." According to Giáp, this siege had started in 1945, and described how the French Army had encircled the Việt Minh, hence the Việt Minh had limited openings to the Communist Bloc. Now, with their new troop capabilities, the Việt Minh had punched larger routes through to their socialist allies, potentially the whole of the Communist Bloc (right into Europe) could become their rear base area. Fighting under siege was a phrase used after the war to describe the Việt Minh's relationship with the Communist Bloc.

With greater access to the Communist Bloc and the French bogged down in a war without boundaries, Giáp concluded that his newly formed army was ready to accelerate the final stage of the war, the counter-offensive as well as the offensive.

Porters: Hồ's Worker Ants

With the Border Campaign period of change now completed, Hồ went back to address Giáp's Westward March. Previous operations into the North-West Autonomous

Zone had helped the Việt Minh penetrate the area, but they still had not gained enough influence there to get the locals to support large battles.

One significant reason why the Communist Party had lost the confidence of the ethnic minorities was explained to officials by one villager, "When the revolutionaries fight the French and win they then withdraw, leaving us vulnerable to reprisals." This statement showed Party members that it was imperative to set up the Revolutionary Infrastructure at all times. If they wanted to keep the villagers on their side, they must not cause serious resentment by leaving them to suffer the consequences of French retribution. Putting this infrastructure in place could be done either before or after military action.

Two of the men made responsible for freeing part of the North-West Autonomous Zone in Lai Châu Province and winning back the locals were Hoàng Đông Tùng and Nông Văn Lạc (1914–199?). Tùng was an experienced commander of armed propaganda, while Lạc had been Giáp's courier at the first battle of Phai Khắt. Giáp instructed them to agitate the masses and build networks from Lào Cai to Phong Thổ, Quỳnh Nhai and Sìn Hồ. Tùng agreed to move westwards to construct the new courier corridors, which would then allow the military to enter the area and if necessary sweep the French out. Lạc arranged to follow on after the military to form the Revolutionary Infrastructure.

This task delighted Lạc because he had read in the works of Phan Bội Châu that early resistance fighters had used roads running through Lai Châu to get to Thailand. Lạc now saw his work as an integral part of this historic struggle. Villagers sent to help Lạc lived in the provinces of Cao Bằng and Bắc Kạn and had a contrary view; they were highlanders terrified of fast-flowing rivers, dreaded mosquitoes, terrestrial leeches, unclean water and vampires. They lived by the general understanding, "If ten men go to Lai Châu only one will come back."

Men such as Tùng and Lạc helped to successfully stabilize the North-West Autonomous Zone and in doing so win the locals over to build a strong porter base. Recruits were mainly females from local ethnic groups, as the men invariably made up the local guerrillas; both were indoctrinated into the ways of the revolution through nationalist talk. During major battles their tasks covered carrying food and military supplies to the front line, bring the wounded back to medical posts and engaging in road building and repairs if damaged by an attack.

The porters had to be discreet. They used a Hoàng Cầm cooking fire, named after the chef who came up with the concept in the early 1950s. He had found a way of dispersing the smoke so the user would not be discovered by the enemy. Việt Minh officials also instructed the porters that, when they resumed their march after sitting down, they had to straighten out the grass that they had just sat on. They even went as far as to weave the branches of trees together over their chosen routes to hide the people from the air.

Even so, there were telltale signs of Việt Minh activity to the highly trained eye. Prior to an attack, villages in the area were deserted, first by the adolescents and men, then by the women and children. The local tribesmen who served as agents for the French ceased to report in, sending their wives on their behalf to make excuses for their absence. Often the French ignored these signs. This meant that the first indication of an attack should have been thousands of Giáp's porters marching like worker ants towards an enemy camp, but because of their subtle ways and tribal instincts, the first inkling for the French was usually a barrage of mortar shells landing on their position. Thanks to

Many of the ethnic groups living within the location of the Westward March were animist and still are today. This is a bamboo blessing to appease the spirits, so that the owner of the paddy field can look forward to a good harvest (Clive A. Hills).

the work of men such as Lạc and Tùng, Giáp had porters to serve his army during larger battles.

Restructuring the Communist Party

To give the revolutionaries greater administrative control, in parallel with the military changes, the Indochinese Communist Party restructured. In 1951, representatives from Vietnam, Lao and Cambodia held the Second Congress. The main purpose was a vote to dissolve the Indochinese Communist Party and in its place have separate groups for Vietnam, Lao and Cambodia. Prior to this change, the Indochinese Communist Party led the revolutionary movement, controlled mainly by the Vietnamese. Now, the revolution of each country would be under the autonomous command of its own communist party. The Vietnamese called their group the Worker's Party of Vietnam, which became overt for the first time, but only in liberated areas. Its mandate was to complete the war of liberation and advance politically towards socialism in Vietnam.

With the new parties formed, Giáp needed to maintain cooperation between the three countries. He had already established military linked fronts, including various inter-zones with Lao, and north-western Cochinchina with north-eastern Cambodia, and he did not want these weakened in any way. Members present at the Second Congress recognized the importance of political and military ties and on 11 March 1951, the Front of Solidarity of the Viet-Cambodian-Lao Alliance formed and members scheduled a conference involving all three countries for September 1952.

The French Push Back

On the French side, in December 1950, General Jean de Lattre de Tassigny (1889–1952) became high commissioner and commander in chief of the French Far East Expeditionary Corps. He had been brought into Vietnam to boost morale after a French defeat at the hands of the Việt Minh during their Border Campaign, which he had done soon after arriving, but also to establish a way forward to find a quick solution to the war.

To achieve these objectives, he had decided on two new approaches. In the first instance General de Lattre built a defense line of bunkers surrounding the Red River Delta to prevent the Việt Minh from re-entering the area once expelled. This would be known as the *De Lattre* Line. His second approach was the "yellowing process" known as the *jaunissement* program or Vietnamization of the war. He believed that the country's own citizens should shoulder the burden of the fighting and play their part in stopping the spread of communism.

Vietnamization led to the creation of a Vietnamese National Army; an easier way to boost troop numbers than asking politicians for the high numbers actually needed.[27] Soldiers of the National Army were much better than the French in pacification; being Vietnamese, they knew the terrain, they had friends and relations within the local populations, they understood how to communicate in different dialects and how to approach tribal customs. This life experience helped them to distinguish between the covert revolutionaries, guerrillas and the ordinary citizens. Clearly, the communists soon worked out highly effective ways of manipulating the National Army, including planting agents in their ranks to sabotage operations against the Việt Minh.

In addition to those two measures, the French designed a counter-guerrilla unit under the cover name *Groupement de Commandos Mixte Aéroportés* (GCMA). This group created a series of fighting units known as *maquis*; each comprised up to 3,000 trained partisans tasked with eliminating the Việt Minh.[28] To form these units, small detachments of partisans were deployed into regions, each with an officer or representative from the French forces. Here they trained locals in guerrilla warfare, radio techniques and basic field intelligence gathering. This work was hazardous because they often deployed deep behind Việt Minh lines and had to live with the ethnic minorities.

General de Lattre produced respectable results, but his time in Vietnam ended abruptly. Just days after awarding his only son his second *Croix de guerre* for valor for his action during the Hà Nam Ninh Campaign, his son died near Ninh Bình. General de Lattre flew back to France in 1951 with his son's body and handed over temporary provisional power of commander in chief to General Raoul Albin Louis Salan (1899–1984). On his return to Vietnam, de Lattre was struck by another tragedy. In late 1951, a doctor diagnosed him with cancer and he left for France. General de Lattre died shortly after.

In January 1952, Salan officially became commander in chief. Hồ and Giáp knew him well, Hồ in the early days even referring to him as "friend." Now on taking this position, Salan was the enemy, facing the next stage of their Westward March.

Confronting New Battlefield Situations

The first major test for Salan was Giáp's North-West Campaign (14 October to 10 December 1952). Including the Border Campaign, this would be the sixth confrontation where the Việt Minh used their main regular army against French troops, and Giáp designed it by drawing upon battle-tested knowledge gained from these other conventional clashes.[29]

The North-West Campaign intended to destroy the French within the North-West Autonomous Zone, primarily so that by 1953 Giáp could then move his troops to the middle and lower regions of Lao. He targeted the provinces of Yên Bái, Lào Cai, Sơn La and Lai Châu; not ideal locations for a large confrontation because the terrain would hinder troop movements and the area was very sparsely populated. Nevertheless, a decision was made to conduct the campaign but there would be two substantial lessons learned: logistics and Salan's new camp design.

To supply the campaign, the Việt Minh recruited thousands of porters. They were given the daunting task of transporting an estimated 120 tons of weapons and ammunition, as well as moving medicine and medical instruments for taking care of a predicted 5,000 wounded soldiers. They also had to carry food to the stores, which were designed to hold 9,000 tons because the villages could not supply such quantities; a vast tonnage when considering that each porter ate on average 92 percent of the food they carried, even though their daily rations were small. This horrific walk to the front had been calculated to be 200–300km in length, longer than those for the Hòa Bình Campaign that finished earlier in 1952.

The opening move of the North-West Campaign destroyed one of the four sub-zones of the North-West Autonomous Zone called Nghĩa Lộ. With this swift success came supply problems; the lines now stretched hundreds of kilometers further than originally calculated. The soldiers in these far-reaching areas lacked their staple diet of rice. Of the 15 tons of rice needed a day, only 6 or 7 tons got through. To avoid the army starving, officials authorized a temporary cessation of all military activities to allow combatants to devote their time to the transportation of rice. It was at this time that a porter named Thanh Hóa came up with the idea of using a "pack bicycle" instead of a shoulder pole: each porter could now carry ten times more goods.

The North-West Campaign not only highlighted logistics issues, but it was the first time that the Việt Minh came across General Salan's new layout of a military camp. Following a sudden and savage surprise attack by the Việt Minh on Nghĩa Lộ, some French forces withdrew to Nà Sản, which had an airstrip protected by military units. When the French forces retreated there, they constructed a large cluster of entrenched camps, connected by trenches and protected by massive firepower and minefields. This new defensive design became known as the "hedgehog," *le hérisson*, and was intended to provoke an enemy to make a frontal assault. The airstrip made the hedgehog an "air-land base," *base aéro-terrestre*, there to ensure regular supplies to the troops.

Where General de Lattre had his *De Lattre* Line, General Salan had his new base system. Both types of fortification gave French forces respite from Việt Minh hit-and-run attacks or walking into Việt Minh ambushes. Nevertheless, Salan's fortification was

Opposite: The author climbing a bamboo ladder in the late 1990s, just as the Việt Minh did, to ascend the limestone karsts in the Westward region (Clive A. Hills).

far less expensive, more flexible and could be constructed in the middle of the very terrain where their enemy felt most comfortable fighting: the forest and mountains.

With the North-West Campaign coming to a close, the Việt Minh controlled all of Sơn La Province, apart from Nà Sản. Giáp made the decision to destroy this last French-held position, but, after days of fighting, most of the assaults upon Nà Sản were unsuccessful and he called off further attacks. On summing up the battle, Giáp noted that the failure to overrun the base could have been because his soldiers were tired or because the units were no longer properly organized due to weeks of fighting. None of this really explained the disastrous outcome of the fighting at Nà Sản.

Giáp believed that the only possible justification was that the French hedgehog was a new defensive class and, because his units had not come across such an outpost before, they simply did not know how to destroy it. He noted that with the cluster of entrenched camps, the French could exploit the fact that it was impossible for the Việt Minh to maintain a great number of combatants in the mountain and forest areas for a long time, because of the eventual shortage of food and limited means of transport. The enemy had only to wait for the Việt Minh to withdrawal and then move from their cluster of entrenched camps to reoccupy the posts the revolutionaries had just left.[30] The cluster of entrenched camps had become a new challenge for the advance of Giáp's army.

At the end of February 1953, the General Staff assembled revolutionaries for a conference to resolve the problem of logistics and to analyze how their troops could attack this new camp arrangement. Those present noted first that to tackle logistics issues, roads had to be repaired or new ones constructed through the North-West Autonomous Zone so that the majority of food, armaments, medicine and soldiers could be taken by truck, at least part of the way. Then they discussed how to attack a big cluster of entrenched camps such as Nà Sản, and concluded that Việt Minh forces had to be supported by weapons, such as anti-aircraft guns. With Soviet help, two new regiments formed, one equipped with howitzers and the other with large caliber 37mm anti-aircraft guns. With these improvements, Giáp could move larger troop formations deeper into the forested mountains of the north-west and upper Lao.

Giáp's Army Threatens Lao

Giáp explained to Hồ that for this next period he had to consolidate a number of guerrilla base areas in Lao into one large liberated zone to give the Lao resistance government their very own Việt Bắc Revolutionary Base. Hồ agreed and Giáp designed the Spring Summer Campaign as a joint Viet-Lao operation.

Giáp knew that he had to strike now. From intelligence gathered in the region of attack, he had been informed that at present 90 percent of enemy troops were weak and poorly trained Lao units, loyal to the Royal Lao government. Although, since the French had lost vital ground during the North-West Campaign, they had sent their own troops to positions in Lao: Xieng Khuang, namely the Plain of Jars, and Sam Neua. It was only a matter of time before the French sent others into Giáp's proposed attack zone.

For the Spring Summer Campaign Giáp planned to attack two regions. Sam Neua was the main target, coordinated with smaller sub-assaults in the direction of Điện Biên Phủ and Mộc Châu. The secondary target Giáp selected as Xieng Khuang. As most of the fighting occurred in Lao, the operation is sometimes known as the Sam Neua Campaign or the Upper Lao Campaign.

The Plain of Jars in Xieng Khuang Province, Lao. This region saw some of the fiercest fighting during the conflicts because of its strategic location between the caves in Vieng Sai and Vientiane, the capital of Lao (Clive A. Hills).

To supply the battles, the General Logistics Department constructed an impressive supply route. They set up a system of depots, wharfs and stations on a 600km route from Lạng Sơn to Sam Neua. They cleared rapids so that heavily laden boats could pass through safely. They assembled horses and porters, both walking and those pushing pack bicycles, to serve the pending battle. Never before had Giáp tried to transport so much food, armaments and fresh troops over such thickly forested mountains.

Although the French had reinforced Sam Neua, Giáp still viewed it as an essential target. The area had been made into a small cluster of entrenched camps, resulting in a small hedgehog design. He believed that by attacking this, his troops and logistics teams could gain first-hand experience in fighting such a configuration, so that in the future he could consider taking Nà Sản. Secrecy was paramount because had the French discovered his plan to attack Sam Neua they then could have reinforced it and made it into a large camp like Nà Sản, which Giáp was not yet ready or confident enough to take on. To divert attention away from Sam Neua, Giáp made Nà Sản a diversion instead as part of the smaller sub-assaults.

Hồ wrote to the combatants about to serve in the campaign, "This is the first time that you have to fulfil such an important and glorious task as this one: to help the people of our ally. Helping our friend is helping ourselves."[31]

The campaign went in the favor of the Việt Minh. They took Sam Neua Province and part of Xieng Khuang and Phongsaly, which enabled Giáp to establish a liberated zone for the Lao resistance.[32] The zone had good connections to the Communist Bloc as well as through the North-West Autonomous Zone to Việt Bắc Revolutionary Base. For

Giáp, now that his goal had been accomplished, he could use this liberated zone to continue his Westward March and swoop down on Cochinchina.

For General Salan, all his long-term planning and effective ideas to win back the initiative had reached an impasse in the eyes of some, leaving him open to criticism by the French government. They did not want a commander who planned to execute a long war. On the contrary, they wanted a swift dramatic victory on the battlefield. Salan was replaced by General Henri Navarre. His future was to be defined by the maelstrom of war; Điện Biên Phủ, a tipping point in colonial history that saw the French Empire begin to implode.

9

The Secrets Behind the Battle of Điện Biên Phủ

All Hopes on Navarre

In May 1953, the communists heard that Salan was to be replaced by General Henri Navarre (1898–1983) as commander in chief of the French Far East Expeditionary Corps. On his arrival in Vietnam, Navarre must have felt confident, partly because the Americans backed the conflict handsomely; their military aid equivalent to more than 70 percent of the cost of the war. From a personal point of view, Navarre was an experienced decorated general, who believed that he could design a military plan to produce a favorable outcome for the military and bureaucrats, and be politically acceptable to the people of France.

Navarre faced conflicting messages. In Indochina, the French Far East Expeditionary Corps had been fighting for years with little possibility of an end in sight. No military fronts seemed to exist. Its units were overstretched. No progress could be measured. However, on the home front, although he had been ordered to create conditions to enable the French government to negotiate an honorable solution, in some instances individual politicians forced their political needs upon him to deny him the freedom to do this. Navarre needed troops, but these politicians knew that they could not authorize the very high numbers needed to end the deadlock and crush Giáp's army; the war was so unpopular it would be political suicide to do so.

With an impasse on both the battlefield and political front, documents relating to the desired honorable solution concept were tabled at a meeting in Paris in July 1953. These documents eventually formed the so-called Navarre Plan and covered future military actions and operations intended for 1953–1954, which were broken down into two major phases.

In phase one, in the south, units would carry out pacification missions, consolidate bases and positions, and implement a strategic offensive in order to occupy the southern delta provinces. In the north, units had to maintain a strategic defensive position and avoid any large-scale confrontations with the Việt Minh; to protect the region Navarre placed a large mobile quick reaction force in the northern delta. Furthermore, in phase one, the French intended to develop the Vietnamese National Army across Vietnam and train the recruits to take over static defense duties and local security roles. By replacing French units bogged down in these roles, Navarre could then add these to any fresh reserves the French government agreed to send from bases outside

Vietnam. This new pool of troops would then be used to strengthen his existing mobile units or form other new large mobile quick reaction forces.

In phase two, these now freed up French forces could then strike Giáp's main regular army in North Vietnam. Navarre aimed to thrust directly into the Việt Minh's rear base area; his desired target was Việt Bắc Revolutionary Base. If this strategy worked, and if a great military campaign triumph against North Vietnam actually materialized, Navarre would regain the initiative both on the battlefield and at any negotiations.

In principle, the Navarre Plan looked forward-thinking and achievable, but Navarre had expressed some unease about how to protect Lao. His well-voiced concerns were heard at the Paris meeting, and although a high-priority matter, members then issued no instructions as to how Lao could be dealt with effectively. This dithering is surprising because those involved with the Navarre Plan knew about French-Lao negotiations for peace.

Indeed, on 22 October 1953, Lao signed a Franco-Lao Treaty of Amity and Association. This finally transferred all residual French powers, except control of military affairs, to the Royal Lao government and completed their independence, albeit within the French Union.[1] The public signing of the Lao pact expressed the conviction of the French authorities that Lao now had to be defended at all costs; to do otherwise would signal to other nations that France did not take its responsibilities as head of their union seriously.

This clear message from the French to the world was needed because they hoped to sign a similar treaty with the pro–French governments of both Cambodia and Vietnam if the outcome of the Navarre Plan proved successful. It is difficult to know whether it was pure naivety or arrogance, but the indecision in Paris over how to protect Lao and the presumption that the Việt Minh would still allow independence under the French Union after years of bloody war were serious failures of judgment that proved very costly.

Westward to Điện Biên Phủ

Navarre's biggest challenge would be the Việt Minh's Winter Spring Campaign of 1953–1954. This campaign was the first time that the Việt Minh had developed such a large-scale coordinated strategy for all of Indochina.[2] Giáp and Hoàng Văn Thái designed a provisional military strategy for this in August 1953 with four clear aims: to step up guerrilla pressure on the rear base areas of the French to foil their attempts to expand their Vietnamese forces; to instruct the main regular army to destroy the French Army; to expand Việt Minh unit numbers in Việt Bắc Revolutionary Base; and to increase activities in the north-west of Vietnam, upper Lao and other locations to disperse the enemy's mobile forces and destroy French troop concentrations in the Red River Delta.

In September, Russian intelligence secured a copy of the Navarre Plan, complete with maps. From this, Giáp further refined his plans for the Winter Spring Campaign. The overarching concept remained that this would be a joint Viet-Lao operation with multiple battlefields. Giáp selected Lai Châu Province as the main direction; the French had only 2,000 soldiers in the area, and by eliminating these, the North-West Autonomous Zone would be liberated. The other directions were upper Lao, central Lao, southern Lao and the Central Highlands in Vietnam. In the south of Vietnam he planned to use guerrilla warfare to destroy French forces whenever they transferred their mobile units to the region.

In November, new intelligence came in that saw further changes to Giáp's campaign strategies. On 19 November, staff at Giáp's headquarters organized a conference for commanders of regimental rank upward to evaluate the implementation of military diversionary battles for the Winter Spring Campaign. Held in Đồng Đau Hamlet, Định Hóa District, during this conference delegates received a telegram from a Việt Minh unit preparing for battle within the north-west. It stated that they had just seen French reconnaissance planes circling over Điện Biên Phủ. On the morning of the second day of the conference, scouts in Phú Thọ Province reported seeing many airplanes, including transport aircraft, flying towards the north-west. Giáp had also received further news on the night of 20 November that a number of French parachute battalions had captured Điện Biên Phủ. Just as Hồ and Giáp predicted, the final confrontation to change the direction of the war looked to be in the north-west of Vietnam. Delegates went from discussing diversionary battles to finalizing the main directions of the Winter Spring Campaign.

After further intelligence gathering, on 6 December the Politburo formally decided that Điện Biên Phủ would be the primary north-west battlefield of the Winter Spring Campaign. First their units would take Lai Châu Town and, once Điện Biên Phủ had been struck, they could advance on into upper Lao to threaten Luang Prabang.

From a French perspective, it is now known that an operation at Điện Biên Phủ had been mentioned at the Paris meeting in July 1953, but only in passing, and so it was not

Luang Prabang was one of three kingdoms formed in the eighteenth century from Lan Xang. When the French reunited the three kingdoms the region was known as the Kingdom of Lao; Luang Prabang being the royal capital. Savang Vatthana served as its last king because he was forced to abdicate when the country fell to the communists in 1975; thus ending a 600-year-old monarchy. Today, Luang Prabang is still referred to as the royal capital. Photographed in the late 1990s (Clive A. Hills).

part of the original Navarre Plan. Failure to have included an operation at Điện Biên Phủ was not an oversight. In Navarre's mind, a heavily defended camp on the initial scale of action proposed in the region lay entirely within his sphere of decision-making.[3]

In late 1953, Navarre ordered Điện Biên Phủ to be occupied, against advice from some senior military officials who thought that the position was just too isolated. Others did endorse Navarre's actions, but what he wanted and what some of his supporters envisaged differed. Navarre did not actually want a major battle at Điện Biên Phủ and they did.

Navarre soon came under increasing pressure to defend the north-west of Vietnam and upper Lao. Finally, he made a decision to defend these two regions and agreed to locate the core of his forces at Điện Biên Phủ. On 20 November, airdrops under Operation Castor facilitated in the construction of a French air-land hedgehog base at Điện Biên Phủ. This base design needed to be considerably larger than the one established at Nà Sản. Navarre stated, "It must be held at all costs." He wanted to "lock the door to Lao" and block Việt Minh forces from reaching Luang Prabang.

Navarre went on to say that Điện Biên Phủ had to become a "boil gathering pus" in the north to draw Việt Minh troops away from other parts of Vietnam and give him a free hand to open an offensive. The offensive Navarre referred to was Operation Atlante, a six-month campaign to be launched on 20 January 1954 in the swampy inlets between Đà Nẵng and Nha Trang. The central initiative of the Navarre Plan, it aimed to flush out 30,000 Việt Minh troops thought to be among the local population.

Both Operation Atlante and a battle at Điện Biên Phủ, in isolation, were not expected to produce total victory. Nevertheless, Navarre hoped that by 1955 French fortunes could be reversed, so putting them in a very much stronger negotiating position and allowing them to see the war end on their own terms.

At the end of November 1953, Việt Minh troops left for their Winter Spring Campaign. By mid–December, the capital of Lai Châu Province was in their hands. This had been the seat of government for the whole of the Tai Federation and, fearing that the Việt Minh might overrun the area, the French had already evacuated their troops and the government of the Federation to Điện Biên Phủ. This evacuation had been recorded by Việt Minh intelligence and showed Giáp that the French planned to establish a large, permanent and heavily fortified camp at Điện Biên Phủ.

Although opposing Operation Atlante was clearly an important part of the Winter Spring Campaign, in late December, Giáp chose Điện Biên Phủ for the decisive battle. On 5 January 1954, Giáp and Việt Minh units marched west for the front with General Wei Guoqing, the head of the delegation of Chinese advisors.

Giáp's Hardest Decision

One of the most hotly debated questions about the Battle of Điện Biên Phủ is why Giáp changed the carefully planned battle tactics originally based upon the Chinese "Fast Strike, Fast Victory" model to his "Steady Fight, Steady Advance" strategy just hours before the operation.

Nghĩa, the head of the Intelligence Department, started:

> For me, what played a crucial part in Brother Giáp changing his mind at the Battle of Điện Biên Phủ was both political and military intelligence.... But there were many other important factors at this time which led to our victory, one being the Navarre Plan itself and French countermeasures to our actions.

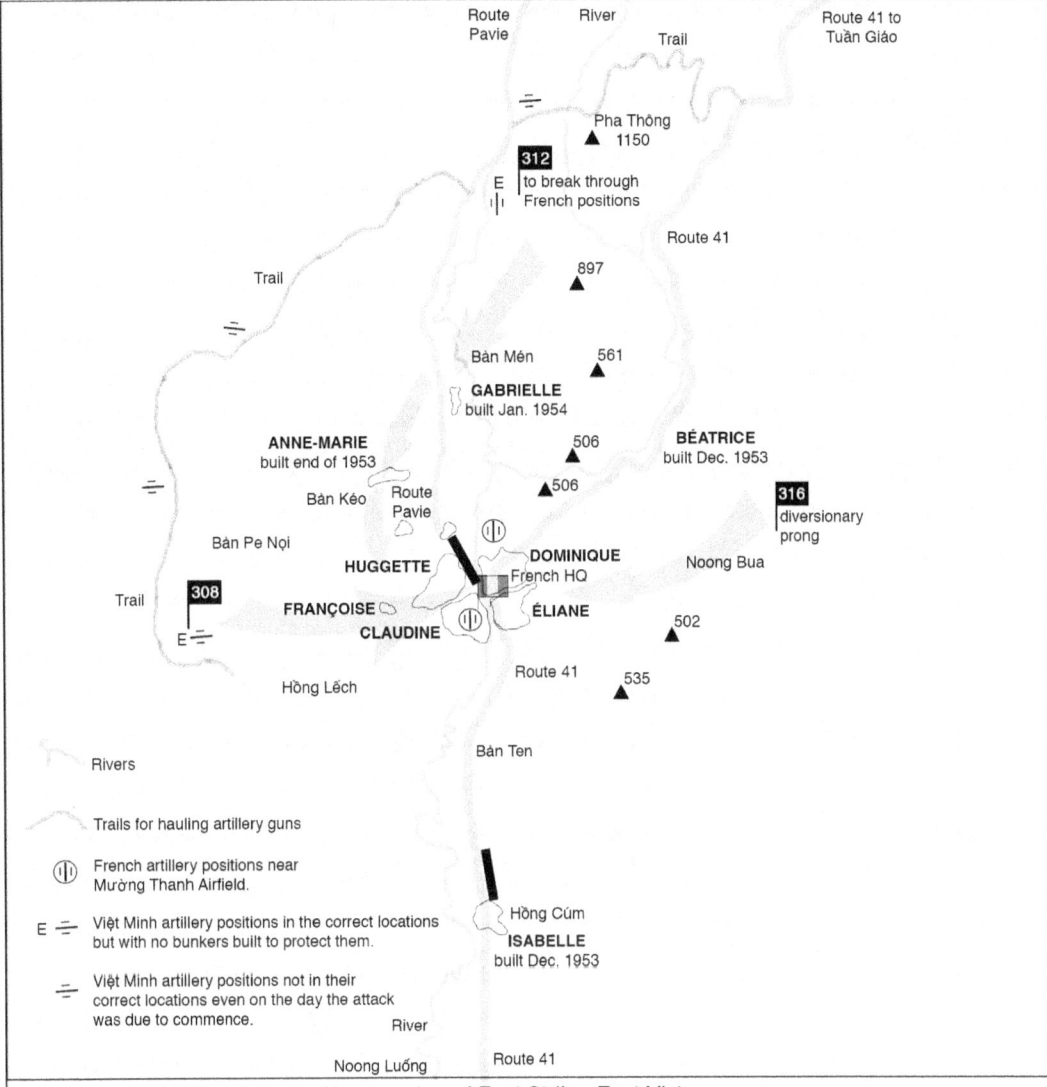

Key reasons for canceling the Chinese plan of Fast Strike, Fast Victory.

1) The French had sufficient time to fortify their positions and the Fast Strike, Fast Victory was not designed for such a situation.
2) The 312th Division had to break through three French fortified positions, and on 23 January, its commander Lê Trọng Tấn expressed concern that his units did not have the strength to do this.
3) In late January, Việt Minh intelligence radio operators had intercepted messages that said Boucher de Crèvecoeur had instructed his units to move on the 308th Division, the Việt Minh's main prong. The intelligence said that on 23 January, he would send a battalion of French paratroopers to drop into their strike zone, with other French troops leaving from Sop Nao, Lao, to attack the 308th Division from behind.
4) When the Fast Strike, Fast Victory was designed, French forces numbered six battalions, just prior to the start date they had ten battalions.
5) The Vietnamese troops had to haul their artillery in by foot, and on 23 January, the units doing this work had stated that they were not ready; they did not have time to build bunkers for their guns and other guns were still too far from their designated firing positions.

Key benefits of Võ Nguyên Giáp's philosophy of Steady Fight, Steady Advance.

1) Việt Minh engineers would have time to build roads so that trucks and soldiers could move the guns into position and then build camouflage bunkers for them.
2) The 308th Division would thrust to Luang Prabang, Lao, so that the French would think that the Việt Minh had abandoned Điện Biên Phủ as the main area of attack.

The informtion for this map and Võ Nguyên Giáp's "hardest decision," was given to the author by Lê Trọng Nghĩa on 26 February 2008; it was first published by the author for a presentation at the National Army Museum, London, on 20 March 2014.

Battle of Điện Biên Phủ 1954, the canceled Fast Strike, Fast Victory battle plan.

> We were due to open the battle at 5 p.m. on 25 January and to finish it three nights and two days later, but this start date was delayed to 26 January because on 21 January our intelligence service had secured important information, this being that the enemy had thoroughly grasped our plans. We worked all hours on the 22 to confirm this.[4] It was not until the morning of 23 January that I was able to report this information to Brother Giáp. Shocking, the enemy knew every detail.[5]

The French did have excellent intelligence on Việt Minh movements, which came from a number of sources such as the external military intelligence agency and French paratroopers.[6] These services had carried out operations to intercept and prevent Việt Minh lines of communications and track their formations as they advanced on Điện Biên Phủ. Other intelligence was thought to have been extracted by the French from a soldier captured in late January from the 308th Division. Intelligence operatives then relayed this to Điện Biên Phủ and its commander, Brigadier General Christian de Castries (1902–1991). Today it is known that the information that the French had gathered about Việt Minh plans predominantly came from the French intercepting several transmissions made by the Điện Biên Phủ Battlefront Logistics Department.

Nghĩa continued:

> During the battle we drew heavily on French-educated Vietnamese, who were fluent in French, understood regional French accents and had studied French military history.
>
> Thanks to this understanding, our intelligence service intercepted French radio communications, which had announced: the start date and time of our attack, the fact we might run out of rice and that the French had designed very comprehensive countermeasures to stop our Fast Strike, Fast Victory assault against Điện Biên Phủ. When I told Brother Giáp of the intelligence, he could not comprehend it straight away.
>
> To understand how I had drawn my conclusions, Brother Giáp came to my headquarters. Here he not only met the officers but also the actual operators who had intercepted the French radio messages and collected the data that informed us that they knew our plans. When he met with the various operatives, including me, Giáp instructed us to check our information again, directly. He even checked it for himself, every telegram and radio message. He then asked them to explain to him how they had come to such a conclusion. Brother Giáp sent me to the front line to see if there was any evidence to be seen on the battlefield of what they had intercepted via the radio traffic. There was, I could see French paratroopers descending, as predicted, into the strict zone of the 308th.
>
> Radio interception was only one part of our intelligence work. Officers could only come to such a conclusion after considering many sources. Our other two main sources were our units who had encircled the enemy's camp and our reconnaissance teams. However, we had also captured documents and gained information from last-minute defectors and spies within French ranks. These people had told us of the initial parachute drops at Điện Biên Phủ and the camp arrangements. Notwithstanding this, our strongest evidence came from the telegrams that our radio operators had intercepted.
>
> I knew what strain Brother Giáp was under. Frequently at that time I had to report to him because I analyzed data at a strategic level, as the head of the Intelligence Department. The deputy head of the Intelligence Department was Cao Pha. He did not have to report to Giáp so often because he conducted reconnaissance work, so was always with an advanced unit, and at that time he had left for the front with one of our divisions.
>
> Brother Giáp had to be very diplomatic and think extremely fast with all this new information coming. In combat all information is sensitive but intelligence information is particularly so. Sharing it compromises the identity of sources. He instructed me not to circulate it to anyone, especially not to leak it to the Chinese advisors, who would not have approved of elitist French speaking Vietnamese working with us. I had to keep it secret unless he instructed otherwise.[7]

With the French undermining the Fast Strike, Fast Victory plans, by late afternoon on 25 January Giáp had convinced all the decision makers to delay the action for twenty-four hours.

There were many general reasons why Giáp delayed the battle, these included: the fast strike plan required an assault to occur during the day across a broad plain, which his army had not been trained to do; they had not been trained to fight such a long battle; his army did not have the capabilities to attack more than one stronghold position at any one time; his soldiers were not as well trained as they needed to be when combining artillery and infantry, in order to attack behind a creeping barrage of artillery fire; the number of artillery guns and shells were limited for such an attack and Giáp was unclear whether his three divisions could destroy the French, who had unlimited air power and cover from artillery. Giáp equally saw that as the planned coordinated battles in the other areas of the country had not yet begun, Navarre's mobile forces had not yet been dispersed thinly across Vietnam. The effect of this last point meant that Navarre could use these forces to counter-attack the Việt Minh at Điện Biên Phủ. With all this in mind, the simple fact was that the food could run out.

In addition to the general points there were five specific reasons for postponing the attack. In the first instance, from the time that French airborne forces first descended by parachute onto the drop zones at Điện Biên Phủ, to the proposed Việt Minh attack date, the French had fortified their positions and expanded the camp. If the Việt Minh had actually struck with sufficient troops in 1953, then they would probably have been victorious, because the fast strike plan was far better at overwhelming temporary enemy bases.

The next three points covered: as a result of additional French fortifications and camp expansion, the Việt Minh's 312th Division would now find it impossible to break through the three fortified positions originally designated to them; Việt Minh reconnaissance teams had seen French troops moving from Sop Nao and Việt Minh intelligence could only conclude that they had left Sop Nao to strike the rear units of the elite 308th Division, which was positioned to assault and overrun Castries' headquarters; and the French forces had now increased their strength from an initial six battalions in November to ten, with tank support to back them up, and although Nghĩa had known of the increase from six to nine battalions he only gathered intelligence on that tenth battalion on 23–24 January.

The fifth point was, because Việt Minh troops had to haul their artillery by foot into positions around the French camp, they had not had time to build gun emplacements or bunkers in which to conceal themselves and their guns from ground and air attack. They were also too far from their ideal firing

An ethnic Akha girl carrying forest products in the late 1990s. Her forefathers would have carried supplies as porters for the Việt Minh in exactly the same way; others pushed pack bicycles laden with supplies (Clive A. Hills).

positions to be effective. This final point was extremely important because if Giáp stopped the attack he needed a clear reason that did not depend on evidence from the Intelligence Department.

Nghĩa explained the diplomacy behind the change of battle plans:

> We were all in place. At their fighting stations were all our key combat officers such as Deputy Chief of General Staff Hoàng Văn Thái, his staff and the staff of the Chinese advisors. In the Front Command Base, presently in an area that belonged to Nà Tấu Village, there was only Giáp as commander of the Battle of Điện Biên Phủ and concurrently the general secretary of the Front Party Committee for the Battle, Trần Văn Quang as the head of the Combat Operations Department, officers from the Political Department, and me.
>
> Releasing this new sensitive information so late was dangerous for me. Our battlefield regulations state that once a combat plan has been made anyone trying to change it questioned a military order, a decision made by the commander in chief, so would be executed. This action is part of Asian history. Traditionally, before an emperor or general went to war, anyone who tried to advise against the action was beheaded, in a ceremony called "Washing the Knife with Blood" to bring luck in the forthcoming battle.
>
> It was 24 January when Brother Giáp summoned Việt Minh officers of the Front Party Committee for an important meeting. The telegram that requested their presence said that they had to come back to the Front Command Base to finalize the fast strike plan. It was written like this so that French intelligence would not notice any changes in circumstances. If they had done so they might have tried to bomb our retreating forces. As a member of the Front Party Committee, Hoàng Văn Thái had been recalled. He had found this message difficult to understand; as chief of staff for the battle he should still be at his Front Headquarters. Hoàng Văn Thái did pull me aside at some point to ask me what was going on, as he was my direct boss, but I had been ordered to say nothing.
>
> Brother Giáp opened the meeting by proposing to postpone the offensive temporarily until 5 p.m. on 26 January. For security reasons he could not say why. The men in the room looked puzzled and did not want to do this. Although Giáp was the general secretary of the Front Party Committee, if he did not get a unanimous decision, the offensive would have to go ahead with the old plan.[8]

In accordance with Communist Party ruling, the Vietnamese were tied to levels of command, but on this occasion Hồ had told Giáp, just prior to him leaving for the front line, "Strike only if you are 100 percent sure of victory." Hồ believed that this gave Giáp the flexibility to achieve victory as he thought possible, when the front line action had been assessed. Hồ's proviso to Giáp; he could only change the plans if all members of the collective leadership on the front line agreed. Fortunately, that January, after much unease, those present did approve the change, although sensitive information had been withheld.

Nghĩa carried on:

> Later on 24 January, Brother Giáp had to persuade the Chinese to halt the battle. Giáp went to see Wei Guoqing, who agreed with Giáp and promised to persuade the other Chinese advisors to accept. They only did so just hours before 5 p.m. on 25 January.
>
> The following day, on 26 January, Giáp went to see Wei Guoqing again and said that they should return to Steady Fight, Steady Advance. Giáp had been weighing up this decision all night. After just a few minutes listening to the reasons, Wei Guoqing said to Giáp that he agreed and that he would get the others to follow.[9]

Guoqing had accepted the change because from 23 January he had kept close watch on Giáp, being the only advisor in his headquarters, he had previously discussed possible battle plan difficulties with him. Guoqing had also reported his apprehension to his superiors in Beijing, about the artillery not being in position, but had said nothing to Giáp. Mei Jiasheng, the chief of staff of the Chinese advisors for the battle, had originally insisted that it could not be done because only the fast victory plan had been cleared by Beijing. He eventually agreed.

Nghĩa said:

> Later on 26 January, the Front Party Committee gathered. Giáp needed to get permission from them all too in order to halt the battle, withdraw and create new tactics to secure victory. Most were reluctant at first, but they knew that with the fast plan they could not give a 100 percent guarantee of victory. Agreement was finally reached at 11 a.m.
>
> The sequence of events was important: first pause so that agreement could be obtained from both the Chinese and the Vietnamese, then look for a united agreement to withdraw and then to draw up a new battle plan. This combination meant that the Chinese advisors did not lose face as they were not put under undue pressure to go against the Beijing authorities. [Although Giáp had been given the authority by Hồ to change his battle plans, the Chinese advisors had not. Any change should have been cleared with Beijing, but there was just no time].
>
> To keep our plans secret, and to stop the French attacking our withdrawing troops, on 26 January, Giáp decided he had to confuse the French. He ordered the 308th Division to slip away from Điện Biên Phủ and to conceal themselves in the jungles of Lao. At the same time he instructed a unit to Mộc Châu District. He asked them to radio in and pretend to be the 308th withdrawing to the Red River Delta. Once satisfied that this operation had run smoothly, he ordered the 308th to make it known to the French that they were moving on the Royal Capital of Lao, Luang Prabang. Giáp hoped that because the 308th was our elite soldiers, the enemy would presume that wherever they were, that location was our main front.
>
> By threatening Luang Prabang, Giáp calculated that the French would think that we had abandoned our plans to attack Điện Biên Phủ, just as we were obliged to against Nà Sản. However, we did not want the French then to withdraw to Nà Sản from Điện Biên Phủ because we still wanted to destroy them there. Hence, Giáp authorized large assaults on Điện Biên Phủ, leading up to our new start date in March. These assaults worked; the French stayed at Điện Biên Phủ but no doubt the French always contemplated whether they should stay, withdraw or chase our troops to Luang Prabang. The French did not know what was what![10]

Giáp's ability to understand failings and learn from them made him stand above other generals. One defining campaign for Giáp was the battle in Đồng Mu, Cao Bằng Province, in February 1945. It was the first company-size attack against a French post but he failed to take it, due to poor intelligence. Out of the disaster came two lessons: keep intelligence fresh on an ever changing battlefield situation by always finding a way to carry out a last-minute reconnaissance mission, and if victory cannot be guaranteed, halt the attack even if it is just before the start time. Using these early failings, and a wealth of experience since, Giáp made the "hardest decision of his career" and changed his battle plan for Điện Biên Phủ.

Giáp's New Strategy

Giáp had spent the last few weeks contemplating a new start time and designing an alternative plan. For his start time, he kept firmly in his mind that he must try and avoid the harsh rainy season, which would not only severely hamper logistics operations but also challenge the fighting spirits of his units. To devise his new battle plan he drew on his experiences from campaigns and battles such as Sam Neua, Hòa Bình and Nà Sản, and combined this with the knowledge the Chinese had gained during the Korean War (1950–1953) and the Battle of Huai Hai, China.[11]

From this research, Giáp formulated his new plan. The original arrangement of Fast Strike, Fast Victory aimed to use all available power to thrust into the base's command center, like the point of a sword penetrating the enemy's heart. This fast surprise strike would create immediate confusion inside the base and, with other parallel thrusts designed to target the enemy's weak points, create confusion both inside and outside their perimeters.

The new Steady Fight, Steady Advance plan proposed to eat away at French-held ground and annihilate the fortified base gradually. Then, as the Việt Minh advanced towards the central area of the camp, they could ultimately gain control of the airstrip and start to suffocate the hedgehog camp configuration. To finish, after surrounding the central area, his troops could then conduct a coordinated general attack from many directions to finish off the enemy troops.

An important example of how the plans had improved included the supply of artillery to the front line; a major reason for halting the original battle. Giáp now instructed Đào Văn Trường, the acting commander of the 351st Engineer and Artillery Division, to have his engineers build camouflaged roads to allow trucks or porters to pull the artillery closer than before to enemy positions, as well as to move supplies to the front. The range of Việt Minh 105mm howitzers was 10km but in the end they hauled their guns to within only 2km of the French positions thanks to the new roads. One artillery officer recorded that he got his gun within 300m of Éliane 2. Moving the guns this close made it easier for the Việt Minh to observe the French, but similarly harder for French planes to attack them for fearing of dropping bombs on their own men.

Trường's brief from Giáp also incorporated artillery positions. Trường ordered that the guns be dispersed around the battle zone with their locations changing regularly, but their overall firepower must still be concentrated on the fixed French positions. This was a tactic the Việt Minh had learned from understanding what the Chinese went through during the Korean War.[12] Trường's location of the guns proved to be very well chosen. Once the siege had begun, the Việt Minh fired at the French supply aircraft when on the ground or landing and taking off, thereby starving the base of urgent equipment, ammunition and food. Likewise, the higher the troop numbers the French sent to reinforce the base, the more they lost to the devastating hail of incoming Vietnamese artillery rounds.

Other contributions to overall victory on the battlefield were made in political education and military proselytizing. Giáp placed great emphasis on the role of the political commissars as supervisory political officers responsible for political education. They targeted the troops and their civilian helpers to motivate them to fight for a socialist-nationalist victory, emphasizing that they must remain loyal to the government, be focused and disciplined, and must not desert or disobey orders. The slogan, Determined to Fight! Determined to Win! was embroidered into flags, and as the campaign accelerated they drove home the following motto, "Three Wells: eat well, sleep well and fight well."

Proselytizing, as an example, was used at the French positions of Anne Marie 1 and 2, enabling Giáp's 36th Regiment to take them without great opposition. To achieve this, agitators offered wounded French and North African prisoners their freedom if all troops abandoned Anne Marie. These prisoners had been taken from Béatrice and Gabrielle in March when these French positions had fallen. Also, for weeks prior to the event, the Việt Minh used loudspeakers and distributed pamphlets to the ethnic Tai at Anne Marie, calling on them to love their country, to not oppose the revolutionaries and return to their villages. This two-pronged approach worked. On 17 March, the Tai did indeed heed Việt Minh propaganda and left, running into the forest. Likewise, the command at Mường Thanh Airfield found it hard to dismiss the offer of having their wounded handed over, so accepted. Prior to handover, the revolutionaries had proselytized detainees, and now some worked for the Việt Minh.

Supply routes for the Battle of Điện Biên Phủ.

The French ability to oppose the siege and the Việt Minh's strength of attack determined the length of fight. Giáp presumed that the Battle of Điện Biên Phủ would be brutal and long.

A Story from the Battle

The Battle of Điện Biên Phủ started on 13 March at 5:05 p.m., with forty heavy Việt Minh weapons ranging from 75mm howitzers to 120mm mortars opening fire in unison. It was a ferocious, highly accurate, artillery barrage that took the French by utter surprise. Never before had the French been attacked in this way. Sergeant Kubiak, who survived the battle for outpost Béatrice, recounted the opening attack on 13 March, "Doomsday arrives all at once…. Béatrice seems to disappear leaving only dust. Rocks and dirt fly all about me. The Legionnaires collapse. Wounded and dead lie everywhere. We are all surprised and ask ourselves how the Viets have been able to find so many guns capable of producing an artillery fire of such power. Shells rain down on us without stopping, like a hailstorm on an autumn evening. Bunker after bunker, trench after trench, collapses, burying under them men and weapons."[13]

This barrage, combined with mass assaults on various French positions, went on for days. One by one, French strongholds fell to the Việt Minh, who used an elaborate web of trenches and underground shelters to move from one position to the next, and ever closer to the center of the camp.

Trường said:

> I would like to share with you one of my happy memories of this time. Our last assault began on 30 April. Two days before this, as commander of artillery, I had to supervise 75mm gun locations. I entered one of our sites located by Dominique 1, a French position which had been built just 200m from their central sub-sector. Our position belonged to Phùng Văn Khầu, a Nùng ethnic minority, who was the commander of the squad. When I arrived, there were just two of them alive, Khầu and a soldier. I first checked the decoy positions around the area, then I entered his post. As I was examining the guns, Comrade Khầu told me, "It's not necessary to use the reflector mirrors, just aim through the barrel." He did not say please, which initially surprised me, but Khầu was from an ethnic minority so not fluent in Vietnamese. I shut the gun cover and we stood observing the enemy camp ahead. Suddenly I heard from Khầu, "Commander, the enemy is raising the barrel—fire." The enemy was about to fire their round just where I stood. I obeyed the command and pulled the lanyard. The 75mm howitzer fired at the enemy position and the enemy artillery stayed silent.
>
> It seemed that a squad commander had given orders to the artillery commander. I was happy, not offended because, although a senior commander, I had had the opportunity to fire at the enemy as a soldier. Only in a revolutionary army could such an event happen without disciplinary consequence. The reason is comradeship for liberation.
>
> Two days before the end of Điện Biên Phủ, our missile battalion joined the battle. When we fired the missiles it puzzled the enemy. We listened into their radios and we overheard them saying, "The Soviet Union firepower has raised its voice. It's Katyusha." This is a multiple rocket launcher, which the enemy called "Stalin's organ," alluding to the sound of the weapon's rockets and visual resemblance of the launch array to a musical church organ. But we did not fire this massive weapon; what we had were BM-13 rocket launchers, made in Red China. This was small. So the enemy became more panic-stricken than they should have![14]

On 7 May, at 5:30 p.m., the 312th Division announced that they had arrested Castries. Although Colonel Pierre Langlais had replaced Castries as commander of Điện Biên Phủ on 24 March, Castries surrendered the forces. Above his French command post the Việt Minh raised a Determined to Fight! Determined to Win! flag. The cream of the French Far East Expeditionary Corps in Indochina had been wiped out. There were thousands of casualties and lives destroyed.

French Failings

The fall of Điện Biên Phủ was the turning point of the war but originally Navarre wanted to attack Việt Bắc Revolutionary Base to cut Việt Minh links with China. Yet after careful reassessment he concluded that his original plans had been too ambitious, he just did not have the military strength because he had not been sent the troops he had requested, so he turned his attention to the weaker north-west area.

Navarre had chosen to build the camp at Điện Biên Phủ to slow Việt Minh advances into Lao. He believed that if they gained control of the upper Mekong region, in unison with their fellow troops in the 5th Zone, they could cut Vietnam in two. Equally, if he lost control of all of Lao, the regions of Cambodia, Cochinchina and Annam might fall into their hands, seeing the French collapse and the spread of communism. He preferred Điện Biên Phủ to Lai Châu Town because it was encircled by rice fields, food the Việt Minh needed, and surrounded by impenetrable mountains; he believed that the Việt Minh could not thrust into Lao easily without controlling Điện Biên Phủ.

Taken at a celebration to mark the fifth anniversary of the Battle of Điện Biên Phủ. Phùng Văn Khâu, in uniform, meets with his former boss, Acting Commander of the 351st Engineer and Artillery Division Đào Văn Trường (courtesy Đào Văn Trường).

Alas, victory did not come, and Navarre is blamed for a catalogue of military and political events, some of which were out of his control. These included that René Cogny (1904–1968), who oversaw French efforts in the Red River Delta, had been instructed to get Castries prepared for First World War style trench warfare, even though both men had neither the specialists nor the necessary engineering equipment for that kind of battle. Likewise, although the hedgehog camp was strong, its design of encircling French troops behind barbed wire and minefields had weakened the capacity of thousands of elite mobile soldiers. Furthermore, both the Americans and French had hesitated about total military support at Điện Biên Phủ. Even though U.S. pilots had flown missions to support the camp, night bomber raids and Operation Vulture (which aimed to use small tactical atomic bombs) were rejected because it was thought that any major attack could lead to a massive assault on Vietnam by China.

For Giáp, Navarre made a strategic miscalculation. Cogny had been offered between three and five more battalions to support Điện Biên Phủ. He had turned down these troops because he did not want units taken away from the Red River Delta. Later, when Điện Biên Phủ fell into difficulty, Cogny and Navarre, his superior, started to argue over the disposition of forces between Điện Biên Phủ, Cogny's own sector, and Navarre's Operation Atlante. When Điện Biên Phủ unquestionably needed saving, Navarre had nothing in reserve. This is cited by Giáp as Navarre's biggest error.

Giáp's thinking concurred with Việt Minh veterans who fought at Điện Biên Phủ. They say that Navarre's main fault was not in choosing this area for a confrontation, but more that he had misjudged Việt Minh logistics capabilities, namely to build secret roads across remote mountainous areas and then for porters and trucks to carry the large amount of supplies and heavy guns the Việt Minh needed to fight a large extended battle. It was a fight that Navarre had not contemplated and so was unprepared for.[15] Failing to understand Việt Minh logistics capabilities could be the result of his intelligence not having been suitably updated since the Battle of Nà Sản. The French General Staff had concluded wrongly, "Việt Minh combat troops cannot operate for a long time in an area 180 kilometers from their own base, where food is scarce."[16]

Trường's French counterpart at Điện Biên Phủ was Lieutenant Colonel Charles Piroth (1906–1954). Trường had said that Piroth had miscalculated the Việt Minh's ability to move heavy weapons and then camouflage them so close to French positions without being compromised. Việt Minh guns had been dug into the hills with such care and intricate camouflage that almost no bush or tree had been disturbed around them. The real artillery pieces were interspersed with decoy emplacements that fired smoke bombs to draw French artillery fire away from the real guns. Thanks to Mother Nature, the flash of the gun and the smoke from the real Việt Minh guns were dispersed so fast by the wind that their location could not be pinpointed. In order to attack the few gun emplacements that were discovered, the French suffered heavy losses because their artillery pounded assumed positions, becoming targets themselves, and their air force had to fly directly into the barrels of anti-aircraft weapons. Wet jungle foliage made napalm worse than useless because under these conditions it produced massive billows of dark smoke, making it even more difficult for the French defenders to locate the Việt Minh. Lieutenant Colonel Piroth committed suicide in his bunker prior to the end of the battle; he had felt he had failed to provide adequate artillery support to the troops during the battle.[17]

Hồ's vision of a Westward March leading to Cochinchina had drawn Navarre to Điện Biên Phủ in his attempt to stop the communists' advance. This countermeasure to Việt Minh actions in Lao ended in French surrender because Navarre had underestimated Việt Minh capabilities and his Navarre Plan had soaked up the troop numbers needed to save the entrenched camp. Ironically, after all the dithering on how to protect Lao, in November 1953 French bureaucrats finally decided that this was not part of Navarre's responsibility. It was a decision delivered to him at the start of December, but by this time his military path had been set.

The Politics Behind the Battle

Not all of Hồ's allies wanted to see Giáp change from the Fast Strike, Fast Victory model to his Steady Fight, Steady Advance and see a final victory for the Việt Minh.

Nghĩa explained:

> At the end of 1953, to the beginning 1954, we can say that the Worker's Party of Vietnam and the Chinese Communist Party were unanimous in their decision to attack the large French encampment formation at Điện Biên Phủ. We can even say that there was joint agreement between Beijing and our

Politburo for using the Fast Strike, Fast Victory military tactic. However, as the battle start time loomed, the only people who wanted the Fast Strike, Fast Victory tactic were in fact the Chinese advisors. They still acted under instructions from Beijing and from our Politburo.[18]

Nghĩa had continued to say that there had been a lesser known story behind why China needed to persist with the Fast Strike, Fast Victory plan. The Chinese, like the Vietnamese, had fought for nearly a decade and during this time they had supplied advisors and material aid to Vietnam. The Chinese now viewed the battle as a great propaganda opportunity; a good way of getting a return on their investment "with interest." Unlike the Soviets, China had openly supported the war against the French and a fast successful outcome at Điện Biên Phủ would increase their status on the world stage because the outcome of the Korean War had damaged their international standing.

China needed the start date of the battle to remain the 25 January and a swift victory because on this date the Berlin Conference was to begin; assigned to run until mid–February 1954. The foreign ministers of the United States, Britain, France and the Soviet Union were to attend and agree to hold a wider international conference, subsequently in Geneva, to discuss Korea and the current Indochina War. The Chinese wanted to be invited to Berlin because if they had been at the negotiations and achieved a fast victory at Điện Biên Phủ they could influence the talks. Their attendance was something that the Soviets had supported, but the other participants did not. Needless to say, they did not attend and the fast strike plan was canceled anyway.[19]

Nghĩa went on to say that he believed that Điện Biên Phủ was the only time that the Chinese actually wanted a big victory for Vietnam, for reasons he had explained, but he did not think that they wanted it to be the final one. China viewed this war as a way of occupying and controlling Vietnam, something that they had wanted to do for a long time, and to achieve this they needed to get the Americans to take over from the French to continue the fight. Some evidence that China wanted to fight the Americans was observed during the Geneva Conference in 1954. At this meeting, China played down Việt Minh successes at Điện Biên Phủ in an attempt to suggest that the French were weak and that if the Americans had fought this battle then the outcome would have been so much different. It was a hint made easier because the Americans had made Vietnam part of their Cold War focus.

Nghĩa clarified:

> To prepare us for having to fight the Americans, the Chinese implied, and actually sometimes stated openly to us, that they wanted Vietnam to fight against the Americans for 100 years. This was then repeated to us throughout the [Vietnam War].[20]
>
> I believe that by getting us to fight the all-powerful Americans during the [Vietnam War], it meant that if the Big Rear base area [North Vietnam] failed to protect the Big Front [South Vietnam], then the Chinese would have a legitimate reason to personally step in to confront America in South Vietnam. To gain access to the South, the Chinese could enter the North; making Vietnam a vassal state of China. Therefore, when we finally took Saigon in 1975, the revolutionaries felt that China was generally unhappy with the end of the Vietnam War because it meant that Vietnam remained Vietnamese.
>
> For us things were more local. Victory at Điện Biên Phủ was vital, regardless if it were fast or not. We knew that if we did not win the revolution would be pushed back for decades because with such intense fighting the majority of our main regular army would be wiped out, taking us years to reestablish it.[21]

For Hồ, the Battle of Điện Biên Phủ held an additional meaning. For him, the Việt Minh had created a turning point in the war in their favor before the Americans became even more deeply involved in Indochina. This sent a strong message to political leaders that the Việt Minh could not be dismissed; they too had a place in the world, which they had the will and determination to fight for.

Peace at Hand

On 26 April 1954, in Geneva, a three-month conference opened to discuss outstanding issues over both Korea and Indochina. Deputy Prime Minister and Foreign Minister Phạm Văn Đồng represented the Democratic Republic of Vietnam; the other communist powers present were China and the Soviet Union. On the other side there was the United States, Britain, France and the French-backed governments of Vietnam, Lao and Cambodia. For Korea, the members present discussed how to settle remaining problems on the peninsula. With regards to Indochina, only after Điện Biên Phủ had fallen was the question raised of how to restore peace in the region.

The Việt Minh knew that they had to maintain military pressure on France. In Annam, they did this by aggressively counter-attacking the French campaign Operation Atlante, a position made easier because their intelligence agents had stolen the plans prior to the start date and the French were still unaware of this.[22] In Saigon, the revolutionaries made preparations to attack a massive arms dump in Phú Thọ Hòa. Organized over many years, it aimed to leave the French weaponry stores empty and unable to supply materials for more battles, a strategy that worked.[23]

During the conference, the Geneva Accords were finalized but the peace agreement did not give the communists an immediate victory or control of Vietnam, Lao and Cambodia as it is believed by some that it should have. The Accords took into account Soviet, Chinese and American interests because the conflict had been dragged into the wider Cold War. One key point agreed at Geneva resulted in Vietnam being divided into two sections at the 17th Parallel, with this division forming a Demilitarized Zone (DMZ). It was planned to unite these two regions through popular elections, to take place two years later. The northern zone above the 17th Parallel was to be governed by the Việt Minh and called the Democratic Republic of Vietnam (North Vietnam, with Hanoi as its capital). The American-backed southern zone was called the State of Vietnam (South Vietnam, with Saigon as its capital, and a year later known as the Republic of Vietnam) and headed by former Emperor Bảo Đại, with his prime minister being Ngô Đình Diệm (1901–1963), a devout Roman Catholic and a fervent anti-communist.

Publicly, this ratified document was presented as a consensus view but neither side welcomed it. For the Việt Minh, the division at the 17th Parallel meant that vast areas once held by them within Cochinchina and Annam now had to be handed over to the State of Vietnam. The Việt Minh were in fact put under pressure by China and the Soviets to agree to the division, both citing that unity could be achieved through the elections, because neither wanted to confront the United States about the terms.

When Hồ first informed Giáp about the Accords he was stunned with what had been agreed, but Hồ assured him that the Việt Minh could make things work. Leading up to the elections they needed to have a free area in which to consolidate if they were to eventually take all of Vietnam. This free area was, in fact, now the whole of North Vietnam, far larger than Việt Bắc Revolutionary Base. It had an established major city, a seaport and an international airport, all of which the Việt Minh had lacked before.

Neither America nor the State of Vietnam ever signed the Accords. The Americans simply put out a government statement saying that they recognized what had been agreed, and promised not to hinder its implementation. This stand-off approach was partly because they never really wanted the proposed election. For their part, they could not support a communist-led Vietnam if the Việt Minh won because Lao and Cambodia would fall like dominos in the same way, according to U.S. President Dwight David Eisenhower's Domino Theory. On the other hand, if the United States rejected the elections it would be viewed as turning its back on a democratic process.

On 21 July 1954, the Accords on the Cessation of Hostilities in Vietnam were signed by those willing to do so, with Lao and Cambodia having their own separate agreements. On the morning of 11 October, Hồ and his revolutionaries returned to Hanoi from the resistance zone. Giáp recalled, that the capital reflected the days of the August Revolution. Red flags overshadowed the sky. Autumn had arrived and the trees along the streets had occasional yellow leaves, although the shrubbery around the Lake of the Restored Sword was still a lush green. The only difference from December 1946, when fighting had broken out in Hanoi, was the absence in the streets of military vehicles, French motor scooters and the sound of the hob-nailed boots that belonged to soldiers in red berets.[24]

The First Victim of Hồ's Blueprint

The surrendered French were the first true victim of Hồ's new form of conflict. He had once said, "Use our own strength to achieve our own liberation." Hồ had done just this; he had designed, implemented and won his All-People's War.

The French could be said to be the first victims because, although some of the strategies were designed and used for the August Revolution, the required blueprint to fight a protracted asymetric war against a superior power had not matured at that point. When examining why the French had lost, crucial to the outcome was that French intelligence had failed from the start to understand that they were fighting a new form of warfare; they planned their deployments and strategies on the basis of inaccurate information. Consequently, the French used mainly conventional warfare to terminate Giáp's army. In doing this, they ended up destroying the people and giving the communists greater recruiting power, so they consumed an ever increasing percentage of the population, making the expansion of Hồ's blueprint self-perpetuating to some degree. When the French finally understood the blueprint it was too late. The blueprint had destroyed France's financial and political capacity to wage a war; their electorate had had enough.

Looking at the blueprint, Hồ's long-term political strategy was fundamental to the outcome of the French War. Initially his book *The Road to Revolution* gave him a platform to politically train recruits and cohesively expand his revolutionary base. When the Vietnamese RYL and later the Communist Party had been established, Hồ made these political groups, rather than an individual such as himself, the highest controlling factor. This principle gave his political groups longevity and an edge above other organizations that had built their party on the personality and ambition of one person. Likewise, he took the brave step of going against cultural history and making all areas of society as equal as he could—men, women and children—which further expanded his pool of revolutionaries.

Political diplomacy was Hồ's greatest personal contribution; the rare skill of uniting two conflicting needs. Hồ recognized that to win he required international help and when relationships with the French left-wing and the Americans broke down he successfully opened diplomatic relations with the Soviet Union and China. This left him balancing the needs of the people and those of his international Communist Bloc allies. Hồ saw his allies would not accept a pure nationalist political party but the face of communism was not acceptable to the general Vietnamese population. To develop a more tolerable facade, he skillfully set up a nationalist front political organization, called the Việt Minh Front, with groups under its umbrella covertly controlled by the Communist Party. This way Hồ softened opinion, encompassed more of the populace and expanded his support base, but without offending his international allies.

Hồ's militarily right-hand man was undoubtedly Giáp, whose carefully thought out strategies were central to the blueprint. Giáp's greatest contribution was his war without boundaries, designed to bog down his opponent. Crucial to this success was his mobile guerrilla warfare concept, which spawned guerrilla combat across Vietnam and enabled him to build two out of the three levels to his army: irregular forces and local regular forces. With this development, came the need to establish extensive improved logistics lines and corridors.

The next phase of Giáp's war without boundaries saw in 1949 the establishment of divisions and with this the third section to his forces, a main regular army. These units enabled Giáp to move on to the counter-offensive as well as the offensive and conduct larger conventional battles. From this position he could expand the land held by the revolutionaries in northern Vietnam, Lao and Cambodia, to create a liberated buffer around southern Annam and Cochinchina. These regular troops, Giáp always maintained, were needed to conclude the war.

Hồ and Giáp were the masterminds behind the propaganda front. Nationalist propaganda played a vital function in keeping nationalism at the heart of the conflict and not communism, because only nationalism could unite the people en masse. Other important areas included targeted propaganda such as at an international level and the issuing of negative messages against the French but to the advantage of the revolutionaries.

These two men designed many forms of proselytizing. Civilian proselytizing meant penetrating opponents' organizations, strategic services in society, political parties and ethnic groups, so that they could be guided either to support, or at least not to oppose, the revolutionaries. Military proselytizing enabled the communists to "win without fighting"; it not only preserved Việt Minh troops and supplies but it actually expanded their support base and fighting strength by persuading elements of the enemy to switch allegiance and join them. A secondary effect was that proselytizing seriously undermined the confidence the French troops had in the auxiliary Vietnamese National Army and the people because they never truly knew if they were friend or foe.

Similarly, Hồ and Giáp worked together to design the Revolutionary Infrastructure. Not only did this enable the other three strategic fronts to operate, but it gave them a shadow government resulting in population control. Specifically, it made it possible to establish base areas; when combined they led to liberated zones. Within liberated areas the infrastructure offered the population services, such as schooling, a working economy, effective law and order and good healthcare, described by the motto, "Both undertake resistance and build the country." The formation of the infrastructure meant that at the right time the communists could harness the power of the masses and guide them to assist, or at least not oppose, the Việt Minh taking power. Then, as the military inflicted

Photographed in the late 1990s, a young lady in Xieng Khuang Province, Lao, is selling metal left over from the wars, including bomb casings and helmets (Clive A. Hills).

their final death blow on the enemy, this hidden administration could emerge from the shadows to form what would be an already established government.

The secrets behind Hồ's blueprint and the final French battle at Điện Biên Phủ did not reveal themselves until decades after the various events. What did become apparent at the time was that these measures undermined the stability of the French empire, eventually leading to its collapse, but furthermore saw Indochina move yet closer to communist rule. This spread of communism was an outcome that clearly jarred with American foreign policy and the Cold War. The Americans made the political decision to step into the boots the French left behind. Giáp stated, "Our people prepared once again for a new stage in the long march toward independence and unification. That long march would turn out to be more miserable than the one we had just completed."[25]

• *The American Vietnam War (1954–1975)* •
10
And So It Begins Again

An Experienced Revolutionary

In 2003, the author drove along the former Hồ Chí Minh Trail in Vietnam to a monument at Đăk Song. This purportedly marked one of the first parts of the trail but, looking at the beginnings of this logistics line, the first routes did not come this far south. After an interview with Nguyễn Trọng Tâm in 2007, it is now known to mark the second point where the northern corridor met the southern corridor, so forming the Hồ Chí Minh Trail along the length of Vietnam; an incredibly significant event because once the two routes met, Hồ's blueprint could be re-established in South Vietnam under Resolution 15. What made things different from the French War is that the Americans used modern weaponry and this conflict became clearly defined as both a civil war and revolution. Sometimes referred to as the Second Indochina War, the revolutionaries called the resulting conflict the American War but it is best recognized as the Vietnam War.

This interview with Tâm (1927–) took place in Biên Hòa City, his story covered his long association with the revolution, focusing on the turbulent period of history leading up to the issuing of Resolution 15, and thereafter its implementation. Born into a poor family in Ý Yên District, Nam Định Province, he was the youngest of seven children. The French deeply distrusted his family as many of them had fought against French rule. In 1943, he had rented a room in the suburbs of Nam Định City to attend school, as his native district did not provide secondary education. During this time he became acquainted with the Việt Minh. By 1944, he had joined a branch of the organization called the National Salvation Youth and he was tasked with distributing leaflets in his local area. After the August Revolution he became commander of his local National Salvation Troops leading a platoon of guerrillas, and at the same time he taught in the literacy program. In 1946, Tâm studied in the Politico-Military School, where he joined the Communist Party.

In 1948, his leaders assigned him to one of the most dangerous jobs of the war: military proselytizing.[1] To prepare for this new role his leaders sent him on a sixty day course in Việt Bắc Revolutionary Base. He studied Việt Minh policy towards enemy POWs and their surrender; how to conduct propaganda among the Vietnamese National Army; the development of revolutionary sympathizers inside enemy ranks; and the infiltration of agents into enemy bases.[2]

Once trained, Tâm's leaders sent him to work within the district, named by the revolutionaries, Thành Mỹ, Nam Định Province.[3] When the local head changed sides and surrendered to the French, Tâm took over his position. After 1951, he worked in Việt Bắc

Revolutionary Base in the Military Proselytizing Department. From there he was sent to Bắc Ninh, a province deemed to be particularly in need of his new skills. In 1953, he was made head of a POW Camp in the Việt Bắc Revolutionary Base area, with inmates mainly of North African origin. Now highly skilled in military proselytizing, he and his fellow officers worked on persuading them to change loyalties and, once won over, form a unit willing to fight against the French; this they named the North African Propaganda and Liberation Army.[4]

Tâm explained:

> Later in 1953, I worked with Comrade Lê Hòa, a renowned military proselytizing officer. Our leaders instructed us to accompany 200 North African POWs to Lai Châu Province, just prior to the Battle of Điện Biên Phủ. They had gone through intense military proselytizing and were now our agents. For two months we journeyed by foot across hostile forested mountains. When we finally arrived we handed over these men to local Việt Minh officers, whose duty was then to infiltrate them back into local French positions to execute further military proselytizing inside their camps. We hoped that when our army surrounded their posts, the men inside would be more inclined to surrender rather than fight, so hoisting a white flag.
>
> Not all our people supported military proselytizing because our army had to pay such a heavy price to capture an enemy soldier alive. They said when I had to accompany 200 North African POWs to Lai Châu Province, "Why should we now put ourselves out further by marching them to Lai Châu, as we can't be sure that they will not just return to the French side. If they had genuinely switched, could we not just take them back to where we had captured them, point them in the right direction and they could walk back to their posts?"
>
> This view was wrong. To begin with, we needed to target certain camps rather than just any one that was near to us. Furthermore, I believed that by developing a fifth column inside French positions, this saved lives in the long run. So I happily spent hours speaking to the POWs in French to switch them over to us, then to escort them to our local agents so that they could be infiltrated by them into targeted French camps. This completed the task.[5]

Tâm would be proved right with proselytizing. Some of these POWs that Tâm worked with did come over to the Việt Minh; the positions where they had been placed fell with fewer losses than expected with such intense fighting. It was this experience that made Tâm an important revolutionary for Hồ.

Facing the South

After the Geneva Accords were signed in 1954, Tâm went back to work with the Military Proselytizing Department, whose offices had just moved to Hanoi. That December, he and a small group of revolutionaries were assigned to go to South Vietnam; this labeled them Reverse Regrouping Men.

Reverse Regrouping Men was an unofficial label used after the war. This title came about because one of the most important parts of the Geneva Accords laid out the requirement for a 300-day period of grace to be established, which allowed people to move freely and regroup within North Vietnam and South Vietnam.[6] This free movement ended in May 1955; thereafter the border would be sealed, paving the way for the elections to be held to see the two Vietnams united. Tâm and colleagues were later unofficially titled Reverse Regrouping Men because they came from the North and should have stayed regrouped there, along with those southern Việt Minh fighters and civilians heading for North Vietnam in accordance with the Geneva Accords. By going south they headed in the opposite direction, so hence their name.

Before leaving, the Reverse Regrouping Men met with Trần Lương (1912–2009), the deputy head of the Vietnamese People's Army Political General Directorate. He ordered them to guide the elections to favor the Việt Minh and, once victory had been achieved, be there to control the handover. They were to do this by infiltrating into the Southern administration and their military. Then once settled they had to find traitors, locate agents planted by foreign intelligence services, weed out any corrupt personnel and identify perceived dead wood. The Party needed this information because once the elections had been won, under the terms of the Geneva Accords, the agencies of government and the military of both North and South Vietnam had to be incorporated into a united system; as an example, the so-called dead wood did not deserve the high salaries being paid by Western nations, which a united Vietnam had to continue paying under the Accords.

One major difficulty facing these men was that they had to understand the new concept of a Southern Army, to be known as the Army of the Republic of Vietnam (ARVN). Hồ eventually named those within this army the "special masses." Traditionally, those who colluded with a foreign invader were traitors, consequently those who joined ARVN could be known as such. However, the Communist Party did not view them that way. First of all, those within ARVN were deemed by the Party not to have taken the official oath; taken by the people who had come to hear the declaration of independence given by Hồ back in September 1945 in Hanoi. This crowd had sworn not to work with the newly invading French, however the Southern youth now in ARVN had not been there to do this. Therefore, the Party regarded them as misguided people, who had not been educated to the nation's cause. In addition, those within ARVN might have once fought for the revolutionaries or at least did not have a long history of fighting against them; they signed up to ARVN because they lived in South Vietnam or had been drafted. Furthermore, at an international level the Geneva Accords stipulated that there must be no discrimination against people who had once sided with the French; not an easy condition to meet because those within ARVN now tried to gain respect from both sides to protect their families from reprisals in case of civil war. By calling those within ARVN special masses it acknowledged these facts and requirements.

To help those operating in South Vietnam, in 1954 Hanoi changed its administrative sections south of the 17th Parallel. They disbanded COSVN and instructed various smaller administrative bodies to form or reform. The 4th Inter-zone Party Committee and the Party Central Committee had to take control of provinces south of the 17th Parallel within Annam, and the Cochinchina Regional Party Committee was re-established to run Cochinchina. This regional committee further subdivided into the Cochinchina Inter-Provincial Party Committees: Eastern (T1), Central (T2), Western (T3) and the Special Zone Party Committee of Saigon-Chợ Lớn-Gia Định-Rừng Sác (T4). To assist the Reverse Regrouping Men each Communist Party committee planned to re-establish local guerrilla and regular armed units as well as expand the infrastructure; the women predominantly did the legal courier work and the men the illegal work.

Tâm operated under the Eastern Zone (T1) and commented:

> When my leaders sent me to the South, I and others secretly boarded a Soviet ship, deployed to travel south to pick up people who were to regroup to North Vietnam. I arrived in Cà Mau Province and left the ship for a local Việt Minh base. There, a female courier called Long the Fourth took me to Biên Hòa City. It was here I became a military proselytizing operative working under Hoàng Minh Đạo.

To operate I needed a new ID [*laissez-passer*] to secure me a legitimate cover. My brother acted as my witness. He had previously reached the South by an American ship and in doing so he was viewed as an ally of the Southern administration, and they issued him with a new ID. What made our new IDs so important was that they had no history connected to them; our previous revolutionary life had been erased and we attracted little or no attention from the local police.

Although I had a good ID I still found it hard to operate in Biên Hoa. Everyone who could, regrouped to the North. So in the South there was a limited infrastructure available and no office remained to serve me, only the local Party stayed, or more specifically the regional military proselytizing cells. This limited manpower made adhering to our compartment rules very difficult.

One of our main compartment rules meant that the head and his deputy, as well as their staff, lived in different places. The head knew where his staff lived but not vice versa. Hoàng Minh Đạo, my direct boss, had several hideouts and even went so far as to establish a fake family life so that no one knew who he was.

Other rules included: the head of a courier system could only be someone who ran a number of large networks, but also a Communist Party member or a professional courier; you were only allowed to know the part of the network that you used; each courier took charge of a certain number of working relationships; high level couriers served just one or two important revolutionaries; a courier did not know the work of the operative whom they served and vice versa; where possible, any courier only guided a secret service operative once. This last rule meant that each time I went on a mission I had the additional pressure of having to remember the route because once there my courier simply disappeared. On occasions I did not even have time to remember their face.

When I had to correspond, this was via coded letters written in invisible ink and left in a dead-letterbox. These letterboxes were mainly located at a courier station, but there were few stations around, and on many occasions they were located more than a day's walk from each other.[7]

Furthermore, the American intelligence service had become very active across the whole country. This meant that the Communist Party temporarily banned the use of radios and all clandestine communications had to be conducted by a limited courier service. The ban all but cut Hanoi off from those areas south of the 17th Parallel.

Faced with all these difficulties these Reverse Regrouping Men sent from North Vietnam to guide the elections and smooth the way for Hồ's party, said that operating in South Vietnam was the same as following an order to "commit suicide."

Proselytizing Dissident Groups

After surviving his reverse regrouping assignment, in 1955 Hoàng Minh Đạo gave Tâm his next task; going into the Rừng Sác Jungle to look for the Bình Xuyên religious sect.

Đạo was one of the most important figures in the newly founded Observing the Enemy Department, established by Hanoi in 1955, with Văn Viên (19??–1955) as its head.[8] The aim of the department was for its members to inform the Cochinchina Regional Party Committee and Hanoi of any policies the Southern administration planned to put in place to oppose the revolutionaries. By using this information they could then guide any situation in their favor to minimize losses.

In March 1955, Đạo instructed military proselytizing operatives to work on the religious sects. Although Đạo was head of the Cochinchina Military Intelligence Department, a subsection of the Observing the Enemy Department and therefore directed by Hanoi, they had not ordered him to approach the sects; he had done so as a result of the changing political climate in the South, and had to act promptly.

Tâm explained:

> We had to get groups such as the Hòa Hảo, Cao Đài and the Bình Xuyên on our side. They had been a highly effective pacification tool for the French in the first half of the 1950s. In fact, their armies

helped the French so effectively that the revolutionary movement in Cochinchina, especially in Saigon, found it hard to rise up.

Before we made our move to win their support, we studied how Diệm targeted them. We noticed that he did not use key people within their group as the French had and seemed to be alienating them thanks to his heavy-handed approach. We also saw that the French and the U.S. were in negotiations with each other, discussing how to transfer the religious sects over to the U.S., after the French had finally left. We concluded that by acting now we could covertly agitate the tense situation between them, and split Diệm from the sects, so destroying one of the most important and proficient war tools at his disposal at that time.

In the case of the Bình Xuyên, we saw an opening we could exploit. Diệm and the Bình Xuyên tolerated each other but it was a tentative partnership with a high degree of tension between them. We agitated this weakness to inflame hatred on both sides. We did this via our secret agents, some of whom were now trusted advisors to Diệm. Thanks to our agitation, Diệm's army fought the Bình Xuyên in the spring of 1955. This forced more of them to look for sanctuary in the Rừng Sác Jungle. Diệm viewed the ousting of the Bình Xuyên as his victory, but in fact he had only superficially gained control of Saigon, as I will explain.

I did not find it easy to get these vicious bandits to switch sides to support the revolution. Viễn the Seventh was the overall commander of the Bình Xuyên, and he had run away to the Rừng Sác Jungle. I had to track him down and make friends with him because if he switched sides so would his men. Thông the Second, who was the secretary of our local Communist Party cell, took Khánh the Seventh, the deputy secretary of the Eastern Zone, and me by boat to the edge of the forest.[9] A Bình Xuyên delegation met us, which comprised Nguyễn Văn Hiếu, Lực the Tenth and Le Paul [son of Viễn the Seventh and who held French citizenship].[10]

In the Rừng Sác Jungle everyone lived in boats and had limited food and no clean water. Everything swarmed with insects. I could see that Viễn the Seventh found this an unbearable situation and he wanted a way out. I played on this and looked for a means for him and Hoàng Minh Đạo to meet. Tough discussions then opened between the two men. Finally, Viễn the Seventh said that he could not return to the revolutionary side because he had betrayed us once before. From this conclusion Đạo strongly advised him to go to France. He fled for Paris in May 1955.

Having removed the leader, I worked on Chief of Staff Nguyễn Văn Hiếu. We got so close to each other that eventually he and his wife treated me as if I were their younger brother. I asked him, "Even with all these weapons, how long do you think you can tolerate living here?" He asked me, "Do you want weapons?" I said, "No we don't need weapons from you." I told him, "You have to look for a way forward. We are only supporting you because you oppose the Americans. We know that you are not revolutionaries who are fighting for liberation; you have your own mission. Yet if you join us, so that the elections are held, then the nation will give you credit for your work. If you do not join us, I can't see you being able to fight the Americans by yourself for two years. The French won't back you, nor will we." On these grounds we only managed to persuade the 3rd Battalion of the Bình Xuyên to change sides at that time, but it was a start.

Although winning over these groups was a small victory for us, it produced big results because it gave us the means to surround Saigon. Not only was the Rừng Sác Jungle ours but we had the rights to use Bình Xuyên camps [for example, from January 1960 the Rừng Sác Jungle would be a base for our water-elite *đặc công* forces].

Consequently, when Diệm, the French and the Americans sided with each other and mistreated the religious sects, they could no longer rely on them or their posts. The "ring of defensive camps" that had once protected Saigon from the revolutionaries would now be the noose to choke the pro–American regime.[11]

Tâm's luck ran out during this period. The person who had taken him to the Rừng Sác Jungle was arrested and he gave Tâm's name to the enemy.

One-Way War

Around the time of Tâm's arrest, the relative peace that Vietnam had enjoyed moved towards greater friction between groups, fueled by Diệm's Denounce the Communists campaign. Started in the summer of 1955, throughout the months that followed communists and other oppositionists were arrested and executed. During this period the term Việt Cộng came into use. This abbreviated the words that had appeared in the warning to kill "Vietnamese communists," issued by Diệm against those who had stayed in the South after 1954. Subsequently, Việt Cộng or VC or Charlie, became universal names for those fighting against the Southern administration; an effective tag to discredit both their nationalist views and the name of the Việt Minh.

Later that year, in October, Diệm added petrol to the smoldering cinders of peace by calling off the promised elections. He had held a referendum to determine the future direction of the South. Both Bảo Đại and Diệm stood as candidates; Bảo Đại advocated the restoration of the monarchy while Diệm ran on a republican platform. Diệm won with more votes than voters and became the head of state, shortly after he proclaimed himself president of the Republic of Vietnam.

Vietnamese revolutionaries called this grim period their "one-way war," because they had been instructed by the Communist Bloc not to fight back once the Geneva Accords had been signed. The principle was that the revolutionaries could not be seen to be derailing any part of the Accords. Understandably, this one-way theory was not always strictly adhered to, especially around the cancellation of the elections. Whereas Diệm tried to legitimize breaking the Accords through his referendum, the revolutionaries sometimes wore the uniform of a religious sect so that any military action could not be linked to them.

The one-way war scenario was linked to the wider communist agendas of the Soviet Union and China. The Soviets had their theory of "peaceful coexistence," developed by them and adopted under Nikita Khrushchev (1894–1971) to keep relations open with capitalist states. Due to this policy, Soviet help to North Vietnam had all but dried up, although they did send some military advisors, a small number of arms and participated in the restructuring of North Vietnam's armed forces. China, too, desired a peaceful international environment after the Korean War to focus on domestic reconstruction. Likewise, China wanted to break the American policy of isolating it, by dissuading armed conflict and encouraging neutralist governments in Lao and Cambodia as well as assisting North Vietnam to consolidate its power and rebuild its economy. For Hanoi to keep any kind of material aid coming from China and the Soviets into North Vietnam, they had to adhere to this new international environment and endure the one-way war.

The one-way war restricted Tâm's ability to operate when incarcerated in Tân Hiệp Prison from October 1955 to 2 December 1956. Tân Hiệp was a center that formed part of Diệm's wider Corrections Program, intended to integrate into modern Southern society those who had not regrouped to the North. Those targeted included former Việt Minh soldiers to be reconditioned by the program to fight in ARVN; Phạm Ngọc Thảo and Vũ Anh used this process as a mask to spy for the communists. Unsurprisingly, the Corrections Program became a cover for a brutal tool of suppression, and expanded to include anyone who opposed Diệm and his regime.

Tâm recalled that, when in Tân Hiệp, his fellow inmates said to him, "Look, the white cars of the International Control Commission [ICC] are passing." The ICC was an international force, established in 1954, to oversee the implementation of the Geneva Accords. Tâm said that he had dreamed of running out to stop the cars to tell those ICC members inside that the inmates were being held illegally and that the Accords had been broken. As political prisoners he and his fellow inmates should not have been in Tân Hiệp but

On May 14, 2007, Nguyễn Trọng Tâm and his wife stand at one of the gates of Tân Hiệp Prison, in which he was incarcerated between late 1955 and late 1956 (Clive A. Hills).

the Diệm regime had purposely wrongly labeled it a correction center under the Corrections Program, knowing that this type of camp did not fall under the ICC remit.

Alas, Tâm could not speak to the ICC and, focusing his anger and feelings of entrapment, he set about planning an escape. As secretary of the Communist Party cell within Tân Hiệp, he organized a breakout.

Tâm continued:

> The regime first put me in a prison, administered under the Counter-Intelligence Department. The CIA ran this. When tortured, I knew that if I gave any information this would not only harm the revolution but it could also lead to my death. Some prisoners naively thought that if they gave some information then their torturers would stop. The opposite happened, the more you gave the more they tortured you. Many prisoners died at the hands of their torturers. What is not said is that we knew that some of the torturers were our agents, there to silence anyone who damaged the revolution. They got nothing from me so they sent me to Catinat Police Station. Here again they tortured me. Here again they got nothing.
>
> I escaped with my life for many reasons but I put most of it down to the fact that I had a new ID and I did not talk. Many revolutionary sympathizers used their old ID cards from the French War so their previous records could be pinned to them. As I did not use my old card they had nothing on me so they moved me to Tân Hiệp, a prison no longer under the Counter-Intelligence Department or police so it was not as harsh.
>
> I credit much of our success in escaping from the jail to one of my first couriers, Long the Fourth, who had taken me from the Soviet ship when I came south. She worked for the Cochinchina Military Proselytizing Department. Her husband was in prison with me and when she visited him she conveyed letters to me from Hoàng Minh Đạo and vice versa. Communication by this means was painstaking. Sometimes the letters were written in invisible ink between the lines of a newspaper story and others were written openly but could be wrapped in small parcels and mixed with goods, or

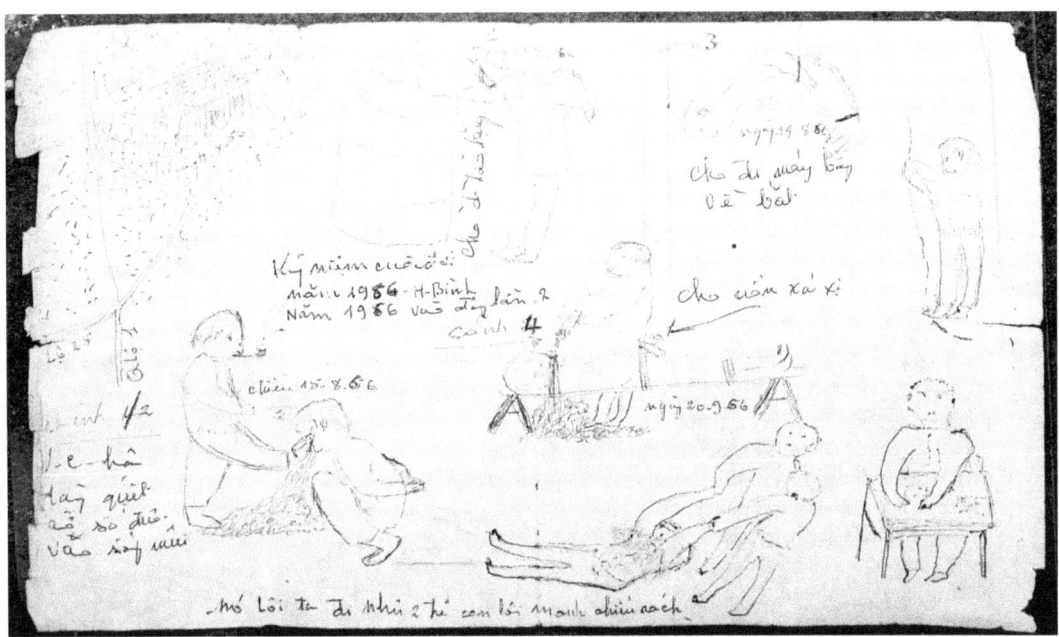

1956 drawings by former prisoners depicting torture techniques. The gruesome names describing each technique were thought up by their guards at Tân Hiệp Prison: "Diving a submarine" meant sinking the head of the prisoner into a barrel of water to choke him; "flying a plane" meant hanging a prisoner upside down by using a rope tied to the ceiling and swinging him from one side of the room to the other; "drinking sarsi" meant stuffing a bottle of soapsuds into a prisoner's mouth; "nose chewing betel" meant striking the prisoner's nose until it bled, as betel is red when chewed; and "hammering nails" meant hamming a pin under a prisoner's nails (courtesy Nguyễn Đức Tâm).

even hidden in shrimp paste. It was through her conveying my messages to Đạo, that I first proposed my breakout plans to him.

The situation in prison was tense; the Cochinchina Regional Party Committee took ages to agree to the breakout. At the time we adhered to the policy of peaceful coexistence and this plan went against that policy. They dithered but finally said, "The secretary of the Biên Hòa Provincial Party Committee should be responsible for this action." Then, one month after asking the consent of the Cochinchina Regional Party Committee, the enemy nearly uncovered our escape plan. In November, we heard that the secretary of the Biên Hòa Provincial Party Committee had died and that seven to eight couriers serving this committee had been arrested, apart from Long the Fourth, because she had been leading Hoàng Minh Đạo's representative to meet me in prison when the arrests were in progress. Nevertheless, when en route to the prison, the representative had been arrested but she managed to escape, he never returned, just vanished. Since she could have been compromised, and we did not know whether or not the man had talked, we had to wait a long time before we could continue.

I was also near to being compromised myself. In prison I ran into Trần Văn Huy, the former head of military proselytizing of Vụ Bản District, Nam Định Province. This province is where I conducted military proselytizing before I went south. He was sent south soon after me. Now in prison, he came up to me and, giving me a slap on the shoulder, he said, "Oh, brother Tâm." I turned back, "Which Tâm?" I pretended to be dazed. He said, "My god. This is brother Tâm. How could I mistake you?" I answered, "Yes. You are mistaken." I could see behind him several "tails" meaning he had been arrested with many others, creating circles of people around him that knew my real identity. This was dangerous for me. Maybe in the end he guessed that I was adhering to our strict Communist Party rule; not doing anything to compromise another. I always said to myself, "When we get out from here, we can be friends again. Please don't get angry with me, my friend Huy." The regime soon sent him to Côn Đảo Island Prison, where he died. Painfully, we could never be friends again.

For the breakout, I had the difficulty of choosing and organizing the prisoners. Leading up to the breakout, I had to build a strong team who, if possible, were good at martial arts. We had no guns to overcome our guards, just our hands. To organize the prisoners and keep them informed I used my courier network that I had built inside the prison. This added risk to the plans, not only because of the numbers of people involved but because I knew that there were traitors amongst us. Nevertheless, by the time we were ready some 300 prisoners had been prepared for the breakout.

Right: **Corpses of female political prisoners tortured to death in Tân Hiệp Prison (courtesy Nguyễn Đức Tâm).**

10. And So It Begins Again

A report issued by the Southern government documenting how the prisoners broke out of Tân Hiệp Prison. It was issued on 3 December 1956 and signed by the commander of the local armed forces of Biên Hòa (courtesy Nguyễn Đức Tâm).

Opposite: Part of the display at Tân Hiệp Prison. This song, composed on February 3, 1955, is "Being Referred to Phú Quốc Prison," written by the prisoners Vân Thủy (music) and Nguyễn Văn Thông (text) (courtesy Nguyễn Đức Tâm).

192 Part II. Evolution and Application of the Blueprint (1954–1975)

Photographs of prisoners who took part in the Tân Hiệp Prison breakout (courtesy Nguyễn Đức Tâm).

The main thrust to the plan was that once the escape had started and the guards overcome, we would take their guns and shoot our way out, taking the guns with us. I remember that it took forty minutes of intense fighting inside the prison before our chosen courier led us to safety. What added further confusion was that some of our people who had agreed to the plan hesitated at the gates. At the last moment they had decided that, because they only had a short time left of their sentence, they would be better off serving this rather than spending the rest of their life on the run.[12]

Tâm had "graduated" from prison; he had not talked under torture and had freed more than 450 prisoners during the sensitive period of the one-way war. Now out, Tâm went to work as the political commissar within the Bình Xuyên unit that he had helped to switch to the revolution. Viễn the Seventh approved this appointment, even though he had already settled in Paris.

Planning for War or Peace

In these early years of tentative peace, the Party Central Committee had to address many complicated issues, other than what the Chinese and Soviets were or were not doing to help.

One of the most problematic issues for the Communist Party was how to strengthen and modernize North Vietnam, not only so that it could become one large revolutionary base area if they needed to attack the South, but so that the Party could build a strong economy and move towards socialism. These were not easy tasks. Agriculture was decentralized and farming methods backward. Industry was small and crippled. Many businesses, water control projects, transportation routes, railroad yards and port facilities had been destroyed during the war. Besides, the French had sabotaged many pieces of machinery as well as supplies before leaving. In the large cities and provincial capitals more than 100,000 people were unemployed, and hundreds of thousands still illiterate.

Politically, the Communist Party implemented an economic recovery plan from 1955 to 1957. Part of this plan was a policy of continuing the Land Reforms, a requirement of the Soviets and Chinese. Another was a policy of integrating newcomers, predominantly those who had operated in the South but who had since May 1955 completed their transfer to regroupment areas in the North, but also Vietnamese volunteer units working in Lao and Cambodia. Not only did these groups have to be vetted, but they had to be re-educated in the need for Land Reforms and made to study the teachings of Marxist-Leninist theory. During this period the Party did achieve stability and successes in many important areas, such as bringing abandoned farmland back into use. Notwithstanding these achievements, in 1956, the Party's supremacy was seriously damaged when the General Secretary Trường Chinh resigned over the now failed Land Reforms.[13] This did not permanently damage the Party's image and they drew up a further three-year plan for economic reform and cultural development to cover 1958 to 1960.

Militarily, North Vietnam recognized that they needed to build a regular army, even though theoretically they were now at peace. Under the guidance of Giáp, now minister of defense and deputy premier, Party members drafted a five-year plan to cover the years from 1955 to 1959.[14] This finally gained approval in March 1957 at the Twelfth Conference and set forward three basic steps: to build a regular and relatively modern army; to establish an initial basic organizational structure to accommodate Navy and Air Force service branches; and finally to create conditions that would modernize the armed forces.[15]

Although during this period Hanoi looked for peace through economic and military stability, since the cancellation of the elections they equally prepared the country for war. In June 1956 the Party Central Committee issued a Resolution regarding their immediate intent in the South. It stated, "Our struggle method throughout the country is presently political, not military. To say this does not mean, however, that we will never employ self-defense measures in limited situations."[16] After studying this Resolution, in December 1956 the Cochinchina Regional Party Committee held a meeting. At this gathering the regional committee issued another Resolution stating it was not the right time to launch a guerrilla war but that they would conduct armed propaganda operations akin to those seen during the French War. Now known as action units, these forces had roughly the same brief as the former armed propaganda teams, and on occasions consisted of religious sect members who had converted to the revolution, such as the Bình Xuyên.

At the Thirteenth Conference in late 1957, Hồ suggested a greater need for military action in the South. In summary he said that the Party had to implement two revolutionary strategies: the popular democratic nationalist revolution in the South and the socialist revolution in the North. Going on to say that both of these revolutionary duties were important, and to disregard either one would be a mistake.

In summer 1958, Hanoi arranged for Lê Duẩn, a member of the Politburo responsible for Cochinchina, to travel to South Vietnam to gather intelligence to confirm the need for a change of strategy. On his return he gave an account of his findings, concluding that a united Vietnam could never be achieved unless North Vietnam engaged in armed resistance. He reported that Diệm's policy of killing and imprisoning opposition members meant that the Communist Party in the South had been weakened significantly. Indeed, in 1955, after regroupment, South Vietnam still had several thousand supporters and Party members based there and every village had a Party cell. By 1957 it was estimated that 70 percent of leading communists in the South had been arrested or killed at commune level, 60 percent at district and 40 percent at provincial level.[17] Fundamentally though, what helped Lê Duẩn draw his conclusions was based on information he had gathered from people who had taken part in the Tân Hiệp Prison breakout in December 1956. They had told him first hand of the rapid imprisonment of revolutionaries and the vast numbers of deaths as a consequence of torture. "There would be no one left if this is allowed to continue," they had said. On his return to the North, Lê Duẩn told Hồ of their words and that the situation in the South was ripe for armed struggle.

In parallel to Lê Duẩn's trip, Giáp, Hoàng Tùng and Trần Quang drafted the Resolution for armed struggle to be heard at the Fifteenth Conference in January 1959. Resolution 15 could be said to be the official declaration by the Party to start hostilities; the main content permitted North Vietnam to complete its socialist revolution and South Vietnam to move from a political struggle to a military one, meaning armed resistance against the Diệm regime in a popular democratic nationalist revolution to unite the country. Hồ summarized the conclusions of the Party Central Committee, by saying we must include South Vietnam in the general revolution of our entire nation and include our nation's revolution in the world revolution.

Those who were present at the Fifteenth Conference forecasted that any conflict

Hồ Chí Minh's house in Hanoi, where he lived and worked from 1958 to 1969. 2003 photograph (Clive A. Hills).

would be a protracted struggle but this time under modern conditions. It was a delicate decision because any advance into South Vietnam must not aggravate the socialist camp by breaking the peaceful coexistence diktat or give the Americans an excuse to become ever more militarily involved in the South. For now, this new All-People's War blueprint would have to be executed covertly.

The American Vietnam War Starts

Once passed, couriers distributed Resolution 15 to departments to act upon; this was done so painfully slowly that this instruction did not reach the Cochinchina Regional Party Committee, in Tây Ninh Province, until September 1959.

The southern revolutionaries performed their first battle of the Vietnam War in 1960. The preparations for this started in November 1959, when the Cochinchina Regional Party Committee held a conference to examine Resolution 15. One of the outcomes of that meeting was that they would direct the Eastern Zone to conduct a large-scale, high-profile attack on an enemy base. This attack was to strengthen the position of the Cochinchina Regional Party Committee; they had to encourage the masses to join the revolution, support the planned Simultaneous Uprising and capture enemy weapons to equip the armed forces.

In early January, military personnel from the Eastern Zone gathered to discuss Resolution 15 and which enemy base to attack. They chose Nguyễn Thái Học Camp at Trảng Sụp, located 7km north-west of Tây Ninh City. Originally known as Tua Hai (*Deuxième Tour*) during the French War, it formed part of a large network of watchtowers there to help the French control regions of the plain through a pacification method known as "oil-spill"; spreading control progressively outward from areas controlled by friendly forces.[18]

The attack known as the Battle of Tua Hai was set for 26 January 1960, a date that coincided with the Tết New Year holiday.[19] The battle could go ahead without approval from the Communist Bloc because Hanoi went out of their way to disguise who took part. Hanoi knew that Western media outlets were reporting clashes between the Diệm regime and the religious sects. Using this to their advantage, Hanoi instructed that any attack on Tua Hai must include one former Bình Xuyên attachment, so that they could trick the Western media into reporting that this was their operation.[20] When these media reports eventually made their way to Moscow and Beijing, Hanoi could confidently reply that they had nothing to do with Tua Hai. "Look," they could say, "it's the Bình Xuyên gangsters." Hanoi could even go as far as saying that the attack was just the religious sect retaliating against Diệm and his efforts to suppress them.

Tâm explained his story:

> The first requirement for armed struggle is weapons. Initially we had been armed with rifles buried in the ground or hidden in villages since 1954. These were old rusty weapons, which malfunctioned, so we needed new modern replacements.
>
> We first had to pinpoint our target. This meant finding a camp located not too far from our existing area of operations, and with regular Southern Army troops based there, armed with new American weapons. This we found in Tua Hai Camp, an ideal choice for two reasons. The Southern unit was going through training there so it meant that they would not be as armed as they could have been. In addition, our leaders decided that, although the unit deployed there was a regimental-sized one with 1,600 men, it was not an entrenched camp. Instead, it was a location that had watchtowers,

A monument celebrating the Battle of Tua Hai. Communist Vietnam now considers this battle to be the official start of hostilities for the American Vietnam War (Clive A. Hills).

there to form a network, or shield, against our army advancing from the North. The camp would not be difficult to attack and seize.

We had many sources of intelligence on the camp. Our elite đặc công forces had carried out their reconnaissance. From this we knew details of weapon locations and the camp layout, such as it was 800m in length and 400m in width and it had a dyke in front of it with no fence. The elite đặc công forces had been aided by our informers within the camp, who had drawn a detailed map of the layout inside. These informers were part of a cell of 120 communists inside the camp. During 1959, this cell had arranged to mount a revolt but their plan had been exposed. The enemy arrested nine agents, but they gave away no information so the cell continued. [Ironically this made conditions favorable for us during our attack. The original revolt had been conducted by South Vietnamese troops who had covertly switched to our side, to guard against further attacks by internal Vietnamese troops the enemy allowed only one of their platoons, the alert platoon, to carry weapons].

Our present plan had four prongs. I led my fifty-three troops to attack the 1st and 2nd Battalions. I had ended up leading them because our commander died in the first few minutes, and as the political commissar of this prong I took control. A second prong attacked the 3rd Battalion using sixty troops and a third prong attacked the regimental headquarters using forty troops. This third prong was the main one and signaled the start of the battle. A fourth prong attacked the arms depot.

Before we started we noticed strange things happening that put us on edge. It was Tết and instead of being quiet, because everyone would be with their family, the enemy arrived at the camp late at night from their homes. Their truck headlights lit up the dark sky. At first we thought that our plan had been compromised so the main prong waited for some thirty minutes. Once confident enough, they opened fire. This was the signal to begin the battle.

This delay did not hinder us too much, and we managed to attack our given posts. Nevertheless, the prong attacking the 3rd Battalion did come across difficulties, which had a knock-on effect at the regimental headquarters and complications were encountered there too. At the same time, the fourth prong attacked the depot. They were commanded by Lê Thanh the Eighth and supported by more than 300 civilian porters. These porters had been instructed to wait outside the camp to carry the ammunition out when needed, either to waiting trucks or away from the fighting by foot. Frustratingly, these waiting trucks were ambushed and the troops protecting them fled so we lost those weapons. Even Lê Thanh the Eighth ran away, having broken his leg!

Though many weapons were lost, later we captured one enemy document that confirmed our attack. It said that General Nguyễn Hữu Có declared that 783 rifles of various kinds were captured including recoilless, heavy machine guns and U.S. rifles. These were the first captured weapons of the American War and we threw away our old guns and replaced them with the new ones.[21]

Although Resolution 15 was the political order to engage in armed struggle, the Battle of Tua Hai showed the military intent. This had led some revolutionaries to say that Tua Hai is the battle that marked the start of the Vietnam War. Even though there had been skirmishes with the enemy before, and some suggest that these should denote the start of the conflict, these had been led by local Communist Party members who had agitated the civilian masses, so had not used regular infantry troops. The Battle of Tua Hai, on the other hand, was conducted mainly by regular infantry troops.

Another reason why Vietnamese scholars take this battle to signify the start of the Vietnam War is that the Battle of Tua Hai has been recorded as the conflict that enabled the Simultaneous Uprising. This was a planned attack executed across many provinces, in accordance with the orders from the Cochinchina Regional Party Committee. Although skirmishes that were associated with the Simultaneous Uprising had started in early 1959, only after the Battle of Tua Hai did the communists have advanced weapons available to them, which boosted morale and enabled those involved to fully obey Communist Party orders. Bến Tre Province benefited from Tua Hai and became the only province that really saw coordinated activities.[22] The Simultaneous Uprising ended in late 1960.

There were other factors that had made the Simultaneous Uprising possible, not just advanced weapons; giving weight to the uprising denoting a start date. Prior to the uprising, Communist Party members had reconnected with those who had once fought for the Việt Minh and they had also recruited some new blood. What assisted the Party is that they had managed to harness the hatred these people had felt for Diệm and his policies. In 1959, for instance, Diệm had authorized the 10/59 Law. This stiffened penalties for those who had communist affiliations, and permitted trial of the accused by special military tribunals and the use of the guillotine, a much-hated symbol of the colonial days.[23]

There were two schools of thought with regards to the outcome of the Simultaneous Uprising: those who believed that an August Revolution style victory could have been achieved and those who were realistic. The former group of people were delusional, according to the realists. These realists knew that the villagers could not rise up as they had done during the August Revolution; this time they mainly fought with sticks and bare hands against a heavily armed enemy. However, as predicted by the realists, the people had managed to eliminate enemy soldiers, spies and local political leaders, and form new fighting villages, snatch advanced weaponry and establish guerrilla fighters.

With all this in mind, most decision-makers saw the uprising and Tua Hai as platforms only, there to re-establish the three strategic fronts and Revolutionary Infrastructure to comply with Resolution 15. The most pressing point to continue this expansion process was to link the North with the South, paving the way for a southern liberation army.

North Vietnam Links to the South

The men chosen to build the framework of a southern military relocated there via a newly founded Southward Strategic Corridor. This route had been one of the first things ordered after Giáp issued Resolution 15 because he had learned the importance of good supply lines from the Battle of Điện Biên Phủ.[24]

To prepare the way for this new Southward March, Giáp instructed that a staff agency be established, under the General Military Party Centre Committee, to research how to establish a strategic corridor from North Vietnam to the South. Võ Bẩm, the Deputy Director of the Army Agricultural Farms Department, was chosen to head this group. Võ Bẩm knew how to proceed because he had spent many years working on the battlefields of the 5th Inter-zone and the Central Highlands. Giáp told Võ Bẩm to research into both land and sea routes.

To transport supplies along this new corridor, a special military communications group was formed, known as the Military Transportation Group 559. It was set up on 19 May 1959 (the 5th month in the year 59). Under Group 559 there were two battalions: the 301st Land Transportation Battalion commanded by Chu Đăng Chữ with Nguyễn Danh as the political commissar, and the 603rd Sea Transportation Battalion commanded by Hà Văn Xá with Lưu Đức as the political commissar. With Võ Bẩm not only conducting research into these two new routes, but also the commander of Group 559, he is therefore recognized as being the first commander of the Hồ Chí Minh Trail and the initial overseer of the Hồ Chí Minh Trail Sea Route.

The 301st Land Transportation Battalion built its launch base at Khe Hó in Vĩnh Linh District and established its first way station in Hàm Nghi Ridge Cave, North Vietnam. The battalion then crossed the Bến Hải River and headed to Route 9 in South Vietnam. From there they traveled along the eastern slopes of the Trường Sơn Mountain

Range down a strategic corridor used by Hướng Hóa District Party members. Eight courier way stations were set up among many different ethnic groups, with a ninth at the hamlet of Pa Lin, near Đa Krông, Quảng Trị Province. This is where the 301st Land Transportation Battalion delivered their first consignment of goods.

With the first journey recorded as a reasonable success, Hanoi deployed other action units to continue the construction of the Southward Strategic Corridor. The 5th Zone created corridors from Pa Lin way station, west through the provinces in central Vietnam and on into the Central Highlands. One of the most important sections of the Southward Strategic Corridor was through the 6th Zone of southern Annam, because once completed, Hanoi then had direct access to Cochinchina and a strategic corridor along the length of Vietnam.

In mid–1960 the Party agreed that Đắk Lắk, in the 6th Zone, must be the "stepping stone" province for both southern and northern action units to meet.[25] The action units from the North were B90 and B500, both had to travel separately to minimize the chances of jeopardizing the mission. B90 left Hanoi on 20 June 1959, headed by Trần Quang Sang with Phạm Văn Lạc and Phùng Đình Ấm as his two deputy commanders.[26] B500 left in December 1959, commanded by Tăng Thiên Kim.[27] Each action unit contained high-ranking officers and soldiers there to build the framework for a future southern liberation army. Those within these action units came from two divisions, the 330th and the 338th. These troops had regrouped to North Vietnam under the Geneva Accords but those chosen also had to have been born in the South or grown up there or been very familiar with the area from the French War. The Party even ordered that no one in the action units could be married or engaged to someone from the North. These were strict rules because the communists needed people who fitted in down in the South, as the North could still not be seen to have any involvement there, even though the one-way war for Hanoi had ceased ever since Resolution 15 had been issued.

Tâm was asked to open the new corridor heading from the South into the 6th Zone to meet with B90. Originally Lâm Quốc Đăng had been tasked with this role.[28] He had left in May 1960 with a detachment from Company 300 that formed an action unit codenamed C300. After several weeks he could not advance past Phước Long Province. Therefore a new action unit formed, codenamed C200, which departed in June 1960 and included eighteen officers and soldiers. Hồng Sơn headed C200, while Tâm was the political commissar and Party secretary of C200.[29]

Tâm explained:

> I could see the importance of the task. D War Zone had no Revolutionary Infrastructure available to us. We had tried to establish it, repeatedly attempting to start networks in the Central Highlands, but the action units that had entered this area clashed with the hill tribes, who killed intruders. Yet the proposed new corridor was needed [because we now could not use E300 as this had been destroyed, nor could we use the way through Cambodia as too many people had been killed, including Nguyễn Bình].
>
> Mai Chí Thọ and Nguyễn Hữu Xuyến summoned me to a meeting.[30] Currently, Thọ was the secretary of the Eastern Zone [7th Zone] located at D War Zone. This meeting had shocked me because I had just been engaged in various battles and they now requested I return to paramilitary work. When they spoke to me they said, "Facing us is an important task, and you Tâm are young, healthy and have already tasted armed struggle." They went on to say, "We will give you a radio. You can form a new action unit, codenamed C200."
>
> Before departure my leaders showed me on a map where to meet my Northern counterparts. They pointed to a place called Bu Puguya. I was told that we must steer clear of the hill tribes, which

meant avoiding using their trails. This instruction was misleading as I had experienced the help of locals when I had conducted armed propaganda during the French War in Lai Châu Province.

When my action unit left D War Zone, we knew difficulty lay ahead because each man could only carry 5kg of rice. Within ten days the inevitable happened and our rice ran out. Not an easy thing to take deep in the jungle. If we went back then we had to walk with no food for ten days and on our arrival D War Zone might not have food for us anyway. We had to continue, a horrific situation because we were walking into the unknown.

Fortunately, on the river bank along the upper reaches of Đồng Nai we found a bulb-like food called *nâng*. Not ideal because, not only was it bitter but toxic, and if you ate just a small bit you got the feeling of being drunk and simply fell asleep. The southerners knew how to treat the bulb by soaking it in salted water for about three days and changing the water as much as twelve times. How could we make the bulb edible when we moved all the time? Where would the salt come from, a rare commodity in the mountains? We could either give up and starve or experiment. So we boiled the bulb until it lost its smell but it did not work and we all ended up drunk. Next, we put it in a basket in a fast-flowing stream and left it overnight. Much to our relief, by morning it was edible. This meant, although horrible in taste, we had food.

Exhausted, we managed to reach Bu Puguya. Thinking that this was our final destination I made radio contact with D War Zone to give them a situation report, only to be told to continue along the banks of the Đồng Nai River. It was like walking with ghosts, as abandoned hamlets came and went. We could only assume that the people had been relocated during the Agroville Plan [implemented to remove the neutral population from guerrilla contact].

It was not easy going, but by the end of August we finally found an inhabited hamlet called Bu Saria. A refreshing sight, but having arrived we now had to go against the advice of our local Party leaders and approach the people. We seemed to have no choice, we were desperately tired and hungry, and we just could not survive on *nâng*. Luckily, I had had experience in the ways of approaching hill tribes and the key to appeasing them was to pay special attention to their customs. With care I approached the chief and to our relief he welcomed us in. Again we were fortunate, I could not speak his language but, like me, he could speak French. That night, in true hill tribe tradition, he slaughtered pigs in our honor and the young played gongs to celebrate.

The following morning the chief suddenly pointed at me saying, "You are the soldiers of the Elder Hồ." Surprised, I tentatively asked how he knew. "I have heard that Elder Hồ's men have arrived in Đắk Lắk. They are having problems crossing the river due to the seasonal downpours." Through his jungle network of tribal whispers he knew that B90 had arrived. Now strangers had come to his village disguised as Southern troops.... He continued, "I knew who you were because no Southern troops would have entered a village with leprosy patients in! This is why we have not been included in the Agroville Plan." After days with the fear of starvation or being killed by a tribesman, I was slightly relieved that our cover had been blown.

Although I kept in radio contact with D War Zone, they had not given me the exact coordinates of B90. D War Zone had only given me a checkpoint location, just in case we had been arrested and our mission intercepted. Now, thanks to this tribe, at least I knew that I was in the right zone. So I asked if we could remain in his village, but he said, "No, if you stay, Southern troops will return and arrest our girls and steal our buffaloes. You must live in another part of the jungle, not the area we are living in now." We moved back into the jungle and made camp in a local cemetery because from experience I recognized that tradition forbade a tribe from returning to one of their ancestors' graves. By staying in the cemetery we reduced our risk of being discovered.

On addressing the need to find B90 I sent a telegram to D War Zone, saying, "If we are not allowed to mobilize the masses to build our infrastructure, we won't be able to link with the units coming from the North." On approval from D War Zone I immediately sent detachments to local villages so

Opposite: **This monument celebrates an important area of D War Zone. Based there were: a courier station for the Eastern Zone to receive aid and personnel from the North; a guard unit of COSVN; a logistics base; a health care station; and a training school for nurses for the Eastern Zone. At first all initial groups from the Orient stayed here before going on to other destinations, and the cabinet of COSVN was stationed here from 1961 to 1962 before moving to the base in Tây Ninh Province. Photographed in 2007 (Clive A. Hills).**

that they could build the infrastructure. D War Zone also informed me where I had to meet with B90. This was to be where the Đồng Nai River flowed south-east, a location where three provinces meet, resulting in less enemy presence. D War Zone instructed me to keep our patrol tactics flexible. We could either go in single file or double file. If we did the first of these patrol formations then only the first person "on point" might be shot and possibly killed. The best approach for moving in thick jungle. The second "staggered double-line formation" was the most efficient when looking for someone hiding. The instructions just stopped dead and gave no advice for the future, just saying, "Don't miss B90!"

I started to look for B90. I sent a group to cross the Vàm Daktih River. They reported that they had found signs that someone had cooked rice on the jungle floor, as if using a Hoàng Cầm cooking fire method to hide the smoke. This was not a cooking method of a local ethnic group, they cooked their rice in a bamboo tube. This was our first sign that B90 had been there and on closer inspection a small trail could be seen going into the trees. An attempt had been made to get rid of these signs, but by observing the ground closely they could be spotted. I radioed D War Zone, who told us to "stay put." So I always had one team waiting on duty there.

Finally, on 30 October at 2 p.m., someone shouted out, "They have arrived." We were so delighted that we forgot to say our passwords. We just hugged each other and burst into tears. For us it was clear that they were from B90 as only armed forces from the North wore that type of uniform. After months C200 had met the 1st attachment of B90, commanded by Comrade Phạm Văn Lạc, at Dak R'tih Commune, Bsa Nia highland village. They said that they had been waiting in Đắk Lắk Province from 30 July 1960 until now. Within the group there were troops from B500 who had met up with B90 in Đắk Lắk.

It was fortunate that we met each other as B90 and the troops from B500 did not have a radio transmitter. They had been halted in their position; although they had attempted to cross the river they had abandoned this idea because Trần Văn Thời had been swept away to his death. To reach us they had taken the decision to go back to the regrouping point in Đắk Lắk to communicate with the 5th Zone. This Zone then radioed the North, who contacted the Eastern Zone by radio. The Eastern Zone then called us and gave us instructions as to where they were. This is how we met. This route was named afterwards D1 corridor.[31]

On 4 November 1960, C300 and the 2nd attachment from B90 and troops from B500 met along Route 14 at the T-junction of Đăk Song. This corridor was given the name D2; in 2003, the author had visited the monument that celebrates this meeting of troops. The Party made D2 the reserve route because Route 14 was too exposed to the enemy, whereas D1's remoteness gave it some form of protection from the enemy. This was also its weakness, as its isolation made rice scarce for those that used it; an issue later resolved when local supplies were sourced and storage facilities built.

Tâm continued:

In November 1960, my group guided the high-ranking officers and soldiers, who we had met from B90 and B500, to Bầu Rã Hamlet [D War Zone] to join the first meeting of the [NLF] so that they could build the framework for a southern liberation army. Later in 1961, our D1 corridor was used by members of other action units who had been instructed by Hanoi to build upon this framework.

Shortly after our route had been developed we listened to *Agence France-Presse* [AFP] on the radio and they announced that a North-South Trail had now opened, and they named the corridor *La Piste de Hồ Chí Minh*, or in English the Hồ Chí Minh Trail. Yes, it was the French who named it the Hồ Chí Minh Trail. We called it the Trường Sơn Trail, after the mountain range where it ran: West Trường Sơn, which ran in Lao, or East Trường Sơn, which ran in Vietnam.[32]

Giáp's new Southward Strategic Corridor built upon what he had started in the 1940s in Tonkin and Phạm Ngọc Thảo had continued later in Annam. Eventually this new corridor expanded beyond what had gone before to become a communications liaison post and transport strategic logistics corridor. On land Hồ's enemy referred to it as the Hồ Chí Minh Trail and those routes that went along the coastline of Vietnam were nicknamed

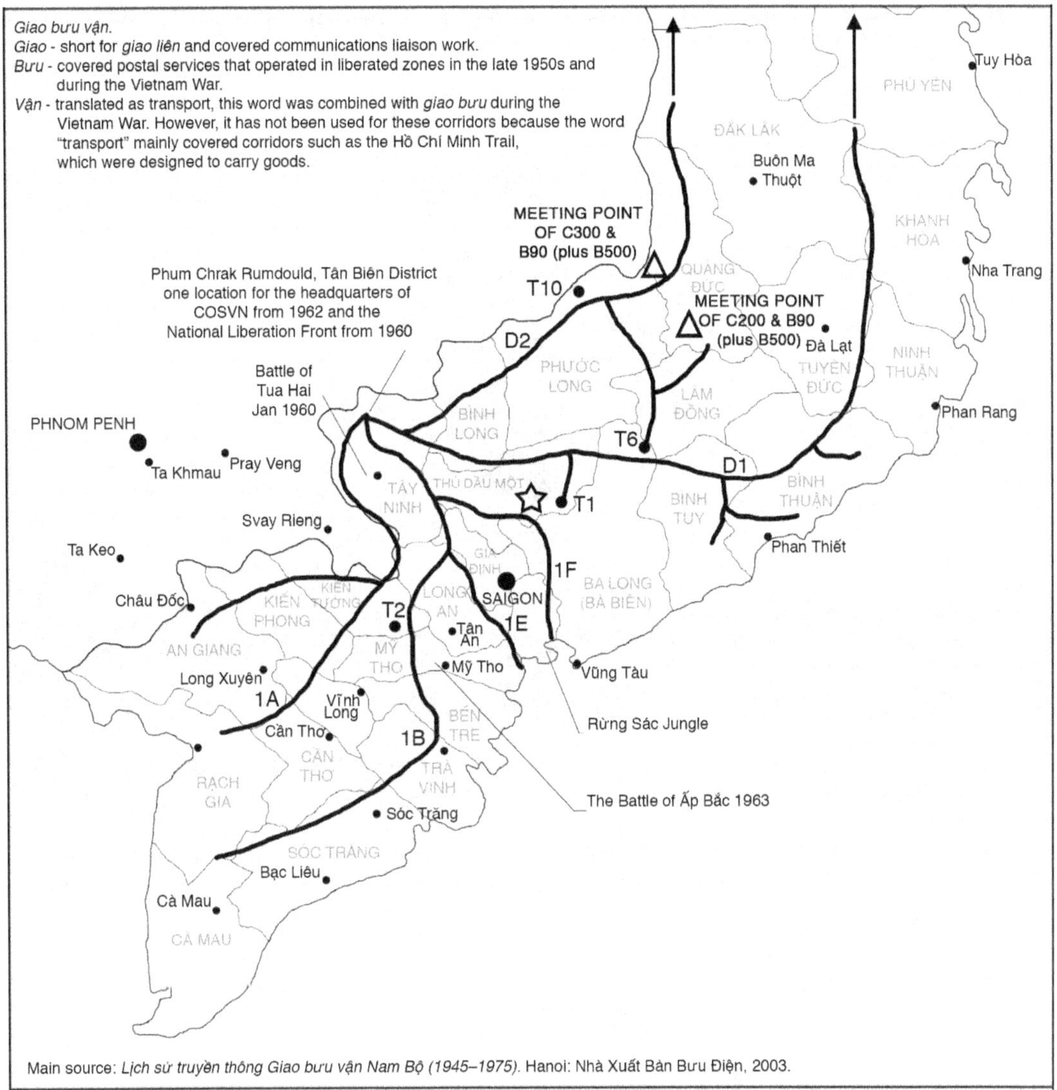

Giao bưu vận.
Giao - short for *giao liên* and covered communications liaison work.
Bưu - covered postal services that operated in liberated zones in the late 1950s and during the Vietnam War.
Vận - translated as transport, this word was combined with *giao bưu* during the Vietnam War. However, it has not been used for these corridors because the word "transport" mainly covered corridors such as the Hồ Chí Minh Trail, which were designed to carry goods.

Main source: *Lịch sử truyền thông Giao bưu vận Nam Bộ (1945–1975)*. Hanoi: Nhà Xuất Bản Bưu Điện, 2003.

— *Giao bưu* corridors
The *Giao Liên* Department for the Cochinchina Regional Party Committee was established in June 1960, four of their initial southern corridors were 1A, 1B, T1 and T4 (T4 being Tây Ninh to Gia Định). Each corridor, and future ones, used the concepts developed from the Southward March of the 1940s.

The *Giao Bưu* Department for COSVN was established in June 1962 and superseded the *Giao Liên* Department. They expanded their network, which included reserve corridors codenamed 1A1, 1B1, 1C1, 1E1, 1D1 and 1D2. As a general rule, 1A1, branched from 1A.

 The original D1 and D2 were established in 1960. Nguyễn Trọng Tâm of C200 met B90 (and troops from B500) from the North in Dak R'tih whereas Lâm Quốc Đăng of C300 met B90 (and troops from B500) at Đăk Song. The meeting points were in Đắk Lắk Province when looking at Hanoi's regional definitions but the Southern administration identified this part of Đắk Lắk as Quảng Đức Province. The routes built by Tâm and Đăng eventually evolved into those shown on this map; some corridors became part of the Hồ Chí Minh Trail.

 The headquarters of Central Office for South Vietnam (COSVN) was in D War Zone until it moved in 1962. COSVN was the American term for North Vietnam's political and military headquarters in the South.

***Giao bưu* corridors from 1962 to 1965.**

204　　Part II. Evolution and Application of the Blueprint (1954–1975)

Monument at Đăk Song along Route 14, erected to celebrate the historic meeting of C300 (from South Vietnam) with those of B90 (from North Vietnam) in 1960 (Clive A. Hills).

the Hồ Chí Minh Trail Sea Route. With the establishment of the Hồ Chí Minh Trail, Hanoi could now create their much-needed southern liberation army, as instructed under Resolution 15.

A Southern Military Force

To administer the formation of a southern liberation army, Nguyễn Hữu Thọ formally established the National Liberation Front (NLF) on 20 December 1960, with its headquarters in Tân Biên District, Tây Ninh Province.

Communist Party members of the NLF wisely established an organizational structure to take advantage of the Vietnamese people's desires for independence and justice. As the Việt Minh had done before, the NLF openly opposed the puppet regime, this time of the Southern administration. Likewise, it strove to incorporate a number of groups from all classes and non-communist backgrounds under one canopy, meaning that the majority of NLF members were not Communist Party members and many had intelligentsia backgrounds. The Communist Party controlled the NLF either directly from the Worker's Party of Vietnam in the North or via its southern branch called the People's Revolutionary Party (PRP), to be established in 1962. The southern branch of the Party Central Committee was COSVN, who ran the PRP. COSVN had been officially re-established on 23 November 1961. Due to communication difficulties, at first COSVN only ran the revolution in Cochinchina, which included Eastern (T1), Central (T2), Western (T3) and Saigon–Chợ Lớn–Gia Định–Rừng Sác (T4). Hanoi administered Annam and the Central Highlands.

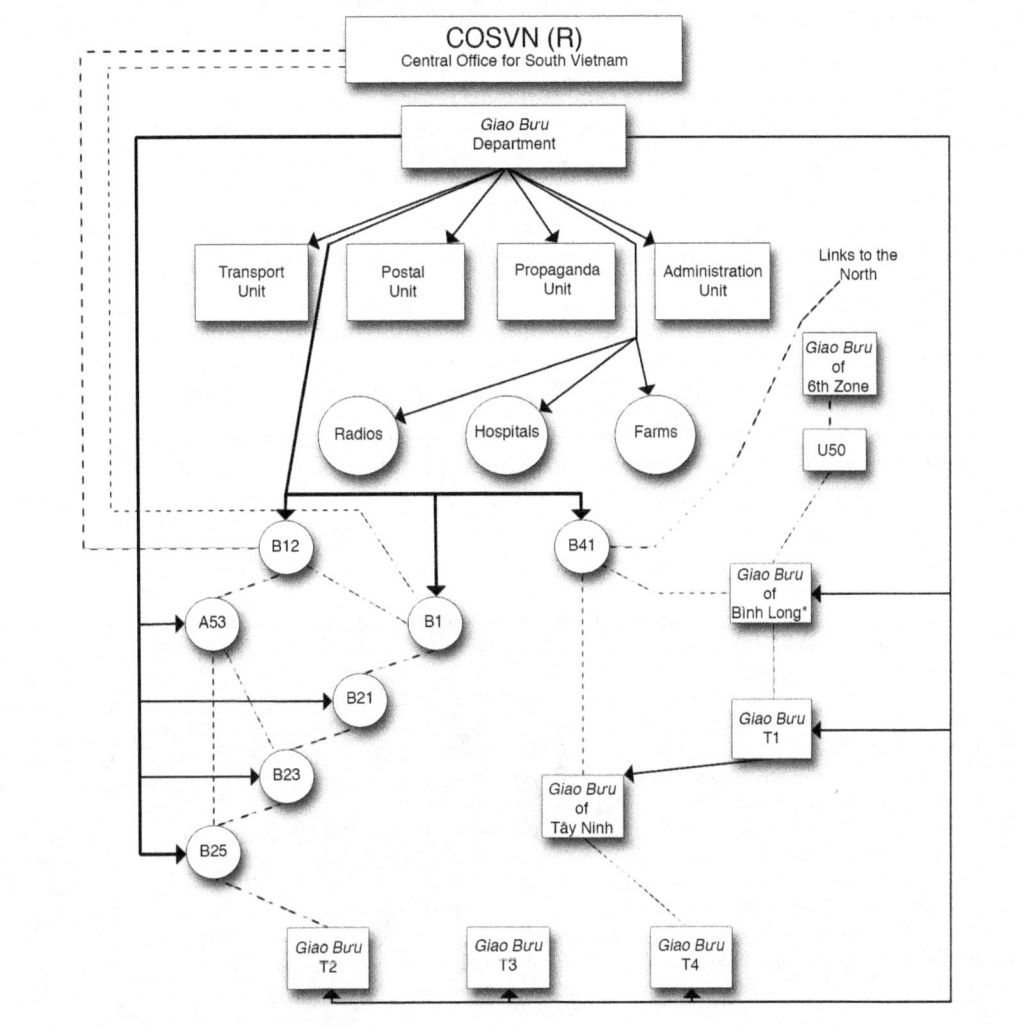

Main source: *Lịch sử truyền thông Giao bưu vận Nam Bộ (1945–1975)*. Hanoi: Nhà Xuất Bản Bưu Điện, 2003.

- *Giao Bưu* Department = Communication Liaison Post Department.
- R is the codename for COSVN, R came from the French word for "région."
- Cochinchina Inter-Provincial Party Committees = (T1) Eastern, (T2) Central, (T3) Western and (T4) Saigon-Chợ Lớn-Gia Định-Rừng Sác.
- The dotted lines represent areas run by COSVN and the *Giao Bưu* Department, and the solid lines are those services run only by the department.
- * Bình Long Province is part of present day Bình Phước Province.

Examples of change:
On 20 June 1962, COSVN issued instruction No 19/CTR, which set boundaries for their new *Giao Bưu* Department. It ordered that,
- the department's structure and hierarchy be defined.
- postal units in liberated areas must construct letterboxes, and deliver and collect the post.
- transport units must develop, monitor and protect corridors; receive delegates such as those sent by Hanoi along the Hồ Chí Minh Trail; and build field depots and warehouses for the military.

Giao Bưu stations of this department were codenamed A53, B1, B12, B21, B23, B25 and B41 and served, for example:
- B1 was for important people, and the main post dispatch point for COSVN and their mail to South Vietnam and Hanoi.
- B41 was responsible for working with the provinces of Bình Long and Tây Ninh (the location of COSVN). It served as a reception place for people and troops from North Vietnam and for recruits from the Mekong Delta and Saigon.
- A53 started in 1965, and was established to connect COSVN with the 8th and 9th Zones. It cut down the time of travel by weeks.
- U50 was a strategic station between T1 and the 6th Zone.
Station locations and names changed throughout this period such as at the end of 1964, B12=V12, B23=V23 and B25=V25.

By mid-1963, there was a *Giao Bưu* Department in each district of around three to five people plus couriers. In each commune there was a courier cell, or a larger station when manpower allowed, which supported any main corridor that ran through their area.

Organizational layout of the *Giao Bưu* Department of COSVN 1962 to 1965.

The military arm in the South was named the Liberation Armed Forces of South Vietnam. Giáp signed the order to establish it and assigned Trần Lương to be the overseer. He was a deputy head of the Political General Directorate and Giáp had first instructed him to start reverse regrouping back in 1954. To blur the connection between this army and the communists, communist propaganda put forward that the NLF controlled the Liberation Army. In fact, the Liberation Army was part of the VNPA and run by Hanoi via COSVN in Cochinchina. The Liberation Army had the three tiers of armed units within its structure.

To expand the Liberation Army, Hanoi ordered further action units to head south in 1961, and later coded the missions the Orient.[33] Trần Văn Quang was the overall commander. His action unit consisted of 500 revolutionaries that were again from the 330th and the 338th Divisions. They traveled down the Hồ Chí Minh Trail in Lao; now the chosen route of Group 559 because areas around Route 9 in Lao had been liberated in April. Trần Văn Quang and his action unit arrived at their assembly area in Bình Long Province on 28 July 1961. He took up his post as deputy military commissar of COSVN. Others within the group were assigned to staff agencies within the Military Affairs Section

The sea trail (photographed in 2007) is recognized to have been established on 23 October 1961, when the 759th Mission officially formed. The first significant North to South journey took place a year later in the wooden boat Orient 1. It left K15 Wharf, Hải Phòng Province and docked at Vàm Lũng Wharf, Cà Mau Province successfully delivering 30 tons of weapons and military equipment. The monument in this image is at Chùm Gọng, near Vàm Lũng Wharf, and it commemorates the location where Bông Văn Dĩa hid his iron vessel when he had been pursued by the enemy, shortly after his first historic trip from the North in Orient 1. Dĩa did not travel back to the North but stayed to be the vice commander of the southern 962 unit, under the 759th Mission (Clive A. Hills).

of COSVN in the 7th, 8th and 9th Military Zones and the Saigon-Chợ Lớn-Gia Định-Rừng Sác Special Zone.

Three other important action units had left for the South in February 1961. Trần Công An led the first advance team, Nguyễn Văn Nhỏ the second and Thà the Tenth the third. Once they had arrived in the South these groups carried out their orders from Hanoi.[34]

In mid–1961 Trần Lương, the military commissar of COSVN, formed the first two battalions of the Liberation Army, one under Trần Công An and the other under Nguyễn Văn Nhỏ.[35] These two battalions created the nucleus of the first regiment of the main regular army, named as Q761, after the seventh month, July 1961. Q761 helped move the headquarters of the Liberation Army from D War Zone to C War Zone, Tây Ninh Province, where they would also be based.[36] Trần Công An stayed at D War Zone to establish COSVN's headquarters there and ran their logistics. Thà the Tenth commanded the second regimental-sized unit of the Liberation Army, known as the 3rd Regiment. With these events, Hồ had opened communications between North and South Vietnam and Giáp had the means to again execute his war without boundaries.

Ready for War

By the beginning of the 1960s, the strategies for a modern All-People's War had been designed in line with Resolution 15. Over the next few years the Military Proselytizing Department in the North sent other men like Tâm to South Vietnam. The first group in 1954 had comprised thirty-four people. The second group added seventeen people. From 1959 to 1964, the department sent a total of 222 people, the majority being military personnel and part of the Orient mission.

What is more, departments other than the Military Proselytizing Department sent people to South Vietnam. Their roles covered the establishment of various parts of the Revolutionary Infrastructure and the three strategic fronts. Now with the French gone, Hồ's blueprint for revolution was again waged, but this time against Americans and South Vietnamese.

11

A Divided Country

The Next Generation

Hanoi aimed to unite Vietnam before the Americans sent in ground troops. The Americans called this period leading up to sending in ground troops, a Special War, and in practical terms this meant that the United States would adopt unconventional warfare, including counterinsurgency and psychological operations, but without the commitment of high numbers of ground troops. Hồ would lead the revolution through some of the Special War era but he later privately told the Soviet ambassador that he had "resigned" from current affairs in 1963, and therefore did not conduct the everyday direction of the country. This had been left to hardline communist Lê Duẩn.

Prior to Hồ's diminishing responsibilities, many of the strategic operations executed by the communists during the Special War were designed by Hồ and Giáp in the late 1950s and early 1960s. The overriding objective was to crush the Saigon regime but also remove U.S. advisors from the South. To create the conditions to do this, one idea proposed was that the communists could try and humiliate the U.S. into leaving by destroying their image and labeling them the "ringleaders of imperialism," as well as fight the United States and the Southern regime with acts of terror and if needed progress to a general offensive and general uprising. During this period it was agreed that any act must only be designed to put just enough pressure on the United States to get them to seek a peaceful solution but not enough to provoke large-scale retaliation and goad them into sending in ground troops. The communists had limited time, if they failed to take Vietnam during the Special War they then had to prepare to win a Limited War or Local War. These latter two terms referred to the fact that the United States would send in high ground troop numbers but not commit their full military strength to Vietnam.

The rare memoirs of Ms. Lê Thị Thu Nguyệt (1944–) typify the voice of the youth during this Special War period. Their stories are similar to those of their forefathers, but what makes them differ to some degree, is this youth had only ever known war and had no adult first-hand experience of the French colonial days; their angry and dismay was detached from the root cause of the revolution. This meant that when the communist propaganda machine sent out negative massages about the United States, the youth absorb them, because an American presence in Vietnam is all they related to. This enabled the communists to blame the United States unjustly for all French errors and the general upheaval in Vietnam.

Born in Saigon, Ms. Nguyệt's father worked for the former government but had secretly joined the Việt Minh in 1936, conducting propaganda among French residents in the city. Her mother gave money to support the cause from her modest takings in Tân Định Market, where she sold clothes. Her mother died when Ms. Nguyệt was six years old, and she was taken to live with her uncle, who had fought for the Việt Minh. She later studied to become a doctor, hoping that one day she could provide people with the treatment that had been denied her mother.

Ms. Nguyệt explained:

The Americans had arrived, my country was not free or at peace, people still lacked good medicine, so when it became impossible for me to study because of the war, I did the right thing and joined the revolution. My father had written to me from Hanoi, where he had regrouped in 1954. Writing to me was no easy task because at that time a letter had to go via Cambodia or Paris. So when my future leaders handed me his letter, which said that as the elections had been canceled only armed struggle was an option, I knew he wanted me to join. I think this all happened because former comrades of my parents had noticed my activities in student demonstrations and strikes.

When I became a courier I was just a teenager. I conveyed secret letters written in invisible ink and coded. On many occasions the text was just a concealed line in a newspaper or on a small piece of paper hidden in my shoe or hair. I had to learn some messages by heart and deliver them verbally, such as before leaving home my handler told me to put on a prearranged colored shirt, and having arrived at the appointed place, I had to find a person wearing a designated colored hat. To be sure they were the correct person, I approached them and said my given password, or conveyed a signal such as sitting down, standing up and so on.

When I had to collect or deposit a letter from a secret box or dead-letter box my handler told me to approach the location exactly as instructed. When I collected from a dead-letter box I never saw the person who left the letter. They went in the morning and I collected the letter in the evening. If I turned up at the wrong time, or worse saw the person who deposited the letter, then the box was abandoned and I would be viewed as a possible informer. I didn't know who my superiors were, all I understood was what the leaders told me, "For every child to go to school we must liberate the country, as the Americans have taken over from the French."

I continued to be a courier and also be very active within the student movement. My leaders liked the fact that I could direct others and they asked me to take on an additional task, of an urban underground elite armed force fighter, around 1959. A huge responsibility because I became a team leader almost straight away. Again it was unpaid so I had to work during the week, and at the weekends I studied or guided revolutionaries back and forth from Saigon to the war zone.

I was excited but nervous when I went to my first war zone, a region near Saigon that had been a Bình Xuyên base. There I saw many local regular forces, of which some were former Bình Xuyên fighters. This made me happy as a baby because I thought that Hanoi was nearby and so was my father, like one big happy family. I ran around the area asking people at random where he was. If we met up he could then send me to school to become a doctor. Then one soldier pulled me aside and gently stroked my hair, and answered, "Just wait, the Americans might wake up and see the situation so that peace will be restored. Then surely you will go to school."

Now that I had a dual role as a courier and fighter, my leaders gave me high-risk tasks. One time they ordered me to guide a group of revolutionaries. These people were seated on a bus and to find my designated person within the group my handler had given me a signal. When I had made contact, the second contacted the third and so on, each person only knowing one of his fellow travelers through a completely different signal. This meant that if the enemy arrested one of us that person could not reveal more than one of their team.

I also took letters to Vietnamese traitors who fought with the Americans. We warned, "If you continue to repress your fellow countrymen, by burning their houses and damaging their villages, you will be punished." If that person did not change their attitudes after several attempts, our urban underground elite armed forces, who specialized in dealing with traitors, were sent in. I only found out how they dealt with the person by reading it in a Saigon newspaper later. The paper might say that a person had been executed by revolutionaries.... To stop someone acting against us was a long process. The revolutionary side had to wait for the wrongdoers to repent their sins or not. If they expressed repentance, then we did not punish them by force. Execution was the ultimate measure.[1]

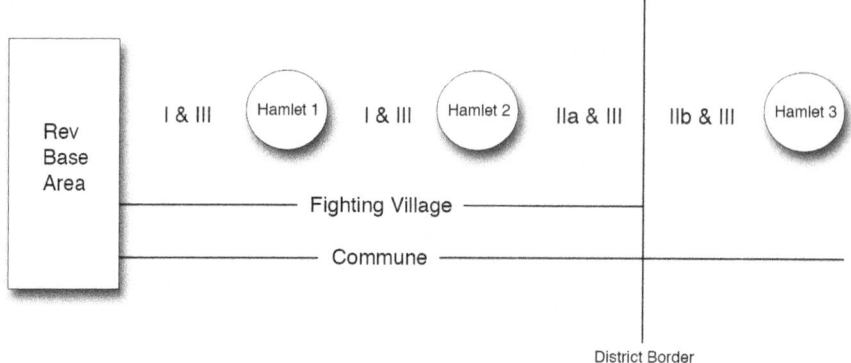

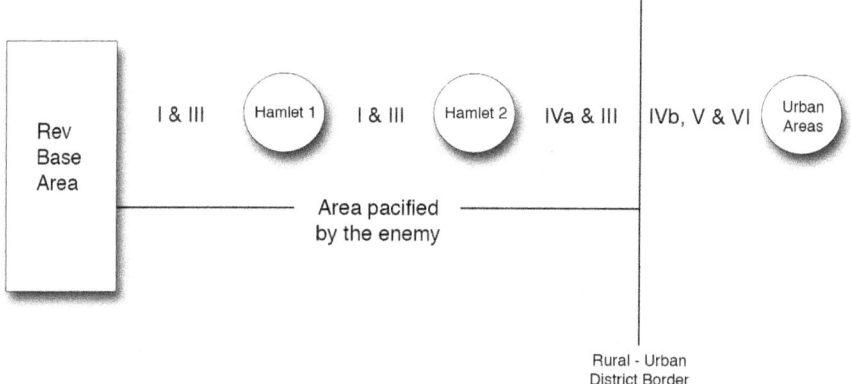

Main source from a book by Đặng Phong reference, *5 đường mòn Hồ Chí Minh*. Hanoi: Tri Thức, 2008.

Key to courier type operating.

I   *Giao liên ấp* - Hamlet communications liaison agent.

II *Giao liên xã* - Commune communications liaison agent.

III *Giao liên du kích* - Communications liaison guerrilla.

IV *Giao liên biệt động* - Communications liaison urban underground elite armed force.

V   *Giao liên hợp pháp* - Communications liaison agent who used legal papers innocently handed out to them by the Southern authority. If the agent used fake papers they were a *giao liên bất hợp pháp* and operated at night.

VI *Giao liên đơn tuyến* - Communications liaison agent who just served one intelligence agent.

Where there is an "a" and a "b" this might be the same courier, but it would depend on where the hamlet was compared to the district border. Between two courier stations or two army stations there was a way station (*cung đường*) every 40km. If this was not possible then there was a smaller post (*bãi khách*) to rest at but hidden within the forest with limited facilities and exposed to the elements.

General principles of courier networks when guiding revolutionaries.

Ms. Nguyệt studied when she could as well as worked part-time in the Institute of Pharmaceutical Products run by Dr. Tính. It was a dangerous but interesting choice because, not only did Dr. Tính's brother-in-law have a job in the Southern regime's secret service, but Dr. Tính himself worked for Diệm as a food taster. Diệm was afraid of being poisoned and just the mere threat of this became a highly effective propaganda ruse for the revolutionaries to keep the war in the headlines of foreign newspapers. It was at this time that Ms. Nguyệt suffered a family tragedy.

Ms. Nguyệt continued:

My first cousin married a revolutionary who had originally been working in Lao during the French War. After the Geneva Accords he returned home but he was arrested by men associated with Ngô Đình Cẩn [1911–1964], the brother of Diệm. While in prison my cousin gave birth to their baby but blood came from my cousin's nose and mouth and because she was married to a political prisoner the staff did nothing, nor did the physicians. I gave up my studies to care for her but she died soon after.

I was just sixteen years old and so naive. I left her body on the hospital bed and ran home to fetch my uncle to help. It was 3 a.m. when we got back to the hospital. We were so late her corpse had been moved to the mortuary and her newborn baby had already been sent to the orphanage. My uncle went off to get a casket. I agreed to enter the morgue. I jumped through a window. Everything was quiet. The guard slept. Only a small dim light lit the way. The condition of the morgue at Hùng Vương Hospital made me sad, with rows of dead bodies wrapped in just mats. I opened each one to look for my cousin. I did this several times before I found her. I burst into tears. Through the dim light I looked down at my feet and there on the floor were the corpses of babies. I felt sick with the thought of ants crawling over their dead bodies. I ran to the window to get out. My uncle had already arrived with the casket. Soon after that we buried her. Just my uncle, her two children and I turned up. So tragic.

I wrote to the Sisters of Mercy at the orphanage asking them to return the baby. When they did I had no idea what to do and all they gave me was a dozen tins of Nestlé Milk. The baby kept me awake and I kept falling asleep in my lessons. My teachers viewed me as a good student, not one to go out dancing all night, and asked me why. I could not tell them that my uncle could not help me because he worked for the revolution. Instead I said that he had taken on a concubine and that he was not prepared to look after his own baby. I decided to give up my studies so that I could work full-time at the pharmacy, pay for childcare and still operate for the revolution. This worked for some time but the babysitters kept stealing the baby's milk to feed their own families. In the end, another cousin in Đà Nẵng cared for the baby.

I hated working for Dr. Tính. He treated us like slaves but this harsh atmosphere posed new opportunities because I guessed from mutterings that some of the workers used to be revolutionaries during the French War. They now worked for Dr. Tính because they had left their villages, mainly in central Vietnam, to avoid Diệm's oppression. I reported these people to my superiors, who asked me to reunite them with the resistance. They agreed to join the ranks of the urban revolutionaries. I felt proud that I had done this.

Distinguishing friend from foe was not easy. I had to be careful because the Southern administration had started to use secret agents to infiltrate into work areas and student movements. I knew that there was an informer at our workplace. It was just a feeling at first but it proved right. I confronted the person and began propaganda against them. I told them directly, "We are not free, the Americans are here. Do not do anything to harm the people's cause. Only the revolution will lead to our liberation and a happier life."[2]

Ms. Nguyệt left the pharmacy after she confronted her work colleague. Frightened of reprisals, she approached her leaders to ask if she could work covertly, but they refused, saying that she had not been compromised to any great extent. Instead, they moved her near to Ngã Bảy, a junction where seven roads met, where she lived in a house belonging to a contractor whose wife worked for the revolution. She shared a room with a girl whose name was similar to hers, which meant that Ms. Nguyệt could use the girl's ID to

Part of the Củ Chi tunnel complex located just outside Hồ Chí Minh City. 2003 photograph (Clive A. Hills).

travel safely. Nevertheless, there were serious complications and each time the police cold-called on the house to check that the numbers living within the dwelling concurred with their register she had to hide in the well because she was not listed as an inhabitant.

She lived a double life for some time until her leaders moved her to a war zone near Củ Chi, a location famous for the Củ Chi tunnels; an immense secret underground warren of rooms and interconnecting passages that eventually ran for more than 325km.[3] The Communist Party tasked Ms. Nguyệt to move revolutionaries back and forth to Saigon from the war zone, using the district of Củ Chi as a springboard. They chose this district not so that she could use the tunnel complex but because a family within the area had agreed to feed her.

Ms. Nguyệt clarified:

> By day I went to the city, at dusk I returned to Củ Chi War Zone. I found it difficult to pay for travel and living because I did not work. My Saigon leaders did give me 5 đồng a month, to buy goods for female hygiene, but I still had to find additional money.[4] So I taught lessons to people in Củ Chi where I stayed, which not only gave me cover but within my classes I conducted propaganda as well.
>
> Out in the fields in Củ Chi, I helped build defenses. I liked being with the local guerrillas, they were more friendly than the city dwellers. My leaders criticized me for doing this because my skin blackened from the sun and I no longer fitted into city life. Each time my leaders saw me helping the local guerrillas they sent me back to Saigon. Each time they sent me back, I returned to the burning sun, not really understanding why I shouldn't.
>
> My task in these days was to guide people and carry letters. I also got involved in conveying weapons into Saigon, to be held at secret armories. It was at this time that the war took on a new phase with another *coup d'etat* against Diệm...[5]

Ms. Nguyệt's story shows how the revolution could transfer to the next generation, nevertheless, recruiting to fight the United States would not be easy. This war focused on South Annam and Cochinchina and, although the Party's message was still one of nationalism, this emotive subject had strong competition: U.S. wealth, the fear of communism and the clear fact that the people of the Mekong Delta did not want socialism because their livelihoods were enriched due to the abundance of fresh fish and rice within the region. These points meant that in order to win over large numbers of Southern people, of any generation, the Party had to dig much deeper than just nationalist propaganda, and further humiliate the United States by damaging the goodies they offered.

Damaging the "Ringleaders of Imperialism"

Since the start of the new John F. Kennedy (1917–1963) administration of January 1961 there had been rising levels of violence in South Vietnam. Prior to that period the main area of concern had not been Vietnam but Lao, a country that the previous administration of Eisenhower had viewed as pivotal to the stability of the region. Eisenhower's thinking was that if Lao became communist then Hanoi could use the country as a launch point to conduct a conventional military attack on Annam, Cochinchina or Cambodia. If Hanoi asked communist China to help in any of these attacks then its Red Army might remain in the area after the initial assault, or even act alone, sweeping through Lao to spread communism to Indonesia.

The ability of Hanoi to take Lao and then to use it as a route to South Vietnam was a genuine threat; the country was poorly defended. During this period Lao had a coalition government with neutralist Souvanna Phouma as prime minister. In 1958 this coalition collapsed, as a result of America suspending aid to Lao following the victory of the political left in supplementary elections. Far from bringing stability to the region, and getting Lao under the influence of the Americans, this move did the opposite and pushed the country further into the hands of the communists.

Kennedy was determined to take the initiative in the struggle against international communism in Vietnam, not just in Lao, something that he believed the previous administration had failed to do. Kennedy said to his National Security Council in April 1961, "We are opposed around the world by a monolithic and ruthless conspiracy that relies primarily on covert means for expanding its sphere of influence—on infiltration instead of invasion, on subversion instead of elections, on intimidation instead of free choice, on guerrillas by night instead of armies by day." He went on to say that to understand this, people should read the works of Mao Zedong and Che Guevara on guerrilla warfare.[6]

That April, a task force, commissioned at the request of the White House, recommended a significant increase in military aid to Diệm. Throughout the rest of the year the United States and the Diệm administration signed a mutual defense treaty. To follow was an agreement to increase the number of U.S. advisors and introduce a small number of combat support troops in Vietnam. This marked the beginning of a period of transition from the use of U.S. advisors to the direct participation of armed forces in combat operations.

In November 1961, Kennedy and the National Security Council officially approved a Special War strategy to pacify South Vietnam within eighteen months. Kennedy went for a counterinsurgency approach because, unlike Eisenhower, he thought that the problem was not just military but political and wanted to create conditions to enable political stability in the South.

Kennedy believed that the Southern administration needed greater control over their population and by providing the populace with economic and social incentives they could be encouraged to support the government. Greater control could be given to the Southern administration through a mixture of military, social, psychological, economic and political measures.

To turn theory into action on the ground, Kennedy wanted to conduct: covert operations in North Vietnam primarily to stop the flow of supplies to South Vietnam; use ARVN soldiers to do sweeping operations using helicopter and armored vehicle assaults; and start rural pacification under the Strategic Hamlet Program. This program meant building secure hamlets for rural communities to stop the communists getting to them. Then, by providing extra foreign aid to support the Southern administration, this in turn could be filtered rapidly down to these hamlets.

The Strategic Hamlet Program was based on previous experiences. In the first instance, during the French War the Việt Minh had successfully established and used fighting villages, communities that were fortified against the enemy. Some of those who had participated in these fighting villages had now switched sides and taken this valuable information with them. Another source of information came from when the British fought the Chinese communists led insurgency in Malaya from 1948 to 1960. One British strategy had been to place the Malayans in fortified villages that were guarded around the clock and thus separated the people from the guerrillas in the jungle. Also, the use of fortified villages was one very successful way to fight Mao Zedong's concept that a guerrilla fighter must move among the people as a fish swims in the sea. This is why fortified villages in Vietnam were referred to as "bail out the water in order to catch the fish."

As a final example, using the principle of fortified villages, Diệm had implemented a Rural Community Development Program in 1959 called Agroville. By 1960, there were more than twenty enclosures each consisting of many thousands of people. It failed partly because some elements of it were driven by Phạm Ngọc Thảo and Vũ Anh. Thảo had established the secret service for the communists in the 1940s and had since got into a position of influence with Diệm. Anh had been Thảo's former *aide de camp*.

Anh got close to Diệm around 1956 after arranging an apparently coincidental meeting with him, and won Diệm over by cutting both the president's and his wife's profiles in silhouette. Anh was able to arrange this meeting because Anh knew Trần Kim Tuyến, a top counter-intelligence officer for Diệm and Ngô Đình Nhu (1910–1963), Diệm's brother.[7] Ironically, Tuyến had some doubts about Anh and had only opened up a friendship with Anh to monitor him. Anh suspected this. To distract attention away from himself, Anh purposely went around to Tuyến's house, under the guise of giving his children art lessons, to monitor Tuyến's feelings on him.

Thảo started to come to the attention of Diệm in 1958 because, under the Corrections Program, his administration accepted seasoned commanders from other armies. Although Thảo had been a commander at battalion level in the Việt Minh, ARVN took him on as a captain, and he worked as the head of the local armed forces in Vĩnh Long Province. Being a captain was a minor posting but as a Catholic in that location it brought him into contact with Archbishop Ngô Đình Thục (1897–1984), another of Diệm's brothers. This meant that when Anh wanted to display his artwork, so that he could mingle

11. A Divided Country

Vũ Anh (middle in a white top and trousers) at a birthday party of an American living in Saigon during the Vietnam War. He often turned up at high society parties, and by cutting the silhouettes of those present, he could fish for information while doing so (courtesy Vũ Anh).

with or spy on high society, Thảo approached Thục and rented a space in his church library. It was not such a hard ask because Anh wanted to display photographs of himself taken with Diệm and Nhu. From these events Thảo and Anh moved up the social ladder.

According to Anh, Thảo was the architect of the Agroville Plan and had persuaded Diệm to adopt it, a task made easier because Diệm had a limited understanding of war. Diệm needed this project so that he could get the Americans committed to South Vietnam along with their money, but without being seen to surrender his independence and rule to them. Diệm saw Agroville as a cash cow and led him to think: no VC, no money. Anh worked in the department founded by Thảo and

Vũ Anh leaving for Cà Mau Province for an exhibition, which had been organized by President Ngô Đình Diệm. This exhibition toured South Vietnam to promote craftwork and homemade goods but also gave this communist agent a legitimate reason to travel (courtesy Vũ Anh).

Vũ Anh (front left) and an unidentified deputy minister of information for the Republic of Vietnam (front right) cut a ribbon to open one of the many galleries Vũ Anh had established in Saigon and Southern provinces in the late 1950s. These galleries were set up on the pretext of raising money for the poor, but were in fact a good cover for his covert work; this was not only because he could meet distinguished people and get information from them, but he could also siphon off any money made and spend it on his covert work (courtesy Vũ Anh).

helped choose camp locations; guiding policymakers to areas where the population hated Agroville. Meanwhile, Thảo worked as an advisor to Diệm and deliberately forced the program forward at an untenable speed; making the camps too big, too far apart and with inadequate communications and coordination between them.

By the time Kennedy announced his Strategic Hamlet Program, millions had already been spent and thousands more people hated Diệm. In fact, by early 1962, Diệm had been the subject of two failed attempted coups. The new program was initiated in early 1962 and aimed to change all this. R.K. Thompson, a former British defense secretary and the official who had conceptualized the anti-terrorist campaign in Malaya, was brought in to advise Diệm. He changed the direction of the program; each camp just housed 100 or 200 people, had well-trained guards protecting them, had efficient coordination between sites, with more aid to the people and better development opportunities than before.

The main failing of the scheme is always cited as the fact that the ethnic groups simply did not want to be taken from their ancestral homes. They believed that living on earth was just a temporary state, whereas their permanent life was in another world, and to earn good merit in order to gain safe passage and position in the permanent world, they had to make offerings to their ancestors. Therefore, when Diệm removed them from their homes they could no longer make these offerings.[8]

One little known reason for its failure, and that of its earlier sister programs, was the misunderstanding of what the metaphorical "water" was. For Mao Zedong, his water was the people. For the Vietnamese communists the "water" was the people and their many other covert services. This meant that, far from bailing out the water in order to catch the fish, these fortified hamlets gave a relatively secure and safe environment for the communists to operate within. This security allowed the communists to recruit and control the people and eventually to engender so much hatred in them that they would rise up and burn down their Strategic Hamlet.

Deputy President Nguyễn Ngọc Thơ of the Republic of Vietnam (right) praises Vũ Anh for his artwork at his gallery in 1956 (courtesy Vũ Anh).

Still, key to foiling the Strategic Hamlet Program was that Diệm still trusted Thảo, and when Nhu employed him to oversee the project, Thảo could direct the program in favor of the communists. Through men like Thảo and Vũ Anh, Hồ could not only damage America's image but stage manage the South through nationalism and fear.

Acts of Terror

The manipulation of the Strategic Hamlet Program became just one part of Hanoi's efforts to push the United States into finding a peaceful solution for Vietnam; another was to attack high-profile targets. The aim of these attacks was to show the Americans that they could not win because the revolutionaries would continue come what may. To conduct these acts of terror, Communist Party leaders instructed urban underground elite armed forces to strike areas such as Tân Sơn Nhất Airport, the Brink Hotel, the Caravelle Hotel, the USNS *Card* aircraft carrier and the My Canh Floating Restaurant.[9]

Ms. Nguyệt described her role:

> Now that the Geneva Accords were not going to be implemented, we had to fight not just the Southern troops but the Americans. This new situation meant that any urban underground elite armed forces were permitted to strike when the opportune moment arose. As an urban underground elite armed force member, I did not want to fight the Southern troops, as they were just misguided people.
>
> To understand the Americans and their weak points, I went to places where they congregated, including big hotels or luxurious restaurants. I sometimes disguised myself as a school girl from a

rich family, or in the evening I dressed as a glamorous young lady. If I had to talk to an American, I had to show him a good time, be a playgirl. My superior also drove me in a luxury car so we fitted in and at the same time he taught me how to conduct reconnaissance, smuggle information or transport light weapons.

My first true battle was on 26 October 1962, the date that Diệm had declared to be our National Day; chosen to commemorate the formation of the Republic of Vietnam. Diệm's regime was planning to celebrate this day by holding a ceremony, which included exhibits shown over several days. Our leaders controlling operations in Saigon instructed us to sabotage the event, but with the strict proviso that we must not harm bystanders.

During these early years any important event that the Southern administration held was conducted in the streets in front of the Presidential Palace. On this occasion the exhibits included weapons. They showed the ones they had captured from us, such as grenades, hand-made crude smoothbores and rifles. They also exhibited their state-of-the-art weapons, which included a UH-1A helicopter, displayed in the street we call Nguyễn Huệ today. The Southern regime promoted helicopter transportation tactics. They wanted to make the people believe that our primitive Việt Cộng weapons were no match for their powerful ones. The authorities similarly drew pictures of our Việt Cộng members looking woefully thin and inadequate. Our group became angry and discussed how to retaliate. At that time I commanded many cells of urban underground elite armed forces [biệt độngs], all of which had around three people in. I had set up and now ran a group called the 159 Biệt Động Unit, which comprised several people, mainly students. All my fighters were under the command of the Saigon Biệt Độngs.

Within my 159 Biệt Động Unit each of us had a code to identify each other, usually a code number. We made our plan. I had to veto one suggestion because it centered on throwing a hand grenade into a pile of mines. I said to this, "The people who have come to see the exhibition are not guilty." So we decided to destroy the UH-1A, the symbol of their modern war and a centerpiece of the exhibition. To destroy this would disrupt their National Day ceremony.

During the conflict the Presidential Palace became an army command control center, and included an underground complex and a heliport on the roof; the helicopter on display in this 2003 photograph is the same model used during the conflict (Clive A. Hills).

I had to take the grenade to a place that only I knew. I would not be directly involved in the attack. This was our protocol. Those who transported the weapons had to be separated from those who executed the attack. This way, if the enemy caught my colleagues, they could not lead them to the weapons or get others into trouble. I dressed in a white oriental robe like a school girl. When I took the grenade, I wrapped it up in a handkerchief on which was a rose that I had embroidered. I'm keen on handicrafts. When my fellow group members were in place, I returned to get the grenade, and handed it over to Comrade Number 2 [Trần Tiên Quang].

I remember the rest well. At the time a plainclothes policeman [Major Phan Bội Ngọc] stood explaining to people viewing the helicopter how weak and ineffectual the Việt Cộng would be against the Americans. Laughing and saying, "If seven Việt Cộng swing on a branch of a papaya tree their bodies wouldn't even make it snap!" With great anger, Comrade Number 2 threw the grenade at the helicopter. It exploded and collapsed, bursting into flames. This injured the policeman but the crowd escaped unhurt. This almighty bang must have made the dignitaries in the Presidential Palace stop. Saigon's National Day holiday was destroyed. We mixed within the crowds and made our escape...

My comrades in my unit went home and I returned to the war zone to report to my leaders. When I arrived back the commander of the Saigon *Biệt Động*s, Trần Hải Phụng, praised our actions and awarded me a certificate of merit.[10] At the time medals were given just as a compliment and in the form of a certificate of merit; there were no bonuses or encouragement via material gains. We did these acts as the new generation of Saigon *Biệt Động*s, there to fight the American War.

After this I continued to convey letters, documents and weapons in and out of Saigon. At the time few young girls in my area did this kind of work; it was sociably unacceptable to be an unmarried women living away from home. Consequently, for the revolution my single status was useful because it made me more flexible but it was not good for my family. Each time I went back to my uncle's house, his wife, bound by the Confucian system, treated me with contempt because my uncle could not tell her that I was a revolutionary. She said, "From which brothel have you come? You live with a bad guy? Our family should not have to tolerate goddamned bad girls like you!" I cried, telling her, "My dear aunt, one day when peace returns, I will tell you the truth and you will understand me." She kept throwing me out but each time I returned.

At the beginning of 1963, my leaders tasked me with another big operation, this time to arrange for a bomb to be planted on a military Boeing 707. The bomb had to be timed to explode over the Pacific Ocean. After the event, our informers within Tân Sơn Nhất Airport said that the bomb had gone off but at a later time in Honolulu. Now we had to ask ourselves why, what had gone wrong?

To gain access to the airport and conduct such a mission took time and careful planning. My leaders told me that I had to start a relationship with a South Vietnamese officer. I picked a man in the logistics service, based at Tân Sơn Nhất Airport. We started to meet like two lovers, sometimes at his home, other times in luxury hotels. Unfortunately, his wife found out and publicly displayed her anger. It was a shameful experience because I was not in this for a relationship but for the revolution. In contrast, the officer loved me, which made his wife even angrier. I went back to my leaders and told them that I could not continue with him, my family might find out and the mission could be compromised. Finally I told my leaders, "I feel bitterly ashamed." My leaders explained that I had to go on, it was imperative that everyone at the gate of the base got used to me loitering there waiting for my lover. They ordered me to return. I continued with my work and through gentle persuasion he finally changed to our side. He was infatuated with me.

The flight to be targeted had been chosen from information gathered by our network inside the base. They had heard that a group of American officers were to leave Vietnam. My boyfriend then found out what type of suitcase they had purchased and we went and bought the same type from the market. We knew from experience that when the Americans boarded the flight they handed their cases to the Vietnamese staff to load them on to the plane. It was at this point, when my boyfriend loaded the cases, he simply switched one of them for our case with the bomb inside.

To say simply is not accurate. The timer had to be calculated to go off at the correct moment, with the aircraft in mid-flight. When scrutinizing events we knew we had done this right, so why did the bomb go off at Honolulu airport? All we could presume was that because we had purchased a cheap alarm clock for the timer, when the plane had climbed to altitude, the clock had stopped due to atmospheric pressure, and when it landed, the clock started and the bomb went off. The American officers had already got out. Only their documents were damaged.

On the one hand our mission had failed, but on the other we had achieved so much more than we could have hoped for. Our achievements were aired on Vietnamese News Agency, Hanoi, who said, "The armed forces and people of Saigon have not only struck the American imperialists in South Vietnam but on American territory as well." My leaders awarded me a second certificate of merit.

In mid–1963, I designed a mission aimed at Military Assistance Advisory Group [MAAG] in Saigon, which was in Trần Hưng Đạo Street at the time. I scouted out MAAG to see who was there and how to approach the place. After my reconnaissance I reported my findings to the command of the Saigon *Biệt Động*s, who gave me permission to conduct it. At that time my 159 *Biệt Động* Unit was located in Củ Chi District.[11]

MAAG was a description given to U.S. military advisors sent to assist in the training of conventional armed forces in Third World countries. The U.S. president claimed that those dispatched to Indochina were not sent as combat troops, but to supervise the use of millions of dollars of American aid given to support the French. When they arrived in Vietnam in 1950, the French did not welcome them and viewed MAAG as stepping on their colonial toes. By the time they decided reluctantly to cooperate with MAAG it was too late; the Battle of Điện Biên Phủ had sealed their fate. In 1955, a conference in Washington, D.C., between officials of the U.S. State Department and the French Minister of Overseas Affairs approved that all U.S. aid be funneled directly to South Vietnam and that all major military responsibilities be transferred from the French to MAAG under the command of Lieutenant General John W. O'Daniel.[12]

A problem arose because the French Far East Expeditionary Corps had to depart from South Vietnam in 1956, as directed by the Geneva Accords, and to fill the void several hundred men joined MAAG by the end of June. For the next few years there was a power struggle. Diệm refused to allot the American advisors high-ranking positions and give them authority over Vietnamese tactical units because he did not want the United States to have control or influence over his forces. This changed because by 1961 the Việt Cộng had become stronger and more active, so Diệm agreed to have American advisors at battalion level. This agreement increased U.S. numbers, so much so that it broke Geneva Accord guidelines.

Ms. Nguyệt said:

As commander of my unit my leaders ordered me to convey the explosives into Saigon, where others would carry out the attack on MAAG. From previous experiences it looked like I would not survive the journey but I wanted to sacrifice my life so that others could live in a liberated country. Comrades I spoke to also agreed that the outcome looked bleak for me and they kindly organized a memorial service for me; a common practice for martyrs, a funeral for yourself that you could attend. Using bamboo, they erected a monument for my war death with a framed banderol of paper that said, "The homeland thanks you for your contribution."

At night I got the go-ahead to advance with a team of supporting revolutionaries. I knew we could not go the most direct way in case we bumped into villagers, so we followed a courier track through Đức Hòa and later on to Đức Huệ, which are small districts you have to travel through to get to Saigon. I had a fair complexion so I covered myself in mud to hide my skin, which meant at each village I had to leave all communications to my fellow revolutionaries. Everything had to be rehearsed in case I met the enemy, because if I did I would have to set off the bomb, and at the same time kill myself, to keep the plan secret. Now do you see why we had my funeral before I died?

We walked across Mỹ Hạnh, a waterlogged field with sharp rushes. As soon as we reached the other side at around 5 a.m., the local guerrillas, who operated mainly at night in each hamlet, said that the enemy had just begun to patrol the area. We had to return to the safe house, only getting there at 11 a.m. The family who cared for us grilled two small fish and served this with rice. It tasted so good. I felt that I had never eaten before. Perhaps I was too hungry. We rested until nightfall, when we set off again. The guerrillas had sent me a message saying that the enemy had withdrawn.

Things had to go to plan this time. If I were delayed, then I might not meet the person I had to, making it impossible to coordinate changes with other agents. It was hard going because I carried the 20kg of plastic explosives in two baskets hung from bamboo, resting on my shoulders, like a farmer. When day broke things became even harder; I had to change my clothing from a peasant farmer to that of a city girl student studying in Saigon. My cover was that I carried gifts from my grandmother, who lived in the countryside, to my family in town. It was important that I had a connection with the countryside because I still carried the explosives as if I was a farmer.

With the explosives, I got a bus heading to the city. The bus soon reached Đức Huệ. Here we stopped at a checkpoint of district guards. The enemy had been attacked several times here, so they checked everyone and everything more closely. They searched students, school girls, rich people and peddlers: everyone.

Now it was my turn. The soldier asked, "Girl, what are you carrying?" I answered, "This is a gift from my grandmother to my mother." He forcefully told me to open my baskets. I refused to do it saying, "This is food. It's not hygienic to open it." I stood my ground because if the soldier forced me to open the baskets I would have no choice but to press the detonator. Only the soldier and I would be killed because everyone else had already got off the bus. To die was simple, to complete my task was difficult. I had a second thought. I stood up and mounted my hands on my hips telling the soldier, "My father is General Trần Tử Oai. If you don't respect our family's affairs, you will be sent to the II Tactical Zone." General Oai was an evil person who had emigrated in 1954 to the South under the American-backed exodus of Catholics from Tonkin. The II Tactical Zone saw some of the worst fighting in the South and the soldier thought that if he upset me he would be sent there. The soldier hesitated before saying, "It appears that we have come across a red ant's nest in this one," and he let me off.

I realized I had had a narrow escape, but now time was my enemy. Before setting off on the bus I had given a secret signal to an agent to say that all was well and I was on my way. I gave various signals when I passed through each secret prearranged liaison point. From these signals my leaders could make sure that I was on track to meet an agent at the bus terminus of Phú Lâm, south-west of Saigon. This agent was there to take the explosives away from me. Now I worried that the agent could have left because they might have thought that I had been captured or followed.

Having got off the bus at the terminus, I tried to hail a pedicab to my meeting point but there were none around. I knew that the agent that waited at the terminus would then have followed me in a pedicab to make sure my cover had not been blown. I had to think quickly. I entered a shop for a drink as a delaying tactic to give the agent time to observe me from afar. Once satisfied he then approached me and with relief and sheer exhaustion I handed him the explosives, which he carried away.

After this I had time to compose myself before meeting the team ordered to carry out the attack. I took a room in a guesthouse. I was nervous. The explosives were to be detonated by a timer that needed an expert to set. I remembered my friend, he had not been that bright and had killed himself accidentally when he misjudged his timing device. Now it was my comrade's time to handle a bomb with a preset timer attached. Would this go off early too?

The attack was divided into three groups, each with a revolutionary carrying a bomb. One was to be disguised as an ARVN captain, another dressed up as a boy hawking bread and the third person's disguise escapes me now. My three comrades walked towards MAAG whilst I watched as commander. MAAG was under tight security but they placed their bombs against the gate and left. We all held our breath but they exploded on time. I don't know how many Americans died. There were almost 100 cars carrying the injured Vietnamese and Americans away. There must have been a high-ranking American who died or was seriously injured because the car with his body was covered with an American flag. Our actions that day showed the enemy that they were not safe even in their base areas.

After the attack my problems continued. I arrived at the address of a revolutionary sympathizer, where I changed my clothes so that I could make my way back to my war zone. Once changed, I traveled more than 30km alone to Củ Chi Base, via the tunnels, arriving at 6 p.m. Here local guerrillas arrested me because according to protocol no one should arrive that late. I begged them, saying that I was from the city going to see my relatives, and I gave them my given secret signal. At the same time, as I found out later, my 159 *Biệt Động* Unit had been watching me from afar, all looking to see if I had been followed. Finally, when I had been given the all-clear, my unit rushed to me and carried me on their shoulders in celebration. One comrade stroked my head, others burst into tears, "We thought you died already." I smiled with delight. I knew I would never betray them, neither soldiers nor revolutionary sympathizers.[13]

Ms. Nguyệt was arrested shortly after this in 1963. One of her colleagues, who had been part of the attack on MAAG dressed as an ARVN captain, had been arrested and given her name under torture. She spent the next decade in various prisons in South Vietnam enduring horrific punishment, of which she still bears the scars to this day. Nevertheless, she survived those dark days because she was a fighter. On one occasion she had arrived at Côn Đảo Island, which at that time was an all male prison. The guards put her in a tiger cage; small barred enclosures lined up in rows in a large prison cell and built by the French to hold political opponents.

Ms. Nguyệt told of the events:

When arriving on Côn Đảo Island, I noticed that the men had lost their will and were dying of neglect. Although they perked up when they saw us women, something needed to be done to change our dreadful lives. Our guards served our food in unwashed rice bowls, which crawled with maggots and flies. The toilet hole in our cell, over which we squatted, never had a cover and the stench and hygiene conditions were disgusting. The enemy refused us a bath for fifty days at a time, even though as women we went through our menstrual cycles.

We demanded to have half an hour out in the fresh air and sun each day but they did not allow this. We confronted them to demand better food, including vegetables twice a week, but they did not accept this either. So we went on hunger strike. To stop us they threw tiny, ground up pieces of some hard substance into our cramped cell, as well as tear gas. It was only when we began to sweat in the intense heat that the tiny pieces of material, which stuck to our skin, became extremely hot and we guessed the powder was phosphorus; this ignites upon contact with water. So our sweat and any water to cool us just made our skins burn more and peel off. For the male prisoners, twelve days of hunger was too long. Some could not continue. Some of them committed suicide. Others went mad.

On the evening of the twelfth day, the enemy went to our cells and said, "OK, we will agree to your demands, due to a new shipment of goods which has just arrived." When they said this, we knew we had won and demanded food. We had to take this slowly because if we ate rice straightaway then we could die. Also, I had been suffering from stomachache ever since they had tortured me by pouring soapy water down my throat and stamping on my stomach to bring it up. On the first day we demanded to be given milk, second day gruel, third rice soup, the fourth mushy rice and from the fifth day, rice. They accepted. I made them sign up to the menu and it was sent to the kitchen, officially.[14]

For her part in these acts of terror, Ms. Nguyệt stayed in prison for a decade. Although she no longer took a lead role in the war, the Communist Party's propaganda on her work helped pave the way for thousands of others to join the revolution. These loyal recruits, and many others across the South, gave the Party the tools they needed to progress to a general offensive and general uprising, and make a strike for victory.

Preparations for the X Plan

At the end of 1964, the General Staff in Hanoi drew up what they called the X Plan, this was then approved by the Party Central Committee under Resolution 11 in March 1965. The X Plan laid out the strategies to execute a general offensive and a general uprising across South Vietnam. The Liberation Army would lead the general offensive and the people the general uprising, agitated and driven to do so by Communist Party cells and paramilitary forces. The aim was to push the Americans into making a decision on Vietnam, namely to get them to leave, and to weaken the Southern regime into unconditional surrender.

The revolutionaries timed the X Plan for December 1965.[15] The thinking behind this period was that the Party had a number of factors in place. They had moved thousands of troops and supplies down the Hồ Chí Minh Trail in 1964 to support the military action. They had succeeded in taking and holding vast parts of rural South Vietnam through military action and their Revolutionary Infrastructure; by the end of 1964, the Party was taking control of an entire district every two weeks. Giáp had begun to establish his forces in the Central Highlands, so that he could order them to advance to the coastal towns and cut the South in two, at an opportune moment during the X Plan. In and around Saigon the communists controlled Bình Xuyên camps, thanks to the work of Nguyễn Trọng Tâm and his colleagues. Likewise, the communists had Phạm Ngọc Thảo. He had one of the best military reputations among the Saigon commanders of ARVN and controlled about 2,000 troops and 150 officers. With this balance of influence within ARVN, when the fighting broke out he could sway the soldiers not to oppose the offensive.

Furthermore, the Communist Party had worked hard on proselytizing. In mid-1964, the Intelligence and Military Proselytizing service of North Vietnam, in coordination with COSVN, ordered that the top personnel within the Saigon authority be targeted. The special agents assigned to the task had to get the targeted people either to side with the revolutionaries, or at least not to oppose them, when the X Plan was implemented. Hanoi also needed the switched Saigon officials to covertly curb Southern government policies to benefit the outcome of the X Plan prior to its execution and then guide the administration into unconditional surrender when events unfolded.

Nguyễn Trọng Tâm, one of the Reverse Regrouping Men, explained:

> Hanoi wanted the proselytizing to be conducted by revolutionaries who had high-ranking Saigon officers or officials as relatives. The strategy was that these revolutionaries would act as special couriers and special propagandists; there to relay messages from our side to the target person on the other side but also put pressure on those they approached to persuade them to become sympathetic to the revolution. They might have already started this work prior to the start of the official program.
>
> For example, Colonel Trần Ngọc Hiền of the Vietnamese People's Army approached his brother, Trần Ngọc Châu, then head of Bến Tre Province. Châu had changed sides to fight for the French in the early 1950s, along with other generals such as Nguyễn Văn Thiệu [1923–2001]. Hiền failed with Châu, who later helped design the American Phoenix Program.
>
> Another example was the nephew of Nguyễn Cao Kỳ [1930–2011], who tried to contact Nguyễn Cao Kỳ. Kỳ was a senior officer in ARVN and very much in league with the Americans. It has been said that the nephew failed to stop Kỳ, in fact Kỳ acted against the revolution during the coup attempt by Phạm Ngọc Thảo in 1965.
>
> Another case was Major Lâm Thị Phấn of the VNPA, who intensified her contact with her brother, Major General Lâm Văn Phát of ARVN. Phấn became a Communist Party member in 1950 and shortly after built the intelligence service in Cần Thơ Province. She then regrouped to the North in 1954. In the second half of the 1950s, she studied economics and intelligence in the Soviet Union. She was sent back to the South in 1962 to operate covertly amongst the upper echelons of the administration, including putting pressure on her brother, Lâm Văn Phát. He did eventually act for the revolution and led two coup attempts against General Nguyễn Khánh [1927–2013] in September 1964 and in early 1965. Phát helped Phạm Ngọc Thảo in these coups but I am unsure whether or not Phát ever knew the real identity of Thảo.
>
> One of my contributions was to contact the brother-in-law of General Nguyễn Văn Vỹ to get him to put pressure on General Vỹ. It was a long-term plan. Vỹ had held many high posts within Bảo Đại's regime in the early 1950s. When Diệm ousted Bảo Đại with U.S. support, Vỹ lost any real power.

Hanoi still kept him as a political card because he opposed Diệm. The problem with these target people, such as Vỹ, was that they swung from one side to another all of their lives. Yet, as I said, it was a long-term plan, and Hanoi used General Vỹ as one of their political cards in early 1975 to help us gain unconditional surrender.

Another person targeted was General Dương Văn Minh [1916–2001] of ARVN, also known as Big Minh due to his size. Captain Dương Thành Nhật of the VNPA was asked to carry out this task. Nhật was ideal because he had started this process of contacting Minh at the end of 1962 and he was his younger brother. This family connection can be seen in the names because Nhật was also known as Dương Văn Nhật.

At the time I worked at zone or provincial level, so I did not participate directly. Nhật and I were friends. I told Nhật's children that their father had arrived in the South. This opened the way for Nhật to meet with his children. From there Nhật asked his children to arrange a meeting between himself and Minh. So the revolutionaries first approached Minh through his brother's children.

Minh knew the real face of Nhật because he had not concealed this from him but it did not mean that proselytizing Minh was easy. In fact, this again was a long-term plan. The aim was not so much to get him to switch

Lâm Thị Phấn (in uniform) conducted proselytizing to prepare for the X Plan. She is pictured here with her daughter, Trần Hồng Hạnh, in 2007 (courtesy Lâm Thị Phấn).

sides, as we knew this was too much to ask, but we wanted him not to oppose us. We played on his nationalist views and the fact that he had tired of working with foreigners. We knew this because the Chinese had tried to switch Minh, but he had rebutted their approaches; after working with the French and Americans he did not want to work with non–Vietnamese any more. These proselytizing efforts on Minh only became clear on 30 April 1975.

Being a special propaganda operative was not easy. The officers assigned were sometimes suspected of colluding with the enemy but it's clear that most of our agents did not betray us. If Nhật had defected before the war ended, then after 1975 he would have lived a life of luxury abroad. Instead, he lived a life of misery. You can't imagine how life was for him.

What made our job harder was the failure to be consistent with our policy on defectors and those who operated within enemy ranks. This policy stated that everyone should be treated fairly but only some were awarded high office. Such as, when Nhật regrouped to the North he was at company level rank only, but when he went to the South to make contact with his brother our leaders promoted him to captain, to encourage him to talk to his brother. Saigon sources say that Nhật was already a captain and promoted to major. [Another example was in the 1940s, when Phan Kế Toại, the King's Special Envoy, switched sides to the Việt Minh thanks to the work of Lê Trọng Nghĩa. Hồ promoted Toại to a high position in his new government; a message to others to follow suit and join the revolutionaries.] However, the Bình Xuyên battalion commanding officer I had persuaded to switch to our side did not get any promotion. In fact, he held the same rank of captain for twenty years in the VNPA; although our leaders did allow him to become a Communist Party member.[16]

Preparations for the X Plan had gained momentum. Now the time had come to eliminate Diệm to enable Hanoi to put their man in place, ready for the anticipated surrender.

Diệm: Not the Man for Hồ

On the political front, the work to weaken the Southern administration in time for the X Plan had started in the early 1960s. Initially, Diệm and his brother, Nhu, had been of use to the revolution. In 1946, Nhu had worked briefly in Hanoi's State Library and knew Hồ and Giáp; in fact Giáp, as minister of interior, had signed the order to appoint him to that post. From knowing important revolutionaries, this meant Nhu could keep political links with Hanoi open for Diệm, which he apparently did via a Polish ambassador. Now time had moved on and the Diệm administration had become more unpredictable and out of control. He had to be removed, and as part of this quest the Communist Party publically demanded Diệm's abolition to undermine confidence in his government.

Privately Hanoi continued their pressure on Diệm. Hồ was aware that both Diệm and Nhu feared U.S. influence in the South and the result of this on their ability to maintain power. Hồ recognized this because to try and secure their powerbase, secretly the brothers had asked their men to approach members of the NLF to negotiate a settlement to see a coalition government formed in the South. This would include the NLF, the Diệm administration and other interested groups referred to as the third segment. Diệm hoped that if the NLF were receptive, talks could then open with the Democratic Republic of Vietnam about the reunification of the entire country. To achieve this coalition, Diệm saw that he had to juggle both Hanoi and the United States. To appease Hanoi he worked knowingly alongside suspected agents including Thảo, and to smooth any difficulties with the United States he recognized that any coalition would comprise people it wanted to appoint. Hồ turned Diệm's suggestion into a political ruse because he saw that the coalition would further damage relations between Diệm and the Americans. Few would see this as a ploy because in June 1962 the Second Coalition government of Lao was established with Souvanna Phouma as prime minister.[17] Why not Vietnam as well? Yet things failed. Diệm had negotiated with communists without informing American officials first and the United States wanted to win the war. For Hồ, Diệm went too far when he made moves to crush the Buddhists. Nevertheless, talk of a coalition was a good scam while it lasted.

Eventually the Americans struck at Diệm, and asked Thảo to conduct a coup against the Southern regime. Part of Thảo's role for Hanoi remained to stage continuous coups in the South, not only to weaken the regime but with the expectation that this would deny the Americans the ability to deploy large troop numbers in South Vietnam or to bomb the North. He had strategically opposed the first two coups against the Southern regime because he was not there to remove Diệm for the Americans. For this third coup though, the CIA put pressure on Thảo to go along with it and he agreed, albeit reluctantly to keep his cover, but this time it fitted in with Hanoi's plans. General Minh had been chosen by the Americans to take over from Diệm and Minh had been targeted by Hanoi through their Intelligence and Military Proselytizing service. Therefore, after the coup, Hanoi would still have direct access to the top man and could put pressure on Minh to kill Diệm.

In early November 1963, Minh overthrew Diệm. A day later, men working for Minh killed both Diệm and Nhu. Minh established a new Armed Forces Council to be chaired by him; members included Trần Thiện Khiêm (1925–) and Nguyễn Văn Thiệu. Hồ had his man in place but ironically due to the instability in South Vietnam at this time, Minh's junta only lasted a few months before being toppled by another military general, Nguyễn Khánh, in January 1964. This weakened Hồ's X Plan but there was still time to make changes.

Thảo's Last Act for Hồ

Hồ saw Thảo as a crucial part of his X Plan, but with so much activity around him the CIA started to keep a watchful eye on his movements. To observe Thảo more closely, and those he contacted, in 1963 the CIA had sent him to Fort Leavenworth in the United States for six months to learn conventional warfare tactics. By the time he returned in 1964, Khánh governed Vietnam. Predictably, the following months saw instability within the Southern regime and that August, Khiêm, Minh and Khánh reluctantly formed a committee to share governance of the country. Khánh prevailed in the ensuing power struggle. Minh was sent on a good will tour so that he could exit the political scene without humiliation, and Khánh dispatched Khiêm to Washington as ambassador, and as Thảo was an associate, he followed him to work as his press attaché. This gave the CIA a second opportunity to watch him.[18]

The CIA did not dispose of Thảo in the early days because he was more valuable to them as a free man. At the time few people in Vietnam could speak both English and Vietnamese, as he could; he was an excellent interpreter at a strategic level both for the CIA and for the Southern government. He had fought for the Việt Minh so he knew about military requirements and had his own troops in ARVN. Nevertheless, with some younger English-speaking generals dubbed the Young Turks coming through the system from Washington in the mid–1960s, the CIA saw Thảo as surplus to requirements. Military Assistance Command Vietnam (MACV), which had now absorbed MAAG, confirmed they no longer needed him.

In late December 1964, Khánh summonsed Thảo back to Saigon. Thảo believed Khánh wanted to kill him because Khánh correctly suspected him and Khiêm of plotting against him. On fearing for his safety the Communist Party asked Thảo to return to a base area, but he refused. Thảo went into hiding to continue his work agitating the Southern government; indeed an American intelligence information cable dated 28 August 1964 stated that Thảo looked to conduct a coup to make himself prime minister of South Vietnam. In 1965, Thảo had to be taken in for questioning and the CIA gave Thiệu the task.[19]

Thảo got in first and conducted his coup shortly before noon on 19 February 1965. Thảo's objective was not to make himself prime minister but to remove Khánh from power and replace him with his colleague, Khiêm, who still resided in America. He timed his actions to blunt any media coverage of the U.S. commitment to bomb the North but also to weaken the Southern regime at this critical time. For Thảo personally, Khánh had to be overthrown because he thought that he had made too many concessions to the Buddhists and had lost prestige with the people. Although the presidency sat with Phan Khắc Sửu, this was in name only in an attempt to show that the government was a civilian one and not military-led. True power still lay with Khánh. On 19 February, Thảo's troops seized vital sites around the city, including the military headquarters, the post office and the Saigon radio station.

Thảo conducted the coup in league with Lâm Văn Phát, who had been targeted as part of Hanoi's proselytized program. The two men wanted to seize the Biên Hòa Air Base to prevent the head of the Vietnamese Air Force, Nguyễn Cao Kỳ, mobilizing air power against them. Kỳ had been approached by Thảo to be a part of the coup but the CIA got to him first. Without Kỳ, the attempt to take the air base failed. Although Thảo's troops still held vital positions in Saigon, Phát and Thảo agreed to surrender but on the condition that Khánh stood down and went into exile. The next morning, South Vietnamese senior officers voted to strip Khánh of his authority, and some days later he left Vietnam for good. Thiệu took power later in the year.

Thảo and Phát were sentenced to death. Phát avoided arrest for the next few years before surrendering and receiving a pardon from Thiệu. Whereas, after the coup, Thảo went into hiding and according to Vu Anh, Thảo's former *aide de camp*, he saw Thảo for the last time in Bà Chiểu Market, Saigon. They had agreed to meet at entrance gate six of the railway station at 6 p.m. but he never showed. Anh later heard Thảo had hidden in Hố Nai Catholic Church but the Americans surrounded the church and as he tried to escape he was shot in the groin and captured. The Americans flew him to hospital. Thiệu ordered him to be taken to the National Police Directorate and tortured, on the grounds that Thảo had refused to promise that he would not try to mutiny again. Here Nguyễn Ngọc Loan, the head of the Social Political Research Department, oversaw proceedings. Thảo died almost at once when his torturer used his hand to crush his testicles. His death was said to have been unintentional and the Saigon press covering the story stated that he had died in a car crash.[20] Thảo had destabilized the regime in time for the X Plan, but for Hồ, he had lost a strategic ally in the South.

Finalizing the X Plan

Thiệu was not the perfect candidate to be in charge of the Southern administration during the execution of the X Plan; being vehemently anti-communist he had a personal mandate against such people. Yet he had once served in the Việt Minh during the French War, so those who knew him understood his shortfalls. These weaknesses, along with the fact that Thảo had given nothing away, meant that preparation for the X Plan could continue.

The communists chose Saigon, the heart of Thiệu's Southern regime, as the main military target; if they could capture the region the rest of the country should follow. In April 1965, the Special Zone Party Committee (T4) held a conference at Suối Đá Base, Tây Ninh Province, to discuss Resolution 11 in relation to Saigon. Those leaders present had to design ways to strengthen the fighting configuration of their local Special Forces, supply weapons, build stores to hide the armaments and provide safe houses for the troops. To assist in this process the Party obtained a map of the city's drainage system; Diên the Third had taken it when he worked as a designer for a U.S. consultancy firm.

On the first point regarding the fighting configuration, the Party established the Group of City Special Forces, codenamed F100, which was made up of 100 urban underground elite armed forces. Nguyễn Đức Hùng was the commander and Võ Tâm Thành the political commissar.[21] Although 100 elite combatants might seem small for such a mission, with the intense program of proselytizing undertaken on ARVN, the Party had been informed that many enemy units had been severely compromised; the soldiers would soon switch allegiances once the fighting had started. For the X Plan, twenty-five targets were listed, which included the regime's strategic military, political and economic positions, as well as important traffic hubs and transport routes.

To support F100, and fulfill other design requirements, the Special Zone Party Committee formed the Supplying Bureau. They created units A20 and A30 to transport weapons and build arms and ammunitions magazines; one to three magazines were constructed for an attack on each target.[22] Those within A20 and A30 had to be the most trusted Communist Party members or sympathizers; the test for this high requirement was surviving the prison system and overcoming torture. Furthermore, they had to be seen to have a good stable job and a safe ID issued by the Southern authorities. When the time came to transport the weapons, the military isolated members of A20 and A30 from current combat actions. Even though the X Plan had many parts, few people actually knew of the plan or indeed the start time.

Despite all the hype and completed preparations, in May 1965 Communist Party members canceled the X Plan; that month the U.S. 173rd Airborne Brigade landed in South Vietnam and launched their first major offensive in June. Their arrival was probably inevitable because in March the 3rd Battalion, 9th Marines, had landed at Đà Nẵng. Some Party officials maintained that despite this, the Special War dragged, so why cancel the X Plan as a general uprising was still possible, believing that they should simply stand up and fight in one big bloody battle. The majority concluded that the U.S. had switched from its Special War to a Limited War and, although to abandon the X Plan was a hard decision, victory had to wait.

U.S. Justification for Ground Troops

The events in late 1964 had already started to sway some Party realists that military action might be premature. Central to them drawing this conclusion was the Gulf of Tonkin Incident, which it is generally cited as the event that escalated the war. The first incident occurred on 2 August 1964; the United States claimed that North Vietnamese patrol boats attacked its destroyer, the *Maddox*. The second incident occurred on 4 August when the *Maddox* and the *Turner Joy* claimed to have come under attack. For decades the United States argued that North Vietnam was the aggressor in these cases. In 2005, the United States declassified an internal National Security Agency historical study that concluded the *Maddox* did fire warning shots at the Vietnamese craft before coming under fire itself and that there may not have been any North Vietnamese naval vessels present on 4 August.

Regardless of the facts now, at the time the effect of this second incident was vast because it saw the passage by Congress of the Gulf of Tonkin Resolution. This granted President Lyndon B. Johnson (1908–1973) the authority to assist any Southeast Asian country whose government was considered to be jeopardized by communist aggression. The Resolution would serve as Johnson's legal justification for deploying U.S. conventional forces and the commencement of open warfare against North Vietnam.

The Gulf of Tonkin Incident did not result in the actual decision for ground troops; the Johnson administration had already determined that it was necessary to Americanize the war. They felt that they could not count on the undisciplined South Vietnamese, who clearly did not possess the will or the capacity, to block what the United States deemed the spread of communism.

A Limited War

Now in 1965, with the X Plan canceled and a peaceful conclusion not expected, Hanoi prepared to fight a Limited War. Hanoi not only had to know how the Americans were to fight, but how to win against their modern technology and advanced tactics. Hanoi drew on numerous events.

Firstly, in September 1962 in Mỹ Tho Province, the 1st Company of the 514th Mỹ Tho Provincial Battalion resisted ARVN sweeps at Cà Nai Canal, Mỹ Long Village, Cái Bè District and at Phú Phong Village, Châu Thành District. Repelling ARVN had been possible because communist troops utilized fighting villages within the area. With this triumph, Party members could see that these fortified villages were still beneficial even under modern conditions, so officials instructed more to be built.

In another case, in October 1962, the same company drove off another sweep mounted by ARVN, and as part of the operation defeated the enemy's helicopter assault tactics by shooting down three of their helicopters. Following on from this action the Mỹ Tho Provincial Party Committee instructed the locals to strengthen their fighting villages. The officials advised the inhabitants to plant wooden stakes in their open fields to prevent enemy troops from landing by helicopter, expand any guerrilla activities, coordinate their actions with the main regular army and use infantry weapons against helicopter assaults.

The most documented event of that early period had been the Battle of Ấp Bắc in January 1963. This is said to be the first large clash that the revolutionaries won against ARVN troops, supported by U.S. air and armored vehicles. On 13 December, communist provincial and main regular units conducted sweeping operations together. These units were stationed at Ấp Bắc, Tân Phú; a fighting village within a contiguous liberated zone formed by the districts of Cai Lậy and Châu Thành. In January, ARVN were ordered to conduct their sweeping operations in the vicinity. Fighting broke out. Of the fifteen American helicopters supporting ARVN, only one escaped undamaged, and five were either downed or destroyed.

This communist victory proved that by coordinating their regular units, irregular forces and the people together, enemy sweep operations and helicopter assaults could be defeated. It too marked the start of being able to crush enemy helicopter transfer tactics and armored personnel carrier assaults. One method used by the communists to do this was to engage so closely with ARVN and U.S. forces that they could not use air attacks on the communists for fear that they would kill their own men, using the slogan, "Holding the enemy by their belt."[23] To defeat helicopter transfers Giáp had advised, wait for the enemy to get out of the helicopter, then strike suddenly, his motto, "Wait for the snail to come out of his shell, then strike." This directive from Giáp had clearly worked.

With a divided country and a Limited War facing the revolutionaries, remarkably there were still divisions within the Communist Party. Hồ and others identified that to force the U.S. to leave and the Southern regime to collapse, they had to master the new battlefield situation, and integrate this knowledge into their blueprint to enable them to build conventional forces supported by a modern southward March. Others within the Party disagreed, still reflecting back almost romantically to the people's uprising of the August Revolution. What gave strength to the argument for a conventional army approach was ultimately that any rational person would conclude that an August Revolution–like method, even with the tactical advances made by their military units, could not defeat the American forces heading for South Vietnam.

12

The Hồ Chí Minh Trail

Outwitting Modern Technology

U.S. ground forces first entered South Vietnam en masse in 1965, starting a period called the Limited War. With them came a new type of conventional combat based on modern technology, far more advanced than that of their predecessors, the French. This did not mean that the revolutionaries' blueprint for asymmetric warfare became obsolete, on the contrary, it was just upgraded to suit. One prime example was the Hồ Chí Minh Trail, Hồ's new Southward March. The U.S. troops who saw some of the worst fighting along the Trail were those in the Studies and Observations Group (SOG) and its supporting services. Jim Burns and John Stryker Meyer disclosed their experiences. Their recollections show the extreme contrast between before and after 1965 and, regardless what advanced military hardware was used, the Americans and South Vietnamese would still become puppets of Hanoi.

What makes the stories of Jim Burns (1941–) and John Stryker Meyer (1946–) so important is that until recently those who operated along the Hồ Chí Minh Trail were very guarded to outsiders about their activities. They operated at the highest level of secrecy and had signed government documentation that made it extremely difficult for them to write about their experiences. Both men served more than one tour in Vietnam and operated in the Secret War, running highly classified missions into Lao, Cambodia and North Vietnam, known as operating "across the fence." Burns was in the U.S. Air Force (USAF) and Meyer a member of SOG. In fact, Burns believes that he escorted Meyer on a flight in 1970, when he flew from Nakhon Phanom Royal Thai Air Force Base (RTAFB), and inserted Meyer into Lao along the Trail.

Burns' story starts much earlier than Meyer's. Burns is a highly decorated veteran whose military career began in 1959 when he enlisted in the Air Force. After extensive training in helicopter maintenance, in February 1964 he reassigned to Clark Air Base in the Philippines as a crew chief and flight mechanic on the Sikorsky H-19B and the Kaman HH-43B. While stationed there he was seconded to a highly classified temporary duty assignment at Nakhon Phanom RTAFB from June 1964 to November 1964. During this period he became a flight mechanic with the first HH-43B unit. He did not see much action on this tour because his primary task was to carry out training exercises in Lao, but without knowing it, he had been stationed in a vipers' nest.

Burns explained:

> I was stationed at Nakhon Phanom with the first USAF Air Rescue Helicopter Unit. They were the first three HH-43B helicopters to be deployed to the Vietnam War. I say the Vietnam War, but in

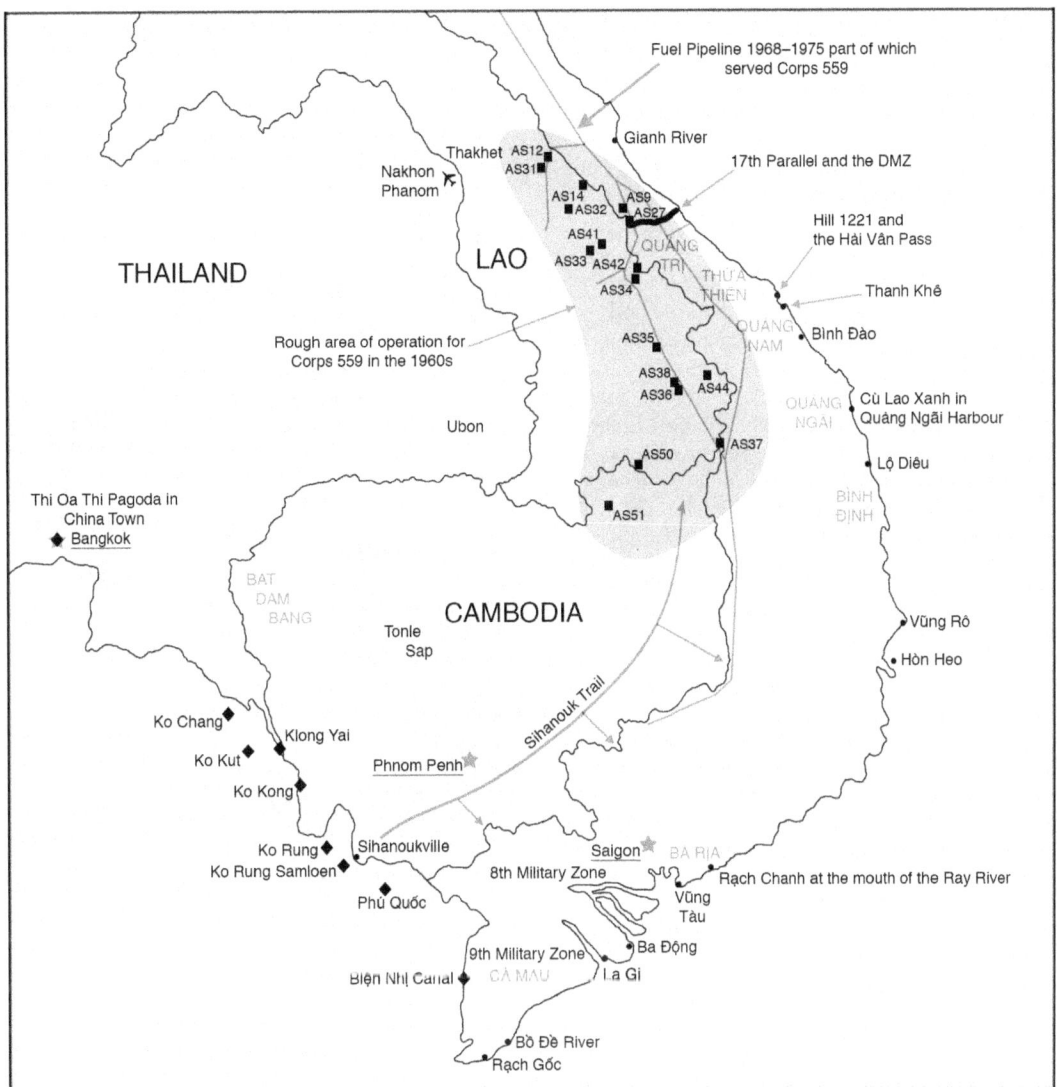

○ The Hồ Chí Minh Trail - 1959 to 1975 (considered by Hanoi to be part of the same network as other logistics land trails).
In 1959, the unit assigned to the Trail was the 301st Land Transportation Battalion and they operated under the Military Transportation Group 559. This group became Corps 559 and generally ran logistics in Lao. In 1970, Corps 559 was given the additional name the Trường Sơn Army and its area of operation covered larger parts of Lao, Vietnam and Cambodia. The army stations (AS) presented here are for the period of the late 1960s (not all have been shown). Today, where Corps 559 worked is considered to be the area of the Hồ Chí Minh Trail.

• The Hồ Chí Minh Trail Sea Route - 1959 to 1975 (not all ports have been shown).
In 1959, the unit assigned to the sea route was the 603rd Sea Transportation Battalion and they operated under Group 559. This unit did only one shipment in 1960 because their boat sunk. In 1961, the 759th Mission officially formed and worked along the route. They operated under the Ministry of Defense, later coming under the Naval Command in 1963. In 1964, the 759th Mission was renamed the 125th Brigade, this unit eventually became the 125th Sea Transportation Corps. Some of the ports used dated from the Trans-West Supply Line.

→ Sihanouk Trail - early 1960s to 1970 (American name, considered by Hanoi to be part of the same network as other logistics land trails).
Run by Corps 17 from 1966, they transported goods from Sihanoukville to areas mainly served by COSVN (the border of South Vietnam, Southern Annam and Corps 559). Logistics units included P100 under the 8th Military Zone and unit 195 under the 9th Military Zone. Some of the ports used dated from the Trans-West Supply Line.

◆ Trans-West Supply Line - 1946 to 1954 (not all ports have been shown).
This line was run by the Cochinchina Maritime Department, which was under the Cochinchina Resistance Administrative Committee and later COSVN. Some of the ports and wharfs were used during the Vietnam War.

Strategic land and sea trails of Hồ Chí Minh.

reality we were there in support of the war that was already taking place in Lao. At the time the base was very bare, with only three or four shacks; the runway and parking ramp were made of pierced steel planking, and there were two Thai Army guards and their families who lived on the base.

There were about twenty of us U.S. Air Force guys and we lived in the town and drove the 16km or so to the base each morning and evening. The Civilize Hotel where we lived was about one block west of the main street through town, which ran next to the Mekong River. We were about two blocks from the centerpiece monument in town, a clock tower, which was a memorial to Hồ Chí Minh. We knew that he had lived very near to Nakhon Phanom sometime in the 1920s and that there were a lot of Vietnamese residing in the area. The hotel owner, Mr. Wandee, opened a restaurant at the hotel for us. The chef was a North Vietnamese who cooked French style, which for us was pretty close to the type of food we were used to, at least much closer than at the Thai restaurants we had been eating in up until then.

I remember one day during that early period that I ended up getting a chewing out from my commander. I had two days off and I had rented a motorcycle and piled the thirteen year old son of Mr. Wandee on the back and I took off and rode the road heading

An HH-43B helicopter hoisting a new water tank in August 1964, Nakhon Phanom RTAFB (courtesy Jim Burns).

north along the Mekong. He was my interpreter and we would stop in villages along the way. We spent the night in one of them before heading back to Nakhon Phanom. When I was telling all the guys about my adventures, my commander informed me that most of the villages north of Nakhon Phanom were occupied by North Vietnamese refugees or sympathizers and I could have been kidnapped or killed and I was never to ride north of Nakhon Phanom again. Heck ... they all seemed pretty nice to me and it was a fun trip. Next time when he and I went riding I went south to Ubon and didn't bother to tell the commander about it. Had a fun trip that time as well![1]

Burns was lucky that day; Nakhon Phanom Province was full of revolutionary sympathizers, there as the eyes and ears of the communists. The Hồ Chí Minh Clock Tower was the clue. In the late 1920s and in 1930, Hồ's area of operation included Nakhon Phanom District capital but also other locations like the district capitals of Na Kae and That Phanom. He had been there to spread propaganda among the masses, writing nationalist articles and plays, as well as organizing training courses for the Vietnamese communities. Nakhon Phanom also saw one of the first cells of the Vietnamese RYL set up there in late 1928, and during the French War and Vietnam War Hanoi kept links with revolutionary sympathizers in the region via their Revolutionary Infrastructure.[2]

Who knows whether or not the North Vietnamese chef who cooked "French style" was part of Hanoi's infrastructure there to monitor Burns and his colleagues. What is known is that the communists did observe the Americans to assess what they needed culturally. Like the French before, the Americans required chefs, waiters and cleaners to

Civilize Hotel in 1964, where American servicemen stayed when in Nakhon Phanom (courtesy Jim Burns).

serve in their bases and to bring in some home comforts. Having now observed any new needs, the communists trained agents through their intelligence, counter-intelligence and public security services to take the jobs and establish communist cells inside enemy safe zones. Not all operatives trained officially; some were the sympathizers Burns' commander had spoken about. What made it easier for Hanoi to infiltrate their operatives into society was that many of them were from the South, so they fitted in, and were employed by South Vietnamese.

When Burns first arrived there in 1964, he might have entered a bare air base with high-tech equipment, but the revolutionaries embedded within and around it were far from sparse, as the next part of his story shows.

Burns continued:

When I was sent on temporary duty to Nakhon Phanom I was prohibited from telling anyone where I was going as it was top secret that we were there. My wife was back in the States and was due to have our first child in early August and she too had not been told where I was. We never talked about our mission when in Nakhon Phanom, or among any of the locals, but we had a gut feeling that our presence and activities were known to the Vietnamese. We obtained solid confirmation of this one day around 7 or 8 August 1964 while sitting on the balcony of the hotel having a few beers after we had returned to town for the day.

That afternoon on the balcony, while we were relaxing and having those beers, we were listening to Hanoi Hannah on Radio Hanoi as she played American music. Of course, we had to put up with her propaganda in between songs but the big shock came to me, and the other guys sitting there, when she made the following announcement after one of the songs. "Now for a special announcement, we want to congratulate Airman James Burns, stationed with the USAF Air Rescue Helicopter Unit at Nakhon Phanom, Thailand, on the birth of his baby girl in the United States. His wife and daughter, born on 6 August, are both doing fine." She went on to give my daughter's birth weight and time of birth, which turned out to be exactly correct and was confirmed about two weeks later when a letter from my wife arrived via my unit back on Clark AB, Philippines. We were all floored when we heard this announcement coming from her ... so much for it being a big secret that we were there![3]

As for how Hanoi Hannah knew of my daughter's birth details, I have always suspected that they got the information by radio intercepts, but that's just a guess. I believe the information on her birth was sent from the Red Cross office in Springfield, Missouri, where she was born, to the Red Cross office at Clark AB. I don't know how this was transmitted, but think it may have been via telegraph. Then I suspect that my squadron on Clark AB was notified by the Red Cross office, maybe by phone or they may have sent a printed copy of the message to them. Next, I believe that the information was radioed to one of the squadron HU-16s that was flying over Vietnam or Lao, and then the HU-16 radioed the message to our communications guys at Nakhon Phanom. Then they brought a short note to me by hand in town when I came in for the night.[4]

I'm not sure where Hanoi picked up on the information, because when I got my short note that night about the birth of my baby it was not clear at all, and did not have the specific detail as Hanoi Hannah had read out. It was kinda like the old parlor game where you sit people in a circle and whisper a

John Wilcox (left) the rescue clerk and Jim Burns (right) in downtown Nakhon Phanom in 1964, standing by the Hồ Chí Minh Clock Tower (courtesy Jim Burns).

story in the ear of the one sitting next to you and so on, and by the time the story gets all the way around the circle, it's not even close to the original story. That's how the note had it. But wherever the communists intercepted it, they had it exactly right!⁵

What happened to Burns was very minor in the bigger picture of the Special War. Nevertheless, it was all part of the psychological measures conducted by the revolutionaries to undermine confidence and instill paranoia in U.S. forces as part of the lead in to the execution of their X Plan. To this day Burns does not really know the answers to his questions on how they got their information on his private life. Although the birth of his daughter was not top secret, what it shows is that, even in those early days, there must have been Revolutionary Infrastructure networks in and around his base. Not only did they know his wife had given birth, but they knew more than he did.

Nakhon Phanom in 1964; in the background across the Mekong River is Lao (courtesy Jim Burns).

Burns went on to serve other tours, including Nha Trang Air Base from June 1967 to March 1968. Then he returned to Nakhon Phanom RTAFB as a Sikorsky CH-3E flight engineer and door gunner for the 21st Special Operations Squadron in 1969. When he went back to Thailand, things had moved on, not only for the Americans but for the maturing communist underground.

Burns went on:

> As I remember, on my return, Nakhon Phanom RTAFB was populated by several thousand U.S. Air Force personnel and several aircraft squadrons. It was well-known that many of the activities on the base and the missions we flew were known to the communists. I also observed that the biggest changes in town from 1964 to my return were the huge increases in the number of bars, bar girls and GIs roaming the streets. I spent very little time in town, maybe going there four or five times in one year, as I didn't want to take a chance of slipping up and saying something that might hurt our missions. I did go to visit Mr. Wandee but did not get to see him, as he was now the mayor of Nakhon Phanom and was out of town on business. I saw his son instead, who was with me on the motorcycle rides in 1964. Some of the men in my squadron, however, had long-term girlfriends, Telocks as we called them, and stayed in town with them a lot, but they all knew not to talk about the missions!⁶

What is so powerful about Burns' story is that it encompasses the difficulties that the general American soldier faced; that your friend might be your enemy. Moreover, it shows how this grave situation put doubts into every soldier as to the effectiveness of their advanced military operations and their so-called top secret status.

Top: First operations building in 1964, Nakhon Phanom RTAFB. *Bottom:* The sign of Nakhon Phanom RTAFB, Thailand, in 1964 (both photographs courtesy Jim Burns).

Top: Nakhon Phanom RTAFB Wing Headquarters in 1969. *Bottom:* A civic action team arrive in their CH-25 to visit a school in Sahatskhan, Thailand, in 1969 (both photographs courtesy Jim Burns).

Westmoreland's Limited War

In 1964, the same year that Burns conducted his first tour of duty, General William Westmoreland (1914–2005) took over from General Paul Harkins (1914–1974) as commander of MACV. Westmoreland had been reluctant to fight in Vietnam. In September 1964, he did not contemplate putting U.S. troops into combat. That "would be a mistake," he had said, because "it is the Vietnamese's war." Later that year in December, again he insisted, "a purely military solution is not possible."

Despite these clear reservations, in 1965 Westmoreland designed a three-stage plan for victory in South Vietnam. The first stage would last until the end of 1965, the objective being to secure populated areas and suppress the enemy's initiative.

A photograph of Bob Hope interviewing Jim Burns at Nakhon Phanom RTAFB in 1969. This was just before Hope's show for the troops was aired on his TV special in America (courtesy Jim Burns).

The second stage he planned for the dry season in early 1966. U.S. forces and ARVN units would launch major search and destroy offensives in high-priority areas to break the hold of the Việt Cộng in the countryside. These search and destroy missions were there to increase body counts, a statistic to measure the progress of the war; the higher the body count the better the United States was thought to be doing. Their operations included deforestation with herbicides, leveling villages with bombardments and resettling the population. If the enemy still persisted, he designed his third and final stage to destroy the enemy within one to one-and-a-half years after the completion of the second stage.

In March 1965, Westmoreland sent in his first battalion-sized ground combat unit; by 31 December, American strength in South Vietnam topped 181,000.[7] The Australian Army and the New Zealand Army joined the United States, to name but two allies committed to the objectives. Even the British arrived; citizens joined allied armies and members of the SAS fought along the Hồ Chí Minh Trail.

To support these troops, in March 1965, Operation Rolling Thunder began, predominantly bombing target areas in Vietnam. In Lao, missions had been started in 1964 and were designated Operation Barrel Roll. In 1965, Lao was split between the northeastern region under Operation Barrel Roll and the southern panhandle missions named Operation Steel Tiger. The sum of these operations became the most intense air-ground battle waged during the Cold War.

Strategically for his Limited War, Westmoreland hoped that the bombing operations and his troops in South Vietnam would reduce the urgency for him to send ground forces into North Vietnam and Lao. Covert operations would play a supporting role.

A Long Road to SOG

Covert operations had been conducted in Vietnam long before Westmoreland's appointment to MACV. Throughout the 1950s and early 1960s, the CIA undertook covert missions against North Vietnam, with limited success. Their programs suffered from recruitment quality control issues; the South Vietnamese did the recruiting, meaning that it was unprofessionally run and the communists abused this fact. There were also no intelligence networks on the ground for operatives to link up with after entering North Vietnam; if they succeeded in avoiding capture, the teams then depended on air drops for resupply. Fundamentally, CIA members felt that Hanoi's intelligence had penetrated their covert missions.

Frustrated that the CIA had not made any headway and embraced covert operations, Kennedy asked the military to take back and oversee large paramilitary missions in Vietnam. Designated Operation Switchback, it began in the early 1960s. Rivalry caused discord between the military and the CIA. William Colby (1920–1996), the chief of the Far East Division of the CIA, stubbornly maintained that covert operations against North Vietnam, regardless of their size or who operated them, would not work. Colby focused on the CIA establishing psychological warfare (psywar); this included fabricating resistance guerrilla movements in North Vietnam, forging documents, kidnapping and then switching the allegiance of these kidnapped Northern citizens, distributing propaganda material and operating falsely attributed radio stations or black radio stations. His rationale was that with the Hanoi leadership paranoid about their internal security, this would infuriate them, building hatred between the North and South.

In 1963, Kennedy finally got his way to make covert operations a central strategy; mainly because of an increase in communist activity in the South and the Buddhists and other groups turning against the Diệm regime. In mid–1963, the Pacific Command drafted a report and sent it to the Joint Chiefs of Staff. It recommended an array of covert operations against Hanoi, all under the rubric Operation Plan 34A (OPLAN 34Alpha). Originally some of the concepts were established by the CIA, but they had to now form part of a joint MACV-CIA strategy.

The intention of OPLAN 34Alpha was for the escalation of covert operations against North Vietnam and efforts against the Hồ Chí Minh Trail. MACV-CIA planners proposed five broad categories of operations to accomplish these goals. The first category involved collecting intelligence on North Vietnam, gathered through the insertion of agents or spies. The second involved psychological operations, targeted at the North Vietnamese leadership and its people to maximize harassment and create divisions. The third involved political pressure, to stir up trouble and escalate costs to make it unworkable for Hanoi to continue their involvement in South Vietnam and Lao. The fourth category planned to develop a resistance movement in North Vietnam. Finally, there would be other destructive operations, such as airborne and seaborne raids. The OPLAN 34Alpha planners believed that the fourth point would be the key to their overall success.

Before progress had been made, Kennedy was assassinated in November, with unknown people behind it. Fortunately the incumbent, President Lyndon B. Johnson, held the same views as Kennedy on covert operations, but he decided to move at a steadier pace with OPLAN 34Alpha and planned to implement those actions of least risk. He cited three key reasons why his government took this approach: Hanoi might escalate the war in the South if Washington interfered with their affairs; China could get involved to save Hanoi; and the Americans would be violating the 1962 Geneva Accords, which recognized the neutrality of Lao.

Sadly for the Americans, if the United States had implemented the full OPLAN 34Alpha program, then over time this plan could have started to undermine Hanoi. Now with the scaled down version some important advisors to the president believed that it would not have any great impact. These advisors included high-ranking generals, who held the view that since ground troops were in South Vietnam it was now best to rely on a conventional strategy, as they had done during the Second World War and the Korean War. They considered covert operations valuable but they would not win the war.

Washington pressed ahead with its scaled down OPLAN 34Alpha program and tasked MACV in Saigon to fulfill the plan. The Special Assistant for Counterinsurgency and Special Activities (SACSA) and Johnson's staff at the Pentagon still had a direct say in the program. To implement OPLAN 34Alpha, MACV in Saigon issued General Order 6 on 24 January 1964; this created the highly secret organization known as Studies and Observations Group (SOG or MACVSOG).

SOG's main objectives would be to plan and then execute responsibilities in four principle mission areas: inserting and running agent teams, psychological warfare, covert

Members of SOG on McGuire Rigs, February 1968 (courtesy Jim Burns).

maritime missions, and cross-border covert missions against the Hồ Chí Minh Trail. With such intense and diverse missions, SOG became the largest and most complex covert operation initiated by the United States since the days of the OSS during the Second World War. One of their earliest missions in very late July 1964 was when four SOG vessels shelled two islands off the coast of North Vietnam. This action could very well have triggered the Gulf of Tonkin Incident, which saw the United States escalate their role in the war.

The first U.S.–led SOG reconnaissance mission into Lao started in October 1965 and was codenamed Shining Brass, renamed Prairie Fire in 1967.[8] The missions were U.S.–led, learning from the earlier failed Vietnamese-led Leaping Lena operations. Nevertheless, the majority of the men within each unit came from hill tribes of various ethnic backgrounds, collectively known as Montagnards. The reconnaissance teams were known as Spike Teams (ST) and later referred to as Recon Teams (RT).[9] There to either support the ST, or to launch their own raids, were exploitation forces; in time these forces consisted of three Haymaker battalions divided into company-sized Hatchet forces, which were further subdivided into Hornet platoons. SOG was part of Westmoreland's covert defense strategy against the Hồ Chí Minh Trail.

SOG: Firepower and the Trail

Meyer was part of SOG. On 1 December 1966, he started his intense training, graduating from the Special Forces Qualification Course a year later. He landed in South Vietnam in April 1968 and a month later arrived at Forward Operating Base 1 (FOB 1) in Phú Bài, where he joined ST Idaho. When FOB 1 closed down in early 1969, his team moved to FOB 4 in Đà Nẵng, redesignated Command and Control North (CCN). It was there that he remained until his return to the United States in April that year. He did not keep out of the war long and returned to CCN in October 1969, staying until April 1970.

Meyer's description of one dangerous mission along the Trail demonstrated the vast amount of back-up technology SOG teams needed. This mission was conducted by one of his best friends, Staff Sergeant Pat Watkins, who had started with ST Moccasin, operating out of Đà Nẵng. When reconnaissance operations at Đà Nẵng were placed on hold through lack of sufficient personnel, Watkins had volunteered to head to the camp at Khe Sanh, which had been under continuous siege since January 1968. At Khe Sanh his officers introduced him to his new team; RT Lion, which consisted of Sergeant George Godwin and seven Bru Montagnards. None of them had run reconnaissance (run recon) before. Watkins took team leader (One-Zero), Godwin radio operator (One-Two) and Lou "Jake Three Zero" DeSeta, who joined later, became his assistant team leader (One-One).

By June 1968, Watkins had been running reconnaissance for more than seven months and had experienced some of the worst of what that could entail. That June, RT Lion was instructed to go into an area of Lao called Tango-6; another name for Oscar-8, a suicidal place in which to operate. The team had to gather intelligence because the information the United States had on the region was very limited. To make matters worse, Watkins had been told that the scheduled over-flight of the area from SOG personnel had been canceled; the anti-aircraft fire was too intense. Covey, the codename for the Forward Air Controller (FAC) covering SOG missions, would therefore select the primary and

General Richard Stillwell (center) inspecting John Stryker Meyer before being inserted into Lao in 1969. Note the jeep bumper, which reads CCN (courtesy John Stryker Meyer).

secondary landing zones. It was said by SOG members that if a Recon Team had a god to which they directed prayers of supplication, it was Covey. It now appeared that RT Lion would be inserted into Oscar-8 at a time and place selected by Covey and not them, but this broke the most fundamental rules of infiltration.

Meyer explained:

With Watkins, Godwin, and the three Bru in the leading 1st Air Cav helicopter and DeSeta and four Bru tailing in the second, the team flew west at just 600ft above the ground. They soon crossed the [Sepon] River into Lao. They could see [VNPA, probably from Corp 559] scattering for cover as they passed over and watched nervously as green tracer rounds tracked their flight...

Watkins got word that they were approaching the landing zone. He looked out and marveled at what he saw below him. Because Oscar-8 had been worked over so many times by B-52s and other bombers, it resembled nothing so much as a cratered moonscape. Trees were almost nonexistent and what cover there was tended to be low and sparse, the exception being elephant grass, which could grow to heights of 6 to 10ft.[10]

Part of the network of Route 20 on the Lao-Vietnam border at Ban Nonggnama. The fence in the center is made from cluster bomb casings. Photograph late 1990s (Clive A. Hills).

Once on the ground, the ten-man team quickly grouped. Watkins made sure that the tail gunner was covering the team's tracks, and then he made his first contact with Covey 265. On this occasion Watkins was told to talk "in the clear" because the Covey pilot did not have the encryption codebook he needed for secure communications. This put the team in even more jeopardy because it allowed the communists to listen in.

Meyer continued:

But what do you do? The team had to know exactly where it was, especially if they had to call in air support. In an additional blow, Covey informed Watkins that one of the gunships had been shot down near Highway 92. Fortunately the crew, including two wounded, had managed to escape and had been picked up. Nonetheless, Covey was going to have to divert an A-1E Skyraider away from RT Lion in order to destroy what was left of the downed Huey. In short, God's eyes were being taken off the ball.

Realizing things were rapidly moving from bad to worse, Watkins instructed DeSeta to set out three claymore mines and get ready for possible enemy contact. He also informed everyone that the crater they had just left behind would be their first rally point should they get hit and separated. The young Bru looked scared and none too confident.

After what seemed a minor eternity, the team heard a large explosion about a kilometer-and-a-half away. Now, thought Watkins, we'll get some covering support. This made him feel a little better, or at least it did until Covey came back on the radio with the news that there was another minor problem. RT Lion had been inserted at the wrong location. One bomb crater looking pretty much like another, it seemed they had been mistakenly inserted very near the junction of Highway 92 and 922. As a result, they were sitting at the pulsing heart of Oscar-8![11]

For the communists, Oscar-8 was the area of operation for Army Station 34.[12] This camp had its headquarters at La Hap, a village located at the junctions of Route 128 (Highway

The author standing next to a bomb crater near Bua La Pha, Lao, in 2002 (Clive A. Hills).

92) and Route B45 (Highway 922). The communists viewed Route 128 as central; it was the main north-south road for trucks in this part of Lao but also the spur road, Route B45, ran into Thừa Thiên Province and trucks using it could supply troops attacking regions such as A Shau Valley and Huế City.

Meyer carried on:

> "But not to worry," Covey said. He was busy talking to the aircrews about the possibility of coming back, picking up the team, and reinserting it at the right landing zone. He suggested the team "hold tight," as if it might inadvertently wander off or relax into beach-party mode.
>
> When it rains trouble, it comes in buckets. As a thoroughly irritated Watkins was explaining the situation to an incredulous Godwin, DeSeta crawled over to tell them that Man-Loi, the tail gunner, had spotted "beaucoup" [many VNPA] swarming around the landing zone. Watkins contacted Covey, informed him of the enemy activity developing around the team, and asked how long it would be before the choppers arrived to get them out. After making a pass over them, Covey helpfully confirmed there was indeed lots of enemy activity around RT Lion, but that all the helicopters were returning to base in order to drop off their wounded and refuel. Sit tight. The only things tight were Watkin's jaws.[13]

With an enemy attack now almost inevitable and night fast approaching, Watkins thought it best to try to move his team to higher ground. They needed every advantage, however slight. Sitting tight was not going to be in their best interests. The team pulled in their anti-personnel claymore mines and began a slow and dangerous trek towards what looked to be a slight rise in the ground. As they moved for ten minutes and listened for ten, which was standard operating procedure for SOG under these conditions, they could hear enemy voices and what was presumed to be movement sounds, on both sides of their line of march. According to Meyer, "Being surrounded has a marvelous way of

Top: Live rockets keeping wood from getting damp at Bua La Pha, Lao. *Bottom:* A house built on cluster bomb casings at Ban Nonggnama, Lao (both late 1990s photographs Clive A. Hills).

focusing the mind," and RT Lion moved with greater stealth. Miraculously, they managed to reach the rise undetected and to secure a perimeter.

Meyer said:

> With the team settled in its RON [Remain Over Night], Watkins told DeSeta and Godwin he was not happy with doing nothing. He didn't like the idea of just sitting and waiting for the enemy to attack. So he'd decided to take two of the Bru and move forward to Highway 92, set up an observation post and see what there was to see...
>
> Before he moved out, however, Watkins checked their commo [communications] situation. Covey had retired for the evening and turned RT Lion's health and happiness over to Moonbeam—codename for the night air force aircraft that fly over the area of operation, the mysterious phantom of the night who always seemed to be there when needed. When finally reached, Moonbeam assured RT Lion he had them loud and clear and that in future commo checks all they need do was break squelch three times to indicate they were alive and well.
>
> The last order of business before moving out was to ensure everyone understood what the night's password was. Watkins didn't want to be hosed down returning to his own team. When the Bru going with him looked confused regarding the password Watkins decided it would be best if he ran point, so he took the lead position in the patrol.
>
> The trio cautiously moved forward about 150 meters, where they ran into Highway 92. They could hear voices and vehicle traffic. Then, their luck continued its dismal descent as the sky cleared and a bright moon came out to cast an iridescent glow over everything, including them.
>
> Even though they had heard voices and vehicle noise, once they reached the road there was no traffic in sight, so Watkins boldly stepped out onto the highway. Several One-Zeros quietly turned over in their graves as Watkins stood there in the moonlight looking around. He could see nothing, but he could hear lots of voices and activity on the opposite side of the road. He immediately melted back into the brush about 10 meters and set up an observation line, with Er [Bru] about 30 meters to his right and Rong [Bru] the same distance to his left. Er and Rong put out claymores facing up and down the road. If they needed to, they would set them off and buy time as they made a run for it.
>
> Watkins was nearly blinded when the first set of headlights rounded the bend not five minutes later. This was stark evidence of [VNPA] confidence in the fact they owned the night, at least in Oscar-8. The first vehicle was soon followed by three trucks packed with supplies. They passed so close to Watkins he could clearly see the soldiers in the cabs, smoking and chatting. He could also make out the foliage that had been draped and fastened across the tops of the trucks to camouflage and conceal them from American aerial reconnaissance flights. The [VNPA] were clearly confident in their control of Oscar-8, and in truth their activities would have gone virtually undetected were it not for SOG reconnaissance operations.
>
> In short order ten more fully loaded trucks passed. Interspersed between them were dozens of soldiers and civilians pushing rickety bicycles piled high with everything imaginable, from live chickens to weapons and ammunition.
>
> To Watkins' utter amazement, the next vehicle was a massive bulldozer, its blade up in the air, and a [VNPA] soldier signaling directions with a flashlight. Watkins was barely over the bulldozer when along came two Russian T-34 tanks, their gun barrels facing aft, and their external fuel tanks mounted just as the manual said.
>
> It took more than three hours for the [VNPA] parade to pass. As the last of its rumblings grew faint, Watkins came out of his daze and looked around. He immediately saw Rong crawling towards him with a panicked look on his face. Watkins had been so mesmerized by all the traffic he had forgotten about the young Bru team members, Er and Rong.
>
> When Rong reached him he could barely talk. Not proficient in English under the very best conditions, what he was now attempting to tell Watkins bordered on the incoherent. Watkins calmed him down as best he could and made him start over. Rong said he'd been watching the traffic, just like Watkins, and had been as taken with it as he was. While he was staring at all the vehicles passing by, a hand had reached out and given his arm a shake. A Montagnard soldier, one of those the [VNPA] had pressed into unwilling service, said "It's your time for guard duty!"
>
> Fortunately Rong was too stunned to do anything but nod his head and grunt a kind of acknowledgement. It was enough, however, and the [VNPA] Montagnard moved off into the brush. Rong was

Trucks along the Hồ Chí Minh Trail in the late 1960s (courtesy Phạm Hồng Cư).

badly rattled and of the definite opinion that the three of them ought to abandon Highway 92 and get back to the rest of the team as fast as possible. Watkins agreed.[14]

Watkins and his team were airlifted out of Lao, but not before they had called a Prairie Fire Emergency. Meyer had said that this emergency gave SOG an astounding kill ratio of hundreds of communists to one SOG member, and at times thousands to one, because once they transmitted for help bombs and napalm dropped like rain on the area to stop the team from being overrun before extraction.

For Watkins and his team, this deluge of firepower first came in the form of 500-pound bombs from F-4 jets; each landed so close that the team lifted off the ground. The next on the scene was a Covey pilot who had been monitoring the team's radio frequency. He flew low over the area looking for a landing zone so that helicopters could come and extract them. Once a landing zone could be identified, the team made their way there, hotly pursued by their enemy. On arriving, the team took up a defensive position in one of the larger craters and quickly started taking incoming mortar fire. Following on, A-1E Skyraiders arrived and covered an area close by with napalm and slowed the enemy's advance. Then two gunships from the 7th Air Cavalry came to extract the team, but as they did so they took casualties so were forced away. Soon after, two A-1Es came to bomb the area. Finally, the South Vietnamese Air Force's 219th Special Operations Squadron sent one of its Sikorsky H-34 Kingbee helicopters; escorted by gunships from Marine Light Attack Helicopter Squadron 367, a group of pilots codenamed Scarface. The helicopters airlifted Watkins and team from the zone. For monitoring the Hồ Chí Minh Trail, SOG and brute firepower were not the only advanced war tool at Westmorland's disposal.

Igloo White

In the early stages of the Vietnam War the Americans started a number of projects that attempted to build a physical and electronic barrier from the coast of Vietnam to

Some of those who attended the School for Army Children of COSVN, located within a COSVN base area. The school was named in honor of Nguyễn Văn Trỗi, a *biệt động* fighter, who had tried to kill Robert McNamara when he had visited Vietnam in the early 1960s. Trỗi was later executed for this act (courtesy Phạm Hồng Cư).

the border of Thailand. The system intended to interdict North Vietnamese infiltration into South Vietnam, a vital target being the Hồ Chí Minh Trail. In 1966, the Secretary of Defense Robert McNamara (1916–2009) approved such a program. Initially called Practice Nine, throughout 1967 it changed names to Illinois City, Dye Marker, Muscle Shoals and finally, in 1968, to Igloo White; sometimes nicknamed the McNamara Line.

By July 1968, the physical part of the barrier had proved to be relatively ineffective; from then Igloo White comprised mainly of an electronic barrier. First, U.S. teams placed electronic movement sensors in strategic locations; when trucks or communist troops went by, these sensors picked up any activity. This information was then relayed to orbiting aircraft, which in turn transmitted the data to a nerve center at Nakhon Phanom for individuals to analyze. Once confident of enemy activity, helicopters airlifted SOG teams into the area or aircraft bombed the hostile location. As the electronic barrier system expanded, Nakhon Phanom changed its codename from Dutch Mill to Sycamore.

Meyer recalled that some of his missions for SOG under Igloo White were to insert these sensors along the A Shau Valley in Vietnam in late 1968. The sensors were highly successful in picking up traffic noise, he had recalled. Nevertheless, no sooner had the Americans implemented new tactics and technology than the communists were close behind with their attempts to derail them. Almost immediately after the VNPA came across their first sensor, just months prior to Meyer's operation, they researched how to destroy or trick them. As a case in point, sensors were given false readings by herding buffalo nearby or buckets of urine were hung in tree branches above the chemical sniffers.

It appeared that the Igloo White project spent hundreds of millions of dollars on a high-tech system that targeted $1,000 trucks protected by buckets of urine. Hồ had once said in August 1945, "We have to win independence at any cost even if the Trường Sơn Mountains burn."[15] The communists would use all means to fight back.

The Trail Maker

The communists said if the couriers and their corridors are the "blood vessels and nervous systems" and the Communist Party the "brains" of the revolution, then the Hồ Chí Minh Trail was their "backbone." U.S. military units or CIA agents had spent years trying to sever this backbone but without success because since Võ Bẩm commanded the Trail there had been two others, Phan Trọng Tuệ and Hoàng Văn Thái, and all three men had been determined to keep it operating.[16]

When Đồng Sĩ Nguyên, the fourth commander of the Hồ Chí Minh Trail, took over in January 1967, the United States now had a bloodier fight. Đồng Sĩ Nguyên turned this so-called backbone from an old low-key covert supply line into a modern strategic overt battlefield. Much of his success stemmed from the fact that he converted most of his forces, which had previously used foot power, bicycles or elephants to carry loads, into vehicle transportation units. He then equipped these troops as fighting units and supported their activities with better supplied and fortified army stations, he installed an advanced communications network to link between stations and constructed a fuel pipeline that stretched across the mountains both in Lao and Vietnam.[17] Later he went on to strengthen anti-aircraft defenses, deployed surface-to-air missile sites at crucial locations to disrupt B-52 missions and designed mobile anti-aircraft detachments.[18] His rational for these changes was that there was no legal justification not to, and the Trail needed to be transformed in order to support what North Vietnam needed to resource the war in the South, a situation partly linked to both China and the Soviets because they had agreed to increase their military aid to North Vietnam.[19]

SOG members had asked the author if Đồng Sĩ Nguyên had taken their operations seriously. "Yes," he had replied, because they could penetrate into any base area at short notice thanks to intelligence data from Igloo White and helicopter transportation. To try to prevent their presence on his battlefield he ordered his strategists to work out how SOG teams operated. He wanted to know how the weather affected their ability to fly, in what way the terrain

Đồng Sĩ Nguyên, when commander of Corps 559, at the Front Headquarters of Corps 559, situated to the west of Sepon, Lao, 15 January 1971 (courtesy Đồng Sĩ Nguyên).

Top: A 37mm anti-aircraft artillery gun captured from the VNPA on the Plain of Jars, Lao, and displayed outside the Nakhon Phanom RTAFB Tactical Unit Operations Center. *Bottom:* A UH-1 helicopter with a member of SOG being extracted out of Cambodia on a McGuire Rig, February 1968 (both photographs courtesy Jim Burns).

dictated their flight path and which U.S. base areas they flew from. Using this information, he deployed spotters, usually local tribesmen, along the Lao border, who could be placed reasonably accurately as a result of his intelligence. The spotters could observe possible landing zones for U.S. helicopters and relay this information to nearby communist army stations, who could then deploy units to attack.

Later in 1967, Đồng Sĩ Nguyên took a decision that saw each army station instructed to have two to three infantry companies within their sphere of operation. He ordered them to defend their area and the region from their army station to the next. Further, on 28 June 1968, the 968th Infantry Division formed as an advisory unit. They taught Vietnamese fighters operating in the south of Lao how to protect themselves against SOG, Thai Special Forces and the Royal Lao Army by using sniffer dogs, tracker teams and radio interception. The division also coordinated with the Pathet Lao to clear southern Lao of enemy troops.

With these new measures in place under Đồng Sĩ Nguyên, it meant that throughout the Limited War the Hồ Chí Minh Trail could expand. It ultimately comprised several routes to South Vietnam: secret roads, bypasses, hard-standing highways, mountain tracks and river systems. These routes supported couriers to truck transportation; some of the goods went by Soviet and North Vietnamese helicopters. Not only did these methods of transport carry thousands of tons of weapons and equipment, but they helped transfer millions of U.S. dollars in cash from Hong Kong to Saigon to fund the revolution

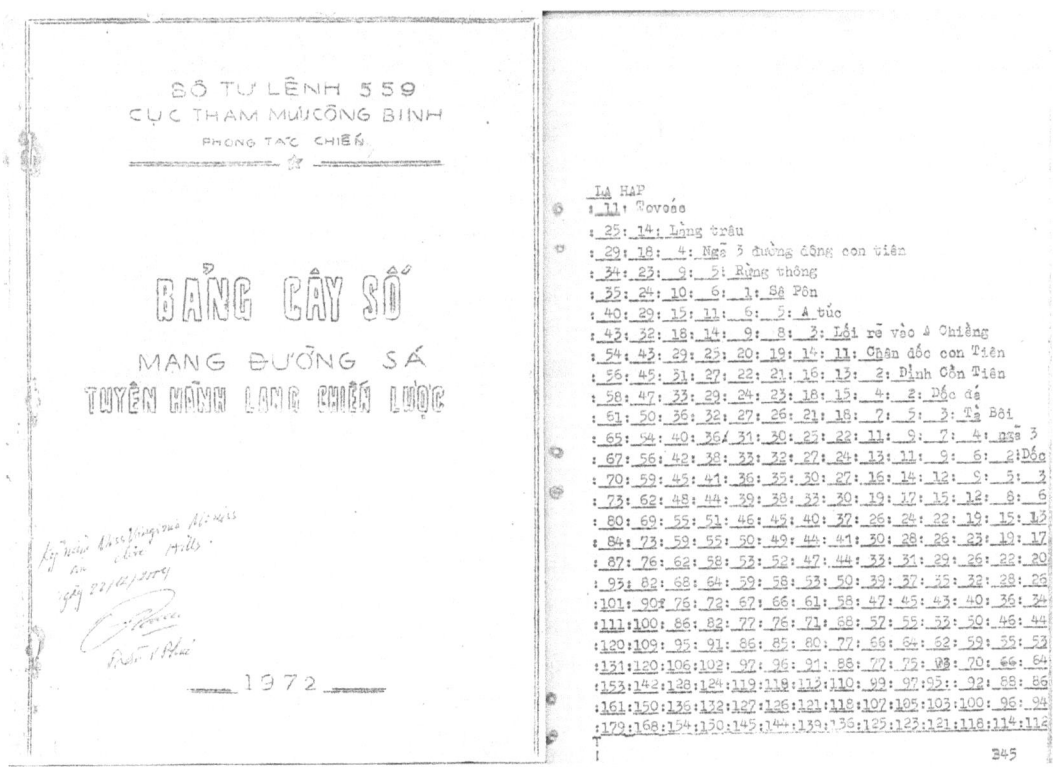

A military record to confirm the distances between strategic locations along the Hồ Chí Minh Trail (courtesy Trần Văn Phúc).

in the South. Đồng Sĩ Nguyên had inherited Corps 559, but by the early 1970s his forces consisted of 100,000 troops and 10,000 Youth Volunteers. A few months prior to the Battle of Lam Sơn 719 in 1971, which was a South Vietnamese–led operation to cut the Trail, they were given the additional name, the Trường Sơn Army.

Đồng Sĩ Nguyên had defended and expanded his overt Trail against the United States might but this was not the only challenge facing U.S. servicemen. This Trail maker knew that the Americans were not only under attack on his battlefield but on their own safe ground.

My Friend Is My Enemy

Meyer had a story that echoed that of Burns' years before, when the communists managed to obtain his daughter's birth details, but this time there were serious consequences. Meyer described when the communists compromised FOB 4, an event that took place on 23 August 1968, and where seven U.S. Special Forces soldiers together with many Vietnamese were killed.

Watkins was there at the time and has always suspected that the attack seemed suspiciously similar to one that had occurred at FOB 4 on 31 December 1967. Little information has come out about these two attacks; not only because this event occurred inside a top secret compound, but there were embarrassing breaches in security. The communists confirmed that Watkins was right. The attack in 1967 had been executed so that around 1,000 POWs being held there could be released but also to help give communist forces practice attacking a U.S. base in readiness for the Tết Offensive. Then, in August 1968, communist forces again attacked FOB 4 using information they had gleaned from 1967. Giáp had not originally made it a target during Tết because since the attack in 1967 the base had seen further fortifications but those in charge had insisted on waves of fighting to incite the people to rise up, and this base became part of Wave III.

For the attack in 1968 the communists used their now standard approach, the starting point being to establish the Revolutionary Infrastructure within the camp. This network could gather intelligence on the camp layout, who was based there, how well armed they were, instigate breaches in camp security and neutralize the most dangerous elements inside the camp before the attack. In addition, the Party cell could conduct extensive proselytizing on civil workers or ARVN troops based at the camp, so that when the battle started, any switched person could, for example, open the gates and show the revolutionaries around the camp. Using the chaos of war, any act they carried out just looked like part of the battle, and if everything ran smoothly, the camp could be overrun, and those who had switched sides, captured with other ARVN soldiers, then released, only to serve again in a U.S. camp ready for the next communist instruction.

From American eyewitness accounts of the 1968 attack, their observations indicate the existences of the Revolutionary Infrastructure within their camp. Americans present that night observed that the communist forces used a hole in the wire fence in the southeast corner of FOB 4 to march into the camp, heavily armed and carrying satchel charges. Prior to the attack, the Americans saw that civilian local helpers who worked at FOB 4 had been returning home daily through this hole for months. This clearly breached security but because only civilian helpers used it, nobody stopped them. In addition, the Americans that night said that the communists appeared to be strong and confident in managing the battle; they clearly knew the camp layout because the enemy troops had used the indigenous mess hall for a pre-attack briefing and they had strategically placed machine guns so that they had clear lines of fire down key pathways to achieve a high kill rate. It was also evident that military proselytizing had been conducted because the local security forces appeared to cooperate with the communists instead of defending the camp.

According to Lieutenant Colonel Lauren Overby, who commanded FOB 4 just prior to the attack, SOG later discovered a scaled replica of the base that the communists had built in the jungle. He noted that it could only have been built with inside help and he suspected a female mess orderly, who disappeared after the attack.[20] What Overby missed is that the Revolutionary Infrastructure had neutralized his modern technology and top secret mission by exploiting human weaknesses and making a so-called friend a covert enemy.

Looking for Answers

One man who helped to question communist actions within covert missions was Robert McKnight, who in January 1968 took over OP34, SOG's Airborne Operations Group. At the end of 1968, this group had three branches: OP34A agent operations, OP34B STRATA operations and OP34C diversionary operations.[21]

McKnight had studied reports of U.S.-run insertions into North Vietnam between April 1964 and October 1967. SOG had put in place around 250 agents and prior to this the CIA had inserted a similar number. They were put into an unknown area and then expected to collect intelligence and sabotage bridges or the like. By late 1967, officials estimated that only a handful of teams still operated, the rest having been either killed or captured shortly after insertion. This failure was disappointing so officials made an assessment of the remaining teams. They found that although the agents still operated, Hanoi now controlled them, and the information they had sent back was being used against MACVSOG.

Key to Robert McKnight's conclusion was that he believed the communists had used the "double-cross system" meaning that they had taken control of U.S. covert operations for seven years.[22] There were many important interconnecting activities needed to make the double-cross system work: take control of all espionage activities run by your enemy in your own country, and from this control, make them think that they are having elements of success so that they do not try to expand or set up another system; use known enemy agents to make contact with and apprehend new agents and spies, so that they can then be turned, killed or captured; obtain information about the personalities and working methods of your enemy's security service; access your enemy's codes and ciphers; understand your enemy's intentions; change the operational intentions of your enemy; and finally, through this system you can send disinformation to your enemy. By way of illustration, in Vietnam, after the first air strikes against the North, one CIA agent who had been inserted into the North in 1961 called enthusiastically for more. He had clearly been switched by Hanoi, because bombing fitted perfectly into portraying the United States as the bloodthirsty "ringleaders of imperialism."[23]

Now McKnight started to see what was happening. SOG might be part of the highest level of security within the U.S. military and taking their directive from the White House, but in fact Hanoi pulled their strings. The next three stories told by Meyer show that

SOG teams understood that they had been compromised, they just did not know how they were or by how much.

Meyer said:

> RT Hawaii left for a mission along the Hồ Chí Minh Trail. It was around fifteen minutes after the helicopters had left the landing zone and could not return to pick the team up without refueling, that a loudspeaker said in English, "Welcome to Ashau Valley members of C and C North RT Hawaii," and then accurately read off the team roster.
>
> In the second story RT Virginia switched primary landing zones at the last minute and inserted on their secondary landing zone, their reserve one. They got into a running fight and made their way to the original primary landing zone, only to discover an anti-aircraft gun positioned there. Location information was supposedly known only to a select few and any messages sent were kept in a secure area, in other words, no South Vietnamese were present.
>
> My third example shows that some SOG teams knew damn well we were being compromised. Some people who didn't take precautions are dead because of it. We knew of one man who was an enemy agent in the highest command levels of SOG in Saigon. Their cover was so deep it was never exposed during the Vietnam War. Then Major General George "Speedy" Gaspard, whilst watching a Hanoi television show in 1996, saw an individual he knew as Francois receive Hanoi's highest military honor for his years of service as a spy in SOG. Francois had access to highly sensitive information while employed by the Americans. Gaspard had said that there was no question that this spy hurt SOG operations.[24]

Gaspard knew first-hand how to protect SOG. He had taken over STRATA operations in October 1967, directing its missions into North Vietnam through September 1968. The unique aspect of STRATA was that the teams launched out of Thailand, flying in U.S. Air Force helicopters. The Air Force performed all insertions and extractions

Udorn RTAFB, Thailand in 1969 (courtesy Jim Burns).

without pre-mission reports to Saigon. Throughout Gaspard's tenure at STRATA 24, he inserted teams into North Vietnam on various intelligence gathering missions. During that time he lost only one and a half teams, meaning that more than 150 STRATA team members were inserted and successfully extracted. He had noted that when looking at the success rate of STRATA teams, it was clear why they succeeded; key was having a separate chain of command, not telling Saigon and working with the Air Force on a need-to-know basis.

To this day, some senior military and government officials still unjustly consider that SOG missions were not as effective as they could have been. Two perceived operational weaknesses cited by critics are that it was hard to disguise a chosen landing zone because the communists just followed the helicopter in, and once there SOG had trouble staying on the ground and completing their missions because the North Vietnamese had such a high level of defense. Critics aired these views even though they knew that SOG did have standard operating procedures to protect their missions, including the use of decoy helicopters, multiple landing zones and switching zones at the last minute.

What the critics had observed did echo the high security measures Đồng Sĩ Nguyên had put in place to protect his Trail. What the critics failed to grasp was that U.S.–led only operations did work for the clear reason that they did not come in contact with Hồ's covert strategies. The critics did not acknowledge it, or did not want to acknowledge it, because Hồ's methods were too complicated and sensitive to deal with. This attitude meant information hemorrhaged out of SOG secure zones, and gave the communists control of U.S. operations.

Shoe-shine boys in Huế City in 2007; a job many couriers adopted because it enabled them to listen in to conversations without raising suspicion (Clive A. Hills).

Echoes from the Past

There is no doubt that Hồ's blueprint had to adapt to the modern technology the United States brought to Vietnam, yet so much of his core principles remained. Meyer and Burns, like their fellow combatants, had fought their whole war by staring their enemy right in the eye but never seeing who they were; sadly these soldiers could not afford to distrust the South Vietnamese as their lives depended on camaraderie.

Their experiences could so easily have been those of their French counterparts. Bernard B. Fall (1926–1967) traveled to Indochina in 1953. He wrote the book *Street Without Joy*, a title taken from the name given to a stretch of Route 1 by French troops, who had fought from Huế to Quảng Trị and had taken appalling casualties there. Fall said, "Of course, the Communists had been informed of the operation, as they usually are, either by the cumbersomeness of our preparations or by spies infiltrating among the Vietnamese cooks and shoe-shine boys and girlfriends and other paraphernalia with which the French units in Indochina are always bogged down."[25]

With the Southward March, the Hồ Chí Minh Trail, ready to supply a large confrontation, the communists launched the Tết Offensive in 1968. This would be the bloodiest and largest city-wide operation conducted by the revolutionaries during the Vietnam War. Now it seemed to be the American soldiers' turn to walk in the footsteps of history, beside an "undetected army" and the ghosts of their French counterparts, to fight along their very own streets without joy.

13

Tết: America's Big Decision

The Start of Lengthy Tết Preparations

The Tết Offensive of 1968 is known as a turning point of the Vietnam War in favor of the communists. Yet few revolutionaries knew the objectives because of the age-old friction within the Communist Party, between those who were realistic and wanted the outcome to have weakened the United States in Vietnam, and those who believed that total victory against the "ringleaders of imperialism" could be achieved by an August Revolution–like approach, a people's uprising, modeled on the X Plan. The latter, although delusional, had their way and as a consequence militarily the communists lost the offensive with catastrophic effects. What saved the Tết Offensive from being a total failure were the gruesome images seen on American televisions, which overwhelmed and demoralized a large part of the U.S. population and accelerated the anti-war demonstrations. From this point on, the U.S. government found it increasingly difficult to persuade its people that it could win, and that right was on their side.

One of the factors that helped to swing the Tết Offensive in Hanoi's favor was the fighting in Huế City. This success can be put down to the work of people such as Phan Nam (1928–2013). At the time of Tết he was a member of both the Huế City Party Committee and the Huế Front. His principal target during Tết was the attack on the West Gate of the Citadel, which enabled the main forces to enter and occupy the city. This attack on an ancient symbolic part of Huế, along with sustained fighting elsewhere, unintentionally guaranteed that bloody images were broadcast into the living rooms of the world for days on end.

Before the Tết Offensive, Phan Nam had accumulated a vast wealth of experience. Born in Phú Lộc District, he had started to participate in revolutionary activities in 1944.[1] Later, as a student, Party members recruited Nam with two others for their handwriting skills and set them to work reproducing Việt Minh documentation in preparation for the August Revolution in 1945. Just months later, he learned to build his first underground network.[2] Impressed with his work, in 1949 his leaders sent him to Huế City, where he joined the Huế City Party Committee. While he built his networks, Nam initially disguised himself as a furniture polisher and used the official documents of a man named Lương Thu, who had died during his covert activities. His successes saw him called to North Vietnam in the early 1950s for further training and re-education. He only returned to the Huế City, under a new alias, in 1960.

As an underground functionary, Nam lived in the forest at the Huế City Party Committee revolutionary base, Kim Phụng Mountain, about 20km out of Huế near Hòn Chén

Temple. There he worked undercover among minority groups, developing and expanding his infrastructure into areas where there had never been communist control. His networks linked to the corridors in A Lưới District, which then interlinked with the Hồ Chí Minh Trail. His infrastructure supported communist military action throughout the 1960s and made U.S. operations in the region highly dangerous.

Nam played his part in preparing for the X Plan of 1965. Although he was not informed about the details of the X Plan, the Communist Party had urged him to hasten his work and open up fresh infrastructure leading down from the mountains into Huế City. Once completed, the Huế City Party Committee could enter the city successfully for the first time since 1957. For his valiant efforts, the Party gave Nam control over parts of the west side of the Perfume River of Huế City. Hoàng Lanh (1926–2008) controlled parts of the southern side. These two men designed agent and courier networks through all levels of society across Huế City, so enabling communist units to move down from the mountains. Although they did not know it at the time, from 1966 they prepared for the 1968 Tết Offensive.

Nam explained:

> To prepare for the Tết Offensive was far more complicated than it would have been if we had wanted to carry out such an operation during the French War. French strategy was not as sophisticated as that of the Americans.
>
> During the French resistance there were three defined regions: enemy controlled areas, disputed areas and liberated areas. The French controlled the cities. The lowland countryside was disputed. The highland mountainous zones belonged to us, liberated.
>
> Looking at Huế, and even Nha Trang, the French might have controlled these areas but we still operated within them and the surrounding lowland countryside. We could do this because the French did not have the ability to correlate data on individuals to the same extent as the Americans did with their computers.
>
> We were safe in the mountainous zones because the French rarely ventured far from their base areas and into the mountains for any great length of time. Within our areas of control our safe houses were more open and could be set up in most locations. When the Americans came with their helicopters all this changed. Now they could operate anywhere at any time, so no region could be deemed safe.[3]

This new high-tech war meant that large parts of the local Communist Party's operations had to be redesigned, such as the transportation of weapons to Huế City. During the French War the supply lines were far less complicated because they ran through liberated areas including the mountain foothills to the Perfume River. For the Vietnam War the Americans actively targeted the Hồ Chí Minh Trail. Therefore, without a change in policy to redesign logistics, weapons could not be shipped at the speed needed to supply the South, and communist losses would be high in both life and equipment.

Two systems altered were the interaction between communist zones and battlefield arrangements. On the first point, for the French War, under the Thừa Thiên Provincial Party Committee, was the Huế City Party Committee and the district party committees. For the Vietnam War, the Party added an additional link between the local and provincial committees to make it harder for the Americans to listen in or to insert an agent into each committee. On the second point, to manipulate U.S. troop movements, the 5th Zone saw its territory divided; some went in 1966 to form the Trị Thiên Military Zone, designated B4, and later that year the Route 9–Northern Quảng Trị Front formed, designated B5.[4]

For Nam, his procedures to arrange for the shipment of weapons changed. From

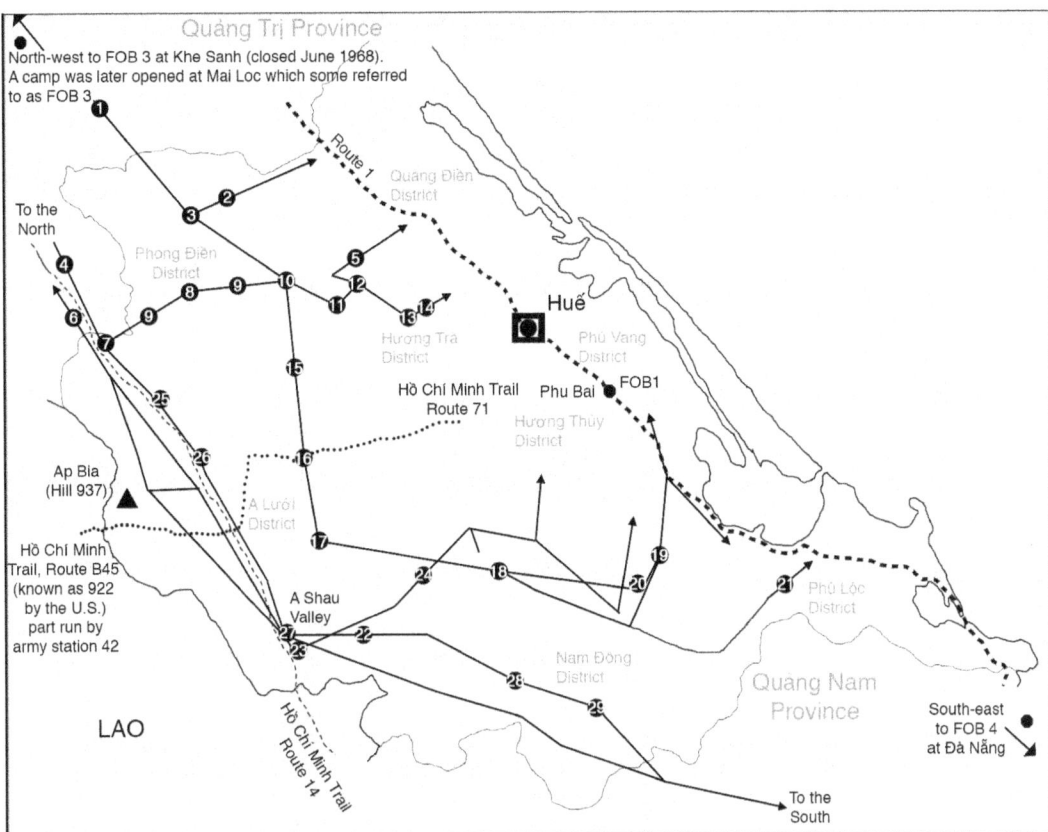

Examples of *giao bưu* corridors and stations for Thừa Thiên Province.

1 - A *giao bưu* corridor from Quảng Trị Province 1956–1967.
2 - A corridor covering Phong Điền District and Quảng Điền District; the *giao bưu* here helped revolutionaries cross Route 1.
3 - Lưu's *giao bưu* station. Lưu established the station.
4 - A main *giao bưu* corridor from 1968–1975, for Quảng Trị Province and Thừa Thiên Province, known as the Trị Thiên Military Zone.
5 - A corridor covering Phong Điền District and Quảng Điền District; the *giao bưu* here helped revolutionaries cross Route 1.
6 - A main *giao bưu* corridor of the Trị Thiên Military Zone from 1956–1967.
7 - The main *giao bưu* station of Trị Thiên Military Zone.
8 - Đà's *giao bưu* station.
9 - A main *giao bưu* corridor for Thừa Thiên Province from 1965–1975.
10 - Vũ's *giao bưu* station.
11 - Hùng's *giao bưu* station.
12 - Hương's *giao bưu* station.
13 - Xu's *giao bưu* station.
14 - The *giao bưu* here helped revolutionaries in Hương Trà District.
15 - A main *giao bưu* corridor for Thừa Thiên Province from 1956–1967.
16 - Lợi's *giao bưu* station.
17 - Hương's *giao bưu* station.
18 - Lan's *giao bưu* station; between 1969 to 1975, the headquarters of the Thừa Thiên Provincial Party Committee was located in a cave nearby.
19 - Hiệp's *giao bưu* station.
20 - Hoàng's *giao bưu* station.
21 - The *giao bưu* here helped revolutionaries in Phú Lộc District.
22 - A main *giao bưu* corridor of the Trị Thiên Military Zone from 1968–1975.
23 - Lợi's *giao bưu* station.
24 - A main *giao bưu* corridor for Thừa Thiên Province from 1968–1975.
25 - Hùng's *giao bưu* station.
26 - Location of the *Giao Bưu* Department of Thừa Thiên Province.
27 - Cường's *giao bưu* station.
28 - Hai's *giao bưu* station.
29 - Diên's *giao bưu* station.

● SOG Forward Operating Bases

***Giao bưu* corridors of Thừa Thiên Province during the Vietnam War.**

1955 to 1960, if he needed weapons the Huế City Party Committee just contacted the 5th Zone or the 4th Zone directly. Once B4 formed and Nam needed supplies, the Huế City Party Committee had to go via the Trị Thiên Party Committee, who then contacted Corps 559, the operators of the Hồ Chí Minh Trail. To coordinate between Corps 559 and the Trị Thiên Party Committee, Provincial Party Committee leaders from Quảng Bình Province in North Vietnam, Quảng Trị Province (DMZ) and the Southern province of Thừa Thiên, met in Thừa Thiên Province at a safe house belonging to Hùng Sơn (1921–), a political man who represented Corps 559.[5]

Nam said:

> On building my infrastructure I realized very quickly that my courier lines had to be unique because our headquarters was about 20km outside the city in the mountains. To get there or further afield we had to go from an urban, predominantly ethnic Vietnamese setting, through countryside villages and on to an ethnic minority mountainous area. I designed three categories of courier lines. My general rule: blend into your surroundings.
>
> Within the first category, lines went through minority areas. I placed my couriers within their native ethnic area so they had the same mannerisms as the people around them and even the same skin tone. Care had to be taken by any revolutionary using these lines, and at all times they had to divert attention away from themselves. If hostile minorities thought they were from the city, then the minority group might think that they were revolutionaries because urban people did not stray into the forest, and they might kill the outsider.
>
> The second category covered lines that traversed the countryside. An operative could either appear to be a farmer or someone visiting the village from the city. As a result, we used many disguises.
>
> The third category of courier lines was within the city; my natural home. I planned my journeys carefully. I could be disguised as a rich or reputable person because such a person could travel around Huế more easily. Or I could be bold and use a road that ran through a Catholic area, since these routes were not policed to the same extent because they thought that the VC did not operate in these areas, so I did![6]

In Huế City, Nam used many different tactics, but whereas Saigon was cosmopolitan, Huế had the atmosphere of a village, so Nam trained his couriers to use this sleepy attitude to their advantage. One example Nam cited was timing. When Nam and his courier had to go via Bao Vinh Bridge, he planned his crossing to coincide with the school girls of Đồng Khánh coming out of class. Nam knew that the soldiers at the checkpoint would just wave him through; frustrated with the swarms of apparently harmless young girls and taking Nam to be a family member escorting one of them home.

Nam continued by saying that he preferred waterways to roads because the Perfume River is vast and has many small waterways and inlets leading from it, which meant that the enemy could not watch the banks all the time. Likewise, Nam considered the look of a girl courier. On occasions she might need to be pretty so that the soldiers watched her and not Nam, whereas at other times she needed to be plain so that she mixed in with the crowd. Nam used to advise his female couriers to sit next to an enemy officer and flirt with him, so that at checkpoints the soldiers thought that the officer and the lady were lovers. If couriers traveled by car he told them to drive an expensive model, because the soldiers presumed that the Việt Cộng were poor. Flirting with an enemy officer was a Nguyễn Bình tactic and using an expensive model car to get around was something Hồ had first taught Lý Phương Đức in the 1920s.

Nam continued:

> Before I recruited or trusted anyone, one of my operatives approached the target person to see if they were receptive. My operative always came from the same social class as the person they approached. If I wanted to talk to students, I used intellectuals to approach them, if I wanted to talk to traders, I

used traders, and so on. Once I had personally observed them, or another trusted colleague had assessed them, I looked to see what the new recruit could do. They might not be any good as a courier but more appropriate for the army.

I put those chosen for covert work through other assessments, including looking at their history to see if they had relatives in the North who had regrouped there. If so, this indicated that they had come from a family of revolutionaries. To take that intelligence further, I might write a letter to their relatives in the North saying, "This is from your sister in a liberated zone." I trained my operative who delivered the letter to observe how the relatives reacted to the news that a family member now worked for the revolution.

What kept me alive? I put that down to being accurate and aware in my work and using what my enemy gave me or turning what he had not done in my favor. For me to travel from the city to the base in the mountains, just 20km away, could take me seven days and many disguises. The Americans flew the same journey in five minutes in their helicopters.[7]

Nam had said that to prepare Huế City for the Tết Offensive was a long dangerous process. He summarized that, in Vietnamese culture, if a person wants to know more and is too inquisitive, then they could be a spy; a person should only know what they need to. Likewise, at all times the measures he put in place were not only done to trick the enemy but to trick the locals who had been asked to look out for suspicious activities. "Details, details, never take your eyes off the details. That's why I survived."[8]

Who to Target

Today Huế City serves as the cultural and intellectual center of Vietnam, a beautiful urban setting divided into the northern and southern sides by the Perfume River. Throughout the Vietnam War, as the third largest city in Vietnam, Huế had a population of 140,000.[9] Two-thirds of the people lived on the northern side secured within the walls of the old city. The southern part of Huế was its modern heart, within which the Thừa Thiên administration buildings, Huế University, the hospital and prisons were located. Although Huế had seen some military action prior to the Tết Offensive it had been treated almost as an open city by both sides, and remained comparatively free from conflict.

What unrest there had been came from women, student or Buddhist movements, the latter having a long history of agitation against the ruling party. The French viewed the Buddhists with suspicion and had done all they could to limit their power and curb the construction of temples. It all came to the surface again during the Vietnam War when, in May 1963, around 20,000 Buddhists assembled in Huế to celebrate the 2,527th birthday of Buddha. Although peaceful at first, things turned violent and people died when government troops opened fire on the crowd. President Diệm later tried to cover up their true cause of death and blamed the incident on the Việt Cộng.[10]

This episode infuriated the Buddhists in Huế, and across the South they pulled together to form a stronger movement against the government. One Buddhist behind the strengthening of this religious group was Thích Trí Quang (1924–), who embarked on a trip around the South to recruit new members. Another Buddhist called Thích Quảng Đức set fire to himself in a street in Saigon. This incredibly famous image was captured by Malcolm Browne, an Associated Press correspondent. Both Buddhists chose different methods but ultimately their actions were united; to urge the Americans to pressurize the Diệm government to reform their policies towards the Buddhists.

To expand his covert networks in Huế City and surrounding areas, Nam studied

Thích Quảng Đức (1897–1963), a Buddhist monk, burned himself to death at a busy Saigon road intersection on 11 June 1963 in protest against the persecution of Buddhists by Ngô Đình Diệm's administration. This is the car in which he was a passenger before he carried out this act. 2007 photograph (Clive A. Hills).

each situation in great detail; not only to see how best to harness any anger towards the Southern regime, but to observe those who were actively against the war or the U.S. presence in Vietnam. He deduced that he could go down two paths: plant agents within enemy ranks, which was very complicated, or look at highly active groups, infiltrate them and steer their activities towards supporting the NLF. On asking how he recruited such a diverse group of people, he said, "It is amazing what you can achieve when you instill nationalism in someone."[11]

Although Nam worked extensively with special propaganda among the upper classes, he credits the speed at which he set up his Revolutionary Infrastructure to the fact that he had approached mainly student and Buddhist movements. Students were highly sought after. Viewed as passionate and at the forefront of change, they played a lead role in Huế City because they could reach out to a spectrum of social classes, mobilize large crowds and influence their teachers, who could further persuade other students to join their line of thinking. Buddhists were in demand as well; people saw them as a predominant high-profile force in South Vietnam and, although difficult to recruit, when they were they added great value. For instance, they were their own entity; they came with temples that could house their covert three-member cells working against the Southern regime. They also had solid strategies for expansion; agitation among relatives in the army and the government, and crash courses in how to entice members into their movement. Students and Buddhists may have been targeted by many political parties, but this had not put Nam off.

A Student's Story

Nam went on to reveal how he approached a student named Hoàng Hoa (1946–). At the time Hoa had an older brother who had regrouped to North Vietnam in the mid-1950s. In about 1963, Hoa's parents received a letter from their son, who resided in the North. Instead of disowning him they replied to him, and it was from this exchange that the Communist Party obtained a strong indication that his parents were willing to join the revolution. In 1964, Nam went to visit them. Hoa was in his first year of training at Huế University and planned to become a mathematics teacher.

Hoa explained:

My father was a skilled carpenter and on his visits Nam would ask him to build various pieces of furniture, ranging from saps to wardrobes; all designed to include secret compartments. Saps are pieces of furniture in people's homes used as a bed or a table, which have a compartment in which to store things. When designing a sap my father constructed a second door in it leading to a secret cell below the floor. Once installed, someone could hide in it, store secret documents and equipment or listen in to conversations surreptitiously. It was from talking to Nam, when he visited my father, that I accepted the line of the NLF.

In my university students were very influenced by the many political stories in the press, but I could see two types of student, those who just wanted to graduate and get a good job, predominately in the Southern government, and those who wanted to do something for their country and oppose the government. In this latter group the students were either pro–NLF or they followed another

Shown here on 10 May 2007, with the exception of Mrs. Khánh, Lê Đỗ Huy and the author, these are veterans who were vital to the resistance in Huế City. From left, Lê Đỗ Huy, Nguyễn Xuân Tốn, Mrs. Trần Thị Kim Khánh (wife of Mr. Vịnh), Lê Quang Vịnh, the author, Hùng Sơn, Hoàng Hoa and Phan Nam (Clive A. Hills).

group such as the Great Viet Party, a Buddhist movement or the Catholic faith. Groups that were not pro–NLF, we called "float" movements. Within each float movement we placed a communist cell, called a "sink" and there to turn the float movement towards the NLF and get individuals to operate directly for us.

Under Nam I became the secretary of a communist cell, instructed to penetrate into student float movements. We had to reach as many people as possible because, although they might not support the NLF, we hoped to persuade them not to join the Southern Army or not to oppose us. I had to arrange demonstrations, a task made easier because the Americans advocated freedom of expression and the right to protest, so they could not stop us. My cell delivered leaflets, carried weapons and conducted special propaganda.

Although at the time life as a student was simple—we went to coffee shops and we did not drink wine and beer—switching people in float movements was hard. When I thought I had a receptive person, I spent months getting closer to them. I talked about their family and political opinions. I did not disclose my communist leanings at first because the people did not accept this political view. I could only reveal this if someone showed strong tendencies towards this line of thinking. To understand them, I went around to their house and pretended to like what they liked to do. If they were good at music I encouraged them to write nationalist songs. Made it fun. I even ran large music festivals such as Sing for the People, and worked with Tôn Thất Lập, an agent of mine and member of the Royal family. He was a famous Royal composer, even in Hanoi after the war. By being with my target person for so long I got to understand if they just spoke of nationalism and opposing the government or if they were actually willing to make sacrifices for their country. So I had two stages: propaganda and sacrifice.

Within the float movements there were those with tendencies towards the NLF and our agents. I operated for four years and during this period I only organized eight agents. I did have other contacts, pro–NLF friends, some I had made myself and others I had met through Nam, who had a list of revolutionary sympathizers across many provinces.[12]

Hoa became one of three leaders of the Huế Civil Affairs Committee for Students (Huế CACS), which was established in 1967, and operated completely covertly under the NLF. The Huế CACS conducted various operations both before and during the 1968 Tết Offensive. In December 1967, with assistance from the Huế CACS, pupils from the college put on a patriotic poem and song performance. From this event the Huế CACS recruited 300 students and sent them to a revolutionary base outside Huế. Here, military and Party types trained them in how to participate in both an uprising and an offensive; at no time were they aware that Tết was the objective.

During the Tết Offensive, the Huế CACS helped set up the Huế Youth Front, a group that intended to bring the youth together. The Party established it just after the Citadel had been taken. Some of the first to join were the 300 students recruited in December. The Huế Youth Front went on to form Civil Defense Teams trained by South Vietnamese officers who had switched sides. Others within the Huế Youth Front encouraged the general uprising. They used jeeps to drive around the city announcing by megaphone that Huế had been liberated, inspiring other students to demonstrate. Then, when the Liberation Army withdrew, the Huế Youth Front helped around 1,000 people to go with them. In July 1968, 700 young people, mostly students, were sent to the North to study.

Hoa stayed at his base area and the enemy arrested him when he returned to the city to rebuild the Revolutionary Infrastructure. He was exiled to the prison on Côn Đảo Island, only being released in 1973.

A Buddhist's Story

Around the same time that Nam had approached Hoa, he engaged with Mrs. Hoàng Thị An (1918–2013), who lived in Xuân Hòa Village and at the time her mother was the

The home of Mrs. Hoàng Thị An, a safe house of Phan Nam, 11 May 2007. From left, Mrs. Nguyễn Quý Hoàng Nhung (daughter of An), Mr. Trung (son of An), Phan Nam, Hoàng Thị An, the author (back) and Lê Đỗ Huy. Just in front of them was the location of the drinking well; this is where Ms. Trâm was beaten when she was being interrogated about the location of Phan Nam (Clive A. Hills).

Buddhist leader of their commune. Born in Phú Yên Province, Mrs. An had been engaged in covert work since 1935. She became a communist during the French War. When her husband, Nguyễn Quý Trọng, regrouped to the North after the Geneva Accords, she took their two children to her parents, who had moved to Huế hoping to avoid persecution. Mrs. An took a job working as the secretary of the Việt Thắng Medical Company. When at this company, she secretly gave the revolutionaries medicine to supplement what herbal products they grew in the forest.

When Mrs. An first moved to Huế, she lost contact with the revolution. Although not intentional, she had not been very keen to get involved from 1955 to 1963 because during this time Diệm had been brutally hunting down activists. She linked with Nam through her relatives, a Mr. Hai and Mr. Châu, who were both from the intelligentsia class and had run networks in Phú Yên Province during the French War. They too had moved to Huế after 1954. On arrival Party functionary Hoàng Lanh recruited them, and Hai and Châu moved to live in the forest working undercover building a revolutionary cell. Nam lived in their forest region and both parties observed one another from afar before they approached each other. Nam was assured of their commitment; he knew that they had both participated in student movements in Hanoi in the early 1950s. Now Nam could work on Mrs. An.

Nam explained:

I started to observe her when building my networks from the mountains into the city. I had a good 100 revolutionary sympathizers in Huế and I was trying to find another agent I could rely on. Although her relatives had tipped me off about her, it was difficult. The Communist Party viewed her with suspicion because we had no file on her when she moved to Huế. So we investigated her husband, brothers and sisters who had stayed in the North to see if she had remained faithful to the revolution. Then we looked at her parents in Huế. We also asked other people in Hanoi if they knew anything about her past.

To move my investigations forward, in 1963 I had to take the risk and visit her. I went to Xuân Hòa Village, a suburb of Huế City. I planned to stay in the area for four days and nights to develop a network there. When we first met we knew nothing of each other, but from this meeting I saw she could speak French, so was well educated. I had to take great care. On the first two occasions we met I said that I was from Huế. If I had told her that I had come from the forest she might have guessed that I was a revolutionary. It was only on my third visit that I disclosed this information. Over time she deduced that I was in the resistance. In 1964 she joined my network.

So much time has passed since then, but even today when I go to her house, the tactics we used flood back to me, the fear, the missions, the sounds.... One technique of knowing that I could enter her house safely was by listening to the sounds of a radio broadcast. The radio is very powerful and rich in information. From Reuters to the BBC our Party employed specialists to listen to national and international radio or TV broadcasts. From these we could get some information about American and Southern troop movements in different areas. Although not enough to act upon, as false information could be given, it did give us the ability to second guess them at opportune moments. Freedom of information can actually be used against you in war.

So, to enter her house safely, I knew from experience that at 6:30 p.m. the BBC broadcast their Radio World Service. For security reasons I had to arrive dead on time at my destination. I could not hang around outside the house. I calculated that it took me ten minutes to cycle to Mrs. An's house from where I was coming. On arrival I rode past the house once. If she was listening to the BBC news, it meant I could enter. If I heard no news it meant that something had happened and I had to go to the next safe house and so on until there was a secure place for me—like an aircraft trying to land in a bad storm. Each place had a different system. I used a coded message to enter a house.

Why the BBC? Before the news, they played the national anthem, so I knew it was the right station. It was also common for those loyal to the Southern regime to be listening to the BBC, so Mrs. An was one of many with the sound of this radio station coming from her house. Equally, Mrs. An had high society friends who listened to the news, so it put her in that class. Conveniently, the BBC aired this just about rush hour, so I went around unnoticed as one of the crowd.[13]

Mrs. An's Buddhist mother became most useful to Nam for the Tết Offensive in Huế City. Mrs. An's mother got her the job at the Việt Thắng Medical Company, whose owner, Mrs. Tuấn Chi, had been an acquaintance of Giáp when they both attended school in Huế.[14] Mrs. An's mother likewise helped her daughter become acquainted with Thích Đôn Hậu, a superior monk. During Tết, both Tuấn Chi and Thích Đôn Hậu became representatives of the Huế Alliance of National, Democracy and Peace Forces, established once the revolutionaries held Huế. Although promoted as being an independent party, it was under the NLF and ultimately controlled by Hanoi. The Huế Alliance intended to attract those in the urban areas who had been alienated by the Thiệu regime, but also entice people who endorsed national independence, democracy, neutrality and peace and were willing to cooperate with the NLF but not join them directly. By drawing these people into the Huế Alliance this new group could isolate the enemy. Mrs. An was an official member of the Huế Alliance covertly representing the Communist Party, and along with Thích Đôn Hậu and Tuấn Chi, she brought the Buddhists into the group.

The Huế Alliance had been part of Hanoi's wider strategy. Prior to Tết, Lê Duẩn had spoken of the need for a second administration in the South; the NLF and another. In April 1968, Hanoi announced the formation of this second administration for South Vietnam, and named it the Alliance of National, Democracy and Peace Forces. They called for the overthrow of the Thiệu regime, the withdrawal of U.S. troops, as well as negotiations to set up a democratic, independent and neutral South Vietnam. The Huế Alliance fell under the new Southern alliance announced that April.

Once the revolutionaries had withdrawn from Huế, Mrs. An helped Thích Đôn Hậu and Tuần Chi to escape from Huế and travel along the Hồ Chí Minh Trail to Hanoi. Mrs. An stayed in the city but the enemy arrested her and sent her to Côn Đảo Island, only being released in 1973.

Westmoreland's Suspicions

Prior to Tết, Việt Cộng activities in Thừa Thiên Province and the neighboring area of Quảng Trị, had not gone unnoticed by the Americans, leading them to fear that the communists planned to strike south of the DMZ and slice the Republic of Vietnam in two, or at least seize the two provinces and use them as bargaining points in any negotiations.

Westmoreland had also aired this apprehension privately months earlier at the Honolulu Conference in 1966, when President Johnson asked him that if he were the enemy then where would he strike. Westmoreland had replied, "Huế."[15] Westmoreland believed that the communists would attack Huế because from early February 1966, U.S. intelligence reports indicated that there had been a significant build up of North Vietnamese troops south of the DMZ in the two provinces of Thừa Thiên and Quảng Trị. He likewise thought that because the city symbolized a unified Vietnam, if the communists took it then this would have a profound psychological impact on the population. To protect Thừa Thiên and Quảng Trị, he sent American troops to the region; Khe Sanh, a former Special Forces camp, became a stronghold for U.S. Marines.

Westmoreland's concerns that the communists planned an attack were further reinforced when, in March 1966, the Buddhist Crises erupted centered on Huế and Đà Nẵng. Predominantly led by Buddhists and students, they tried to oust the government because they felt that after all the work they had done to help overthrow Diệm, the ruling military party did not show any gratitude nor represent their needs. It turned out to be the largest political upheaval since the downfall of Diệm. Westmoreland jittered because he saw that if these demonstrations had coincided with a sustained North Vietnamese offensive, it could have resulted in the loss of the northern provinces south of the DMZ. As he stated, "It might have done South Vietnam in."[16]

The Việt Cộng did not plan the civil unrest in Huế and Đà Nẵng but Nam and his networks played a lead role in stirring the disturbances in his region. Hoa agitated student groups and Mrs. An did the same to the Buddhists. It is not surprising therefore, that after the unrest had died down in June 1966 that the government retaliated and went all out to capture opposition and Việt Cộng suspects for months after. Mrs. Nguyễn Quý Hoàng Nhung, the daughter of Mrs. An and a revolutionary sympathizer, explained one of these brutal encounters with the enemy.

Mrs. Nhung said:

> Nam was nearly caught on a number of occasions, but I remember one horrendous time in April or May 1967. Southern troops, led by American officers, swarmed into our area at about 3 a.m. It was very tense. They knocked on doors. We could hear them getting closer to us, eventually knocking on

ours demanding Nam. I said I knew nothing of his whereabouts and they left. An hour later soldiers came banging on our door again, "Is Ms. Trâm here?" She had a German father, he had defected to the Việt Minh and married a Vietnamese woman. The enemy knew she worked for us. My mother is Trâm's godmother, and in fact Ms. Trâm is her adopted daughter from Phú Yên. So Trâm is my older sister.

The soldiers barged their way into our house with their guns ready to fire. I was frightened, young, and still at high school, about sixteen or seventeen years old. Nam was sleeping on a bed. On hearing them enter he flew off the bed and slipped into the secret hideout at the back of the cupboard. To hide the variation in cupboard depth, between the outside and the inside dimensions, a bookshelf had been built at the back of the cupboard. [This hideout was a cupboard built by Hoa's father].

Trâm was in her room. The soldier called, "Trâm, come out!" She did and the soldiers shouted, "No one move." If we had they would have shot us. I froze. They mistreated Trâm saying, "Someone has said that you are hiding a VC. Where is the secret cell?"

While they questioned Trâm, the soldiers started to search the house vigorously, pulling things down, opening doors, even searching the salt jar! Then a dozen Vietnamese soldiers rushed into Trâm's room where Nam hid and pulled down every book from the shelf, but no one noticed that the inside dimensions of the cupboard were different from the outside ones, as the compartment was so slim. They only found revolutionary documents, books and newspapers on her bed, as she read them at night.

"Where is he?" they demanded. When they could get nothing from Trâm they pulled her outside and beat her so severely that she was totally unrecognizable, insisting, "If you denounce the VC we will release you." It was so dreadful watching. They pulled water from our well and mixed soap powder in. Dragging her to a corner of the garden, they beat her blue, her clothes were all tattered and the grass beneath her torn up. With the force, a revolutionary newspaper fell out of her clothing, "Now you can't deny you are VC." She still protected Nam. They poured chili into the soapy water and forced it into her mouth. She vomited up the mix. Streaks of blood came up with it as they jumped on her stomach.

They stayed from 4 a.m. till 8 a.m. in the morning. Ms. Trâm worried that if the soldiers stayed searching the house any longer, too much would be compromised. So at around 8 a.m. she tricked the soldiers and said that she would show them the cell. She led them away. Predictably they found nothing and they took her to the police department and arrested her. This was a real blow because the revolution lost a key agent and a *biệt động* fighter in the Lê Quang Vịnh Unit who operated inside the city. She was also the head of a Buddhist sect as well as having a secret cell at Lê Đình Toán's house. He later became part of Nam's assault on the West Gate during the Tết Offensive.

They kept her in Thừa Phủ Prison and tortured her using electric shocks. She said nothing and even continued to work inside, sending out information that was later used for the prison breakout during Tết. She too was part of this breakout and ran to freedom, only to be captured again because the enemy found revolutionary documentation on her. They only released her after the Paris Accords of 1973. Thereafter her leaders sent her to North Vietnam, where she married a man from Bình Định Province. They had three children before he died, and to this day she still lives in his province.[17]

Saigon had also been affected by the Buddhist Crises. To stop the Việt Cộng agitating the people and to crush their increased activity in and around the city, Westmoreland had to stab at their heartland. In 1967, two large operations were waged: Operation Cedar Falls in January and Operation Junction City from February to May. The former operation targeted the Iron Triangle located north of Saigon near C War Zone and D War Zone, with Operation Junction City seeing activity in C War Zone. Between these two operations, the United States planned to destroy COSVN, the main Việt Cộng forces, and help ease threats to Saigon.

In fact, Hanoi had been warned about Junction City, information thought to have been obtained via the intelligence network of Colonel Đinh Thị Vân in Saigon. Some of her group worked as TV repairmen for high-ranking Southern officers. Once they had gained access to their offices her repairmen then smuggled out the battle plans.[18] The information she and her associates gleaned meant that the core members of COSVN did not retreat to Cambodia from their headquarters at Phum Chrak Rumdould during the battle, as is commonly believed, they had withdrawn to D War Zone beforehand. Here, those members of COSVN consolidated themselves before moving to Katum to lead the Tết Offensive.[19]

Operation Cedar Falls and Operation Junction City did not destroy COSVN, the main Việt Cộng forces or ease threats to Saigon. On the contrary, for Giáp the fighting to repel these two operations mirrored his success against the French in Operation Léa back in October 1947. This French operation targeted the region of Việt Bắc to destroy the leadership of the Việt Minh and their army; in fact, the revolutionaries had protected their political base and their armed units had grown in strength and numbers. Now, during Operation Cedar Falls and Operation Junction City, the Party leadership had again been protected. Giáp went on to state on this matter that, although the U.S. Army was a far more formidable machine than that of the French, since U.S. ground troops had first entered the war, his army had gained in strength. That is why as the war had moved on he had been confident in using larger troop formations.

Giáp's age-old motto from the French War, "The more we fight, the stronger we become," was still relevant. Westmoreland had suspected trouble; within months he was about to feel the force of Giáp's stronger armed units, and see his gut feeling realized.

Mixed Strategic Planning

Hanoi's response to those years after the X Plan had been canceled was to look for another opportunity to strike their enemy. The Politburo only chose the year of the monkey of 1968 at their conference in October 1967.

The year 1968 had drawbacks. The Americans had conducted aggressive sweep operations against communist forces and guerrilla units across South Vietnam, which had a direct effect on Hanoi's ability to operate in some areas. The bombing of the North in Operation Rolling Thunder was highly restrictive. The United States had more than 500,000 well-trained and highly equipped troops deployed in South Vietnam, and although communist forces had become stronger they still had not destroyed a U.S. regimental-sized unit to date because the United States used fortified positions.[20]

The negative side to 1968 did not outweigh the positives. The Soviet Union and China now provided weapons to North Vietnam, which had been a change in direction for the two powers. Communist-led battles in the mountainous regions had gone well, such as the fighting around Khe Sanh, and as planned had drawn U.S. troops away from their comfort zone. In the United States, not only were the anti-war demonstrators growing louder but the offensive coincided with the 1969 U.S. elections, meaning that Tết would keep the war on the election agenda. Most importantly, Hanoi knew that there was a serious disconnect between what some senior U.S. officials in Washington stated publically to what the communists saw on the ground; U.S. officials stated victory but in fact it was stalemate.[21]

With Hanoi confident of their position, what were their objectives for the Tết Offensive: total victory or to weaken the enemy and go for total victory at a later date? Strategically, Hanoi always said that winning the war had to be done step by step.

When Giáp designed the plan for Tết and tabled it at the Politburo Conference in

This 2007 photograph is a typical view of the Mekong Delta in the region of Rạch Xẻo Giá, Cà Mau Province. It was at Rạch Xẻo Giá on 1 January 1967, that a fierce battle with ARVN Marines broke out because a Hồ Chí Minh Trail Sea Route boat had been discovered. Captain Nguyễn Hữu Phước of the 125th Sea Transportation Corps was trying to head back to the North in his large wooden craft, Ship 69, but after becoming embroiled in the fighting, to stop his vessel falling into enemy hands, he sunk Ship 69 with the hope that he could refloat it. After this engagement it became almost impossible to carry goods along the sea trail in the region, making supplying weapons to this area for the Tết Offensive difficult. Today at low tide you can still see Ship 69 (Clive A. Hills).

October 1967 he had titled it *A Surprise Attack at a Strategic Level*, and it was not for final victory; his forces did not have the strength and firepower to beat the Americans nor could he trap the United States as effectively as he had managed to do against the French at Điện Biên Phủ. Giáp designed his strategic level plan to execute surprise attacks on his enemies' nerve centers, namely the big cities. He hoped to draw them out of the countryside to defend the cities so that at a strategic moment his forces could then withdraw to a now empty countryside and take large previously occupied regions with fewer troop losses. Using this methodology Giáp could: send a strong psychological and physical message to U.S. politicians and the American public, give Hanoi the upper hand at any peace talks, and push the United States into a change of strategy to end the stalemate.

There were a number of ways that this stalemate could end. Giáp's strategy could force the United States to reduce troop numbers and see them implement Vietnamization, so weakening U.S. influence over the South. His strategy could see a new policy implemented for Vietnam, going from the Domino Theory to Decent Interval, meaning Washington tolerating a communist regime in the South as long as there was a two to three year period between U.S. troops withdrawing and a communist takeover. In addition, if

Tết went Hồ's way, not only would it give U.S. politicians the opportunity to withdraw their troops, but they could do so with American public support as they could see through media reports that the forces of the NLF were stronger than thought and the war could now not be won. Giáp knew the main direction of U.S. thinking because at the end of 1967 the Americans had sent messages to Hồ to indicate their desire to leave Vietnam.

No, total victory was all that some high-ranking Communist Party members wanted the Tết Offensive to achieve, reflecting the X Plan of 1965. Lê Duẩn had led this split in thinking saying, "I am not a coward, I will seize final victory." Those who refused this line were scheduled for removal from office, including Hồ and Giáp. For Hồ, he had "resigned" from current affairs in 1963, which meant theoretically no one would miss him. Nevertheless, practical militant officials pointed out that to totally dismiss him meant handing America a psychological victory; why oust him now, they argued, he was old and would die soon anyway. Giáp retained his place for some of the same reasons as Hồ, but in addition these officials identified that if the desired uprising did not occur during Tết, they needed the VNPA for a final death blow at a later date. Giáp understood the modern technology the army needed and the army was better off being commanded by a general not by politicians. Besides, both Giáp and Hồ had connections with Moscow and therefore access to military aid. To keep Giáp unaware of the change in the final decision-making of the Tết Offensive, from his plan titled *A Surprise Attack at a Strategic Level*, to launching an immediate final blow through a general offensive and general uprising, Lê Duẩn sent Giáp for a so-called emergency operation in Hungary at the end of 1967.

On top of his reckless requirement of victory over the South, Lê Duẩn made other senseless errors. He insisted that the military be credited for logistics only, leaving the Party to lead the final offensive. In practical terms, this meant that the Communist Party could be credited for a Tết triumph and not the military, as they had been at Điện Biên Phủ. Lê Duẩn put himself as commander in chief and instructed his political comrades to rework Giáp's plan. Being politically driven it meant that they overlooked strategic targets that the military knew had to be taken and the units instructed to carry out chosen tasks were not suitable for the role. In particular, in Huế City, Giáp had wanted the 1st ARVN Division's Headquarters at Mang Cá Base to be a main objective. However, as part of the new plan the units requested to attack this position were not listed to be dispatched early enough, and they were inexperienced and too weak to have any great impact.

On another point, as Lê Duẩn had instructed final victory, the participating units, Communist Party members, agents and civilians were under pressure to take additional risks, leading to more being killed or exposed. Indeed, during the offensive itself Communist Party members openly organized their administrations and those civilians who rose up revealed their intentions to the enemy. Even long-term secret agents who had infiltrated into enemy ranks joined the fight; an agent's position that had cost so many lives in the first instance to achieve.

Lê Duẩn's next blunder was that he gave commanding military roles to local Communist Party secretaries who should have only been given responsibility for the people's uprising. Phan Nam was the secretary of the Left Bank District Party Committee during the Tết Offensive, and consequently commanded the Northern Wing.[22] Hoàng Lanh was deputy political commissar of the Southern Wing and commanded a flank of the Southern Wing. This was despite the fact that both men had never been trained to take on such a military role. Lê Duẩn's divisive political emphasis meant that politicians led the Tết Offensive and not experienced military veterans.

The Final Plan

The idea to launch a general offensive and general uprising was tabled in January 1968 at the Fourteenth Conference of the Party Central Committee. Prior to this Conference the Politburo was unanimous in their decision that operations should commence on the eve of Tết.[23] They chose this date because there had been a temporary ceasefire approved by both sides for the holiday; the South would not be expecting an attack.

The Politburo agreed that the start time, "H hour," included the early hours of the morning up to daybreak, before celebrations started for the Tết holiday itself. This seemed a defined start time. What confused things was that at the end of 1967, the Communist Party had decreed to change North Vietnam's calendar, and so this change made Tết New Year a day earlier. The Party no longer wanted to be in line with the Chinese, a decision partly to distance Vietnam from the bloody Cultural Revolution happening in China at the time. Hanoi planned this change to be implemented across the whole of Vietnam but this had not been communicated to all members in the South.[24] In jest, people in the North said that Lê Duẩn brought forward Tết by a day so that he could spend the real New Year in Saigon.

Couriers delivered the H hour message to senior Communist Party members but none knew the information they carried. What made things unusual was the message issuer, Chief of General Staff Văn Tiến Dũng, had not grasped that Vietnam now had two Tết eves. His message did not mention any date, only a coded message saying *"giao thừa"* translated as "New Year's Eve." So for the southern zones under close control of Hanoi, H hour was the early hours of the morning up to daybreak on 30 January but for those under COSVN, H hour was the early hours of the morning up to daybreak on 31 January 1968. Hence, some regions under Hanoi's control in the southern part of Annam were confused; should they use the old Southern Tết calendar or new Northern one? The action taken in accordance with the new Northern Tết calendar has been recorded in history books as starting a day early.

These two different start times caused serious failings; the element of surprise had been lost. Historians from both sides say that if the attacks had started all at once, the NLF could very well have occupied many more important areas, thus causing a larger psychological blow. NLF veterans say that this critical start time failure was because Văn Tiến Dũng held a position too high for his intellect. His fast-tracked promotion to chief of general staff had been linked to the Chinese aid in the 1950s and the fact that, as a weaver, he represented the worker class. Hoàng Văn Thái, whom Dũng replaced owing to his intelligentsia background, had been demoted to the deputy chief of general staff from 1953; according to veterans he was a real staff officer and would not have confused such an important instruction.[25]

In January 1968, members at the Fourteenth Conference approved the final Tết Offensive plan titled *The General Offensive and General Uprising*. Presented in Resolution 14, it reworked Giáp's original *A Surprise Attack at a Strategic Level* plan.[26] Lê Duẩn based the new Vietnamese Tết Offensive on the Russian Revolution in 1917, which had the motto, "Workers, farmers, soldiers unite"; soldiers meant from the enemy's side. Collectively these people would rise up to take political power and defend the land, incited to do so through political violence; a recent case being Mao and his Red Army.

The practical aim of *The General Offensive and General Uprising* sought victory through an August Revolution–like people's uprising. Initially, the army would give the enemy a full-on blow, and once this blow had crippled the enemy, the masses could rise, and armed through their own means with home-made or seized weaponry, they could defend the land. From these actions a new political power could emerge, the core of which would be formed from top members of the Revolutionary Infrastructure, such as Phan Nam and Hoàng Lanh.

Some delegates and key revolutionaries felt deeply uncomfortable about any general uprising theory, especially the ones that actually mobilized the masses in the main cities during the August Revolution. Not only in paperwork terms did it go against what had been originally agreed in Resolution 15 back in 1959, which looked for total victory through a military solution, but an uprising seemed too rudimentary against a modern army and those few who might rise would be too weak against conventional units and their military firepower. Lê Duẩn pushed ahead with his final plan, leaving the people he so desperately needed exposed to disaster.

Huế City: Westmoreland's Fear

In mid-1967, Đặng Kinh, the chief of staff of the Trị Thiên Military Zone, went to Hanoi to discuss with Giáp preparations for the Tết Offensive in the southern part of Annam. He told Giáp that Huế City should be targeted.

Locally, Huế was surrounded by regions with good revolutionary ties. The provinces of Quảng Bình, Quảng Trị and Thừa Thiên had traditionally fought with the Việt Minh, and that is why at the 1954 Geneva talks the communists proposed that the border between North and South to be at the 13th not the 17th Parallel. Strategically, Huế City was close to the Lao border so any supply lines to the battlefield in Vietnam stayed short, and if Huế City was captured it would be a psychological blow against the West.

Taking Kinh's views on board, when Giáp had designed his *A Surprise Attack at a Strategic Level* plan, he made Khe Sanh and the Trị Thiên Military Zone key regions. Giáp chose Khe Sanh to be attacked as a diversionary target. He had battered the region for months, to slowly entice the finest U.S. and South Vietnamese mobile units away from the Mekong Delta and the cities that they protected. He did this before the start of the Tết Offensive and to date this had worked.[27]

For the Trị Thiên Military Zone, Giáp made their main target Huế City. Their objective was to establish local political power and if possible break away from the rest of South Vietnam. Giáp expressed that this must not be done at any cost, to preserve manpower. To realize this plan Giáp proposed to send a division to the 5th Military Zone. Kinh, as representative of the zone, was hesitant; he believed that the zone could not hide such a high number of troops prior to the battle, fearing U.S. aerial and electronic reconnaissance missions might discover them. Kinh went on to say that he was a guerrilla commander and was uneasy fighting in a divisional arrangement. Giáp never concluded the discussion because he was sent abroad for surgery; he and his close aides did criticize the decision of the 5th Military Zone, saying that they clung to guerrilla warfare when they should now go conventional.

In October 1967, the Party Central Committee sent Lê Ngọc Hiền to the DMZ to give Lê Chưởng, the political commissar of the Trị Thiên Military Zone, the region's final plan for the Tết Offensive. This was titled, *Huế's Uprising to Coordinate with the Whole of the South*. When Hồ and Giáp were not around to protest, Lê Duẩn authorized the alteration of the plan from a surprise blow at a strategic scale to final victory.

On 20 December, Hanoi asked members of the Trị Thiên Military Zone to report on their preparations they had made to execute the final plan, and their guarantees on a completion date of 25 January 1968. Those members asked listed their arrangements: uprising training programs for locals had been established; Communist Party members and guerrilla fighters had been sent to Huế City so that the former could guide the locals through the uprising and the guerrillas could be activated when Tết started; they had specially trained around 200 couriers to take on any new roles such as fighting; field hospitals had been constructed and medical supplies stockpiled both in and outside the city; and they had amassed a reserve of 2,000 tons of rice. The food stock was not higher because the locals had no more food to give but the Party officials had calculated that a soldier could fight for seven days without substantial food by drinking only tea and eating New Year jam. It seems all the while Westmoreland expressed concerns over an attack on Huế City, the communists prepared to deliver his nightmare.

Huế Front

Party leaders established the Huế Front in January 1968, a military unit that commanded the local armed forces of the Trị Thiên Military Zone. Under the Huế Front sat the Huế City Party Committee.

Đặng Kinh was now chief of staff of the Trị Thiên Military Zone and the Huế Front. Based at Kim Phụng Mountain, he commanded the Tết Offensive for the Trị Thiên Military Zone as part of his chief of staff duties, and dealt with the regular forces. Lê Minh, who was the Party secretary for both the Thừa Thiên Provincial Party Committee and the Huế City Party Committee, resided at the same headquarters. Instead of a military person promoted to be the commander of the Huế Front, Lê Duẩn assigned Lê Minh to the role, which meant that as a Party leader he commanded both the political and military aspects of the battle for Huế City and its suburbs. This promotion surprised Lê Minh, and was an error by Lê Duẩn, but he did it in his attempt to get the Communist Party credited for total victory.

Party leaders divided the Huế Front into two areas that reflected the side of the Perfume River they were on: the Southern Wing and the Northern Wing. Within these two wings there were four directions of attack. In addition, each of the eight wards within Huế City and some land from neighboring districts had their own Communist Party committees running events. When the Tết Offensive started these Communist Party leaders were ordered to open fire at the same time, so that the enemy did not know that the Northern Wing was the main area to be attacked.

The communist units there to conduct the Tết Offensive in Huế City encompassed the 6th Regiment, units of the 9th Regiment and the 5th Group. This latter group included: the 4th, 10th and 815th Infantry Battalions, three independent infantry companies, the 1st and 2nd Elite Battalions known as K1 and K2 and a number of *biệt động* and elite *đặc công* forces.[28] Party leaders had instructed the 5th Group to "kill tyrants and eliminate traitors" to clear the area prior to the Tết Offensive. In total on the communists' side there were around 5,000 regular troops with their supporting services. This number did not include units such as guerrilla fighters, which in the three surrounding districts of Huế totaled some 1,000 personnel. Although a sizable number of units took part, during the battle they got into serious trouble. Even with fresh reserves sent, Đặng

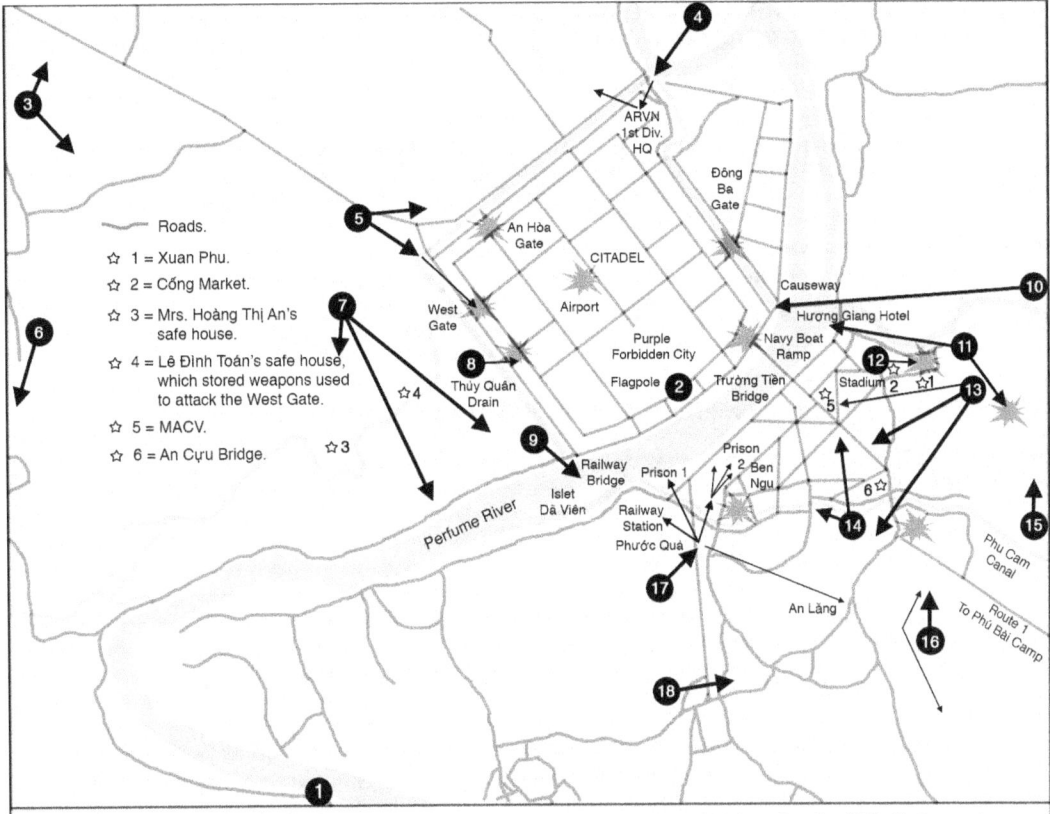

1 - Kim Phụng Mountain. One of the headquarters of the Huế City Party Committee, the front headquarters of the Huế Front and the headquarters of the Trị Thiên Military Zone. The start time for Tết in Huế was set for 02:30hrs on 31 January 1968.

2 - Units from the 6th Regt. thrust through the West Gate to reach the Purple Forbidden City. At 09:00hrs on 31 January Nguyễn Văn Tuyên raised the flag of the Liberation Army up the flagpole.

3 - 116th Battalion, 9th Regt, 304 Div. strike to the south-east (La Chữ Hamlet) and to the north-east (Quế Chữ Hamlet).

4 - 1st Elite Company (đặc công) and the 2nd Infantry Company, 6th Regt. attack south-west against ARVN's 1st Division. ARVN's 7th Battalion failed to counter-attack. Still only a small team of the 1st Elite Company penetrated the western section of Mang Cá; they fought for a further five hours before withdrawing at 08:00.

5 - A city elite unit (biệt động) leads companies of the 6th Regt. to strike An Hòa Gate and penetrate the West Gate. Once penetrated they split into two groups. One group pushed north-east to the north end of Tây Lộc Airport. The second group pushed south-east to the Thủy Quân Drain to attack the south end of the airport.

6 - 116th Battalion, 9th Regt, 304 Div. continue to push south through Bốn Phố Hamlet and to Bốn Trị Hamlet.

7 - Companies of the 6th Regt. head south and south-east from An Hòa to the banks of the Perfume River.

8 - In the early hours of 30 January the 2nd Elite Company (đặc công), 2nd Elite Battalion (K2) penetrated through the Thủy Quân Drain to attack the airport. This attack was premature due to the confusion with dates.

9 - From the banks of the Perfume River companies of the 6th Regt. push across the railway bridge from Kẻ Vạn to Islet Dã Viên.

10 - Companies of the 10th Infantry Battalion (K10), 5th Group advance west to occupy Gia Hội. Detachments from the 6th Regt. and the 9th Regt. advance from Đông Ba Gate.

11 - Units of the 2nd Elite Battalion fought battles around Hương Giang Hotel; both sides wanted to occupy the causeway there.

12 - On 12 Feb companies of the 10th Infantry Battalion, 5th Group plus a squad of eleven girl couriers clash with the 2nd Battalion of U.S. Marines who had come via the Perfume River to MACV. The girls were known as the Eleven Perfume River Girls.

13 - 2nd Elite Company, 1st Elite Battalion (K1) advance in three directions. West in an abortive attack on MACV but successfully to the railway station and towards the south-west to An Cựu.

14 - 4th Infantry Battalion, 5th Group advance north to the river bank and north-west to the bridge at Nam Hamlet.

15 - Units of the 10th Infantry Battalion, 5th Group attack the 1st Battalion, 3rd Regt. of ARVN at Đồng Di and the 4th Battalion, 3rd Regt. of ARVN at Tam Đồng. They did this with units from the 2nd Elite Battalion.

16 - Companies of the 1st Elite Battalion successfully attack north against ARVN's 7th Armoured Regt. before returning south to Ngũ Tây Hamlet to consolidate.

17 - Companies of the 815th Infantry Battalion, 5th Group and a detachment of the 2nd Elite Battalion advance on Phước Quả. Here they split heading north-west toward Ga Huế (railway station), north-north-west to attack prison 1, north-north-east to Thừa Thiên Province administration buildings near prison 2 and south-east to attack a South Korean company at An Lăng Hamlet.

18 - Companies of the 1st Elite Battalion attack east against an ARVN engineering battalion.

The Tết Offensive of 1968 in Huế City, communist occupation and the first phase of their defense.

Kinh must have recognized that it was far too late and wished he had taken the division first offered by Giáp.

Several high-ranking commanders in the U.S. military had seriously underestimated the communists' ability to sustain a lengthy attack on Huế City. This meant that on the northern side of the city there was only the 1st ARVN Division's Headquarters at Mang Cá Base, commanded by Ngô Quang Trưởng (1929–2007). This headquarters held garrison troops but had no combat units of battalion-size. On the southern side of the Perfume River there were limited American-run operations. These included MACV and the Civil Operations and Revolutionary Development Support (CORDS) compound. Just outside Huế City, down Route 1, there was a U.S. base at Phú Bài that housed the Forward Headquarters of the 1st Marine Division. With this misjudgment of forces the city was barely secure.

The Northern Side of Huế

Phan Nam commanded the Northern Wing as the secretary of the Left Bank District Party Committee. He had been instructed to breach the West Gate, to allow the 6th Regiment to take and occupy the Citadel. If he failed, the Tết Offensive in Huế City would stall.

Nam had been one of the initial people to know the general plan for the offensive because some of the first units sent to breach the West Gate were to be armed police.

A 2007 view of the restored West Gate on the outer wall of the Citadel. This is the gate attacked by the units that had been supplied by Phan Nam with weapons (Clive A. Hills).

These police operated under the security section of the Huế City Party Committee, whose secretary was Lê Minh. Nam had known him for many years and they worked closely together. Generally speaking, Nam said, the secretaries of all the districts near to the city knew about the coming attack on Huế. They just did not know when the start time or date was, only finding out some five days beforehand.

Nam explained,

> It took years to prepare for the Tết Offensive. At the time of these preparations we did not know what we prepared for. Some of the events I supported in preparation were attacks on the Hương Giang Hotel and the West Gate. I remember some of our new units were frightened at first, holding hand grenades was alien to them. After three years though they became professionals.
>
> I ran seven courier networks during Tết. One of my operatives was Lê Đình Toán, a vital person in enabling the communists to breach the West Gate. Initially he agreed to receive and store weapons for me, although unaware what they were for. They had been sent from our revolutionary base at Khe Trai Mountain, about 26km north-west of Huế. To get them to his house, those responsible for doing so had a laborious journey from the mountains to a station in Hương Trà District.
>
> Eight crates arrived full of weapons and explosives, including hand grenades, pistols and AK47s. Two crates were for the attack on the West Gate and six for units to control the region where Lê Đình Toán's house was. His house was perfect because we hid them in a cemetery that backed on to his garden. No one went there, least of all inquisitive children, frightened of ghosts!
>
> I had to take our two crates into the city on the afternoon of 30 January. Lê Đình Toán loaded the two crates into my car. This had been driven to his house earlier in the day by another man. I arrived at Lê Đình Toán's once everything had been completed. It was late afternoon by now.
>
> I took a driver, who was a special courier, and a young child, and we drove into Huế. The child knew nothing of our mission other than that we headed to his house. He was there because he knew the people and the roads well. Our car did not match the profile of what a VC drove. It was smart and modern, done up for Tết. Revelers swarmed the streets with the noise of good cheer. I feared getting through the West Gate, but the guards recognized the child and casually waved us on. The enemy unit stationed at the West Gate was the South Vietnamese Black Panther Company.
>
> On arriving at the child's house I strolled around nervously as the driver unloaded the weapons. At 9:30 p.m. an elite *đặc công* squad came to the house to arm themselves. There I briefed them to liaise with the 6th Regiment of the regular army. This was important because the *đặc công* had to attack from the inside of the Citadel and to secure the West Gate so that the 6th Regiment could enter. Lê Đình Toán had guided this *đặc công* squad into the Citadel after he had loaded my vehicle earlier that day. This squad now hid with their weapons in a safe house. As night fell Lê Đình Toán guided the *đặc công* to the West Gate to lay in wait for H hour. As planned, the charge had been set and the gates blasted open.[29]

Once the West Gate had been cleared of the Black Panther Company, the 66D and 66E armed police and the *biệt động* units of the Left Bank attacked locations to clear the way for the 6th Regiment to occupy the city.[30] The 66E attacked Tây Lộc Airport, the Citadel and the Purple Forbidden City. The 66D and a *biệt động* unit of the Left Bank attacked Thượng Tứ Gate, Tràng Tiền Bridge and other locations within the Citadel.

Nam continued:

> A DKB shot fired, which signaled for the 6th Regiment to make their drive into the Citadel.[31] A *biệt động* unit of the Left Bank led the regiment into battle. At the same time all our units opened fire to confuse the enemy. After our units seized their targets, they fought against any counter-attack.
>
> We achieved great things and our flag finally flew above the city. This iconic image captivated the attention of the world, telling them: Huế had fallen. It was near here that we established our headquarters for the Northern Wing.[32]

Things might have been so different for Nam. In the early morning of 30 January the 2nd Elite Company attacked Thủy Quân Drain, just a short distance from the West

Top: This is Ngọ Môn Gate opposite the flagpole and the main entrance into the Citadel. *Bottom:* The flagpole where on 31 January 1968, Nguyễn Văn Tuyên of the 6th Regiment hoisted the Liberation Army flag. On 21 August 1945, Đặng Văn Việt and Cao Pha had hoisted a Việt Minh flag here when in the Frontline Youth (both photographs 2007 Clive A. Hills).

Gate; a mishap resulting from the mix-up in New Year dates. Fortunately, this had not phased Nam, who held steady to prevent Tết stalling in the Northern Wing. Now it was for those on the southern side of Huế City to challenge their foes.

The Southern Side of Huế

Hoàng Lanh was deputy political commissar of the Southern Wing.[33] This wing had two out of the four directions of attack, and Lanh ran the north-east one leading both the political and military activities. It had been Lê Minh, the commander of the Huế Front, who gave Lanh this position; both long-standing acquaintances of Nam.

Lê Minh knew Lanh well and respected his knowledge. In 1949, Lê Minh had instructed Lanh to move to Huế and build a secret unit there for the 1950 offensive and, although it had been canceled, Lê Minh had seen Lanh's good work. In addition, Lê Minh saw Lanh was very familiar with Huế; out of the eight wards, Lanh had served as the secretary of the 6th Ward and later the 3rd. Lanh had also been trained overseas; in 1959 he went to China for medical treatment and to study, he later went to Moscow for training. In 1960 he moved back to Huế.

Before Lanh spoke of his role in the Tết Offensive he recalled two memorable events. Just prior to going back to Huế he had realized his ambition and met with Hồ in Hanoi.

Hoàng Lanh (seated) was the deputy political commissar of the Southern Wing in Huế City for the Tết Offensive. Standing from left, Nguyễn Thị Hoa, the author and Hoàng Thị Nở on 9 May 2007. Both Vietnamese women were specially trained Tết couriers who formed part of the Eleven Perfume River Girls (Clive A. Hills).

Lanh noted that Hồ had asked in great detail about Huế City, as he had once taught there, and on leaving Hồ gave their group cigarettes and candy. The second memorable event was on a more serious note. Lanh had said that he was extremely fortunate because from 1950 to 1975 he had never been arrested but the enemy did put a price on his head: dead or alive.

Lanh said of the Tết Offensive:

President Hồ Chí Minh sent a New Year poem to the Trị Thiên Military Zone and Trị Thiên Party Committee to wish us luck. It read, "This New Year will be better than the past New Years, victory and good news will sweep the nation, South and North unite with each other in fighting the Americans, Advance: total victory is ours."

For the Tết Offensive there were three main approaches: military, political and military proselytizing. Military proselytizing held the least significance. For us, the most important aspect to prepare was our local city forces, including guerrillas and self-defense teams. During the offensive I was ordered to conduct military attacks within a region of Huế that had a high concentration of official buildings called "the triangle" covering an area between Phú Bài, Ấp Năm [Fifth Hamlet] and Động Toàn.

Five days before the offensive I moved my local forces from their base area in Quảng Điền, Phong Điền District to Phú Vang just outside Huế, so that they could be trained. I had to rely entirely on my specially trained courier to help my troops weave through the inhospitable terrain. At each border the district secretary had greeted us, so that the secretary could transfer us to the next district and so on.

The troops arrived at Phú Vang on 30 January at 7:30 p.m. Now everyone saw that Huế City was the target. The district secretary had prepared the area for the arrival of thousands of troops. To keep them busy the people of the district engaged them in their Tết New Year celebrations.

For the north-east direction our troops marched to a location near Hùng Vương Street. Here we waited for the order to attack. Before this came, the Southern militia shot our chief of staff, Lê Túc, straight through the heart. I remember that his body could not be retrieved in fear of compromising our positions.

The signal for us to open fire was a shot fired at Phú Bài Airport, another fired at the 1st ARVN Division's Headquarters at Mang Cá Base and a shot fired at the area known as the triangle. This occurred at 2:33 am on 31 January.

Our troops attacked a prison, being well defended we attacked five or six times. We called on ARVN to surrender, but they didn't. One man had escaped from the prison through a tunnel, a Mr. Lanh, and we forced him to guide us back inside. Now we could attack from both the inside and outside of the prison. We attacked the interrogation department, where they questioned our people. We liberated thousands of political prisoners, some of whom were high-ranking such as Nguyễn Khoa Điềm.[34]

One of Lanh's main targets for that night was the MACV compound. Inside there were heavily armed Americans and Australians. Although the communists fought long and hard, those inside MACV held off the attack. Apart from MACV, most of the other administrative buildings on that first day fell under communist control or remained empty.

The men inside MACV could not identify with the situation at the time because they had limited communications to the outside world. Their immediate priority was to get their wounded evacuated by helicopter, but because any radio call had to go through many operators, by the time it got to Phú Bài Camp the request was garbled, so produced little result. This should not have occurred; on this first day of the offensive commanders at Phú Bài Camp had received radio messages that informed them of unrest in their area of operation. Finally, III Marine Amphibious Force instructed the command at Phú Bài to send their Marines to assist. Since those at Phú Bài Camp had still not understood the gravity of the message they just sent A Company, 1st Marine Division.[35]

The troops from A Company headed for MACV and linked up with G Company. Their command ordered both companies to cross the river to the Citadel to assist Ngô Quang Trưởng, because the 1st ARVN Division's headquarters was under heavy fire. They made it, but with so many killed or wounded they wanted to retreat back to MACV. On their return journey they met a young Vietnamese man wearing an ARVN uniform and claiming to be a doctor home on Tết leave. With limited outside help coming, the commander took him back to MACV.[36] By the end of the first day everyone was exhausted. Then the arguments erupted within the compound, was this ARVN medic a Việt Cộng spy or not?[37]

The Americans did send in more support to save Huế City. By air the helicopters landed at the university sports field, by boat they docked at the navy boat ramp and by Route 1 reinforcements now came in from Phú Bài. It was within these first few days that the commander of the 2nd Battalion, 5th Marine Regiment, 1st Marine Division, a Lieutenant Colonel Ernest Cheatham, arrived to lead his troops in Huế City: companies F, G and H.

Frantic firefights continued across the city and Cheatham knew that to take the southern area of Huế every single alley, street, house and building held by his enemy had to be checked and fought over. Strangely, many U.S. Marines welcomed the opportunity finally to have revenge and see their enemy face to face. All too often in the past they had seen their friends injured or killed by booby traps planted by the "undetected army" who had long since disappeared back into the forest. The Americans fought hard, especially around Phú Cam Canal, along Lê Lợi Street and within the region of the Capitol.

On 6 February, H Company raised the Stars and Stripes over the Capitol, the building the communists had used as a command post. H Company had taken pleasure in removing the communist flag because this had been raised on the first day and for them it had fluttered over the fighting in the area for far too long.

It was at this stage that Cheatham's units met Lanh's couriers. Cheatham's 2nd Battalion had taken the area from Phú Cam Canal to MACV and on 10 February were ordered to push to the stadium area. Lanh's 10th Infantry Battalion (K10) had fought from Đập Đá to the Hương Giang Hotel in order to overrun it, yet they had taken heavy casualties.[38] Lanh ordered eleven female couriers to take up arms to help continue the fight. Mrs. Hoàng Thị Nở and Mrs. Nguyễn Thị Hoa were two of those eleven.

Mrs. Nguyễn Thị Hoa explained:

Comrade Hoàng Thị Nở and I grew up in the same village. We became involved in the revolution in different ways. I joined because my extended family asked me to, I was sixteen. It was 1965. It had been important for me because in 1963 the enemy attacked a camp near my home in Huế. I saw many terrible things. When I was first approached to join the revolution, I did not know the people. One person just said that by joining I would be sent to school so that I could learn to read and write. This was exciting for me because the Southern regime still adhered to the old feudal system. The leaders could also see how distressed I had become with the war and all the barbaric scenes. Comrade Hoàng Thị Nở came from a well-off family so she went to school.

After I had been carrying letters, Mr. Pha took me on and trained me to become a courier. Mr. Pha was a standing member of the Thừa Thiên Provincial Party Committee. I supported myself by making conical hats. With my confidence growing my leaders taught me how to set mines and traps and become a guerrilla fighter. Now I lived at the base just outside the city, operating in a legal capacity. My team set traps to catch out the enemy. If an enemy soldier was killed, we ran away to the city until the atmosphere settled, then we returned to continue. I was very young and held no fear of dying. I did not care about myself, such as when my trousers were torn off crossing a river I just put parachute fabric around me, and because I had no needle and thread I used banana string to secure them. I was here to help the revolution.

I did many things to help prepare for the Tết Offensive but at the time we were unaware of the battle. In the daytime I carried on my normal life. At night I went into the city or villages with my comrades to buy supplies such as food, or we tried to persuade the locals to stockpile food. By doing this, when the battle started we did not have to burden them because what we needed was already there. Unfortunately, it turned out that we had not stockpiled enough. The first aim of the offensive was to attack, which we did. The second was to hold the city, being told, "hold the city at any cost," but this became impossible. One reason was that after twenty days we had no food.

To prepare for the offensive my unit attacked the Hương Giang Hotel. This, as I know now, was a trial to see how I and others reacted under fire, so if our leaders called upon us to join the actual attack upon Huế City we had been battle-trained. I had been ordered to guide the elite đặc công forces to assault the hotel. On 20 October 1967, I led them from our base in Vân Khê Village, Hương Thủy District, to Đập Đá. Here we poisoned the dogs to kill them to stop them barking. Then the đặc công used lifejackets to cross a waterway to the hotel. This battle had been very successful, but because of this the Americans fortified the place with bunkers, so during the Tết Offensive K10 failed to take it and they lost many lives.[39]

Both Nguyễn Thị Hoa and Hoàng Thị Nở became part of the Eleven Perfume River Girls, a name given to their unit during the Tết Offensive. The group had originally formed two years previously and was part of the new generation of around 200 couriers in Huế specially trained in additional tasks in preparation for the Tết Offensive. These duties included being taught to be *biệt động* fighters in 1966, going on to operate as such in October 1967; being expected to guide soldiers; to collect any wounded and take them to the suburbs for treatment; and to protect the Southern Wing's headquarters where Lanh was.

Mrs. Hoàng Thị Nở continued:

Before the Tết Offensive I went in and out of the city to inform my leaders of enemy activity. I conducted propaganda among teenagers to persuade them to join the militia or guerrilla forces.

For the Tết Offensive itself my main role was in the defense of Huế, as one of many female couriers who guided our soldiers, because I knew the streets well. I was in a squad under the command of Miss Phạm Thị Liên, and we shadowed a unit known as K10. When K10 tried to overrun Hương Giang Hotel they ran into trouble, coming under heavy fire and taking many casualties, so they failed to achieve this. Commander Lanh could see that K10 was reduced in strength. He ordered us to arm ourselves with our fallen comrades weapons, which included K10s B40s, B41s, AK47s and K44s and any captured American weapons, and "fight to the death if need be." He ordered us to try to help our comrades halt the advancing U.S. Marines.

We took up our combat positions on 12 February at 5 a.m., but the Marines came from all directions, being reinforced by troops stationed at the Hương Giang Hotel, and who had now landed at the navy boat ramp to attack us. During the day they fought; at night they returned to the hotel. We first fought the Marines at Xuan Phu. To avoid heavy casualties we withdrew to Cống Market but we lost two girls. We then moved to the soccer stadium, surrounded by rice fields with U.S. units camped there. Our unit fought with guns, but the Americans had tanks, air support and threw tear gas at us. To cover our faces we took clothing from local houses. We were firing just 10m away from each other. All we could do was build barricades to try and slow down their advance.

In total we lost four girls during those days, six throughout the war. They did not die in vain. We succeeded in halting a battalion of American troops. We believe that part of our success was because we used a ditch along the Thủy Dương Canal. From this ditch we could pick off the enemy troops.

After we withdrew from Huế to Phú Vang we asked for permission to form a new squad called the Võ Thị Sáu Unit. She was a courier hero of the French War. Arrested by the French for throwing a hand grenade that killed a French officer, they tortured her and then moved her to Côn Đảo Island. They executed her; she was in her teens. Our leaders agreed to the name, we had earned the right to do so. Our unit now comprised around thirty to forty people under Miss Phạm Thị Liên. Our first task was to resist enemy attacks on Phú Vang, which saw us fight for around twenty days.[40]

Although the girls changed their group name to Võ Thị Sáu Unit, the title Eleven Perfume River Girls and the story of what the girls did were used during Tết as propaganda. Their unit might have only achieved small gains, however, because they were brave they served as a good example across Vietnam, and as they were women, people said, "If girls can fight so can we."

When Lanh met Hồ and explained to him about the girls and their bravery, this prompted Hồ to write a poem in their honor. In March 1968, Hồ sent this to them, it read, "Self-confidence with rifle in arms. Smart natured in the city. Uncle respects our guerrilla nieces who fought the U.S. troops until these troops fell down."[41] Today there is a small memorial at Cống Market, built by the locals, for the soldiers of K10 as well as for the two girls who died there. At the stadium there is a larger state-built monument for all eleven girls.

Lanh finished his interview by saying, "The three principle theatres of the Tết Offensive were Saigon, Đà Nẵng and Huế City. However, Huế City was the lead city as fighting started here first. It also saw twenty-six days of continuous fighting. Then, on the night of 26 February, Hanoi ordered us to withdraw. It was so sudden, we were in shock, so consequently our withdrawal was not as precise as it should have been. Some began to retreat as early as 21 February."[42] Hanoi gave the order because, although they had supported Huế, it was evident that the city could not split away from the rest of South Vietnam.

Fighting in Saigon

Huế City saw continuous fighting rather than there being any waves of combat, whereas Saigon was meant to see three waves. These waves had not been mentioned in the original Resolution 14, although it did state that there could be months of heavy fighting. In Saigon, Wave I started in January and peaked at the end of February, a peak now referred to as Wave II. Wave III was meant to occur in May.[43]

The waves came about because there was no people's rising in arms and therefore no total victory in sight as Lê Duẩn had wanted. These waves were ordered after a meeting held on 2 February 1968 between Hồ, Giáp and Lê Duẩn. They had met in Giáp's headquarters at the Dragon House, Hanoi. Here Giáp announced bluntly, "See, the uprising has not occurred." Lê Duẩn could not see Giáp's point despite the evidence presented. Against advice, the Communist Party imprudently went on to agree further waves of fighting, to incite a people's uprising. With others, Giáp and Hồ vigorously opposed this, fearing revolutionary obliteration in the South.

Ms. Võ Thị Tâm (1950–) took part mainly in the first two waves of fighting in Saigon. Born in Bến Tre Province, she became a courier after the Simultaneous Uprising in 1960. She noted that to be a courier, "You must not fear death."[44] Then, in 1964, she was assigned to Saigon, and from that time until 1968 she took on an additional role of a *biệt động* fighter. To build up a network of supporters around her she conducted propaganda, saying, "We have to fight the American invaders and their puppets, to liberate the country. Only then there will be no more death and misery."[45] Tâm became one of the specially trained couriers in Saigon for the Tết Offensive.

Ms. Tâm said:

> For Wave I of the Tết Offensive our leaders ordered my unit of *biệt động* fighters to strike Tân Sơn Nhất Airport, as part of the opening of the offensive. This battle occurred at the same time as attacks

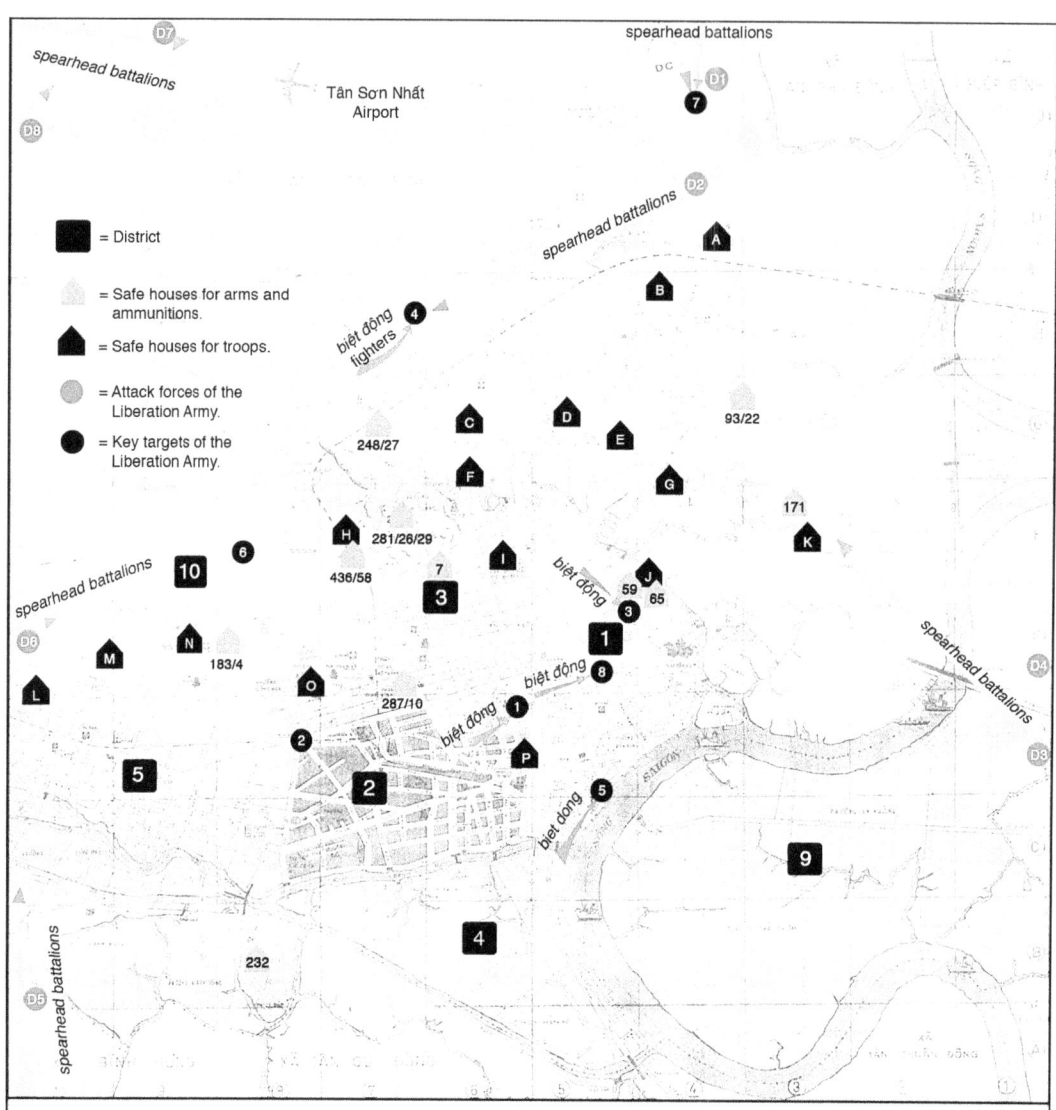

Examples of houses used as covert arms and ammunition magazines (used in 1968 but built for the X Plan in the early 1960s). In general each pit held 100kg of explosives as that was the estimated need for most targets.

65 Nguyễn Bỉnh Khiêm St. or Quốc Anh Tailors - owned by Trần Phú Cương (Mộc the Fifth) and his wife Mrs. Trần Thị Út. They were both elite troops (biệt động) and attacked the Saigon radio station; Cương was deputy commander of the battle and died in action.

436/58 Lê Văn Duyệt (now Cách Mạng Tháng Tám) - owned by Lê Tấn Quốc. The house served the attack on the Presidential Palace. Quốc was deputy commander of the 11th Elite Force and died in action at the American Embassy.

287/10 Trần Quý Cáp St. (now Võ Văn Tần) - the home of Trần Văn Lai (Mai Hồng Quế or USOM the Fifth). The house served the attack on the Presidential Palace.

248/27 Nguyễn Huỳnh Đức St. (now Huỳnh Văn Bánh) - owned by Mrs. Bùi Thị Lý. The house served the attack on the General Staff of the Army of the Republic of Vietnam (ARVN).

281/ 26/29 Trương Minh Ký (now Lê Văn Sỹ) - owned by Phan Văn Bảy and his daughter Mrs. Phan Thị Thúy. The house served the attack on the General Staff of ARVN.

59 Phan Thanh Giản - owned by Mrs. Nguyễn Thị Huệ (Phê the Second). The house served the attack on the American Embassy.

93/22 Cường Để (now Ngô Đức Kế). The house served the attack on the headquarters of ARVN Marines.

171 Bạch Đằng St, - owned by Vũ Bá Tài. This house served as a safe house for eight radio operators during the Tết Offensive.

7 Yên Đỗ St. (now Lý Chính Thắng) - a noodle shop owned by Ngô Toại. This premises served as the Front Headquarters of the 6th Sub-Zone. During Wave I of the Tết Offensive Võ Văn Thạnh was the political commissar of the 6th Sub-Zone and Nguyễn Đức Hùng the chief of staff, both commanded *biệt động* troops from here.

183/4 Trần Quốc Toản St. (now 3rd February St.) - owned by Đỗ Văn Căn (Latex the Third). This house was to serve the attack on the General Office of the Saigon Police. This attack did not take place and the arms and ammunitions remained hidden for the next seven years until 1975. Đỗ Văn Căn was originally from Hanoi and was sent by Hanoi's secret service to intermingle with the Catholics who had regrouped from the North to the South in the mid-1950s. Having been a silversmith, Đỗ Văn Căn changed occupation to that of a latex worker as this provided better cover to transport weapons and to keep them hidden. His wife Mrs. Nguyễn Thị Cúc and his sister were both *biệt động* troop members. Both Đỗ Văn Căn and Mrs. Nguyễn Thị Cúc each had a house used as a weapons and ammunition magazine. In accordance with policy, each of these houses were developed secretly without the other knowing.

232 Dương Bá Trạc - owned by Phạm Văn Đầy a latex worker, whose mentor was Đỗ Văn Căn (Latex the Third).

▲ Examples of safe house cells used to shelter troops.
Started for the X Plan, by the end of 1967 there were 19 cells - a cell contained several safe houses in the same neighborhood and provided shelter for tens of troops. There were some 300 families involved providing 400 places for troops to hide. The following are a few examples:

A - a cell at Nguyễn Trung Trực St.

B - a cell at Lê Quang Định St., Cây Quéo area.

C - a cell at the corner of Võ Di Nguy St. and Monk Nguyễn Minh Chiểu St.

D - a cell in Đông Ba Hamlet.

E - a cell at the junction of Trần Tế Xương St, Vạn Kiếp St. and Hàng Keo Police Post.

F - a cell in the Labor Market between Cầu Kho Hamlet and Công Lý Bridge (now Nam Kỳ Khởi Nghĩa and Nguyễn Văn Trỗi St.).

G - a cell in the area of Lê Văn Duyệt St. (now Đinh Tiên Hoàng St.) and Bùi Hữu Nghĩa St., Bà Chiểu area.

H - a cell in the Hòa Hưng area.

I - a cell in Tân Định, Xóm Chùa (Temple Hamlet).

J - a cell at 65 Nguyễn Bỉnh Khiêm St.

K - a cell in the Hang Xanh area at the junction of Bạch Đằng St. and Red Cross (now Xô Viết Nghệ Tĩnh and Bình Thạnh St.).

L - a cell at Thuận Kiều St.

M - a cell at Triệu Đà St. (now Ngô Quyền St.)

N - a cell at the junction of Trần Quốc Toản St. (now 3rd February St.) and Lý Thái Tổ St.

O - a cell in the Bàn Cờ area.

P - a cell in the area of Lê Thánh Tôn St. and Gia Long St. (now Lý Tự Trọng).

● There were twenty-five targets listed to be attacked. Not all were because the units failed to get to them on time; partly because of the reworked Tết plan. The following are a few examples:

1 = Presidential Palace.

2 = General Office of the Saigon Police, the attack by the *biệt động* fighters failed to take place as they never arrived.

3 = Saigon radio station.

4 = General Staff of ARVN.

5 = Headquarters of ARVN Marines.

6 = Chí Hòa Prison, the attack failed to take place as the troops never arrived.

7 = Artillery Command and Armored Command headquarters and the Signals Station.

8 = American Embassy, only put on the list of places to attack a week before by the *biệt động* fighters.

● Examples of attack units on the first day/night of the Tết Offensive. The *biệt động* units were meant to hold their positions for an hour until the spearhead battalions (*đặc công*) arrived; the *đặc công* did not arrive because they had consumed all their energy in the fighting beforehand.

D1 - The Củ Chi Battalion a local force, a *đặc công* battalion and one battalion of the 11th Regiment.

D2 - The 2nd Battalion of the 1st Sub-Zone.

D3 - The Dĩ An District Battalion, a local force of the 5th Sub-Zone.

D4 - The Thủ Đức Battalion, a local force of the 4th Sub-Zone.

D5 - The Nhà Bè Battalion, a local force of the 3rd Sub-Zone.

D6 - The Bình Tân Battalion, a local force of the 6th Sub-Zone.

D7 and D8 - 2 battalions of the 2nd Sub-Zone.

At the end of 1967, standing members of COSVN dissolved Eastern Cochinchina (T1) and the Special Zone - Saigon-Chợ Lớn-Gia Định-Rừng Sác (T4). In their place they formed a Focal Point Region that consisted six sub-zones; the sixth being inner city Saigon and the area of the Front Headquarters for the Tết Offensive under COSVN.

Opposite and above: **The Tết Offensive of 1968 in Saigon, examples of communist safe houses and their initial attacks.**

This was the house of Đỗ Văn Căn (Latex the Third) but it is now owned by his son, who is in the 2007 photo entering the secret hideout. When his father built this hideout, he disposed of the unwanted soil by raising the kitchen floor. His house was ideally located near dwellings owned by senior members of the Southern government and important government offices, which gave it good cover as people did not expect the communists to be so close (Clive A. Hills).

on other strategic targets such as the U.S. Embassy. Initially we shelled the airport with thirty-seven mortars and as we did so our soldiers across Saigon began to fight.

My leaders then instructed me to guide an infantry regiment, stationed under the command of the 2nd Sub-Zone. They asked me because I worked there so knew the streets well. The regiment had to strike the city from the south-west. I had to lead them through the 6th, 5th and then the 3rd District. They then held out in the 5th District and 10th District for a week.

We had been told, "When the fighting starts, attack and destroy enemy military posts from the suburbs into the inner city, stand and fight whenever the enemy resists heavily, so that we can keep advancing." Our soldiers were not made of steel so they died or were wounded in successive battles.

By February, for Wave II, the Americans had strengthened their positions in Saigon. They had better road blocks and they used airpower. For us to thrust into the city center we had to fight in the streets. This was very dangerous. To avoid their massive firepower we decided to go from house to house by boring holes through the walls. They fired at us in the houses and we fired at them from the houses. The fighting was so fierce. Our troops looked in despair as they could see no way out, the enemy was waiting for us with tanks, artillery and helicopters ... our leaders ordered us to withdraw.[46]

For Wave III, veterans of this event say it did occur, whereas officially it is not recorded as such. For this so-called phantom Wave III, skirmishes did take place around Saigon. Why it is said not to have occurred, is Saigon saw brutal fighting from the outset because the United States threw its military power at the city in order to hold it. This meant that Saigon only really saw two official waves of fighting because the communist

Top: The harbor in Saigon, which was once the headquarters of the ARVN Marines. During the Tết Offensive it was attacked by a unit headed by Nguyễn Văn Lém, who was later arrested and shot by General Nguyễn Ngọc Loan. *Bottom:* The Saigon radio station building in Saigon, attacked during the Tết Offensive (both photographs 2007 Clive A. Hills).

troops by then had become too exhausted and they had limited ammunition to fight with. On top of this, the Revolutionary Infrastructure had been destroyed, meaning that the troops had no help. Although leaders in the South had been given strict instructions by Hanoi not to expose their strategic intelligence networks, this had not been extended to the wider infrastructure. To save what was left, both troops and infrastructure, the Communist Party allowed their prized security courier lines to be used so that troops could withdraw from inner city Saigon to the outskirts, prior to when Wave III should have happened.

Tâm explained her part in these skirmishes:

> On 26 May, our leaders ordered us to strike again, but we had limited numbers. Then in one attack a brick wall fell on me. It knocked me out and when I came round I realized my legs were trapped. I had wounds all over my body and my eyeball had come out. I am now blind in that eye. I was very lucky, my friends thought I was dead but they came back to help me. They took me back to my base and I spent two months in hospital. Although my wounds had not healed, when my leaders asked for people to go back to fight in the outskirts of Saigon, I volunteered.
>
> On my return to Saigon the enemy stopped me at a checkpoint and arrested me. They took me to Băng Ky Interrogation Centre and tortured me. I said, "I am a patriot, patriotism is not a crime and I'm not guilty." They stopped this line of questioning when I said this, but they changed tack and forced me to salute their flag. I refused to do so. They asked, "Why?" I said, "I do not respect this flag so I will not salute it. I respect only the red flag with a yellow star on it." Again they ruthlessly beat me. This did not help them get anything from me.[47]

Tâm ended her war on Côn Đảo Island in a tiger cage. She was detained for six years and one month. What helped her to get through was her belief that the revolutionaries would win.

Missed Opportunity

The three waves, or in some cases more, gave the impression of a chaotic state across the whole of South Vietnam. It is hardly surprising then that when a reporter interviewed General Westmoreland about the offensive he replied, "I have no hesitation in saying that the enemy was inviting defeat."[48] This was a U.S. victory.

Regardless of first impressions, what was the outcome of the Tết Offensive for the communists since total victory had not been achieved? As the dust settled on the fighting, would Giáp get his wish of a weaker U.S. presence in Vietnam or could the Americans use Tết to gain the initiative?

For Hanoi, the offensive nearly destroyed Hồ's blueprint in South Vietnam because of the waves of fighting insisted upon by Lê Duẩn. This was a serious blow; not only because of the numbers dead and injured but because the knowledge base had vanished. Those who had been instructed to build the Revolutionary Infrastructure prior to Tết but had been burdened with military affairs had since died on the battlefield. Others within the blueprint who were veterans of the French War had been exposed, killed or imprisoned and could only be replaced with individuals who had limited experience.

On trying to reduce the losses during the fighting, Giáp had successfully won over some top leaders. They agreed that Giáp should not commit more than 20 percent of his main regular forces from North Vietnam to the South. One of the key reasons Giáp gave was that, because the Chinese Red Army had massed on Vietnam's northern border, he feared that they might cross into Vietnam. If this was to happen, Giáp needed his army to be in place to repel them.

Hồ had to rebuild his blueprint in the South before the Americans struck. Fortunately, thanks to Giáp's thinking, he had some of the means to do this. Giáp informed Hồ that he would fall back on one of his old mottos from the French War: independent companies–concentrated battalions. During the Vietnam War, this meant that Giáp divided his regimental-sized units into local regular forces of company-sized or battalion-sized units as well as guerrilla fighters. He then instructed them to travel down the Hồ Chí Minh Trail to operate in the enemy's rear base area. Giáp foresaw problems. This time, instead of sending southerners he had to send mainly northerners, because most natives had already been sent back South in the late 1950s and early 1960s. Now these new arrivals in the South were not at all familiar with the area, nor looked like a southerner, this alone might see the United States make further claims that Hanoi had not respected the Geneva Accords or had invaded the South.

For the Americans, this was their big decision, because the Tết Offensive could be Washington's strategic opportunity to take the initiative at any peace talks. It was at this time that Washington should have authorized the invasion of Cambodia, to cut the Sihanouk Trail. This did occur, but much later in 1970, and Hanoi did indeed change their logistics strategy. Washington should have instructed an invasion of Lao, to cut the Hồ Chí Minh Trail. Again this took place but much later on in 1971 and was a South Vietnamese-led land force operation, but it failed to make an impact at this time. Bold military action should have been taken soon after Tết. This probably would have needed more ground troops, and might not have been in line with the Geneva Accords, but it would have further crippled Hanoi at a time when they were seriously wounded.

The problem lay with the American public. They had not seen a U.S. victory, just waves of bloody fighting, images that they were not used to seeing. The photographs of Việt Cộng bodies strewn across the gardens of the American Embassy in Saigon was too close to home. The images of Nguyễn Văn Lém being shot in the head by South Vietnamese General Nguyễn Ngọc Loan looked callous. All these images kept the offensive in TV and newspaper headlines across the world day in and day out. The American Embassy debacle infuriated Westmoreland. According to him, the reporters and television cameramen were everywhere, their faces mirroring dismay and incredulity as if the end of the world was at hand. He insisted, "This was war, people died!"

The revolutionaries had used the "fog of war" and the media to turn a military defeat into a political victory. Instead of going for the kill, the Washington government went with public opinion to defend its political future. They ordered a step change in strategy. General Creighton W. Abrams, who succeeded Westmoreland as commander in June 1968, oversaw these policies. Naming just two examples: on point one, go from a Limited War to De-Americanization of the war and see a reduction in U.S. troop numbers, and on point two, implement covert tactics. Point one played into the hands of the communists and supported Giáp's original *A Surprise Attack at a Strategic Level* plan. Point two was far less advantageous because the Americans had finally seen the need to destroy the Revolutionary Infrastructure, known to them as the Việt Cộng Infrastructure (VCI), a decision critical to the development of the Phoenix Program.

The likes of Phan Nam and Hoàng Lanh had succeeded in changing American strategy and weakening their presence in Vietnam, thanks in part to the bloody images of Huế City. Interestingly, the two men were never truly recognized for what they did. Lanh said that some people would whisper spitefully, "How could he have worked in Huế for so long without being caught?" He had replied, "The people protected me."[49] Nam had credited his war survival not only to the people, but to his skill and luck. He too said that people questioned his honor saying, "How can such a senior operative escape capture; this is to insinuate," he continued, "that I must have been an agent for the CIA."[50] Ironically, if you went to prison and survived without giving information to the enemy you earned respect from the Communist Party. If you did not go to prison you must have been in an arrangement with the CIA. Today neither of the men are around to clear their names.

14

The Phoenix Program: Targeting the VCI

The Start of Phoenix

Hồ died on 2 September 1969, but before he passed away he left strategies and a forecast for the people, relayed to them in his New Year's greeting of 1969. Part of this message said, "Fight so the Americans leave. Fight so the puppets collapse." Many years prior to this collapse, the Vietnamese people had to overcome America's new strategy.

The U.S. had tried to realize for South Vietnam: a military powerful enough to subdue its enemy, majority support by the people for the political movement offered, and strong economic growth. The Tết Offensive gave the impression that this approach had failed. In 1969, Richard Nixon took over from Johnson as president of the United States. Later that year, he laid out a new worldwide strategy called the Nixon Doctrine.[1] Through this, he formally altered the De-Americanization of the war policy that Johnson had approved and replaced it with what he believed to be the more powerful strategy of Vietnamization, which meant reducing U.S. troop numbers, but strengthening Southern forces and pacification. To support Vietnamization he reinforced the need to eliminate the Revolutionary Infrastructure, his driving strategy being the Phoenix Program.

The Americans had been forewarned about the Revolutionary Infrastructure by a number of people long before they became heavily involved in the war. Trần Ngọc Châu had been one such person but he was not taken seriously. This dismissive approach was regrettable. Châu had good reason to understand its significance for the communists because his revolutionary training dated back to the days of Vũ Anh, when they both attended the Quảng Ngãi Land Force School in 1946 to learn the art of covert work. Châu then went on to fight for the Việt Minh and used the infrastructure to operate. He switched sides to fight against them in the 1950s; potentially disillusioned after the Chinese insisted that those from a privileged background could no longer take high office. In the early 1960s, as head of Bến Tre Province for the Southern regime, Châu now tackled the infrastructure in his own region; ironically he took the position from Hanoi's spy guru Phạm Ngọc Thảo.

Châu's knowledge of the infrastructure put him into a different class from his colleagues but also at loggerheads with high-ranking Americans. Châu believed that there was more to winning the war than body counts, an outlook that conflicted with general U.S. attitudes. Whereas the Americans wanted to kill as many Việt Cộng as possible, and viewed body counts as a benchmark for success, Châu favored the use of both political

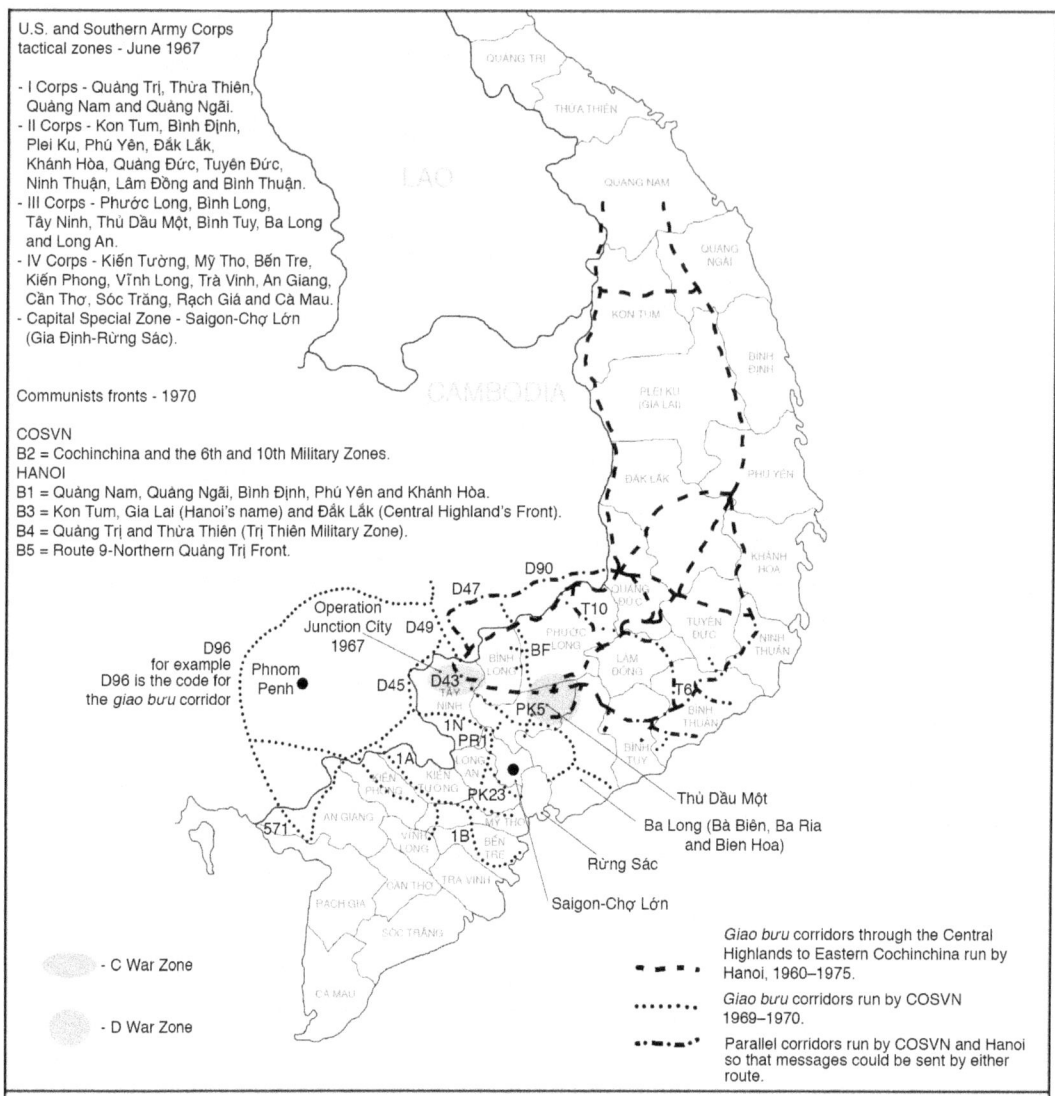

U.S. and Southern Army Corps tactical zones - June 1967

- I Corps - Quảng Trị, Thừa Thiên, Quảng Nam and Quảng Ngãi.
- II Corps - Kon Tum, Bình Định, Plei Ku, Phú Yên, Đắk Lắk, Khánh Hòa, Quảng Đức, Tuyên Đức, Ninh Thuận, Lâm Đồng and Bình Thuận.
- III Corps - Phước Long, Bình Long, Tây Ninh, Thủ Dầu Một, Bình Tuy, Ba Long and Long An.
- IV Corps - Kiến Tường, Mỹ Tho, Bến Tre, Kiến Phong, Vĩnh Long, Trà Vinh, An Giang, Cần Thơ, Sóc Trăng, Rạch Giá and Cà Mau.
- Capital Special Zone - Saigon-Chợ Lớn (Gia Định-Rừng Sác).

Communists fronts - 1970

COSVN
B2 = Cochinchina and the 6th and 10th Military Zones.
HANOI
B1 = Quảng Nam, Quảng Ngãi, Bình Định, Phú Yên and Khánh Hòa.
B3 = Kon Tum, Gia Lai (Hanoi's name) and Đắk Lắk (Central Highland's Front).
B4 = Quảng Trị and Thừa Thiên (Trị Thiên Military Zone).
B5 = Route 9-Northern Quảng Trị Front.

D96 for example D96 is the code for the *giao bưu* corridor

Giao bưu corridors through the Central Highlands to Eastern Cochinchina run by Hanoi, 1960–1975.

Giao bưu corridors run by COSVN 1969–1970.

Parallel corridors run by COSVN and Hanoi so that messages could be sent by either route.

- For example, T1, Eastern Cochinchina or 7th Zone were names for the same administrative area and were run by the Party Committee of the zone.
- Each Front or Military Zone had its own Military Intelligence Section and each province and "T" zone had a Military Proselytizing Department.
- Each "T" zone had its own Public Security Department.
- COSVN had a Guard and Security Department.
- Hanoi had its own Public Security Ministry, which ran its own services in the 5th Military Zone and the Trị Thiên Military Zone.

COSVN
T1, Eastern Cochinchina (or 7th Zone) = 7th Military Zone - Tây Ninh, Thủ Dầu Một and Ba Long.
T2, Central Cochinchina (or 8th Zone) = 8th Military Zone - An Giang, Kiến Phong, Kiến Tường, Long An, Mỹ Tho and Bến Tre.
T3, Western Cochinchina (or 9th Zone) = 9th Military Zone - Rạch Giá, Cần Thơ, Vĩnh Long, Trà Vinh, Sóc Trăng and Cà Mau.
T4, Special Zone - Sài Gòn-Chợ Lớn-Gia Định-Rừng Sác.
T6, Southernmost of Annam (or 6th Zone) = 6th Military Zone - Tuyên Đức, Ninh Thuận, Lâm Đồng, Bình Thuận and Bình Tuy.
T10, Southernmost of Annam (or 10th Zone) = 10th Military Zone - Quảng Đức, Phước Long and Bình Long (lasting from 1966–1972 otherwise part of T6 or T1).

Hanoi
T5, Southern Annam (or 5th Zone) = 5th Military Zone - Quảng Trị, Thừa Thiên, Quảng Nam, Kon Tum, Quảng Ngãi, Gia Lai, Bình Định, Đắk Lắk, Phú Yên and Khánh Hòa. Note the 5th Military Zone would be divided into different fronts B1, B3, B4 and B5. Hanoi ran these provinces because of communication issues such as radio signal strength.
In March 1962, the Public Security Ministry of Hanoi set up intelligence centers. A1 = Saigon, A2 = Nha Trang, A3 = Quảng Đà (Quảng Nam-Đà Nẵng), A4 = Thừa Thiên-Huế, A5 = Quảng Trị as well as Z17 = 17th Parallel.
In 1965 these centers came under COSVN at a provincial level, but A5 and Z17 merged to form T65 and remained with Hanoi.

and military action. Force alone upset the locals, giving them reasons to join the Việt Cộng. He contended that by giving the locals cause for supporting the Southern administration, the farmers would leave the sphere of the communists, thus starving them of recruits.

When head of Bến Tre, Châu set about finding ways to eliminate the infrastructure, and designed two teams to deal with the issue. He called one group Census Grievance Teams, and sent them into every village in his province to solve local problems, thereby encouraging farmers to join him rather than the communists. These teams made it known that any Việt Cộng members who turned themselves in would not be persecuted but helped back into society through work. Not everything went smoothly; when he brought in a school teacher his counterpart in the infrastructure undermined the teacher's work, killing the teacher if need be. To support the work of his Census Grievance Teams, Châu used intelligence techniques to locate senior members of the infrastructure. He then sent in three-man teams to capture or kill them. Since he believed that the Việt Cộng used terror as a weapon to dominate the rice farmers, Châu called his three-man units Counter Terror Teams (CTT).[2]

Although few people could see the worth of his political military methods, Edward Lansdale (1908–1987) did.[3] No one thought that pacification alone could win the war, but some believed that a combined approach with the military would be the most effective. Lansdale linked with Châu to nurture what he could see was a way forward for the Americans. There had been other pacification methods around since the 1950s but not directed specifically at the Revolutionary Infrastructure. They included the Civil Guards and the Village Self-Defense Corps, which later became the Regional Forces and the People's Self-Defense Forces respectively and were used mainly for local village security.[4] Yet it was largely due to the efforts of Lansdale and other like-minded Americans that adaptations of Châu's systems were rolled out countrywide.

Sadly for Châu, he did not see his systems through to the end. In 1970, President Thiệu accused him of spying and had him arrested, on the grounds that Châu's brother, Trần Ngọc Hiển, was a communist intelligence officer and since the two brothers had met they must have exchanged confidential information to the benefit of the communists. The reality was, Thiệu had to deliberately undermine Châu's pacification methods because they consumed too much of the money that Washington sent to Vietnam. By discrediting Châu and his programs, the money could be legitimately channeled to other areas and spent on elevating Thiệu's powerbase.

Châu was released from prison in 1974. Even though his brother took part in the revolution, when Saigon fell, Châu still went to re-education; his camp ironically being in Vũng Tàu where he had once worked. He had a miserable few years. His background of both fighting and later opposing the revolution, and then being accused of spying, seemed to make him a traitor to all sides. He finally escaped with his family as a boat refugee in 1979. After a horrific voyage the craft washed up on a small island off Indonesia. Eventually, the U.S. granted Châu and his family permission to stay in America.

In parallel to the efforts of Lansdale and Châu, there had been an incident that helped focus the United States on the Revolutionary Infrastructure. In 1964, infrastructure activities around the town of Qui Nhơn, in the I Corps area, so enraged residents that they requested their local officials act. Those sent to help were ARVN soldiers and U.S.

Opposite: Important communist corridors and secret service divisions from 1960 to 1975.

military personnel, who harnessed local anger and formed an armed unit made up of villagers.[5] Peer De Silva of the CIA sent one of his men down to investigate how effective this unit had been. The conclusion was positive and led to the formation of more of these armed units, which became known as People's Action Teams (PATs). To train more PATs, the United States established a center at Vũng Tàu, Phước Tuy Province, known as the Long Hải Military Training School.[6] Vũng Tàu became a hub for covert work.[7]

Peer De Silva's enthusiasm for his PATs niggled at other CIA operators; they too had been working on this type of approach for months. To stop any in-house fighting between CIA operatives, the CTTs, PATs and others similar teams were consolidated to form other CTTs and run countrywide, becoming known as Provincial Reconnaissance Units (PRUs) in November 1966.[8] These PRUs comprised Việt Cộng personnel who had switched sides, and their terms of reference expanded to include intelligence gathering.

In 1966, the enduring problem of who should run pacification was handed over to Robert W. Komer (1922–2000), a member of the National Security staff in Washington. He had to unite American government agencies involved in pacification projects into a unified effort. He argued that success could only be achieved by integrating three tasks. The first and most basic requirement for pacification had to be security because the rural population needed to feel safe and kept isolated from the insurgent forces. The second point had to look at weakening the insurgents' forces by destroying their infrastructure, and by developing programs to win over the people's sympathy for the Southern government and the U.S. forces. The third condition was that the new strategy had to be applied on a large scale to turn around what had been up until then, at best, an indecisive war.

For the scale required for anything to work, Komer recommended the responsibility for pacification be vested in MACV. General Westmoreland would head the program, with a civilian deputy head commanding both military and civilian U.S. pacification efforts. Agencies complained but Komer pressed forward, supported by Johnson. In November 1966, the Office of Civil Operations (OCO) was set up with civilian governance as an intermediate measure to organize all civilian pacification programs, but it failed. This reinforced Johnson's and Komer's view that only the U.S. military had the resources and personnel to implement a large-scale pacification plan.

In May 1967, the Americans created CORDS (Civil Operations and Revolutionary Development Support). Komer became one of Westmoreland's three deputy commanders, being given the title of ambassador and the equivalent rank of a three-star general. William Colby, the boss of the CIA's Far East Division, became Komer's deputy; eventually in late 1968, Colby took over the running of CORDS.

The data collection part of CORDS was known as the Intelligence Coordination and Exploitation Program (ICEX) and provided a central clearing house for intelligence. Komer computerized data collection, which gave ICEX extensive processing capacity. When the data was collected and used properly operatives within ICEX built a meaningful picture of the Việt Cộng Infrastructure (VCI) so that named individuals could be killed, captured, arrested, induced to desert or compromised, thus neutralizing the infrastructure.

When Komer tried to drum up support for these pacification efforts, U.S. advisors in the I Corps area suggested a new name for any package under CORDS: the Phoenix Program.[9] This name probably came about because those in Quảng Ngãi Province already called their program Phượng Hoàng, in English "phoenix," the bird that rose from the ashes bearing news of peace.

CORDS struggled to make an impact. The major problems listed included insufficient security, lack of management between the U.S., the South Vietnamese military and civilian operations, and the absence of any commitment and competence on the part of the South Vietnamese government and army. To resolve issues, Komer developed an ambitious eight-point program called Project Takeoff. It was approved by the White House in the summer of 1967 and then by President Thiệu in December, and it gave consent for South Vietnamese pacification efforts to be far better linked to U.S. outfits and promoted long-standing projects, including attacks on the VCI. In late 1968, Komer officially listed Phoenix as one of the eight points of the 1969 pacification campaign plan.

On 24 January 1969, Samuel A. Adams, an analyst for the CIA, drafted a top secret report titled "Intelligence Failures in Vietnam: Suggestions for Reform." His report summarized the conduct of U.S. intelligence, which he characterized as having a lack of foresight, a neglect of fundamentals and an absence of clear central direction. These qualities, he argued, caused massive intelligence failures. In the first instance, U.S. intelligence had failed to gauge the scope of the war, which had always been larger than the intelligence had portrayed it. On another point, he cited the frequent inability of the United States to fathom the enemy's intentions.

Adams continued, "[another] basic failure has been—until very recently—the relative neglect by U.S. intelligence of the [origin] of the enemy's power, the Communist Party and its related bureaucracies, collectively called the 'infrastructure'.... In misunderstanding where the enemy's main strength lay, the U.S. devoted a disproportionate share of its resources to attacking the enemy's army.... The Allies' best conceived and most ambitious scheme to attack the infrastructure, the Phoenix Program, did not begin to get off the ground until some time last year." Adams then further noted, "that the United States has never systematically addressed the implications of the infrastructure and that this has produced many imbalances. It has allowed the enemy to deploy his forces far more efficiently than the United States; it has given the enemy the intuitive, and therefore allowed him to control his losses; it tends to be self-reinforcing because the more counter-intelligence penetrations the enemy has into the Southern government, the harder it is for the United States to recruit agents among the communists; and a final result of the imbalance may be that the Phoenix Program is so penetrated with communist agents that it has little hope of success, except in the very long-term."[10]

Project Takeoff might have been the most ambitious pacification project in Vietnam, but Adams' report went on to say that the basic problem in estimating the size of the infrastructure and defining it had not been resolved; a tight analysis might yield a number of a few thousand but a loose interpretation might end up with a total in the hundreds of thousands.[11] From the outset the Phoenix Program was not without its problems, but it needed to be radical in its approach if it was to change American fortunes in Vietnam.

Recruited by the CIA

Since Phoenix was a product of the secretive world of intelligence and special operations, few people speak of their involvement. Mark Smith is one of a small number of ex-operatives to do so. His stories highlight both the pitfalls and the successes of Phoenix.[12]

Smith arrived in Vietnam in December 1965, on temporary duty. He held various

A 1 March 2008 photograph of Mrs. Phuong and Mark A. Smith, who were both part of the Phoenix Program (Clive A. Hills).

posts in the country, giving him extensive knowledge of Vietnam that set him apart from the average soldier. His Vietnam War ended when communist forces captured him and later released him from a prison in Cambodia on 12 February 1973, when he was sent home to the United States as part of the prisoner exchange agreement.

In 1969, spymaster Colby asked Smith to be part of the Phoenix Program. Its major two components were the PRUs and the Regional Interrogation Centers. Smith said that it was rarely referred to as the Phoenix Program but usually called Phượng Hoàng or the PRU Program. As a regular soldier, he was an advisor to two Vietnamese Ranger battalions in parallel with his secondary covert work. Even his senior Ranger bosses did not know about his dual life, although Ranger High Command did.

When under Phoenix, Smith was an evaluation team leader of the PRU Program. His work included analyzing data collected from the Hamlet Evaluation Survey (HES), a statistical system that measured the success of rural pacification, and part of the data collected for ICEX. As well as being team leader, Smith ran a Special Purpose Unit, which operated throughout Vietnam and in the border areas, carrying out tasks such as hunting down identified communists within the VCI.[13] For his covert work, Smith answered directly to Colby.

Smith recalled:

> I honestly believed that I was a soldier from December 1963 to May 1985. But during this time I was asked by some pretty significant people to participate in something out of the ordinary, starting in 1967 and then on and off until into 1969.
>
> Here is how it all happened. I had been selected to be a colonel's driver in Special Forces. That's why a lot of guys say, "Mark Smith got into Special Forces by being a colonel's driver, he was too

young!" You had to be twenty. I was eighteen. The difference between Special Forces and other military guys is the maturity level. I was not really mature. I evolved rather quickly though in my new role. It became evident that I was a "shooter" by nature. I don't like the word "assassin" because it misrepresents what we did, and plays into the hands of the media.

But I started to get connected with Military Intelligence and the CIA in 1967, when I met Captain Jones. At that time I was in a Reconnaissance Platoon as a staff sergeant and platoon sergeant, and there to provide security for operations being run out of Bến Cát District by Jones and his PRUs. I had been assigned to the U.S. 28th Infantry in Lai Khê, Bến Cát District, just up the road. I got onto the intelligence radar because I thought what he did was pretty unique stuff and I got into a habit of going down to talk to him and his team. Also, on one mission, an ambush-type operation, my superiors wanted more details of it after the event. I obliged, and when I gave my account I met a guy I had not been aquatinted with before who worked for Colby.

However, it was the event on 16 October 1967 that started my journey into covert work. Captain Jones and his PRUs came into Ông Thạnh to operate with the 2nd Battalion, 28th Infantry. It was Operation Shenandoah II, and I was there in the capacity of recon platoon sergeant. Jones was out on an operation with Captain Clark Welch, who commanded D Company, 2nd Battalion, 28th Infantry. On 16 October, Jones was killed in the opening fight of the Battle of Ông Thạnh, which occurred a day later. His PRUs did not know anyone else there but me, and they were not allowing anybody to touch his body other than them. So I got involved at that point until an American from MACV showed up and handled everything with Captain Jones' body and his PRUs. I had previously met the man from MACV, and about three or four weeks later a guy in civilian clothes came and said, "Thank you for what you did for Captain Jones." He told me about a new unit that had recently been formed, called the B-36 5th Special Forces Group, and that they wanted me involved. In the end I stayed with the 28th Infantry.

These sporadic contacts continued on and off until I got slightly wounded in 1968, and went back to the States. I was finally assigned to go to Military Assistance Training Advisory [MATA] run by Special Forces at Fort Bragg North Carolina in the fall of 1968.[14] Those who trained there were Special Forces, but called by MACV provincial or district military forces, and there to advise ARVN units, Regional Forces or the Popular Forces in Vietnam. So I am there, and I then spend an extra two weeks training in Washington before going to Fort Bliss, Texas, to take a Vietnamese test to see if I spoke it well enough.

When in Washington I met a couple of guys that I had been seeing down the years. I was still a 2nd lieutenant, almost promotable to 1st lieutenant. These guys had a little "charm school" that they had arranged for me to attend. This was separate and secondary to my MATA work. They trained me in a number of disciplines such as how to set up an agent net, how to do dead drops and so on. We did dead drops into Peoples Drug stores, this is when you put a message some place…. I found the best way to make a dead drop in a drug store was to leave an envelope in a box of many types of envelopes that were for sale. That is, before they plastic wrapped everything. I would open a box of envelopes and place a message inside one of them and put a little mark on the box and then put it back. Whoever came in to pick up the dead drop would see the little mark and purchase the box of envelopes that had my message in it. It shocked me when I found out that many of my friends used what I thought was my unique system as well. Then, the last four days I went up to northern Virginia and got into all kinds of explosives, and how to make strange bullets. Things like that. And that was it. Afterwards I went back to finish the MATA Sector/Unit Course.

On my return to Vietnam in January 1969, I went to MACV/CMAC. As a regular soldier I was assigned to advise the Vietnamese 31st Ranger Battalion and to assist with an advisor problem in the Vietnamese 37th Ranger Battalion. I answered to Capital Military Assistance Command [CMAC]. That was where complications set in; me being there sometimes, not being there at other times. Usually at night I would be called away as part of the [Phoenix Program] to work on the evaluation of data about people. Then I could be sent out to kill a specific person or sent on another predetermined mission with my Special Purpose Unit, made up of the "little people" there to assist me.[15] However, then during the day, or even at night I was expected to go out with the Rangers. Not even my immediate boss knew where I had been, I would even take a swig of beer sometimes to make out that I had been downtown all night. In truth, I could have just stepped off a plane that had taken me to a place a couple of provinces away.

One of my less conventional assignments was hunting down a high-ranking military VC coming down the Hồ Chí Minh Trail. Lots of people were unhappy that the mission was not just given to a reconnaissance team to do, however, on the other hand they could not find anyone else to do it so they sent my Special Purpose Unit in. The mission had to be done, as from our intelligence we knew that he was carrying a large bag of "goodies" because he visited different way stations recording their activities, so pretty valuable stuff. He was not supposed to be killed because he was a really good snatch target. Instead of being taken by helicopter, we walked in; we knew this man's exact position close to the Lao-Vietnam border because a SOG team had wiretapped the communist lines.

When we tracked him down we doped him immediately after he was seized to calm him down. We were told that it was Scopolamine mixed with an opiate. This latter drug is present in opium poppy plants. During tests it was found that in limited use the combination made people obey but it was all dependent on other factors such as age. The drug was rarely used because of side effects noted during trials. Once subdued, we took this man back across the border to a waiting helicopter so that he could be taken for interrogation. There were no exchanges of fire and we were out of there before anyone knew he was missing. He was arrogant, knew the place well and just moved about on his own. This made him a valuable target. Our intelligence also indicated that he might be making some money on the side and so his disappearance, conveniently, might be blamed on his own internal security apparatus.

Frankly a SOG team could have done this, they were the experts. I am embarrassed by the entire baloney of walking back across the border because nobody wanted to ask for SOG lift assets. I even needed to borrow a decent pistol. To further compound my embarrassment, I was supposed to be constructing the Vietnamese Ranger, Rest and Recreation Center (R&R) in the city port of Vũng Tàu. When I came back, after three days, I got the glory for building the thing!

One of my most memorable operations to disrupt the VCI was in 1969, when my Special Purpose Unit raided a gangster meeting in a hotel in Saigon-Chợ Lớn Special Zone at midnight. We had to break it up because those present were from the VCI and a Bình Xuyên gang, and were meeting to discuss how to coordinate smuggling weapons for operations in Chợ Lớn and the Rừng Sác Special Zone.[16] We went in with M-3s, nicknamed "grease-guns," along with .22-caliber Colt automatic pistols, both types with suppressors fitted. The M-3 was an American submachine gun that entered the U.S. Army during the Second World War. As it was a .45 caliber, the heavy bolt made a distinctive "clack, clack, clack" sound when fired, even with the suppressor. With such rudimentary weapons it made out they had done each other in: criminals killing criminals over the spoils of war. There was no link to American involvement, you understand. I saw numbers later in the newspapers saying approximately ten to twenty people died. But it was fifty-eight people. We had destroyed a sizeable cell of the VCI and their criminal helpers.[17]

By 1970, there were around 700 U.S. Phoenix advisors throughout South Vietnam; supported by many hundreds of South Vietnamese.

Working Within Phoenix

Smith introduced the author to Mrs. Phuong in Bangkok in 2008. She had worked in the Phoenix Program and knew all too well how complicated it was to tackle the infrastructure. She had first heard about covert work from her father, David W. Jones. Born in Houston, Texas, he was an American citizen but ethnically Chinese. During the Second World War, he had been sent to China to work for the nationalist Kuomintang by the U.S. government. He would say, "Forget the army marching into Beijing; it is the man selling soda in the market who is the real problem." In 1949, due to his work in China, the U.S. government transferred him to Vietnam to protect him from the Chinese Red Army.

Born on 8 June 1945, in Guangzhou, China, Mrs. Phuong moved to Saigon with her father. She received a good education while her father continued his work for the

Top: Street stall sellers in Rạch Giá Town, Rạch Giá Province; couriers who sold fresh goods as a cover used merchandise that were all the same in which to hide the message because this minimized the risk of the wrong person buying the item with the note in. *Bottom:* These women in a market in Rạch Giá Town, Rạch Giá Province could have so easily been couriers during the wars. If they both had been it is likely that neither would have known the other was, owing to this compartment rule of the underground system (both 2007 photographs Clive A. Hills).

community. Later, her father ran the Amerasian Program, which he had established for children fathered by American citizens in Vietnam. He took the ones that no one wanted, protecting them and giving them an education. Mrs. Phuong used the program to give her a cover story; building trust between sides so that she could operate covertly for the Americans. The Amerasian Program also allowed her father to raise money for the war effort. He was murdered in 1966 in Texas, it is assumed because of his connections to the OSS and later the CIA. After his death, she took over the program.

In 1967, Mrs. Phuong was a lieutenant in ARVN and trained in intelligence. During this period she worked in the office of President Thiệu, in Gò Vấp District, Gia Định Province. She reported to him directly, drawing on the intelligence that she received or had found by translating documents and looking at codes. In late 1968/early 1969, she joined the Phoenix Program, one of her trainers was Lieutenant General Hiep, who knew Smith.

When Mrs. Phuong joined Phoenix, she studied at a number of institutes, including Vũng Tàu. At Vũng Tàu, people could be streamed into two groups. The first, "agent handling," saw a person being taught how to form a covert network, and gather information and sift through it. The second group Smith called "shooters," who would go into the field. Her teachers assigned her to the first group; her main role after she had finished her training was to gather intelligence on people she thought were part of the VCI. She fell under CORDS and was called a security officer; most of her intelligence went to assist the PRUs, National Police Directorate, ARVN or the U.S. military.

Mrs. Phuong said:

> My team had to gather the intelligence on individuals who had been brought to our attention. We looked for "indicators" and to get these I set up a network of people I trusted. Either I inherited them from others or I found them myself.
>
> Like the VCI, we too tried to penetrate our agents into various groups in the community to look for indicators. My agent could have been a teacher, there to observe, but just as importantly to listen in on the children's conversations; they repeat what their parents say and do and we built some of our evidence from this. I placed my agents within restaurants or even pharmacies. Việt Cộng agents had opened such shops so that they had access to drugs or rice to smuggle to their troops. Who would question a restaurant owner ordering a few too many bags of rice? It was my job, and that of my networks, to question these sorts of activities.
>
> From the intelligence, if you had one clear indicator then you could start to look for other telltale signs. If you found three indicators, then they could be Việt Cộng. If you had seven indictor matches then you are probably looking at a Việt Cộng. This process of elimination could take months.
>
> An indicator can be pretty much anything, such as if a man is home every night apart from Wednesdays, why? This is an indicator. He might have been seeing his girlfriend or that might be the night that the Communist Party meets. Who did he go to school with, are any of them now out in the forest, does he have scratches on his legs, and if so, where are they from? If you think that the scratches are from the forest, only VC go there. Sometimes we just asked them if they liked the government, or we said that we didn't like the government, and we observed how they reacted. These are indicators. We had to find out who these people were. Most importantly, our teachers at Vũng Tàu said intuition is also an indicator; look at him, is something wrong?
>
> We mainly focused on senior revolutionaries not couriers; they were of limited importance because they only knew a few people, although we occasionally followed the couriers because by doing so we could sometimes capture the main person they led us to.
>
> A typical case when we decided to arrest a courier was when she took on the role of what we referred to as a "Swallow." Just like this small bird, which has the ability to fly through the smallest of gaps, a seemingly innocent and delicate girl could evade security and get through checkpoints or to Americans in their camps; a farmer, a laundry woman or a girlfriend.[18] We say that during Tết 1968, these Swallows tried to take South Vietnam, but after that time, the Phoenix came and they flew away.[19]

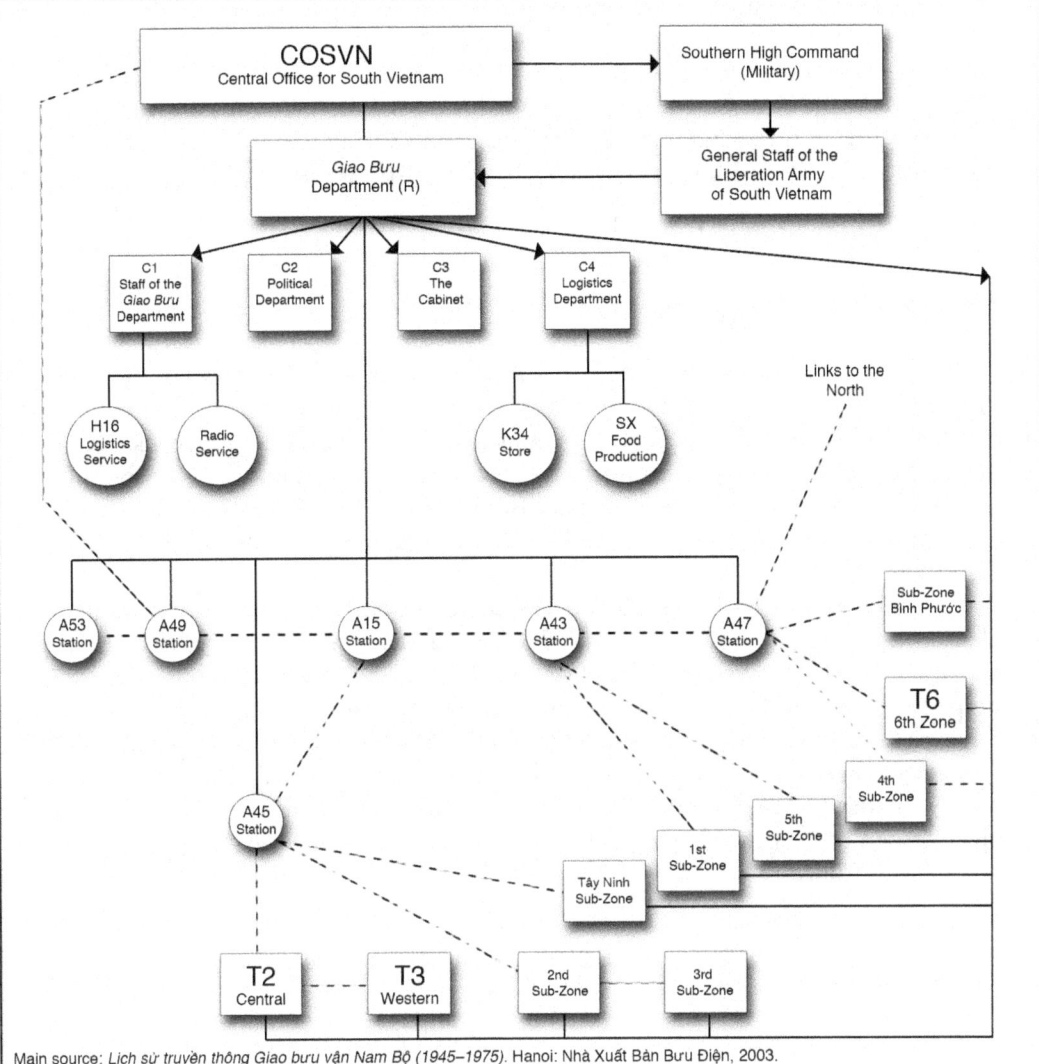

Main source: *Lịch sử truyền thông Giao bưu vận Nam Bộ (1945–1975).* Hanoi: Nhà Xuất Bản Bưu Điện, 2003.

- The dotted lines represent areas run by COSVN and the *Giao Bưu* Department, and the solid lines are those services run only by the department.
- At the end of 1967, the standing members of COSVN temporarily dissolved T1 & T4 in preparations for the coming Tết Offensive in 1968 and in their place they formed six sub-zones.

Examples of changes to courier security during this period.

As a result of American troops arriving in South Vietnam, in September 1965 the standing members of COSVN issued instruction No 27/CT-65. This gave the *giao bưu* permission to defend their individual corridors; to support this directive they were armed and authorized to fight.
In June 1966, the *Giao Bưu* Bureau was formally upgraded to the *Giao Bưu* Department, to be administered under the General Staff of the People's Liberation Armed Forces Southern Command Headquarters. The *giao bưu* were issued extra military hardware and ordered to hold military ranks.

As a result of the U.S. Phoenix Program, on 5 September 1970 the standing members of COSVN issued instruction No 01/QD. This stated that the,
- *Giao bưu* must switch back to being civilians and be run by the Party.
- A *Giao Bưu* Department must be established under COSVN.
- A Military *Giao Bưu* Department must be established under the General Staff. This department had to run "unity" corridors: routes from North Vietnam to Cochinchina, which terminated at stations coded C10, C20 and C30.
- Although civilians again, supplies of ordnance and food to the *giao bưu*, must not alter from the way they were being supplied to the *giao bưu* by the military.

Organizational layout of the *Giao Bưu* Department of COSVN, 1966–1970.

When the United States acted against the VCI, the revolutionaries changed their policies. After the Phoenix Program, COSVN instructed their couriers to switch back to being civilians to save what was left of their crippled infrastructure. Hồ's Swallows had not flown away as Mrs. Phuong alluded to, they were still there, but they now hid within the civilian flock.

Underestimating Couriers

Mrs. Phuong had made it clear that they might observe couriers but did not see the worth in eliminating most because they played a limited role in the war compared to others. Hồ viewed all his couriers as important because even in a high-tech conflict only certain roles could be completed by them. Ms. Lê Thị Thu (1930–) told of her activities working as a so-called Swallow and Ms. Trần Thị Thu (1952–) spoke of her times on the front line couriering soldiers; both women added value to the revolution before and after Phoenix.

Born in Đà Nẵng, Ms. Lê Thị Thu was fourteen or fifteen when she joined the revolution as a courier. Her mother had died when she was a child and her father was killed later fighting for the revolution. She worked during the French War as a courier spreading propaganda among the female population. For the Vietnam War, at the age of twenty-three, she couriered documents and guns. She did not participate to any great extent in propaganda because by then women had become more liberated. This new approach made it harder for women to outwit soldiers because they could search a courier more openly, but a courier could now publicly take advantage of male weaknesses.[20]

Ms. Lê Thị Thu said:

I operated between the countryside and Saigon serving our secret agents, coded K41, K42, K43 and K44, who worked within the city and the Southern administration. I supported many low-ranking agents. If they had been at a more senior strategic level then they would have been allocated just one courier for their tasks. From the moment I started operating in this manner the enemy watched me. Some wanted me to leave for my own safety and theirs, but I felt a duty to others and so stayed.

In 1962, my leaders ordered me to move four weapons out of a home of one of our agent's because we had been tipped off that the enemy might search it. I put the four pistols in a hand basket used to take goods home from the market. I packed it strategically so that I put vegetables at the bottom, green bean sprouts at the top and fish in the middle, and sandwiched between all of that were these guns. I was nervous. I met a group of thirty to forty policemen, who surrounded me and asked in an aggressive tone, "Hey, madam where're you going?" "I have been to the market," I replied. "What are you carrying?" "Fish," I replied. I thought my life might end. They asked, "What is underneath?" I knew they hated smelly fish and would not want to probe the bag, or that's what I hoped, so I said, "Please look." They lazily poked my things before one said, "Just let her go." For a moment there was silence, then they waved me on. I ran as if I had four legs to carry me. From that point on I held no fear when passing a checkpoint. Be bold and they will let you through.

My leaders saw that I had the strength to conduct such a task, so I returned to carry twelve guns. As they were big and heavy I could not move them all at once. I took eight at first and placed them in two baskets on a bamboo pole slung over my shoulder, as if a farmer carrying goods to the market. I passed all the checkpoints because at that time, to live or die, I feared nothing. Even my superiors thought that I would be arrested and killed. They could not believe that I had survived the journey. To show gratitude to me they gave me a chicken.

I became a courier for a revolutionary who conducted military proselytizing within an ARVN unit, of which he was a member. After a few days I went to visit him, under the cover of being his sister. We swapped codes to confirm our identities and pretended to discuss going out for drinks, but all the while we exchanged information. I then went back to our base area and described what he had told me. For example, that his unit planned troop movements and where. From this my superiors could now counter them. Proselytizing was important so we had one or two of these operatives in each enemy post; served by couriers.

I even conducted military proselytizing myself. On one occasion my leaders instructed me to find a lonely man in enemy ranks, flirt with him, and be his lover. I first talked about love, then I slowly spoke about the revolution, before revealing my true identity, saying, "Avoid death and come to our side."

It was when I delivered documents for Wave II of the Tết Offensive that I thought my time had run out. I had to pass an enemy post carrying documents for a Communist Party member. I wore two sets of clothes so I could hide the papers between the layers. As I approached, two policemen saw me and called me over. I did not know them but when they saw my face, they said, "You are Thu." I said, "You must be joking, this is my ID card, I do not know who Thu is!" The policemen had me on their wanted list. "You don't say," he said, and grabbed me and took me to their command post. When we went inside I asked to go and pee. I entered the cubical and took the bundles of documents out, putting them into the rubbish bin. I did not pee as I did not have time. The officers asked, "Why do you have heavy clothes on today?" I made an excuse that I was going to the rice fields and I had to wear these clothes because otherwise the sun would burn my skin. They said, "Take off your trousers!" They found no documents because I had already disposed of them in the bin toilet. I was lucky, the policeman who had originally allowed me to go off to relieve myself was one of our agents. I knew this because once I had been taken into the post I asked each policeman questions, such as, "What fruit would you like today?" I had to try and find out if they knew the password such as "orange" or "mango." I asked several questions, and depending on how they replied, it meant I could secretly identify who the policeman worked for. This method saved my life.

This boat in An Giang Province was the type of craft the couriers used to transport weapons or messages around the Mekong Delta, either in one of the pots or in a false bottom in the boat (Clive A. Hills).

This is one of the many types of boats that the couriers used to ship operatives or supplies around the Mekong Delta. The waterweed in these waters was a rich source of food but also gave cover to the water-elite *đặc công* forces before a battle because, by using a bamboo tube to breathe, they were able to hide below it underwater for hours (Clive A. Hills).

> When I think back to those days, I sometimes lie on my bed shaking from fear of what might have happened. I think of my husband who died, and my only child. I had sent her to work for the revolution to set an example, in the hope that others would do the same with their children. I thought it best that she died for the revolution, rather than marrying one of the enemy. This would have been so shameful. I have cried so much; she was very young, seventeen when I sent her away. She died just six years after in Quảng Nam at the Battle of Bồ Bồ in 1967, she was a military nurse. Now I am alone and find it difficult to sleep.[21]

The other woman, Ms. Trần Thị Thu, originally joined at the age of fourteen and worked as a courier from 1966 to 1973, living either in Huế City or in a base nearby. Educated in medicine by the revolution, she went on to be a propaganda operative until 1975. One of her key memories was that she and her fellow colleagues were always happy-go-lucky and joking, although they could have been killed at any time. She said that they had joined after witnessing horrific things but had been young and naïve about the overall picture.

Ms. Trần Thị Thu explained:

> I was just a small girl. I saw these scenes but I did not know what to do. I just followed the revolution. One of my most vivid memories, which haunts me to this day, is that of the sixteen couriers in my station outside Huế. I was the only woman, and all fifteen men died protecting me. Why did I live and they did not?
>
> After Tết things became very hard. I lost contact with my agent, maybe until 1970 or 1971. This happened across the South. We had lost a high percentage of our guerrilla base and those who hadn't been killed were disorganized.

Cao Lãnh ferry traveling across the Tiền Giang (Front River), which goes from Cao Lãnh, Đồng Tháp Province, where Hồ Chí Minh's father's grave is, to An Giang Province. During regrouping, Soviet ships docked at Cao Lãnh to take people to the North, and throughout the Vietnam War the ferry crossing was a courier route to reach the regions of Central (T2) and Western (T3) (Clive A. Hills).

To expand our forces in the South, the North sent troops from the VNPA down the Hồ Chí Minh Trail. They had been trained in North Vietnam for three months prior to their departure, but how can you change a Northern dialect? They would just arrive at a courier station to take further instructions. Although they had a Southern map, with their general area of operation, without a courier the new arrivals were unable to travel to and then attack enemy positions safely. We had to guide them.

I too guided top Communist Party members coming from the North. These Party members wore masks. This had to be done after Tết because there were so few people left. By wearing masks, if anyone were caught they could not identify anyone.

New arrivals needed to adjust to the more open Southern ways. This was very evident when I had to lead some fresh-faced elite *đặc công* forces, who had just arrived from the North, to conduct a reconnaissance mission on Đồng Lâm Military Post, Thừa Thiên Province, so that others could attack it later. This was in a strategic location and blocked our way from Quảng Trị, but the enemy protected it well with infantry units, tanks, helicopters and armored forces. I and one other led the *đặc công* forces to the base. We divided into two groups: one went to the northern side and the other to the southern. We led them to the barbed wire fence. They were meant to be back in a couple of hours but they did not return until 3 a.m. I was so worried. I only found out later that these boys from the North had been watching the Swan girls singing in a performance for the enemy soldiers. Swan girls were secret policewomen.[22] The *đặc công* boys had hidden in rubbish holes in the ground, under banana leaves. Some of them had been peed on by troops relieving themselves of excess beer. But they endured this part of the mission to secretly gawp at the pretty girls.

Contrary to that story, in 1969, I led a group of young *đặc công* boys to an enemy camp. I lay down in the grass as a sign that it was now time for them to attack. When each of the young men passed me to enter the camp, they said "See you again." In the pitch black one pinched me. I knew who he was because he fancied me. He never returned and only now when I think of that night do I realize that he had never felt a woman before.

To guide both new arrivals from the North and those established in the South required great knowledge of an area. One such time we had to pass two enemy positions. As experienced couriers we knew that the safest route was passing between them, because sometimes the enemy did not extend their defensive patrols to include this overlapping area of responsibility, each thinking that the other camp was doing so. To compensate for this grey area they laid mines, though. We split our formation into several groups; each went all the way through before the next started. I led the first group, and my comrade led the last. These mines cut off your leg and if one detonated they might all then blow in a chain reaction. Sometimes, if the mines had been laid too close to each other, we would send in trained dogs first. Then, when the first person went through, they secured the path by leaving something such as lime on each of their footprints so the next one could see this and follow safely.

We not only guided our own but took ARVN deserters. This happened to me after the liberation of Quảng Trị Town in 1972, during the Easter Offensive. An ARVN infantry battalion revolted against the Southern regime. Maybe they had just lost the will to fight. The commander of this unit, Lê Quang Ninh, was a secret agent of ours. At the time we did not know this, but later we learned that he had converted around 2,000 troops to our side during the war. My group comprised just two couriers and one liberation soldier, and we had to lead some of them from their camp to our base in the forest. I could not believe that we controlled so many men. ARVN battalions are twice the size of ours so there were a lot of men, around 900. At first they had been frightened, uneasy about switching to the Việt Cộng, because they did not know if we would kill them. As I led them, their heads hung low, they were respectful and obedient. We were so nervous as we let them carry their guns because we did not have the ability to do it ourselves. We walked for around two or three days through our liberated areas. I asked our own troops if they had spare rice to feed them, which the deserters then cooked for themselves. I did this to show them that we were human and that even deserters are treated well. On arrival we handed them over to a political commissar and they were taken off for re-education, with some later fighting in the Hồ Chí Minh Campaign.

One of my closest friends died just prior to that campaign. We were like blood brothers because he saved my life and I had saved his. Before the Hồ Chí Minh Campaign, the enemy heavily bombed our base in Phong Điền and we had to move to Nhi Bridge, the other side of the Ô Lâu River, Quảng Trị Province. I guided him and another soldier in the Vầy area, a zone that was highly anti-revolutionary. In Vầy, the villages had been destroyed and I had to guide them through one of the abandoned ones. The enemy chased us with ground troops and a helicopter. I flung open one of the doors of a house and the enemy, on the other side, shot dead one of my comrades. My friend gave me cover so that I could flee. He too was wounded but created a diversion. We ran separately but both to the Ô Lâu River. I grabbed at the bamboo by the bank and made a breathing straw so I could submerge myself as the helicopter flew above. I stayed there all day wondering what had happened to my friend. When the sun set I made my way to our prearranged meeting point. When we met I could see that he could barely walk. I carried him and two guns the 10km to our base in the dark. I could feel his blood dripping down my back. We had survived but he soon returned to the front line, and that is when he died at the beginning of March 1975. I can't forget this.[23]

It is understandable that U.S. intelligence did not have the resources to investigate everyone and only targeted high up VCI operatives or occasionally so-called Swallow couriers. Nevertheless, this was a serious misjudgment and as the war rolled on it became part of the reason why the United States could not achieve more in Vietnam.

Problems with Phoenix

Phoenix did not turn out to be the silver bullet the United States had hoped it would be. It had many serious fundamental issues that influenced the day-to-day workings of the program, problems that could also be found in more conventional U.S. operations.

One main issue was that Phoenix relied on a series of linked data collection efforts, the Hamlet Evaluation Survey (HES) being of most importance. Established in 1963, this was now the bedrock of Phoenix and probably America's most important indicator in influencing the direction of the war. HES rated the status of pacification in South Vietnam on a monthly and quarterly basis. Each province, district, village and hamlet was given a unique HES identification number, which came from a multiple choice questionnaire filled out by officials and covered subjects such as the military, political and economic position of each hamlet under their supervision. Officials then put this data into a computer and each hamlet was classed A for secure, B for contested or C for Việt Cộng-controlled.

HES was flawed. Much of the information correlated was more than a month old before it was disseminated and the monthly reporting cycle did not have the ability to react to natural fluctuations, such as agricultural production seasons. Officials also weighted all indicators equally, which skewed the HES number. An example of this would be, if a hamlet had been secure for a long time, and so had a high positive security rating, this high reading might hide a lagging development program, which made the people dissatisfied with progress and drift to the Việt Cộng.

For all these reasons, HES figures could simply not be relied upon. According to Smith, "Some people looked at HES as a never-ending exercise in gathering data and manipulating lists, with little direct action taken."[24] The data that came out of HES at the end of 1972 claimed that more than 90 percent of the people in South Vietnam were secured and under ARVN control. This contradicted Pentagon figures. They secretly believed that the VCI existed in around 71 percent of the population.[25] This led some within HES to say that the garbage you put into a computer equals the garbage you get out.

Just even understanding Vietnam became an issue. For U.S. Special Forces or CIA agents, their tour of duty in Vietnam was too short to give any continuity and cultural understanding of Vietnam, so each time new personnel arrived in the country there was a degree of starting from scratch. Furthermore, few CIA case officers in the field could actually speak Vietnamese and those assigned to the provinces prior to August 1968 seldom had more than two hours of instruction on Việt Cộng organization and dynamics before arriving.

Vietnamization also influenced the day-to-day workings of Phoenix; this concept cannot work effectively when used in a protracted civil war. When the French first brought in their version of Vietnamization after the Border Campaign in 1950, it had some early success. However, once the communists had worked out ways to use Vietnamization to their advantage, it was a key factor in destroying French chances of any type of victory. Now, during the Vietnam War, the communists used Vietnamization to their advantage from the outset. Although the United States did use lie detectors and other means to try to weed out the enemy, with so many people to deal with, it became impossible to tell friend from foe.

Smith said:

> It was not uncommon for Vietnamese troops who were supposedly fighting against the Việt Cộng to call in resupplies and then simply hand the weapons straight to communist forces. Or, on other occasions, that only the leader survived an ambush and then showed his true colors by running back to his communist buddies soon after.[26]

Mrs. Phuong also remarked:

> Our work was very complicated, with matters made worse by the fact that there was a feeling of denial by some. For example, Colby trusted a man called Nguyễn Văn Hoàng. This man managed to convince the CIA that he was the man for them. He told the CIA what they wanted to know, and how he could destroy the VCI. The CIA gave him a high post in the [Phoenix Program] and promoted him to colonel. The secretaries would say that his eyes were all wrong. The PRU men, mainly former Việt Cộng, pointed out that Hoàng was a spy but officials ignored them. Not everyone could see it, and some of our superiors simply turned a blind eye. I reported directly to Hoàng. That is why I always tried to go around him, against our standard operating procedures, and report my findings directly to an American. In the end, those who did not trust him were proved right. His real name was Vũ Văn Hoàn and he was born in 1947. His cover identity when he served in the American military was Nguyễn Văn Hoàng, born in 1942. When all the Americans and high-ranking Vietnamese fled Vietnam in 1975, they left him to destroy their documents. Instead of doing this and jumping on a helicopter out of Saigon, he changed clothes into his North Vietnamese uniform and betrayed us by handing over our highly classified information to his communist leaders. So not only had we been betrayed by him but also by those on our own side.[27]

Although Phoenix had its operational issues, what further undermined it was the fact that, just as the Americans started to target the Revolutionary Infrastructure relentlessly, the U.S. government ordered their troops to begin withdrawing. This command caused serious morale problems as U.S. forces began to doubt their overall purpose in Vietnam and whether any of their efforts had worked.

Success or Failure

Success is judged by results, but because the Phoenix Program was one of the most controversial operations of the Vietnam War, its success seems more linked to public opinion. The argument even to this day, Smith said, is whether the Phoenix Program was engaged in "planned assassination" or in "legitimate conflict management."

NLF veterans favor assassination because Phoenix was the main part of what they called the "extermination war"; the Americans looking to eliminate the communists. American officials, on the other hand, say that Phoenix was "legitimate conflict management."[28] To clarify this, the military command in Vietnam issued a directive that stated it had based the anti–VCI campaign on South Vietnamese law, that the program was in compliance with the laws of land warfare, and that U.S. personnel had the responsibility to report breaches of the law.

Smith commented:

> Something my evaluation did show was that in nearly every province the program worked, but success hinged on good intelligence, filtering out who should or should not be on the "list." The reason why people say that [Phoenix] was an assassination program was simply because there were too many lists of people to target. At district and provincial levels, officials had started their own list, meaning that the people to be targeted had not been sufficiently scrutinized.
>
> An individual could be on the list because of ulterior and highly dubious reasons. He could have been named by a third party because he owed a large sum of money and his death would be used as a warning to others, or alternatively someone put the person he owed money to on the list, to avoid paying. Love triangles played a larger role than anyone wished to admit. Even if you had paperwork evidence to prove the accused was a communist you had to ask yourself, "Who drew up that paperwork?" In addition, after the Tết Offensive, people were trying to position themselves just in case the communists rose up again. These people told stories to protect themselves or went further and had to eliminate anyone who knew that they had worked for us.

This is a 2007 photograph of Tức Dụp Revolutionary Base of An Giang Provincial Party Committee; the staircase partly indicates the size of the cave complex this rock face hides. The Americans and Southern government labeled it the nerve center of the communists in Châu Đốc; the U.S. attacked it in the middle of 1968 during the Tết Offensive but failed to close it down (Clive A. Hills).

> A big mistake made by some was that they thought that anyone talking to a Việt Cộng was a communist. This might not have been the case. They could have been forced to talk to them while handing over supplies of rice demanded from them. That didn't make them Việt Cộng, it could just have been that they were scared.
> So we had to weed out the faulty information from what was actually factual. That is why most of the real work on the [Phoenix Program] was done by agents such as Mrs. Phuong.[29]

Robert G. Kaiser Jr., a *Washington Post* reporter who was skeptical of the war, seemed to concur with what Smith had said and the wrongful public perception of Phoenix. Kaiser had decided to scrutinize the work of Phoenix and went on to publish an article on 17 February 1970, "US Aides in Vietnam Scorn Phoenix Project" stating, "Many of the accusations against Phoenix cannot be verified here. Some seem to be based on misunderstandings of Phoenix terminology and statistics." Other journalists concluded the same, that kill figures, and some of the dark stories surrounding Phoenix, could be traced to other units conducting independent snatch patrols, or that, if a senior political figure died on the battlefield, his death had been recorded as a Phoenix statistic.

Smith continued:

> When we found a senior Việt Cộng member we analyzed things to see what to do with him, and once things had been agreed, the job was usually assigned to the PRUs, assisted by American advisors. The PRUs would move into a hamlet dressed as Việt Cộng, then drag off or kill the targeted individual. This led to a cartoon I saw in Mr. Colby's office showing a group of PRUs dressed as VC, and killing a

member of the VCI, as villagers peeked out of their homes saying, "The Việt Cộng even kill their own!"

Hell, Vietnam was so confusing, even my own brother-in-law's brother was a colonel in the North's intelligence service.[30]

When looking at the results of the Phoenix Program, it appears to have been successful. A report dated 1970 stated that 22,341 targets had been neutralized.[31] This figure included those who had been killed, captured, arrested, induced to desert or falsely set up and compromised as if traitors to their own side. The final figure of infrastructure members neutralized between 1968 and 1972 is believed to be more than 81,000, of whom over 26,000 were killed. Smith, however, gave a simple example of how difficult it was to get accurate figures.

Smith said:

> When William Colby issued his thank you to me, detailing that thanks to me 2,834 VCI had been neutralized, I knew that many of these same VCI had been double recorded at district or provincial levels by their own Interrogation Centers, therefore, the numbers at the higher headquarters did in fact gibe with reality. My function was to be an evaluation team leader of the PRU Program analyzing data, and many listed as my personal targets were actually carried out by my team. I just got the credit because I was the team leader.[32]

Perhaps the real test of success is not the numbers neutralized or public opinion, but how the opposition viewed the program. When asked, veterans recognize that the 1968 Tết Offensive did serious damage to the infrastructure but likewise from 1969–1971 it sustained its heaviest losses ever as a direct consequence of American counter-espionage strategies. Tết and Phoenix destroyed many senior people, and although there was always a willing person to fill the vacant position, the underground never operated as effectively again. Problems arose because the knowledge base had gone. Replacements did not have the experience needed to hold such a post, nor were they educated in the ways of the revolution, and they were even divisive with their own agenda. In the main the unpredictable replacements damaged the revolutionaries but their irrational behavior also made it more dangerous for any U.S. personnel wishing to destroy them.

The Phoenix Program will always be controversial. Nevertheless, what people at home in the United States did not appreciate was that this type of operation had to be conducted if the Americans were ever going to overcome Hồ's new form of warfare. Phoenix might have undermined the infrastructure but the United States failed to convince the public that it was not an abuse of human rights. So again, propaganda-wise, Hồ's revolutionaries won.

Smith looked for normality:

> It was two months after the Bình Xuyên gang shooting when Colby asked me to drop in for a chat. He said to me, "You're really good at this, you are always off somewhere new." He and a handful of other senior officers at MACV/CMAC and staff at the U.S. Embassy knew what I was doing. He had called me in because after six months I had gone in and said to my superiors, "It is overwhelming, I can't do two things at once." Colby now said that I needed to make a choice of what I wanted to be: a shooter or a soldier. In the end he said to me, "I know what your choice is…" That's because I had stayed with him many times. It is also when he said to me, "90 percent of what the CIA does is very mundane."
>
> All I wanted to be was in the regular army. So after 179 days I returned to normal duty, and went on to become a company commander of C Company, 1st Battalion, 506th Infantry, 101st Airborne Division.[33]

The Phoenix Program was more of a success than people credit it to be, thanks to the work of people such as Smith and Mrs. Phuong. In 1972, the program closed, the same year the revolutionaries switched to rely predominately on high-tech conventional warfare. Now, as a normal soldier, Smith would encounter these forces.

Changing the Battlefield Situation

It was when Smith served on the MACV Advisory Team 70, connected to the 9th Infantry Regiment, that he fought the encounter of his career, the Battle of Lộc Ninh, Bình Long Province, in April 1972. At the time, both the 9th Infantry Regiment and a battalion of ARVN Rangers defended the region. The attack on Lộc Ninh opened when the 5th Division and the 203rd Armored Regiment of B2 Front launched into Vietnam from their communist base in Cambodian. After three days of heavy fighting, the vastly outnumbered South Vietnamese forces, supported by U.S. airpower, were forced to abandon their positions. Ironically, a member of the Revolutionary Infrastructure helped to save Smith's life.

Smith noted:

In 1969, I was shocked to find out that my favorite beef soup maker was one of the main VCI members in Lộc Ninh Village. He had been compromised by PRUs who operated out of Bình Long Province. I knew who he was and he in return knew of my covert role but also that I had carried out popular work that had helped the locals. We kept our distance and did not kill each other; call it professional courtesy.

The day before the battle actually started I returned to Lộc Ninh from Saigon and visited Combined Intelligence Center, Vietnam. While there, we had a mini debate over whether any pending offensive would come through Tây Ninh or straight down Route 13 through Lộc Ninh and then An Lộc towards Saigon itself. I considered any enemy moves into Tây Ninh to be at worst a feint, and simply noted, "Hồ Chí Minh said that Lộc Ninh was the soul of Vietnam and they always go through there." When I stopped for soup the old man pulled me aside, "Go back to Lai Khê." He had already warned the French who still lived in the village and they had gone. I knew this was true because I had met one of them from the plantation, and he had dramatically waved his arms in an attempt to stop us proceeding further as he was rushing out of town with his driver.

After the opening rounds of the battle Lieutenant General Minh, the III Corps commander, and Major General James Hollingsworth, a III Corps senior advisor, placed me in command of all forces in Lộc Ninh District, although I was the junior officer present. This decision was driven by the fact that Colonel Vinh, the 9th Infantry Regiment commander, talked surrender.

During the fight I was captured and taken to the 9th Division's Headquarters located south of our camp. There I saw the soup man and he interceded when the political commissar cracked me across the nose with a stick. General Trần Văn Trà also rushed in to save me and invited me to breakfast. General Trà was the commander of B2 Front.

When the fighting stopped, they took me to the Corps' headquarters of General Trần Văn Trà in Snoul, Cambodia. We drove there in one of my own jeeps from Lộc Ninh. The soup man had come with us as a passenger in the front seat. They took me to a prison near Kratie, where they chained me inside a log cage, as well as held me in a hole in the ground for months. Fellow prisoners had counted thirty-eight wounds on my body.

I believed that the soup man became instrumental in smoothing my stay. On one occasion when my guards took me out of my hole in the ground, he again interceded when political types brought some villagers to see me, and they had sticks in their hands. Also, in October 1972, General Trà came to see me with the soup man in tow and interviewed me for release in front of the other American prisoners. I turned him down and told him to release Captain Dave Baker instead. I was the only POW to whom he talked about release, but he said, "No matter what you retort, you are still alive

Top: An ARVN and American fortified defense position protecting a bridge into Tây Ninh Town (2007 photograph Clive A. Hills). *Bottom:* Sitting in the front, from left, Nguyễn Văn Linh and General Trần Văn Trà, two heads of COSVN at the 1st Conference titled "Agitation and Propaganda among Women" in August 1973 (courtesy Phạm Hồng Cư).

with all those wounds." General Trà said I would live and that he would personally check on my well-being. A medic gave me rudimentary medical treatment and I was filmed bent over a log as a surgeon cleaned and bandaged a large wound in my behind.[34]

Smith's battle was part of the communists' wider Easter Offensive. Executed between March and October 1972, it aimed to regain former liberated land, create a capital for the revolutionary government and give the communists the advantage at the Paris peace talks by defeating Vietnamization. Giáp's main attack front was the provinces of Quảng Trị and Thừa Thiên, to be known as the Battle of Trị Thiên, with the core target being Huế. Secondary confrontations included attacks in the Central Highlands as well as Eastern Cochinchina to form the new capital, where Smith fought.

Giáp designed the Battle of Trị Thiên to emulate the success he had seen against the French at Đông Khê during the Border Campaign in 1950. This had been a turning point in the French War as it ended what Giáp called fighting under siege; it opened up the Chinese border to Vietnam. For the Easter Offensive, like Đông Khê, Giáp wanted to use the classical maneuver called "cutting off the lizard's tail."[35] Many lizards have developed a defense mechanism called autotomy, which means that if a predator has got hold of their tail they are able to drop it so that they can flee. By capturing Đông Khê, Giáp had forced the French command in Hanoi to drop their chain of outposts fanning north because, as Route 4A ran through Đông Khê, they had no means to send in supplies to support them.[36]

Giáp planned the Battle of Trị Thiên with Lê Duẩn in mind; he had wanted his native province of Quảng Trị back from enemy hands. To realize this, Giáp decided that he had to build a secret road to the south-west of Huế to enable his troops to conduct a surprise attack on a town along Route 1, and then hold it. To unnerve ARVN units within the area of Trị Thiên, Giáp would order other troops to attack enemy outposts near the DMZ. Although U.S. air supplies, of ammunition and troop reinforcements, could support some ARVN positions, there would be no resupply along Route 1 leaving ARVN vulnerable. Anticipating that high communist troop numbers could now sweep down through the DMZ, Giáp predicted that ARVN would flee Trị Thiên in retreat. By holding part of Route 1, Giáp would create the effect of "cutting off the lizard's tail" and see Vietnam severed in two, with Huế in communist hands.

Whereas Đông Khê had been successful, the Easter Offensive had not entirely met its objectives. The Easter Offensive suffered the same split in thinking as the Tết Offensive. Giáp designed the Easter Offensive to influence the Paris peace talks, whereas Lê Duẩn and his men wanted total victory: a people's uprising in arms. To reinforce his uprising vision, operations in Eastern Cochinchina, the region Lê Duẩn had been responsible for during the French War, were named the Nguyễn Huệ Offensive, after an emperor who had once united Vietnam. Lê Duẩn elevated the Nguyễn Huệ Offensive to the same status as the Battle of Trị Thiên because a triumphant win in Eastern Cochinchina could then see a military push to Saigon.

Lê Duẩn and his men managed to rework Giáp's plan because, just prior to the start of the Easter Offensive, a group of doctors conveniently deemed it necessary for Giáp to go to Eastern Europe for medical treatment. This was a calculated scenario that paralleled Giáp's absences prior to the Tết Offensive.[37] When Giáp returned from Europe the Easter Offensive had already started and he discovered his battle plans had been changed. Giáp had been furious, even more enraged than when he heard about the reworked plans for the Tết Offensive.

Lê Duẩn made three fundamental errors. In the first instance, the new plan meant that the VNPA had to strike head-on. Giáp never aimed to strike head-on but for his soldiers to use flank tactics because, by attacking the sides of an opposing force, it did not leave his troops so exposed. The second error was, that after the first offensive the soldiers had to have time to build a line of defense to hold the ground they had just fought for. Lê Duẩn wanted non-stop fighting. Giáp knew that his forces did not have U.S. levels of supplying power to maintain such a request. Giáp had tried to contact the commanders to switch to the defense but to no avail.

The third error was the failure to complete the secret road south-west of Huế to support the Battle of Trị Thiên. When Giáp asked why, officials told him that Lê Duẩn and Văn Tiến Dũng had nursed a plan to elevate the attack on the Central Highlands to the same status as that of the Battle of Trị Thiên and the Nguyễn Huệ Offensive. In their belief, whoever took the Central Highlands would take Vietnam. Although the two men wanted to take Huế, with Lê Duẩn's excitement of moving to high-tech conventional warfare, he had viewed this as an overt convoy of firepower moving on the city, without the need of a secret road. Hence, to conduct the new Central Highlands battle, Lê Duẩn had ordered the two engineering regiments, originally dedicated to Giáp's secret road, to the region. It turned out that such a large-scale attack could not go ahead; the rainy season had set in and the troops had limited rice to eat and ammunition to fire. Although the two regiments came back to finish building Giáp's road, the opportunity had been lost; the rain hindered progress and there was no means to supply the troops to build the road under a barrage of enemy fire.

By not finishing this secret road, the VNPA had lost their ability to cut Route 1 and achieve a similar result to that at Đông Khê for which Giáp had hoped. Giáp did advise Nguyễn Hữu An to construct an artillery barrage to sever Huế from the rest of South Vietnam and stop ARVN resupplies moving along Route 1, but the secret road was too short for his troops to do this. This shortfall likewise meant that enemy convoys moving south through Trị Thiên were out of range of VNPA artillery. Without this actual and physiological blow of cutting Route 1, Giáp's troops, who had won the first period of their maneuvers around the DMZ, were in difficulties. His army now pushed southwards from Quảng Trị through relentless air attacks and strong ARVN units, with limited ammunition to fight back with.

The Easter Offensive had too many so-called commanders, who had spread their forces too thinly across three main fronts, to achieve too many core objectives. While the offensive failed to cut off the lizard's tail this time, Giáp did learn from the errors and successfully used this strategy at the Battle of Buôn Ma Thuột in 1975. In addition, the Easter Offensive did produce results. Giáp showed that without direct U.S. firepower Vietnamization had not worked as effectively against his troops as the United States had hoped. The countryside of Quảng Trị Province resided in the hands of the liberation forces and as for Smith's battle at Lộc Ninh, the area had been taken and occupied as the revolutionary capital. Now at the Paris peace talks the Easter Offensive had shown the Americans to some degree that the VNPA still had a very real ability to fight.

America: No More Vietnam

Hồ predicted at the beginning of 1968 to those at the Air Defense Headquarters, Hanoi, "Sooner or later the Americans will send their B-52s to strike Hanoi. They will accept defeat only after they have lost in that effort." These would be known as the Christmas Bombings, the Điện Biên Phủ of the air, but to realize this prophecy there would be years of peace talks and bloody fighting.

The Americans had been calling for peace talks for years but North Vietnam had not engaged in the idea. The Americans believed that the North finally came to the negotiation table because President Johnson halted Operation Rolling Thunder in March 1968, opening the way for both sides to meet in Paris in May. From Hanoi's point of view, the talks were a way of giving the United States an honorable exit from Vietnam, and they regarded them as a formal process that needed to be followed when the right opportunity presented itself. Hanoi became receptive to the idea of talks because at the end of 1967 Washington representatives had sent Hồ messages to imply that they wanted to leave Vietnam. Hanoi had been encouraged by this and in 1968 decided to agree to American requests but, unbeknown to the United States, they planned to use the formal process as a ruse and a way of distracting it during the Tết Offensive.

For months the negotiations stalled. North Vietnam wanted all bombing of its territory to be stopped and the United States demanded that the North agree to a reciprocal de-escalation in South Vietnam. It was not until October 1968 that Johnson permitted the end to the air strikes and that progressive negotiations began. By then Hanoi knew that Tết had not gone entirely their way, so the Party no longer viewed the talks as a ruse.

Luckily for Hanoi they had more tricks ongoing. At the negotiating table, in order to limit the Southern regime's influence and to try and get the United States to leave on Hanoi's terms, the North knew that they had to deal with the Americans directly. To achieve this goal, Hanoi had instructed the NLF to refuse to recognize the Southern administration at any negotiations. As anticipated by Hanoi, in retaliation, the United States and the Southern administration refused to accept the authority of the NLF. To resolve a stand-off, both parties agreed that North Vietnam and the United States be the named parties. NLF officials joined North Vietnam's team while Saigon's representatives joined their U.S. allies.

In 1969, Nixon became president; extremely anti-communist, the revolutionaries wondered how he would deal with Vietnam. Within his first year, Nixon started his Madman Theory, there to make the leaders of other countries think that his behavior was irrational and unstable in the hope of stopping hostile Communist Bloc nations provoking America. It worked; through this Nixon successfully kept the North Vietnamese focused on the negotiations.

Furthermore, Nixon started the process of Vietnamization, one principle of this was to create a responsible government in South Vietnam. Hanoi saw that if they generated an official opposition to the U.S.-backed regime in the South, their new party would be a great opportunity to elevate their mandate for unification and weaken the Southern government. To be part of Vietnamization any aspiring group required government status. In June 1969, Communist Party delegates attended a conference to form the Provisional Revolutionary Government of the Republic of South Vietnam (PRG). Representatives included those from the NLF, the Alliance of National, Democracy and Peace Forces, the People's Revolutionary Party (PRP) and many other smaller groups. Once formed, NLF leaders sent PRG members to the Paris peace talks to give the group government prominence. Now formally part of Vietnamization, the PRG promoted the new name, the Republic of South Vietnam, and started to influence international and Vietnamese public opinion to support liberation their way.

Under Nixon, the most important negotiations that led to the initial peace agreement did not occur at the peace conference at all, but were carried out during secret negotiations between Henry Kissinger, the U.S. National Security Advisor, and Lê Đức Thọ, a North Vietnamese Politburo member. These talks had begun in August 1969 but had not progressed well.[38] For three years North Vietnam insisted that no agreement could be concluded unless the United States approved the removal of President Thiệu from power, but Nixon and Kissinger were unwilling to oust a U.S.-backed government that the communists had failed to overthrow by force of arms. Determined to break the deadlock at the secret negotiations, in May 1972 Nixon decided to blunt the ongoing Easter Offensive and announced the mining and bombing of Hanoi and Hải Phòng, in a campaign known as Operation Linebacker I (May to October 1972). Fortunately, this did indeed set in motion diplomatic events that focused all parties on a ceasefire.

Hanoi quickly responded with a suggested plan. They had to make this appealing and realistic. The Easter Offensive had not gone their way and if Nixon's efforts at détente significantly improved U.S. relations with the Soviet Union and China, Hanoi feared increased isolation. In fact, Hanoi was in such a poor situation, worse than after the Tết Offensive, that some within the Communist Party concluded that the negotiations were now the only way to get the U.S. to exit Vietnam, if that be on Hanoi's terms or not. Part of Hanoi's plan proposed a three-part government in South Vietnam to include South Vietnam (but without President Thiệu), North Vietnam and a neutralist third segment holding the balance. A third segment concept had been around for some time and was seen as an immensely inclusive category that incorporated a variety of groups. Unsurprisingly, this coalition concept was another deception by Hanoi. Present communist leaders had no plans to continue it; they controlled many of the parties under the third segment and time was on their side. The Nixon administration may have increased the bombing against the North, but he was also reducing U.S. troop numbers.

Finally, on 8 October 1972, in a secret meeting with Kissinger, Lê Đức Thọ gave him the text of the first completed draft treaty presented by any side since the start of the war. Thọ had greatly modified his bargaining line. In particular, he agreed that the Saigon regime could remain in power and that negotiations between the PRG and the Southern administration could lead to a final settlement. Nevertheless, he said nothing on VNPA troop withdrawals from the South and a coalition government. During this period, to keep the pressure on Hanoi, the United States dropped tens of thousands of tons of bombs on the North in the most intense period of daily bombing on that region since the start of U.S. involvement. Within days, the people who attended these secret talks had drawn up a final draft. Kissinger held a press conference in Washington during which he announced, "We believe that peace is at hand."

Not everyone felt jubilant; President Thiệu had not even been informed of the secret negotiations. When presented with the draft of the new agreement he became irate with Kissinger and Nixon and refused to accept it without significant changes. He insisted on his program of four nos: no abandonment of territory, no coalition, no negotiations and no communist or neutralist activities in South Vietnam. He then made numerous public and radio addresses to undermine the proposed agreement. Hanoi were stunned at Thiệu's reactions and believed that they had been duped in a propaganda ploy by Kissinger. At the end of October, to counter Thiệu, Radio Hanoi broadcast key details of the draft agreement.

Frustrated with President Thiệu, the U.S. government put diplomatic and economic pressure on him; he had to agree to the peace treaty even if his concessions could not be

14. The Phoenix Program

Mark A. Smith, front row third from left, with fellow POWs at Lộc Ninh on 12 February 1973, the date that they were released from their prison camp (courtesy Mark A. Smith).

met. To help Thiệu decide, Nixon pledged continued substantial aid to South Vietnam. Given Nixon's landslide victory in the presidential election he felt confident that he could follow through on that pledge. To show intent, Nixon ordered Operation Linebacker II, commonly referred to as the Christmas Bombings, in December 1972. With the U.S. committed to disengagement, Thiệu had little choice but to accede.

On 27 January 1973, officials signed the Paris Peace Accords. Just days earlier Nixon had announced a suspension of offensive actions against North Vietnam. Smith and many other POWs including Ms. Lê Thị Thu Nguyệt were released through Lộc Ninh. Hồ had predicted that the bombing of Hanoi with B-52s would lead to a U.S. downfall. America's Vietnam War was over.

The Second Victim of Hồ's Blueprint

The Nixon administration had taken the Vietnam War from a Limited War to De-Americanization to Vietnamization of the war. Hồ's New Year's greeting of 1969 had been realized, "Fight so the Americans leave." Now the Non-American War could start, but that was not the end for some U.S. troops. For many there was an element of deep unease and apprehension, not only for their Vietnamese friends who wanted them to stay, but there were, and still are, U.S. veterans genuinely haunted by the fact that they "failed to win," as articulated by one SOG member.

The United States suffered similar intelligence failings to the French, the predominant one being not grasping that they fought a new form of warfare, so they used mainly conventional warfare to terminate Giáp's army and in doing so destroyed the people. American decision-making politicians had been told. After the fall of Điện Biên Phủ in 1954, Robert Kennedy said that the United States should not intervene in Vietnam, "since you cannot fight an enemy that is nowhere and is everywhere at the same time." Brigadier General Castries told the French Assembly that you can resist an army but you cannot resist a nation, a message relayed to the Americans. The Phoenix Program was one strategy that tried to solve U.S. fortunes but by then it was again too late because, like the French before, the financial and political capacity to wage a war had dried up; the U.S. public wanted their boys back home. Nevertheless, there were differences between the French and American conflicts. Namely, for the Vietnam War Hồ did not look to beat the U.S. Army, as the communists had defeated the French, but to force the Americans home because he knew that his forces were no match for its stronger and better equipped troops. Whereas the French had Điện Biên Phủ, the United States was left with no grand conclusion. This fact adds to the plight of veterans and their ability to put closure to their war.

If the U.S. government had understood Hồ's blueprint from the beginning, might the United States have decided not to intervene at all? The U.S. did not see that the war could be impossible to win, even though it had been warned that this would probably be the outcome without a change of mindset and strategic thinking. After days of talking Smith concluded, "We lost a whole damned war through not listening,"[39] and the "ring leaders of imperialism," as Hồ had branded the Americans, became the second victim of Hồ's model.

15

Total Victory

The South: Positioning for Control

With the Americans gone, a new phase of the conflict started called the Non-American War. There were now two possibilities for the revolution: victory through primarily political struggle or as a result of a continuation of war. The Communist Party additionally debated what to do when they had gained victory; a concern dating back to May 1941 and the Eighth Conference when delegates deliberated class struggle and nationalism. After victory, Party members would have to ask themselves to what extent socialist principles should be implemented. Nguyễn Hữu Thái played his part in ending the pro-American Southern government. His story typifies that of many of his fellow countrymen in South Vietnam; torn between the hopes of nationalism and the fears of communism.

Thái is a progressive, outspoken Vietnamese national. During the war, he had learned first-hand what it was like to love his country and its people so strongly that he was willing to risk his life and, having done so, found himself bitterly disappointed by those whom he had helped bring to power.[1] When asked, he described the post-war years as tough; difficulties brought on by paranoid officials as well as mismanagement and corruption of the new communist government. Today, he is a member of the Vietnam Association of Architects and a guest lecturer at universities.

In 1963, Thái was well-known as the president of the Saigon Student Union and, being pro–Western, he aspired to go to America for further education. When Thích Quảng Đức burned himself alive, this image of a monk left a lasting impact on Thái, and even as an anti-communist nationalist, he moved towards the revolution. Instead of going to America for further education, he became a Buddhist militant in June 1963, and joined the student struggle against President Diệm. Soon afterwards, he made his first visit to an NLF–controlled area. Impressed with their cause and fighting spirit, he still questioned if he could live under agrarian socialism.

Thái was eventually imprisoned for his activities. His first period in custody covered December 1964 to March 1965. He recalled that the jails were "revolutionary schools that saw the graduation of many compatriots."[2] He was imprisoned three times, spending a total of four years in jail, years that gave him the rare opportunity to meet Vietnamese from all social strata. Prison, and those he had met there, only reinforced his determination to fight against the Americans. After his second period of incarceration from June 1967 to January 1968, the Southern government forced him to enlist in ARVN. During this time members of the NLF assigned to him small covert political tasks to see his suitability to join their ranks. He played a variety of difficult roles including psychological warfare officer and anti-war journalist. These duties resulted in him being thought of as a "leftie" by the Southern government, but the NLF similarly became suspicious of him, leading them to investigate his loyalty to the revolution.

Satisfied that Thái could be trusted, in 1971 when the Republic of Vietnam held elections for its Congress, members from the NLF suggested that Thái run as an independent. They advised that he stand on issues of neutrality and peace, so preparing the ground for a third segment, an inclusive category that incorporated a variety of groups. Standing for the elections was important, and indeed the communists viewed it as another political front line to attack. The Paris peace talks had not yet been settled and the neutralists hoped to be the pacifying factor in a future Dương Văn Minh administration. Minh himself backed Thái because they had worked together many times; especially when Thái was president of the Saigon Student Union.

It soon dawned on Thái that running as an independent candidate was too tough. While well-known to many people, he was a small fish and being penniless he believed it to be a fruitless task. He discussed this issue with his local party and suggested that he might run instead for elections in his homeland of Đà Nẵng with the support of the Buddhist Provincial Association there. That way he could enjoy the support of Minh, who was running for president to keep his name in the public domain, but also of Thích Trí Quang, the superior monk, who had recruited new members in the early 1960s after the Buddhists had been targeted by Diệm in Huế. Unfortunately for Thái, the Buddhist Provincial Association refused to support his application; some high-ranking Buddhist members in Saigon feared he was communist. In the end, neither Thái nor Minh stood, Minh clearly saving himself for a better opportunity. Then, just prior to the signing of the Paris Peace Accords, Thái was arrested for the third time in October 1972.

Thái said:

> I was freed from jail in April 1974, but could not find my old NLF apparatus as it had been broken up by the Saigon police. When waiting to be reconnected with my previous organization, former pro–NLF Buddhists, who were acquaintances from Đà Nẵng, suggested that I join them in the Buddhist National Concord and Reconciliation Movement. I agreed as it was compatible with my current situation. The movement was led by people such as Senator Vũ Văn Mẫu [1914–1998], later Minh's prime minister.
>
> I was asked to re-establish contact with my old acquaintances, such as people working around Thích Trí Quang, a superior monk, and Minh, and even with these two personalities themselves. My mission was to promote the National Concord and Reconciliation Movement. The strongest opposition newspaper to the war, *Tin Sáng*, had been shut down, so I began to write for *Điện Tín*, which was run by Minh's group in Saigon. I was put in charge of the international page. The peace and reconciliation policy of the Minh group had attracted attention from most of the opposition deputies in the National Assembly. Some had NLF connections.
>
> On the eve of Tết New Year in 1974, President Thiệu moved to arrest opposition people accused of belonging to the "dangerous neutralist left third segment." I was on the black list but managed to escape the police round-up. I had just gone out when the police rushed in to search my parents' house in the military housing compound at Bắc Hải. At the same time, they searched my wife's family's home in downtown Saigon. The police operation was quick and drastic. Few of the targeted people avoided arrest. Among the detainees was Prof. Châu Tâm Luân, and writers and journalists such as Sơn Nam and Kiên Giang. Luân was a Catholic and a high school classmate. He had studied agriculture in the United States on a scholarship but had been disappointed by American actions in Vietnam. He had become an anti-war activist and participated in the Committee for the Implementation of the Paris Peace Accords, led by Attorney Trần Ngọc Liễn. The writer Sơn Nam specialized in writing magazine and newspaper serials and was considered by the Southern government to be a covert Việt Cộng activist. Kiên Giang was well-known for his broadcasts of poetry on Saigon radio.

INVITE NGUYEN HUU THAI

as ASSU Guest Professor

Nguyen Huu Thai, 36 years old.

Endorsed by

Congressman Pete McCloskey

Kevin O'Grady, Beth Garfield
Jim Friend, Charles Ogletree,
current ASSU Council
of Presidents

Lee Zeigler, Director
International Center

Robert Textor, Professor,
Anthropology

Michael Closson, Assistant
Dean of Undergraduate Studies

The Chaparral

Mr. Thai's background:
- Vietnamese journalist for the last ten years
- Graduate sudies in Architecture and Urban Planning at the University of Saigon
- Former president of the Union of University Students of Vietnam
- Leader in peace movement in Vietnam since 1963.

- A PRISONER OF CONSCIENCE. For publishing articles advocating negotiation and coalition government and criticizing the repressive Thieu regime, Thai was arrested and jailed in October, 1972. He is still in prison. He has never been formally charged with a crime or tried in court.

What Can Nguyen Huu Thai Share With Stanford Students?
Mr. Thai can teach in a variety of areas grounded in his intensive experience of the Vietnamese social and political situation. He is especially prepared to conduct seminars on journalism and urban planning in developing Asian countries.

What Can Stanford Students Do For Nguyen Huu Thai?
We can help free Mr. Thai by inviting him here as ASSU Guest Professor. Public pressure could contribute to his release, as it has for other political prisoners.

Vote for Nguyen Huu Thai for ASSU Guest Professor April 17 and 18.

Also Vote for the $1.00 Refundable Fee Assessment to Fund the ASSU Guest Professor Program.

This flyer, printed by students at Stanford University in California in 1974, called for Nguyễn Hữu Thái to be released from prison. Near the end of the war Thái was invited to teach at Stanford University and the Free University of Berlin, thanks to the support of Amnesty International and influential American politicians, but he remained in Saigon (courtesy Nguyễn Hữu Thái).

My Buddhist contacts found me a hiding place in the residence of a National Assembly representative affiliated to Thích Trí Quang. But since I needed to be informed about new developments politically, some friends suggested that I hide in Minh's residence, the Orchid Palace in Saigon. This turned out to be too public, so I moved to the home of Lý Quý Chung [1940–2005], a colleague of Minh's and later his information minister. Chung was very well informed, and I could receive visitors at his house without attracting attention. The people surrounding Minh were busily working for a political solution, one that involved replacing Thiệu with Minh. They believed that this would make it possible to deal with the NLF. Minh was seen as a personality who would be acceptable to all sides in this war. Thanks to my "observation post" I was able to stay abreast of new political developments and act accordingly.

At this time I had frequent contact with a poor student named Huỳnh Bá Thành from an area near Đà Nẵng, who had started working at Điện Tín as a layout designer. He had come to Saigon to study at the National Administration Institute. He ended up working in publishing and became well-known for his political cartoons under the pen name Ớt [Hot Pepper]. His attacks on the regime of Thiệu could be very funny, and were full of cutting sarcasm. I always discussed political events with Huỳnh Bá Thành. After 1975 he was revealed to be an agent of A10, a branch of T4 [Special Zone] specializing in running a spy network to penetrate high-ranking government officials.

The war was picking up pace at the start of 1975, with the fall of Phước Long Province north of Saigon. This was followed by the sudden collapse of ARVN in the Central Highlands, beginning with the loss of Buôn Ma Thuột. At this point we did not know whether there had been a change of plans by Hanoi for the war in South Vietnam. Had the revolutionaries been given the green light for a general offensive and general uprising earlier than previous plans had foreseen? Until this time we had been receiving orders to consolidate the third segment for the implementation of a coalition government in line with the negotiations at the Paris peace talks.

It was only later that we learned some events that occurred were just a smokescreen for the coming final offensive. One event was the mass arrests on the eve of Tết New Year of 1974. Now we know that these had been a consequence of intentional leaks from NLF intelligence to deceive the Southern government. Then, in early 1975 and by the start of Tết, we heard that the idea of a coalition government was pure deception spread by the NLF.[3]

In the period after Tết 1975, while Thái still hid from the Southern authorities, both Thái and Minh positioned themselves for the battle of Saigon.

Designing Total Victory

In 1973, when delegates signed the Paris Peace Accords, Hanoi did not want to aggravate the situation. They ordered their military units to resort to armed force only if attacked, but told the various movements under their control that they should use every possible means to weaken the enemy. Confrontations did occur but in general Hanoi appeared on the surface to be implementing the Accords.

Still supported by the United States, President Thiệu refused to compromise with Hanoi. He insisted on his program of four nos expressed during the Paris talks: no abandonment of territory, no coalition, no negotiations and no communist or neutralist activities in South Vietnam. Taking advantage of Hanoi's passive approach, Thiệu ordered sweeping operations in the Mekong Delta and along the central coastal region. According to COSVN estimates, the amount of land under PRG control had reduced to no more than 20 percent of South Vietnam.

Moscow and Beijing also pressurized the North. There was bitterness in Hanoi at the Soviets, not only at their general attitude towards the Vietnamese revolutionaries but because the Soviets no longer supplied them with the quantity of weapons they needed, mainly as a result of U.S. pressure. Relations with China were particularly unpleasant. Beijing was irritated that Hanoi depended on the Soviets too much and that against their advice Hanoi planned to escalate military action in the South. On the other hand, Hanoi resented Beijing's decision not to provide adequate aid and support to the Vietnamese revolution, largely as a consequence of President Nixon's visit to China in 1972. Hanoi also felt threatened by China and feared that it might enter Vietnamese territory.

Regardless of hostile international politics, Hanoi went ahead and designed a

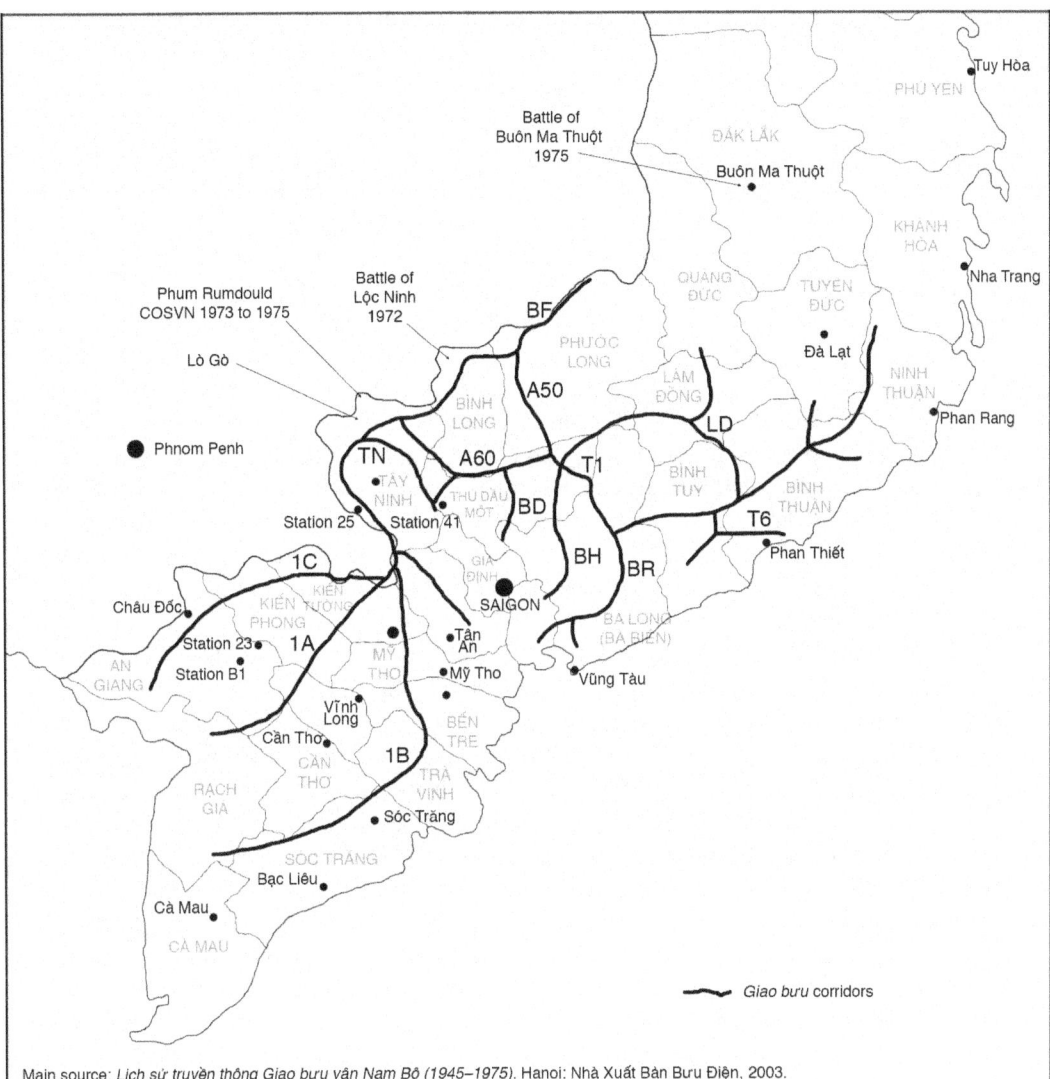

Main source: *Lịch sử truyền thông Giao bưu vận Nam Bộ (1945–1975)*. Hanoi: Nhà Xuất Bản Bưu Điện, 2003.

Examples of change:

After the Paris Peace Accords the *Giao Bưu* Department of COSVN moved to Lò Gò, near Thiện Ngôn Airport. To serve the cabinet of COSVN, the department established a new station at Phum Rumdould so that this station could facilitate any documents coming or going to the "T" zones and provinces; for security reasons Station B1 at Cần Đăng Hamlet received the documents first. Station 23 at Ba Chàm Hamlet and Station 25 in Nhum Jungle served corridors to T3 and T2 zones and areas of the T1 zone, which belonged to the southern area of Saigon. Station 41 at Tha La served T4 zone and areas of the T1 zone, which belonged to the sub-zones that served the eastern and north-eastern areas of Saigon.

At the end of 1973, COSVN's *Giao Bưu* Department (1) established a transportation group codenamed 571, their aim was to serve all the transportation needs of COSVN and coordinate with the Logistics Department and General Staff of COSVN as well as the 470th Group of the Hồ Chí Minh Trail; (2) established a *Giao Bưu* Department for the Provisional Revolutionary Government; (3) worked closely with T2 and T3 party committees to upgrade corridors 1A, 1B and 1C; and (4) developed bridgehead stations for accessing T1, T2, T3 and T4 zones and the sub-zones of the provinces of Tây Ninh and Bình Phước.

After the Battle of Buôn Ma Thuột in March 1975, the *giao bưu* troops were divided into two groups. The first were instructed to lead the push into areas occupied by the Army of the Republic of Vietnam in order to serve the Front Headquarters and complete combat liaison tasks. The second group were instructed to be in the rear base area to maintain the corridors and conduct postal and telecommunications work.

Giao bưu corridors from 1973 to 1974.

military plan to be ready for any strategic opportunity. In April 1973, they established a group called Central Team, which included Hoàng Văn Thái, Lê Trọng Tấn (1914–1986), Lê Hữu Đức (1925–?) and Võ Quang Hồ (1922–2016). They had to identify regions in the South, which if targeted, could be used to inflict a decisive blow on ARVN. The four men began by examining Vietnam's long history of fighting invaders to see what lessons could be learned. They came up with four areas: Saigon, Kon Tum, Plei Ku and Buôn Ma Thuột. With the support of Giáp and Hoàng Minh Thảo (1921–2008), they chose Buôn Ma Thuột to be the main region to attack. Unlike during the Easter Offensive, where the Central Highlands were targeted in the hope of taking Vietnam, these present analysts knew Buôn Ma Thuột had to be seized to start this process. Hoàng Minh Thảo was the commander of B3 Front (the Central Highlands Front).

In March and April 1974, Hanoi hosted two high level military conferences to review the battlefield situation and to discuss strategies to take the South. The conferences concluded that the VNPA had regained the initiative in the South for the first time since the failed 1972 Easter Offensive. Following on from these conferences, the General Staff in Hanoi completed a draft study in May titled, *Outline Study of a Plan to Win the War in the South*, which Giáp reviewed.

On 18 July 1974, Giáp held a meeting with Deputy Chief of General Staff Hoàng Văn Thái and issued him orders to prepare a campaign plan designed at securing total victory in the South by the end of 1976. Giáp told Hoàng Văn Thái that his overall theory was for a two-stage offensive: a major assault in the Central Highlands followed by a push south to take Saigon. A month later, the General Staff completed the requested document called, *Strategic Plan for 1975–76*, and presented it to Communist Party leaders for approval at a lengthy Politburo session in October 1974. The General Staff members summarized: to start there would be a limited probing offensive in COSVN's region to measure the enemy's strength, if weak, troops would conduct a major attack in March 1975 on Buôn Ma Thuột, followed by a push towards the coast to divide South Vietnam in two and then attacks in northern central Vietnam from August to October. The final battle would see an assault on Saigon in 1976.

The plan was cautious as Hanoi still had problems. Their rural guerrilla base and Revolutionary Infrastructure was still very weak in places, partly as a consequence of the failings during the Tết Offensive but also because of South Vietnam's F-6 Campaign, which had targeted the infrastructure since the Phoenix Program ended. Hanoi likewise feared that the United States would come back and that Red China would invade as it now occupied the Vietnamese Paracel Islands. Equally, although the Hồ Chí Minh Trail had been functioning efficiently since the end of U.S. bombing, the VNPA faced serious shortages of heavy weapons and ammunition.

Nevertheless, towards the end of 1974, Giáp could see that Hanoi's position had got stronger, so he re-addressed the *Strategic Plan for 1975–76*. He now believed that victory could be achieved in 1975 and called the new proposal the Spring Offensive. There were three main reasons why Giáp, and those he confided in, thought that victory could be achieved earlier, and that any battles would not mirror the failed 1972 Easter Offensive.

Primarily, the Communist Party leadership could see that the people had started to move against President Thiệu, partly because of the growing uncertainty in the South was causing mass migration into the cities from rural areas and increasing urban unemployment. In the second instance, Republican Gerald Ford had succeeded as U.S. president in August 1974 after President Nixon had resigned due to the Watergate scandal. That

The team at COSVN responsible for military proselytizing. The photograph is dated after the Paris talks of 1973 because all within the image are showing their faces and some are wearing North Vietnamese uniforms. Lê Hòa, standing second from left, had traveled with Nguyễn Trọng Tâm to Lai Châu when they were escorting African POWs before the Battle of Điện Biên Phủ (courtesy Phạm Hồng Cư).

November, the people voted in a Democrat-controlled Congress at the mid-term elections. Congress immediately imposed limits on funding and military activities in Vietnam, to be phased in through 1975 and culminating in a total cut-off in 1976. They had the authority to do this because in 1973, the *War Powers Resolution* had been approved, which checked the president's power to commit the United States to an armed conflict without the consent of Congress. That November, Congress used this document to limit Ford's ability to save the Thiệu regime.

Lastly, there would be no reworked plan. Giáp's conventional forces were ready for a symmetrical fight: units of the VNPA against units of ARVN. Giáp made it very clear to those he spoke to, who still drummed on about an August Revolution–like people's uprising, that the Spring Offensive did not incorporate any such event. Giáp stressed that the soldiers and officers who had been sent to liberate the South had always maintained that no such uprising was being contemplated in the minds of the population; economically they lived well due to U.S. aid as well as other factors. Giáp only felt confident that conventional action could now conclude the war because in late 1974 communist units had overrun the small ARVN outposts at Bù Đăng and Bù Na on Route 14, and in doing so they had seized a treasure trove of 7,000 rounds of artillery ammunition and four 105mm howitzers. Using these weapons they had conducted further probing

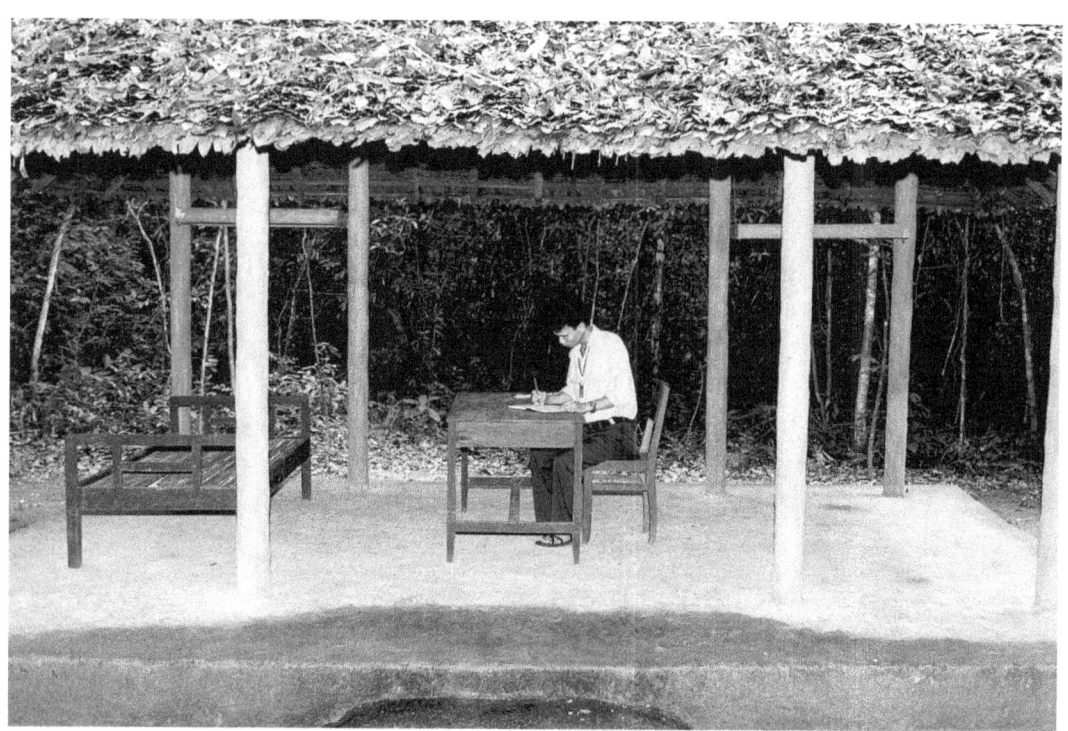

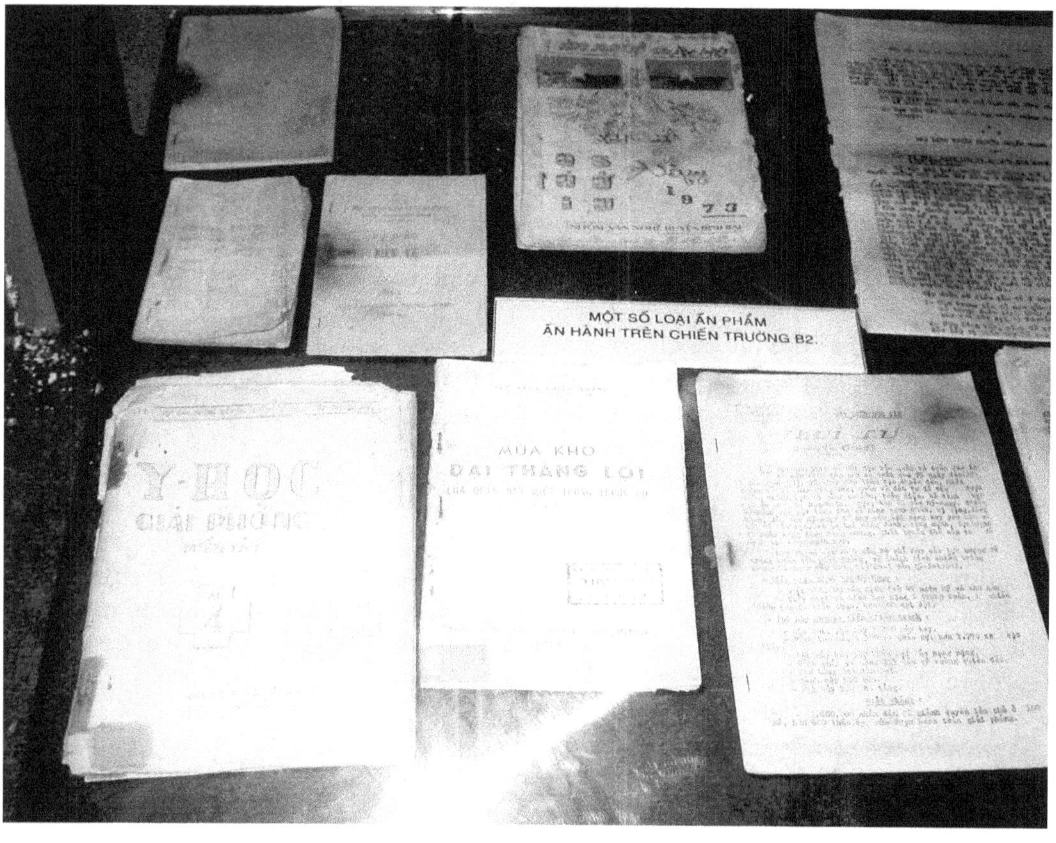
MỘT SỐ LOẠI ẤN PHẨM
ẤN HÀNH TRÊN CHIẾN TRƯỜNG B2.
MÙA KHÔ
ĐẠI THẮNG LỢI

military attacks to see how ARVN or indeed the Americans would react. Little came from either camp, so Giáp privately geared up for a 1975 victory.

A Story from the Battle of Huế

The Spring Offensive started on 13 December 1974. The main attacks executed to gauge when to push to Saigon included assaults on Buôn Ma Thuột (Central Highlands Campaign or Campaign 275) and the coastal towns (Huế-Đà Nẵng Campaign). In February, Giáp's military attacked the diversionary regions of Plei Ku and Kon Tum to pave the way for the Battle of Buôn Ma Thuột. This fierce battle started in early March and just days later this strategic region fell; Giáp had successfully cut off the lizard's tail. Hanoi, surprised by the speed of progress in the Central Highlands Campaign, ordered their units to focus on the coastal areas.

President Thiệu feared that without extensive U.S. money he needed to re-address what he could afford to do. With less money coming in, less territory could be controlled. Thiệu decided to abandon remote and hard to defend provinces, mostly in the north of South Vietnam. When he ordered the retreat, he declared this to be a "lighten the top and keep the bottom" strategy. As ARVN tried to disengage from the enemy, refugees and poor bridge and road conditions slowed the rush back south. On 20 March, President Thiệu instructed Huế to be held at all costs as the VNPA began an assault on the city.

Mrs. Nguyễn Quý Hoàng Nhung, whose mother had worked with Phan Nam, spoke of their experience during this time:

> The Southern regime had so many people under surveillance, from the Tết Offensive to the end of the war. This is why, although the Party begged me to work for them, I refused.
>
> In 1972, my younger brother Trung had been forced to enlist in ARVN when in his second year at college in Huế. This was part of the general mobilization order from President Thiệu, saying that all students must join the military to protect their country. This further complicated things. Senior Communist Party members said that they wanted a meeting with me to talk about Trung. They said that I should not let Trung join ARVN because our house was used for the revolution.
>
> I kept being approached by the Party and eventually the Southern regime's police arrested me. They took me to a temporary detention cell, where they kept me for ten days. On the table they placed many tools for torture. They asked me if I wanted to "fly a plane" or wanted electric shocks instead. They kept me in a large room, all alone, to send me mad. The other rooms were full of prisoners. They shoved disgusting undercooked rice meals through a small door. At 12 o'clock each night they interrogated me. They spoke of my brother Trung. They threatened to put him in prison. A soldier in ARVN could not have a VC family member. Trung was now fighting with the local armed forces near the 17th Parallel. In the end I went crazy and got so sick that they took me to hospital. I had a fever and my body swelled. We were both in a difficult situation. Trung wanted to fight for the revolution and once I was released, because they had no evidence against me, I was under surveillance all the time. Ms. Trâm had been arrested too and taken back to Thừa Phủ Prison. Eventually, after the Party kept approaching me, I agreed to help Phan Nam.
>
> In 1975, the fall of Huế was a frightening experience. You could work for the revolutionaries but the soldiers of the Liberation Army would not know this, and your handler might not be around to verify your story. Things became chaotic and unsafe for those working covertly, you now had to hope

Opposite, top: A 2007 mock-up of a courier station in the main part of COSVN's revolutionary base at Phum Rumdould, Tân Lap Commune, Tân Bien District, which is now a museum. *Bottom:* COSVN documents record various periods throughout the Vietnam War, which served B2 Front, displayed at the museum at Phum Rumdould (both photographs Clive A. Hills).

This monument commemorates the Battle of Buôn Ma Thuột, which took place here in 1975. This communist victory provoked the collapse of the South's defenses in the region, which in turn led to the fall of Saigon. 2003 photograph (Clive A. Hills).

that you would be exposed at the right time to the right person, otherwise you could be killed as a collaborator of the Southern government.

The revolutionaries had taken coastal towns and the people in Huế had fled to Saigon. Only my grandmother and I stayed at home. We waited and hoped Trung would come. One night, at about 12 o'clock, he came through the door with a local army officer friend. Trung said that their unit had been beaten near Huế. After seeing the Việt Cộng making progress, the Southern government ordered their military back to Saigon, hoping that this would allow ARVN to build a defensive line around the capital.

Trung had sent his unit to board a boat to Saigon, and although he and his friend had to get on the boat, they wanted to return to their homes instead. I was very anxious but happy to see Trung. It turned out that his friend wanted him to go to Đà Nẵng. Trung did not want to go, but he was afraid that if he did not, he could be shot by his friend for desertion. Yes, his friend had the right to shoot him. I decided that we had to go with him because there were rumors going around that those who stayed in Huế waited for the VC. I was so sad to leave my grandma.

We all jumped in the car. The streets were full of confused people. They clung to our vehicle. Across the sky you could hear the sound of exploding bombs. People lay dead or dying. We drove to the college. On our way we came across a group of paratroopers. They stopped us and pointed a gun at us. "Give us your vehicle," one said. Trung had two guns, one of which was his friend's and the other his. If they shot at us Trung would not have the time to get to the guns as they were draped around his shoulders. They demanded the car. Fortunately there was an armored vehicle behind us with soldiers in it. I shouted at them to help their fellow soldiers. Trung's friend was determined to keep the car, so he ordered Trung to open fire on the paratroopers. Trung got out and showed the soldiers in the armored vehicle his papers. These soldiers asked why he was not with his unit. I stepped in and said that I was ill and he was just taking me home. We walked back to the car and drove back home to our grandma, and his friend left for Đà Nẵng.

There was an uneasy feeling in Huế. I asked Trung to go out onto the street and see what was going on. Suddenly a jeep drove up and stopped at our house, revolutionary soldiers jumped out and pointed guns in our direction, and shouted, "Who lives here? We will come in and look." "Oh my God, Uncle Phúc," I said. We were so happy and hugged. My mother had adopted him as her child and he had become a VC agent. By chance Uncle Phúc and his group had come to our house. He said that we were so lucky. Somebody had reported that an ARVN soldier lived in the house. They had been authorized to shoot us. He asked about Trung's situation. When he knew that Trung was an ARVN army officer, but wanted to fight for liberation, he allowed him to join the revolutionary army. In late March Huế fell.[4]

With the coastal regions falling to the revolutionaries, this led to the complete destruction of ARVN's units in these areas and began the chain of events that would lead to a final assault on Saigon.

The Hồ Chí Minh Campaign

Giáp's southward military action had gone to plan, giving him the confidence to announce in a Politburo session on 18 March 1975 that their long awaited strategic opportunity had arrived to unite Vietnam. Up to this point only Giáp actually knew that his army was ready to take Saigon; most Party members still thought this could not happen until 1976.

To seize Saigon, he recommended that the VNPA immediately launch a nationwide general offensive against the city, to be called the Hồ Chí Minh Campaign.[5] Giáp ordered General Văn Tiến Dũng to prepare his units for a start date in April and see Saigon captured before May to avoid the coming monsoon. Dũng set up his new headquarters near to the city, which replaced COSVN.

Top: General Hồ Đệ, the commander of the 10th Division of the Central Highlands Front, on 6 May 2007. His division overran Đức Lập and in 1975 destroyed the 23rd Division of ARVN, which had been sent in to take Buôn Ma Thuột. He later became chief of staff for the 3rd Corps during the Hồ Chí Minh Campaign in 1975. *Bottom:* The identity card of Major Elliott, shown to the author by General Hồ Đệ. Elliott was captured by members of the 66th Regiment, 10th Division, when the regiment attacked Đắk Siêng Special Forces Camp in April 1970. General Hồ Đệ was commander of the regiment at the time. Major Elliott returned to America in the prisoner exchange agreement after the Paris Peace Accords (both photographs Clive A. Hills).

15. Total Victory

Sitting on the left, Vũ Anh talks with staff from the U.S. Embassy in Saigon after 1973, trying to establish if the United States would return to Vietnam if Saigon fell (courtesy Vũ Anh).

A final military death blow against Saigon could now be inflicted. In the first instance, Hanoi saw that the Americans had no intention of returning to save Saigon because from the beginning of 1975, NLF agents had intensified efforts to fish around among U.S. Embassy staff to obtain this information. On another point, Giáp needed the Hồ Chí Minh Trail completed. From his experience in fighting the French, he foresaw that victory could not be achieved until this had been done. It now had, thus concluding his logistics needs.

In Saigon, hopes that the situation could be stabilized rapidly disappeared. Any dream of a defensive line of ARVN troops to protect the lower part of South Vietnam quickly evaporated. On 21 April, an embittered President Thiệu resigned, declaring that the United States had betrayed South Vietnam. In a scathing attack, he suggested that Kissinger had tricked him into signing the Paris Peace Accords two years before; promising military aid that failed to materialize. Having transferred power to Trần Văn Hương (1902–1982), Thiệu left for Taiwan on 25 April. Huong resigned on 27 April. General Minh took over and ordered all U.S. personnel to be removed from South Vietnam within twenty-four hours to ease negotiations with the communists. On the morning of 29 April, the evacuation by helicopter of the last U.S. diplomatic, military and civilian personnel started.

Thái takes up the story:

> When the Liberation Army shelled Tân Sơn Nhất Airport at midnight on 29 April, I knew that the final battle had begun. In a concluding meeting with Huỳnh Bá Thành, he suggested, "We can save Saigon from bloodshed and devastation only by persuading and pushing the Southern administration to surrender in the spirit of concord and reconciliation!" No one, including me, knew at this point that Thành was an active NLF secret agent. I later learnt that at this time, in the final days of

fighting, Thành had met Minh himself and told him straight out that he was from the NLF. He asked Minh to take the initiative himself to declare a ceasefire.

Meanwhile, at the end of April our militant student group, including young anti-war officers and soldiers, secretly settled in at the Vạn Hạnh Buddhist University, Saigon, which was on a main road leading out towards the airport. We decided to turn it into a stronghold, where we could stock small arms, as well as clothing and paint for slogans. We foresaw a drawn-out fight for Saigon and knew that we must immediately set up a reconciliation committee, transforming pagodas into refugee centers. I had learned that a lot of armed bandits, supporters of the Southern administration, had vowed to stand and fight. At the same time, we knew that the Liberation Army would be eager to end the war at any cost, even the destruction of Saigon. We all thought that the fighting would last a relatively long time, at least until the official birthday of President Hồ Chí Minh on 19 May.

Early on the morning of 30 April, I rode my Honda motorcycle to the Ấn Quang Pagoda, headquarters of the Unified Buddhist Church, to meet Thích Trí Quang. I still kept up good relations with him, despite the fact that he knew for sure what side I was on. I asked him, "The situation is pressing, how can you persuade Minh's people to end this war, to avoid useless bloodshed and devastation in Saigon? The liaison networks with the other side have all been disrupted, we can't propose any new negotiating proposals to them now." He seemed to understand the situation and went immediately to the phone. I heard some exchanges of conversation, then he hurried back and said, "You can be assured. I could not reach General Minh himself. But I have spoken to Prof. Vũ Văn Mẫu, his new prime minister. Perhaps they will act in that direction."

I returned to Vạn Hạnh Buddhist University and settled down with my friends to discuss a plan of action. At 9 a.m., Minh declared on the Saigon radio, "Our policy is for national concord and reconciliation, to save our compatriots lives. I believe deeply in the reconciliation between Vietnamese to save Vietnamese blood. For this reason, I request all our brother ARVN combatants to stay calm. Do not fire and stay in place where you are. We also request our brother combatants, of the PRG, to stop fighting. We are here, waiting for the PRG to meet us to discuss a ceremony to transfer power so as to avoid the useless bloodshed of our compatriots."

I suddenly saw a unit of ARVN Rangers at the gate of the university, led by a lieutenant colonel who was planning to establish a resistance post in the university compound. I rushed out to talk with the colonel, and informed him of Minh's recent declaration. Other students talked to the officers and soldiers, to persuade them to lay down their arms. They finally agreed to disband, leaving behind a lot of weapons.

I told the student group that the most pressing objective was to take the broadcasting station. Our priority had to be to announce the revolution's policy of reconciliation, to avoid any more useless and bloody clashes. Since there was a whole armed police company stationed in the radio and television compound, we divided our group into two teams. The ones armed with small arms got into a van heading for the nearby agriculture school, from where they could prepare to occupy the radio station. I led the journalist Cung Văn and Prof. Huỳnh Văn Tòng toward the Presidential Palace, where we hoped to persuade Minh's government to transfer power smoothly.

I had known Huỳnh Văn Tòng since his return from France some years earlier, with his leftist stand on the war. His situation was similar to that of Châu Tâm Luân insofar that he was disillusioned with the Southern government. Tòng was an intellectual working actively in the National Concord and Reconciliation Movement and opposition press. He had graduated in history and taught media courses at various Saigon and regional universities. He was very popular among students, who were attracted by his flamboyant, progressive courses and his very critical and persuasive articles in the Saigon papers. Cung Văn was the pen name of journalist Nguyễn Vạn Hồng, who worked in the Vietnam Press Office. He had developed a reputation, thanks to his humorous political verses, as a critic of the Southern government. He came across as a reckless playboy and was involved with all kinds of people, even with strongly anti-communist ones, but this image was probably a cover for his real work as an NLF agent.

We rushed to Cung Văn's blue Renault 8 sedan to head for the Presidential Palace. As a journalist, he had a special safe conduct pass, which would make things easier for us. We entered by the left side gate on Nguyễn Du Street. Everything seemed quiet and we went straight to the palace steps. We ran into a British television crew, who saw our armbands with blue and red colors. Guessing that we were NLF members, they tried to interview us. I did not reveal much as I was focused on the search for Lý

15. Total Victory

Clive A. Hills and the author standing in the grounds of the former Presidential Palace next to one of two tanks used to break through the gates of the palace by the Liberation Army on 30 April 1975. Photograph taken 2003 (Clive A. Hills).

Quý Chung, the new information minister. When we found Chung, he agreed to take us to the Saigon radio station. Not one driver dared to venture out in an official car at that moment, however.

We were debating alternatives as to how we would go to the radio station, when suddenly our attention was caught by what was happening on Thống Nhất Boulevard. It was a great sight: a tank column was advancing rapidly on the Presidential Palace. All of a sudden, the palace gates were smashed and the tanks ploughed across the carpet of grass surrounding the palace. They stopped at the palace steps. A Northern soldier, later identified as Bùi Quang Thận, detached the antenna of the lead tank, which flew a tiny triangular NLF flag of red and blue, dirtied with dust and battle smoke, and dashed to the palace.[6]

I was standing at the entry porch to the palace as the tanks lined up in battle formation. Perhaps Bùi Quang Thận had noticed that I was wearing the red and blue armband of the popular uprising force of the NLF, since he followed me when I offered to lead him. I actually did not know the palace layout or which elevator to take to reach the roof. A man in civilian clothes passed us, maybe one of the high-ranking officers of the Palace Guard. I asked him to take us up to the top floor. I helped Thận fold the tank aerial that had the flag on it, to fit it into the smaller secondary elevator located in the aisle of the entrance hall, as Bùi Quang Thận did not allow us to carry it up to the roof. When we got up on the roof, we had to climb a wooden ladder to reach the flagpole. We pulled down the Southern regime's flag, a huge one attached with hard polyester wire. It took us some minutes to get it down and raise the tiny NLF flag, amidst shouts of joy and bursts of machine gun fire.

Was it just a quirk of fate that at this historical moment at the top of this building, where the French governor's palace had once stood, there were three young men from three parts of Vietnam: Bùi Quang Thận from the Red River Delta, Prof. Huỳnh Văn Tòng from the South Vietnamese province of Tây Ninh, and myself, from Đà Nẵng, a seaport city of central Vietnam? This historic moment marked the end of 117 years of colonial and imperialist domination, and opened the way to a new period of independence and reunification for Vietnam. We could not hold back our tears of joy and pride. At this moment, it was certain that all of Saigon had been liberated, peace re-established, and our people would be unified in one country. No force could ever divide it again.[7]

Total Victory

From the roof of the Presidential Palace, Thái looked down at a Saigon in utter chaos. Terrified people ran through the streets looking for answers. The city had been their last bastion; now the communists had arrived.

Thái continued:

I can't remember how I got down to the front lawn of the palace. Our main task of securing the Saigon radio station had not yet been accomplished. I knew that I had to get there right away. The first high-ranking NLF officer to reach the Presidential Palace was the tank group's political commissar, Bùi Văn Tùng. As he later recalled these events, he decided to bring Minh to the radio station to declare the surrender. That would be the most effective way of shortening the fighting. He was conscious of the dangers, but there was no other choice. I got into his jeep with a few journalists, among them the West German correspondent Borries Von Gallasch [ZDF German Television] and the freelancer Hà Huy Đình, to escort President Minh, his Prime Minister Vũ Văn Mẫu and Information Minister Lý Quý Chung to the radio station.

Our students and NLF fighters had already occupied the radio station but could not get the equipment to work. Moreover, no one knew what to say on the first broadcast. The German journalist lent us a cassette to record Minh's declaration of surrender, and its acceptance by Political Commissar Bùi Văn Tùng.

Perhaps Minh recognized me among the crowd and became more relaxed. He seemed tired and did not show any signs of joy. His body was as imposing as ever, but his face was haunted. He was forced to sacrifice his general's honor to save the city from devastation. Later, I learned that he and his staff had already decided to surrender, in spite of possible maltreatment by the other side. It was a valiant act by a Buddhist in his last moment of power. He may never have been successful in politics, but his character was a personality that was needed in difficult situations. In 1963, there was no one except him who had the credibility to gather competing generals and lead the military coup to topple President Diệm. At this time, the Southern administration had no other personality who had the respect needed to end the war smoothly. At least he was able to keep Saigon intact and spare the rest of South Vietnam from useless bloodshed and destruction, in what everyone knew was the final act of the war.

I took a glance at Prof. Vũ Văn Mẫu, who was unobtrusive in his teacher's suit. While studying at the law faculty, I had admired his way of teaching the history of legal institutions, which was clear and eloquent but also humorous. He was descended from North Vietnamese mandarins, had emigrated in 1954 to the South, and served as foreign minister under the Diệm regime. In 1963, he had challenged the Diệm regime by shaving his head in protest against the repression of Buddhists, and he had resigned from his post. I realized that when he had accepted the job of prime minister, it would have been in the hope of bringing about peace, national concord and reconciliation.

My friend, Lý Quý Chung, was considered to be a playboy by many people, but was very conscious of our national history. Originally a supporter of the independent Cochinchina spirit in line with the thinking of the conservative Trần Văn Hương, he soon joined the opposition and became a promoter of national reconciliation. I did not think he was pro–French. However, in the Southern government's last moments, the French possibly considered Minh's group to be the best hope to conclude the war, favoring a neutral South Vietnam. To me, Minh and others, including the French, were supporting an aspect of the PRG's policy until the very end of this war. This had called for the establishment of a neutral government, in line with the Paris Peace Accords. This government would then negotiate with the Northern government for unification. But by the end of April 1975 this policy had clearly been overtaken by events.

The attorney, Nguyễn Văn Huyền [1911–1995], was a member of Minh's inner circle. He had been made deputy president. He was a politician from the southern moderate Catholics, representing the Catholic Church alongside the Buddhists Minh and Vũ Văn Mẫu.

15. Total Victory

Our student group had played a key role at that historic moment. We had led the Liberation Army to the Saigon broadcasting station and helped at the Presidential Palace. At the radio station, we had hurriedly found a replacement battery for the cassette player, as well as technicians to start the broadcast. Political Commissar Bùi Văn Tùng himself acknowledged it, "If we had not had the help of the students who found a battery, and the broadcast technicians who aired General Minh's surrender speech, we cannot say for sure what would have happened." We had found the broadcast technician Trần Văn Bảng living in the vicinity. He had then called other experts to help him get the station working.

I witnessed a short argument between General Minh and Political Commissar Tùng about the contents of the surrender speech. Minh did not want to use the word "president" and preferred the more intimate word "general." However, Bùi Văn Tùng firmly rejected it. He thought that since Minh was the last president of the South, he needed to make his declaration in that capacity. That way the NLF would have jurisdiction over both civilian and military personnel. Many attempts were required before they got the declaration of surrender right, but Prime Minister Vũ Văn Mẫu was able to speak live when he made his announcements.

Toiling until 2 p.m., Saigon time [which was at that time one hour later than today], we finally got the first statements from the revolution on the air. This was my original opening speech, "We are representatives of the Saigon-Chợ Lớn-Gia Định Revolutionary Popular Committee. We have been the first people present at the Presidential Palace before noon today, and helped the liberation combatants plant the NLF flag on it. We are Prof. Huỳnh Văn Tòng, and Thái, the former president of the Saigon Student Union. Normal life has recovered. Saigon, the new Hồ Chí Minh City, the city beloved by Uncle Hồ, is now liberated. We would like to present the declaration of Messrs Dương Văn Minh and Vũ Văn Mẫu on the surrender of this city."

General Minh's speech followed, "I, Dương Văn Minh, president of the Southern government, call on the Armed Forces of the Republic of Vietnam to lay down their arms and to surrender without condition to the Liberation Army. I declare that the Southern government, from the central to regional levels, must be dissolved completely. All central and regional authorities must hand over to the PRG of South Vietnam."

Then Political Commissar Bùi Văn Tùng spoke, "Representing the Liberation Army, we solemnly declare that the city of Saigon is completely liberated. We accept the unconditional surrender of Mr. Dương Văn Minh, the Southern government's president."

Finally, the voice of Vũ Văn Mẫu was heard, "In the spirit of concord and reconciliation, I, Prof. Vũ Văn Mẫu, prime minister, call on all compatriots to hail in joy this national day of peace, and to return to normal activity. All administrative officials must return to their own offices under the guidance of the Revolutionary Government."

I then continued to relate the story, "The Liberation Army has entered the Presidential Palace and occupied all military and civilian bases of the Saigon-Chợ Lớn-Gia Định area…" These speeches were greeted with tears of joy in many different areas. People had longed for an end to the fighting for so many years!

The Liberation Army escorted Minh and his colleagues back to the Presidential Palace. I took charge of the continuing broadcast. I borrowed a copy of the revolutionary policy for newly liberated areas from a Liberation Army officer and read it on the air. I intentionally mentioned our names, Huỳnh Văn Tòng's and my own, to reassure the people of Saigon.

At that time the South Vietnamese had been panicked by American and Saigon black propaganda, which circulated false rumors about bloodshed and mistreatment of the population in the provinces of central Vietnam, which had been liberated earlier. The people of Saigon were really terrified, and had been rushing to find ways to escape at any cost! We hoped that if they heard our names on the air, they would be reassured, "Ah, if petty bourgeois intellectuals like Tòng and Thái are involved, then things may be all right!" I later learned that some people already on the high seas had returned when they heard the broadcast. When later they were sent to re-education camps, they most certainly blamed us for deceiving them![8]

When Hồ had died in 1969, it left some to question, "Now that Uncle is dead, how can we beat the enemy?" Remarkably, the communists had completed their Southward March, started back in the 1940s by Giáp. Hồ's mastery, even from the grave, had secured total victory.

The Third Victim of Hồ's Blueprint

The Minh regime had become the third victim of Hồ's blueprint, again for much of the same reasons the French and the Americans had, but this time victory had led to a geographically united country. Did Minh have a choice, could he have carried on with the fight? He had to weight up many factors. On a human level, he did not want to continue the misery and bloodshed, a swift end remained his preferred goal. Equally, covert communist members of the third segment had put pressure on him to end the fighting. Minh later confirmed that their persistence had influenced how he viewed his ability to get support in opposing the advances from the VNPA. Nevertheless, an overwhelming factor was Minh knew that, long before any tanks rolled through the gates of the Presidential Palace, the communists not only controlled the people of the South but ran much of his government and army.

Looking at those who had worked against the ruling Southern regime, pro-revolutionaries included Prime Minister Vũ Văn Mẫu, Deputy President Nguyễn Văn Huyền and Information Minister Lý Quý Chung. Those who held Communist Party membership comprised Nguyễn Văn Diệp, the minister for trade and the economy and for

This photograph was taken on 30 April 1975. The three men in the front are, from left, President Dương Văn Minh, Information Minister Lý Quý Chung and Prime Minister Vũ Văn Mẫu. All three men of the Southern regime were in fact pro-revolutionaries (courtesy Nguyễn Hữu Thái).

many years part of the Revolutionary Infrastructure, Brigadier General Nguyễn Hữu Hạnh (1926–?) and Triệu Quốc Mạnh. The latter two men had been secret agents for some fifteen years before they took up strategic posts just before the fall of Saigon.

Minh had appointed Nguyễn Hữu Hạnh as assistant to Chief of Staff Nguyễn Phước Vĩnh Lộc (1923–2009), with orders to lead ARVN if anything happened to Vĩnh Lộc. As the communists circled Saigon, Vĩnh Lộc went off to inspect areas of unease, but he appeared preoccupied and seemed more concerned with the evacuation of his family than his job. It is now known that he had already handed power over to Hạnh, who had immediately contacted ARVN field commanders to agree battlefield conditions that secretly favored the VNPA. As one example, he instructed ARVN soldiers not to destroy bridges (to make it easier for the communist troops to move on Saigon). Ultimately, Hạnh ordered ARVN to lay down their arms.

Whereas Hạnh was military, on 28 April President Minh made Triệu Quốc Mạnh the police chief of Saigon-Gia Định, with the instructions to negotiate favorable conditions with revolutionary leaders. Instead of following Minh's orders, Mạnh persuaded him to dissolve the brutal city police force and by doing so Minh authorized the release of hundreds of political prisoners, some of whom then rejoined the revolution.[9]

What gave the communists a big advantage was that Minh himself, although not pro-communist, was pro-revolution. Hanoi had started proselytizing him back in the early 1960s through his brother, Dương Thành Nhật. Now, just prior to the fall of Saigon, his brother, along with NLF members, visited him again to emphasize why he should not oppose the advances of the revolutionaries. Minh had tried to negotiate, influenced to do so by French Intelligence and the Chinese, but his conscience told him that it had to end. Minh's regime was destined to become Hồ's third victim.

War Concludes for Some

The war is officially recorded as ending on 30 April 1975, but not everyone enjoyed liberation on that day. Nguyễn Xuân Tốn (1920–?) and Lê Quang Vịnh (1936–?) were two prisoners sent to Côn Đảo Island and held in tiger cages. Their stories highlight why so many people had mental health problems long after the fighting and any physical restraints had gone.

Tốn had been a high-ranking Communist Party leader when arrested in 1957, during Diệm's Denounce the Communists campaign. To understand the gravity of his prison sentence duration, the U.S. public saw a string of presidents—Eisenhower, Kennedy, Johnson, Nixon and Ford—while he was incarcerated.

Tốn described prison:

> When the International Red Cross visited the tiger cages in 1970, the enemy did not allow them to see them at first. The enemy told them that these were only for normal prisoners, not political ones. The commander of the island had to ask the police department in Saigon for authorization. When the people of the Red Cross finally entered our room, they fled. The smell was so strong. They requested fans to blow the smell away. Once inside, they asked us many questions. We refused to answer how they wanted. One question they asked, "In a place that is one meter in width and two meters in length, with six of you and all your sanitary waste inside, how do you cope?" As it was still the war we could not say anything but "We love our country, we love liberty and we are eager to sacrifice. That is why we can stand this, we will not surrender." The Red Cross people knew that every day we were manacled, even at night they handcuffed our hands and legs as we lay down. The enemy only

released the manacles when we ate. The Red Cross people said, "Although your answer is acceptable, it is not scientific. However, if your survival was based purely on science you would probably not be able to survive this horror."

We could not tell them about our secret agents inside enemy ranks. For instance, at night our agents used to stand on top of the iron net that covered the cage and drop vitamin C tablets to us. By breaking this tablet into four we could make it last that many days. We also pierced a hole in the wall, so that the people who worked in the kitchen could give us dry rice with sugar on through it. We then stored these supplies by concealing them in the lime brick wall. When someone was sick we used the food to keep them alive. Likewise, when the enemy did not give us drinking water we used our water-soaked towels to drink from. This was possible because the guards used a bucket of water to flush the toilet. Those sympathetic to us kept some water in the bucket and allowed us to drop our towels in it to soak up the water unnoticed. In extreme cases, when we did not receive any supplies, we had to drink each other's urine.

We also had other means of survival. The enemy did not let us have trousers, shirts or tops, only shorts. We tore the shorts we had so that we could place the cloth over our chests at night to keep the cold out and during the day we used it to hold our rice or as a fan to cool ourselves. When very hot we used the cloth to rub all the grime off our bodies, we called this a sauna. We had to do that because they did not allow us a shower. Thanks to our agents and to our will, we could survive. We could not tell this to the International Red Cross, but this was our life in a tiger cage.

One small bit of happiness was that we used poems, like Lê Quang Vịnh's. He used a brick to write the sentences on the floor. Our group then discussed each line until it formed a poem, this is what kept our hopes alive. We would tell ourselves victory is at hand, if we did not we would have gone mad waiting. All the time we would say, "Our victory is near." In 1960 we said, "Our victory is near." In 1972 we said, "Our victory is near." I was freed in April 1975![10]

The second man, Lê Quang Vịnh, joined the revolution for many reasons, but he remembers vividly the moment a French soldier shot his lawyer father dead. Vịnh and his elder sister were full of hate and anger, and they swore to revenge their father's death. Both joined the revolution. Within seven months, at just fourteen years old, the enemy arrested Vịnh; on release, he again operated for the Việt Minh. Once the French left, Vịnh and his sister resisted the Americans. In 1955, he was again captured and on release he left Huế and moved to operate in Saigon. He studied for a bachelor's degree in mathematics for five years and during this time he directed a student cell covertly; he then graduated and became a teacher. Vịnh had just started a career as a teacher when he was captured in 1961; he had been attending a Party conference that the enemy overran.

Vịnh explained:

In 1961, the enemy arrested me but this time they sentenced me to death. During these days the Southern regime used the guillotine, but I escaped execution because an American officer had been arrested by the Liberation Army; a lieutenant colonel. The Liberation Army announced on the radio that if the Southern regime used the guillotine on us, they would shoot the American officer. The enemy transferred me to Côn Đảo Island and took me off death row, but put me in a camp for prisoners who had been handed down a death sentence.

After four years they changed my sentence to penal servitude for life. My life became even more intolerable because the Southern regime had guidelines to kill political prisoners little by little, their minds, their hopes.... They forced us to shout out, "Down with communist Hồ Chí Minh." If we didn't, they beat us. To force us to shout this, they used pistols to beat our knees, which then swelled; if we didn't shout out, they continued to beat us. If someone fell unconscious, they stopped, then brought them back to the cell, only to continue after a few days. After this hell they put me into solitary confinement where I sat in a cave or cell for eight years. To communicate with the outside world I used secret codes such as Morse code.

The first full day of liberation for Vietnam was 1 May 1975. I was almost dead, with my stomach bleeding and my legs paralyzed. On the night of 30 April 1975, prisoners rose up, and those who could, came and helped those who could not move. My friend came to help me. I heard the sound of him beating on the door, "Is Vịnh inside?" I replied, "Vịnh is here but in manacles." He released me from the manacles, which were being secured by a pole outside my cell. The door flung open. My friend jumped in and shouted, "Vịnh, liberation, liberation." I tried real hard to stand up but I kept falling over at the threshold of the door because my legs were paralyzed.

I was unconscious. When I recovered consciousness, I cried. Then a captain in the Southern regime, who worked covertly for the revolutionaries, came and saluted me and said, "On behalf of the Liberation Committee, I invite you out of this place." People guided me with their hands to the Liberation Committee room where the chairman of the island used to reside. I sat down with tears streaming down my face. I had composed a song, "Great Liberty." I remember singing it so proudly because finally I was a free man. I had dreamt of this day, of freedom. One of my dreams was to taste a bowl of fresh hot noodle soup-*phở*. I had just spent fourteen years in hell and I couldn't even eat this. Those who did so died as their bodies could not take it.[11]

	1	2	3	4	5
I	a	b	c	d	d
II	e	f	g	h	i
III	j	k	l	m	n
IV	o	p	q	r	s
V	t	u	v	x	y

A secret code sheet that inmates used to communicate while at Côn Đảo Island Prison. Words were formed by using different knocking techniques. For instance a knock with a stone and a tap by a hand would be "a," two knocks with a stone and a tap by a hand would be "b." It could take months to agree among prisoners any coordinated disorder in the camp (courtesy Lê Quang Vịnh).

Not all fighting across former French Indochina stopped when Saigon fell. Lao was taken by the communist Pathet Lao later in 1975. Although the Khmer Rouge had seized Cambodia a few days before Saigon fell, they went on to invade the southern provinces of Vietnam in 1978, with the VNPA having to push them back to Phnom Penh in 1979.

The biggest problem was China. Before Saigon fell, the Communist Party had instructed that when the strategic opportunity appeared, all communist forces must launch an all-out offensive aimed at securing total victory in the shortest possible time. They needed a swift victory so that countries inclined towards intervention, such as China or the United States, had insufficient time to react. Hanoi took the threat from China much more seriously than a new U.S. presence. In 1974, China had taken a small group of islands in the South China Sea known as the Paracel Islands, which were historically part of Vietnam. Later, unmarked Chinese warships threatened the Spratly Islands, again historically connected to Vietnam. To save the Spratly Islands from a possible Chinese takeover, in April 1975, the Vietnamese communists snatched them back from the Southern troops. Then, just prior to the fall of Saigon, intelligence reports had indicated that Chinese forces were near the northern Vietnamese border; China finally invaded parts of Vietnam in 1979.

The longest fight for the new owners of Vietnam was with the United Front for the Liberation of Oppressed Races (FULRO). Their objective was autonomy for the Montagnards and hostilities continued until 1992. Although unrest did persist throughout the region, overcoming barriers preventing nation building their way became a Party priority.

The liberation song Lê Quang Vịnh wrote while in prison (Clive A. Hills).

Hồ's Women Couriers: A Legacy

With the fall of Saigon the couriers unofficially disbanded, but what happened to Hồ's most important element for victory? To reduce the risk of alienating areas of society, the government did put policy measures in place to ease the couriers back into normal life. They sent the youth to schools to study either at home or overseas in Eastern Bloc countries and paid known former southern couriers higher wages than if they had worked in the North during the war. This inflated pay aided their transition from a comfortable lifestyle supported by the Americans to the lower conditions that now existed. This nurturing did assist a few couriers to reach high positions, such as former Deputy President Ms. Trương Mỹ Hoa.

Generally though in this new society, former couriers faced a bleak future. By the very nature of their work, many of the women relied on jobs within the structure of the former Southern regime, so they had limited success when applying for military or civilian careers. This left them vulnerable to the mass unemployment sweeping the country. Having been unpaid as couriers and now jobless they had limited resources to buy land to sustain themselves by growing food. A few had been compensated with fields during the Land Reform Program but the majority were not. On top of these financial woes, although Hanoi paid pensions to their known regular armed forces, they did not pay couriers; there were too many to compensate and most could not be verified as couriers because their handlers had died or vanished.

On a feminine level, things became personal. With no partner and sometimes ill or

15. *Total Victory* 341

Top: A monument to those who died serving in the Trường Sơn Army (the Hồ Chí Minh Trail), taken at their cemetery near Route 9. *Bottom:* These are the graves of Chinese revolutionaries who lost their lives in support of the Vietnamese revolution, located on the outskirts of COSVN's revolutionary base at Phum Rumdould (both photographs Clive A. Hills).

aged, numerous women had no children. Those who had left their offspring to be cared for by others, whilst they carried out their work, on return found them difficult to track down, and many a mother and child were sadly never reunited. This childless status marked them as outcasts in a conservative, family orientated society, especially in the countryside where villagers relied on their youth to care for them in sickness or old age.

For the couriers, their harsh wartime experiences continued into their post-war lives. Nevertheless, the freedom the conflict had given them now allowed them to throw off some of the shackles of an oppressive Confucian feudal society. The couriers interviewed for this book did not dwell on that achievement; they were just content to be alive and had joined the revolution to liberate their country, not themselves. They graciously handed over the small growth of women's liberation to the next generation; another part of Hồ's legacy.

The Last Divide

To build a stable socialist nation, the Communist Party had to re-educate the population to unite behind the principles of the new government. This process led to great upset, fear and paranoia within society. Two main problems arose: who to select for socialist training and where should they be sent? Wrong-doers could have been branded disloyal to the new regime, displayed a tendency to be too capitalist or become too economically reliant on handouts. Once processed, they then could be incarcerated, sent to a re-education camp or directed to toil in the harsh environment of a New Economic Area.[12]

The fear of being sent for socialist training fueled a rise in people leaving Vietnam. This problem was a highly sensitive and contentious issue within the Party, not only because they needed to know how to control Vietnamese abroad but also how to stop people leaving in the first place. On the former point, when the tens of thousands of boat people left, Hanoi had to prevent the rise of any overseas opposition movements or simply stop people airing vocal protests aimed at prizing Vietnam from Party control. To do this, Hanoi sent agents abroad to control those who had left. To stop people leaving in the first place, moderates within the regime wanted the concept of re-education addressed. They believed that those who had worked for the Southern regime should be persuaded rather than forced to think as the revolutionaries. In this way, the brain drain from Vietnam could be slowed.

Thái explained:

We hated both the war and the thought of a Stalinist or Maoist style of communism. We opposed the widespread murder of innocent people by the U.S. military, and despised the corrupt and undemocratic pro–American regimes. But we also hated the very idea of Stalin's communism—a one-party state, lack of a free press and free speech, and all the rest. We knew full well how we would be treated under a communist regime. Feeling loyalty toward America, and not knowing any actual Việt Cộng or North Vietnamese ourselves, we were deeply torn—who should we follow?

In the aftermath of the war, until 1979, I became part of the Communist Youth League. My duties included implementing successive campaigns for socialist transformation to build a new society, erase the corrupt culture of the past, oppose capitalists who had profited from the war and mobilize the masses for reconstruction. Urban youth was again in the vanguard of the social revolution in the newly liberated South.

Throughout the 1980s, isolation and encirclement put a heavy toll on post-war Vietnam, including a siege mentality fostered by the Hanoi leadership, and the tragedies of re-education camps, starvation and the exodus of the boat people. The country's tragedy paralleled that of my divided family, typical of thousands of other urban middle-class households. I was disillusioned with agrarian socialism and shared the sorry fate of many urban NLF fighters from the South. "To go or stay?" was the question on everyone's mind at the time. The new authorities distrusted me and scrutinized my past activities. I often felt disoriented and discouraged. Finally, I had to decide: to go or to stay? I chose to emigrate to Canada in 1990. Five years later, I returned home to the homeland to work. Whether at home or abroad, I remained a patriot working for the well-being of my people.[13]

Yet what of those people whose loyalty should have been unquestionable? It is now known that the new government's security apparatus did hunt down and imprison people who had at one time worked covertly, such as within the infrastructure, been an intelligence agent or a military proselytizing operative. Phạm Xuân Ẩn was one such agent who had seen many couriers die protecting his cover and so professional that not even his own wife knew of his other life. He had been a reporter for Reuters, *Time* magazine and the *New York Herald Tribune* but had simultaneously spied for the revolutionaries. Giáp even went as far as to say on receiving intelligence from him, "We are now in the United States war rooms!"[14] It had been Phạm Xuân Ẩn who had secured the intelligence on the Battle of Lam Sơn 719 in 1971, a South Vietnamese–led operation to cut the Hồ Chí Minh Trail; they failed thanks to him. Nevertheless, the Party sent him for re-education. They accused him of having a relationship with the CIA and being too capitalist because he had worked so closely with the Americans.

Nguyễn Trọng Tâm, one of the Reverse Regrouping Men, became another victim of Hanoi's rules and ended up in political training and suffering years of incarceration. He believes that a spy left by the Americans had plotted against him. Nevertheless, few came to his rescue, he simply knew too much; who had double-crossed the revolutionaries and who had talked under torture in Tân Hiệp Prison. Now these traitors held high positions in government and when Tâm's name came up for review, they happily sent him away to silence him to keep out of jail themselves.

Others under suspicion by members of the Party or who were envied and needed to be removed when appropriate included Giáp, Lê Trọng Nghĩa, Đào Văn Trường, Vũ Anh, Lê Quang Vịnh and even one of the first communist children and couriers of Uncle Hồ, Ms. Đức.[15] It seemed in the Socialist Republic of Vietnam, no one was immune to accusations, opening a new division between the people.

Welcoming a New Dawn

Probably the most important question that needs answering is, was this all about the spread of communism? The answer to this depends on who you are talking about. The Party implemented communism across Vietnam after Saigon fell but high-ranking members had been split on the future of the country. Even Party members who had expressed moderate views were in different camps; some wanted to see socialist change but on Vietnamese terms only and not those of world revolution, and others argued that, while long-term plans were being finalized, instead of dismantling capitalism straight away why not use the wealth of the South to rebuild the North.

The moderate Party members were at loggerheads with Lê Duẩn's group, who saw the Vietnamese revolution as a class struggle for socialist change leading to world revolution, or in Western terms, the spread of communism.[16] With Lê Duẩn holding the power, he ruthlessly spread communism across the country and dismantled capitalism in the South. On top of this debacle, because he had set no clear role for the intelligentsia, he left the economy to be run by inexperienced people and his entire government apparatus became bogged down in bureaucratic and corrupt management. If a moderate had been in control then things might have been very different.

Notwithstanding splits in local Party thinking, changing Vietnam into a socialist state on its own terms in 1975 was made much harder due to pressure from the USSR and China. For instance, for Vietnam to get aid from the USSR, Hanoi had to declare their loyalty to Moscow. When Hanoi did this, although they got aid, in return Vietnam unwittingly became a Soviet outpost to stop Chinese expansionism. In contrast to the USSR, China reduced aid to Vietnam. Instead, China formed greater ties with the United States and its allies, leading some Chinese officials to admit that this alliance was a treacherous thrust into the back of its long-time friend, Vietnam. The frosty relationship between China and Vietnam not only arose because Vietnam had declared loyalty to the USSR, but because China had wanted it to continue fighting the United States for 100 years; this clearly had not materialized. Without the Party having the capabilities to adopt a neutral policy towards the Soviets and China, this left Vietnam wedged between two super-states.

Although Vietnam still has to deal with international personalities, today, with a progressive new government in control, the Socialist Republic of Vietnam has become one of Asia's emerging economies. It is a wonderful tourist destination that is starting to redefine Vietnam in Western minds as a place of rich culture rather than of war. Yet the personal wounds of the wars across Indochina will require further generations to heal. Families and fellow citizens have to come to terms with the horrors of the fighting but moreover the sense of betrayal by some of those around them. The people of Vietnam will recover from these tensions and divisions, not only because of the passing away of the wartime generation, but more importantly with the emergence of a forgiving youth.

Epilogue: Eyes Wide Open

Vital Elements to the Blueprint

The author's last appointment in Vietnam was not so much an interview but a thank you to Phạm Hồng Cư and his wife, Mrs. Đặng Thị Hạnh. They had arranged access to the Vietnamese veterans. Đặng Thị Hạnh had taught French literature during the wars. Phạm Hồng Cư's revolutionary path had started in the early 1940s during his student days and he went on to become a seasoned political commissar and a highly distinguished general. When the author met him in Hanoi, he was still involved closely in governmental affairs, which gave her the opportunity to circumnavigate officialdom and bring forward this book to a time when the veterans were still alive. His contacts ranged from his connections to Hồ Chí Minh, and Hồ's wider family, and to his personal relationship with one of the most important generals, Võ Nguyên Giáp. He then advised the author on her conclusions regarding the wars in Vietnam.

Phạm Hồng Cư opened the interview by asking, "After working alongside senior Vietnamese war veterans for so many years what was the key piece of information which led to your understanding of our All-People's War?"[1] The author explained that scrutinizing their strategies was exhausting and as complicated as piecing together a large glass vase that had been smashed into tiny parts decades earlier. One vital shard of the broken vase that enabled her to understand Hồ's blueprint came from Lê Trọng Nghĩa, the former head of the Intelligence Department. He had concluded, "If we had lost at Điện Biên Phủ, it would have set us back for years; it would not have stopped us."[2] Nghĩa's words seemed like propaganda at the time: we will never surrender. Over time the author understood what he actually meant; the blueprint was made up of many parts, therefore even if the main regular army had been destroyed, the rest of the blueprint remained intact not only to rebuild the damaged part but to continue the fight.

The All-People's War is a blueprint to fight a protracted asymmetric conflict against a superior power. It comprised four main parts: the Revolutionary Infrastructure and the three strategic fronts of political, propaganda and the military. It is not the place for this conclusion to list all aspects again, but if the author were to choose vital parts of the blueprint they would be as follows. Have a clear objective and robust strategy on how to achieve it. Have a vision for after victory. Create a strong brand. Use the people and utilize their traits, strengths and weaknesses. Exploit nationalism. Form a war without boundaries. Build local fighters and a main regular army. Have great logistics networks.

Mrs. Đặng Thị Hạnh, Phạm Hồng Cư (real name Lê Đỗ Nguyên), the author, the author's husband, Clive A. Hills, and their daughter, Bluebelle. The family visited Hạnh and Cư on 27 February 2010 to thank them for all their help as the project came to an end (Clive A. Hills).

Establish the means to gain access to military supplies and goods. Found liberated zones. Form a main political party. Create an infrastructure. Establish law and order. Conduct extensive propaganda across all mediums. Have a strong covert and overt section to the war. Exercise military and civilian proselytizing. Form and control many groups to draw in all areas of the population. Infiltrate key operatives into your groups and all opposing systems and organs of power. Use local and international events to your advantage. Exploit your enemies' systems: democracy, their legal process, human rights and freedom of speech. Be diplomatic. Form alliances. Seek international support. Have a means to fund the war. In summary, using the words of Hồ, "If you have the people, you'll have everything."

Phạm Hồng Cư went on to say to the author, "What have you learned from us?"[3] The author replied that she understood how the revolutionaries had won and that she could never have achieved this without speaking directly to those who had designed and built the blueprint, from the top generals to the people on the battlefield. She went on to say that, by being privileged to learn Hồ's strategies, this knowledge had given her a good appreciation of how terrorists were impregnating countries today. She made it clear that it was the strategies only, not the cause, which had similarities.

From All-People's War to All-People's Terrorism

People will always theorize why the Americans lost Vietnam. Moving away from focusing purely on strategies, could a factor be because the American soldiers were

13,000km from home and simply could not have been as dedicated as the communists who fought for their homeland? Could it be that many of the American soldiers were young, uneducated and came from poor backgrounds? Or those who had an education were disillusioned with the stated political aim of the war; to fight the spread of communism and bring democracy to the Vietnamese? Or perhaps, as a result of this disillusionment and hatred of the war by the American population, military order broke down?

The communist interviewees gave two main reasons for U.S. failings in Vietnam. In the first instance, by continually bombing the locals the United States had pushed them into the hands of the revolutionaries. Secondly, American politicians were dictated to by financial and political restraints; this prevented them from keeping to their stated military aim: staying until the job was done.

Notwithstanding these points, perhaps the Americans failed in their aims because they simply did not understand an All-People's War, or did they understand more than history has recorded? The ironic twist is that the Americans did teach other groups strategies that had been part of Hồ's blueprint. Although Hồ's methods were not all unique, how Hồ used them was important, and the Americans learned from this. The Soviet War in the 1980s in Afghanistan is a case in point.

An Afghan sympathetic to the Mujahideen's fight had told the author that they had been given manuals describing Mao Zedong's, Hồ Chí Minh's and Võ Nguyên Giáp's revolutionary strategies. From these, the Mujahideen leadership had studied and then integrated adaptations of Mao's, Hồ's and Giáp's strategies into their very own existing people's fight and ancient tribal systems. The Mujahideen got this classified information from a number of sources, including the United States when they had supported the Mujahideen against the Soviets.

During the 1980s, Soviet conscripts besieged by CIA-supplied Afghan rebels called these insurgents "ghosts" because they could never quite grasp and hold their enemy.[4] One explanation of how the Mujahideen achieved this ghost-like presence was that it had been shown how to establish and then run a shadow government, or ghost government. The Mujahideen's shadow government had not been as effective as Hồ's shadow government; known as his Revolutionary Infrastructure. Like Hồ's Việt Minh or NLF, the Mujahideen had many groups operating under the name. Unlike the Việt Minh, these individual groups wanted their own government representative in each village. This division within the various Mujahideen groups did cause difficulties and tensions. Nevertheless, the shadow government was efficient enough to have controlled and administered the population as well as supported and supplied the war effort.

Afghanistan became what most CIA officers regarded as one of the proudest achievements in the agency's history; the repulsion of the invading Soviet forces by covert action.[5] Yet how the United States interfaced with the Mujahideen and the Inter-Service Intelligence Directorate (ISI), the Pakistani intelligence service, would come back to haunt it years later.[6]

The next high-profile time the United States came across a shadow government was as part of its Global War on Terrorism, also known as the War on Terror, terms applied to an international military campaign that started after the 11 September 2001 (9/11) terrorist attacks launched by the Islamic group Al-Qaeda on New York and Washington.[7] Supported by their allies, the United States responded by launching this global war, and invaded Afghanistan to destroy the Taliban, who it believed harbored Al-Qaeda.

One problem facing the United States in Afghanistan was the strategies it had helped established for the Mujahideen years earlier. Members of the Mujahideen now formed part of the Taliban; an organization far more complicated, both in their strategies used and levels of power. Today, one faction under the Taliban could be best described as local nationalist Afghans fighting to free their country from foreigners, and another faction self-interested Afghans who had their own agenda. Although difficult to fight, these local groups were not the entire picture; a good percentage of the problem lay with the brutal Pakistan Taliban, some of which allegedly had links to the Pakistani ISI.[8] The strategies once fed to the Mujahideen had now been mastered by the Taliban, including creating a war without boundaries, proselytizing and how to establish an effective shadow government.

The Americans quickly used elements of the Phoenix Program against the Taliban, a tactic they had once established in Vietnam to eliminate Hồ's infrastructure. Now named Kill/Capture, the United States generally targeted the mid- and high-ranking officials. Kill/Capture did not reach expectations. The Taliban operatives were so ingrained over generations within society that they became extremely difficult to identify. If identified, once eliminated, these deceased Taliban officials were often replaced by uncontrollable, untested radicals.

The most high profile person neutralized through Kill/Capture was the top man, the leader of Al-Qaeda, Osama bin Laden. This occurred in 2011, after he had been in hiding for a number of years. Navy SEALs of the United States Naval Special Warfare Development Group were given the task, a mission based on intelligence gathered predominately by the CIA. They, among other sources, had been monitoring his shadow government, more specifically the activities of his so-called personal courier, a man named Abu Ahmed al-Kuwaiti, who is believed to have been a computer expert and helped train the 9/11 hijackers.

The Americans were not the only ones who taught the Afghans covert strategies. Throughout the 1960s and 1970s, the Soviet KGB, had secretly funded and nurtured communist leadership networks at Kabul University, and in the Afghan army it trained and indoctrinated some 3,725 military personnel on Soviet soil.[9] One crucial Vietnamese military concept used by the Russians and taught to the Afghans was the *biệt động* fighting approach, first established by Nguyễn Bình in the 1940s.

The Mujahideen adopted the strategies taught to the Soviet-backed Afghan communist forces because there was such a high desertion rate from the communist forces to the Mujahideen. Like the United States before them in Vietnam, the Soviets now had to distinguish the Mujahideen from the population. Out of shear frustration, the Soviets adopted the same failed strategy as the United States did and bombed the country. By 1987, the populace of Afghanistan was in the order of 15 million. Up to this point it is estimated the Soviet occupation had led to the deaths of almost 1.5 million Afghans with a further 6 million people being displaced, fleeing to Iran and Pakistan.[10] This bombing further pushed more Afghans into the hands of the Mujahideen and undermined any attempts the Soviets made to establish a local government the people believed in. This cycle of destruction and death continued and became a principal factor that led to the Soviets total failure in the country and their withdrawal in 1989.

The Soviets invaded Afghanistan for many reasons but one factor was to preserve their vision of world revolution. After the end of the Vietnam War, China seized Cambodia as a vassal state so that it had, among other things, more land for its expanding population. The Soviets took Vietnam and Lao into their sphere of influence. When the Vietnamese went into Cambodia in 1979, to protect their borders from the Chinese-influenced Khmer Rouge, Moscow did not object. This in effect expanded the Soviets' influence but without their full-scale military involvement.

With Indochina now predominantly under the Soviets, they could focus their efforts on Afghanistan, but was this a decision that ended their vision of world revolution? Possibly. With the Soviets damaged by their defeat in Afghanistan, the political dominance of the USSR faded. One scenario was that their old rival, China, saw a weaker USSR and became more ambitious over the former French colonies, especially over Vietnam and Lao.

The question remains then, did the United States use the strategies it had once fought bitterly against in Vietnam, to stop communism in Afghanistan? This could be an ironic twist but is a complicated concept and not for this research. What is more relevant today is that the people who were once U.S. allies, in this case the Mujahideen, may now be using the strategies against America and its Western partners.

The United States and its allies have gone from total victory during the Second World War to total defeat during the Vietnam War, to success against the Soviets in Afghanistan. However, the Americans have never defeated the All-People's War model, because you cannot destroy what you cannot define. Hồ designed it for liberation and a means of defense, not for an invading force, but could the strategies be adapted to suit a shadow or ghostly slow invasion? If so, this could be one of the biggest threats to the world today and the winning of a global war on terror, better described as a fight against an All-People's Terrorism.

Thank You and Goodbye

Đặng Thị Hạnh had listened to her husband and the author converse as her son, Lê Đỗ Huy, translated. It was her final words that brought the conversation back to Vietnam and a personal level. "What you have to remember, is that hundreds of citizens sacrificed everything without being able to foresee the outcome."[11] This to the author was of greatest significance. The revolutionaries would have fought to the bitter end; Vietnam is their home. They did all this without knowing the outcome; victory or annihilation. Indeed, the United States had considered the nuclear option to assist the French at the Battle of Điện Biên Phủ.

To give up your entire life, without benefiting directly and without an end point, is something that few of us will ever understand. It illustrates that those involved had to have shown collective sacrifice and be bonded through an unshakable, deep-rooted vision, a reason to endure the pain; essentially achieved by the revolutionaries keeping some form of nationalism at the heart of their message. This dedication led to the revolutionaries accomplishing their final goal of total victory, giving them independence and the ability to implement socialist political change in Vietnam.

Today, many of those who helped with this book have passed away. Among those are the daughter of Ms. Đức, who translated documents from Chinese to Vietnamese to tell the memories of her parents. Out of gratitude to those who are no longer here, the architects and the women whose stories were used as the connecting thread, the author hopes that she has gone some way to thanking them for revealing their very personal accounts, so she could understand and disclose Hồ's blueprint for revolution.

Appendix I: Abbreviations and Acronyms

ARVN	Army of the Republic of Vietnam
ATK	*An toàn khu*
CCN	Command and Control North
CIA	Central Intelligence Agency
Comintern	Communist International
CORDS	Civil Operations and Revolutionary Development Support
COSVN	Central Office for South Vietnam
DGER	*Direction Générale des Études et Recherches*
DMZ	Demilitarized Zone
FOB	Forward Operating Base
HES	Hamlet Evaluation Survey
Huế CACS	Huế Civil Affairs Committee for Students
ICEX	Intelligence Coordination and Exploitation Program
ISI	Inter-Service Intelligence Directorate
MAAG	Military Assistance Advisory Group
MACV	Military Assistance Command Vietnam
MACV/CMAC	Military Assistance Command Vietnam/Capital Military Assistance Command
MATA	Military Assistance Training Advisory
NLF	National Liberation Front
OSS	Office of Strategic Services
PRG	Provisional Revolutionary Government
PRU	Provincial Reconnaissance Unit
RT	Reconnaissance Team (Recon Team)
RTAFB	Royal Thai Air Force Base
SOG	Studies and Observations Group
TW	Communist Party Headquarters (TW is a code only)
VC	Việt Cộng
VCI	Việt Cộng Infrastructure
Vietnamese RYL	Vietnamese Revolutionary Youth League
VNPA	Vietnamese People's Army
ZANO	*Zone Autonome du Nord-Ouest*
ZONO	*Zone Opérationnel du Nord-Ouest*

Appendix II: Translation of Vietnamese Terms

Advancing propaganda team	*Tuyên truyền xung phong*
Advancing Southwards Bureau	*Ban xung phong Nam tiến*
Agitation and propaganda among the enemy	*Địch vận*
Agitation and propaganda among the intelligentsia	*Trí vận*
Agitation and propaganda within the Chinese communities	*Hoa vận*
Annamese Communist Party	*An Nam Cộng sản Đảng*
Armed propaganda team	*Đội vũ trang tuyên truyền*
Army station	*Binh trạm*
Business-Finance	*Kinh-Tài*
Central Office for South Vietnam	*Văn phòng Trung ương Cục miền Nam*
City Action Unit Department	*Ban Công tác Thành*
City liaison agent	*Liên lạc thành*
Cochinchina Resistance Administrative Committee	*Uỷ ban Kháng chiến Hành chính Nam Bộ*
Cochinchina Secret Service Department	*Phòng Mật vụ Nam Bộ*
Commune communications liaison agent	*Giao liên xã*
Communications agent (courier)	*Giao thông*
Communications liaison agent (courier)	*Giao thông liên lạc (giao liên)*
Communications liaison agent who just served one intelligence agent	*Giao liên đơn tuyến*
Communications liaison agent who used fake papers and who operates only at night	*Giao liên bất hợp pháp*
Communications liaison agent who used legal papers innocently handed out to them by the Southern authority	*Giao liên hợp pháp*
Communications liaison guerrilla	*Giao liên du kích*
Communications liaison post agent	*Giao bưu*
Communications liaison post transport agent	*Giao bưu vận*
Communications and Liaison Service	*Thông tin Liên lạc*
Communications liaison urban underground elite armed force	*Giao liên biệt động*
Elite force	*Đặc công*
Frontline Youth	*Thanh niên Tiền Tuyến*

Great Viet	*Đại Việt*
Hamlet communications liaison agent	*Giao liên ấp*
Honorary fighting team	*Danh dự trừ gian*
Indochinese Communist League	*Đông Dương Cộng sản Liên đoàn*
Indochinese Communist Party	*Đông Dương Cộng sản Đảng*
League for Revolution	*Đồng Minh Hội*
League for the Independence of Vietnam	*Việt Nam Độc lập Đồng Minh Hội*
Liaison agent or liaison soldier	*Liên lạc*
Military postman	*Quân bưu*
Military proselytizing	*Binh vận*
Military Proselytizing Department	*Cục Địch vận*
Modernization Movement	*Duy Tân*
National Defense Guard	*Vệ Quốc Đoàn*
National Salvation Troops	*Cứu Quốc quân*
New Vietnamese Revolutionary Party	*Tân Việt cách mạng Đảng*
Observing the Enemy Department	*Ban Nghiên cứu địch tình*
People's Public Security	*Công an*
People's Revolutionary Party	*Đảng Nhân dân cách mạng*
Plain of Reeds	*Đồng Tháp Mười*
Porter	*Dân công*
Provincial Party Committee	*Tỉnh Ủy*
Regional Party Committee	*Xứ Ủy*
Revolutionary Infrastructure	*Hạ tầng cơ sở cách mạng*
The Road to Revolution	*Đường Cách Mệnh*
Self-defense team	*Tự vệ*
Simultaneous Uprising	*Đồng Khởi*
Society of Hearts	*Tâm Tâm Xã*
Soldier	*Bộ đội*
Southern Intelligence Department	*Phòng Tình báo Miền Nam*
Southward March	*Nam tiến*
Special masses	*Quần chúng đặc biệt*
Special propaganda	*Tuyên truyền đặc biệt*
Strategic Hamlet Program	*Ấp Chiến lược*
Union of Vietnamese Communists	*Việt Nam Cộng sản Liên đoàn*
Urban underground elite armed force	*Biệt động*
Vanguard Youth	*Thanh niên Tiền Phong*
Vietnam Liberation Army	*Việt Nam Giải phóng Quân*
Vietnam Modernization Association	*Việt Nam Duy tân Hội*
Vietnam Propaganda and Liberation Army	*Việt Nam Tuyên truyền Giải phóng Quân*
Vietnamese Communist Party	*Việt Nam Cộng sản Đảng*
Vietnamese Kuomintang	*Việt Nam Quốc dân Đảng*
Vietnamese Restoration League	*Việt Nam Quang Phục Hội*
Vietnamese Revolutionary Youth League	*Hội Việt Nam Cách mạng Thanh Niên*
Westward Front	*Tây Tiến*

Chapter Notes

Introduction

1. Lê Trọng Nghĩa, interview with the author, 26 February 2008.

Chapter 1

1. Kim Liên Village, Nghệ An Province, was known as Sen Village by the Vietnamese; today Kim Liên is a commune.
2. French Indochina included Lao only after the Franco–Siamese War of 1893.
3. The Party Central Committee's Research Bureau, *President Hồ Chí Minh: Life's History and Work*. Hanoi: Truth Publishing, 1975.
4. In 1885, Emperor Hàm Nghi attacked the French in Huế City, but failed. The emperor, his family and his followers reluctantly fled to the hills and jungles on the Lao–Vietnam border. The regent, Tôn Thất Thuyết, who had helped the emperor escape, persuaded him to make an announcement, calling for the people to wage a guerrilla war against the French; this they called the Save the King Movement. Tran My-Van quotes the end of the movement as 1895, whereas others use 1889, but former members kept it going unofficially until the beginning of the new century. My-Van, Tran. *A Vietnamese Royal Exile in Japan: Prince Cuong De (1882–1951)*. Oxford: Routledge, 2005.
5. Prince Cường Để was a royal relative of the Nguyễn Dynasty and according to the rule of primogeniture, the heir of the dynasty. He never took the throne because the French sidelined him.
6. Japan went on to become the first Asian force in modern times to defeat a European power, causing Russia to abandon its expansionist policy in the Far East.
7. Sơn, Phạm Văn. *Việt Nam chiến sử*. Saigon: Self-published, 1972.
8. Chau, Phan Boi. *Overturned Chariot: The Autobiography of Phan-Boi-Chau*. Hawai'i: University of Hawai'i Press, 1999.
9. Lý Tuệ—real name Nguyễn Hữu Tuệ (1871–1938).
10. Previously, trainees going to Hong Kong had to use a number of hazardous routes. They could take a small sailing craft and skirt the dangerous shores around the Gulf of Tonkin, or they could go by land across Lao and Siam before sailing to Hong Kong, and then on to Japan.
11. Khoan, Nguyễn Văn. "The Work of the Giao Thông Liên Lạc which Served the Propagation of Marxism–Leninism to Indochina in the Early Years of the 20th Century." PhD diss., Hanoi University, 1985.
12. Duiker, William J. *Ho Chi Minh: A Life*. New York: Theia, 2000.
13. The Kuomintang Army (National Revolutionary Army, and known as the Republic of China Army after the 1947 Constitution) is the military arm of the Kuomintang. The Kuomintang is a political party in Taiwan (the Republic of China). Its predecessor, the Revolutionary Alliance, was one of the major advocates that ended the Qing Dynasty to establish the Republic of China, which at the time covered just a small area of mainland China. In 1928, the Kuomintang became the ruling party of an expanded Republic of China. It had to retreat to the island of Taiwan in 1949 after being defeated by the Chinese Communist Party during the Chinese Civil War, which saw the establishment of the People's Republic of China on the mainland.
14. When the Go East Movement students were expelled from Japan, Hồ Học Lãm went to study at the Baoding Military Academy in China; Lãm graduated in 1911. Bai Chongxi had been his classmate and he went on to become an important nationalist Chinese Kuomintang general and politician in China in the years to follow, and therefore a very good contact for Lãm.
15. Sun Yat-sen was a Chinese revolutionary. In 1905, he joined forces with other anti-monarchist societies in Tokyo and formed a group called Tongmenghui, which sponsored uprisings in China. He played a key role in the overthrow of the Qing Dynasty, and as a pioneer of the Republic of China he served as its provisional president when the republic formed in 1912. Later in the same year he co-founded the Kuomintang and served as its first leader. Sun Yat-sen's chief legacy, and later guiding ideology of the Kuomintang,

Great Viet	Đại Việt
Hamlet communications liaison agent	Giao liên ấp
Honorary fighting team	Danh dự trừ gian
Indochinese Communist League	Đông Dương Cộng sản Liên đoàn
Indochinese Communist Party	Đông Dương Cộng sản Đảng
League for Revolution	Đồng Minh Hội
League for the Independence of Vietnam	Việt Nam Độc lập Đồng Minh Hội
Liaison agent or liaison soldier	Liên lạc
Military postman	Quân bưu
Military proselytizing	Binh vận
Military Proselytizing Department	Cục Địch vận
Modernization Movement	Duy Tân
National Defense Guard	Vệ Quốc Đoàn
National Salvation Troops	Cứu Quốc quân
New Vietnamese Revolutionary Party	Tân Việt cách mạng Đảng
Observing the Enemy Department	Ban Nghiên cứu địch tình
People's Public Security	Công an
People's Revolutionary Party	Đảng Nhân dân cách mạng
Plain of Reeds	Đồng Tháp Mười
Porter	Dân công
Provincial Party Committee	Tỉnh Ủy
Regional Party Committee	Xứ Ủy
Revolutionary Infrastructure	Hạ tầng cơ sở cách mạng
The Road to Revolution	Đường Cách Mệnh
Self-defense team	Tự vệ
Simultaneous Uprising	Đồng Khởi
Society of Hearts	Tâm Tâm Xã
Soldier	Bộ đội
Southern Intelligence Department	Phòng Tình báo Miền Nam
Southward March	Nam tiến
Special masses	Quần chúng đặc biệt
Special propaganda	Tuyên truyền đặc biệt
Strategic Hamlet Program	Ấp Chiến lược
Union of Vietnamese Communists	Việt Nam Cộng sản Liên đoàn
Urban underground elite armed force	Biệt động
Vanguard Youth	Thanh niên Tiền Phong
Vietnam Liberation Army	Việt Nam Giải phóng Quân
Vietnam Modernization Association	Việt Nam Duy tân Hội
Vietnam Propaganda and Liberation Army	Việt Nam Tuyên truyền Giải phóng Quân
Vietnamese Communist Party	Việt Nam Cộng sản Đảng
Vietnamese Kuomintang	Việt Nam Quốc dân Đảng
Vietnamese Restoration League	Việt Nam Quang Phục Hội
Vietnamese Revolutionary Youth League	Hội Việt Nam Cách mạng Thanh Niên
Westward Front	Tây Tiến

Chapter Notes

Introduction

1. Lê Trọng Nghĩa, interview with the author, 26 February 2008.

Chapter 1

1. Kim Liên Village, Nghệ An Province, was known as Sen Village by the Vietnamese; today Kim Liên is a commune.
2. French Indochina included Lao only after the Franco–Siamese War of 1893.
3. The Party Central Committee's Research Bureau, *President Hồ Chí Minh: Life's History and Work*. Hanoi: Truth Publishing, 1975.
4. In 1885, Emperor Hàm Nghi attacked the French in Huế City, but failed. The emperor, his family and his followers reluctantly fled to the hills and jungles on the Lao–Vietnam border. The regent, Tôn Thất Thuyết, who had helped the emperor escape, persuaded him to make an announcement, calling for the people to wage a guerrilla war against the French; this they called the Save the King Movement. Tran My-Van quotes the end of the movement as 1895, whereas others use 1889, but former members kept it going unofficially until the beginning of the new century. My-Van, Tran. *A Vietnamese Royal Exile in Japan: Prince Cuong De (1882–1951)*. Oxford: Routledge, 2005.
5. Prince Cường Để was a royal relative of the Nguyễn Dynasty and according to the rule of primogeniture, the heir of the dynasty. He never took the throne because the French sidelined him.
6. Japan went on to become the first Asian force in modern times to defeat a European power, causing Russia to abandon its expansionist policy in the Far East.
7. Sơn, Phạm Văn. *Việt Nam chiến sử*. Saigon: Self-published, 1972.
8. Chau, Phan Boi. *Overturned Chariot: The Autobiography of Phan-Boi-Chau*. Hawai'i: University of Hawai'i Press, 1999.
9. Lý Tuệ—real name Nguyễn Hữu Tuệ (1871–1938).
10. Previously, trainees going to Hong Kong had to use a number of hazardous routes. They could take a small sailing craft and skirt the dangerous shores around the Gulf of Tonkin, or they could go by land across Lao and Siam before sailing to Hong Kong, and then on to Japan.
11. Khoan, Nguyễn Văn. "The Work of the Giao Thông Liên Lạc which Served the Propagation of Marxism–Leninism to Indochina in the Early Years of the 20th Century." PhD diss., Hanoi University, 1985.
12. Duiker, William J. *Ho Chi Minh: A Life*. New York: Theia, 2000.
13. The Kuomintang Army (National Revolutionary Army, and known as the Republic of China Army after the 1947 Constitution) is the military arm of the Kuomintang. The Kuomintang is a political party in Taiwan (the Republic of China). Its predecessor, the Revolutionary Alliance, was one of the major advocates that ended the Qing Dynasty to establish the Republic of China, which at the time covered just a small area of mainland China. In 1928, the Kuomintang became the ruling party of an expanded Republic of China. It had to retreat to the island of Taiwan in 1949 after being defeated by the Chinese Communist Party during the Chinese Civil War, which saw the establishment of the People's Republic of China on the mainland.
14. When the Go East Movement students were expelled from Japan, Hồ Học Lãm went to study at the Baoding Military Academy in China; Lãm graduated in 1911. Bai Chongxi had been his classmate and he went on to become an important nationalist Chinese Kuomintang general and politician in China in the years to follow, and therefore a very good contact for Lãm.
15. Sun Yat-sen was a Chinese revolutionary. In 1905, he joined forces with other anti-monarchist societies in Tokyo and formed a group called Tongmenghui, which sponsored uprisings in China. He played a key role in the overthrow of the Qing Dynasty, and as a pioneer of the Republic of China he served as its provisional president when the republic formed in 1912. Later in the same year he co-founded the Kuomintang and served as its first leader. Sun Yat-sen's chief legacy, and later guiding ideology of the Kuomintang,

was the political philosophy known as the Three Principles of the People.

16. Hải, Siêu. *With the Alias Ebony.* Hải Phòng: Hải Phòng Publishing, 1993.

17. The name of the passenger was Mai.

18. Tiên, Trần Dân. *Hồ Chí Minh: The Founder of Independent Vietnam.* Hanoi: Thế Giới, 1997.

19. Quinn-Judge, Sophie. *Ho Chi Minh: The Missing Years, 1919–1941.* Berkeley: University of California Press, 2003.

20. The Modernization Movement of Phan Chu Trinh's was an entirely different group to that of the Vietnam Modernization Association of Phan Bội Châu.

21. Cư, Phạm Hồng. *General Giáp: His Youth.* Hanoi: Youth Publishing, 2007.

22. For the Vietnamese Restoration League, Phan Bội Châu was deputy president and minister of foreign affairs and Prince Cường Để was president and chairman.

23. At the end of the First World War, other central powers on the German side were dealt with under different treaties.

24. The general association of nations became the League of Nations in January 1920, there as an international organization to provide a forum for resolving international disputes.

25. My-Van, Tran. *A Vietnamese Royal Exile in Japan: Prince Cuong De (1882–1951).* Oxford: Routledge, 2005.

26. Annamese was often used to address the people of Tonkin, Annam and Cochinchina because from 1802 to 1945, the emperors of the Nguyễn Dynasty, who ruled these people, had their seat in Huế City and Huế was in Annam.

27. Khoan, Nguyễn Văn. "The Work of the *Giao Thông Liên Lạc* which Served the Propagation of Marxism–Leninism to Indochina in the Early Years of the 20th Century." PhD diss., Hanoi University, 1985.

28. The French called Vũng Tàu, Cape Saint Jacques, and wealthy Vietnamese abbreviated the name to Ô Cấp.

29. *Lịch sử truyền thông Giao bưu vận Nam Bộ (1945–1975).* Hanoi: Nhà Xuất Bản Bưu Điện, 2003.

30. In this case "courier" meant *giao thông liên lạc* translated as "communications liaison agent." The mention of legal and illegal referred to their courier groupings and how they operated. *Lịch sử truyền thông Giao bưu vận Nam Bộ (1945–1975).* Hanoi: Nhà Xuất Bản Bưu Điện, 2003.

31. Tom Mann had become a communist after reading the *Communist Manifesto* in 1886, which had been written by Karl Marx and his friend Friedrich Engels. From there he worked directly for the revolution as a colleague of Marx. Hồ met Mann again when they both attended the Fifth Congress of the Comintern in Moscow in 1924. Hồng, Việt. "Stories about Karl Marx told on the Trail." *Vietnamese Communist Party Newspaper,* 5 May 1968.

32. Duiker, William J. *Ho Chi Minh: A Life.* New York: Theia, 2000.

33. Quinn-Judge, Sophie. *Ho Chi Minh: The Missing Years, 1919–1941.* Berkeley: University of California Press, 2003.

34. Hồng, Việt. "Stories about Karl Marx told on the Trail." *Vietnamese Communist Party Newspaper,* 5 May 1968.

35. Hồng, Việt. "Stories about Karl Marx told on the Trail." *Vietnamese Communist Party Newspaper,* 5 May 1968.

36. Borton, Lady. *Hồ Chí Minh: A Journey.* Hanoi: Thế Giới, 2007.

37. The French Communist Party was called the French Section of the Communist International (SFIC).

Chapter 2

1. The Trưng Sisters were Vietnamese military leaders who ruled for three years after rebelling against Chinese rule in AD 40, and are regarded as national heroines of Vietnam.

2. Khoan, Nguyễn Văn. *Giao Thông Liên Lạc Thông Tin.* Hanoi: Lao Động Publishing, 1997.

3. The Four Virtues in Vietnamese translates to *tứ đức* and the Three Submissions *tam tòng.* Nguyễn Thị Hoa, interview with the author, 10 May 2007.

4. Marr, David G. *Vietnamese Tradition on Trial, 1920–1945.* Berkeley: University of California Press, 1984.

5. Đức, Lý Phương. *Following Uncle Hồ to Work for the Revolution.* Hanoi: Unpublished memoir, 1984.

6. Siam changed its name to Thailand in 1939. Thailand was renamed Siam from 1945 to 1949, after which it again reverted to Thailand; now the most common name for the region.

7. Lý Tự Trọng—real name Lê Văn Trọng; Lý Phương Thuận—real name Nguyễn Thị Tích; Lý Phương Đức—real name Nguyễn Thị Đức; and Lý Trí Thông—real name Hoàng Nam.

8. *Quốc ngữ* is a Latinized Vietnamese script created by Western missionaries in the sixteenth century, and Hồ Chí Minh established it as the official Vietnamese alphabet in 1945.

9. The friendship between Ms. Lý Phương Đức's family and the headmaster and his deputy continued. These two school officials visited them in China just before the Guangzhou Commune Uprising in December 1927 and met Hồ, Lê Hồng Sơn and Hồ Tùng Mậu on the third floor of a house in Hui Ai Street, Guangzhou. After 1930, they both joined the Siamese Communist Party.

10. Đức, Lý Phương. *Following Uncle Hồ to Work for the Revolution.* Hanoi: Unpublished memoir, 1984.

11. Hà Tĩnh and Quảng Bình had been under the leadership of Phan Đình Phùng (1844–1896), a noted warrior who had organized a guerrilla army in these provinces.

12. Cựu Tuấn had fled to Siam at the turn of the century with a few fellow compatriots after a revolt led by Phan Đình Phùng collapsed. Surprisingly, it was not until a later attempt by patriots to perform a

similar action in 1908 that the French sought revenge. This latter attempt intended to poison French soldiers in the Citadel in Hanoi, while the troops of Hoàng Hoa Thám simultaneously assaulted them. The French soldiers repulsed the attack and defended themselves, and none were seriously poisoned. The subsequent continuing repression by the French was called White Terror by the revolutionaries. Many of the revolutionaries now known to the French were imprisoned or executed. Others followed the example of Tuấn and fled to Siam, and, in doing so, they further expanded the revolutionary area of influence in the region. On arriving in Siam, Tuấn stayed in the first Vietnamese village of the area, named Vat Pa, in Nakhon Phanom Province. Tuấn instantly adopted a revolutionary lifestyle because the village was a courier way station and part of Phan Bội Châu's underground system. Tuấn and Châu became further acquainted because Tuấn now worked with Đặng Thúc Hứa (1870–1931), Châu's very much trusted ambassador in Siam for the Vietnamese Restoration League. Tuấn and Hứa expanded the courier networks across the provinces of Nakhon Phanom and Phichit. By 1925, these new networks ran from Vietnam through Lao and on into Siam, and became the most heavily used by the eager youth wishing to join the Vietnamese revolutionaries in China.

13. Ms. Lý Phương Thuận married Hồ Tùng Mậu (first husband).

14. Đức, Lý Phương. *Following Uncle Hồ to Work for the Revolution.* Hanoi: Unpublished memoir, 1984.

15. First established by Phan Bội Châu, this courier sea route to Guangzhou had been used extensively by Vietnamese patriots. It became harder to use during the 1930s because the French cracked down on Vietnamese nationalists in Bangkok.

16. Đức, Lý Phương. *Following Uncle Hồ to Work for the Revolution.* Hanoi: Unpublished memoir, 1984.

17. Vietnamese RYL was founded by Hồ and is considered the first pro–Marxist organization in Indochina. At its heart were eight men: (1) Lê Hồng Phong, executed in 1942, (2) Lâm Đức Thụ—real name Nguyễn Công Viễn (188?–1947), (3) Trương Văn Lĩnh (1902–1946), (4) Lý Thụy (Hồ Chí Minh), (5) Lê Quảng Đạt, died 193?, (6) Ngô Chính Quốc (1903–1990), the brother of Ms. Lý Phương Đức (7), Lê Hồng Sơn, executed in the early 1930s, and (8) Hồ Tùng Mậu, who died during a French air raid in 1951. Hồ headed the Vietnamese RYL. Lâm Đức Thụ hosted the first meeting of the group at his house in Guangzhou in June 1925. Lê Hồng Sơn and Hồ Tùng Mậu were pivotal in recruiting young couriers for Hồ, such as Lý Phương Đức.

18. Đức, Lý Phương. *Following Uncle Hồ to Work for the Revolution.* Hanoi: Unpublished memoir, 1984.

19. Khoan, Nguyễn Văn. *Lý Phương Đức: The Female Giao Thông of Uncle Hồ.* Hanoi: People's Public Security Publishing, 2006.

20. Khoan, Nguyễn Văn. *Lý Phương Đức: The Female Giao Thông of Uncle Hồ.* Hanoi: People's Public Security Publishing, 2006.

21. Lý Phương Đức, interviews with Nguyễn Văn Khoan, 1980s.

22. *Hồ Chí Minh: A Biography by Years, 1890–1930, Volume 1.* Hanoi: National Political Publishers, 1993.

23. Nguyễn Văn Lém is best known from the iconic image captured by the Associated Press photographer Eddie Adams. Lém is the prisoner photographed wincing just before he was shot in the head at point-blank range with a pistol by South Vietnamese General Nguyễn Ngọc Loan at the height of the Tết Offensive in 1968. Lém was a commander of a *biệt động* unit that attacked the headquarters of the Republic of Vietnam Marines and had committed civilian atrocities.

24. Lý Văn Minh went to Siam. It is believed that Lý Thúc Chất and Lý Thúc Tự ended up in Moscow, only to be killed defending the city in 1941. Both Ms. Lý Phương Đức and Ms. Lý Phương Thuận joined the Chinese Communist Party at Hồ's request, Đức joined in 1927 and Thuận shortly after.

25. Phan Bội changed names to Hoàng Hữu Nam and served as deputy minister of interior in Hồ's government in 1946.

26. Borton, Lady. *Hồ Chí Minh: A Journey.* Hanoi: Thế Giới, 2007.

27. Chất was also linked to the old-time revolutionary Phan Bội Châu; Chất's real name was Vương Thúc Thoại, making him a relation of Vương Thúc Oánh, the son-in-law of Châu.

28. Liên Mạc Hamlet was also called Mạc, Thụy Phương was known as Chèm and Hoàng Mạc was referred to as Hoàng.

29. *19 August Revolution Is Creation.* Hanoi: Association of Vietnamese Historians, 1995.

30. *19 August Revolution Is Creation.* Hanoi: Association of Vietnamese Historians, 1995.

31. *19 August Revolution Is Creation.* Hanoi: Association of Vietnamese Historians, 1995.

32. *19 August Revolution Is Creation.* Hanoi: Association of Vietnamese Historians, 1995.

33. *19 August Revolution Is Creation.* Hanoi: Association of Vietnamese Historians, 1995.

34. Trust Bills, translated into Vietnamese as *tín phiếu*.

35. Đặng Xuân Khu was best known as Trường Chinh (Long March), a name he took after 1946. Trường Chinh became the acting general secretary of the Communist Party at the Seventh Conference in November 1940 and the general secretary after the Eighth Conference in May 1941.

36. *19 August Revolution Is Creation.* Hanoi: Association of Vietnamese Historians, 1995.

37. Prior to 1945, ATKs were in regions not controlled by revolutionaries but after the August Revolution the revolutionaries set up ATKs, where possible, in communist-controlled areas. Initially, ATKs stretched across the rural provinces of Cao Bằng, Bắc Kạn, Lạng Sơn, Thái Nguyên, Tuyên Quang, Hà Giang, Bắc Giang and the outskirts of Hanoi but as the war continued they spread.

38. Officially the revolutionary administration

would become known as the Revolutionary Infrastructure.

39. The TW changed locations. Just prior to the August Revolution both the general secretary and Hồ moved to Tân Trào Commune, Tuyên Quang Province. Once Hồ controlled the country his first Provisional Government of the Democratic Republic of Vietnam located to Hanoi. During the French War the TW returned to Việt Bắc Revolutionary Base area; Hồ's headquarters was generally situated within Sơn Dương District, Tuyên Quang Province. In 1955, the Party Central Committee and the government moved back to Hanoi.

40. The department established in 1942 was the forerunner of both the Security Office and the Police Office of Tonkin. These two offices formed on 23 August 1945 under the Ministry of Interior governed by Võ Nguyên Giáp. Then, on 21 February 1946, Hồ signed a decree to establish the People's Public Security Department of Vietnam; this was created by uniting the Security Office and the Police Office in each administrative region. Sáu's action unit first came under the Security Office and then the People's Public Security Department.

41. Võng La is another name for Kẻ Chài Hamlet, a name used two centuries ago.

42. *19 August Revolution Is Creation*. Hanoi: Association of Vietnamese Historians, 1995.

43. *19 August Revolution Is Creation*. Hanoi: Association of Vietnamese Historians, 1995.

44. Đào Văn Trường recalled to the author during his interview in Hanoi that Hoàng Văn Thụ had been arrested for military proselytizing activities, a crime punishable by death. Although Đào Văn Trường also had a death sentence hanging over him when arrested in 1942, it appears that his wealthy family used their money, as was common practice, and successfully lobbied the French for a reprieve. Unfortunately for some prisoners, another common approach by the French was to lift only one of, say, two death sentences, and then simply carry out the other one. Because of his affluent family background, Đào Văn Trường might not have been promoted to where he should have been within the Communist Party, but he lived into his nineties thanks to his wealth.

Chapter 3

1. *Hồ Chí Minh: A Biography by Years, 1890–1930, Volume 1*. Hanoi: National Political Publishers, 1993.

2. Henri Merlin was the governor general of Indochina from 1922–1925. Phạm Hồng Thái—real name Phạm Thành Tích. A monument was erected in honor of Phạm Hồng Thái, authorized by the government of Sun Yat-sen.

3. Albert Sarraut was the governor general of Indochina from 1911–1914 and again from 1916–1919.

4. Marr, David G. *Vietnamese Tradition on Trial 1920–1945*. Berkeley: University of California Press, 1984.

5. Quinn-Judge, Sophie. *Ho Chi Minh: The Missing Years, 1919–1941*. Berkeley: University of California Press, 2003.

6. The Vietnamese Kuomintang was also known as the Vietnamese Nationalist Party or VNQDD. When the group was created, it took time to establish, and it continually reinvented itself over the years under different guises.

7. *Vietnamese Revolutionary Youth League*. Hanoi: Political Theory Publishing, 1985.

8. The Nationalist Party of the Chinese Army Officer Academy in Guangzhou was commonly known as the Whampoa Military Academy. It had been opened by Sun Yat-sen in June 1924, with the inauguration ceremony conducted on Changzhou Island, offshore from the Whampoa dock, hence the academy's familiar name.

9. *The Party's Precursor Organizations, Volume 1*. Hanoi: Party Central Committee's Research Bureau, 1977.

10. The *Road to Revolution* had fifteen chapters written in simple question and answer format, and defined revolutionary needs under the following headings: The Status of a Revolutionary; Why should this Book be Written?; Revolution; History of the American Revolution; French History; History of the Russian Revolution; Internationality; International Communist Women; International Workers; International Communist Youth; International Help; International Red Assistance; Methods of Building a Labor Union; Organizing the Peasants; The Co-operatives. *The Legal Case of Nguyễn Ái Quốc (Hồ Chí Minh) in Hong Kong 1931–1933 (Documents and Photographs)*. Hanoi: National Political Publishers, 2006.

11. Hoàng Văn Hoan worked with Võ Nguyên Giáp, becoming responsible for the Eastward March. He became a member of the politburo for nearly twenty years. During the war with China in 1979, he fled to China and is now considered a traitor in Vietnam.

12. Hoan, Hoàng Văn. *A Drop in the Ocean, Hoàng Văn Hoan's Revolutionary Reminiscences*. Beijing: Foreign Languages, 1988.

13. Hoan, Hoàng Văn. *A Drop in the Ocean: Hoàng Văn Hoan's Revolutionary Reminiscences*. Beijing: Foreign Languages Press, 1988.

14. Ms. Bảo Lương—real name Nguyễn Trung Nguyệt.

15. Tôn Đức Thắng was a prominent leader of the Vietnamese RYL, who in April 1927 set up their Courier Department in Cochinchina. He became the president of Vietnam after Hồ Chí Minh passed away in 1969, holding the post until his death in 1980.

16. Tai, Hue-Tam Ho. *Passion, Betrayal, and Revolution in Colonial Saigon: The Memoirs of Bao Luong*. Berkeley: University of California Press, 2010.

17. Lương, Bảo and Trang, Vân. *A Cochinchinese Girl: Memoirs of Bảo Lương Nguyễn Trung Nguyệt*. Hanoi: Literature Publishing, 2004.

18. Trầm Hương, interview with the author, 15 June 2006.

19. Khoan, Nguyễn Văn and Vượng, Đức. *Hồ Chí*

Minh's Trip Abroad for Vietnam's National Salvation. Hanoi: Truth Publishing, 1990.

20. The two couriers sent to track Hồ down were Lê Duy Điếm and Cao Hoài Nghĩa; for security reasons each traveled separately.

21. The origin of the Communist Party networks dated back to those established under the Vietnamese RYL. Nguyễn Công Thu (born in Thái Bình Province, alias Red Spring, 1894–1976) founded the first cell of the Vietnamese RYL in Hanoi, in Dịch Vọng Village, Từ Liêm District, and then operated a courier line between China and Hanoi. He built all this on his return to Vietnam in 1926, after he had trained at the second course of the Vietnamese RYL in Guangzhou. This first cell comprised himself and eleven other members, whom he had personally trained. This first cell soon expanded and when enough members enrolled, it divided into a total of ten new cells, making eleven in total. Each of these eleven cells had three members. Some of the members were responsible for courier lines while others focused on recruitment.

22. *The Torch: Memoirs.* Hanoi: Literature Publishing, 1980.

23. Macau was formerly a Portuguese territory but today it is part of China.

24. *The History of the Post Office of Vietnam, Volume 1.* Hanoi: Post Office Publishing, 2002.

25. Trường Chinh, who would work with Sáu, also contributed to *Le Travail* after his release from prison in late 1936.

26. The revolutionaries did not always start newspapers; another tactic they employed was to buy a weak or failing privately run newspaper, such as from a rival group. They would then put their slant on the articles and publish it until the French shut the publication down. By setting up or purchasing newspapers, the revolutionaries could reach out to a wider readership, which might not be traditionally aligned with their views.

27. To implement in practice the work of the Courier Department, in December 1939, the Party Civil Affairs Committee of B-Inter-Provincial Zone, instructed loyal agents to operate within their territory, which stretched across north-east Tonkin. The main areas within B-Inter-Provincial Zone were the coal mining regions of Hồng Gai, Cẩm Phả, Uông Bí and Vàng Danh. The four initial agents sent were Lê Trung Đình, Nguyễn Văn Cương, Nguyễn Văn Phúc and Hoàng Minh Đạo, others included Hoàng Văn Trạch, Lê Hoàng and Hoàng Quốc Việt (real name Hạ Bá Cang). The main station for communications with Hanoi was Tràng Xá, however, in 1940, agents established a courier station in Văn Điển, a town near Hanoi, to facilitate communications between the Tonkin Regional Party Committee and the provincial party committees of Hà Đông and Hà Nam.

28. The Second Sino-Japanese conflict saw Japan expand its influence and territorial holdings to other parts of China.

29. Đào Văn Trường—real name Thành Ngọc Quản.

30. Đào Văn Trường, interview with the author, 27 February 2008.

31. Greater East Asia Co-Prosperity Sphere was formally recognized in 1940.

32. Đào Văn Trường, interview with the author, 27 February 2008.

33. The Second World War started in 1939 and Germany invaded France in 1940. The Franco-German Armistice of 22 June 1940 divided France into two zones: one to be under German military occupation and one to be left to the French in full sovereignty, at least nominally. The French zone, known as Vichy France, officially the French State, was governed by Marshal Philippe Pétain's regime and based in the small city of Vichy.

34. Phan Đăng Lưu met a number of Communist Party leaders in Tonkin including Hoàng Văn Thụ, Trường Chinh and Hoàng Quốc Việt. The former two were close associates of courier Trần Thị Sáu.

35. Đào Văn Trường, interview with the author, 27 February 2008.

36. Đào Văn Trường, interview with the author, 27 February 2008.

37. Đào Văn Trường, interview with the author, 27 February 2008.

38. Đào Văn Trường, interview with the author, 27 February 2008.

39. Trường Chinh and Hoàng Văn Thụ also attended the conference in May 1941, escorted there by Chu Văn Tấn and a squad of Bắc Sơn guerrillas.

40. Duiker, William J. *The Communist Road to Power in Vietnam.* Boulder, CO: Westview, 1996.

41. Phùng Chí Kiên—real name Nguyễn Vĩ (other names included Mạch Văn Liễu and Võ Văn Như).

42. Hoàng Văn Thái—real name Hoàng Văn Xiêm, became Vietnam's first chief of general staff of the army, appointed to the post in September 1945.

43. Đào Văn Trường, interview with the author, 27 February 2008.

44. Đào Văn Trường, interview with the author, 27 February 2008.

45. While incarcerated, Đào Văn Trường became the secretary of the secret prisoner Communist Party cell. First in Hanoi Central Prison and then later on Côn Đảo Island, where one of the cell members was Lê Duẩn, a future general secretary of the Party. Trường, Đào Văn. *The History of Armed Struggle and the First Armed Forces of the Party.* Hanoi: Self-published, 1956.

46. Tai, Hue-Tam Ho. *Passion, Betrayal, and Revolution in Colonial Saigon: The Memoirs of Bao Luong.* Berkeley: University of California Press, 2010.

47. Hải, Siêu. *With the Alias Ebony.* Hải Phòng: Hải Phòng Publishing, 1993.

48. These so-called New Revolutionaries were people who had taken advantage of the departure of the French in the mid-1950s and now attempted to earn favor with the emerging Việt Minh administration. One way to do this was to eliminate presumed traitors. By being able to pinpoint these traitors it gave the

impression that the New Revolutionaries had always sided with the Việt Minh, which in turn helped position themselves more favorably while Land Reforms were being implemented. Nguyễn Công Thu's poor relationship with the Communist Party became compounded when in 1955, New Revolutionaries branded him a traitor, captured him and sentenced him to death. At the last moment a Soviet-made car, loaded with Party members, rushed to the local execution grounds and snatched him away. Taken to Hanoi, he went on to lead a secluded life.

49. Trần Tư Chính—allies Bàng Thống and Chính the Fifth.

50. There are differing explanations as to what happened in the Rue Barbier case. Dương Quang Đông (also known as Dương Văn Phúc or Đông the Fifth) gave one account of who might have killed Lê Văn Phát and their motive. Phát was hated by his rival and classmate, Ngô Thiêm, as well as by Đỗ Đình Thọ. Phát and Thọ loved the same woman; Phát being involved with her even though he was married. (Some sources say that the woman was the sister of Cao Hoài Nghĩa, a veteran courier of the Vietnamese RYL.) According to Vietnamese RYL protocol, Phát's affair was damaging, and his removal was a possible solution. A different explanation comes from Ms. Bảo Lương. She recalls that at the Saigon headquarters of the Vietnamese RYL, a number of members hated Phát. He had abused his position of power, he had been lax with security and rumors circulated that he had mistreated a young girl. Unfortunately, the Vietnamese RYL Party Central Committee in Guangzhou had chosen Phát to represent them in the south of Vietnam, so they defended him, and sent a telegram to Saigon to explain why. This telegram clearly added friction between the two Vietnamese RYL groups, and the southern group took matters into their own hands. Neither stories can be truly verified, what is known is that at the time if a person mistreated a young girl it was punishable by death through being tied up and thrown into the sea. Phát, however, was killed by a person or people inflicting blows.

51. Trần Tư Chính had been ordered to buy a gun for a member of the Vietnamese RYL and to meet at a safe house to hand it over. The first two attempts to convene at the safe house failed as the French swarmed too close to the meeting place. On the third try the French were actually waiting. Revolutionaries concluded that Trần Tư Chính had informed the French of his actions and the location of the safe house. Others members, however, think that Trần Tư Chính became yet another victim of a French plot to covertly discredit his reputation. Regardless, with another accusation now hanging over him he was viewed with suspicion by revolutionaries thereafter.

52. The Battle of Điện Biên Phủ was codenamed by the Việt Minh—*Tran Dinh*.

53. B Department was a strategic-level organization supplying the southern battlefield with civilian goods such as food.

Chapter 4

1. Võ Nguyên Giáp—nickname Brother Văn.
2. Võ Quang Nghiêm's birth date is unknown; he died in 1948 from being tortured by the French in a prison located near Huế.
3. Cư, Phạm Hồng. *General Giáp: His Youth*. Hanoi: Youth Publishing, 2007.
4. From 1902 to 1939 and from 1947 to 1954, Hanoi served as the capital of French Indochina. Nevertheless it was Huế City to which the poem referred, as this was the Imperial Capital of Vietnam.
5. Cư, Phạm Hồng. *General Giáp: His Youth*. Hanoi: Youth Publishing, 2007.
6. The New Việt Party's full name was the New Vietnamese Revolutionary Party.
7. An "alternate member" meant that the person was not a full member of the Central Executive Committee.
8. Giáp's work for the New Việt included supporting women who had opened a shop, not only to act as a front for a courier way station but to become a source of revenue that did not attract suspicion.
9. Phan Đăng Lưu was an ideal candidate to be sent to China to unite the Vietnamese RYL with the New Việt. He had attended the third course of the Vietnamese RYL and knew the characters involved.
10. Bloc National, also called Bloc of National Unity.
11. Minh the Teacher—real name Bùi Đức Minh (1900–1963). He was called Minh the Teacher in reference to his original occupation.
12. Giáp, Võ Nguyên. *From the People Onwards: The Historical Stages, Part I*. Hanoi: National Political Publishers, 1994.
13. Võ Nguyên Giáp's house had been a courier way station, first in Henry d'Orleau (now Dường Thành Street) and later on the second floor of 42 Nam Ngư Street.
14. *Two Sisters, Revolutionary Martyrs*. Hanoi: Youth Publishing, 2007.
15. Khoan, Nguyễn Văn. *Lý Phương Đức: The Female Giao Thông of Uncle Hồ*. Hanoi: People's Public Security Publishing, 2006.
16. *Two Sisters, Revolutionary Martyrs*. Hanoi: Youth Publishing, 2007.
17. Phạm Văn Đồng went on to become the prime minister of North Vietnam 1955–1976 and chairman of the Council of Ministers of a reunified Vietnam from 1976 until his retirement in 1987.
18. One book Võ Nguyên Giáp had written in 1938–1939 was titled *The Current Military Situation in China*.
19. Hồ searched for a commander of his new army for an entire year before the Bắc Sơn Uprising which saw the Bắc Sơn guerrillas formed in October 1940.
20. Giáp, Võ Nguyên. *From the People Onwards: The Historical Stages, Part I*. Hanoi: National Political Publishers, 1994.
21. Giáp, Võ Nguyên. *From the People Onwards: The Historical Stages, Part I*. Hanoi: National Political Publishers, 1994.

22. The Sun Yat-sen clothing would be known worldwide as the Mao suit because generally whenever Mao was seen in public he had one on.

23. Giáp, Võ Nguyên. *From the People Onwards: The Historical Stages, Part I*. Hanoi: National Political Publishers, 1994.

24. Giáp, Võ Nguyên. *From the People Onwards: The Historical Stages, Part I*. Hanoi: National Political Publishers, 1994.

25. *Memories of Vũ Anh: The Riverhead*. Hanoi: Literature Publishing, 1977.

26. Giáp, Võ Nguyên. *Memoirs of War: Fighting Under Siege*. Hanoi: Thế Giới, 2004.

27. Xích Thắng—real name Dương Mạc Thạch. On many occasions he had hosted Hồ in his home; later he became the political commissar of the first unit of the Vietnam Propaganda and Liberation Army.

28. Gia Bằng is today Minh Tâm Commune.

29. Lũng Hoài is today in Hồng Việt Commune.

30. The *Vietnam's Independence* translates to *Việt Lập*.

31. Giáp, Võ Nguyên. *From the People Onwards: The Historical Stages, Part I*. Hanoi: National Political Publishers, 1994.

32. Quang, Nông Văn. *The Southward Routes*. Hanoi: National Culture Publishing, 1995.

33. Kim Mã and Tam Kim have today joined to form Tam Kim Commune.

34. Armed propaganda teams were disbanded at the end of the French War but re-established during the early stages of the Vietnam War under the wider title of action units. These operated mainly in the Central Highlands; their duties being akin to those of their armed propaganda predecessors. During the French War they were known as *công tác đội* and for the Vietnam War *đội công tác*.

35. Vượng, Đức. *Comrade Trường Chinh, Volume 2*. Hanoi: Truth Publishing, 1991.

Chapter 5

1. Chinh, Trường. *The August Revolution*. Hanoi: Thế Giới, 1962.

2. Chinh, Trường. *The August Revolution*. Hanoi: Thế Giới, 1962.

3. At the conference of 9 to 12 March 1945, the Party Central Committee discussed the need to improve the Revolutionary Infrastructure in Cochinchina. After the conference, the Party sent two couriers to Saigon, Mrs. Nguyễn Thị Kỳ (real name Cài Thị Tám) and Lý Chính Thắng (real name Nguyễn Đức Huỳnh), but both were unaware of the other's presence for security reasons. They met with the Cochinchina Regional Party Committee, initially to see if their shaky courier network could at least deliver some of the appeal leaflets from the conference that they had carried south, but in addition for the Cochinchina Regional Party Committee to write a report on courier improvements. On their return, they couriered this important report back to the Party Central Committee. The report highlighted four principles that had to be adopted in order for the courier service in the south to survive. In some instances these were principles already used in the north but had yet to be implemented in the south. The first of these principles was headed "Parallel." It said that any message needing to be delivered must be taken by at least two couriers using separate routes, with each courier not knowing of the other's task. There should be several courier routes established for any given destination, using both land and water routes. Between stations there should be one main line and another in reserve, as well as bypass routes in use as a last resort. These rules were to be implemented in all areas, including connecting the TW to the regional party committees and the provincial party committees, and connecting the Party to other friendly groups such as the French Communist Party, the Chinese Communist Party and the Comintern (until 1943). The second principle was headed "Independence." It said that when two couriers meet they must not be known to each other, that any courier must not be known to any low-ranking revolutionary, and that a courier must have a clean record with the enemy. Each courier system should operate independently from every other one; Party members and those of other revolutionary organizations should not use the same courier lines. The third principle was headed "Specialization." It said that courier stations should be used for no reason other than this work. The fourth principle was headed "Indirectness." It said when a courier worked for a leader and returned from delivering the leader's message, that courier could not go directly back to the leader but must send any reply via an intermediate courier. *Resolution from the 1st Indochinese Communist Party Central Committee Conference, October 1930, Volume 1*. Hanoi: Truth Publishing, 1964. *Resolution from the First National Party Congress of the Indochinese Communist Party, March 1935*. Hanoi: Truth Publishing, 1977. *The History Files of the Vietnamese Communist Party, Volume 1*. Hanoi: Marxism–Leninism Textbook Publishing, 1978.

4. Vượng, Đức. *Comrade Trường Chinh, Volume 2*. Hanoi: Truth Publishing, 1991.

5. Phan Kế Toại was Bảo Đại's government representative in Tonkin, so that the emperor could stay in Huế to continue his royal duties.

6. In addition to his anti-colonial view, Roosevelt was unhappy with Vichy France and its past collaboration with the Japanese; in some cases this had been outrageously overt, with officers from both sides wining and dining each other. Hence Roosevelt had little sympathy for the French soldiers on 9 March and the reprisals from the Japanese and local Vietnamese thereafter.

7. The Free French agents operated under the DGER, the French foreign intelligence service formed in November 1944. This body had ties with Force 136, a branch of the British Special Operations Executive (SOE) that operated in Indochina.

8. The OSS was the predecessor of the American CIA.

9. Tài, Phùng Thế. *The First Bodyguard of Hồ Chí Minh*. Hanoi: Youth Publishing and People's Army Publishing, 2000.

10. According to Charles Fenn, Hồ saved seventeen U.S. pilots before the war ended.

11. In 1945, Archimedes Patti headed OSS operations in Kunming; his mission in Vietnam was to establish an intelligence network. In mid-1945, a French officer said that if the OSS wanted to infiltrate and build a network, then the OSS should meet with Hồ, so Patti did.

12. In Vietnam, the Chinese were often looked at with suspicion.

13. Lê Trọng Nghĩa—real name Đoàn Xuân Tín.

14. Nguyễn Đình Thi (1924–2003) was a famous composer.

15. Lê Trọng Nghĩa, interview with the author, 26 February 2008.

16. Hồ Chí Minh ordered the establishment of the Democratic Party in 1944. It coexisted in the north of Vietnam with the ruling Party until 1988.

17. Vũ Quý (?–1945)—alias Kiên, died in Tân Trào. He had been summoned to Tan Trào to join the National People's Congress, to be held there in August 1945. It is thought that his mysterious death was a direct result of various people branding him a mole, accusations that stemmed from the fact that some revolutionaries were arrested soon after he had been released from a spell in prison. Therefore, when a radio transmitter was found on him, this was the evidence some needed to prove his collaboration with the French. Others however, defended him because a so-called "boy scout" might have possessed such a "toy." Still, his elimination was seen to be essential to the survival of those who worked closely with him.

18. Rue Rollande is today Hai Bà Trưng Street.

19. Rue Gambetta is today Trần Hưng Đạo Street.

20. Lê Trọng Nghĩa, interview with the author, 26 February 2008.

21. Ms. Bảo Lương married Hồ Hữu Tường.

22. Lê Trọng Nghĩa, interview with the author, 26 February 2008.

23. In control of the National People's Congress was the Provisional Commanding Committee of the Liberated Zone, but the Provisional Commanding Committee got temporarily sidetracked as events unfolded.

24. One of the most important parts of the Indochinese Communist Party Resolution issued at the All Country Conference was headed *The Courier Problem*. In March 1945, the Cochinchina Regional Party Committee had highlighted four principles that had to be adopted to strengthen the couriers in the south. This new Resolution built on these principles but stated that the courier lines between the Cochinchina Party Regional Committee and the provincial party committees had to be strengthened further and a Specialized Communication Board Department must be established and dedicated to the work of the couriers across Vietnam. After the Vietnam War, officials decided to choose 15 August 1945 as the symbolic day that the Post and Telecommunications service of Vietnam was founded, in recognition of the Specialized Communication Board Department and the imperative role of the couriers. *The History Files of the Vietnamese Communist Party, Volume 1*. Hanoi: Marxism-Leninism Textbook Publishing, 1978. *History of Communication, Post and Transportation in Cochinchina (1945–1975)*. Hanoi: Post Office Publishing, 2003.

25. Võ Nguyên Giáp signed Military Order No 1. It is now recognized that the order should have been expanded and been clearer on what was meant by "fight," and should have stated: cut off their routes of retreat, seize their weapons, take political power and control the offices of government, but do not directly fight or encounter the enemy, namely the Japanese Army. Fortunately, some districts in Bắc Ninh Province did take political power because there were no Japanese troops in an area, even before Hanoi, because they just seized the opportunity.

26. Marr, David G. *Vietnam 1945: The Quest for Power*. Berkeley: University of California Press, 1995.

27. Lê Trọng Nghĩa, interview with the author, 26 February 2008.

28. During these meetings with Phan Kế Toại, Lê Trọng Nghĩa used the alias Prof. Lê Ngọc.

29. Nguyễn Huy Khôi (1922–1995) was also known as Trần Quang Huy.

30. Lê Trọng Nghĩa, interview with the author, 26 February 2008.

31. Hoàng Xuân Hãn had contacted Lê Trọng Nghĩa with his desires to meet, through a courier called Thụy; later Thụy was known as Nguyễn Thành Lê and became spokesman for the Democratic Republic of Vietnam at the Paris Peace talks in the 1970s.

32. At this point, Nguyễn Xuân Chữ was both the head of the Political Committee of the Great Việt Party for Tonkin and the King's Special Envoy.

33. The offices of the King's Special Envoy later became a government-run guesthouse.

34. Nguyễn Xuân Chữ was arrested but released a few days later when Hồ Chí Minh arrived in Hanoi.

35. Lê Trọng Nghĩa, interview with the author, 26 February 2008.

36. *19 August Revolution is Creation*. Hanoi: Association of Vietnamese Historians, 1995.

37. Rue de la Concession is today called Phạm Ngũ Lão Street.

38. Lê Trọng Nghĩa, interview with the author, 26 February 2008.

39. The *Kempeitai* were the military police branch of the Imperial Japanese Army.

40. Lê Trọng Nghĩa, interview with the author, 26 February 2008.

41. Marr, David G. *Vietnam 1945: The Quest for Power*. Berkeley: University of California Press, 1995.

42. Pierre Messmer later became the prime minister of France.

43. Dunn, Peter. M, *The First Vietnam War*, C. Hurst & Company, 1985.

44. Lê Trọng Nghĩa, interview with the author, 26 February 2008.
45. Lê Trọng Nghĩa, interview with the author, 26 February 2008.
46. Lê Trọng Nghĩa, interview with the author, 26 February 2008.
47. Lê Trọng Nghĩa, interview with the author, 26 February 2008.
48. Lê Trọng Nghĩa, interview with the author, 26 February 2008.
49. Giáp, Võ Nguyên. *Unforgettable Days*. Hanoi: Thế Giới, 1975.
50. Cao Pha—real name Nguyễn Thế Lương (1919–2006). He became a famous intelligence officer during both the French War and the Vietnam War. He was deputy to Lê Trọng Nghĩa for many years until 1968, when he became the commander of a newly formed Elite Force (*Bộ đội Đặc công*). Đặng Văn Việt was a regimental commander during the battles for Route 4 leading up to the Border Campaign in 1950.
51. Marr, David G. *Vietnam 1945: The Quest for Power*. Berkeley: University of California Press, 1995.
52. Mrs. Ngô Thị Huệ, interview with the author, 15 June 2006.
53. The Vietnamese Kuomintang had just crossed the border from China and were in fact still too isolated at that time to do any harm.
54. Lê Trọng Nghĩa, interview with the author, 26 February 2008.
55. Fighting in the city was one of many areas that distinguished Việt Minh strategies from those of Mao Zedong. Mao had stated that the rural areas must be used to encircle the urban regions and not to fall into the trap of actually fighting in them. In contrast, the Vietnamese regarded both the urban areas and rural countryside as areas for operating in.
56. Hồ became president in 1945 but he had expressed a desire not to. One reason was that Hồ (Nguyễn Tất Thành) had served in the British Army as a baker from 1914–1918, and he feared that his enemies might use this information to undermine him.
57. Those present at the Potsdam Conference in Germany included President Harry S. Truman (1884–1972), Prime Minister Winston Churchill and Joseph Stalin (1878–1953).
58. Hoàng Đạo Thúy ran the Communications Liaison Service, and at the time of appointment was the head of the Boy Scouts. He went on to use communications equipment either captured from or given by, the Americans, French or Japanese. To man the newly formed service, liaison foot soldiers were co-opted from the army as well as from his Boy Scouts, for example. These individuals were not referred to as military couriers but known as liaison soldiers (*liên lạc*), their main role being liaison work. The troops were therefore guided by either civilian couriers when operating within the enemy's rural rear base areas or by military liaison soldiers when within the mountainous regions.

Chapter 6

1. Hồ always maintained that retaining power for the Communist Party must not be done at any cost to human life because it would turn the people against them.
2. Mack, Andrew J. R. "Why Big Nations Lose Small Wars: The Politics of Asymmetric Conflict." *World Politics* (January 1975).
3. Arreguin-Toft, Ivan. *How the Weak Win Wars: A Theory of Asymmetric Conflict*. Cambridge: Cambridge University Press, 2005.
4. Windrow, Martin. *The Last Valley, Dien Bien Phu and the French Defeat in Vietnam*. London: Cassell, 2005.
5. Tax reductions and the seizure of land from French colonials were first tabled in Tân Trào in mid–August at the All Country Conference.
6. Duiker, William J. *The Communist Road to Power in Vietnam*. Boulder, CO: Westview, 1996.
7. Once this diplomatic event between the Chinese Kuomintang and the Việt Minh had finished, on 22 May 1946, the Communist Party renamed the National Defense Guard the National Army of Vietnam.
8. "Political human shields" were people the revolutionaries knew to be weak and ineffectual when challenging their rule.
9. The French Union was the equivalent of the British Commonwealth and was established after the Second World War.
10. Giáp, Võ Nguyên. *Unforgettable Days*. Hanoi: Thế Giới, 1975.
11. Sweeteners came in the form of gold collected during Gold Week. Organized by Hồ's Provisional Government, Gold Week ran from 17 to 24 September 1945, and aimed to amass valuables from the population to buy weapons, etc., because the treasury was empty.
12. Nguyễn Bình—real name Nguyễn Phương Thảo (also known as Bình the Third).
13. Giáp, Võ Nguyên. *Memoirs of War: Fighting Under Siege*. Hanoi: Thế Giới, 2004.
14. Marr, David G. *Vietnamese Tradition on Trial, 1920–1945*. Berkeley: University of California Press, 1984.
15. Trần Văn Giàu's guise was as an official representative of the Vietnamese News Agency; a post he used from early 1946 to the end of 1947 for his covert work.
Vietnamese in Thailand, 1910–1960. Hanoi: People's Public Security Publishing, 2008.
16. Dương Quang Đông came from Trà Vinh Province. He started his anti-government activities in the 1920s as a member of the Labor Union. In April 1927, he was appointed head of the Courier Department for the Vietnamese RYL of the Cochinchina Regional Party Committee. From this point on he became an important figure for the revolution, establishing courier lines throughout Cochinchina. Đông worked closely with Trần Văn Giàu throughout this part of the colonial period. Originally, Đông's task to buy weapons

in 1946 had been given to Nguyễn Thanh Sơn but he had not succeeded because his advance courier boat had been intercepted by the French. This initial disappointment led to a split in thinking in Cochinchina. Vũ Đức (real name Hoàng Đình Giong, 1904–1947) advocated they go cap-in-hand to Hanoi; he was an experienced operative and was one of the six Vietnamese trained to infiltrate Japanese positions by British intelligence before the August Revolution. Phan Trọng Tuệ (1917–1991) said that they must continue with Siam; Tuệ was well versed in covert work and eventually took up the post of the commander and political commissar of the Hồ Chí Minh Trail in the mid-1960s. The leaders were persuaded by the second option, and Đông was given gold, again collected during Gold Week, and reached Bangkok on 25 February 1946.

17. Sơn Ngọc Minh became the general secretary of the Communist Party in Cambodia when the Indochinese Communist Party divided into three separate parties in 1951.

18. Abel Rene (1921–1982) was among the crew of the newly purchased 20-ton sailing boat. He was a Vietnamese patriot but a French citizen and had trained in France as a navigator. His Vietnamese name after 1945 was Lê Văn Một.

19. Hùng, Nguyên. *Dương Quang Đông and his Trans-West Supply Line.* Hanoi: Youth Publishing, 2004.

20. Name changes are steeped in tradition. For instance, in Cochinchina a number is often added to a name, as with Bình the Third. The actual first child is called the second and so on, with the last child being called the little one (*út*). This number is added to confuse evil spirits thought to have a list of people to take from the earth. In Tonkin, on the other hand, a married man or woman frequently took their first son's or daughter's name to deceive the devil. This labyrinth of cultural practice made tracing operatives through their names nearly impossible for any foe hunting them.

21. Hùng, Nguyên. *Nguyễn Bình, The Myth and Reality.* Hanoi: Literature Publishing, 1995.

22. Hùng, Nguyên. *Nguyễn Bình, The Myth and Reality.* Hanoi: Literature Publishing, 1995.

23. It is now known why the Japanese acted as they did to Nguyên Bình. Prior to this encounter they had captured documentation, signed by Giáp, which had laid out Bình's role as Hồ's ambassador in Cochinchina.

24. Hùng, Nguyên. *Nguyễn Bình, The Myth and Reality.* Hanoi: Literature Publishing, 1995.

25. Nguyễn Bình's position of commander was officially ratified by Hồ in January 1948, when he promoted Nguyễn Bình to the rank of Lieutenant General for his work in forming the Armed Force of Cochinchina.

26. Vĩnh Lộc is in present day Bình Chánh District.

27. One prominent commander of a Saigon *Biệt Động* unit in 1948 was Phạm Ngọc Thảo, the man who helped to bring down the Southern regime during the Vietnam War.

28. Hùng, Nguyên. *Nguyễn Bình, The Myth and Reality.* Hanoi: Literature Publishing, 1995.

29. The Cochinchina Communications Liaison Department was a crude arrangement based at the Red Flag Base, the nerve center of the southern resistance and located in Đồng Tháp Mười War Zone. Operations were conducted from a thatched hut on the banks of the Dương Văn Dương Canal, a waterway named after the deceased Bình Xuyên commander, Dương Văn Dương (Dương the Third). The head of the department was Nguyễn Văn Thức. He had an initial staff of roughly fifty communications liaison agents and a network of ten lines connecting Saigon, the provinces and Cambodia together. His department served a system of mailboxes, all coded using names that each courier had to learn by heart. For the Party Central Committee, the codename for their mailbox was Independent Military Unit No. 61 or Maternity No. 36. One of the longest and most grueling lines to traverse was the one to the Việt Bắc Revolutionary Base area. This could take six months, going from Đồng Tháp Mười War Zone through Trà Cú near the Vàm Cỏ Tây River, across the Bồ Bồ River to reach Vàm Cỏ Đông, to An Nhơn Tây (Củ Chi District) and An Thạnh (Thủ Dầu Một Province and Bình Dương Province today). It then crossed the 6th Zone using the coastal corridor known as E300, developed by Phạm Ngọc Thảo, on to the 5th Zone, the provinces of Thừa Thiên, Quảng Trị and Quảng Bình before arriving at Việt Bắc. Within this vast network, although radio eventually took some of the travel time away, courier principles still applied. In particular, important messages such as the battle plans issued for the Tết Offensive would always be taken by foot and via two or more routes, for security reasons.

Chapter 7

1. Hoàng Minh Đạo (real name Đào Phúc Lộc, 1923–1969) was chosen to head the Intelligence Department because he not only spoke good Chinese but was a highly accomplished expert in covert activities, having started courier duties in the 1930s. His department covered military issues, the main objective being to gather intelligence not only on the Chinese Kuomintang in Vietnam, the Vietnamese Kuomintang, the Japanese and the French but even on the Việt Minh themselves. *The Untold Story about a Hero.* Hanoi: People's Public Security Publishing, 2005.

2. After the northern Border Campaign in 1950, the intelligence service divided into two: the Strategic Intelligence Department and the Military Intelligence Department. The Strategic Intelligence Department, codenamed the Liaison Department, was run for a time by Nguyễn Văn Địch (better known as Trần Hiệu) and dealt with intelligence and security, including some special propaganda. The Military Intelligence Department was run by Lê Trọng Nghĩa and dealt with strategic intelligence and military intelligence for both the army and the Politburo (the Politburo being referred

to as the standing members of the Party Central Committee from 1930 to 1951).

3. Lucien Phạm Ngọc Thuần later became known as Phạm Ngọc Hùng.

4. Nguyễn Thanh Sơn—real name Nguyễn Văn Tây. Born in Vĩnh Long Province. Trained at the third course of the Vietnamese RYL in Guangzhou. He became commander and concurrently political commissar of Vietnam's Volunteer Armed Force in Cambodia (1950–1954) and later deputy minister of finance of the Democratic Republic of Vietnam (1958–1976).

5. Nguyễn Sơn—real name Võ Nguyên Bác (also known as Hồng Thủy). Trained at the second course of the Vietnamese RYL in Guangzhou. Took part in the 1927 Guangzhou uprising then fled to Siam. Held the rank of general in Vietnam but also in China's Red Army as he took part in the Long March.

6. One task of the Southern Military Command was to track down and gather up defeated Việt Minh units retreating northward. These soldiers would be regrouped into new detachments, retrained and then sent back to Cochinchina for further fighting.

7. Vũ Anh also known as Nguyễn Quốc Tài.

8. Vũ Anh, interview with the author, 19 May 2007.

9. Vũ Anh unpublished memoir.

10. Vũ Anh, interview with the author, 19 May 2007.

11. Dương the Third Battalion was a unit named after its deceased field commander, Dương Văn Dương. Under him, the Bình Xuyên sided with the revolutionaries until he was killed by the French in 1946. Thereafter, some of the troops under Lê Văn Viễn (alias Viễn the Seventh, 1904–1971) drifted away, finally surrendering to the French in 1948.

12. Võ Sĩ (1910–1948) was better known as Lê Văn Sĩ. From late 1945, he was political commissar of the 8th Zone with Đào Văn Trường as commander. He was the most influential Communist Party leader in Cochinchina at the time but was killed in a French raid.

13. Vũ Anh, interview with the author, 19 May 2007.

14. Y Blok Edan had been a sergeant in the French Army and later became a general in the VNPA.

15. For much of the French War the French intelligence service in Indochina did not run at its full capacity. One issue was that many of the original operatives were now in prison or dismissed because they had served in the Vichy government in Indochina during the Second World War and were considered traitors. In addition, there was a shortage of Vietnamese interpreters to join the French intelligence service, but when employed, on many occasions they turned out to be agents for the Việt Minh.

16. Vũ Anh, interview with the author, 19 May 2007.

17. Đồng Tháp Mười War Zone was not far from the Vàm Cỏ River, an area made famous by the sinking of the French vessel L'Espérance. This attack had been led by a fisherman named Nguyễn Trung Trực (1839–1868) in 1861, and saw the boat set on fire and scuttled. The French frequently used Vàm Cỏ River for their operations and through this attack the locals felt that they had struck a damaging blow against their enemy. Later, during the wars, it would become a communist courier route.

18. *60 Years of the People's Army of Vietnam*. Hanoi: Military Institute of the Ministry of Defense and People's Army Publishing, 2004.

19. Cochinchina Secret Service Department was codenamed Lê Minh Regiment, Lê Minh being the nickname of Thảo.

20. Colonel Đinh Thị Vân (1916–1995), of the Military Intelligence Department, led its strategic-level networks in Saigon until Tết of 1968.

21. Vũ Anh, unpublished memoir.

22. Hương, Trầm. "Half a Century of Inconclusive Affairs of General Nguyễn Bình." *Journal of Hồn Việt* (November 2008).

23. Hồ Chí Minh used the invisible ink technique when imprisoned in Hong Kong in the 1930s but his ink was made from rice water.

24. The Cryptography Department traced its roots back to the Military Cryptography Department first set up after the August Revolution.

25. Hương, Trầm. "Half a Century of Inconclusive Affairs of General Nguyễn Bình." *Journal of Hồn Việt* (November 2008).

26. *The History of the Post Office of Vietnam, Volume 1*. Hanoi: Post Office Publishing, 2002.

27. Miss Vương Thị Trinh, interview with Trầm Hương, 2001.

28. Vũ Anh, interview with the author, 19 May 2007.

29. Vũ Anh, interview with the author, 19 May 2007.

Chapter 8

1. Some of the Vietnamese generals who Giáp studied were: Lý Thường Kiệt, Trần Hưng Đạo, Nguyễn Trãi and Nguyễn Huệ.

2. During the French War the corridors that pushed west into Lao and Thailand were part of the Westward March (*Tây Tiến*) and later referred to as the Westward Strategic Corridor. Historically, the Westward March used some courier routes that had been first established during the Save the King Movement. During the Vietnam War, elements of the Westward Strategic Corridor formed part of the Southward Strategic Corridor as Giáp pushed south through Lao along the Trường Sơn Mountain Range, a region that forms the natural border between Lao and Vietnam. The Southward Strategic Corridor was more commonly known as the Hồ Chí Minh Trail. For both the French War and later the Vietnam War, Giáp believed that his strategic corridors would lead to victory.

3. Lai Châu Province was never taken by the Việt Minh in August 1945 because at the time of the Japanese coup in March 1945, thousands of French troops under Major General Marcel Alessandri had been based there. Although they had briefly retreated to Yunnan in China, after the political issues around the coup had settled, they had started to return.

4. Lê Hiến Mai—real name Dương Quốc Chính.

5. Sam Neua Province is present day Hua Phan Province.

6. *The Westward Once and Forever*. Hanoi: Thế Giới, 2008.

7. Hoàng Sâm—real name Trần Văn Kỳ.

8. The 2nd Zone was one of nine areas established in October 1945 and comprised Sơn La, Hòa Bình, Sơn Tây, Hà Đông, Hà Nam, Nam Định, Ninh Bình and Lai Châu. At the time the latter province included the region of Điện Biên Phủ.

9. Lê Hiến Mai and Nguyễn Anh Đệ were on their way back from Lao after seizing Mường Lát.

10. Giáp, Võ Nguyên. *Memoirs of War: Fighting Under Siege*. Hanoi: Thế Giới, 2004.

11. Battalion-sized mobile guerrilla units fought at a strategic level and were under the control of the General Staff headquarters and the headquarters of individual zones.

12. The ATK comprised the districts of Sơn Dương, Chiêm Hóa and Na Hang in Tuyên Quang Province, Định Hóa, Đại Từ and Phú Lương in Thái Nguyên Province as well as Chợ Đồn and Ba Bể in Bắc Kạn Province.

13. Việt, Đặng Văn. *Highway 4: The Border Campaign (1947–1950)*. Hanoi: Thế Giới, 1990.

14. Nguyễn Danh Lộc was a *liên lạc*. He received the first ever medal awarded to an army man during the wars in Vietnam.

15. The French Far East Expeditionary Corps included enlisted and volunteer troops from the French Union colonial territories; French professional troops; and the French Foreign Legion, this last group being made up mostly of Europeans.

16. Giáp, Võ Nguyên. *Memoirs of War: Fighting Under Siege*. Hanoi: Thế Giới, 2004.

17. Giáp, Võ Nguyên. *Memoirs of War: Fighting Under Siege*. Hanoi: Thế Giới, 2004.

18. Sip Song Chau Tai was a confederation of the Tai ethnic group chiefdoms in the north-west of Vietnam, dating back at least to the seventeenth century, and became an autonomous part of the French protectorate of Tonkin in 1889. In 1948, the French declared the region to be the Tai Federation; an independent component of the French Union with its own flag, constitution and parliament. The Tai Federation sat within the region of the French North-West Autonomous Zone (*Zone Autonome du Nord-Ouest*, ZANO), which was divided into four sub-zones: Nghĩa Lộ, Sông Đà, Sơn La and Lai Châu.

19. The Pathet Lao became the most known resistance group; from 1955 the political arm was the Lao People's Party, which changed in 1972 to the Lao People's Revolutionary Party. Two men that held high posts within the Pathet Lao were Prince Souphanouvong (1909–1995), called the Red Prince because he had aligned himself with the Việt Minh, and Kaysone Phomvihane. After the war when the Pathet Lao came to power in the newly named Lao People's Democratic Republic, Souphanouvong became president 1975–1991 and Kaysone his prime minister 1975–1991 and in 1991 president until his death in 1992.

20. *Northwest Battlefields in the First Days of the Resistance War against the French Invasion*. Hanoi: Military History Institute, 1988.

21. The Thao River is the upper stretch of the Red River. The waters originate from China and flow to Hanoi through the Vietnamese provinces of Lào Cai, Yên Bái and Phú Thọ.

22. Giáp, Võ Nguyên. *Memoirs of War: The Road to Điện Biên Phủ*. Hanoi: Thế Giới, 2004.

23. Giáp, Võ Nguyên. *Memoirs of War: The Road to Điện Biên Phủ*. Hanoi: Thế Giới, 2004.

24. The first military divisions of the VNPA. In 1949, the 308th Division was formed. On 10 March 1950, the 304th was established followed by the 312th on 25 December 1950. On 11 March 1951, the 325th was created and a few days later, on 27 March, the 351st Engineer and Artillery Division was founded. Giáp created the 320th Division on 16 April 1951, part of which was the 52nd Regiment, known as the Westward Regiment. Finally, on 1 May 1951, the 316th Division was set up.

25. Giáp, Võ Nguyên. *Memoirs of War: Fighting Under Siege*. Hanoi: Thế Giới, 2004.

26. North-West Campaign was also known as Lê Hồng Phong I.

27. Vietnamese National Army translates to *Armée Nationale Vietnamienne*.

28. Harclerode, Peter. *Fighting Dirty, The Inside Story of Covert Operations from Ho Chi Minh to Osama Bin Laden*. London: Phoenix, 2002.

29. The five confrontations prior to the North-West Campaign of 1952, where the Việt Minh used their main regular army against French troops, were: the Border Campaign 1950, the Trần Hưng Đạo Campaign in December 1950, the Hoàng Hoa Thám Campaign in early 1951, the Hà Nam Ninh Campaign later in 1951 and the Hòa Bình Campaign, which finished in early 1952.

30. Giáp, Võ Nguyên. *Memoirs of War: The Road to Điện Biên Phủ*. Hanoi: Thế Giới, 2004.

31. Giáp, Võ Nguyên. *Memoirs of War: The Road to Điện Biên Phủ*. Hanoi: Thế Giới, 2004.

32. Due to its strategic location, Sam Neua Province remained in the hands of the Lao communists until the end of the French War. Once the war had concluded, Sam Neua and Phongsaly became a critical part of the 1954 Geneva Accords, where it was agreed that the Pathet Lao could use these two northern provinces as regroupment areas. The long-term aim of those at Geneva in 1954 was to see elections across Lao that would lead to these two provinces being reintegrated into the Kingdom of Lao.

Chapter 9

1. Stuart-Fox, Martin, and Mary Kooyman. *Historical Dictionary of Laos*. Lanham, MD: Scarecrow, 1992.

2. Giáp, Võ Nguyên. *Điện Biên Phủ, Rendezvous with History*. Hanoi: Thế Giới, 2008.

3. Fall, Bernard B. *The Siege of Dien Bien Phu, Hell in a Very Small Place*. London: Da Capo, 1986.

4. The original start date of the Battle of Điện Biên Phủ was 20 January 1954, but the artillery guns were not in place.

5. Lê Trọng Nghĩa, interview with the author, 26 February 2008.

6. France's external military intelligence agency was called *Groupement de Commandos Mixtes Aéroportés* (GCMA). In December 1953, it was renamed the *Groupement Mixte d'Intervention* (GMI).

7. Lê Trọng Nghĩa, interview with the author, 26 February 2008.

8. Lê Trọng Nghĩa, interview with the author, 26 February 2008.

9. Lê Trọng Nghĩa, interview with the author, 26 February 2008.

10. Lê Trọng Nghĩa, interview with the author, 26 February 2008.

11. The part of the Battle of Huai Hai that took Huai Hai (November 1948 to January 1949) is considered by the Chinese revolutionaries to be their decisive one, which led to the overthrow of the Kuomintang.

12. Đào Văn Trường, interview with the author, 27 February 2008.

13. Giáp, Võ Nguyên. *Điện Biên Phủ, Rendezvous with History*. Hanoi: Thế Giới, 2008.

14. Đào Văn Trường, interview with the author, 27 February 2008.

15. Đào Văn Trường, interview with the author, 27 February 2008.

16. Giáp, Võ Nguyên. *Memoirs of War: The Road to Điện Biên Phủ*. Hanoi: Thế Giới, 2004.

17. Đào Văn Trường, interview with the author, 27 February 2008.

18. Lê Trọng Nghĩa, interview with the author, 26 February 2008.

19. Lê Trọng Nghĩa, interview with the author, 26 February 2008.

20. Some Vietnamese Communist Party members believed that in 1950, when the Chinese insisted on the removal of privileged Vietnamese from high office, this was part of their plan to undermine Vietnamese talent so that those who remained did not have the ability needed to end the war.

21. Lê Trọng Nghĩa, interview with the author, 26 February 2008.

22. One of the agents who stole the plans for Operation Atlante worked at the French Headquarters in Nha Trang, and was probably one of Phạm Ngọc Thảo's recruits.

23. The Phú Thọ Hòa operation started on the night of 1 June and carried on until the morning of 2 June 1954. What made this event so significant was that it has been officially recorded as the first major battle of the elite *đặc công* forces. One of two spies planted within Phú Thọ Hòa was Nguyễn Văn Lém, who had been sent to operate covertly as a porter inside the arms dump to record the camp layout, but also to glean technical details regarding the performance and abilities of any weapon technology that could be used against the Việt Minh, or that they could copy and use themselves. The reconnaissance motto was, "Hear by your own ears, see by your own eyes, touch by your own hands." When regrouped to the North in 1954, Nguyễn Văn Lém trained in courier work and returned south in 1962. Nguyễn Văn Lém was shot in the head by South Vietnamese General Nguyễn Ngọc Loan at the height of the Tết Offensive in 1968.

24. Giáp, Võ Nguyên. *Điện Biên Phủ, Rendezvous with History*. Hanoi: Thế Giới, 2008.

25. Giáp, Võ Nguyên. *Điện Biên Phủ, Rendezvous with History*. Hanoi: Thế Giới, 2008.

Chapter 10

1. In 1948, military proselytizing was officially under the Military Party Committee but after 1950 it formed as a department under the Political General Directorate. This change was a result of Chinese advisors arriving in Vietnam.

2. Nguyễn Trọng Tâm's teachers in military proselytizing work, when at Việt Bắc Revolutionary Base in 1948, were celebrated communists such as Lưu Quyên (real name Lưu Đức Hiếu) and Lưu Văn Lợi. This latter revolutionary was the secretary to Lê Đức Thọ when Thọ represented North Vietnam at the Paris Peace talks, which started in the late 1960s.

3. Thành Mỹ District is present day Mỹ Lộc District.

4. North African Propaganda and Liberation Army is translated to *Détachement International Nord-Africain* (DINA). From records it is now known that after the war some of these POWs who had been influenced by Nguyễn Trọng Tâm, and other Việt Minh proselytizing operatives, became distinguished commanders and leaders back in their home countries.

5. Nguyễn Trọng Tâm, interview with author, 14 May 2007.

6. During the Geneva Accords' 300-day period of grace it was estimated that around one million northerners fled communist rule and went to South Vietnam. Since many of these were Catholics, they were urged on by the CIA with slogans such as "The Virgin Mary is going South." A widely diverse estimate of 10,000 to 50,000 civilians and about 100,000 Việt Minh fighters moved in the opposite direction and regrouped in North Vietnam.

7. Nguyễn Trọng Tâm, interview with author, 14 May 2007.

8. The Observing the Enemy Department temporarily took over from the Intelligence Directorate and, although run by Hanoi, it was firmly rooted in the provinces of Cochinchina where intelligence gathering was most needed. Observing the Enemy Department reverted back to the Intelligence Directorate when COSVN officially returned to serve Cochinchina in 1961, with Hanoi administering the provinces of Annam that lay south of the 17th Parallel. The deputies of the Observing the Enemy Department ran the

following departments. Mai Chí Thọ (real name Phan Đình Đồng 1922–2007, one of the brothers of Lê Đức Thọ) became head of the Political Intelligence Department, which operated within opposition groups and governmental institutions. He ran six networks, OT1 to OT6. Cao Đăng Chiếm (1921–2007) was head of the Counter-Intelligence Department. He ran five networks, MQ1 to MQ5. Trần Quốc Hương (real name Trần Ngọc Ban, 1924–) was one of the key Reverse Regrouping Men and led the espionage group. He ran ten networks, GH1 to GH10. Hoàng Minh Đạo was the head of the Cochinchina Military Intelligence Department. He ran six networks, NB1 to NB6. Đạo was arrested in 24 December 1956, but soon escaped and in 1957 ran the Military Proselytizing Department of Cochinchina. He had to switch departments because under department rules, any agent who had been arrested, once released, could no longer work directly for the intelligence service. Hanoi hoped to have operating not only the main Observing the Enemy Department but a subsidiary in each province as well. *The Untold Story about a Hero*. Hanoi: People's Public Security Publishing, 2005.

9. Khánh the Seventh—real name Võ Văn Khánh.

10. Lực the Tenth—real name Ngô Văn Lực. Nguyễn Văn Hiếu also known as Nhỏ the Fourth.

11. Nguyễn Trọng Tâm, interview with author, 14 May 2007.

12. Nguyễn Trọng Tâm, interview with author, 14 May 2007.

13. Land Reforms had officially started in early 1953 and ran until 1956 in areas under the Việt Minh. They were part of the Communist Party's democratic revolution to address exploitation of peasants by feudalistic landlords. In some cases landlords were subjected to witch hunts due to the land that they had once owned. Trường Chinh resigned over the many failings of the scheme in 1956. To try to prevent any more persecution, the Party did run a correction program until 1958.

14. The structure of the new VNPA under the initial five-year plan (1955 to 1959) was as follows. The existing divisions that remained were: the 308th, the 304th, the 312th, the 316th, the 320th and the 325th. The 351st disbanded and divided to form artillery and engineering units. Other units were established. Troops from the Việt Bắc area and the 3rd Inter-zone formed three divisions: the 350th in September 1954 and the 328th and the 332nd in June 1955. Regrouped soldiers from the 5th Inter-zone formed two divisions: the 305th in September 1954 and the 324th in June 1955. Regrouped soldiers from Cochinchina formed two divisions: the 330th in January 1955 and the 338th in December 1956. Vietnamese volunteer troops from Lao and Cambodia formed the 335th in June 1955. Other new units were the three artillery divisions of the 675th, the 45th and the 349th, with the anti-aircraft division being the 367th. The VNPA also included three battalions of signal forces, which were directly subordinate to the Communications Liaison Service. Military transportation had two truck regiments subordinate to the General Rear Services Department and the Military Communications Office of the General Staff. These were not the only units or departments formed because Giáp built or upgraded military schools and colleges, for example, driver training schools.

15. In 1958, the military plan was extended by a year from 1959 to 1960, which meant that it matched the time scale of the new three-year economic reform and cultural development plan. The military plan was modified to see a reduction in troop numbers in the VNPA to reflect the relative peace Vietnam now enjoyed. Many soldiers transferred from active to reserve duties and were ordered to rebuild the country as well as work in state government agencies and on state farms. Although predominantly civilian jobs, those who did them were kept as reservists in case war broke out. Within what remained of the army the infantry was still the primary specialty branch and was reorganized into seven divisions, six brigades and twelve independent regiments not attached to a division. By the end of the restructuring, the army consisted of 160,000 soldiers. Even though the army had been streamlined, the firepower of one infantry division in 1960 was equal to the firepower of the entire communist army at Điện Biên Phủ in 1954. Many of these advanced weapons had been made by the Chinese and the Soviets.

16. Military History Institute of Vietnam, *Victory in Vietnam: The Official History of the People's Army of Vietnam, 1954–1975*. Lawrence: University Press of Kansas, 2002.

17. Thọ, Nguyễn Hữu. *Under the Same Flag*. Hồ Chí Minh City: National Political Publishers, 1993.

18. Griffin, Christopher. "A Revolution in Colonial Military Affairs: Gallieni, Lyautey, and the Tache d'huile." Paper presented at the annual conference for the British International Studies Association, Leicester, 14–16 December 2009.

19. *Vietnam: The Anti-U.S. Resistance War for National Salvation 1954–1975: Military Events*. Hanoi: People's Army Publishing, 1982.

20. The Bình Xuyên chosen for the attack on Tua Hai were those that had been switched over to the revolution by Nguyễn Trọng Tâm; at the time Tâm was better known as BK the Seventh, BK was short for Bắc Kỳ.

21. Nguyễn Trọng Tâm, interview with author, 14 May 2007.

22. During the Vietnam War, Bến Tre Province was called by the Southern regime Kiến Hòa.

23. Định, Nguyễn Thị, *No Other Road to Take*. New York: Cornell University, 1976.

24. Võ Nguyên Giáp, interview with the author, 30 December 2004.

25. The Southern authorities named part of Đắk Lắk Province, Quảng Đức Province.

26. Trần Quang Sang, was also known as Phước the Third. Phạm Văn Lạc, was also known as Lạc the Fourth.

27. *The Orient Mission*. Hanoi: People's Army Publishing, 2004.

28. Lâm Quốc Đăng—real name Nguyen Van Thuoc.
29. Hồng Sơn was also known as Hồng Sơn the Second. The author is unable to verify if he was the same person who had worked with Phạm Ngọc Thảo and Vũ Anh in the late 1940s.
30. Kiến Quốc the Eighth—real name Nguyen Hữu Xuyển. He was Giáp's commander of Armed Forces in Cochinchina until the end of 1960, and the first commanding officer of the southern liberation army from 1961 to 1963.
31. Nguyễn Trọng Tâm, interview with author, 14 May 2007.
32. Nguyễn Trọng Tâm, interview with author, 14 May 2007.
33. The Orient (*Phương Đông*) was a name given by Võ Nguyên Giáp to Trần Văn Quang's action unit. Giáp announced it at the banquet thrown for Quang before his unit departed in May 1961. Giáp got the name from Vostok-1 (Orient or East-1); the first human space flight launched in April 1961 by the USSR. Orient became a wider title given to those groups which were sent south both before and after May 1961 to establish the framework of the Liberation Army; although not all individuals who traveled appear on the official list.
34. Trần Công An—alias Ca the Second. Nguyễn Văn Nhỏ—alias Nhỏ the Second. Nguyễn Việt Hoa—alias Thà the Tenth.
35. Trần Lương—real name Trần Khuy and later known as Trần Nam Trung. He first came to Cochinchina in 1959 to reorganize the Cochinchina Regional Party Committee to form COSVN, he then returned to the North. In 1961 he went back to Cochinchina as part of the Orient mission.
36. C War Zone, also known as Dương Minh Châu War Zone.

Chapter 11

1. Mrs. Lê Thị Thu Nguyệt, interview with the author, 16 June 2006.
2. Mrs. Lê Thị Thu Nguyệt, interview with the author, 16 June 2006.
3. The Củ Chi tunnels were established during the French War by the Việt Minh. This network would be critical for conducting attacks on Saigon throughout the Vietnam War. Today, the Củ Chi tunnels are one of Vietnam's most famous tourist attractions.
4. At the time $1 was approximately 70 *đồng*.
5. Mrs. Lê Thị Thu Nguyệt, interview with the author, 16 June 2006.
6. Shultz, Richard H. Jr. *The Secret War Against Hanoi*. London: HarperCollins, 1999.
7. Ngô Đình Nhu was widely regarded as the architect of the Ngô family's nepotistic and autocratic rule.
8. Some reasons the Strategic Hamlet Program failed were: (1) the scheme placed too much emphasis on the military side, whereas the people wanted physical and economic security as well as confidence in any legal system; (2) the scheme failed to have a long-term comprehensive defense strategy for the hamlets; (3) the scheme started to exploit the human and material resources of each hamlet too early; (4) some of the staff who operated the hamlets were too corrupt; and (5) although the Southern government did run high-profile propaganda campaigns to encourage people to take part such as "We would rather leave our birth place than live under the communists," unsurprisingly the communists used reverse psychology to get the people to oppose the scheme. They claimed that the American and Southern governments were building "concentration camps" to hold innocent Vietnamese farmers and peasants in confinement.
9. Brink Hotel was also known as the Brink Bachelor Officers Quarters (BOQ).
10. Trần Hải Phụng had been a commander under Nguyễn Bình in the initial stages of the French War.
11. Mrs. Lê Thị Thu Nguyệt, interview with the author, 16 June 2006.
12. MAAG was renamed MAAG Vietnam in 1955.
13. Mrs. Lê Thị Thu Nguyệt, interview with the author, 16 June 2006.
14. Mrs. Lê Thị Thu Nguyệt, interview with the author, 16 June 2006.
15. Some sources record that the start date of the X Plan was to be 19 May 1965; Hồ Chí Minh's birthday.
16. Nguyễn Trọng Tâm, interview with author, 14 May 2007.
17. The Second Coalition government of Lao formed as a condition for international endorsement of the neutrality of Lao at Geneva in July 1962. Both the Democratic Republic of Vietnam and the Lao government had agreed to these terms.

This model used for Lao was the one that some of those who were involved in signing these Geneva Accords had hoped to draw up for Vietnam. Sadly for those people by the end of the year they saw their hopes fade away. Part of the Geneva Accords specified that all foreign military personnel had to leave Lao by 7 October. Both sides now violated this; Hanoi sent troops down the Hồ Chí Minh Trail and Souvanna Phouma requested American assistance.
18. One of the main reasons the CIA suspected Phạm Ngọc Thảo of being an agent of Hanoi's was that his brother, Gaston Phạm Ngọc Thuần, had been appointed North Vietnam's ambassador to East Germany and in 1963 Thảo had visited him. In those days it was extremely difficult to enter the Communist Bloc unless you were from another socialist country.
19. In 1964, the Americans had made Nguyễn Văn Thiệu chairman of the Committee of State Leaders, with the potential of becoming president. He was one of a number of American-backed South Vietnamese men being groomed to take high office. He eventually became the longest serving president of South Vietnam.
20. Vũ Anh believes that Trần Kim Tuyến, the counter-intelligence officer who had monitored him, played a part in Phạm Ngọc Thảo's death. Tuyến had been arrested when the Diệm administration fell, but

was released from prison by Thiệu shortly after Thảo died.

21. Nguyễn Đức Hùng (1928–2012), also known as Chu the Fourth, went on to become the chief of staff of the 6th Sub-Zone during the Tết Offensive in Saigon.

22. A20 and A30 were renamed J8 and J9 respectively in 1967.

23. The slogan, "holding the enemy by their belt," had its roots in 1953, when the Việt Minh pursued pro-French Thai soldiers in upper Lao, during the Upper Lao Campaign. Instead of killing these fleeing Thai soldiers the Việt Minh kept pace with them, captured their weapons, and then released them after proselytizing. The Việt Minh engaged so closely with the Thai soldiers that the Việt Minh fighters said that they held onto their belts.

Chapter 12

1. Jim Burns, email message to author, 31 December 2009.

2. To keep in contact with sympathizers in Thailand, after 1945 Võ Nguyên Giáp re-established courier corridors to Nakhon Phanom. (They were first set up in the 1920s by the likes of Phan Bội Châu and Cựu Tuấn.) Giáp said to his commanders in Thailand and Lao, "These courier corridors must be built as civilian routes." Eventually, they became part of the Trans-Indochina Link during the French War. Giáp maintained links to Nakhon Phanom for the Vietnam War; on the Lao–Vietnam border these corridors became part of the Hồ Chí Minh Trail. Revolutionary activities in Thailand came under Hanoi's jurisdiction. These lines of communications enabled elite đặc công forces to design and execute attacks on U.S. bases there because American bombers flew from them to strike North Vietnam. There are records of attacks on Udorn RTAFB and Nakhon Phanom RTAFB. At all times Hanoi took care not to aggravate the Thai authorities as this might have expanded the war. Vick, Alan, *Snakes in the Eagle's Nest: A History of Ground Attacks on Air Bases*. Santa Monica, CA: Rand, 1995.

3. Jim Burns, email message to author, 31 December 2009.

4. Jim Burns, email message to author, 3 January 2010.

5. Jim Burns, email message to author, 31 December 2009.

6. Jim Burns, email message to author, 31 December 2009.

7. Bond, Ray. *The Vietnam War, The Illustrated History of the Conflict in Southeast Asia*. London: Salamander, 1987.

8. Shining Brass operations followed in the footsteps of those who had carried out U.S.-led covert missions before, under Operation Hotfoot, which started in 1959. Hotfoot was later renamed Operation White Star. Operations formally halted on the signing of the second Geneva Accords in 1962 with the neutrality of Lao. It took until 1964 for covert missions, codenamed Project Leaping Lena, to reconvene along the Hồ Chí Minh Trail. However, these were restricted in their area of operation and Vietnamese-led, and on insertion into Lao the teams were compromised and attacked, with just a handful of men making it back. No more teams were sent in until Shining Brass.

9. Greco, Frank. *Running Recon: A Photo Journey with SOG Special Ops Along the Ho Chi Minh Trail*. Boulder, CO: Paladin, 2004.

10. Meyer, John Stryker. *On the Ground: The Secret War in Vietnam*. Oceanside, CA: Levin, 2007.

11. Meyer, John Stryker. *On the Ground: The Secret War in Vietnam*. Oceanside, CA: Levin, 2007.

12. Located in Lao, Army Station 34 took responsibility from La Hap to the north of Bac along Route 128, and from La Hap to A Tuc along Route B45. Within this station were: the 39th Engineer Battalion and 45th Engineer Battalion, the 57th Truck Transport Battalion, the 10th Anti-aircraft Artillery Battalion, the 1st Infantry Battalion, the 11th Courier Battalion and units to deal with supplies and medical care. *Lịch Sử Đoàn 559 Bộ Đội Trường Sơn Đường Hồ Chí Minh*. Hanoi: People's Army Publishing, 1999.

13. Meyer, John Stryker. *On the Ground: The Secret War in Vietnam*. Oceanside, CA: Levin, 2007.

14. Meyer, John Stryker. *On the Ground: The Secret War in Vietnam*. Oceanside, CA: Levin, 2007.

15. Võ Nguyên Giáp, interview with the author, 30 December 2004.

16. Hoàng Văn Thái, who became commander of the Hồ Chí Minh Trail, was not the same Hoàng Văn Thái who became chief of staff during the first stages of the French War.

17. Đồng Sĩ Nguyên, interview with the author, 3 September 2003.

18. Prados, John. *The Blood Road: The Ho Chi Minh Trail and the Vietnam War*. New York: John Wiley & Sons, 1998.

19. In the early 1960s, the Chinese had been the first to support the escalation of the war in Vietnam. In 1963, Zhou Enlai stated that if North Vietnam was attacked China could be used as a rear base area by the Vietnamese revolutionaries. Zhou Enlai was now the prime minister of the People's Republic of China and this pledge gave Hanoi access to greater troop training programs, for example. The Soviets' loyalty had been very different. They had only really been accommodating since 1964, when Russian leader Nikita Khrushchev lost his office. Khrushchev's support for Hanoi, after the Geneva Accords in 1954, was more in the form of information, technical advisors and moral support. Now, with Leonid Brezhnev in power, the Soviets resumed aiding North Vietnam, following the new doctrine of supporting the liberation movement of the world. Nevertheless, supplies from the Soviets were at times threatened when the Soviets accused China of stealing consignments transiting their country.

20. Shultz, Richard H. Jr. *The Secret War Against Hanoi*. London: HarperCollins, 1999.

21. STRATA operations stood for Short-Term Roadwatch and Target Acquisition.

22. The "double-cross system" was what John Cecil Masterman had called this type of work during the Second World War. Masterman had chaired the Twenty Committee and had run such an operation against Nazi Germany for MI5; double-cross was named after the Roman numerals for twenty, XX. Masterman explained that this system was more than just conducting a few isolated covert incidents. Through double-cross agents, MI5 had actively run and controlled the entire German espionage system in Britain.

23. Shultz, Richard H. Jr. *The Secret War Against Hanoi*. London: HarperCollins, 1999.

24. John Stryker Meyer, interview with the author, 2 January 2012.

25. Fall, Bernard B. *Street Without Joy: The French Debacle in Indochina*. Mechanicsburg, PA: Stackpole, 1989.

Chapter 13

1. Lê Minh, also known as Tư Minh and Minh the Fourth (1915–1990) encouraged Phan Nam to join the revolution. Phan Nam only used the name Phan Nam after 1975 when he became chairman of the People's Committee (mayor) of Huế City.

2. In the 1940s, Phan Nam had been asked to enter covert activities because he was a member of the Phú Lộc District Party Committee, and the Party wanted to promote the youth.

3. Phan Nam, interview with the author, 10 May 2007.

4. B4 covered the provinces of Quảng Trị and Thừa Thiên, with the administrative arm being the Trị Thiên Party Committee. The main objective of B4 was to draw American troops closer to the DMZ so that the communists could fight them nearer to communist supply lines. This enabled the communists to supply their troops as well as to keep them operationally effective. B5 was under the command of B4. Its area of operation was Route 9, which included Khe Sanh. B5 was there to force the Americans to further disperse their strategic mobile units and draw them into the mountains. This took them away from the cities and Cochinchina, where the revolutionaries were at their weakest.

5. Hùng Sơn had built the Revolutionary Infrastructure in the region during the French War, and for the Vietnam War he expanded upon it.

6. Phan Nam, interview with the author, 10 May 2007.

7. Phan Nam, interview with the author, 10 May 2007.

8. Phan Nam, interview with the author, 10 May 2007.

9. Willbanks, James H. *The Tet Offensive: A Concise History*. New York: Columbia University Press, 2006.

10. Most positions of power were held by the Catholics, and Ngô Đình Diệm and his government made every effort to undermine Buddhist celebrations.

11. Phan Nam, interview with the author, 10 May 2007.

12. Hoàng Hoa, interview with the author, 10 May 2007.

13. Phan Nam, interview with the author, 10 May 2007.

14. Mrs. Tuấn Chi—real name Đào Thị Xuân Yến (1909–1997).

15. Westmoreland, William C. *A Soldier Reports*. London: Da Capo, 1989.

16. Westmoreland, William C. *A Soldier Reports*. London: Da Capo, 1989.

17. Mrs. Nguyễn Quý Hoàng Nhung, interview with the author, 11 May 2007.

18. In the 1954 exodus, Colonel Đinh Thị Vân had been sent south by Hanoi to infiltrate the Southern administration.

19. After the Tết Offensive COSVN continued to move locations, including going back to Phum Chrak Rumdould, before finally establishing a new base nearby, at Phum Rumdould, from 1973.

20. Hồ Đệ, interview with the author, 6 May 2007.

21. "Vietnam: The Signs of Stalemate," an article written by R. W. Apple Jr., special correspondent to the *New York Times* on 7 August 1967, stated why those in Washington needed to tell the truth. "The Americans and their Allies, having killed by their own count 200,000 enemy troops, now face the largest enemy force they have ever faced: 297,000 men, again by their own count. The enemy has progressed from captured rifles and skimpy supplies to rockets, artillery, heavy mortars, a family of automatic infantry weapons and flame throwers, most of which has been brought into South Vietnam in the face of American air power, 1.2 million Allied troops have been able to secure only a fraction of a country less than one and a half times the size of New York State. The Allies are reaching the bottom of their ready manpower pool, while the North Vietnamese have committed only one-fifth of their regular army. Above all, if the North Vietnamese and American troops were magically whisked away, the South Vietnamese regime would almost certainly crumble within months, so little have the root problems been touched."

22. Left Bank was the historic name for the northern bank of the Perfume River.

23. Tết eve for a launch date or fighting over the New Year holiday had not been agreed to by Hồ or Giáp, who were abroad at the time.

24. The change of calendar for Tết New Year was only implemented in South Vietnam after 1975.

25. Evidence that Hoàng Văn Thái could think fast on his feet was seen during the Tết Offensive. Prior to Tết, he had been told by Giáp to travel from Annam (where he was the commander of the 5th Military Zone) to Cochinchina (and become the commander of B2 Front). Giáp's order was not transmitted by radio but in autumn 1967 Hanoi sent a military delegation

to the 5th Military Zone to deliver the instruction; a journey that took them two months to complete. Now based in Cochinchina for Tết, Hoàng Văn Thái could see that he had to implement Giáp's philosophy of not to fight at any cost, to prevent parts of the revolutionary forces, especially the secret service, from being exposed. His actions saved strategic agents from death or imprisonment, including Phạm Xuân Ẩn, enabling them to be available to fight in the final offensive of 1975. Other leaders were not confident decision-makers and consequently their agents perished.

26. Resolution 14 was also known as the Quang Trung Resolution. Nguyễn Huệ defeated the Qing Army from China in 1789. He became Emperor Quang Trung and presided over a united Vietnam. Emperor Quang Trung came to power in 1789 and Hồ came to power after the August Revolution in 1945; both the Year of the Rooster. It was hoped that the Rooster was a good omen because 1969 was also the Year of the Rooster, which again could see the first full year of a united Vietnam.

27. To keep the U.S. Marines at Khe Sanh, in order to take vital U.S. military manpower from other strategic locations during Tết, Giáp not only attacked the camp in January 1968 but spread rumors saying that this was America's Điện Biên Phủ. Giáp's plan worked because to stop a disaster happening like Điện Biên Phủ, the U.S. Marines stationed there stubbornly defended Khe Sanh until their planned withdrawal in June.

28. The three independent infantry companies were linked to Hương Trà, Hương Thủy and Phú Vang districts.

29. Phan Nam, interview with the author, 10 May 2007.

30. The 66D, the 66E and the *biệt động* units of the Left Bank were three units who operated under the security section of the Huế City Party Committee.

31. This DKB was a Soviet made Grad-P single tube launcher system.

32. Phan Nam, interview with the author, 10 May 2007.

33. Thân Trọng Một was the commander of the Southern Wing and Nguyễn Vạn the political commissar.

34. Hoàng Lanh, interview with the author, 9 May 2007.

35. A Company was part of the 1st Battalion, 1st Marine Regiment, 1st Marine Division.

36. Nolan, Keith William. *Battle for Hue: Tet, 1968.* Novato, CA: Presidio, 1996.

37. It has been recorded by American soldiers fighting in Huế City that some battle-hardened South Vietnamese soldiers ceased to oppose the communists even when ordered to fight them, although they still remained within their Southern unit. Porch, Douglas. *The French Foreign Legion, A Complete History of the Legendary Fighting Force.* New York: Harper Perennial, 1992.

38. K10, K referred to battalion.

39. Mrs. Nguyễn Thị Hoa, interview with the author, 9 May 2007.

40. Mrs. Hoàng Thị Nở, interview with the author, 9 May 2007.

41. Hoàng Lanh, interview with the author, 9 May 2007.

42. Hoàng Lanh, interview with the author, 9 May 2007.

43. In other areas for Tết, Wave I started in January, Wave II in May and Wave III in August, although the February Wave II attacks in Saigon also occurred in other cities. The wave numbering only officially took place after the Tết Offensive had concluded and Communist Party members needed to define events.

44. Mrs. Võ Thị Tâm, interview with the author, 16 June 2006.

45. Mrs. Võ Thị Tâm, interview with the author, 16 June 2006.

46. Mrs. Võ Thị Tâm, interview with the author, 16 June 2006.

47. Mrs. Võ Thị Tâm, interview with the author, 16 June 2006.

48. Westmoreland, William C. *A Soldier Reports.* London: Da Capo, 1989.

49. Hoàng Lanh, interview with the author, 9 May 2007.

50. Phan Nam, interview with the author, 10 May 2007.

Chapter 14

1. The Nixon Doctrine meant that the U.S. would supply arms but not military forces to its allies in Asia and elsewhere. It was put forward during a press conference in Guam on 25 July 1969 by Nixon and later formalized in his speech on Vietnamization on 3 November 1969.

2. Grant, Zalin. *Facing the Phoenix: The CIA and the Political Defeat of the United States in Vietnam.* New York: W. W. Norton, 1991.

3. Edward Lansdale was one of the first specialists brought into Vietnam in the early 1950s to look at covert activities. He had originally been in the Philippines where, in the 1950s, covert operations, political reform and economic development played a significant role in defeating the communist insurgency there, and he had been credited by some for America's success there. Now in Vietnam his initial mission was to train, equip and infiltrate a handful of small paramilitary teams into North Vietnam. The problem he faced was that the North Vietnamese paid particular attention to their internal security and population control. Like the French before them with their *maquis* covert operatives, he would find building resistance movements and agent networks inside North Vietnam a daunting if not a fruitless task.

4. People's Self-Defense Forces were also known as the Popular Forces.

5. Prados, John. *Lost Crusader: The Secret Wars of CIA Director William Colby: The True Story of One of*

America's Most Controversial Spymasters. Oxford: Oxford University Press, 2003.

6. Phước Tuy Province was formerly Ninh Thuận Province.

7. Prados, John. *The Hidden History of the Vietnam War.* Chicago: Elephant, 1998.

8. PRUs dropped the word terror because it was not seen as appropriate.

9. Prados, John. *Lost Crusader: The Secret Wars of CIA Director William Colby, The True Story of One of America's Most Controversial Spymasters.* Oxford: Oxford University Press, 2003.

10. Adams, Samuel. "Intelligence Failures in Vietnam: Suggestions for Reform." Paper presented at a meeting for the CIA, Washington DC, 24 January 1969.

11. Adams stated that one initial definition agreed upon for the VCI was, "As the political and administrative organization through which the Việt Cộng control, or seek to control, the South Vietnamese People. It embodies the Party control structure, which includes a command and an administrative apparatus (COSVN) at the national level, and the leadership and administration of a parallel front organization (NLF), both of which extend from the national level down to the hamlet level." Adams, Samuel. "Intelligence Failures in Vietnam: Suggestions for Reform." Paper presented at a meeting for the CIA, Washington, DC, 24 January 1969.

12. Major Mark A. Smith is now retired from the U.S. Army. He first enlisted into the military in December 1963, but was not brought to active duty until February 1964 when he was sent to Fort Ord, California, for basic training and advanced infantry training. Today, he is a military intelligence advisor in Asia, looking at extremists and their infrastructures.

13. Special Purpose Unit was known as *Biệt Đội* in Vietnamese.

14. Fort Bragg North Carolina was also where Phạm Ngọc Thảo had done some of his training.

15. Little people meant the Vietnamese.

16. Rừng Sác Special Zone was sometimes spelt Rung Sat Special Zone and was the name given by the South Vietnamese and Americans to a large area of the Sác Forest, *Rừng Sác*.

17. Mark Smith, interviews with the author, 29 February–1 March 2008 and 4 March–10 March 2010.

18. One American interrogator stated, "The Việt Cộng men always gave him the information he asked for but the Việt Cộng women were another thing. They were the hardest to turn into police informers, but when one did, it broke the back of their VC Communist cell." Games, Ben R. *Confession of a CIA Interrogator.* Bloomington, IN: Author House, 2007.

19. Mrs. Phuong, interviews with the author, 29 February–1 March 2008 and 4 March–10 March 2010.

20. The liberation and perception of women changed between the French and the American conflicts. The French saw women as delicate, and the Vietnamese men were reluctant to search females due to social protocol but also in fear that they might find women's essentials or worse that she was having her menstrual cycle and deemed untouchable. The Americans had no such inhibitions and Vietnamese attitudes were forced to change, albeit slowly.

21. Lê Thị Thu, interview with the author, 15 June 2006.

22. Swan girls (*thiên nga*) were secret policewomen who infiltrated communist positions or operated very close by. They used radios to call in heliborne Special Forces ranger units to destroy areas or they acted as a form of forward observation officer to direct ground-based heavy artillery or a helicopter's on-board firepower on to communist areas.

23. Trần Thị Thu, interview with the author, 10 May 2007.

24. Mark Smith, interviews with the author, 29 February–1 March 2008 and 4 March–10 March 2010.

25. Kolko, Gabriel, *Anatomy of a War, Vietnam, The United States and the Modern Historical Experience.* London: Phoenix, 2001.

26. Mark Smith, interviews with the author, 29 February–1 March 2008 and 4 March–10 March 2010.

27. Mrs. Phuong, interviews with the author, 29 February–1 March 2008 and 4 March–10 March 2010.

28. Mark Smith, interviews with the author, 29 February–1 March 2008 and 4 March–10 March 2010.

29. Mark Smith, interviews with the author, 29 February–1 March 2008 and 4 March–10 March 2010.

30. Mark Smith, interviews with the author, 29 February–1 March 2008 and 4 March–10 March 2010.

31. Prados, John. *Lost Crusader: The Secret Wars of CIA Director William Colby, The True Story of One of America's Most Controversial Spymasters.* Oxford: Oxford University Press, 2003.

32. Mark Smith, interviews with the author, 29 February–1 March 2008 and 4 March–10 March 2010.

33. Mark Smith, interviews with the author, 29 February–1 March 2008 and 4 March–10 March 2010.

34. Mark Smith, interviews with the author, 29 February–1 March 2008 and 4 March–10 March 2010.

35. "Cutting off the lizard's tail," was an expression used by Giáp after the wars and came from an ancient Vietnamese saying. Giáp's motto during the war was, "Strike enemy posts that are difficult to access, but important to the enemy, to force them to defend their positions." It was an important strategy because those enemy troops making up the so-called lizard's tail were still able to fight but might not have the stomach to do so, be unable to take directions from their command, fail to make rational decisions and be forced to withdraw. If the enemy sent in reinforcements, Giáp could attack them when they were not ready to fight, his motto being, "Lay in ambush so that the few can confront the many." Giáp used this type of attack to gain a strategic effect: if he failed to take the posts he would have tied up the enemy as they made a push to save the situation, but if he did achieve his goals it would force enemy headquarters to build another belt of outposts, thus draining valuable resources.

36. The chain of outposts cut off by the VNPA when

they took Đông Khê included those situated in both cities and towns: Cao Bằng, Đông Khê, Thất Khê, Na Sầm, Đồng Đăng, Lạng Sơn, Tiên Yên, Móng Cái and some small post such as Đồng Lập.

37. The doctors who sent Giáp to Eastern Europe for medical treatment, prior to the Easter Offensive, were appointed especially to serve Politburo members. In certain instances their decisions were driven by Communist Party needs.

38. It was these secret meetings in China in 1969 that led people such as Mrs. Phuong to mistakenly conclude that Kissinger was a communist and there to double-cross the South.

39. Mark Smith, interviews with the author, 29 February–1 March 2008 and 4 March–10 March 2010.

Chapter 15

1. Letter by Fred Branfman for Nguyễn Hữu Thái, 9 August 2006.
2. Thái, Nguyễn Hữu. *Choices: An Insider's Account of War and Peace in Vietnam, told by a Former Saigon Student and Leader.* Hanoi: Self-published, 2005.
3. Thái, Nguyễn Hữu. *Choices: An Insider's Account of War and Peace in Vietnam, told by a Former Saigon Student and Leader.* Hanoi: Self-published, 2005.
4. Mrs. Nguyễn Quý Hoàng Nhung, interview with the author, 11 May 2007.
5. The name Hồ Chí Minh Campaign was only chosen a few days before the campaign started.
6. Bùi Quang Thận was commander of the 4th Tank Company, 1st Tank Battalion, 203rd Tank Armor Brigade, 2nd Corps.
7. Thái, Nguyễn Hữu. *Choices: An Insider's Account of War and Peace in Vietnam, told by a Former Saigon Student and Leader.* Hanoi: Self-published, 2005.
8. Thái, Nguyễn Hữu. *Choices: An Insider's Account of War and Peace in Vietnam, told by a Former Saigon Student and Leader.* Hanoi: Self-published, 2005.
9. Nhương, Hà Bình. *Magnificent Camouflage, Stories of Secret Agents in the Saigon Administration.* Hanoi: Thế Giới, 2008.
10. Nguyễn Xuân Tốn, interview with the author, 10 May 2007.
11. Lê Quang Vịnh, interview with the author, 10 May 2007.
12. The New Economic Areas were originally set up in good faith because after the war there were nearly three million urban unemployed in the south who needed help to get back to work. However, they were established on uncultivated land in under-populated rural provinces, so conditions were harsh and over time the areas became a mass way of punishing or re-educating people.
13. Thái, Nguyễn Hữu. *Choices: An Insider's Account of War and Peace in Vietnam, told by a Former Saigon Student and Leader.* Hanoi: Self-published, 2005.
14. Bass, Thomas A. *The Spy Who Loved Us, The Vietnam War and Pham Xuan An's Dangerous Game.* New York: Public Affairs, 2009.
15. Ms. Đức and her brother Ngô Chính Quốc were branded traitors by the Communist Party. No evidence has been found to prove their guilt but they are thought to be victims of the divide-and-rule tactics of the French.
16. Lê Duẩn's group were called dogmatic opportunists by so-called proper communists. In other words, they might have flown the flag of communist ideology but secretly they followed their own interests and authority. Lenin designated people or groups who put their interests first as enemies of socialism, communism and internationalism.

Epilogue

1. Phạm Hồng Cư and Mrs. Đặng Thị Hạnh, interview with the author, 27 February 2010.
2. Lê Trọng Nghĩa, interview with the author, 26 February 2008.
3. Phạm Hồng Cư and Mrs. Đặng Thị Hạnh, interview with the author, 27 February 2010.
4. Coll, Steve. *Ghost Wars, The Secret History of the CIA, Afghanistan and Bin Laden, from the Soviet Invasion to September 10, 2001.* London: Penguin, 2004.
5. Coll, Steve. *Ghost Wars, The Secret History of the CIA, Afghanistan and Bin Laden, from the Soviet Invasion to September 10, 2001.* London: Penguin, 2004.
6. The situation in Afghanistan was very complicated. The official agreement was that the funds and weapons supplied by the CIA to the Mujahideen had to go via Pakistan and that no CIA officer must establish contact with any high level Mujahideen leaders without the permission and presence of an operative from the ISI, the Pakistani intelligence service. This arrangement meant that Pakistani military generals allocated the funds and weapons to various Mujahideen leaders. A situation that has led some to believe that the money and supplies were distributed more to control events in Afghanistan to meet the agenda and long-term strategic needs of Pakistan, which may or may not have suited the CIA or the Afghans. Dr. Aziz Shahab, email message to author, 17 July 2014.
7. Al-Qaeda cited U.S. support of Israel, the presence of U.S. troops in Saudi Arabia and sanctions against Iraq as motives for the attacks.
8. Dr. Aziz Shahab, interview with the author, 9 February 2014.
9. Coll, Steve. *Ghost Wars, The Secret History of the CIA, Afghanistan and Bin Laden, from the Soviet Invasion to September 10, 2001.* London: Penguin, 2004.
10. Arreguin-Toft, Ivan. *How the Weak Win Wars: A Theory of Asymmetric Conflict.* Cambridge: Cambridge University Press, 2005.
11. Phạm Hồng Cư and Mrs. Đặng Thị Hạnh, interview with the author, 27 February 2010.

Bibliography

Books

Arreguin-Toft, Ivan. *How the Weak Win Wars: A Theory of Asymmetric Conflict.* Cambridge: Cambridge University Press, 2005.

Bass, Thomas A. *The Spy Who Loved Us: The Vietnam War and Pham Xuan An's Dangerous Game.* New York: Public Affairs, 2009.

Bond, Ray. *The Vietnam War: The Illustrated History of the Conflict in Southeast Asia.* London: Salamander, 1987.

Borton, Lady. *Hồ Chí Minh: A Journey.* Hanoi: Thế Giới, 2007.

Chau, Phan Boi. *Overturned Chariot: The Autobiography of Phan-Boi-Chau.* Hawai'i: University of Hawai'i Press, 1999.

Chinh, Trường. *The August Revolution.* Hanoi: Thế Giới, 1962.

Coll, Steve. *Ghost Wars: The Secret History of the CIA, Afghanistan and Bin Laden, from the Soviet Invasion to September 10, 2001.* London: Penguin, 2004.

Cư, Phạm Hồng. *General Giáp: His Youth.* Hanoi: Youth Publishing House, 2007.

Định, Nguyễn Thi. *No Other Road to Take.* New York: Cornell University, 1976.

Đức, Lý Phương. *Following Uncle Hồ to Work for the Revolution.* Hanoi: Unpublished memoir, 1984.

Duiker, William J. *The Communist Road to Power in Vietnam.* Boulder, CO: Westview, 1996.

Duiker, William J. *Ho Chi Minh: A Life.* New York: Theia, 2000.

Fall, Bernard B. *The Siege of Dien Bien Phu: Hell in a Very Small Place.* London: Da Capo, 1986.

Fall, Bernard B. *Street Without Joy: The French Debacle in Indochina.* Mechanicsburg, PA: Stackpole, 1989.

Games, Ben R. *Confession of a CIA Interrogator.* Bloomington, IN: Author House, 2007.

Giáp, Võ Nguyên. *Điện Biên Phủ: Rendezvous with History.* Hanoi: Thế Giới, 2008.

Giáp, Võ Nguyên. *From the People Onwards: The Historical Stages, Part I.* Hanoi: National Political Publishers, 1994.

Giáp, Võ Nguyên. *Memoirs of War: Fighting Under Siege.* Hanoi: Thế Giới, 2004.

Giáp, Võ Nguyên. *Memoirs of War: The Road to Điện Biên Phủ.* Hanoi: Thế Giới, 2004.

Giáp, Võ Nguyên. *Unforgettable Days.* Hanoi: Thế Giới, 1975.

Grant, Zalin. *Facing the Phoenix: The CIA and the Political Defeat of the United States in Vietnam.* New York: W.W. Norton, 1991.

Greco, Frank. *Running Recon: A Photo Journey with SOG Special Ops Along the Ho Chi Minh Trail.* Boulder, CO: Paladin, 2004.

Hải, Siêu. *With the Alias Ebony.* Hải Phòng: Hải Phòng Publishing, 1993.

Harclerode, Peter. *Fighting Dirty: The Inside Story of Covert Operations from Ho Chi Minh to Osama bin Laden.* London: Phoenix, 2002.

The History Files of the Vietnamese Communist Party, Volume 1. Hanoi: Marxism–Leninism Textbook Publishing, 1978.

History of Communication, Post and Transportation in Cochinchina (1945–1975). Hanoi: Post Office Publishing, 2003.

The History of the Post Office of Vietnam, Volume 1. Hanoi: Post Office Publishing, 2002.

History of the Vietnamese People's Army, Volume 1. Hanoi: People's Army Publishing, 1974.

Hồ Chí Minh: A Biography by Years 1890–1930, Volume 1. Hanoi: National Political Publishers, 1993.

Hoan, Hoàng Văn. *A Drop in the Ocean: Hoàng Văn Hoan's Revolutionary Reminiscences.* Beijing: Foreign Languages, 1988.

Hùng, Nguyên. *Dương Quang Đông and His Trans-West Supply Line.* Hanoi: Youth Publishing, 2004.

Hùng, Nguyên. *Nguyễn Bình, The Myth and Reality.* Hanoi: Literature Publishing, 1995.

Khoan, Nguyễn Văn. *Giao Thông Liên Lạc Thông Tin.* Hanoi: Lao Động Publishing, 1997.

Khoan, Nguyễn Văn. *Lý Phương Đức: The Female

Giao Thông of Uncle Hồ. Hanoi: People's Public Security Publishing, 2006.

Khoan, Nguyễn Văn, and Vượng, Đức. *Hồ Chí Minh's Trip Abroad for Vietnam's National Salvation*. Hanoi: Truth Publishing, 1990.

Kolko, Gabriel. *Anatomy of a War: Vietnam, the United States and the Modern Historical Experience*. London: Phoenix, 2001.

The Legal Case of Nguyễn Ái Quốc (Hồ Chí Minh) in Hong Kong 1931–1933 (Documents and Photographs). Hanoi: National Political Publishers, 2006.

Lịch Sử Đoàn 559 Bộ Đội Trường Sơn Đường Hồ Chí Minh. Hanoi: People's Army Publishing, 1999.

Lịch sử truyền thông Giao bưu vận Nam Bộ (1945–1975). Hanoi: Nhà Xuất Bản Bưu Điện, 2003.

Lockhart, Greg. *Nation in Arms: The Origins of the People's Army of Vietnam*. Sydney, Australia: ASAA Southeast Asia Publications Series, 1989.

Lương, Bảo, and Trang, Vân. *A Cochinchinese Girl: Memoirs of Bảo Lương Nguyễn Trung Nguyệt*. Hanoi: Literature Publishing, 2004.

Marr, David G. *Vietnam 1945: The Quest for Power*. Berkeley: University of California Press, 1995.

Marr, David G. *Vietnamese Tradition on Trial, 1920–1945*. Berkeley: University of California Press, 1984.

Memories of Vũ Anh: The Riverhead. Hanoi: Literature Publishing, 1977.

Meyer, John Stryker. *On the Ground: The Secret War in Vietnam*. Oceanside, CA: Levin, 2007.

Military History Institute of Vietnam. *Victory in Vietnam: The Official History of the People's Army of Vietnam, 1954–1975*. Lawrence: University Press of Kansas, 2002.

My-Van, Tran. *A Vietnamese Royal Exile in Japan: Prince Cuong De (1882–1951)*. Oxford: Routledge, 2005.

Nhưỡng, Hà Bình. *Magnificent Camouflage: Stories of Secret Agents in the Saigon Administration*. Hanoi: Thế Giới, 2008.

19 August Revolution Is Creation. Hanoi: Association of Vietnamese Historians, 1995.

Nolan, Keith William. *Battle for Hue: Tet, 1968*. Novato, CA: Presidio, 1996.

Northwest Battlefields in the First Days of the Resistance War against the French Invasion. Hanoi: Military History Institute, 1988.

The Orient Mission. Hanoi: People's Army Publishing, 2004.

Party Central Committee's Research Bureau. *President Hồ Chí Minh: Life's History and Work*. Hanoi: Truth Publishing, 1975.

The Party's Precursor Organizations, Volume 1. Hanoi: Party Central Committee's Research Bureau, 1977.

Phong, Đặng. *5 đường mòn Hồ Chí Minh*. Hanoi: Tri Thức, 2008.

Porch, Douglas. *The French Foreign Legion: A Complete History of the Legendary Fighting Force*. New York: Harper Perennial, 1992.

Prados, John. *The Blood Road: The Ho Chi Minh Trail and the Vietnam War*. New York: John Wiley & Sons, 1998.

Prados, John. *The Hidden History of the Vietnam War*. Chicago: Elephant, 1998.

Prados, John. *Lost Crusader: The Secret Wars of CIA Director William Colby, The True Story of One of America's Most Controversial Spymasters*. Oxford: Oxford University Press, 2003.

Quang, Nông Văn. *The Southward Routes*. Hanoi: National Culture Publishing, 1995.

Quinn-Judge, Sophie. *Ho Chi Minh: The Missing Years, 1919–1941*. Berkeley: University of California Press, 2003.

Resolution from the 1st Indochinese Communist Party Central Committee Conference, October 1930, Volume 1. Hanoi: Truth Publishing, 1964.

Resolution from the First National Party Congress of the Indochinese Communist Party, March 1935. Hanoi: Truth Publishing, 1977.

Revolutionary Newspapers in Vietnam, 1925–1945. Hanoi: Social Science Publishing, 1984.

Shultz, Richard H., Jr. *The Secret War Against Hanoi*. London: HarperCollins, 1999.

60 Years of the People's Army of Vietnam. Hanoi: Military Institute of the Ministry of Defense and People's Army Publishing, 2004.

Sơn, Phạm Văn. *Việt Nam chiến sử*. Saigon: Self-published, 1972.

Stuart-Fox, Martin, and Mary Kooyman. *Historical Dictionary of Laos*. Lanham, MD: Scarecrow, 1992.

Tai, Hue-Tam Ho. *Passion, Betrayal, and Revolution in Colonial Saigon: The Memoirs of Bao Luong*. Berkeley: University of California Press, 2010.

Tài, Phùng Thế. *The First Bodyguard of Hồ Chí Minh*. Hanoi: Youth Publishing and People's Army Publishing, 2000.

Thái, Nguyễn Hữu. *Choices: An Insider's Account of War and Peace in Vietnam, Told by a Former Saigon Student and Leader*. Hanoi: Self-published, 2005.

Thọ, Nguyễn Hữu. *Under the Same Flag*. Hồ Chí Minh City: National Political Publishers, 1993.

Tiên, Trần Dân. *Hồ Chí Minh: The Founder of Independent Vietnam*. Hanoi: Thế Giới, 1997.

The Torch: Memoirs. Hanoi: Literature Publishing, 1980.

Trường, Đào Văn. *The History of Armed Struggle and the First Armed Forces of the Party*. Hanoi: Self-published, 1956.

Two Sisters, Revolutionary Martyrs. Hanoi: Youth Publishing, 2007.

The Untold Story about a Hero. Hanoi: People's Public Security Publishing, 2005.

Vick, Alan. *Snakes in the Eagle's Nest: A History of Ground Attacks on Air Bases.* Santa Monica, CA: Rand, 1995.

Việt, Đặng Văn. *Highway 4: The Border Campaign (1947–1950).* Hanoi: Thế Giới, 1990.

Vietnam: The Anti-U.S. Resistance War for National Salvation, 1954–1975: Military Events. Hanoi: People's Army Publishing, 1982.

Vietnamese in Thailand, 1910–1960. Hanoi: People's Public Security Publishing, 2008.

Vietnamese Revolutionary Youth League. Hanoi: Political Theory Publishing, 1985.

Vượng, Đức. *Comrade Trường Chinh, Volume 2.* Hanoi: Truth Publishing, 1991.

Westmoreland, William C. *A Soldier Reports.* London: Da Capo, 1989.

The Westward Once and Forever. Hanoi: Thế Giới, 2008.

Willbanks, James H. *The Tet Offensive: A Concise History.* New York: Columbia University Press, 2006.

Windrow, Martin. *The Last Valley, Dien Bien Phu and the French Defeat in Vietnam.* London: Cassell, 2005.

Articles

Adams, Samuel. "Intelligence Failures in Vietnam: Suggestions for Reform." Paper presented at a meeting for the CIA, Washington, D.C., 24 January 1969.

Apple, R. W., Jr. "Vietnam: The Signs of Stalemate." *New York Times*, 7 August 1967.

Griffin, Christopher. "A Revolution in Colonial Military Affairs: Gallieni, Lyautey, and the Tache d'huile." Paper presented at the annual conference for the British International Studies Association, Leicester, 14–16 December 2009.

Hồng, Việt. "Stories about Karl Marx Told on the Trail." *Vietnamese Communist Party Newspaper*, 5 May 1968.

Hương, Trầm. "Half a Century of Inconclusive Affairs of General Nguyễn Bình." *Journal of Hồn Việt* (November 2008).

Kaiser, Robert G., Jr. "U.S. Aides in Vietnam Scorn Phoenix Project." *Washington Post*, 17 February 1970.

Khoan, Nguyễn Văn. "The Work of the *Giao Thông Liên Lạc* which Served the Propagation of Marxism-Leninism to Indochina in the Early Years of the 20th Century." PhD diss., Hanoi University, 1985.

Mack, Andrew J. R. "Why Big Nations Lose Small Wars: The Politics of Asymmetric Conflict." *World Politics* (January 1975).

Morris, Virginia. "The Genius of General *Giáp*." *Outlook, Volume XI, Number 121*, November 2013.

Morris, Virginia. "Uncle Hồ's Revolutionary Government Was Unique." *Việt Nam News*, 19 May 2015.

Morris, Virginia. "We Were Waiting for Them." *The Guardian*, 25 August 2006.

Index

Numbers in **_bold italics_** indicate pages with illustrations

Abrams, Creighton W. 289
action unit 35–36, 112–114, 124, 126, 199, 201–202, 206, 207, 352, 357n40, 360n34 368n33; advancing propaganda team 72–73, 76, 87, 352; honorary fighting team 72, 87, 353; self-defense team 72, 87, 141, 143, 280, 353; *see also* armed propaganda team; Orient
Adams, Samuel A. 295, 372n10
Afghanistan 3, 347–349, 373epn6
agitprop 36–37, **_44_**, 73
Agroville Plan 201, 215
Ái, Hoàng Thị **_48_**
Alessandri, Marcel 133, 364ch8n3
All-People's Terrorism 346, 349
All-People's War 3, 6, 153, 195, 207, 347, 349; aim of 101; definition of the blueprint 78, 345; first victim of the blueprint 179–181; second victim 317–318; third victim 336–337; vital elements of the blueprint 345–346
Alliance of National, Democratic and Peace Forces 266, 315
Al-Qaeda 347–348, 373epn7
Ấm, Phùng Đình 199
An, Hoàng Thị 264, **_265_**, 266–267
An, Nguyễn Hữu 314
Ẩn, Phạm Xuân 343, 370ch13n25
An, Trần Công 207, 368n34
Anh, Đào Duy 65
Ánh, Trần Hồng **_5_**
Anh, Vũ 69
Anh, Vũ (worked with Thảo) **_119_**, 121, **_121_**, 122, **_123_**, 124–125, 127, 129–130, 187, 214–215, **_215–216_**, 217, **_217_**, 227, 297, **_331_**, 343, 364n7, 368n20, 368n29
Annam Regional Party Committee **_48_**, 66
Annamese Communist Party 43, 59, 352
armed propaganda team 73, 125, 141, **_142_**, 146, 148, 155, 193, 201, 352, 360n34; *see also* action unit

Army of the Republic of Vietnam (ARVN) 184, 187, 214, 221–224, 226–227, 229, 238, 252, **_270_**, 271, **_275_**, 276, 280–281, **_284–285_**, **_287_**, **_292_**, 293, 297, 300, 302, 306–307, 311, **_312_**, 313–314, 319, 322, **_323_**, 324–325, 327, 329, **_330_**, 331–332, 337, 351
Association of Annamese Patriots 13
asymmetric war 1, 3, 6, 100–101, 118, 179, 230
ATK (safe zone) 35–36, 70, 76, 87, 90, 145, 351, 356n37, 365n12; TW 35–36, 128, 351, 357n39, 360n3
August Revolution 1, 6, 35, 40, 62, 78–79, 86, **_89_**, 90, 93, 96–100, 118, 133, 143, 179, 182, 198, 229, 257, 272–273, 325, 356n37, 357n39, 362n16, 364n24, 371n26; General Uprising Order 88; Hanoi City Party Committee **_29_**, 87, 90–91; Hanoi Revolutionary Military Committee 90–91; Military Order No 1 88, 94, 96, 361n25
Australia 238, 280

B-52 242, 249, 314, 317
Ba, Nguyễn Ngọc **_44_**
Bắc Sơn Uprising 52–54, 56–58, 359n19
Bạch, Phạm Văn 115
Bái, Phí Văn **_29_**
Bẩm, Võ 198, 249
Bằng, Nguyễn Lương **_44_**
Bằng, Trần Văn 335
Banomyong, Pridi 107–108
Báo, Trần **_48_**
base aéro-terrestre (air-land base) 158, 166
Battle of Ấp Bắc **_203_**, 229
Battle of Buôn Ma Thuột 314, 322, **_323_**, 324, 327, **_328_**, **_330_**; *see also* Spring Offensive
Battle of Điện Biên Phủ (and area) 4, 62–63, **_77_**, 86, 101, 105, **_119_**,

_134–135_, 154, 160, 162–165, 169, **_173_**, 175, **_175_**, 178, 181, 183, 198, 220, 270–271, 315, 318, **_325_**, 345, 349, 359n52, 365n8, 366ch9n4, 367n15, 371n27; Anne Marie **_167_**, 172; Béatrice **_167_**, 172, 174; Dominique **_167_**, 174; Fast Strike, Fast Victory 166, **_167_**, 168, 171, **_173_**, 176–177; Gabrielle **_167_**, 172; Steady Fight, Steady Advance 166, **_167_**, 170, 172, **_173_**, 176; *see also* French War; Giáp, Võ Nguyên
Battle of Lam Sơn 719 252, 343
Battle of Lộc Ninh 4, 311, 314, **_317_**, **_323_**; *see also* Easter Offensive
Battle of Nà Sản (and area) 158, 160–161, 166, 171, 176
Battle of Ông Thạnh 297
Battle of Trị Thiên 313–314; *see also* Easter Offensive
Battle of Tua Hai 195, **_196_**, 197, **_203_**, 367n20
Bảy, Phan Văn **_284_**
Bernard, Harry 81, 82
biệt động (elite force) 113, 129–130, 209, 217–218, 221, 227, **_248_**, 268, 274, **_275_**, 277, 282–283, **_284–285_**, 348, 352–353, 356n23, 363n27, 371n30
Bình, Nguyễn 105, 110, 128, 199, 260, 348, 362n12, 363n23, 363n25, 368n10
Bình, Phan Trọng **_44_**
Bình, Trần Tử 90–91
Bình Xuyên 110, 185–186, 192–193, 195, 209, 223–224, 298, 310, 363n29, 364n11, 367n20
Blueprint *see* All-People's War
boat people 342–343
Border Campaign 117, **_134_**, 154, 157–158, 307, 313, 362n50, 363n2, 365n29
Brezhnev, Leonid 369n19
Britain 3, 10, 14, **_17_**, 22–23, 25, 41, 81, 91, 94, 98, 102, 105–107, 111, 118, 128–129, 177–178, 202, 214, 216, 226, 238, 246, 254, 294, 332,

377

360n7, 362n9, 362n56, 362n16, 370ch12n22
Bưng, Nguyễn Thới 3, **5**
Burns, Jim 230, 232–234, **234**, 235, 238, **238**, 252, 256; *see also* Studies and Observations Group

C War Zone **119**, 207, 268, **292**, 368n36
Cambodia 1, **4**, 7, **29**, **44**, 70, 99, 107–108, 117, **121**, 130, 133, 146, 156–157, 164, 175, 178–180, 187, 193, 199, 209, 213, 230, **231**, **250**, 269, 289, 296, 311, 339, 348, 363n17, 363n29, 364n4, 367n14; Khmer Rouge 1, 339, 349
Căn, Đỗ Văn **285**, **286**
Cẩn, Ngô Đình 211
Cao Đài **106** 107, 110, 185
Capital Military Assistance Command (CMAC) 297, 310, 351
Catholicism 107, 121–122, 178, 214, 221, 227, 260, 264, 320, 334, 366n6, 370n10
Cầu Ngang Campaign **119**, 130
Central Highlands 138, 164, 198–199, 204, 223, 313–314, 322, 324, **330**, 360n34
Central Intelligence Agency (CIA) 3, 188, 225–227, 239, 249, 253, 290, **292**, 294–295, 297, 300, 307–308, 310, 343, 347–348, 351, 360n8, 366ch10n6, 368n18, 372n11, 373epn6
Central Office for South Vietnam (COSVN) 130, 184, **201**, **203**, 204, **205**, 206–207, 223, **248**, 268–269, 272, **285**, **292**, **301**, 302, **312**, 322, **323**, 324, **325**, **327**–**328**, **231**, 329, **341**, 351–352, 366ch10n8, 368n35, 370n19, 372n11
Chánh, Phan Văn **33**
Chắt, Lý Thúc 23, 27, 356n24
Châu, Minh **29**
Châu, Nguyễn Văn 127
Châu, Phan Bội 8–10, 12–14, 19–20, 22–23, 39–41, **44**, 64–65, 139, 155, 355n20, 355n22, 355n12, 356n15, 356n27, 369n2
Châu, Trần Ngọc 122, 223, 291, 293
Cheatham, Ernest 281
Chennault, Claire 82
Chi, Lương Văn 55–56
Chi, Tuấn 266–67, 370n14
Chiang Kai-shek 11, 40, 55
Chiếm, Cao Đăng 366ch10n8
China **8**, 9–12, **22**, 19–27, **28**, 39–43, **44**, 45–46, **48**, 49, 52, 54–58, **60**, 62–63, 65–72, **74**, 76, 79–82, 84, 91, 98, 102–105, 110–112, 117, 125, 132–133, 136, 138–139, 145–146, 149, 151–154, 166, **167**, 168, 170–172, **173**, 174–178, 180, 187, 192–193, 195, 214, 224, 240, 249, 269, 272, 279, 288, 291, 298, 316, 322, 324, 337, 339, **341**, 344, 348–349, 352, 354n13, 354n14,

354n15, 355n1, 355n9, 355n12, 356n24, 357n8, 357n11, 358n21, 358n23, 358n28, 359n9, 360n3, 361n12, 362n7, 362n53, 363n1, 364ch8n3, 364n5, 365n21, 366n1, 366n11, 366n20, 367n15, 369n19, 371n26, 373n38; People's Republic of China 151, 354n13, 369n19; Red China **45**, 117, 122, 149, 174, 213, 272, 288, 298, 324, 364n5
Chinese Communist Party 11, 25, 40, 176, 354n13, 356n24, 360n3
Chinese Kuomintang 10–11, **22**, 26, 41, 43, **44**, 52, 54–55, 69–72, 80–82, 91, 98, 103, 105, 136, 138, 151, 298, 354n13, 354n14, 354n15, 362n7, 363n1, 366n11
Chinh, Nguyễn Bá 87
Chính, Trần Tư **45**, 59, 62, 359n49, 359n51
Chinh, Trường **29**, 34–37, 49, 51, 57, 77, 79, 88, 102, 145, 193, 356n35, 358n25, 358n34, 358n39, 367n13
Chữ, Chu Đăng 198
Chữ, Nguyễn Xuân 91, 361n32, 361n34
Chu, Trần Tích **44**
Chung, Lý Quý 321, 334, 336, **336**
Chưởng, Lê 273
Churchill, Winston 80, 362n57
Civil Operations and Revolutionary Development Support (CORDS) 276, 294–295, 300, 351
Có, Nguyễn Hữu 197
Cochinchina Regional Party Committee **48**, 53, 106–107, 115, 130, 184–185, 189, 193, 195, 197, **203**, 360, 361n24, 362n16, 368n35
Cochinchina Resistance Administrative Committee 115, 120, 124, 352
Cochinchina Secret Service Department 118, 122, 126–127, 129–130, 352, 364n19
Cochinchina Uprising 52–53, 58, 88, 97, 107
Cogny, René 175–176
Colby, William 239, 294, 296–297, 308–310
Cold War 19, 100, 149, 152, 177–178, 181, 238; Communist Bloc 151, 153–154, 161, 180, 187, 195, 315, 340, 368n18
Combined Intelligence Center, Vietnam 311
Comintern 16, 19, 24–26, **31**–**33**, 40, 43, 45–46, 351, 355n31, 360n3
Côn Đảo Island Prison 12, **28**, 68, 190, 222, 264, 267, 282, 288, 337–338, **339**, 358n45
Corrections Program 187–188, 214
Cử, Nguyễn Văn **28**, 51
Cư, Phạm Hồng 345–346, **346**
Củ Chi tunnels 212, **212**, 368n3
Cúc, Nguyễn Thị **285**
Cung, Trần Văn 43, **45**
Cương, Nguyễn Văn **48**, 358n27
Cương, Trần Phú **284**

D War Zone 112, **119**, 126, 199, **200**, 201, **201**, 202, **203**, 207, 268–269, **292**
Đắc, Nguyễn Văn **28**, **45**
đặc công (elite force) 113–114, 186, 197, 274, **275**, 277, 282, **304**, 305, 352, 362n50, 366n23, 369n2
Đại, Bảo 80, 87, 95, 114, 127, 178, 187, 223, 360n5
Đăng, Lâm Quốc 199, 368n28
Danh, Nguyễn 198
Đạo, Hoàng Minh **48**, 118, 130, 184–186, 188–189, 358n27, 363n1, 366n8
Đạo, Trần Hưng 364n1
d'Argenlieu, Thierry 93, 105
Đạt, Lê Quảng **44**
Đầy, Phạm Văn **285**
Đệ, Hồ **330**
Đệ, Nguyễn Anh 13 6, 365n9
Đế, Nguyễn Cường 8, 13, 19, 40–41, 52, 80, 354n5, 355n22
de Castries, Christian 168–169, 174–175, 318
Decent Interval 270
de Crevecoeur, Boucher **167**
Deer Team 84, 89
Demands of the Annamese People 13–14, 25
Demilitarized Zone (DMZ) **4**, 178, 184–185, **231**, 260, 267, 273, 313–314, 327, 351, 366ch10n8, 370n4
Democratic Party 87, 90, 93, 361n16
Democratic Republic of Vietnam 63, 76, 98, **98**, 99, 104, 151, 178, 225, 357n39, 361n31, 364ch7n4, 368n17
Denounce the Communists 186, 337
DeSeta, Lou 241–244, 246
de Tassigny, Jean de Lattre **134**, 157–158
Dĩa, Bông Văn 108, **206**
Địch, Nguyễn Văn 118, 363n2
Điểm, Lê Duy **44**
Diệm, Ngô Đình 178, 186–187, 194–195, 198, 211–215, **215**, 216–218, 220, 223–225, 239, 261, **262**, 265, 267, 319–320, 334, 337, 368n20, 370n10
Diên, Nguyễn Thành 54
Diệp, Nguyễn Văn 336
Diểu, Nguyễn Chí 65
Đinh, Hà Huy 334
Đính, Lê Trung **48**
Độ, Trần Hữu **32**
Đời, Nguyễn Danh **45**
Domino Theory 179, 270; spread of communism 6, 16, 19, 152, 157, 175, 181, 228, 343, 347
Đông, Dương Quang **48**, 105, 107–108, 359n50, 362n16
Đồng, Phạm Văn **45**, 67, 69, **74**, 102, **119**, 133, 178, 359n17
Đồng Tháp Mười War Zone 126, 363n29, 364n17
Donovan, William 81
double-cross system 253, 370ch12n22

Dư, Trần Thị 48
Duẩn, Le 66–67, 115, 117, 120–121, 130–131, 193–194, 208, 266, 271–274, 283, 288, 313–314, 343, 358n45, 373n16
Dực, Đặng Hồng 5
Đức, Lê Hữu 324
Đức, Lưu 198
Đức, Lý Phương 21–22, *22*, 23–24, 27, 31, 34, 37–38, 41, 67, 260, 343, 349, 355n7, 355n9, 356n17, 356n24, 373n15
Đức, Thích Quảng 261, *262*, 319
Đức, Vũ 362n16
Ducoroy, Maurice 95–96
Dũng, Văn Tiến 272, 314, 329
Dương, Dương Văn 363n29, 364n11

Easter Offensive 306, 313–314, 316, 324, 373n37; *see also* Battle of Lộc Ninh; Battle of Trị Thiên; Nguyễn Huệ Offensive
Eastward March 48, *74*, 357n11
Eisenhower, Dwight David 179, 213–214, 337
Engels, Friedrich 16, *17*, 355n31

Fenn, Charles 81–82, 361n10
fighting village 143, 198, 214, 229
Ford, Gerald 324–325, 337
French Communist Party 16, 40, 105, 355n37, 360n3
French Far East Expeditionary Corps 145, 157, 163, 175, 220, 365n15
French Foreign Legion 132, 365n15
French Indochina 4, 7, 43, 52, 86, 98, 339, 354n2, 359n4
French *Sûreté* 14, 25, *26*, 34, 37, 49, 58, 68
French Union 104, 164, 362n9, 365n15, 365n18
French Vichy government 52, 69, 80, 358n33, 360n6, 364n15
French War (start of) 105; First Vietnamese American Hostilities 114; key activities in Tonkin **134–135, 137, *142*, *147*, *150*–*151***; Việt Minh regions in Cochinchina and parts of southern Annam **118–119**; *see also* Battle of Điện Biên Phủ
Frontline Youth 95, *278*, 352

Gallasch, Borries Von 334
Gaspard, George 254–255
GBT 81–82
Geneva Accords *148*, 178–179, 183–184, 187, 199, 211, 217, 220, 240, 265, 289, 365n32, 366n6, 368n17, 369n8, 369n19; Geneva Conference 177
Giải, Trần Ngọc 45
Giám, Hoàng Minh 29
Giang, Kiên 320
Giao, Trần Bá 44
Giáp, Võ Nguyên 5, *29*, 47, 49, 62–73, *74*, 75–77, *77*, 78, 82, **83**, 86, 88–89, 94, 101–102, 114, 117–118, 128, 130, 132–133, 136, 138–141, 143–146, 148–149, 151, *151*, 152–158, 160–166, 168–172, 174–176, 178–181, 193–194, 198, 202, 206–208, 223, 225, 229, 252, 266, 269–273, 276, 283, 288–289, 313–314, 318, 324–325, 327, 329, 331, 335, 343, 345, 347, 357n11, 357n40, 359n1, 359n8, 359n13, 359n18, 361n25, 363n23, 364n1, 364n2, 365n24, 367n14, 368n30, 368n33, 369n2, 370n23, 370n25, 371n27, 372n35, 373n37; Hà, Đặng Bích (second wife of) *64*; Kiên, Nguyễn Thị (mother of) 63; Nghiêm, Võ Quang (father of) 63–64, 359n2; Thái, Nguyễn Thị Quang (first wife of) *28*, 49, 65–66, *66*, 67; *see also* Battle of Điện Biên Phủ
Giàu, Trần Văn 96, 105–106, *106*, 107–108, 110, 114–115, 117, *119*, 362n15, 362n16
Global War on Terrorism 347
Go East Movement 10, 12, 354n14
Godwin, George 241–242, 244, 246
Gold Week 122, 362n11, 362n16
Gracey, Douglas 105
Great Việt 91, 129, 264, 353, 361n32
Greater East Asia Co-Prosperity Sphere 49, 80–81, 358n31
guerrilla in-front warfare 139–140

Hà, Hoàng 122, 124–125
Hamlet Evaluation Survey (HES) 296, 307, 351
Hãn, Hoàng Xuân 91, 361n31
Han, Lu 103
Hạnh, Đặng Thị 345, *346*, 349
Hạnh, Nguyễn Hữu 337
Hanoi Hannah 102, 234
Hào, Song 82
Harkins, Paul 238
Hậu, Thích Đôn 266, 267
le hérisson (hedgehog) 158, 160–161, 166, 172, 175
Hiền, Lê Ngọc 273
Hiền, Trần Ngọc 223, 293
Hiền, Vũ Văn 132
Hiểu, Nguyễn Văn *77*, 186
hill tribes 70–73, 75, 124–125, *136*, 143, 155, *156*, 157, *169*, 172, 174, 180, 199, 201–202, 216, 241, 251, 260, 365n18; Montagnards 241, 246, 339
Hồ, Võ Quang 324
Hồ Chí Minh Campaign 4, 306, 329, *330*, 373ch15n5; *see also* Spring Offensive
Hồ Chí Minh Trail 1, 4, 6, *61*, 102, 108, 139, *146*, 182, *203*, 204, *205*, 223, 230, 238–239, 241, 247, *247*, 248–249, 251, *251*, 254, 256, 258, *259*, 260, 267, 289, 298, 305, *323*, 324, 331, *341*, 343, 362n16, 368n17, 369n2, 369n8, 369n16; Group 559 198, 206, **231**; *La Piste de Hồ Chí Minh* 202; Route of Hồ Chí Minh *119*, 124, 126; Southward Strategic Corridor 198–199, 202, 364n2; Trường Sơn Army **231**, 252, ***341***; Trường Sơn Trail 202; *see also* Vietnam War
Hồ Chí Minh Trail Sea Route 4, 108, *109*, 126, *127*, 198, 204, **231**, *270*
Hoa, Hoàng 263, *263*, 264, 267–268
Hoa, Nguyễn Thị *279*, 281–282
Hòa Hảo 107, 110, 185
Hoan, Hoàng Văn 40, 69–70, 357n11
Hoàn, Nguyễn Tôn 129
Hoàng, Lê 48
Hoàng, Nguyễn Văn 308
Học, Ngô Chính 44
Hollingsworth, James 311
Huệ, Ngô Thị 5
Huệ, Nguyễn 364n1
Huệ, Nguyễn Thị *284*
Hứa, Đặng Thúc 22–23, 355n12
Huế Alliance of National, Democratic and Peace Forces 266–267
Huế Civil Affairs Committee for Students 264, 351
Huế Youth Front 264
Hùm, Phan Văn 33
Hùng, Lê Thiết 11, *22*, 44, 59, 62, 71–72, *74*, 75
Hùng, Nguyễn Đức 227, *285*, 369n21
Hưng, Quang 75
Hương, Trâm 5, 42
Hương, Trần Quốc 366ch10n8
Hương, Trần Văn 331, 334
Huy, Lê Đỗ *263*, *265*, 349
Huyền, Nguyễn Văn 334, 336

Igloo White 247–249
independent companies 141, *142*, 143–144, 146, 148, *150*, 152, 289
Indochinese Communist League 43, 45, 65, 353
Indochinese Communist Party **28–29**, *32*, 43, **44**, 46, 48, 53, 56, 97–98, 103, 107, 156, 353, 361n24, 363n17; founded 45; *see also* Vietnamese Communist Party; Worker's Party of Vietnam
Indochinese Democratic Front 46, 55; Indochinese Democratic Youth **29**, 49
Intelligence Coordination and Exploitation Program (ICEX) 294, 296, 351
International Control Commission (ICC) 187, 188
Iron Triangle 268

Japan 1, 3, 5, 9–10, 12, 27, 39–40, 47, 49, *51*, 52–54, 68, 70, *74*, 79–82, **83**, 84, 87–89, 91–98, 103, 105, 107, 110–112, 132, 136, 139,

143, 354*n*6, 354*n*10, 354*n*14, 354*n*15, 358*n*28, 360*n*6, 361*n*25, 362*n*16, 362*n*58, 363*n*1, 363*n*23, 364*ch*8*n*3; Hiroshima and Nagasaki 88, 96; Japanese Army 52, 88, 91–92, 94, 361*n*25, 361*n*39
Johnson, Lyndon B. 228, 240, 267, 291, 294, 315, 337
Jones, David W. 298

Kennedy, John F. 213–214, 216, 239–240, 337
Kennedy, Robert 318
Khai, Nguyễn Thị Minh 66–67
Khâm, Nguyễn Duy 121
Khang, Nguyễn 90–91
Khánh, Nguyễn 223, 226–227
Khánh, Trần Thị Kim **263**
Khánh the Seventh 186, 367*n*9
Khẩu, Phùng Văn 174, **175**
Khe Sanh 241, 267, 269, 273, 370*n*4, 371*n*27
Khiêm, Trần Thiện 225–226
Khiết, Trần Đình 136
Khoan, Nguyễn Văn 21, 27, 37
Khôi, Nguyễn Huy 90, 361*n*29
Khrushchev, Nikita 187, 369*n*19
Kiên, Phùng Chí 56–57, 69, 358*n*41
Kiến, Trần Quảng 86
Kiệt, Lý Thường 364*n*1
Kill/Capture 348; *see also* Phoenix Program
Kim, Tăng Thiên 199
Kim, Trần Trọng 80, 90, 95
King Sisavangvong 146
Kingdom of Lao **165**, 365*n*32; Royal Lao Army 251; Royal Lao government 146, 160, 164; *see also* Lao
Kinh, Đặng 273–274, 276
Kissinger, Henry 316, 331, 373*n*38
Komer, Robert W. 294–295
Korea 40, 171–172, 177–178, 187, 240, **275**
Kỳ, Bùi **29**
Kỳ, Đào Duy **29**
Kỳ, Nguyễn Cao 223, 227

Labor Union 41, 46, 357*n*10, 362*n*16
Lạc, Phạm Văn 199, 202, 367*n*26
Laden, Osama bin 348
Lai, Trần Văn 87, **284**
Lâm, Hồ Học 10–11, 27, 55, 59, 69–71, 354*n*14
Lâm, Mai Trung **74**
Land Reforms 38, 151, 193, 358*n*48, 367*n*13
Lăng, Lê Văn 87
Lãng, Trần Thị Nguyệt **29**
Langlais, Pierre 174
Lanh, Hoàng 258, 265, 271, 273, 279, **279**, 280–284, 289
Lansdale, Edward 293, 371*n*3
Lao 1, **4**, **29**, **44**, **60**, 99, 133, **134**–**135**, 136, 138, 142, **143**, 146, **146**, 148, **148**, 149, **149**, 156–158, 160–161, **161**, 164–165, **165**, 166, **167**,

171, **173**, 175–176, 178–180, **181**, 187, 193, 202, 206, 211, 213, 225, 230, **231**, 232, 234, **235**, 238–242, **242**–**243**, 244, **244**–**245**, 247, 249, **249**–**250**, 251, 273, 289, 298, 339, 348–349, 354*n*2, 354*n*4, 354*n*10, 355*n*12, 364*n*2, 365*n*9, 365*n*19, 365*n*32, 367*n*14, 368*n*17, 369*n*2, 369*n*23, 369*n*8, 369*n*12; *see also* Kingdom of Lao; Pathet Lao
Lập, Lê Hữu **44**
Lập, Tôn Thất 264
De Lattre Line **134**, 157–158
League for Revolution 104, 353
Leaping Lena 241, 369*n*8
Lê Hồng Phong Campaign **119**, 130
Lém, Nguyễn Văn 25, **287**, 289, 356*n*23, 366*n*23
Lenin, Vladimir Ilyich 16, 19, 39, 62, 65, 193, 354*n*11, 355*n*27, 361*n*24, 373*n*16; *Thesis on the National and Colonial Questions* 15
Liberation Army 198, 199, 202, 204, 207, 222, 264, **278**, **284**, **301**, 327, 331–332, **333**, 335, 338, 368*n*30, 368*n*33; Liberation Armed Forces of South Vietnam 206; *see also* Vietnamese People's Army
Liên, Phạm Thị 282
Liễn, Trần Ngọc 320
Limited War 208, 228–230, 238–239, 251, 289, 317
Linh, Nguyễn Văn **5**, 312
literacy program 102, 182
Lo-o Jungle 126
Lộc, Nguyễn Danh 145, 365*n*14
Lộc, Nguyễn Phước Vĩnh 337
Lợi, Nguyễn Văn **44**
Long, Trần Đình 90–92
Lúa, Hoàng Văn 33
Luân, Châu Tâm 320, 332
Lực the Tenth 186, 367*n*10
Lương, Bảo 41–42, **45**, 59, 62, 357*n*14, 359*n*50, 361*n*21
Lương, Trần 184, 206–207, 368*n*35
Lưu, Nguyễn Thị **48**
Lưu, Phan Đăng 53, 65, 358*n*34, 359*n*9
Lý, Bùi Thị **284**

Madman Theory 315
Mai, Đặng Thai **29**, 65
Mai, Dương Bạch **33**, 96, 111
Mai, Lê Hiến 133, 364*ch*8*n*4, 365*n*9
Mạnh, Triệu Quốc 337
Mann, Tom 14, 355*n*31
Mao Zedong 97, 117–118, 132, 151–152, 154, 213–214, 217, 272, 342, 347, 362*n*55*maquis* 157, 371*n*3
Marx, Karl 14, **17**, 39–40, 49, 62, 65, 71, 81, 90, 132, 141, 193, 355*n*31, 356*n*17, 355*n*31; Longuet, Jean (grandson) 15–16
Mậu, Hồ Tùng **22**, 23–24, 41–42, 355*n*9, 356*n*13, 356*n*17

Mẫu, Vũ Văn 320, 332, 334–336, **336**
McKnight, Robert 253
McNamara, Robert 248, **248**
McNamara Line 248
Mei Jiasheng 170
Mercy Team 92
Merlin, Martial Henri 39, 41–42, 59, 357*n*2
Messmer, Pierre 93–94, 361*n*42
Meyer, John Stryker 6, 230, 241, **242**, 243–244, 246–248, 252–254, 256; *see also* Studies and Observations Group
Military Assistance Advisory Group (MAAG) 220–222, 226, 351, 368*n*12
Military Assistance Command Vietnam (MACV) 226, 238–240, 253, **275**, 276, 280–281, 294, 297, 311, 351
Military Assistance Training Advisory (MATA) 297, 351
military proselytizing 57, **58**, 102, 113, 141, **150**, 172, 180, 182–185, 188–189, 207, 223, 225, 253, 280, **292**, 302–303, **325**, 343, 353, 357*n*44, 366*n*1, 366*n*2, 366*n*8
Minh, Dương Văn 224–226, 320–322, 331–332, 334–336, **336**, 337
Minh, Hồ Chí: First Bold Revolutionary Act 12–14; Lenin's *Thesis* 15–16; Loan, Hoàng Thị (mother) 7; Sắc, Nguyen Sinh (father) 7–8, 10, **18**, 59
Minh, Lê 274, 277, 279, 370*n*1
Minh, Le An **32**
Minh, Lý Văn 23, 356*n*24
Minh, Sơn Ngọc 108, 363*n*17
Minh the Teacher **28**, 66–69, 359*n*11
mobile guerrilla warfare 140–141, 144, 153, 180, 365*n*11
Modernization Movement 11–12, 353
modus vivendi 104–105, 115, 138–139
Mujahideen 3, 347–349, 373*ep*n*6

Nakhon Phanom Royal Thai Air Force Base (RTAFB) 230, **232**, 235, **236**–**238**, **250**, 369*n*2
Nam, Phan 257–258, 260–263, **263**, **265**, 267–268, 271, 273, 276, **276**, 277, 279, 289–290, 327, 370*n*1, 370*n*2
Nam, Sơn 320
National Concord and Reconciliation Movement 320, 332, 334
National Liberation Front (NLF) 26, 202, 204, 206, 225, 262–264, 266, 271–272, 308, 315, 319–320, 322, 331–335, 337, 343, 347, 351, 372*n*11
National Salvation Organizations 55
National Salvation Troops **29**, 55–57, **74**, 76, 82, 182, 353; *see also* Vietnamese People's Army

Navarre, Henri 162–164, 166, 169, 175–176
Navarre Plan 163–164, 166, 168, 176
New Economic Area 342, 373n12
New Việt Party 65, 353, 359n6, 359n8, 359n9
New Zealand 238
newspapers (of the revolution) 25, *28–29*, *32–33*, 36, 47, 49, *50*, 51, *51*, 71, 128, 268, 358n26
Ngân, Hoàng *48*, 49
Nghệ, Huỳnh Văn 111
Nghị, Lê Thanh 88
Nghĩa, Lê Trọng 6, *77*, 86, *86*, 87–94, 97, 166, 168–171, 176–177, 224, 343, 345, 361n13, 361n28, 361n31, 362n50, 363n2
Nghĩa, Nguyễn Thị *48*
Nghĩa, Phan Tứ *29*
Ngọc, Phan Bội 219
Nguyên, Đồng Sĩ *61*, 249, *249*, 251–252, 255
Nguyên, Nguyễn Văn *32*
Nguyễn Huệ Offensive 313–314; see also Easter Offensive
Nguyệt, Lê Thị Thu *5*, 208–209, 211–213, 217, 220, 222, 317
Nha Trang Air Base 235
Nhật, Dương Thành 224, 337
Nhật, Lý Hồng *45*
Nhỏ, Nguyễn Văn 207, 368n34
Nhơn, Ngô Tấn 124
Nhu, Ngô Đình 214–215, 217, 225, 368n7
Nhung, Nguyễn Quý Hoàng *265*, 267, 327
Ninh, Lê Quang 306
Ninh, Nguyễn An *33*
Ninh, Trần Đăng 54, 88
Nixon, Richard 315–317, 322, 324, 337 Nixon Doctrine 291, 371n1
Nở, Hoàng Thị *279*, 281–282
Non-American War 317
North-West Autonomous Zone *134*, 146, 149, 153–155, 158, 160–161, 164, 365n18
North-West Campaign (1950) 153, 365n26,
North-West Campaign (1952) 158, 160, 365n29
Northward March *48*, *74*, 76

Oánh, Vương Thúc *45*, 65, 356n27
Observing the Enemy Department 185, 353, 366n8
O'Daniel, John W. 220
Office of Civil Operations 294
Office of Strategic Services (OSS) *29*, 81, 84, *89*, 92, 351
one-way war 186–187, 192, 199
Operation Atlante *119*, 166, 176, 178, 366n22
Operation Barrel Roll 238
Operation Castor 166
Operation Cedar Falls 268–269
Operation Ceinture 145
Operation Hotfoot 369n8

Operation Junction City 268–269, *292*
Operation Léa 145–146, 269
Operation Linebacker I 316
Operation Linebacker II 317
Operation Rolling Thunder 238, 269, 315
Operation Shenandoah II 297
Operation Steel Tiger 238
Operation Switchback 239
Operation White Star 369n8
Orient *201*, 206, *206*, 207, 368n33, 368n35; see also action unit
Overby, Lauren 253

Pác Bó *48*, 55, 71, *74*, 81, *83*
pack bicycle 158, 161, *169*
Paris peace talks 313–315, 366n2; Paris Peace Accords 317, 320, 322, *330*, 331, *323*, 334; see also Vietnam War
Pathet Lao *142*, 148, 251, 339, 365n19, 365n32; Lao People's Democratic Republic 365n19; Lao People's Liberation Army 149; see also Lao
Patti, Archimedes 92–93, 361n11
Paul, Le 186
peaceful coexistence 187, 189, 195
People's Revolutionary Party (PRP) 204, 315, 353
Pha, Cao 95, 168, *278*, 362n50
Phấn, Lâm Thị 223, *224*
Phát, Lâm Văn 223, 226
Phoenix Program 6, 122, 223, 289, 291, 295, *296*, 298, *301*, 302, 318, 348; Census Grievance Team 293; Counter Terror Team 293; F-6 Campaign 324; People's Action Team 294; Provincial Reconnaissance Unit (PRU) 294, 296–297, 300, 308–311, 351, 372n8; Vũng Tàu 293–294, 298, 300, 355n28; see also Kill/Capture; Phuong; Smith, Mark A.; Vietnam War
Phomvihane, Kaysone *142*, 148, *149*, 365n19
Phouma, Souvanna 213, 225, 368n17
Phú, Trần *44*
Phúc, Nguyễn Văn *48*
Phùng, Phan Đình 27, 355n11, 355n12
Phụng, Trần Hải 219, 368n10
Phước, Nguyễn Hữu *270*
Phuong *296*, 298, 300, 302, 308–309, 311, 373n38; see also Phoenix Program
Phương, Huỳnh Văn *33*
Piroth, Charles 176
Plain of Jars 160, *161*, *250*
Plain of Reeds 107, 128, *119*, 353
political human shield 104, 362n8
porter 154–156, 158, 161, *169*, 172, 176, 197, 353, 366n23
Prairie Fire 241, 247; see also Shining Brass
Prince Souphanouvong *149*, 365n19

Project Leaping Lena 241, 369n8
Project Takeoff 295
Provisional Revolutionary Government (PRG) 315–316, 322, *323*, 332, 334–335, 351

Quảng, Phan Trọng *44*
Quang, Thích Trí 261, 320–321, 332
Quang, Trần Tiên 219
Quang, Trần Văn 170, 206, 368n33
Quốc, Lê Tấn *284*
Quốc, Ngô Chính 22, *22*, 23, 27, 356n17, 373n15
Quý, Vũ *29*, 86–87, 361n17
Quyết, Nguyễn 90–91

re-education 62, 73, 257, 293, 306, 335, 342–343
Regional Interrogation Centers 296
Republic of Vietnam 184, 187, *216–217*, 218, 267, 320, 335, 356n23; State of Vietnam 178–179
Resolution 15 182, 194–195, 197–199, 204, 207, 273
Reverse Regrouping Men 183–185, 206, 223, 343, 366n8
Revolutionary Infrastructure 5, 67, *74–75*, 76–78, 88, 97, 118, 125, 128, 131, 133, 141, 146, 148, 155, 184–185, 198–199, 201–202, 207, 223, 232, 235, 252–253, 258, 260, 262, 264, 273, 288–289, 291, 293–295, 298, 302, 308, 310–311, 324, 337, 343, 345–346, 356n38, 360n3, 370n5; courier definitions 115, *210*, 352–353; l'infrastructure Clandestine Việt Minh 73; infrastructure definition 73, 114–115; shadow government 73, 101, 180, 347–348; shadow nation 73, 75; see also Việt Cộng Infrastructure
The Road to Liberation (book) 70
The Road to Revolution (book) 40, 59, 179, 353, 357n10
Roosevelt, F.D. 80, 360n6
Route 9-Northern Quảng Trị Front 258
Rue Barbier case *45*, 62, 359n50
Rừng Sác Jungle 185–186, *203*, *292*

Sách, Nguyễn Sĩ *45*
Sainteny, Jean 93
Salan, Raoul Albin Louis 157–158, 162–163
Sâm, Hoàng 136, 365n7
Sang, Trần Quang 199, 367n26
Sarraut, Albert 39, 47, 357n3
Sáu, Trần Thị 27, 31, 33–38, 55, 67, 358n34
Save the King Movement 8, 23, 27, 64, 354n4, 364n2
Secret War 230
Shaw, Rudolph 81, 96
Shin, Mac 82, *82–83*, 84, 89
Shining Brass 241, 369n8; see also Prairie Fire
Sĩ, Võ 124, 364n12

Siam 4, 21–23, 27, 43, **44–45**, 107–108, 354n2, 354n10, 355n6, 355n9, 355n12, 356n24, 364n5; *see also* Thailand
Siamese Communist Party **44**, 355n9
Sihanouk Trail 108, **231**, 289
Simultaneous Uprising 195, 197–198, 283, 353
Smith, Mark A. 6, 295–296, **296**, 298, 300, 307–311, 313–314, 317, **317**, 318, 372n12; *see also* Phoenix Program
Socialist Republic of Vietnam 343–344
Society of Hearts 39–40, 353
Sơn, Hùng 260, **263**, 370n5
Sơn, Lê Hồng 22, 23–25, 34, 355n9, 356n17
Sơn, Nguyễn **22**, 120–122, 364n5
Sơn, Nguyễn Thanh 120, 122, 129–130, 362n16, 364n4
Sơn, Việt 127, 129
Song, Nguyễn Bá **29**
Southward March **4**, **48**, 63, 69–70, 72–73, **74**, 76, 78, 82, **83**, 118, 133, 198, 229–230, 256, 335, 353
Soviet Union 3, 14, 21, 25, 27, **29**, **32**, 39–43, **44**, 46, 54, 56, 63, 69, 80, 82, 88, 90, 102, 107, 117, 138, 151–152, 160, 164, **173**, 174, 177–178, 180, 184, 187–188, 192–193, 195, 208, 223, 246, 249, 251, 269, 271–272, 279, **305**, 316, 322, 344, 347–349, 354n6, 355n31, 356n24, 357n10, 358n48, 367n15, 368n33, 369n19, 371n31; KGB 348
special masses 184, 353
special propaganda 102, 129, 223–224, 262, 264, 353, 363n2
Special War 208, 213, 228, 235, 348
Spring Offensive 325; Central Highlands Campaign 327; Huế–Đà Nẵng Campaign 327; *Outline Study of a Plan to Win the War in the South* 324; *Strategic Plan for 1975–76* 324; *see also* Battle of Buôn Ma Thuột; Hồ Chí Minh Campaign
Spring Summer Campaign 160
Stalin, Joseph 151, 154, 342, 362n57; Stalin School 107; the Stalin organ 174
Strategic Hamlet Program 214, 216–217, 353, 368n8
Studies and Observations Group (SOG) 230, 239, 240, **240**, 241–242, 244, 246–249, **250**, **259**, 251, 254–255, 298, 351; Operation Plan 34A 239–240, 253; Oscar-8 241–243, 246; *see also* Burns, Jim; Meyer, John Stryker
Sun Yat-sen 11, 19, 69, 354n15, 357n2, 357n8, 360n22
Swan girls 305, 372n22

Tài, Vũ Bá **284**
Tai Federation **134**, **136**, 146, 166, 365n18
"The Tale of Kiều" (poem) 117
Taliban 3, 347–348
Tâm, Nguyễn Trọng 182–188, **188**, 189, 192, 195, 199, 202, **203**, 207, 223, **325**, 343, 366n2, 366n4, 367n20
Tâm, Võ Thị **5**, 283, 288
Tấn, Chu Văn 54, 56–58, **74**, 76–77, 82, 88, 358n39
Tan, Frank 81–82, **82–83**
Tấn, Lê Trọng **167**, 324
Tân Hiệp Prison 187, 188, **188–192**, 194, 343
Tân Trào **29**, 57, **74**, 82, **82–83**, 84; 88–89, **89**, 90, 94, 97, 139, 357n39, 361n17, 362n5
Tạo, Nguyễn Văn **33**
Tập, Hà Huy **32–33**
Tây, Nguyễn Văn **45**
Tết Offensive **4**, 26, 113–114, 144, 252, 256–258, 261, 264, 266–269, **270**, 274, **275**, 276–277, 279–281, **284–285**, **287**, 288, 291, 300, **301**, 303–305, 308, **309**, 310, 313, 315–316, 324, 327, 356n23, 363n29, 364n20, 366n23, 369n21, 370n19, 370n23, 370n24, 370n25, 370n27, 371n43; Eleven Perfume River Girls **275**, **279**, 282–283; *The General Offensive and General Uprising* 272; *Huế's Uprising to Coordinate with the Whole of the South* 273; *A Surprise Attack at a Strategic Level* 270–273, 289; *see also* Vietnam War
Thà the Tenth 207, 368n34
Thạch, Phạm Ngọc 95–96
Thạch, Trần Văn **33**
Thái, Hoàng Văn 56, 118, 164, 170, 249, 272, 324, 358n42, 369n16, 370n25
Thái, Nguyễn **45**
Thái, Nguyễn Hữu 319–320, **321**, 322, 331, 334–335, 342, 373n1
Thái, Phạm Hồng 39, 41, 357n2
Thai Special Forces 251
Thailand **4**, 21, 23, 25, 40, **44**, 108, 133, 138–139, 146, 155, 230, **231**, 232, 234–235, **236–237**, 248, 251, 254, **254**, 298, 351, 355n6, 356n15, 362n16, 364n2, 369n2, 369n23; *also see* Siam
Thận, Bùi Quang 333, 373ch15n6
Thần, Nguyễn Hải 71
Thần, Nguyễn Sinh **44**
Thắng, Tôn Đức 41, 62, 357n15
Thành, Hoàng 129
Thanh, Hoàng Thị 110–112, 117, 128
Thành, Huỳnh Bá 322, 331–332
Thành, Phan **29**
Thanh, Trần Thị **29**
Thành, Võ Tâm 227
Thạnh, Võ Văn **285**
Lê Thanh the Eighth 197
Thảo, Hoàng Minh 324
Thảo, Phạm Ngọc 115, 118, **119**, 120, **120–121**, 122, 124–130, 187, 202, 214–217, 223, 225–227, 291, 363n27, 363n29, 366n22, 368n18, 368n20, 368n29, 372n14
Thao River Campaign 149, **150–151**
Thâu, Tạ Thu 33
Thị, Nguyễn Đình 86, 361n14
Thiêm, Ngô **45**
Thiện, Lương Khánh **28**
Thiệu, Nguyễn Văn 223, 225–227, 266–267, 293, 295, 300, 316–317, 320–322, 324–325, 327, 331, 368n19, 368n20
Thinh, Ca Văn 124
Thọ, Lê Đức 86–87, 316, 366n2, 366n8
Thọ, Mai Chí 199, 366n8
Thomas, Allison 84, 89, **89**, 94
Thompson, R.K. 216
Thông, Lý Trí 22, **22**, 23–24, 41, 355n7
Thông the Second 186
Thụ, Hoàng Văn **29**, 33–35, 37, 55, 57, 67–68, 357n44, 358n34, 358n39
Thụ, Lâm Đức 41–42, 59, 62, 356n17
Thu, Lê Thị **5**, 302
Thu, Nguyễn Công 59, 358n21
Thu, Trần Thị 302, 304
Thủ Dầu Một War Zone 126
Thuấn, Gaston Phạm Ngọc 115, 120, 127, 368n18
Thuấn, Lucien Phạm Ngọc 120, 364n3
Thuận, Lý Phương 22–26, 41, 355n7, 356n13, 356n24
Thục, Ngô Đình 214–215
Thức, Nguyễn Văn 363n29
Thường, Trần Quang 136
Thúy, Hoàng Đạo 118, 362n58
Thúy, Phan Thị **284**
Thuyến, Đặng Thái **44**
Toại, Ngô **285**
Toại, Phan Kế 80, 87, 90–91, 224, 360n5, 361n28
Toán, Lê Đình 268, 277
Tốn, Nguyễn Xuân **263**, 337
Tòng, Huỳnh Văn 332, 333, 335
Tonkin Regional Party Committee **28–29**, 33, 51, 54–55, 57–58, 67, 87, 90, 358n27
Trà, Trần Văn 311, **312**
Trạch, Hoàng Văn **48**
Trãi, Nguyễn 102
Trân, Nguyễn Văn **33**
Trans-Indochina Link 133, **134**, 138, 369n2
Trans-West Supply Line **4**,108, **109**, **119**, **231**
Trị Thiên Military Zone 258, 273–274, **275**, 280, **292**
Triêm, Phan 127
Trinh, Lê Mạnh **45**
Trinh, Phan Chu 11–14, 16, 19, 40, 65, 99, 114, 355n20
Trinh, Vương Thị 127–128
Trỗi, Nguyễn Văn 248
Trọng, Lý Tự 22–26, 41, 355n7
Trotskyites **33**, 87

Truman, Harry S 362n57
Trung, Đàm Quang 94
Trường, Đào Văn 5, **29**, 47, 49, **49–51**, 52–58, **58**, 59, **60–61**, 62, **77**, 172, 174, **175**, 176, 343, 357n44, 358n29, 358n45, 364n12
Trường, Ngô Quang 276, 281
Trường, Phan Văn 12–13
Trường Sơn Mountain Range 198, 249, 364n2
Trust Bills 34, 73, 356n34
Tsuchihashi, Yuitsu 92
Tu, Kiều Văn **29**
Tự, Lý Thúc 23, 27, 356n24
Tử, Phạm Việt 81
Tuấn, Cựu 21–23, 27, 139, 355n12, 369n2
Tuệ, Phan Trọng 249, 362n16
Tùng, Bùi Văn 334–335
Tùng, Hoàng Đông **142**
Tùng, Võ **44**
Tường, Hồ Hữu **33**, 87, 361n21
Tuyên, Nguyễn Văn **278**
Tuyến, Trần Kim 214, 368n20
two-faced puppet local administrator 37, 141

U Minh forest 107, **119**
Udorn Royal Thai Air Force Base (RTAFB) **254**, 369n2
Union of Vietnamese Communists 65, 353
United Front for the Liberation of Oppressed Races (FULRO) 339
United States (early involvement) 1, 3–4, 6, 11, 13, 26, 52, 70, 73, 75–76, 80–82, 84, **85**, 86, 88, 92–94, 96–98, 100, 102, 113–114, 126, 132, 138, 152, 163, 175, 177–182, 185 187, 195; *see also* Vietnam War
Upper Lao Campaign 160, 369n23
Út, Trần Thị **284**

Valluy, Jean Etienne 145
Văn, Cung 332
Vân, Đinh Thị 127, 268, 364n20, 370n18
Vàng, Trịnh Khánh 111–112
Vanguard Youth 95–96, 353
Vĩ, Nguyễn **45**
Viễn, Lê Văn 364n11
Viễn 185
Viễn the Seventh 186, 192, 364n11
Vientiane **44**, **135**, **161**
Việt Bắc Revolutionary Base 35, **77**, 78, **83**, 88, 117, 126, 133, **137**, 145, **147**, 149, 151, 154, 160–161, 164, 175, 178, 182–183, 269, 357n39, 363n29, 366n2, 367n14; Bắc Sơn-Võ Nhai **48**, 56–57, 70, **74**; Cao Bằng **48**, 56, 70
Việt Cộng (VC) 187, 218–220, 238, 260–261, 267–269, 281, 289, 291, 293–294, 300, 306–310, 320, 329, 342, 351, 372n11, 372n18
Việt Cộng Infrastructure (VCI) 73, 289, 291, 294, 296, 298, 300, 302, 306–308, 310–311, 351, 372n11; *see also* Revolutionary Infrastructure
Việt, Đặng Văn 95, 154, **278**, 362n50
Việt, Hoàng Quốc **48**, 49, 57, 358n27, 358n34
Việt Minh 26, 71–73, 76–77, **77**, 79–82, 84, **85**, 86–89, **89**, 90–97, 103–105, **106**, 107, 110–111, 113–114, 118, **118–119**, 124–125, 128–130, 132–133, **134**, 136, **137**, 138–139, 145, **147**, 149, **150**, 151–155, 157–158, **158**, 160–161, 163–166, **167**, 168–169, **169**, 170, 172, 174–180, 182–184, 187, 198, 204, 208–209, 214, 224, 226–227, 257, 268–269, 273, **278**, 291, 338, 347, 358n48, 359n52, 362n55, 362n7, 363n1, 364n6, 364n15, 364n3, 365n19, 365n29, 366n23, 366n4, 366n6, 367n13, 368n3, 369n23; Eighth Conference 55–57, 70, 319, 356n35; League for the Independence of Vietnam 55, 353; Việt Minh (non-communist) 70–71
Vietnam Liberation Army 77, 89, 97–98, 103, 353; Vietnam Propaganda and Liberation Army 76, 77, 353, 360n27; *see also* Vietnamese People's Army
Vietnam Modernization Association 8–10, 12, 353, 355n20
Vietnam War (start of) 195, **196**, 197–198; Gulf of Tonkin Incident 228, 241; Gulf of Tonkin Resolution 228; *see also* Hồ Chí Minh Trail; Paris peace talks; Phoenix Program; Tết Offensive; United States; X Plan
Vietnamese Communist Party 2–3, 45, 65, 353, 366n20; founded 43; *see also* Indochinese Communist Party; Worker's Party of Vietnam
Vietnamese Kuomintang 40, 96, 104, 110, 117, 353, 357n6, 362n53, 363n1
Vietnamese National Army 157, 163, 180, 182, 365n27
Vietnamese People's Army (VNPA) 62, **64**, 77, 113, 184, 206, 223–224, 242, 244, 246, 248, **250**, 271, **292**, 305, 314, 316, 324–325, 327, 329, 336–337, 339, 351, 364n14, 365n24, 367n14, 367n15, 372n36; Armed Force of Cochinchina 110, 112, 363n25; National Defense Guard 103, 353, 362n7; Three-Layered Military 152–153; *see also* Liberation Army; National Salvation Troops; Vietnam Liberation Army
Vietnamese Restoration League 12, 22, 39–40, **44**, 353, 355n12, 355n22
Vietnamese Revolutionary Youth League (RYL) 24–25, **28**, 40–43, **44–45**, 46, 54, 56, 59, 62, 65, 120, 179, 232, 351, 353, 356n17, 357n15, 358n21, 359n9, 359n50, 359n51, 362n16, 364n4, 364n5
Vietnamization 270, 291, 307, 313–315, 317, 371n1; De-Americanization 289, 291; *jaunissement* program 157
Vịnh, Lê Quang **263**, 337–339, **339–340**, 343
Vỹ, Nguyễn Văn 223–224

war without boundaries 139–140, 153–154, 180, 207, 345, 348
Watkins, Pat 241–244, 246–247, 252
Wei Guoqing 166, 170
Welch, Clark 297
Westmoreland, William 238–239, 241, 267–269, 273–274, 288–289, 294
Westward March **48**, **74**, 76, 132–133, **135–136**, **143**, 146, **146**, 148, 153–154, **156**, 157, 162, 176, 364n2
Whampoa Military Academy **22**, 40–41, 54–55, 56, 139, 357n8
White Terror 43, 47, 58, 75, 355n12
Wilson, Woodrow 13
Winter Spring Campaign 164–166
Worker's Party of Vietnam 176, 204; founded 156; *see also* Indochinese Communist Party; Vietnamese Communist Party.
World War I 12–14, 175, 355n23
World War II 47, 49, 79–80, 89, 96, 100, 140, 149, 240–241, 298, 349, 358n33, 362n9, 364n15, 370n22

X Plan 222–224, **224**, 225–229, 235, 257–258, 269, 271, **284–285**, 368n15; *see also* Vietnam War
Xá, Hà Văn 198
Xiao Wen 103
Xuyến, Nguyễn Hữu 199, 368n30

Yong, Pradi Phnom 107

Zhou Enlai 151, 369n19
Zhuang Tian 151

www.ingramcontent.com/pod-product-compliance
Lightning Source LLC
Chambersburg PA
CBHW080755300426
44114CB00020B/2733